CHINA

FACTS & FIGURES

ANNUAL

Related Titles From

ACADEMIC INTERNATIONAL PRESS

China Documents Annual

Sino-Soviet Documents Annual

CHINA
FACTS & FIGURES
ANNUAL * HANDBOOK

Edited by
Gary Bennett

VOLUME 20

Academic International Press
1996

CHINA FACTS & FIGURES ANNUAL
Volume 20

ISBN: 0-87569-182-X

Composition by Janice Frye

By direct subscription with the publisher.

A list of Academic International Press publications is found at the end of this volume.

ACADEMIC INTERNATIONAL PRESS
POB 1111 • Gulf Breeze • Florida • 32562-1111 • USA

CONTENTS

ABBREVIATIONS OF TERMS

ADB—Asian Development Bank
ASEAN—Association of Southeast Asian Nations
b—barrels
bd—barrels per day
bn—billion
BOP—Balance of Power
BOT—Balance of Trade
CAS—Chinese Academy of Sciences
CC—Central Committee
CCP—Chinese Communist Party
CIS—Commonwealth of Independent States
CMC—Central Military Commission
CNPC—China National Petroleum Corporation
CPC—Communist Party of China
CPPCC—Chinese People's Political Consultative Conference
CSA—Canadian Standard Association
CTDF—China Tibet Development Foundation
cu—cubic
DPRK—Democratic People's Republic of Korea
EAEC—East Asia Economic Caucus
EFTA—European Free Trade Association
ESCAP—Economic and Social Commission for Asia and the Pacific
ETDA—Economic and Technological Development Zone
EU—European Union
FIE—Foreign Investment Enterprise
FTC—Foreign Trade Company/Corporation
GAC—General Administration of Customs
GATT—General Agreement on Tariffs and Trade
GDP—Gross Domestic Product
GNP—Gross National Product
GPD—General Political Department
GSP—Generalized System of Preferences
ha—hectare

HK—Hong Kong
IAEA—International Atomic Energy Agency
IDA—International Development Association
IMF—International Monetary Fund
INTELSAT—International Telecommunication Satellite Organization
JV—Joint Venture
kg—kilogram(s)
km—kilometer(s)
kw—kilowatt
kwh—kilowatt hour
m—meter(s)
MD—Military District
MFN—Most Favored Nation
mn—million
MOFTEC—Ministry of Foreign Trade and Economic Cooperation
MR—Military Region
MW—megawatt
NPC—National People's Congress
NPT—Nuclear Non-Proliferation treaty
PB—Political Bureau
PER—Price Earnings Ratio
PLA—People's Liberation Army
PRC—People's Republic of China
Rmb—renminbi
ROC—Republic of China
ROK—Republic of Korea
SEC—State Education Commission
SEZ—Special Economic Zone
SPC—Supreme People's Court
TVE—town and village enterprise
UK—United Kingdom
UN—United Nations
UNCTAD—United Nations Conference on Trade and Development
UNDP—United Nations Development Program
US—United States
WB—World Bank
yn—yuan

ABBREVIATIONS OF SOURCES

AAR—American Asian Review
OGJ—Oil and Gas Journal
AB—Asian Business
AMF—Asia Money and Finance
AMM—Asian Monetary Monitor
AJ—Atlanta Journal
BCT—Beijing Central Television
BR—Business Review
BW—Business Week
CBR—The China Business Review

CD—China Daily
CMR—China Monthly Review
CN—China Now
CNA—China News Analysis
CNS—China News Service
CTR—China Trade Report
CSM—Christian Science Monitor
ED—Economic Daily
ER—Economic Reporter
ECR—Economic Research

FEER—Far Eastern Economic Review
IMR—International Monetary Review
LD—Literature Daily
MB—The Military Balance, International Institute for Strategic Studies
NYT—New York Times
PB—Population Bulletin
RGB—Renmin Gongan Bao
TK—Tokyo Kyodo

UNB—United Nations, Monthly Bulletin of Statistics
WD—Workers Daily
WSQ—World Statistics Quarterly
WP—Washington Post
YTS—Yearbook of Tourism, World Tourism Organization
X—Xinhua

I SURVEY

China entered 1995 at the center of controversy and remained there throughout the year. Major items of contention were the "one China policy," ownership of the Spratly Islands, intellectual property rights and the trade balance.

Chinese leadership demanded that all nations recognize the Peoples Republic of China (PRC) as the only legitimate Chinese government. This was at odds with US policy to recognize and trade with Taiwan and caused a diplomatic fracture between China and the US. In April, 1995 China registered a formal protest with the US government when a Taiwanese official visited a US university. Following that protest Australia refused entry to a Taiwanese diplomat and made a formal statement declaring recognition of the PRC's "one China" policy. Japan made a similar declaration of recognition in mid-year and in September Cambodia followed suit.

As 1995 progressed China's relations with Taiwan became increasingly strained leading to China's open intimidation of the island nation. In November and December of 1995 China conducted military exercises involving unprecedented large numbers of ships, aircraft, artillery and troops in waters off Taiwan's coast and nearby strategic locations. This action came as a surprise to world leaders after China's rare attitude of compromise with Taipei in August of 1994. Part of the breakdown of relations was blamed on fatal incidents involving Taiwanese commercial fishermen and the issue of illegal Chinese immigrants in Taiwan. At stake in these issues was China's refusal to recognize Taiwan's jurisdiction, or the authority of its laws and enforcement agencies.

China also refused to recognize the right of other Pacific Rim countries to inhabit land or fish the waters of the Spratly Islands. This position led to confrontations with the Philippines, Vietnam, Malaysia and Indonesia. At the close of 1995 the matter remained unresolved.

Balance of trade with other nations, particularly the US, came to the forefront in 1995 with a US attempt to slow the flow of Chinese imports until China agreed to purchase more US agricultural and industrial products. Another point of contention between the two countries was China's seeming disregard for the proprietary rights of owners of intellectual property. A reflection of this disregard was China's failure to arrest and prosecute compact disc counterfeiters. The US viewed China's efforts to contain an illegal multimillion dollar world-wide operation as "feeble at best and non-existent at worst." By December of 1995 little occurred to curb illegal intellectual property activities. Even so, and although no formal balance of trade agreement was completed, trade between the US and China continued unchanged. China-UK trade temporarily halted when UK-Hong Kong officials reformed Hong Kong's constitution against China's wishes. Trade resumed with a compromise on the issue and British officials pointed to robust trade growth to show that neither the UK's nor China's commercial interests suffered from poor relations.

Although the economy continued to boom, the Chinese government was somewhat successful in its efforts to slow it without stopping it entirely. The growing economy was led by demand side increases in investment in fixed assets, most pointedly in property, and by a mini-boom in consumer goods. By the end of 1995 these upward trends had subsided. The fourth quarter saw investment in fixed assets grow by just 25 percent and retail sales increase by a comparatively small 6 percent.

Leadership was concerned about serious social unrest if prices rose unduly. Complicating matters was the widening wealth gap between coastal and interior China. Official estimates indicated there were 80 million Chinese living below the poverty line of Rmb200. Most were in the central areas of the country and many were from China's ethnic minorities.

Unemployment continued as a problem in all areas, although government officials felt that inflation was a greater danger than unemployment. Of special concern was the price of food.

continued...

Food prices were driven up by a less abundant crop yield than 1993 or 1994 as bad weather exacerbated the effects of the continuing loss of arable land.

On the plus side was the growth of specialized sideline activities such as truck farms but they could not offset a smaller total harvest, and some economic reform plans were temporarily abandoned to stabilize food prices. This was not seen as a long-term solution, but so concerned was the leadership with staying in power and so uncertain was the political climate that the short term was the focus of attention during 1995.

Another of Chinese leadership's problems was a power shortage highlighted when Beijing authorities rationed electricity to cope with a surge in demand. The supply for 100 large factories was affected. Electricity production has been a serious bottleneck for Chinese industry. But even with electricity shortages industry registered 16 percent growth. Short strides were made toward lessening electrical power shortages with plans for two more nuclear power stations in Guangdong province.

To decrease its reliance on foreign oil China signed agreements with western oil companies to prospect for oil in interior areas. In the meantime a black market developed to offset quotas for oil products. Quotas were illegally sold by government officials to end-users.

Governmental concern over corruption and graft at the national and regional level was ameliorated by crackdowns on criminal activities within the government. This led to the investigation, arrest and prosecution of several regional officials who were tried then either imprisoned or executed. Illegal drug sales and use grew to near epidemic proportions in China's cities despite harsh punishments for those convicted of trafficking and use.

Associated with higher drug use was an increase in the number of AIDS cases in China. A lack of education, sexual promiscuity especially between young men and prostitutes, and a shortage of trained medical professional contributed to growth in the number of Chinese infected with the disease. In other areas of medicine China moved forward in 1995 with a greater number of people being vaccinated against disease than during any other year in its history. Chinese research into the causes of high blood pressure was lauded by medical practitioners world-wide.

China's greater society continued to enjoy more freedom than in past years. An indication of increased freedom was expanded numbers of media outlets and satellite and non-satellite television and radio receivers throughout the country. On the other hand laws restricting access to the global telecommunications network were enacted. Laws regulating travel outside China and those allowing tourists inside were less restrictive exposing the Chinese population to a broader view of the world. Even though human rights remained a concern there was little evidence of a return to the more repressive government restrictions of the past, at least for the immediate future.

II SUMMARY OF SOCIAL AND ECONOMIC INDICATORS, 1995

MAP OF CHINA

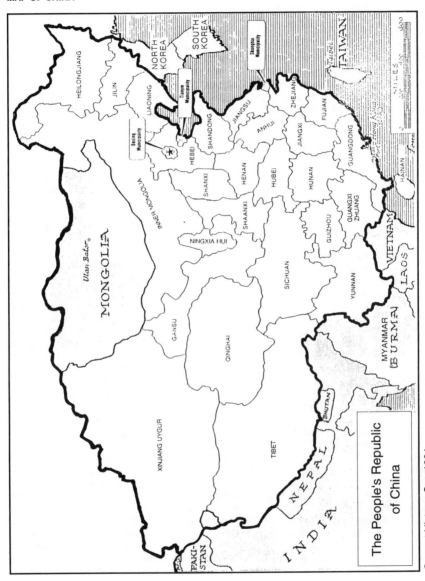

The People's Republic of China

Current History, Sep 1991.

CHINA BASIC STATISTICS, 1995

Location, Climate, Language, Religion, Flag, Capital
The People's Republic of China covers a vast area of eastern Asia, with Mongolia and Russia to the north, Tajikistan, Kyrgyzstan and Kazakhstan to the northwest, Afghanistan and Pakistan to the west, and India, Nepal, Bhutan, Myanmar (formerly Burma); Laos and Viet Nam to the south. The country borders the Democratic People's Republic of Korea in the northeast, and has a long coastline on the Pacific Ocean. The climate ranges from sub-tropical in the far south to an annual average temperature of below 10°C (50°F) in the north, and from the monsoon climate of eastern China to the aridity of the northwest. The principal language is Northern Chinese (Mandarin); in the south and south-east local dialects are spoken. The Xizangzu (Tibetans), Wei Wuer (Uighurs), Menggus (Mongols) and other groups have their own languages. The traditional religions and philosophies of life are Confucianism, Buddhism and Daoism. There are also small Muslim and Christian minorities. The national flag (proportions 3 by 2) is plain red, with one large five-pointed gold star and four similar but smaller stars, arranged in an arc, in the upper hoist. The capital is Beijing (Peking).

Recent History
The People's Republic of China was proclaimed on 1 October 1949, following the victory of Communist forces over the Kuomintang government, which fled to the island province of Taiwan. The new Communist regime received widespread international recognition, but it was not until 1971 that the People's Republic was admitted to the United Nations, in place of the Kuomintang regime, as the representative of China. Most countries now recognize the People's Republic.

With the establishment of the People's Republic, the leading figure in China's political affairs was Mao Zedong, who was Chairman of the Chinese Communist Party (CCP) from 1935 until his death in 1976. Chairman Mao, as he was known, also became Head of State in October 1949, but he relinquished this post in December 1958. His successor was Liu Shaoqi, First Vice-Chairman of the CCP, who was elected Head of State in April 1959. Liu was dismissed in October 1968, during the Cultural Revolution (see below), and died in prison in 1969. The post of Head of State was left vacant, and was formally abolished in January 1975, when a new constitution was adopted. The first Premier (Head of Government) of the People's Republic was Zhou Enlai, who held this office from October 1949 until his death in 1976. Zhou was also Minister of Foreign Affairs from 1949 to 1958, and subsequently remained largely responsible for China's international relations.

The economic progress which was achieved during the early years of Communist rule enabled China to withstand the effects of the industrialization programs of the late 1950s (called the "Great Leap Forward"), the drought of 1960-62 and the withdrawal of Soviet aid in 1960. To prevent the establishment of a ruling class, Chairman Mao launched the Great Proletarian Cultural Revolution in 1966. The ensuing excesses of the Red Guards caused the army to intervene; Liu Shaoqi, Head of State, and Deng Xiaoping, General Secretary of the CCP, were disgraced. In 1971 an attempted coup by the Defense Minister, Marshal Lin Biao, was unsuccessful, and by 1973 it was apparent that Chairman Mao and Premier Zhou Enlai had retained power. In 1975 Deng Xiaoping re-emerged as first Vice-Premier and Chief of the General Staff. Zhou Enlai died in January 1976. Hua Guofeng, hitherto Minister of Public Security, was appointed Premier, and Deng was dismissed. Mao died in September 1976. His widow, Jiang Qing, tried unsuccessfully to seize power, with the help of three radical members of the CCP's Politburo. The "gang of four" and six associates of Lin Biao were tried in November 1980. All were found guilty. (Jiang Qing committed suicide in May 1991.) The 10th anniversary of Mao's death was marked in September 1986 by an official reassessment of his life; while his accomplishments were praised, it was now acknowledged that he had made mistakes, although most of the criticism was directed at the "gang of four".

In October 1976 Hua Guofeng succeeded Mao as Chairman of the CCP and Commander-in-Chief of the People's Liberation Army. The 11th Congress of the CCP, held in August 1977, restored Deng Xiaoping to his former posts. In September 1980 Hua Guofeng resigned as

continued...

CHINA BASIC STATISTICS, 1995 (continued)

Premier but retained his chairmanship of the CCP. The appointment of Zhao Ziyang a Deputy Premier since April 1980, to succeed Hua as Premier confirmed the dominance of the moderate faction of Deng Xiaoping. In June 1981 Hua Guofeng was replaced as Chairman of the CCP by Hu Yaobang, former Secretary-General of the Politburo, and as Chairman of the party's Central Military Commission by Deng Xiaoping. A sustained campaign by Deng to purge the Politburo of leftist elements led to Hua's demotion to a Vice-Chairman of the CCP and, in September 1982, to his exclusion from the Politburo.

In September 1982 the CCP was reorganized and the post of Party Chairman abolished. Hu Yaobang became, instead, General Secretary of the CCP. A year later a "rectification" (purge) of the CCP was launched, aimed at expelling "Maoists", who had risen to power during the Cultural Revolution, and those opposed to the pragmatic policies of Deng. China's new Constitution, adopted in December 1982, restored the office of Head of State, and in June 1982 Li Xiannian, a former Minister of Finance, became President of China.

Following the announcement of a major anti-crime drive in late 1982, thousands of people were reported to have been executed, while at the same time a campaign was launched against "spiritual pollution"; stricter censorship was introduced to limit the effects of Western cultural influences. The reorganization of the CCP and of the Government continued. During 1984-85 a program of modernization for the armed forces was undertaken. In September 1986 the sixth plenary session of the 12th CCP Central Committee adopted a detailed resolution of the "guiding principles for building a socialist society", which redefined the general ideology of the CCP, to provide a theoretical basis for the program of modernization and the "open door" policy of economic reform.

In January 1986 a high-level "anti-corruption" campaign was launched, to investigate reports that many officials had exploited the program of economic reform for their own gain. In the field of culture and the arts, however, there was a significant liberalization in 1986, with a revival of the "Hundred Flowers" movement of 1956-57, which had encouraged the development of intellectual debate. However, a wave of student demonstrations in major cities in late 1986 was regarded by China's leaders as an indication of excessive "bourgeois liberalization", and in the ensuing government clamp-down, in January 1987, Hu Yaobang unexpectedly resigned as CCP General Secretary, being accused of "mistakes on major issues of political principles". Zhao Ziyang became acting General Secretary.

The campaign against "bourgeois liberalization" was widely regarded as part of a broader, ideological struggle between those Chinese leaders who sought to extend Deng's reforms and those, generally elderly, "conservative" leaders who opposed the reforms and the "open door" policy. At the 13th National Congress of the CCP, which opened in October 1987, it became clear that the "reformist" faction within the Chinese leadership had prevailed. The "work report", delivered to the Congress by Zhao Ziyang, emphasized the need for further reform and the extension of the "open door" policy. Deng Xiaoping retired from the Central Committee, but amendments to the Constitution of the CCP permitted him to retain the influential position of Chairman of the Central Military Commission.

The composition of the new Politburo, appointed by the Central Committee in November 1987, represented the fulfillment of another of Deng's goals: the promotion of his supporters within the CCP. The majority of its 18 members were relatively young officials, including the mayors, or party secretaries, of China's major industrial cities, which had been the forefront of the urban reform program. The membership of the new Politburo also indicated a decline in military influence in Chinese politics. The newly-appointed Standing Committee of the Politburo was regarded, on balance, as being "pro-reform" In late November Li Peng was appointed Acting Premier of the State Council, in place of Zhao Ziyang. At the first session of the Seventh National People's Congress (NPC), held in March-April 1988, Li Peng was confirmed as Premier, and Yang Shangkun (a member of the CCP Politburo) was elected President.

The death of Hu Yaobang, in Beijing on 15 April 1989, served as a catalyst for the most serious student demonstrations ever seen in the People's Republic of China. The students'

continued...

CHINA BASIC STATISTICS, 1995 (continued)

demands were addressed mainly at the alleged prevalence of corruption and nepotism within the Government and sought a limited degree of Soviet-style *glasnost* in public life. The protests were initially tolerated by the Government, but, when they persisted beyond Hu's funeral ceremony, Deng authorized the inclusion of an editorial in the *People's Daily* newspaper condemning the students' actions. On the following day, the demonstrations resumed in Beijing, and, after negotiations between government officials and the students' leaders had failed to satisfy the protesters' demands, workers from various professions joined the demonstrations in Tiananmen Square, which had now become the focal point of the protests. At one stage more than 1 mn people congregated in the Square, as demonstrations spread to more than 20 other Chinese cities. As May progressed, the Government became increasingly anxious to terminate the protests, in view of the imminent arrival of President Gorbachev of the USSR, who was to attend a "summit" meeting with Deng (see below). On 13 May, however, some 3,000 students began a hunger strike in Tiananmen Square, while protesters demanded the resignation of both Deng Xiaoping and Li Peng, and invited President Gorbachev to address them. Gorbachev arrived on 15 May, but his visit was largely overshadowed by the events in Tiananmen Square. The students ended their hunger strike some four days later, at the request of Zhao Ziyang, who was generally regarded as being sympathetic to the students' demands and had argued within the Politburo for serious discussions with the students' leaders. On 20 May a state of martial law was declared in Beijing. This was widely interpreted as an indication that known political "hard-liners" in the leadership (principally President Yang, Li Peng and, latterly, Deng) had prevailed in a struggle against the reformist faction, led by Zhou. Within days, some 300,000 troops had assembled around Beijing, but the process of troop convoys towards Tiananmen Square was halted by crowds of people acting in support of the students. At the end of May the students erected a 30-m high replica of the US Statue of Liberty in the Square, entitled the Goddess of Democracy and Freedom. On 3 June a further unsuccessful attempt was made to dislodge the demonstrators, but on the following day troops of the 27th army of the People's Liberation Army attacked protesters on and around the Square, killing an unspecified number of people. Television evidence and eye-witness accounts estimated the total dead at somewhere between 1,000 and 5,000, although the Government immediately rejected these figures and claimed, furthermore, that the larger part of the casualties had been soldiers.

Following the armed suppression of the demonstrations, the Government initiated a large-scale propaganda campaign, alleging that a counter-revolutionary rebellion had been taking place and portraying members of the army as innocent victims. A wave of arrests and executions ensued, although some student leaders eluded capture and fled to Hong Kong, and those involved in the protests were compelled to undergo televised self-criticism. At a session of the CCP Central Committee on 23 June 1989, Zhao Ziyang was dismissed from all his party posts and replaced as General Secretary of the CCP by Jiang Zemin, hitherto the secretary of the Shanghai municipal party committee. Zhao was described as a proponent of "bourgeois liberalization" and accused of participating in a political conspiracy to overthrow the CCP and to establish a bourgeois republic in China. Zhao had not been seen in public since the declaration of martial law and was apparently under house arrest. In November Deng resigned as Chairman of the CCP Central Military Commission, his sole remaining party position, and was succeeded by Jiang Zemin. A personality cult was immediately fostered around Jiang, who was hailed as the first of China's "third generation" of communist leaders (Mao being representative of the first, and Deng of the second). However, despite Deng's assertion that he would no longer interfere in political affairs, it was conjectured that he would retain effective power.

In January 1990 martial law was lifted in Beijing, and it was announced that a total of 573 prisoners, detained following the pro-democracy demonstrations, had been released. Further groups of detainees were released during the course of the year. In June Fang Lizhi, the prominent astrophysicist and dissident (who, although required to stand trial on charges of participation in the pro-democracy protests, had been granted refuge in the US embassy in Beijing), was permitted to leave the country for the United Kingdom. In October Wang Ruowang,

continued...

CHINA BASIC STATISTICS, 1995 (continued)

the eminent writer and dissident, was released from prison after 13 months in detention. In late 1990, however, human rights organizations estimated that hundreds of pro-democracy activists remained in prison. Furthermore, the authorities were proceeding with the prosecution of prominent dissidents. In January 1991 the trials of many of those arrested during the pro-democracy protests of 1989 commenced. Most activists received relatively short prison sentences.

Meanwhile, in March 1990 Deng Xiaoping resigned from his last official post, that of Chairman of the State Central Military Commission, being succeeded by Jiang Zemin. During April and May an extensive military reshuffle was carried out. The changes included the replacement of six of the country's seven regional commanders. In September Premier Li Peng resigned from the position of Minister in Charge of the State Commission for Restructuring the Economy. In December, at the seventh plenary session of the 13th Central Committee of the CCP, proposals for the Eighth Five-Year Plan (1991-1995) and for the 10-year development program (1991-2000) were approved. The Ministers of Public Security and of Foreign Economic Relations and Trade were replaced. The fourth plenary session of the Seventh NPC opened in March 1991. Emphasis was placed on the promotion of political stability in China. In the following month government changes included the appointment of two new Vice-Premiers. In July a large rally to commemorate the 70th anniversary of the founding of the CCP was held in Beijing.

In September 1991 a report released by Amnesty International repeated the human rights organization's severe criticism of China's record. Thousands of citizens, including those detained for their alleged involvement in the anti-Government demonstrations of 1989, were believed to remain in detention without trial.

In January 1992 Deng Xiaoping toured the special economic zones (SEZs) of southern China, where he emphasized the importance of reform, thus initiating a period of intense debate between reformists and "hard-liners" within the CCP. In March, at a session of the NPC, Premier Li Peng affirmed China's commitment to rapid economic reform, but stressed the need for stability. In September government changes included the replacement of the Minister of Finance. At the CCP's 14th National Congress, held in October 1992, a new 319-member Central Committee was elected. The Politburo was expanded and a new Secretariat was also chosen by the incoming Central Committee. Many opponents of Deng Xiaoping's support for a "socialist market economy" were replaced.

At the first session of the Eighth NPC, convened in March 1993, Jiang Zemin was elected as the country's President, remaining CCP General Secretary. Li Peng was reappointed as Premier, and an extensive reorganization of the State Council was announced. The Congress also approved amendments to the 1982 Constitution. Changes included confirmation of the State's practice of a "socialist market economy".

During 1993 the Government became concerned at the growing disparity between urban and rural incomes (exacerbated by the heavy taxes imposed on farmers) and the decline in support for the CCP in the countryside. In June thousands of peasants took part in demonstrations in Sichuan Province to protest against excessive official levies. In response to the ensuing riots, the central Government banned the imposition of additional local taxes.

Public disquiet over corruption within the CCP and the state bureaucracy was acknowledged in August 1993, when the Party initiated an anti-corruption campaign. CCP officials were forbidden to trade on the stock market and to hold private business interests.

Meanwhile, the trials of pro-democracy activists had continued. In July 1992 Bao Tong, a senior aide of Zhao Ziyang, the former General Secretary of the CCP, was found guilty of involvement in the pro-democracy unrest of mid-1989. Zhao himself remained under house arrest. In early September, following his return to China from exile in the USA, Shen Tong, a leader of the pro-democracy movement, was arrested and later deported. Several prominent dissidents were subsequently released from prison. In February 1993 Wang Dan and Guo Haifeng, leading student activists in the 1989 demonstrations, were freed. In May, having

continued...

CHINA BASIC STATISTICS, 1995 (continued)

served 12 years of a 15-year sentence, Xu Wenli was released from prison. In August the arrest and expulsion from China of Han Dongfang, a trade union activist who had attempted to return to his homeland after a year in the USA, attracted much international attention. In the following month, shortly before the International Olympic Committee was due to vote upon the venue for the 2000 Games, for which Beijing was bidding, Wei Jingsheng, another long-serving political prisoner, was released.

Tibet (Xizang), a semi-independent region of western China, was occupied in 1950 by Chinese Communist forces. In March 1959 there was an unsuccessful armed uprising by Tibetans opposed to Chinese rule. As a result, the Dalai Lama, the head of Tibet's Buddhist clergy and thus the region's spiritual leader, fled with some 100,000 supporters to northern India, where a government-in-exile was established. The Chinese ended the former dominance of the lamas (Buddhist monks) and destroyed many monasteries. Tibet became an "Autonomous Region" of China in September 1965, but the majority of Tibetans have continued to regard the Dalai Lama as their "god-king," and to resent the Chinese presence. In October 1987, shortly before the 37th anniversary of China's occupation of Tibet, violent clashes occurred in Lhasa (the regional capital) between the Chinese authorities and Tibetans seeking independence. Further demonstrations during a religious festival in March 1988 resulted in a riot and several deaths, and a number of Tibetan separatists were arrested and detained without trial. The Dalai Lama, however, renounced demands for independence, and in 1988 proposed that Tibet become a self-governing Chinese territory, in all respects except foreign affairs. In December 1988 an offer from the Dalai Lama to meet Chinese representatives in Geneva was rejected, and later that month two more demonstrators were killed by security forces during a march to commemorate the 40th anniversary of the UN General Assembly's adoption of the Universal Declaration of Human Rights. On 7 March 1989 martial law was imposed in Lhasa for the first time since 1959, after further violent clashes between separatists and the Chinese police. The violence ensued when a pro-independence demonstration was dispersed by police, resulting in the deaths of 16 protesters. In October the Chinese Government condemned as an interference in its internal affairs the award of the Nobel Peace Prize to the Dalai Lama. In November 1989 several Tibetan Buddhist nuns claimed to have been severely tortured for their part in the demonstrations in March of that year. In early May 1990 martial law was lifted in Lhasa. At the end of the month, following the resignation of Doje Cering, Gyaincain Norbu became Chairman of the Xizang Autonomous Region. Human rights groups claimed that during the last six months of the period of martial law as many as 2,000 persons had been executed. Furthermore, political and religious repression and torture were reported to be continuing throughout 1990. In December, renouncing his insistence on complete separation, the Dalai Lama proposed a "loose confederation" for Tibet. Renewed anti-Chinese protests were reported in October 1991. In March 1992 a pro-independence demonstration in Lhasa was reported to have been violently dispersed by the security forces. In May a report issued by Amnesty International was critical of the Chinese authorities' violations of the human rights of the monks and nuns of Tibet. A document entitled *Tibet—Its Ownership and Human Rights Situation* was published by the Chinese Government in September, attempting to prove that historically the region is part of China. There was further unrest in 1993. In May several thousand Tibetans were reported to have demonstrated in Lhasa against Chinese rule. A number of protesters were believed to have been killed by the security forces. In August the Dalai Lama affirmed that he sought only limited autonomy for Tibet.

In the Xinjiang Uygur Autonomous Region anti-Chinese sentiment continued to increase. Unrest intensified in early 1990, and in April as many as 60 people were reported to have been killed when government troops opened fire on Muslim protesters. Following the uprising, the Communist authorities initiated a new campaign to repress the Islamic separatist movement. Nevertheless, Muslim activity continued. In October 1993 protests by thousands of Muslims in Qinghai Province were brutally suppressed by the authorities.

In the early years of the People's Republic, China was dependent on the USSR for economic and military aid, and Chinese planning was based on the Soviet model, with highly centralized

continued…

control. From 1955 onwards, however, Mao Zedong set out to develop a distinctively Chinese form of socialism. As a result of increasingly strained relations between Chinese and Soviet leaders, caused partly by ideological differences, the USSR withdrew all technical aid to China in August 1960. Chinese hostility to the USSR increased, and was aggravated by territorial disputes between the two countries, and by the Soviet invasion of Afghanistan and the Soviet-backed Vietnamese invasion of Cambodia. Sino-Soviet relations remained strained until 1987, when representatives of the two countries signed a partial agreement concerning the exact demarcation of the disputed Sino-Soviet border at the Amur river. The withdrawal of Soviet troops from Afghanistan (completed in February 1989) and Vietnam's assurance that it would end its military presence in Cambodia by September 1989 resulted in a further *rapprochement.* In May 1989 the Soviet President, Mikhail Gorbachev, attended a full "summit" meeting with Deng Xiaoping in Beijing, at which state and party relations between the two countries were formally normalized. However, the massacre in Tiananmen Square in June 1989 limited subsequent Sino-Soviet contacts, although Gorbachev proposed the creation of joint economic zones on the Sino-Soviet border. In April 1990 Li Peng paid an official visit to the USSR, the first by a Chinese Premier for 26 years. Jiang Zemin, CCP General Secretary, visited Moscow in May 1991. In December 1991, upon the dissolution of the USSR, China recognized the newly-independent states of the former union. The President of Russia, Boris Yeltsin, visited China in December 1992.

During the 1970s Sino-Soviet friction was accompanied by an improvement in China's relations with Japan and the West. Almost all Western countries had recognized the Government of the People's Republic as the sole legitimate government of China, and had consequently withdrawn recognition from the "Republic of China", which had been confined to Taiwan since 1949. The People's Republic claimed Taiwan as an integral part of its territory, although the island remained to be "liberated". For many years, however, the USA refused to recognize the People's Republic but, instead, regarded the Taiwan administration as the legitimate Chinese government. In February 1972 President Richard Nixon of the USA visited the People's Republic and acknowledged that "Taiwan is a part of China". In January 1979 the USA recognized the People's Republic and severed diplomatic relations with Taiwan. For its part, Taiwan has repeatedly rejected China's proposals for reunification, whereby Taiwan would become a "special administrative region", and has sought reunification under its own terms. China threatened military intervention, in the event that Taiwan should declare itself independent of the mainland. Trade and reciprocal visits greatly increased in 1988, as relations improved. Reconciliation initiatives were abruptly halted, however, by the violent suppression of the Pro-Democracy Movement in June 1989. The actions of the Chinese Government were strongly condemned by Taiwan, although it was indicated that there would be no consequent change in official policy towards China. In May 1990 President Lee of Taiwan suggested the opening of direct dialogue on a government-to-government basis with the People's Republic. Beijing, however, rejected the proposal, maintaining that it would negotiate only on a party-to-party basis with the Kuomintang. In April 1991 a delegation from the Straits Exchange Foundation (SEF) of Taiwan, established in late 1990 to handle bilateral issues, traveled to China for discussions, the first such delegation ever to visit the People's Republic. The Association for Relations across the Taiwan Straits (ARATS) was established in Beijing in December 1991. In May 1992 the People's Republic rejected Taiwan's proposal for a non-aggression pact. Nevertheless, in April 1993 historic talks between the Chairmen of the ARATS and SEF took place in Singapore, where a formal structure for future negotiations on economic and social issues was agreed. In August, however, the People's Republic issued a document entitled *The Taiwan Question and the Reunification of China,* reaffirming its claim to sovereignty over the island. Relations were further strained by a series of aircraft hijackings from the mainland to Taiwan. An ARATS-SEF meeting, held in Taiwan in December 1993, attempted to address the issue of hijacker repatriation.

continued...

CHINA BASIC STATISTICS, 1995 (continued)

China will re-establish sovereignty over Hong Kong when the existing lease on most of the British dependent territory expires in 1997. In September 1984, following protracted negotiations, China reached agreement with the British Government over the terms of Chinese administration of the territory after that date. In 1985 a Basic Law Drafting Committee (BLDC), including 25 representatives from Hong Kong, was established in Beijing to prepare a new Basic Law (Constitution) for Hong Kong. Consultations on the Committee s second draft were temporarily suspended in 1989, following the student massacre in Tiananmen Square. The Basic Law for Hong Kong was approved by the NPC in April 1990. In July a Minister of State at the Foreign and Commonwealth Office of the United Kingdom visited Beijing for consultations on the future of Hong Kong. The Governor of Hong Kong visited China for discussions in January 1991. In September, during a visit to China by the British Prime Minister, a Memorandum of Understanding on the construction of a new airport in Hong Kong was signed. In October 1992 the new Governor of Hong Kong traveled to Beijing for discussions, relations between China and the United Kingdom having been strained by the announcement of ambitious plans for democratic reform in Hong Kong prior to 1997. In January 1993 a senior Chinese official warned that Hong Kong would experience "hardship" if the program of political reform were pursued. In April China and the United Kingdom resumed negotiations on the future of the territory, thus ending an impasse of several months. By the end of the year, however, no progress had been made, and in December, following Hong Kong's decision to press ahead with electoral reform, China declared that it would regard as null and void any laws enacted by the territory's Legislative Council.

In June 1986 China and Portugal opened formal negotiations for the return of the Portuguese overseas territory of Macau to full Chinese sovereignty. In January 1987 Portugal agreed that withdrawal from Macau should take place in 1999. The agreement is based upon the "one country, two systems" principle, which formed the basis of China's negotiated settlement regarding the return of Hong Kong. In March 1993 the final draft of the Basic Law for Macau was approved by the NPC.

China condemned Vietnam's invasion of Kampuchea (now Cambodia) in December 1978, and launched a punitive attack into northern Viet Nam in February 1979. Armed clashes across the border continued, and negotiations between the two countries failed to resolve the dispute. China continued to give sustained financial and military support to Cambodian resistance organizations, notably the communist Khmer Rouge, despite the Vietnamese troop withdrawal (completed in September 1989), as it refused to accept Vietnam's assurance that its military presence in Cambodia had ended. However, in November 1990, following an improvement in Sino-Vietnamese relations, China announced that it had ceased supplying weapons to the Khmer Rouge. Following the holding of elections in Cambodia in May 1993, China welcomed the establishment of a national government. The restoration of normal relations between China and Viet Nam was announced in late 1991. The Chinese Premier visited Hanoi for discussions in December 1992. In October 1993 China and Viet Nam signed a preliminary agreement to facilitate the settlement of their border dispute by peaceful means. The question of the sovereignty of the Spratly (Nansha) Islands, situated in the South China Sea and claimed by six countries (including China and Viet Nam), remained unresolved.

China's relations with the USA improved steadily throughout the 1980s, but were seriously impaired by the student massacre in 1989. In 1984 Premier Zhao Ziyang visited Washington, and in the same year President Ronald Reagan visited Beijing, where a bilateral agreement on industrial and technological cooperation was signed. Following the suppression of the pro-democracy movement, however, the new US President, George Bush, suspended all high-level government exchanges and banned the export of weapons to China. In November 1989, at a meeting in Beijing with the former US President, Richard Nixon, Deng accused the USA of being deeply involved in the "counter-revolutionary rebellion" in June, and indicated that the USA, and not China, was responsible for the deterioration in relations between the two countries. In the same month the US Congress approved a proposal to

continued...

CHINA BASIC STATISTICS, 1995 (continued)

extend the sanctions that President Bush had imposed in June. In December representatives of the US Government conferred with Deng in Beijing, and it was revealed that secret, Sino-US negotiations had taken place in July of that year. In November 1990 President Bush received the Chinese Minister of Foreign Affairs in Washington, thereby resuming contact at the most senior level. Nevertheless, in January 1991 a report published by the US State Department was critical of China s record on human rights. This concern was reiterated in November, when the US Secretary of State visited Beijing. In May 1993 President Bill Clinton renewed China's most-favored-nation (MFN) trade status, guaranteeing privileged Chinese access to US markets, for a further year, but warned that future renewals would be dependent upon an improvement in China's record on human rights. In August the USA imposed sanctions on China, in response to the latter's sales of technology for nuclear-capable missiles to Pakistan, in alleged violation of international non-proliferation guidelines. Another obstacle to good relations between China and the USA is the question of Taiwan, and, in particular, the continued sale of US armaments to Taiwan. Sino-US relations deteriorated in September 1992, upon President Bush's announcement of the sale of 150 F-16 fighter aircraft to Taiwan.

China's relations with Japan, a major trading partner, began to deteriorate in 1982, after China complained that passages in Japanese school textbooks sought to justify the Japanese invasion of China in 1937. In June 1989 the Japanese Government criticized the Chinese Government's suppression of the pro-democracy movement and suspended (until late 1990) a five-year aid program to China. The Prime Minister of Japan visited Beijing for discussions with his Chinese counterpart in August 1991. In April 1992 Jiang Zemin traveled to Japan, the first visit by the General Secretary of the CCP for nine years. In October Emperor Akihito made the first ever imperial visit to the People's Republic. Japan was one of many countries to criticize China's resumption of nuclear testing in October 1993.

The long-standing border dispute with India, which gave rise to a short military conflict in 1962, remained unresolved in 1992 (see chapter on India). The Indian Prime Minister traveled to China for discussions in December 1988, and the Chinese Premier visited New Delhi in December 1991. Sino-Indian discussions on the issue continued, and in September 1993 the two countries signed an agreement to reduce their troops along the frontier and to resolve the dispute by peaceful means. Diplomatic relations with Indonesia, severed in 1967, were formally restored in August 1990, and in October diplomatic relations between China and Singapore were established. During 1992 China established diplomatic relations with Israel and with the Republic of Korea.

In July 1990 Saudi Arabia transferred its recognition from Taiwan to the People's Republic, and in September, as the Gulf crisis continued, China expressed its support for Saudi Arabia in its defense against Iraq. In November, hoping to secure a peaceful solution, the Chinese Minister of Foreign Affairs (the most senior representative of the five permanent members of the UN Security Council to visit Iraq since the onset of the crisis) traveled to Baghdad in an attempt to persuade Saddam Hussein to withdraw his forces from Kuwait.

Government

China is a unitary state. Directly under the Central Government there are 22 provinces, five autonomous regions, including Xizang (Tibet), and three municipalities (Beijing, Shanghai and Tianjin). The highest organ of state power is the National People's Congress (NPC). In March 1993 the first session of the Eighth NPC was attended by 2,921 deputies, indirectly elected for five years by the people's congresses of the provinces, autonomous regions, municipalities directly under the Central Government, and the People's Liberation Army. The NPC elects a Standing Committee to be its permanent organ. The current Constitution, adopted by the NPC in December 1982 and amended in 1993, was China's fourth since 1949. It restored the office of Head of State (President of the Republic). Executive power is exercised by the State Council (Cabinet), comprising the Premier, Vice-Premiers and other Ministers heading ministries and commissions. The State Council is appointed by, and accountable to, the NPC.

continued...

CHINA BASIC STATISTICS, 1995 (continued)

Political power, is held by the Chinese Communist Party (CCP). The CCP's highest authority is the Party Congress, convened every five years. In October 1992 the CCP's 14th National Congress elected a Central Committee of 189 full members and 130 alternate members. To direct policy, the Central Committee elected a 22-member Politburo.

Local people's congresses are the local organs of state power. Local revolutionary committees, created during the Cultural Revolution, were abolished in January 1980 and replaced by local people's governments.

Defense
China is divided into seven major military units. All armed services are grouped in the People's Liberation Army (PLA). In June 1993, according to Western estimates, the regular forces totaled 3,030,000, of whom 1,275,000 were conscripts: the army numbered 2,300,000, the navy 260,000 (including a naval air force of 25,000), and the air force 470,000 (including 220,000 air defense personnel). There are also strategic rocket forces of 90,000 and about 1.2 mn in paramilitary forces. Military service is by selective conscription, and lasts for three years in the army and marines, and for four years in the air force and navy. Defense expenditure for 1993 was budgeted at 41,800 mn yuan.

Economic Affairs
In 1992, according to estimates by the World Bank, China's gross national product (GNP), measured at average 1990-92 prices, was US $442,346 mn, equivalent to some $380 per head. During 1985-92, it was estimated, GNP per head increased, in real terms, at an average annual rate of 6.0%, one of the highest growth rates in the world. Over the same period, the population grew by an average annual rate of 1.5%. China's gross domestic product (GDP) grew, in real terms, by an average annual rate of 9.4% in 1980-91. According to official sources, compared with the previous year GDP increased by 12.8% in 1992, to total 2,393,800 mn yuan.

Agriculture (including forestry and fishing) contributed 24.2% of GDP in 1991. Agricultural GDP increased by an average annual rate of 5.7% in 1980-91. Compared with the previous year, in 1992 agricultural GDP increased, in real terms, by 3.7%. About 60% of the labor force were employed in agriculture in 1991. China's principal crops are rice (production of which accounted for an estimated 36% of the total world harvest in 1992), sweet potatoes, wheat, maize, soybeans, sugar cane, tobacco, cotton and jute. The harvest of grain (cereals, pulses, soybeans and tubers in "grain equivalent") increased from 435.24 mn metric tons in 1991 to 442.58 mn tons in 1992.

Industry (including mining, manufacturing, construction and power) contributed 42% of GDP in 1991. Industrial GDP increased by an average annual rate of 11.0% in 1980-1991. In 1992, compared with the previous year, industrial GDP grew by 20.8%; the sector accounted for 42.3% of GDP. Growth was estimated at 23.6% in 1993. China is the world's largest producer of coal and natural graphite. Coal output reached an estimated 1,110 mn metric tons in 1992. Other important minerals include tungsten, molybdenum, antimony, tin, lead, mercury, bauxite, phosphate rock, iron ore and manganese. China is also the world's largest producer of raw cotton, cloth and cement, with output in 1992 totaling an estimated 4.9 mn metric tons, 18,500 mn m and 304 mn metric tons respectively.

Energy is derived principally from coal (74.1% in 1991), petroleum (19.2%) and hydroelectric power (4.7%). In 1992 crude petroleum output totaled an estimated 142 mn tons. Mineral fuels and lubricants accounted for only 3.3% of the cost of total imports in 1991.

Receipts from tourism are of growing importance, reaching US $3,950 mn in 1992.

In 1992 China recorded a trade surplus of US $5,183 mn and there was a surplus of $6,401 mn on the current account of the balance of payments. A trade deficit of more than $12,000 mn was recorded in 1993. In 1992 the principal trading partners were Hong Kong (which provided 25.5% of imports and received 44.1% of exports), Japan (17.0% of imports and 13.7% of exports) and the USA (11.0% of imports and 10.1% of exports). Indirect trade with Taiwan is of increasing significance. The principal imports in 1991 were machinery and transport equipment, basic manufactures and chemicals and related products. The principal exports were

continued...

CHINA BASIC STATISTICS, 1995 (continued)

basic manufactures, miscellaneous manufactured articles and food and live animals. In an effort to increase exports, China devalued its currency by 21.2% and 9.6% against the US dollar in December 1989 and November 1.990 respectively. A series of minor devaluations followed. A unified floating exchange rate was introduced in January 1994.

In 1993 the budget deficit was projected at 84,400 mn yuan. China's total external debt at the end of 1992 was estimated to be US $69,321 mn of which $58,475 mn was long-term debt. In 1992 the cost of debt-servicing was equivalent to 9.6% of revenue from exports of goods and services. The annual rate of inflation averaged 7.5% in 1985-92. In 1992 the national rate was 6%, rising to an estimated 15% in 1993. In some urban areas, however, the inflation rate was in excess of 20%. An estimated 2.3% of the urban labor force were unemployed in mid-1993. Surplus rural laborers totaled 100 mn.

China is a member of the Asian Development Bank and joined the Asia-Pacific Economic Co-operation forum (APEC) in 1991. In 1993 China became a member of the Association of Tin Producing Countries (ATPC).

The Chinese economy was, from 1953, subject to central control within the framework of five-year plans. The Eighth Five-Year Plan (1991-95) and 10-year development program for 1991-2000 envisaged average annual GNP growth of 6%. It was hoped that, over the decade, the rate of population increase could be restricted to an average of 1.25% per year. Economic reforms were to continue, the planned economy being combined with market regulation. In 1978 a process of reform, known as the "open door" policy, was introduced to decentralize the economic system and to attract overseas investment to China. The state monopoly on foreign trade was gradually relinquished, commercial links were diversified, and several "special economic zones" were established. Measures to reduce the resultant high level of inflation were introduced in September 1988. A further austerity program, aimed at curbing the unrestrained economic growth and countering the high rate of inflation, was announced in July 1993. Speculative loans were called in, interest rates were raised, government expenditure was cut by 20% and investment projects were to be reassessed. Nevertheless, GNP growth in 1993 was estimated at 13%. In November a new economic restructuring plan was adopted. This involved radical reforms in the banking, taxation, investment and foreign trade sectors.

Social Welfare
Western and traditional Chinese medical attention is available in the cities and, to a lesser degree, in rural areas. A fee is charged. In December 1992 there were 1.81 mn doctors and 1.04 mn nurses. In 1991 there were 209,036 health establishments. About 1.3 mn "barefoot doctors", semi-professional peasant physicians, assist with simple cures, treatment and the distribution of contraceptives. There were more than 2.74 mn hospital beds in December 1992. Large factories and other enterprises provide social services for their employees. Industrial wage-earners qualify for pensions. It was announced in 1986 that China was to introduce a social security system to provide assistance to retired people and unemployed contract workers, as part of the planned reform in the labor system.

Education
The education system expanded rapidly after 1949. Fees are charged at all levels. Much importance is attached to kindergartens. Primary education begins for most children at seven years of age and lasts for five years. Secondary education usually begins at 12 years of age and lasts for a further five years, comprising a first cycle of three years and a second cycle of two years. Free higher education was abolished in 1985; instead, college students have to compete for scholarships, which are awarded according to academic ability. As a result of the student disturbances in May and June 1989, college students are required to complete one year's political education, prior to entering college. In November 1989 it was announced that post-graduate students were to be selected on the basis of assessments of moral and physical fitness, as well as academic ability. Since 1979 education has been included as one of the main priorities for modernization. The whole educational system was to be reformed, with the aim

continued...

CHINA BASIC STATISTICS, 1995 (continued)

of introducing nine-year compulsory education in 75% of the country by 1995. The establishment of private schools has been permitted since the early 1980s. As a proportion of the total school-age population, enrollment at primary, and secondary schools in 1991 was 86% (boys 91%; girls 81%). In that year 100% of both boys and girls in the relevant age-group were enrolled at primary schools.

International Year Book, 1993–1994.

NATIONAL ECONOMIC PERFORMANCE, 1994

I. Agriculture
A fairly good agricultural harvest was reaped after overcoming serious natural disasters. Among the output of major farm produce, there was a slight decrease in grain; in cotton output began to pick up after the decreased production trend was stopped; and oil-bearing crop output hit an all-time high. Vegetable and fruit output increased considerably while that of sugar-bearing crops, jute and hemp, and cured tobacco declined. In comparison with the rapidly growing national economy and people's rising living standards, the problem of stagnation in agricultural production has become serious.

Output of Major Farm Produce

	1994 (tn)	Increase Over 1993 (percent)
Grain	444,500,000	-2.5
Of which: cereals	393,970,000	-2.8
Oil-bearing crops	19,840,000	10.0
Of which: peanuts	9,640,000	14.4
Rapeseed	7,460,000	7.5
Cotton	4,250,000	13.6
Jute, ambry hemp	380,000	-44.1
Sugarcane	60,860,000	-5.2
Beetroot	12,530,000	4.0
Cured tobacco	1,950,000	-35.2
Tea	580,000	-2.9
Fruit	34,780,000	15.5

New progress was made in forestry. The quality of afforestation improved further. Newly afforested areas in 1994 covered 5.9 million hectares. State key forestry projects made noticeable headway; and measures against forest fires, for the prevention and control of forest diseases, and for protection of resources were reinforced. Forest cover increased to 13.9 percent. Animal husbandry production developed in an all-round way; and the output of meat, poultry, eggs, milk, and other livestock products also increased.

Output of Major Animal Products and Heads of Livestock in Stock

	1994	Increase Over 1993 (percent)
Meat (tn)	43,000,000	11.9
Of which pork, beef, and mutton (tn)	36,700,000	13.8
Cow milk (tn)	5,300,000	6.2
Sheep wool (tn)	260,000	6.2
Silkworm cocoons (tn)	830,000	10.2
Pigs in stock at yearend (head)	412,180,000	4.9
Sheep & goats in stock at yearend (head)	239,590,000	10.2
Draught animals in stock at yearend (head)	150,320,000	7.5

continued...

NATIONAL ECONOMIC PERFORMANCE, 1994 (continued)

Fishery developed steadily. Aquatic product output in 1994 amounted to 20.98 million tons, an increase of 15.1 percent over 1993. Of this total, the output of fresh-water products was 8.9 million tons, up 19.1 percent; and that of marine products was 12.08 million tons, up 12.3 percent.

Further improvement was made in agricultural production conditions. By the end of 1994, the aggregate power of the country's farm machinery reached 336.85 million kw, increasing 5.9 percent over the end of the previous year. There were 690,000 large and medium tractors, a drop of 4.6 percent; 8.21 million small and walking tractors, up 4.1 percent; and 760,000 trucks, up 9.9 percent. A total of 33.13 million tons of chemical fertilizers (in terms of 100 percent active ingredients) were applied, up 5.1 percent. Rural consumption of electricity in the year totaled 151.1 billion kwh, up 21.4 percent. Construction of rural water conservancy projects were further stepped up, thus expanding the area of farmland under effective irrigation.

II. Industry and Building Industry

Industrial production continued its rapid growth. In 1994, added value of industry amounted to 1.8359 trillion yuan, up 18 percent over the previous year. Of this total, the growth of state-owned enterprises was 5.5 percent (the growth rate was 6.8 percent if state-owned holding enterprises were included); that of collective enterprises was 21.4 percent, of which township industrial growth took 27.3 percent; and Sino-foreign joint ventures, cooperative enterprises, and solely foreign-funded enterprises grew 28 percent. Large and medium enterprises maintained their momentum of steady development, with a growth rate of 12 percent.

In 1994, light industry grew faster than heavy industry. The added value of light industry was 766.8 billion, up 19.9 percent over the previous year, and that of heavy industry came to 1.0691 trillion yuan, up 16.5 percent. There were ups and downs in the production of key industrial products.

Output of Major Industrial Products

	1994	Increase Over 1993 (percent)
Chemical fibers (tn)	2,690,000	13.3
Yarn (tn)	4,700,000	-6.3
Cloth (m)	20,000,000,000	-1.5
Machine-made paper and paperboard (tn)	20,000,000	4.5
Sugar (tn)	5,819,000	-24.6
Salt (tn)	29,746,000	1.1
Cigarettes (cases)	34,213,000	1.4
Synthetic detergents (tn)	1,964,000	4.3
Color TV sets (units)	16,895,000	17.7
Household washing machines (units)	10,964,000	22.4
Household refrigerators (units)	7,645,000	28.1
Total energy production (in terms of standard fuel, tn)	1,120,000,000	4.7
Coal (tn)	1,210,000,000	5.3
Crude oil (tn)	146,000,000	1.0
Electricity (kwh)	920,000,000,000	9.6
Steel (tn)	91,530,000	2.2
Rolled steel (tn)	80,036,000	3.7
Ten kinds of nonferrous metals (tn)	3,752,000	7.5
Cement (tn)	400,050,000	10.1
Timber (cu m)	61,000,000	-4.5
Sulfuric acid (tn)	14,947,000	11.8

continued...

NATIONAL ECONOMIC PERFORMANCE, 1994 (continued)

	1994	Increase Over 1993 (percent)
Soda ash (tn)	5,684,000	6.3
Chemical fertilizers (in terms of 100% active ingredients, tn)	22,760,000	16.3
Farm chemicals (in terms of 100% active ingredients, tn)	268,000	4.4
Power-generating equipment (kw)	17,069,000	15.9
Metal cutting machine tools (units)	192,000	-26.8
Motor vehicles (units)	1,402,000	8.0
Tractors (units)	46,000	21.8

The economic returns of industrial enterprises improved. In 1994, the industrial enterprise composite efficiency index rose to 97, up 0.4 percentage points over the previous year. However, the stockpiling of industrial goods increased; the number of losing enterprises increased; and the problem of arrears among enterprises was fairly serious. The industrial enterprises' general level of economic performance has yet to be raised.

The construction industry continued to develop steadily. In 1994, this sector's added value totaled 290 billion yuan, up 12 percent over the previous year. The floor space of buildings under construction by state-owned construction enterprises was 307 million square meters, up 15.1 percent over the previous year, with 120 million square meters completed during the year, about the same as the previous year. Per capita labor productivity was 8,968 yuan, an increase of 21.5 percent over the previous year, and the per capita profit and tax payment exceeded 1,660 yuan, but the number of losing enterprises in this sector increased slightly.

New progress was made in geological surveys. During the year, 150 principal mineral deposits were discovered or proven as industrial deposits; and major progress was made in surveying 58 mining areas. Seven hundred and ninety important geological reports that could be used for development were completed. Thirty minerals were found to have increased reserves, of which coal reserves increased 8.2 billion tons; copper, 1.2 million tons; pyrite, 53.3 million tons; and phosphorus, 90.61 million tons. A total of 15.9 billion yuan was spent as operating expenses in geological surveys. A total of 3.84 million meters of machine-driven core exploration drilling was completed.

III. Investment in Fixed Assets

Investment in fixed assets was brought under control to a certain extent. Investment in fixed assets completed during the year was 1.5926 trillion yuan, up 27.8 percent over the previous year (up 15.8 percent in terms of the actual work completed, when price increases were factored in), representing a drop of 30.8 percentage points in growth rate. Of this total, investment of state-owned units (including joint ventures, joint operations, and investment in the form of stock-holding between state-owned units and overseas entities; similarly hereinafter) was 1.1354 trillion yuan, up 34.2 percent; that of collective units was 275.8 billion yuan, up 23.6 percent; and individual investment by urban and rural residents was 181.4 billion yuan, up 22.9 percent.

Of the investment of state-owned units, capital construction investment was 628.7 billion yuan, up 35.3 percent over the previous year; technical innovation and transformation project investment was 284.2 billion yuan, up 29.6 percent; real estate investment was 179.6 billion yuan, up 41.3 percent; and investment in other fields was 42.9 billion yuan, up 24.8 percent. Investment in central government projects was 354.4 billion yuan, up 37.7; and investment in local government projects was 601.5 billion yuan, up 34.5 percent.

During the year, 76,492 capital construction and technical innovation and transformation projects costing more than 50,000 yuan were started, or 1,768 projects fewer than in the previous year. However, total investment in projects under construction was still too large.

continued...

NATIONAL ECONOMIC PERFORMANCE, 1994 (continued)

Planned investment in capital construction and technical innovation and transformation projects still under construction by the end of the year totaled 3,057.4 billion yuan, up 31.4 percent over the previous year.

The investment structure continued to improve. Of the investments of state-owned units, the proportion of investment in the energy sector was up from 20.7 percent to 21.8 percent; that in raw and semifinished materials was 11.9 percent, about the same as in the previous year; and that in posts and telecommunications projects rose from 4 percent to 5.3 percent. However, the proportion of investment in agriculture continued to decline and dropped to 1.9 percent, down 0.3 percentage points from the previous year. The proportion of investment in transportation fell from 16.2 in 1993 to 15.4 percent.

New progress was made in the construction of key projects. During the year, 105.1 billion yuan was invested in 151 key projects listed in the state plan, surpassing the planned investment target for the year. Of the key state projects, 72, including single-item projects, were completed and put into operation. A total of 137 large and medium capital construction projects and 244 above-norm technical innovation and transformation projects were completed and put into operation in various parts of the country.

The nation's capital construction led to increases in production capacity in the following major categories: 4.77 million tons of coal, 15.27 million kw in power generating capacity, 15.45 million tons in oil, 1.134 billion cubic meters in natural gas (including capacity increased as a result of technical innovation and other investments), 810,000 tons in steel, 92,200 motor vehicles, 480,000 tons in chemical fertilizers, 148,000 cubic meters in timber felling and transporting, 278.6 kilometers [km] of newly built railway lines, 1,342 km of double-track railway lines, 25.8 million tons of cargo handling capacity in coastal harbors, 16.22 million telephone lines in cities, 30,000 km of optical fibers, 10,000 km of new microwave circuits, and 493 km of expressway.

IV. Transportation, Posts and Telecommunications

Transportation and communications registered steady progress. The sector's added value was 224.7 billion yuan, an increase of 6 percent over 1993. However, the imbalance between transportation capacity and demand still remained.

Volume of Transportation by Various Means

	1994	Increase Over 1993 (percent)
Freight transport volume (bn tn-km)	3,327.5	9.1
Railway (bn tn-km)	1,246.2	4.1
Highway (bn tn-km)	448.1	10.1
Waterway (bn tn-km)	1,570.4	13.9
Airways (bn tn-km)	1.95	17.4
Pipelines (bn tn-km)	60.8	0.0
Passenger transport volume (bn person-km)	849.2	8.1
Railway (bn person-km)	363.7	4.4
Highway (bn person-km)	414.7	12.0
Waterway (bn person-km)	17.5	-10.8
Airways (bn person-km)	53.3	11.6
Cargo handled at major coastal ports (mn tn)	730	6.2
Of which: volume of exports and imports (mn tn)	270	11.1

Posts and telecommunications service maintained rapid growth. Total business transactions in 1994 came to 69.3 billion yuan, an increase of 50.2 percent over the previous year. New telephone subscribers in both urban and rural areas topped the 10 million mark, thus expanding the ratio of telephone subscribers in the country to 3.2 percent. Public telecommunications

continued...

NATIONAL ECONOMIC PERFORMANCE, 1994 (continued)

service improved. The number of ordinary telephone lines installed has reached 48.78 million, while the number of long-distance exchangers was 2.2 million. The telephone network's technical level was further improved. The ratio of long-distance transmission through digital control reached 80 percent, while that of numerical controlled city telephone exchangers was 97 percent. Block exchanger networks and public digital data networks were able to provide information needed by the national economy at the present stage. More than 2.9 million km of new postal roads were added to the old ones, and more computers were used to manage postal affairs.

V. Domestic and Market Prices

The domestic market for consumer goods remained flourishing. The retail sales of consumer goods in 1994 was 1,605.3 billion yuan, up 31.2 percent over the previous year, or an actual increase of 7.8 percent after allowing for price increases. Of this total, urban market sales amounted to 955.5 billion yuan, up 33.2 percent, while sales in rural areas came to 649.8 billion yuan, an increase of 28.4 percent.

Among the various economic sectors, retail sales of consumer goods in the nonstate-owned sector was brisk, with its ratio to total volume of retail sales increasing from 60.3 percent in 1993 to 66.3, while the volume of retail sales by state-owned commercial enterprises dropped from 39.7 percent in 1993 to 33.7 percent.

The means of production market was stable. The total volume of means of production marketed in 1994 came to 2,298 billion yuan, up 21.2 percent over the previous year, or an actual increase of 12 percent after allowing for price increases.

In the past two years, demands in society grew excessively fast, and the amount of currency issued exceeded the economy's capacity. The negative effects of these, plus the reduction in the output of some farm produce caused by natural disasters, the state's price adjustment made for policy implementation, and the promulgation of a number of price-sensitive macroeconomic reform measures combined to cause large increases in market prices, which became a prominent issue in the nation's economic life.

Increase (percent) in Prices Over the Previous Year by Category

Cost of living for residents	24.1
Of which: Urban areas	25.0
35 large and medium cities	24.8
Rural areas	23.4
Of which: food	31.8
Grain	50.7
Meat, poultry, and manufactured products	41.6
Edible vegetable oil	64.1
Eggs and egg products	15.0
Aquatic products	20.3
Fresh vegetable	38.2
Clothing	17.1
Household equipment and appliances	12.0
Medical and health products	11.7
Transportation and telecommunications equipment	7.8
Entertainment, education, and cultural products	12.5
Dwelling commodities	21.3
Service items	25.7
Retail price	21.7
Of which: Urban areas	20.9
35 large and medium cities	20.7
Rural areas	22.9
Retail price of agricultural capital goods	21.6
Farm produce procurement prices	39.9
Producer price of manufactured goods	19.5

continued...

NATIONAL ECONOMIC PERFORMANCE, 1994 (continued)

VI. Foreign Economic Relations

Foreign trade developed rapidly. Customs statistics showed that the value of exports in 1994 was US$121 billion, up 31.9 percent over the previous year, and the value of imports was US$115.7 billion, up 11.2 percent. Further improvement was made in the import and export structure. The proportion of machinery and electronic products in the export mix rose from 24.7 percent in 1993 to 26.4 percent. Of the products imported, the share of raw and semifinished materials and machinery and transportation equipment that were in short supply on the domestic market increased. The export of foreign-funded enterprises continued to grow by a big margin, with an annual export value of US$34.7 billion, up 37.6 percent, and its share in the total export rose from 27.5 percent in 1993 to 28.7 percent.

The amount of foreign capital actually utilized continued to increase. A total of $45.8 billion was actually used in 1994, an increase of 17.6 percent over the previous year. Of this total, $33.8 billion was in the form of direct foreign investment, up 22.8 percent. By the end of 1994, some 206,000 foreign-invested enterprises had been registered in China, 40,000 more than at the end of 1993.

Considerable progress was made in economic and technical cooperation with foreign countries. In 1994, overseas construction and labor projects contracted by China totaled US$7.99 billion, up 17.5 percent, and operational revenue reached US$5.97 billion, up 31.5 percent.

International tourism performed well. In 1994, 43.68 million foreigners; compatriots from Taiwan, Hong Kong, and Macao; and overseas Chinese came to China for tourism, visiting, business, or other purposes, up 5.2 percent from 1993. Foreign exchange revenue from tourism was US$7.323 billion, showing a fairly large increase over the previous year.

VII. Banking and Insurance

The financial situation was basically stable, savings deposits grew rather rapidly, and more credits were granted to support key state construction projects, industrial restructuring, efficient state-owned enterprises with marketable goods, and import and storage of major state materials.

At the end of 1994, savings deposits in various forms in state banks totaled 2,932.8 billion yuan, an increase of 794 billion yuan or 37.1 percent over the figure at the end of 1993. Of the total, enterprises' savings accounted for 1.1467 trillion yuan, up 273.5 billion yuan or 31.3 percent from the figure at the end of 1993. By the end of 1994, the banks had extended 3.1603 trillion yuan worth of loans, 516.1 billion yuan or 19.5 percent more than the amount extended by the end of 1993. Of the total, short- and medium-term loans accounted for 2.3428 trillion yuan, 19.3 percent higher than 1993, and medium- and long-term loans accounted for 717.3 billion yuan, 20 percent higher than 1993. At the end of 1994, the total money in circulation came to 728.9 billion yuan, up 24.3 percent over the previous year, while the amount of money supplied in 1994 was 142.4 billion yuan, and broad money (M2) rose 34.4 percent over the previous year. By the end of 1994, urban and rural residents' savings deposits had reached 2.1519 trillion yuan, an increase of 631.5 billion yuan or 41.5 percent over the end of 1993.

China's foreign exchange reserves increased by a large margin. The state had $51.6 billion in cash at the end of last year, $30.4 billion more than the beginning of the year.

The insurance sector made considerable progress. Insurance coverage of various kinds [cheng bao zong e 2110 0202 4920 7345] totaled 11.1735 trillion yuan last year, up 30.1 percent over the previous year. Income from insurance premiums [bao fei shou ru 0202 6316 2392 0354] reached 49.8 billion yuan, increasing 22.7 percent over 1993. Of the total, 33.6 billion yuan was from property insurance, and 16.2 billion yuan from life insurance. Indemnities for property insurance totaled 19.5 billion yuan, and those for life insurance totaled 10.1 billion yuan.

VIII. Science, Education, Culture, Public Health, and Sports

The ranks of scientific and technical personnel expanded. There were 26.58 million professionals and technicians of all specializations working in state-owned enterprises and institutions by

continued...

NATIONAL ECONOMIC PERFORMANCE, 1994 (continued)

the end of 1994, up 2.4 percent over the figure at the end of 1993. Nationwide, there were 5,860 state-owned independent research and development institutions at and above the county level, 3,000 university-affiliated research institutions, and 11,656 research institutions under large and medium industrial enterprises. A total of 2.415 million people were engaged in scientific and technological work, of whom 1.529 million were scientists and engineers.

Financial input for scientific and technological activities increased. Nationwide, units such as scientific and technological institutions, universities, and large and medium industrial enterprises spent 63 billion yuan on scientific and technological activities in 1994, of which 22.2 billion yuan went to research and development. The money spent on research and development was 13.3 percent higher than that spent in 1993 and accounted for 0.5 percent of the GDP.

New progress was made in science and technology. At the provincial and departmental levels, 26,000 key scientific and technological successes were made nationwide in 1994. These were the major scientific and technological successes: Our country had the world's most advanced atomic manipulation and processing capability, the national computer and network facility (NCFC) [abbreviation as received] linked up with domestic and international networks, 270 new strains of crops were cultivated, and the country invented a standard high-speed locomotive that travels 160 km per hour and the Dongfeng-4E heavy internal-combustion engine. The State Natural Science Fund provided 310 million yuan in funds for 3,537 scientific projects. Our country constructed another key state laboratory, 15 state engineering research centers, six state industrial experimental bases, and 60 state-level industrial technology centers. In 1994, the state planned and completed 100 industrial experiment projects that developed, promoted, and absorbed new technology; and developed and put to use upon assessment 17 types of major technological equipment.

Quality inspection, standardization, patent application, and weather forecasting further improved. There were 3,000 organs in charge of supervising and testing product quality across China by the end of the year. Among them were 234 national centers for inspecting and testing product quality. A total of 1,414 national standards of all sorts were formulated and modified in the year. In 1994, China processed 78,000 patent applications from applicants both at home and abroad and approved 43,000. A total of 1,894 ultra-shortwave transmitting stations, constituting a weather warning system, were set up in China. Topographic departments surveyed and drew 67,761 maps of various scales and published 893 kinds of maps.

Technology markets enjoyed better business than any previous year. A total of 212,000 technological contracts with a total transaction amount of 22.88 billion yuan were signed in China in the year. In 1994, 33,997 units participated in "production-school-research" cooperation and established 12,844 projects for development through cooperation. A total of 454,000 people participated in these projects.

Various educational undertakings made new progress. A total of 51,000 postgraduate students were enrolled across the country, an increase of 9,000 postgraduate students over the previous year. There were 128,000 postgraduate students still attending school, an increase of 21,000 students over the previous year. Ordinary colleges and universities enrolled 900,000 students studying either regular college courses or professional training courses, a decrease of 2.6 percent from the previous year. There were 2.799 million college or university undergraduates, more than the previous year by 264,000 students. Vocational and technical secondary school education continued to develop. Various vocational and technical secondary schools boasted a total of 8.446 million undergraduates (including 1.822 million students at skilled workers' schools), accounting for 56 percent of the total number of undergraduates at the level of senior middle schools, which stood at 15.09 million.

The work to make nine-year compulsory education universal further developed. There were 43.17 million junior middle school students and 130 million primary school students in China. The attendance rate of primary school-age children reached 98.4 percent and the rate of primary school graduating students entering schools of a higher grade rose from the previous year's 81.8 percent to 86.6 percent. The rate of ordinary junior middle school students

continued...

NATIONAL ECONOMIC PERFORMANCE, 1994 (continued)

discontinuing their studies was 5.11 percent and that of primary school students discontinuing their studies was 1.85 percent. Conditions for running middle and primary schools continued to improve.

Adult education for formal schooling of a higher grade developed rapidly. Various forms of technical training were vigorously conducted. Colleges and universities for adults enrolled 1.017 million students studying either regular college courses or professional training courses (including students admitted into ordinary classes of the TV, Correspondence, and Evening Universities), a growth rate of 17.9 percent over the previous year; such colleges and universities boasted a total of 2.352 million undergraduates, a growth rate of 26.3 percent over the previous year; technical secondary schools for adults boasted 2.214 million undergraduates, more than the previous year by 146,000; the number of students attending technical training schools for adults increased 66.25 million; and there were 7.615 million adult students attending middle and primary schools. As a result, China obliterated the illiteracy of 4.862 million people in the year.

Cultural undertakings developed steadily. By the end of the year, there were 2,681 theatrical performance troupes, 2,875 cultural halls, 2,597 public libraries, 1,140 museums, 3,585 archive establishments, 1,108 broadcasting stations, 748 mediumwave and shortwave broadcast transmitting stations and relay stations, 764 TV stations, and 1,123 TV transmitting stations and broadcast stations with a an output power of more than 1 kw in China. Broadcast and TV covered 77.4 and 83.3 percent of the population respectively. There were 109,000 units for showing all kinds of films. In 1994, 148 feature films were produced and 213 various new (long) motion pictures released; 16 films won (16) awards at international film festivals. A total of 18.67 billion copies of national and provincial-level newspapers, 2.25 billion volumes of various magazines, and 5.93 billion volumes (sheets) of books and publications came off the press.

Medical care and public health conditions improved. As of the end of 1994, there were 2.832 million hospital beds, an increase of 1.3 percent as compared with the previous year. There were 4.191 million professional medical workers and technicians, an increase of 2 percent over the previous year. Of this number, 1.882 million were physicians (including 1.425 million Chinese traditional and Western medical doctors [zhong xi yi shi 0022 6007 6829 1597]), an increase of 2.8 percent; and the number of senior and junior nurses was 1.094 million, an increase of 3.6 percent.

Physical culture and sports activities achieved marked results. In major competitions at home and abroad, Chinese athletes won 79 world championships. Twenty-six athletes and four teams set world records 72 times in 41 kinds of competition; 24 athletes and five teams set Asian records 44 times in 37 kinds of competition; and 73 athletes and 21 teams set national records 131 times in 89 kinds of competition. At the 12th Asian Games, the Chinese sports delegation scored first in both total number of gold medals and total number of medals. Mass physical culture and sports activities developed in an orderly manner under the national health program's guidance, with 87 percent of students of various schools reaching "national standards for physical culture and sports training.

IX. Population and the People's Living Condition

Positive results were achieved in family planning work. In 1994, the annual population growth rate was 1.77 percent, the death rate was 0.649 percent, and the natural growth rate was 1.121 percent. As of end the of 1994, the total population was 1.1985 billion, increasing by 13.33 million as compared with the end of 1993.

People's incomes increased steadily. The average annual living income of urban residents was 3,179 yuan, an increase of 36 percent over the previous year; after allowing for price increases, the actual increase was 8.8 percent. The average annual net income of rural residents was 1,220 yuan, an increase of 32 percent over the previous year; after allowing for price increases, the annual increase was 5 percent. However, the gap between regions and between urban and rural areas expanded, and the actual income of some residents decreased.

continued...

NATIONAL ECONOMIC PERFORMANCE, 1994 (continued)

Employment for workers developed steadily. There were over 170,000 employment offices of various types. The number of employed people in urban areas increased 7.15 million during 1994. As of the end of 1994, the number of unemployed people was 4.8 million, an unemployment rate of 2.9 percent. As of the end of 1994, there were 151 million staff members and workers in China's urban areas, an increase of 2.5 million. Some 13.22 million people were engaged in the work of private enterprises or were individual workers in urban areas, an increase of 2.06 million. Some 120 million people were engaged in the work of rural village and town enterprises, an increase of 7.22 million. Some 24.38 million people were engaged in the work of private enterprises or were individual workers in rural areas, an increase of 2.42 million.

Reform of the social security insurance system made new progress. Over 95 million staff members and workers joined unemployment insurance; over 80 million staff members and workers of various enterprises joined basic pension insurance; and over 18.5 million retired workers joined social insurance, which combines mutual assistance funds with individual accounts. Labor departments in various localities provided assistance to more than 1.8 million unemployed people and helped 1.06 million unemployed staff members and workers find jobs.

Wages for staff members and workers were raised relatively fast. The total amount of wages for staff members and workers in urban areas was 665 billion yuan, an increase of 35 percent over the previous year, and the average annual wage of staff members and workers was 4,510 yuan, an increase of 34 percent over the previous year; after allowing for price increases, the actual increases were 8 and 7.2 percent respectively.

Urban and rural living conditions improved further. A total of 200 million square meters of new buildings was completed in urban areas and 580 million square meters of new houses were built in rural areas in 1994.

Social welfare work further developed with each passing day. At the end of 1994, there were 940,000 beds in social welfare institutions of various types in China, with 730,000 clients. Some 43 million people in need received relief from the state. A social security system was established in 32 percent of rural townships. In 1994, there was a comparatively large development of an urban community service network/with 101,000 community service facilities established.

Further development was done in environmental protection. At the end of 1994, the nation's environmental protection department had 85,000 employees; there were 2,306 environment monitoring stations at various levels across the country, with 34,000 environment monitors. China now has 763 nature protection zones, 90 at the state level, covering 66.18 million hectares, accounting for 6.8 percent of the country's total area. As of the end of 1994, 325 sets of environmental protection standards had been formulated; 3,134 smoke and dust control zones, covering 11,588 square km, were built in 647 cities; and 1,928 noise control zones, covering 4,683 square km, were built in 573 cities. In 1994, 6,285 projects fighting environmental pollution were completed on schedule as required, absorbing an investment of 2.62 billion yuan.

1. All figures in this communique are preliminary, it does not include data for Taiwan Province and Hong Kong and Macao Regions.
2. Absolute values of GDP and added values of industries quoted in the communique are at current prices, whereas growth rates are at comparable prices.

X, 28 Feb 1995.

MAP OF ECONOMIC ZONES, 1995

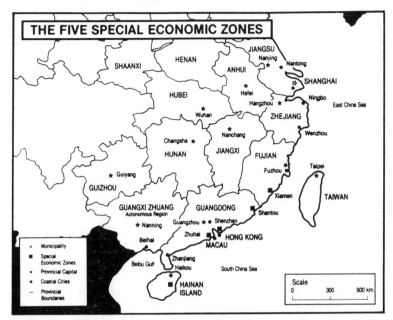

Asia Money and Finance, Jun 1995.

MARKET PRICES, 1995 (percent price over previous year)

	Percent
Consumer prices	24.1
City consumer prices	25.0
35 large and medium-sized city consumer prices	24.8
Rural consumer prices	23.4
Food in general	31.8
Grain	50.7
Meat, poultry, and other products	41.6
Vegetable oil	64.1
Egg products	15.0
Aquatic products	20.3
Fresh vegetables	38.2
Clothing	17.1
Household appliances and necessities	12.0
Medical treatment and health-care articles	11.7
Transportation and communications equipment	7.8
Entertainment, educational, and cultural items	12.5
Housing	21.3
Services	25.7
Commodity retail prices	21.7
City commodity retail prices	20.9
35 large and medium-sized city commodity retail prices	20.7
Rural commodity retail prices	22.9
Retail prices of agricultural means of production	21.6
Agricultural product procurement prices	39.9
Industrial goods ex-factory prices	19.5

Zhongguo Xinxi Bao, 18 Apr 1995.

III CHRONOLOGY, 1995

January
15 Chinese Vice-Premier and Foreign Minister Qian Qichen met with former US Secretary of State Henry Kissinger. In a friendly atmosphere, they exchanged views on Sino-US relations and international issues of common concern.

16 The Council of Agriculture guaranteed a donation of US$9,470 to sponsor an Asian "Tiger Ride". The bicycle ride through 15 tiger reserves in India, Butan and Nepal was to raise tiger conservation awareness.

17 Workers at the Japanese owned Panasonic Motor Factory in Zhuhai ended a one day strike after management opened wage negotiations.

19 A Chinese government spokesman denied that Deng Xiaoping was dying. Foreign ministry spokesman Shen Guofang said: "In general for an old man in his 90s, Deng Xiaoping is in good health."

20 Chinese Vice Premier and Foreign Minister Qian Qichen visited five African countries. The purpose of the visit was to show Africa that China attaches great importance to its relations with African nations.

February
7 China planned to hold 26 industrial exhibitions of various kinds in Tokyo, Paris, Chicago, Seoul, Sao Paulo and Frankfurt and twenty other cities in 1995.

10 A ceremony was held in Osaka, Japan to mourn 21 Chinese students killed in the Hanshin earthquake in Japan.

12 The Chinese Envoy to the UN told delegates that his government is firmly opposed to the exploitation of human rights for political purposes.

14 A well informed source in Beijing revealed that Deng Xiaoping, the supreme leader of China is unconscious and is barely alive with the help of an oxygen mask.

15 Catholics from two mountain villages in Hebei's Liangshou county fled their homes to escape brutal torture they claimed officials meted out under the Government compulsory birth-control program.

March
6 Chen Jinjua, minister in charge of the State Planning Commission called for stricter supervision and control of market prices.

11 State Council Premier Li Peng met with the Japanese Prime Minister Tomiichi Murayama. Li Peng said he appreciated Japan's continued support of the Sino-Japanese Joint Declaration and persisting in its one China policy.

22 Chinese scientists met to discuss artificially affecting the weather during the past 30 years. This meeting was part of an on-going program to help relieve natural disasters.

29 China signed agreements on two international loans totaling US$150 million. The loans were partially underwritten by the World Bank.

April
5 Wu Guofang, vice premier of the PRC State Council, met with a Republic of Korea (ROK) delegation to discuss China-ROK trade and economic relations.

10 Wang Jianye, a former section head of the Shenzhen Planning Commission, was sentenced to death after being convicted of taking bribes totaling more than 10 million yuan, bigamy and illegally crossing the border.

17 Chinese Vice-Premier and Foreign Minister Qian Qichen met with Dutch Deputy Prime Minister and Minister of Foreign Affairs Hans Van Mierlo to discuss economic affairs. The Netherlands is China's fifth largest trade partner in Western Europe.

26 The Swiss consulate general in Shanghai was inaugurated, making it the 24th consulate general in the city.

continued...

May

4   Officials pointed to the development of Chain Stores as evidence of structural reform. Stores grew at the rate of 200 annually and were popular with the people.

6   According to a unnamed source China's million strong armed police were a barrier to social reform and a source of fear in the general populace.

15   Heavy rains eased the drought which afflicted the country for months and was particularly hard on north China.

19   China announced it will open its archives on Japan's germ warfare research in northeastern China during WWII.

30   Taiwan scholar Li Teng-hui was denied entry to Australia. Australian Foreign Minister Gareth Evans said that a visit to Australia by Taiwan's Li Teng-hui was out of the question. He said Australia's policy of one-China had not changed.

June

1   The Music Copyright Society of China signed a mutual representation agreement with the British Performing Rights Society.

7   Research by Chinese medical specialists determined that hypertension or high blood pressure, may be the result of salt sensitivity, besides inheritance factors.

12   A total of 21 domestic airlines named Wuhan as a destination since the opening of Tianhe International Airport.

29   According to Hong Hu, vice-minister of the State Commission for Restructuring the Economy, improving the state-owned sector and speeding the structural readjustment of State-owned businesses is key to enterprise restructuring.

July

3   Shandong Branch of China's Dongfang Airline Company opened scheduled international flights between Quingdao and Osaka, Japan. This air service will carry 244 passengers per trip in a wide airframe passenger plane.

13   China's inflation rate was on a month-by-month downward trend in the first six months of 1995. This according to a July, 1995 bulletin from the State Statistics Bureau.

18   China's Minister of Agriculture said natural disasters in the southern provinces will not affect overall grain output in 1995. Further, the minister said China will import only a small amount of grain in 1995 and that only for variety.

27   The Bank of China announced individual deposits of 205 billion yuan. The BOC saw the fastest growth in renminbi yuan individual savings growing from 100 billion yuan to 205 billion.

August

6   China and Zambia signed a special loan agreement to boost operations of the China-aided Tanzania-Zambia Railway.

7   Securities Administration Director Zhou Daojiong stated that despite rumors to the contrary China has no plans to open a new stock exchange.

20   One of Australia's largest companies, Broken Hill Propriety, has showed an interest in China's geological prospecting industry. The major BHP undertaking was lead and zinc prospecting in Sichuan.

29   Vice-Premier Qian Qichen called for a freeze on Hong Kong's laws to assist the peaceful transition of the territory to the Chinese authorities in 1997.

September

1   China led the world in cement production for the tenth year. Production was at an annual rate of 50 million tons.

8   The Indian Warships INS Knanjar and INS Saryu, a guided missile corvette and offshore cruiser, visited Shanghai. This constituted the first Indian ship visits to China since 1958.

15   The United Nations Fourth World Conference on Women ended at Beijing International Convention Center after adopting a Platform for Action and Beijing Declaration.

continued...

21   A Beijing source disclosed that CPC elder Deng Xiaoping's health was declining and that his mind was not clear. The source said medical opinion was that Deng given proper care and treatment could live another two years.

October
19   Circulation of counterfeit banknotes was rampant in the first half of 1995 with bogus notes to the value of RMB 84 million being seized. During the entire year of 1994 the same RMB amount of counterfeit banknotes was confiscated.
21   A "South China Morning Post" editorial stated China's planned emasculation of the Bill of Rights is an outrageous act which raises doubts about Hong Kong's promised autonomy after 1997.
23   Taiwan's Premier Lien Chan said the Chinese government has clear guidelines for relations between the two sides of the Taiwan Strait, and the lack of consensus among Mainland China's leadership means the development of cross-strait ties may be stalled for some time.
27   Mr. Hung Huot, foreign minister of the Royal government of Cambodia said that Cambodia follows a foreign policy of "only one China."

November
2   The Chinese military issued a general order banning fishermen along the coast of the East China Sea from entering and operating on the East China Sea fishing ground as of November 1995.
16   China and the United States settled a dispute over the principle of non-discrimination among the 18 members of the Asia Pacific Economic Cooperation forum.
23   Hong Kong's governor vowed to reject any mainland moves to establish a shadow Hong Kong government ahead of the 1997 transfer of sovereignty.
26   Sixteen million people in east China's Shandong Province have taken out old-age insurance since the rural pension system began in 1991. Over 24,000 received a monthly pension in 1995.

December
1   An international drug baron was ordered to hand over HK$57 million in the biggest confiscation order in Hong Kong history. Chun Yeung also received a 25 year prison sentence.
8   Shandong province authorities planned to close, transform or merge 350 enterprises within two years in an effort to lessen the province's pollution problem.
13   The trial for dissident, Wei Jingsheng opened. Mr. Wei who is defending himself was charged with planning to overthrow the state. He faced a minimum sentence of 10 years or possible execution.
27   Russia confirmed that Russian President Boris Yeltsin was scheduled to visit China in 1996. Earlier reports by Russian and Chinese officials had denied the visit was scheduled.

GOVERNMENT LEADERS, 1995

HEAD OF STATE

President: JIANG ZEMIN (elected by the Eighth National People's Congress on 27 March 1993).
Vice-President: RONG YIREN.

STATE COUNCIL
(January 1994)

Premier: LI PENG.

Vice-Premiers: ZHU RONGJI, ZOU JIAHUA, QIAN QICHEN, LI LANQING.

State Councillors:

LI TIEYING	CHEN JUNSHENG
Gen. CHI HAOTIAN	ISMAIL AMAT
SONG JIAN	PENG PEIYUN
LI GUIXIAN	LUO GAN

Secretary-General: LUO GAN.

Minister of Foreign Affairs: QIAN QICHEN.

Minister of National Defence: Gen. CHI HAOTIAN.

Minister of State Economic and Trade Commission: WANG ZHONGYU.

Minister of State Planning Commission: CHEN JINHUA.

Minister of State Commission for Economic Restructuring: LI TIEYING.

Minister of State Education Commission: ZHU KAIXUAN.

Minister of State Science and Technology Commission: SONG JIAN.

Minister of State Commission of Science, Technology and Industry for National Defence: DING HENGGAO.

Minister of State Nationalities Affairs Commission: ISMAIL AMAT.

Minister of Machine-Building Industry: HE GUANGYUAN.

Minister of Public Security: TAO SIJU.

Minister of State Security: JIA CHUNWANG.

Minister of Civil Affairs: DOJE CERING.

Minister of Justice: XIAO YANG.

Minister of Supervision: CAO QINGZE.

Minister of Finance: LIU ZHONGLI.

Minister of Internal Trade: ZHANG HAORUO.

Minister of Foreign Trade and Economic Co-operation: WU YI.

Minister of Agriculture: LIU JIANG.

Minister of Forestry: XU YOUFANG.

Minister of Power Industry: SHI DAZHEN.

Minister of Coal Industry: WANG SENHAO.

Minister of Electronics Industry: HU QILI.

Minister of Water Resources: NIU MAOSHENG.

Minister of Construction: HOU JIE.

Minister of Geology and Mineral Resources: ZHU XUN.

Minister of Metallurgical Industry: LIU QI.

continued...

GOVERNMENT LEADERS, 1995 (continued)

Minister of Chemical Industry: Ms GU XIULIAN.
Minister of Railways: HAN ZHUBIN.
Minister of Communications: HUANG ZHENDONG.

Minister of Posts and Telecommunications: WU JICHUAN.
Minister of Personnel: SONG DEFU.
Minister of Labour: LI BOYONG.
Minister of Culture: LIU ZHONGDE.
Minister of Radio, Film and Television: AI ZHISHENG.
Minister of Public Health: CHEN MINZHANG.
Minister of State Physical Culture and Sports Commission: WU SHAOZU.
Minister of State Family Planning Commission: Ms PENG PEIYUN.
Governor of the People's Bank of China: ZHU RONGJI.
Auditor-General of Auditing Administration: LU PEIJIAN.

MINISTRIES

Ministry of Agriculture: Fuxing Lu, B 15, Beijing 100862; tel. (1) 8512594; telex 22349; fax (1) 8515048.

Ministry of Chemical Industry: Liupukang, Andingmenwai, Beijing; tel. (1) 446561; fax (1) 4215982.

Ministry of Civil Affairs: 9 Xihuangchenggennan Jie, Xicheng Qu, Beijing; tel. (1) 551731.

Ministry of Coal Industry: Beijing.

Ministry of Commerce: 45 Fuxingmennei Dajie, Xicheng Qu, Beijing 100801; tel. (1) 668581; telex 20032.

Ministry of Communications: 10 Fuxing Lu, Haidian Qu, Beijing; tel. (1) 8642371; telex 22462.

Ministry of Construction: Baiwanzhuang, Western Suburb, Beijing; tel. (1) 8992833; telex 222302.

Ministry of Culture: Jia 83, Donganmen Bei Jie, Beijing; tel. (1) 442131.

Ministry of Electronics Industry: Beijing.

Ministry of Finance: 3 Nansanxiang, Sanlihe, Xicheng Qu, Beijing; tel. (1) 868731; telex 222308.

Ministry of Foreign Affairs: 225 Chaoyangmennei Dajie, Dongsi, Beijing; tel. (1) 553831.

Ministry of Foreign Trade and Economic Co-operation: 2 Dongchangan Jie, Dongcheng Qu, Beijing 100731; tel. (1) 553031; telex 22168.

Ministry of Forestry: 18 Hepingli Dongjie, Dongcheng Qu, Beijing; tel. (1) 463061; telex 22237.

Ministry of Geology and Mineral Resources: 64 Funei Dajie, Beijing 100812; tel. (1) 6031144; telex 22531.

Ministry of Internal Trade: 25 Yuetanbei Jie, Xicheng Qu, Beijing.

Ministry of Justice: 11 Xiaguangli, Sanyuanqiao, Chaoyang Qu, Beijing; tel. (1) 668971.

Ministry of Labour: 12 Hepinglizhong Jie, Dongcheng Qu, Beijing.

Ministry of Machine-Building Industry: Sanlihe, Xicheng Qu, Beijing.

Ministry of Metallurgical Industry: 46 Dongsixi Dajie, Beijing; tel. (1) 557431.

continued...

GOVERNMENT LEADERS, 1995 (continued)

Ministry of National Defence: Beijing; tel. (1) 667343.

Ministry of Personnel: 12 Hepinglizhong Jie, Beijing.

Ministry of Posts and Telecommunications: 13 Xichangan Jie, Beijing 100804; tel. (1) 660540; telex 222187.

Ministry of Power Industry: 1 Baiguang Lu, Ertiao, Xuanwu Qu, Beijing.

Ministry of Public Health: 44 Houhaibeiyan, Xicheng Qu, Beijing 100725; tel. (1) 4034433; telex 22193.

Ministry of Public Security: 14 Dongchangan Jie, Beijing; tel. (1) 553871.

Ministry of Radio, Film and Television: Fu Xing Men Wai Dajie 2, POB 4501, Beijing; tel. (1) 862753; telex 22236; fax (1) 8012174.

Ministry of Railways: 10 Fuxing Lu, Haidian Qu, Beijing; tel. (1) 864061; telex 22483.

Ministry of State Security: 14 Dongchangan Jie, Beijing; tel. (1) 553871.

Ministry of Supervision: 35 Huayuanbei Lu, Haidian Qu, Beijing 100083; tel. (1) 2016113.

Ministry of Water Resources: 1 Baiguang Lu, Ertiao, Xuanwu Qu, Beijing 100761; tel. (1) 3260495; telex 22466; fax (1) 3260365.

STATE COMMISSIONS

State Commission for Economic Restructuring: 22 Xianmen Jie, Beijing.

State Commission of Science, Technology and Industry for National Defence: Beijing.

State Economic and Trade Commission: Beijing.

State Education Commission: 37 Damucang Hutong, Xicheng Qu, Beijing; tel. (1) 658731.

State Family Planning Commission: 4 Cixiansi, Xizhimenwai, Haidian Qu, Beijing; tel. (1) 668971.

State Nationalities Affairs Commission: 252 Taipingqiao Jie, Beijing; tel. (1) 666931.

State Physical Culture and Sports Commission: 9 Tiyuguan Lu, Chongwen Qu, Beijing 100763; tel. (1) 7012233; telex 22323; fax (1) 7015858.

State Planning Commission: 38 Yuetannan Jie, Xicheng Qu, Beijing.

State Science and Technology Commission: 54 Sanlihe, Fuxingmenwai, 100862 Beijing; tel. (1) 8012594; telex 22349; fax (1) 8012594.

Legislature

QUANGUO RENMIN DIABIAO DAHUI
(National People's Congress)

The National People's Congress (NPC) is the highest organ of state power, and is indirectly elected for a five-year term. The first plenary session of the Eighth NPC was convened in Beijing in March 1993, and was attended by 2,921 deputies. The first session of the Eighth National Committee of the Chinese People's Political Consultative Conference (CPPCC, Chair. LI RUIHUAN), a revolutionary united front organization led by the Communist Party, took place simultaneously. The CPPCC holds discussions and consultations on the important affairs in the nation's political life. Members of the CPPCC National Committee or of its Standing

continued...

GOVERNMENT LEADERS, 1995 (continued)

Committee may be invited to attend the NPC or its Standing Committee as observers.

Standing Committee

In March 1993 134 members were elected to the Standing Committee, in addition to the following.

Chairman: QIAO SHI.

Vice-Chairmen:

TIAN JIYUN	WANG BINGQIAN
WANG HANBIN	PAGBALHA GELEG NAMGYAI
NI ZHIFU	WANG GUANGYING
Ms CHEN MUHUA	CHENG SIYUAN
FEI XIAOTONG	LU JIAXI
SUN QIMENG	BUHE
LEI JIEQIONG	TOMUR DAWAMAT
QIN JIWEI	LI PEIYAO
LI XIMING	WU JIEPING

Secretary-General: CAO ZHI.

Provincial People's Congresses

Province	Chairman of Standing Committee of People's Congress
Anhui	MENG FULIN
Fujian	(vacant)
Gansu	LU KEJIAN
Guangdong	LIN RUO
Guizhou	(vacant)
Hainan	DU QINGLIN
Hebei	LU CHUANZAN
Heilongjiang	SUN WEIBEN
Henan	LI CHANGCHUN
Hubei	GUAN GUANGFU
Hunan	LIU FUSHENG
Jiangsu	SHEN DAREN
Jiangxi	MAO ZHIYONG
Jilin	HE ZHUKANG
Liaoning	QUAN SHUREN
Qinghai	HUANJUE CENAM
Shaanxi	ZHANG BOXING
Shandong	LI ZHEN
Shanxi	LU GONGXUN
Sichuan	YANG XIZONG
Yunnan	YIN JUN
Zhejiang	LI ZEMIN

Special Municipalities	
Beijing	ZHANG JIANMIN
Shanghai	YE GONGQI
Tianjin	NIE BICHU

continued…

GOVERNMENT LEADERS, 1995 (continued)

Autonomous Regions

Guangxi Zhuang	LIU MINGZU
Nei Monggol	WANG QUN
Ningxia Hui	MA SIZHONG
Tibet (Xizang)	RAIDI
Xinjiang Uygur	AMUDUN NIYAZ

People's Governments

Province	Governor
Anhui	FU XISHOU
Fujian	JIA QINGLIN
Gansu	ZHANG WULE (acting)
Guangdong	ZHU SENLIN
Guizhou	CHEN SHINENG
Hainan	RUAN CHONGWU
Hebei	YE LIANSONG
Heilongjiang	SHAO QIHUI
Henan	MA ZHONGCHEN
Hubei	JIA ZHIJIE
Hunan	CHEN BANGZHU
Jiangsu	CHEN HUANYOU
Jiangxi	WU GUANZHENG
Jilin	GAO YAN
Liaoning	YUE QIFENG
Qinghai	TIAN CHENGPING
Shaanxi	BAI QINGCAI
Shandong	ZHAO ZHIHAO
Shanxi	SUN WENSHENG (acting)
Sichuan	XIAO YANG
Yunnan	HE ZHIQIANG
Zhejiang	WAN XUEYUAN

Special Municipalities	Mayor
Beijing	LI QIYAN
Shanghai	HUANG JU
Tianjin	ZHANG LICHANG

Autonomous Regions	Chairman
Guangxi Zhuang	CHENG KEJIE
Nei Monggol	WU LIJI
Ningxia Hui	BAI LICHEN
Tibet (Xizang)	GYAINCAIN NORBU
Xinjiang Uygur	ABULAIDI AMUDUREXITI (acting)

Political Organizations

COMMUNIST PARTY

Zhongguo Gongchan Dang (Chinese Communist Party—CCP): Beijing; f. 1921; 50.32m. mems in 1991; at the 14th Nat. Congress of the CCP, in October 1992, a new Cen. Cttee of 189 full mems and 130 alternate mems was elected; at its first plenary session the 14th Cen. Cttee appointed a new Politburo.

Fourteenth Central Committee

General Secretary: JIANG ZEMIN.

continued...

GOVERNMENT LEADERS, 1995 (continued)

Politburo

Members of the Standing Committee:

JIANG ZEMIN
LI PENG
QIAO SHI
LI RUIHUAN

ZHU RONGJI
Gen. LIU HUAQING
HU JINTAO

Other Full Members:

DING GUANGEN
TIAN JIYUN
LI LANQING
LI TIEYING
Gen. YANG BAIBING
WU BANGGUO

ZOU JIAHUA
CHEN XITONG
JIANG CHUNYUN
QIAN QICHEN
WEI JIANXING
XIE FEI

Alternate Members: WEN JIABAO, WANG HANBIN.

Secretariat

HU JINTAO
DING GUANGEN
WEI JIANXING

WEN JIABAO
REN JIANXIN

OTHER POLITICAL ORGANIZATIONS

China Association for Promoting Democracy: 98 Xinanli Guloufangzhuangchang, Beijing 100009; tel. (1) 4033452; f. 1945; mems drawn mainly from literary, cultural and educational circles; Chair. LEI JIEQIONG; Sec.-Gen. CHEN YIQUN.

China Democratic League: 1 Beixing Dongchang Hutong, Beijing 100006; tel. (1) 5137983; telex 211246; fax (1) 5125090; f. 1941; formed from reorganization of League of Democratic Parties and Organizations of China; mems mainly intellectuals active in education, science and culture; Chair. FEI XIAOTONG; Sec.-Gen. YU ZEYOU.

China Democratic National Construction Association: 93 Beiheyan Dajie, 100006 Beijing; tel. (1) 5136677; telex 22044; f. 1945; mems mainly industrialists and businessmen; Chair. SUN QIMENG.

China Zhi Gong Dang (Party for Public Interests): Beijing; f. 1925; reorg. 1947; party for public interests; mems are mainly returned overseas Chinese; Chair. DONG YINCHU; Sec.-Gen. WANG SONGDA.

Chinese Communist Youth League: 10 Qianmen Dongdajie, Beijing 100051; tel. (1) 7012288; fax (1) 7018131; f. 1922; 56m. mems; First Sec. of Cen. Cttee LI KEQIANG.

Chinese Peasants' and Workers' Democratic Party: f. 1930 as the Provisional Action Cttee of the Kuomintang; took present name in 1947; 47,000 mems, active mainly in public health and medicine; Chair. LU JIAXI; Sec.-Gen. SONG JINSHENG.

Jiu San (3 September) Society: f. 1946; fmrly Democratic and Science Soc.; mems mainly scientists and technologists; Chair. WU JIEPING; Sec.-Gen. LIU RONGHAN.

Revolutionary Committee of the Chinese Kuomintang: tel. (1) 550388; f. 1948; mainly fmr Kuomintang mems, and those in cultural, educational, health and financial fields; Chair. LI PEIYAO.

Taiwan Democratic Self-Government League: f. 1947; recruits Taiwanese living on the mainland; Chair. CAI ZIMIN; Sec.-Gen. PAN YUANJING.

continued...

GOVERNMENT LEADERS, 1995 (continued)

Diplomatic Representation

EMBASSIES IN THE PEOPLE'S REPUBLIC OF CHINA

Afghanistan: 8 Dong Zhi Men Wai Dajie, Chao Yang Qu, Beijing; tel. (1) 5321582; Ambassador: (vacant).

Albania: 28 Guang Hua Lu, Beijing; tel. (1) 5321120; telex 211207; Ambassador: TAHIR BAJRAM ELEZI.

Algeria: Dong Zhi Men Wai Dajie, 7 San Li Tun, Beijing; tel. (1) 5321231; telex 22437; Ambassador: ABED MAHIEDDINE.

Argentina: Bldg 11, 5 Dong Jie, San Li Tun, Beijing; tel. (1) 5322090; telex 22269; Ambassador: CARLOS LUCAS BLANCO.

Australia: 21 Dong Zhi Men Wai Dajie, Beijing 100600; tel. (1) 5322331; telex 22263; fax (1) 5324605; Ambassador: MICHAEL LIGHTOWLER.

Austria: 5 Xiu Shui Nan Jie, Jian Guo Men Wai, Beijing; tel. (1) 5322061; telex 22258; fax (1) 5321505; Ambassador: DIETRICH BUKOWSKI.

Bangladesh: 42 Guang Hua Lu, Beijing; tel. (1) 5321819; telex 22143; fax (1) 5324346; Ambassador: C. M. SHAFI SAMI.

Belgium: 6 San Li Tun Lu, Beijing 100600; tel. (1) 5321736; telex 22260; fax (1) 5325097; Ambassador: CLAIRE KIRSCHEN.

Benin: 38 Guang Hua Lu, Beijing 100600; tel. (1) 5322741; telex 22599; fax (1) 5325103; Ambassador: AUGUSTE ALAVO.

Bolivia: 2-3-1 Tayuan Diplomatic Office Bldg, Beijing 100600; tel. (1) 5323074; telex 210415; fax (1) 5324686; Ambassador: CARLOS BOHRT IRAHOLA.

Brazil: 27 Guang Hua Lu, Beijing; tel. (1) 5322881; telex 22117; fax (1) 5322751; Ambassador: ROBERTO ABDENUR.

Bulgaria: 4 Xiu Shui Bei Jie, Jian Guo Men Wai, Beijing; tel. (1) 5322231; Ambassador: STEFAN GABEROV.

Burkina Faso: 9 Dong Liu Jie, San Li Tun, Beijing; tel. (1) 5322550; telex 22666; fax (1) 5323343; Ambassador: RAYMOND EDOUARD OUEDRAOGO. (Relations suspended, February 1994.)

Burundi: 25 Guang Hua Lu, Beijing 100600; tel. (1) 5321801; telex 22271; fax (1) 5322381; Ambassador: THARCISSE NTAKIBIRORA.

Cameroon: 7 San Li Tun, Dong Wu Jie, Beijing; tel. (1) 5321771; telex 22256; Ambassador: ELEIH ELLE ETIAN.

Canada: 19 Dong Zhi Men Wai Da Jie, Beijing 100600; tel. (1) 5323536; telex 222445; fax (1) 5324072; Ambassador: FRED BILD.

Chad: 21 Guang Hua Lu, Jianguo Men Wai, Beijing; telex 22287; Ambassador: HELENA TCHIOUNA.

Chile: 1 Dong Si Jie, San Li Tun, Beijing; tel. (1) 5321641; telex 22252; fax (1) 5323170; Ambassador: EDUARDO BRAVO.

Colombia: 34 Guang Hua Lu, Beijing 100600; tel. (1) 5321713; telex 22460; fax (1) 5321969; Ambassador: ALVARO ESCALLÓN.

Congo: 7 San Li Tun, Dong Si Jie, Beijing; tel. (1) 5321644; telex 20428; Ambassador: ALPHONSE MOUISSOU-POUATI.

Côte d'Ivoire: Beijing; tel. (1) 5321482; telex 22723; Ambassador: ANET N'ZI NANAN KOLIABO.

Croatia: 2-2-22 Jian Guo Men Wai, Beijing 100600; tel. (1) 5326241; fax (1) 5326257; Ambassador: ANDRIJA KOJAKOVIĆ.

Cuba: 1 Xiu Shui Nan Jie, Jian Guo Men Wai, Beijing; tel. (1) 5321714; telex 22249; Ambassador: JOSÉ ARMANDO GUERRA MENCHERO.

continued...

GOVERNMENT LEADERS, 1995 (continued)

Cyprus: 2-13-2, Tayuan Diplomatic Office Bldg, Liang Ma He Nan Lu, Chao Yang Qu, Beijing 100600; tel. (1) 5325057; fax (1) 5325060; Ambassador: MYRNA Y. KLEOPAS.

Czech Republic: Ri Tan Lu, Jian Guo Men Wai, Beijing; tel. (1) 5321531; telex 222553.

Denmark: 1 Dong Wu Jie, San Li Tun, Beijing; tel. (1) 5322431; telex 22255; fax (1) 5322439; Ambassador: WILLIAM FRIIS-MØLLER.

Ecuador: 2-41 San Li Tun, Beijing; tel. (1) 5322264; telex 22710; fax (1) 5323158; Ambassador: CÉSAR ENRIQUE ROMÁN GONZÁLEZ.

Egypt: 2 Ri Tan Dong Lu, Beijing; tel. (1) 5322541; telex 22134; Ambassador: SAMIR BORHAN RAGUEB.

Equatorial Guinea: 2 Dong Si Jie, San Li Tun, Beijing; tel. (1) 5323709; Ambassador: LINO-SIMA EKUA AVOMO.

Eritrea: Beijing; Ambassador: ERMIAS DEBESSAI HIDAD.

Ethiopia: 3 Xiu Shui Nan Jie, Jian Guo Men Wai, Beijing; telex 22306; Ambassador: HAILE GIORGIS BROUK.

Finland: Tayuan Diplomatic Office Bldg, 1-10-1, Beijing 100600; tel. (1) 5321806; telex 22129; fax (1) 5321884; Ambassador: ILKKA RISTIMÄKI.

France: 3 Dong San Jie, San Li Tun, Beijing; tel. (1) 5321331; telex 22183; Ambassador: FRANÇOIS MARCEL PLAISANT.

Gabon: 36 Guang Hua Lu, Beijing; tel. (1) 5322810; telex 22110; fax (1) 532-2621; Ambassador: BENJAMIN LEGNONGO-NDUMBA.

Germany: 5 Dong Zhi Men Wai Dajie, Beijing 100600; tel. (1) 5322161; telex 22259; fax (1) 5325336; Ambassador: Dr ARMIN FREITAG.

Ghana: 8 San Li Tun Lu, Beijing; tel. (1) 5321319; telex 210462; fax (1) 5323602; Ambassador: (vacant).

Greece: 19 Guang Hua Lu, Beijing; tel. (1) 5321317; telex 22267; Ambassador: PANDELIS S. MENGLIDES.

Guinea: 7 Dong San Jie, San Li Tun, Beijing; tel. (1) 5323649; telex 22706; Ambassador: ABOU CAMARA.

Guyana: 1 Xiu Shui Dong Jie, Jian Guo Men Wai, Beijing 100600; tel. (1) 5321601; telex 22295; Ambassador: RONALD MORTIMER AUSTIN.

Hungary: 10 Dong Zhi Men Wai Dajie, Beijing 100600; tel. (1) 5321431; fax (1) 5325053; Ambassador: KLÁRA MÉSZÁROS.

Iceland: Beijing; Ambassador: INGVI S. INGVARSSON.

India: 1 Ri Tan Dong Lu, Beijing; tel. (1) 5321927; telex 22126; Ambassador: CHANDRASHEKAR DASGUPTA.

Indonesia: San Li Tun, Diplomatic Office, Bldg B, Beijing 100600; tel. (1) 5325484; fax (1) 5325368; Ambassador: ABDURRAHMAN GUNA-DIRDJA.

Iran: Dong Liu Ji, San Li Tun, Beijing; tel. (1) 5322040; telex 22253; fax (1) 5321403; Ambassador: M. H. TAROMI RAD.

Iraq: 3 Ri Tan Dong Lu, Chao Yang Qu, Beijing; tel. (1) 5321950; telex 22288; Ambassador: MOHAMED AMIN AHMED AL-JAF.

Ireland: 3 Ri Tan Dong Lu, Beijing 100600; tel. (1) 5322691; telex 22425; fax (1) 5322168; Ambassador: THELMA M. DORAN.

Israel: 1 Jian Guo Men Wai Dajie, Beijing 100004; tel. (1) 5052970; fax (1) 5050328; Ambassador: ZE'EV SUFOT.

continued...

GOVERNMENT LEADERS, 1995 (continued)

Italy: 2 Dong Er Jie, San Li Tun, Beijing 100600; tel. (1) 5322131; telex 22414; fax (1) 5324676; Ambassador: OLIVIERO ROSSI.

Japan: 7 Ri Tan Lu, Jian Guo Men Wai, Beijing; tel. (1) 5322361; telex 22275; Ambassador: MICHIHIKO KUNIHIRO.

Jordan: 54 Dong Liu Jie, San Li Tun, Beijing; tel. (1) 5323906; telex 22651; Ambassador: S. ALFARAJ.

Kazakhstan: Beijing; Ambassador: MURAT M. AUEZOV.

Kenya: 4 Xi Liu Jie, San Li Tun, Beijing; tel. (1) 5323381; telex 22311; Ambassador: JAMES SIMANI.

Korea, Democratic People's Republic: Ri Tan Bei Lu, Jian Guo Men Wai, Beijing; telex 20448; Ambassador: CHU CHANG JUN.

Korea, Republic: Beijing; Ambassador: HWANG PYONG-TAE.

Kuwait: 23 Guang Hua Lu, Beijing 100600; tel. (1) 5322216; telex 22127; fax (1) 5321607; Ambassador: GHAZI AL-RAYES.

Kyrgyzstan: Beijing; Ambassador: M. S. IMANALIEV.

Laos: 11 Dong Jie, San Li Tun, Chao Yang Qu, Beijing 100600; tel. (1) 5321244; telex 22144; Ambassador: PONMEK DALALOI.

Lebanon: 51 Dong Liu Jie, San Li Tun, Beijing; tel. (1) 5322770; telex 22113; Ambassador: FARID SAMAHA.

Libya: 55 Dong Liu Jie, San Li Tun, Beijing; telex 22310; Secretary of the People's Bureau: MUFTAH OTMAN MADI.

Luxembourg: 21 Nei Wu Bu Jie, Beijing 100600; tel. (1) 5135937; telex 22638; fax (1) 5137268; Ambassador: GEORGES SANTER.

Madagascar: 3 Dong Jie, San Li Tun, Beijing; tel. (1) 5321353; telex 22140; Ambassador: JEAN-JACQUES MAURICE.

Malaysia: 13 Dong Zhi Men Wai Dajie, San Li Tun, Beijing; tel. (1) 5322531; telex 22122; Ambassador: Dato NOOR ADLAN YAHAYAUDDIN.

Mali: 8 Dong Si Jie, San Li Tun, Beijing 100600; tel. (1) 5321704; telex 22257; fax (1) 5321618; Ambassador: KAFOUGOUNA KONE.

Malta: 2-1-22, Tayuan Diplomatic Compound, Beijing 100600; tel. (1) 5323114; telex 22670; fax (1) 5326125; Chargé d'affaires: Dr JOSEPH PIROTTA.

Marshall Islands: Beijing; Ambassador: LAURENCE EDWARDS.

Mauritania: 9 Dong San Jie, San Li Tun, Beijing; tel. (1) 5321346; telex 22514; Ambassador: HAMOUD OULD ELY.

Mexico: 5 Dong Wu Jie, San Li Tun, Beijing 100600; tel. (1) 5322122; telex 22262; fax (1) 5323744; Ambassador: MANUEL RODRÍGUEZ ARRIAGA.

Mongolia: 2 Xiu Shui Bei Jie, Jian Guo Men Wai, Beijing; tel. (1) 5321203; telex 22262; Ambassador: KH. OLZVOY.

Morocco: 16 San Li Tun Lu, Beijing; tel. (1) 5321489; telex 22268; Ambassador: ABDERRAHMAN BOUCHAARA.

Mozambique: Ta Yuan 1-7-1, Beijing; tel. (1) 5323664; telex 22705; fax (1) 5325189; Ambassador: DANIEL SAUL MBANZA.

Myanmar: 6 Dong Zhi Men Wai Dajie, Chao Yang Qu, Beijing; tel. (1) 5321584; telex 10416; Ambassador: U SET.

Nepal: 1 Xi Liu Jie, San Li Tun Lu, Beijing; tel. (1) 5321795; telex 210408; fax (1) 5323251; Ambassador: Prof. BASUDEV CHANDRA MALLA.

continued...

GOVERNMENT LEADERS, 1995 (continued)

Netherlands: 1-15-2 Tayuan Diplomatic Office Bldg, 14 Liang Ma He Nan Lu, Beijing 100600; tel. (1) 5321131; telex 22277; fax (1) 5324689; Ambassador: D. J. VAN HOUTEN.

New Zealand: 1 Ri Tan, Dong Er Jie, Chaoyang Qu, Beijing 100600; tel. (1) 5322731; fax (1) 5324317; Ambassador: CHRIS ELDER.

Nigeria: 2 Dong Wu Jie, San Li Tun, Beijing; telex 22274; fax (1) 5321650; Chargé d'affaires a.i.: E. O. AMBODE.

Norway: 1 Dong Yi Jie, San Li Tun, Beijing; tel. (1) 5322261; telex 22266; fax (1) 5322392; Ambassador: JAN TORE HOLVIK.

Oman: 6 Liang Ma He Nan Lu, San Li Tun, Beijing; tel. (1) 5323956; telex 22192; Ambassador: (vacant).

Pakistan: 1 Dong Zhi Men Wai Dajie, Beijing; tel. (1) 5322504; Ambassador: KHALID MAHMOOD.

Peru: 2-82 San Li Tun, Bangonglou, Beijing 100600; tel. (1) 5324658; telex 22278; fax (1) 5322178; Ambassador: GABRIEL GARCÍA PIKE.

Philippines: 23 Xiu Shui Bei Jie, Jian Guo Men Wai, Beijing; tel. (1) 5321872; telex 22132; Ambassador: FELIPE MABILANGAN.

Poland: 1 Ri Tan Lu, Jian Guo Men Wai, Beijing; tel. (1) 5321235; telex 210288; fax (1) 5325364; Ambassador: ZBIGNIEW DEMBOWSKI.

Portugal: 2-72 Bangonglou, San Li Tun, Beijing; tel. (1) 5323220; telex 22326; fax (1) 5324637; Ambassador: JOSÉ MANUEL VILLAS-BOAS.

Qatar: 2-9-2 Tayuan Diplomatic Office Bldg, 14 Liang Ma He Nan Lu, Beijing 100600; tel. (1) 5322231; telex 20434; Ambassador: ABDURAHMAN M. AL-KHALIFI.

Romania: Ri Tan Lu Dong Er Jie, Beijing; tel. (1) 5323255; telex 22250; fax (1) 5325728; Ambassador: ROMULUS I. BUDURA.

Russia: 4 Dong Zhi Men Nei, Bei Zhong Jie, Beijing 100600; tel. (1) 5321291; telex 22247; fax (1) 5324853; Ambassador: IGOR ROGACHEV.

Rwanda: 30 Xiu Shui Bei Jie, Beijing; tel. (1) 5322193; telex 22104; fax (1) 5322006; Ambassador: ISIDORE JEAN BAPTISTE RUKIRA.

Saudi Arabia: Beijing; Ambassador: TAWFIQ AL-ALAMDAR.

Senegal: 1 Ri Tan Dong Yi Jie, Jian Guo Men Wai, Beijing; tel. (1) 5322576; telex 22100; Ambassador: MADY NDAO.

Sierra Leone: 7 Dong Zhi Men Wai Dajie, Beijing; tel. (1) 5321222; telex 22166; Ambassador: SHEKU BADARA BASTRU DUMBUYA.

Singapore: 1 Xiu Shui Bei Jie, Jian Guo Men Wai, Beijing 100600; tel. (1) 5323926; fax (1) 5322215; Ambassador: CHENG TONG FATT.

Slovakia: Ri Tan Lu, Jian Guo Men Wai, Beijing 100600; tel. (1) 5321531; telex 222553; fax (1) 5324814.

Somalia: 2 San Li Tun Lu, Beijing; tel. (1) 5321752; telex 22121; Ambassador: MOHAMED HASSAN SAID.

Spain: 9 San Li Tun Lu, Beijing; tel. (1) 5323742; telex 22108; fax (1) 5323401; Ambassador: JUAN LEÑA.

continued...

GOVERNMENT LEADERS, 1995 (continued)

Sri Lanka: 3 Jian Hua Lu, Jian Guo Men Wai, Beijing 100600; tel. (1) 5321861; telex 22136; fax (1) 5325426; Ambassador: SUHITA GAUTAMADASA.

Sudan: 1 Dong Er Jie, San Li Tun, Beijing; telex 22116; Ambassador: ALI YOUSUF AHMED.

Sweden: 3 Dong Zhi Men Wai Dajie, Beijing; tel. (1) 5323331; telex 22261; fax (1) 5325008; Ambassador: SVEN G. LINDER.

Switzerland: 3 Dong Wu Jie, San Li Tun, Beijing 100600; tel. (1) 5322736; telex 22251; fax (1) 5324353; Ambassador: Dr ERWIN SCHURTENBERGER.

Syria: 6 Dong Si Jie, San Li Tun, Beijing 100600; tel. (1) 5321563; telex 22138; fax (1) 5321575; Ambassador: LOUTOF ALLAH HAYDAR.

Tanzania: 53 Dong Liu Jie, San Li Tun, Beijing; tel. (1) 5321408; telex 22749; Ambassador: SEIF ALI IDDI.

Thailand: 40 Guang Hua Lu, Beijing; tel. (1) 5321903; telex 22145; fax (1) 5323986; Ambassador: MONTRI JALICHANDRA.

Togo: 11 Dong Zhi Men Wai Dajie, Beijing; tel. (1) 5322202; telex 22130; Ambassador: YAO BLOUA AGBO.

Tunisia: 1 Dong Jie, San Li Tun, Beijing; tel. (1) 5322435; telex 22103; Ambassador: MOHAMMED HABIB KAABACHI.

Turkey: 9 Dong Wu Jie, San Li Tun, Beijing; tel. (1) 5322650; telex 210168; fax (1) 5323268; Ambassador: RESAT ARIM.

Uganda: 5 Dong Jie, San Li Tun, Beijing; tel. (1) 5322370; telex 22272; fax (1) 5322242; Ambassador: F. A. OKECHO.

Ukraine: 11 Dong Wu Jie, San Li Tun, Beijing; tel. (1) 5326369; telex 210082; Ambassador: ANATOLY PLYUSHKO.

United Kingdom: 11 Guang Hua Lu, Jian Guo Men Wai, Beijing; tel. (1) 5321961; telex 22191; fax (1) 5321939; Ambassador: Sir ROBIN MCLAREN.

USA: 3 Xiu Shui Bei Jie, Beijing 100600; tel. (1) 5323831; telex 22701; fax (1) 5323178; Ambassador: J. STAPLETON ROY.

Uruguay: 2-7-2 Tayuan Bldg, Beijing; tel. (1) 5324445; telex 211237; fax (1) 5324357; Ambassador: JULIO DURAÑONA.

Venezuela: 14 San Li Tun Lu, Beijing 100600; tel. (1) 5321295; telex 22137; fax (1) 5323817; Ambassador: EDUARDO SOTO-ALVAREZ.

Viet Nam: 32 Guang Hua Lu, Jian Guo Men Wai, Beijing; Ambassador: DANG NGHIEM HOANH.

Yemen: 5 Dong San Jie, San Li Tun, Beijing 100600; tel. (1) 5321558; telex 210297; fax (1) 5324305; Ambassador: GHALEB SAEED AL-ADOOFI.

Yugoslavia: 1 Dong Liu Jie, San Li Tun, Beijing 100600; tel. (1) 5323516; telex 22403; fax (1) 5321207; Ambassador: (vacant).

Zaire: 6 Dong Wu Jie, San Li Tun, Beijing; tel. (1) 5321995; telex 22273; Ambassador: LOMBO LO MANGAMANGA.

Zambia: 5 Dong Si Jie, San Li Tun, Beijing 100600; tel. (1) 5321554; telex 22388; fax (1) 5321891; Ambassador: PETER LESA KASANDA.

Zimbabwe: 7 Dong San Jie, San Li Tun, Beijing 100600; tel. (1) 5323795; telex 22671; fax (1) 5325383; Ambassador: BONIFACE GUWA CHIDYAUSIKU.

Chiefs of State and Cabinet Members of Foreign Governments, 1995.

THE CONSTITUTION OF CHINA, 1992

The Constitution
A new constitution was adopted on 4 December 1982 by the Fifth Session of the Fifth National People's Congress. Its principal provisions, including amendments made in 1993, are detailed below. The Preamble, which is not included here, states that 'Taiwan is part of the sacred territory of the People's Republic of China'.

General Principles
Article 1: The People's Republic of China is a socialist state under the people's democratic dictatorship led by the working class and based on the alliance of workers and peasants.

The socialist system is the basic system of the People's Republic of China. Sabotage of the socialist system by any organization or individual is prohibited.

Article 2: All power in the People's Republic of China belongs to the people.

The organs through which the people exercise state power are the National People's Congress and the local people's congresses at different levels.

The people administer state affairs and manage economic, cultural and social affairs through various channels and in various ways in accordance with the law.

Article 3: The state organs of the People's Republic of China apply the principle of democratic centralism.

The National People's Congress and the local people's congresses at different levels are instituted through democratic election. They are responsible to the people and subject to their supervision.

All administrative, judicial and procuratorial organs of the State are created by the people's congresses to which they are responsible and under whose supervision they operate.

The division of functions and powers between the central and local state organs is guided by the principle of giving full play to the initiative and enthusiasm of the local authorities under the unified leadership of the central authorities.

Article 4: All nationalities in the People's Republic of China are equal. The State protects the lawful rights and interests of the minority nationalities and upholds and develops the relationship of equality, unity and mutual assistance among all of China's nationalities. Discrimination against and oppression of any nationality are prohibited; any acts that undermine the unity of the nationalities or instigate their secession are prohibited.

The State helps the areas inhabited by minority nationalities speed up their economic and cultural development in accordance with the peculiarities and needs of the different minority nationalities.

Regional autonomy is practiced in areas where people of minority nationalities live in compact communities; in these areas organs of self-government are established for the exercise of the right of autonomy. All the national autonomous areas are inalienable parts of the People's Republic of China.

The people of all nationalities have the freedom to use and develop their own spoken and written languages, and to preserve or reform their own ways and customs.

Article 5: The State upholds the uniformity and dignity of the socialist legal system.

No law or administrative or local rules and regulations shall contravene the Constitution.

All state organs, the armed forces, all political parties and public organizations and all enterprises and undertakings must abide by the Constitution and the law. All acts in violation of the Constitution and the law must be looked into.

No organization or individual may enjoy the privilege of being above the Constitution and the law.

Article 6: The basis of the socialist economic system of the People's Republic of China is socialist public ownership of the means of production, namely, ownership by the whole people and collective ownership by the working people.

World Governments, 1992.

NUMBER OF GOVERNMENT STAFF AND WORKERS BY REGION, 1995 (10,000 persons)

Region	Total	State-Owned	Number of Staff and Workers Collective-Owned of Township	Other
National Total	14,753.0	10,872.6	3,363.9	516.5
Beijing	467.4	369.2	78.4	19.8
Tianjin	289.5	204.4	68.7	16.4
Hebei	699.1	538.3	146.9	13.9
Shanxi	460.1	359.7	96.1	4.3
Inner Mongolia	386.8	303.7	80.0	3.1
Liaoning	1,029.4	678.8	313.9	36.7
Jilin	529.0	375.1	142.9	11.0
Heilongjiang	860.4	639.7	209.6	11.1
Shanghai	485.7	354.5	86.9	44.3
Jiangsu	907.4	571.7	289.9	45.8
Zhejiang	502.4	297.6	178.0	26.8
Anhui	492.3	348.7	134.0	9.6
Fujian	341.0	219.0	72.5	49.5
Jiangxi	409.3	324.5	79.8	5.0
Shandong	862.8	621.5	215.5	25.8
Henan	771.4	599.4	161.8	10.2
Hubei	734.7	563.8	156.0	14.9
Hunan	586.4	452.8	125.6	8.0
Guangdong	871.4	558.9	200.2	112.3
Guangxi	330.8	273.6	48.5	8.7
Hainan	108.5	96.4	8.1	4.0
Sichuan	974.7	729.0	220.8	24.9
Guizhou	234.8	194.1	39.1	1.6
Yunnan	304.6	258.0	44.2	2.4
Tibet	16.9	15.7	1.1	0.1
Shaanxi	391.1	325.3	62.9	2.9
Gansu	253.2	208.3	43.9	1.0
Qinghai	65.1	56.6	8.4	0.1
Ningxia	71.4	60.4	10.4	0.6
Xinjiang	315.4	273.9	39.8	1.7

China Monthly, 19 Jul 1995.

VICE PREMIERS FACE OPPOSITION, 1995

The Chinese parliament approved two new vice premiers Friday [17 March], but the vote caused huge embarrassment to the country's leaders by revealing unprecedented opposition to one of the sole candidates. The promotion of Wu Bangguo and Jiang Chunyun had been widely expected, but the failure of party whips to minimize negative votes for Jiang will have disconcerted the government—specially the man who nominated both candidates, Premier Li Peng.

Wu, the 53-year-old former party chief of Shanghai, received "yes" votes from 86 percent of the 2,752 deputies present, but Jiang could only muster 63 percent, with 36 percent either opposing his candidacy or abstaining.

The National People's Congress (NPC), still regarded as a rubber-stamp parliament, has witnessed grass-roots opposition to candidates before—most notably during Premier Li's re-election in 1993, when 10 percent of the deputies voted against him or abstained.

continued...

VICE PREMIERS FACE OPPOSITION, 1995 (continued)

Jiang, 64, and Wu—both members of the Communist Party politburo and secretariat—will be given special responsibility for agriculture and industry respectively. Their election now brings the number of vice premiers to six. The four incumbents are Li Lanqing, Qian Qichen, Zhu Rongji and Zou Jiahua.

The announcement of the unusually high "no" vote for Jiang caused a considerable stir among the deputies on the floor of the Great Hall of the People. Indications that deputies were unhappy with the candidates had caused concern within the leadership and forced Premier Li to go to unusual lengths in his nomination papers to praise both candidates.

Wu, a member of the so-called "Shanghai faction" led by President Jiang Zemin, is considered a mainstream technocrat, although some doubts have been raised about his lack of experience in economic matters. Jiang Chunyun oversaw a period of rapid economic growth in Shandong after taking over as party chief of the province in 1988, but he has been criticized for failing to stem an equally rapid swell of corruption there and is not noted for his agricultural expertise.

Analysts voiced surprise at the degree of opposition, especially to Jiang's nomination. "It's pretty embarrassing for the leadership as a whole," said one diplomat, adding, however, that the result did not necessarily amount to a vote of no-confidence in the government. "Jiang is a relative non-entity, and I think a lot of deputies wanted to register their opposition to a candidate they didn't know and one who has no proven record in agriculture," she said.

At the same time, the vote was a reflection of the effect China's economic reforms and policy of opening to the outside world have had in a country where until recently such a public display of dissent would have been inconceivable.

Another source of dismay has been Li's plan to build a dam on the Yangtze River's Three Gorges site, causing the displacement of around a million people and overriding warnings from environmentalists. "It's a sign of the times in China," said another diplomat. "There is more discontent, especially in the provinces, and people are no longer happy to just toe the party line for the sake of it."

While Wu's relatively high profile term as Shanghai party chief helped him garner a substantial "yes" vote, observers here said the 371 abstentions and votes against signaled annoyance with what some regard as the city's over-representation within the upper echelons of the party and government.

There had been speculation that the promotions might coincide with the removal of one of the incumbent vice premiers. The decision to retain the current line-up reflects 'the leadership's desire to avoid any personnel changes that smack of political maneuvering and promote an image of stability as the country awaits the demise of patriarch Deng Xiaoping.

Friday's voting procedures did not entail any visual display of dissent, by a show of hands or lining up by the delegates to cast their vote. Delegates pressed a button in front of their seats to cast their vote electronically.

Hong Kong AFP, 17 Mar 1995.

MINISTRY RESTRICTED EXIT APPLICATIONS, 1995

China's Public Security Ministry recently issued a circular calling on public security organs in all localities to carefully examine applications to leave the country (territory) for sightseeing abroad, strictly enforce rules and regulations, and crack down on practices of changing the location of exit visa applications.

The Public Security Ministry's circular said: All authorized travel agencies should operate their tourist businesses abroad strictly according to relevant government regulations. A travel agency whose poor management leads to serious consequences, such as tourists overstaying their visas abroad or sneaking into third countries, shall have its power of handling exit visa applications suspended temporarily or revoked, depending on the degree of seriousness of

continued...

MINISTRY RESTRICTED EXIT APPLICATIONS, 1995 (continued)

each case. Units not authorized to operate tourist businesses abroad should not engage in such businesses in any form. Violators shall be severely punished.

The Public Security Ministry reiterated: Units and personnel involved in exit application fraud or practices of changing the location of exit applications shall be investigated to affix their responsibilities and shall be duly punished.

Hong Kong SHE, 24 Sep 1995.

CHINA'S DOORS OPEN WIDER, 1995

Wei Jianxing, Secretary of the Beijing Municipal Committee of the Chinese Communist Party (CPC), said today that the Chinese Capital will open wider to the outside world.

Wei, also a member of the Political Bureau of the CPC Central Committee, made the remarks when meeting Shih-ping Zhuang, Honorary Chairman of the Nanyang Commercial Bank, Ltd., Hong Kong, here this afternoon.

Beijing will try to raise its level of opening up, further improve its investment environment and attract more foreign funds and technology for its development, Wei said.

He described the current situation in Beijing as stable, both politically and socially, saying that the economy is witnessing fast, sustained growth and all work are proceeding in a normal and orderly way.

Wei spoke highly of late Vice-Mayor Li Runwu, who died of heart attack on November 2 while at work. As an outstanding official loved and respected by the public, he said, Li Runwu is symbolic of the essence and mainstream of the ranks of cadres in the Capital.

The overwhelming majority of officials in the city are good or relatively good, Wei said, dismissing speculations about reshuffle in Beijing's municipal leadership as "groundless."

Shih-ping Zhuang said he felt encouraged and more at ease after hearing Wei's briefing on the situation in Beijing, and expressed the hope to make more contributions to the city's reform and opening up.

The Beijing branch of the Nanyang Commercial Bank, Ltd., the fourth overseas bank approved by Beijing City. will start operation next Monday [18 December].

X, 15 Dec 1995.

GOVERNMENT'S EMPLOYMENT STRATEGY, 1995

How is unemployment manifested in China? And what sound strategy will the Chinese Government adopt to deal with this virtually global problem? Two recent news items from the Chinese Ministry of Labor may serve to shed some light on this issue.

The first cites statistics which put the late 1994 rate of urban unemployment in China at 2.8 percent, a 0.2 percentage point increase over 1993, with the number of unemployed increasing to approximately 5 million from the 1993 figure of 4.2 million. An official from the Ministry of Labor said that an analysis of the cause and development trend of unemployment indicates the situation is rather grim, and the problem has become a major problem affecting China's social progress and stability.

The second mentions some significant achievements and valuable experiences gained in the 1994 re-employment project trial implemented in 30 Chinese cities. The project will be promoted nationwide this year. Experts note that the development of the re employment project and the adoption of a series of other employment promotion measures clearly demonstrate the Chinese Government's efforts to reduce the impact of unemployment on society.

Along with the deepening of reform, one of the most outstanding problems is the need to place redundant personnel currently employed in state-owned enterprises. People have high hopes for the measures taken by the state, including the re-employment project, to control unemployment and re-employ redundant workers. However, as the unemployment problem

continued...

GOVERNMENT'S EMPLOYMENT STRATEGY, 1995 (continued)

today is a chronic social malady facing many countries, an intelligent assessment tells us that a proper solution can by no means be achieved overnight. In China, many problems unique to the country must be addressed.

Moreover, according to a recent forecast, the rate of China's urban unemployment during the Ninth Five-Year Plan period will equal that of the Eighth Five-Year Plan period and urban and rural employment will face great pressure. Data from the State Statistical Bureau provide an analysis of the employment situation in China over the next several years:

Toward the end of the Ninth Five-Year Plan, the growth of China's labor resources will reach new highs. The number of unemployed urban workers and rural laborers shifting to cities and towns will increase considerably.

Plus the laborers generated by natural growth, the number of urban laborers to be employed will stand at 50 million, or 10 million annually, during the Ninth Five-Year Plan period; at the same time, there will be some 15 million redundant workers.

In light of the new employment situation, the Chinese Government will set new goals for itself, based on China's own experiences as well as international successes.

Specifically, the goals are these: During the Ninth Five-Year Plan period, efforts will be made to keep the urban employment rate at above 90 percent, the unemployment rate at around 5 percent, and the rate of those not fully employed down to 5 percent, thereby addressing to a certain extent both the chronically unemployed and those having difficulty getting and holding jobs; in the rural areas, efforts will be made to keep the transfer of surplus rural laborers to non-agricultural sectors at around 10 percent.

To achieve this goal, the state will adopt the following five concrete measures:

—Improve the unemployment insurance system, and implement the re-employment project. China will gradually establish an unemployment insurance system to cover all workers at all levels; a three-party responsibility system for expenses to be shared by the state, the work unit and individual will be implemented; unemployment relief will be closely linked with re-employment; and the system will be implemented through state legislation. At the same time, the functions of unemployment insurance will be given full play to guarantee daily necessities of life and to support the employment effort; measures such as job recommendation and guidance counseling will be adopted; job re-training will be introduced and methods of organizing the unemployed to engage in production will be adopted, along with appropriate support policies to accelerate the re-employment of the chronically unemployed.

—Implement "the orderly transregional flow of rural laborers" in a planned and orderly manner.

—Establish an unemployment forecasting and warning system, strengthen the monitoring and control of the labor market, ensure that labor resources (supply) are equitably balanced with labor market demands.

—Promote economic development and open up more employment avenues.

—Expedite the development of the employment system and employment service and form a new labor market mechanism.

Beijing Review, 5 Nov 1995.

AGENDA FOR NPC COMMITTEE SESSION, 1995

The Eighth National People's Congress [NPC] Standing Committee held a chairmanship meeting this morning at the Great Hall of the People and decided to hold the 17th session of the Eighth NPC Standing Committee from 20 to 28 December in Beijing.

Chairman Qiao Shi presided over the meeting.

The meeting first heard and approved a report by Cao Zhi, secretary general of the NPC Standing Committee, on the proposal for the draft agenda and daily program arrangement for the 17th session of the Eighth NPC Standing Committee.

continued...

AGENDA FOR NPC COMMITTEE SESSION, 1995 (continued)

The chairmanship meeting proposed the following main agenda for the session: deliberating on the draft electric power law and draft amendment to the criminal procedure law; deliberating on a motion by the NPC's Education, Science, Culture, and Public Health Committee to study the draft law on promoting transfer of scientific and technological achievements; deliberating on martial law; deliberating on a motion by the State Council to study the vocational education law, administration supervision law, and auction law; deliberating on a motion by the Central Military Commission to study the draft amendment to the provisional regulations on punishing soldiers for criminal dereliction of duties and responsibilities; deliberating on the draft decision of the NPC Standing Committee on convening the Fourth Session of the Eighth NPC; deliberating on the draft name list of component members of the Preparatory Committee of the Hong Kong Special Administrative Region [SAR] for the NPC; hearing and deliberating on the State Council reports on reform of large- and medium-sized state enterprises and the UN Fourth World Conference of Women; hearing the work report of the Preliminary Working Committee of the Preparatory Committee of the Hong Kong SAR; and hearing reports by NPC Standing Committee inspection groups on investigating enforcement of the agriculture law, Taiwan compatriots' investment protection law, and resolution on deepening the propaganda and education of the legal system.

Today's chairmanship meeting also heard Cao Zhi's explanation of the draft decision on convening the Fourth Session of the Eighth NPC; a report by NPC Law Committee Chairman Xue Ju on an amendment to the draft electric power law, and explanations by NPC Legislative Affairs Commission Chairman Gu Angran on the draft curfew law and the draft amendment to the criminal procedure law.

Vice chairmen Tian Jiyun, Wang Hanbin, Ni Zhifu, Chen Muhua, Fei Xiaotong, Sun Qimeng, Li Ximing, Wang Guangying, Chen Siyuan, Lu Jiaxi, Buhe, Tomur Dawamat, Li Peiyao, and Wu Jieping attended the meeting.

X, 13 Dec 1995.

LU PING REQUESTS HONG KONG CIVIL SERVICE DATA, 1995

China's top Hong Kong official blasted the Hong Kong Government's refusal to provide Beijing with personal information on top civil servants. Hong Kong and Macao Affairs Office director Lu Ping said it would hinder Beijing's ability to appoint the principal officials who will serve after 1997. "The central Government cannot possibly appoint the principal officials with our eyes closed," he said in a strongly-worded attack at the Preliminary Working Committee meetings in Beijing. "We must have all the details."

The Hong Kong Government insisted it would only supply the details to the future Chief Executive, who would head the government of the Special Administrative Region. This official was to be chosen in late 1996.

Mr. Lu denied Beijing's demand would damage the morale of local civil servants. It would be more demoralizing, he said, if those who hold senior posts in the civil service lost the chance to become principal officials in the post-1997 administration because Beijing was barred from receiving information about them.

South China Sunday Morning Post, 15 Jan 1995.

LEADERSHIP OF THE PRC, 1995

The Main National Leadership of the PRC

(Changes are underlined)

Liu Jen-Kai

Abbreviations and Explanatory Notes

CC	=	Central Committee
CCa	=	Central Committee, alternate member
CCm	=	Central Committee, member
CCSm	=	Central Committee Secretariat, member
CCP	=	Chinese Communist Party
PBa	=	Politburo, alternate member
PBm	=	Politburo, member
Cdr.	=	Commander
CPPCC	=	Chinese People's Political Consultative Conference
CYL	=	Communist Youth League
Dep.Cdr.	=	Deputy Commander
Dep.Ch.	=	Deputy Chief
Dep.Dir.	=	Deputy Director
Dep.Eds.-in-Chief	=	Deputy Editors-in-Chief
Dep.Head	=	Deputy Head
Dep.P.C.	=	Deputy Political Commissar
Dep.Sec.	=	Deputy Secretary
exec.	=	executive
f	=	female
Gen.Sec.	=	General Secretary
Hon.Chm.	=	Honorary Chairman
H.V.-Ch.	=	Honorary Vice-Chairman
NPC	=	National People's Congress
PLA	=	People's Liberation Army
Pol.Com.	=	Political Commissar
PPC Chm.	=	Provincial People's Congress Chairman
Sec.	=	Secretary
Sec.-Gen.	=	Secretary-General
V.-Chm.	=	Vice-Chairman
V.-Gov.	=	Vice-Governor
V.-Min.	=	Vice-Minister
V.-Pres.	=	Vice-President
Vice-M.	=	Vice-Mayor

* Chairmen and vice-chairmen of autonomous regional governments are equivalent to governors and vice-governors of provinces and to mayors and vice-mayors of Beijing, Shanghai and Tianjin.

Year and month behind a name indicate the date the person assumed the post or was identified in this position.

STATE PRESIDENT

President	Jiang Zemin	PBm	93/03
Vice-Pres.	Rong Yiren		93/03

NATIONAL PEOPLE'S CONGRESS

Chairman	Qiao Shi	PBm	93/03
V.-Chm.	Buhe		93/03
	Chen Muhua (f)	CCm	88/04
	Cheng Siyuan		93/03
	Fei Xiaotong		88/04
	Lei Jieqiong (f)		88/04
	Li Peiyao		93/03
	Li Ximing		93/03
	Lu Jiaxi		93/03
	Ni Zhifu	CCm	88/04
	Pagbalha Geleg Namgyai		93/03
	Qin Jiwei		93/03
	Sun Qimeng		88/04
	Tian Jiyun	PBm	93/03
	Tomur Dawamat	CCm	93/03
	Wang Bingqian		93/03
	Wang Guangying		93/03
	Wang Hanbin	PBa	88/04
	Wu Jieping		93/03
Sec.-Gen.	Cao Zhi		93/03

NPC Standing Committee
Legislative Affairs Commission

Chairman	Gu Angran		93/07

Education, Science, Culture and Public Health Committee

Chairman	Zhao Dongwan		93/03
V.-Chm.	Han Huaizhi		94/03
	Hao Yichun (f)		93/03
	Li Xu'e		93/03
	Nie Dajiang		93/03
	Yang Haibo		93/03

Environmental and Resources Protection Committee

Chairman	Qu Geping		93/03
V.-Chm.	Lin Zongtang		93/03
	Qi Yuanjing	CCm	93/03
	Qin Zhongda		93/03
	Yang Jike		93/03
	Yang Zhenhuai	CCa	93/03

Financial and Economic Committee

Chairman	Liu Suinian		93/03
V.-Chm.	Chi Haibin		93/03
	Dai Jie		93/03
	Dong Fureng		88/03
	Huang Yicheng		93/03
	Li Hao		93/03
	Zeng Xianlin	CCa	93/03
	Zhang Xuwu		93/03

Foreign Affairs Committee

Chairman	Zhu Liang		93/03
V.-Chm.	Yang Zhenya		93/03
	Zhou Jue		93/03
	Zhu Qizhen		93/03

Internal and Judicial Affairs Committee

Chairman	Meng Liankun		93/03
V.-Chm.	Gu Linfang		93/03
	Peng Qingyuan		88/03
	Zhang Kehui		93/03
	Zhu Guang		93/03

Law Committee

Chairman	Xue Ju		93/03
V.-Chm.	Cai Cheng		93/03
	Li Yining		93/03
	Wang Shuwen		93/03
	Xiang Chunyi		83/06

Nationalities Committee

Chairman	Wang Chaowen	CCm	93/03
V.-Chm.	Huanjue Cenam		93/03
	Li Xuezhi		88/03
	Tao Aiying		88/03
	Wu Jinghua		93/03
	Yu Xinglong		94/03

Overseas Chinese Affairs Committee

Chairman	Yang Taifang		93/03
V.-Chm.	Huang Changxi		94/03
	Lin Liyun (f)	CCm	91/03
	Liu Zhenhua		93/03
	Wan Shaofen (f)		93/03
	Wang Songda		93/03

STATE COUNCIL

Premier	Li Peng	PBm	88/04
Vice-Premiers			
	Li Lanqing	PBm	93/03
	Qian Qichen	PBm	93/03
	Zhu Rongji (exec.)	PBm	91/04
	Zou Jiahua	PBm	91/04
State Councillors			
	Chen Junsheng	CCm	88/04
	Chi Haotian	CCm	93/03
	Ismail Amat	CCm	93/03
	Li Guixian	CCm	88/04
	Li Tieying	PBm	88/04
	Luo Gan	CCm	93/03
	Peng Peiyun (f)	CCm	93/03
	Song Jian	CCm	86/04
Sec.-Gen.	Luo Gan	CCm	88/12

ORGANS OF THE STATE COUNCIL

State Council's General Office

Head	Luo Gan	CCm	88/12

COMMISSIONS

Economic and Trade

Chairman	Wang Zhongyu	CCm	93/03
V.-Chm.	Chen Qingtai		93/05
	Shi Wanpeng		93/05
	Xu Penghang		93/05
	Yang Changji (exec.)		93/05
	Yu Xiaosong		93/05

Education

Chairman	Zhu Kaixuan	CCa	93/03
V.-Chm.	Liu Bin		85/05
	Wang Mingda		85/05
	Wei Yu (f)		93/05
	Zhang Tianbao		93/05
	Zhang Xiaowen	CCa	93/05

Family Planning

Chairman	Peng Peiyun (f)	CCm	88/01
V.-Chm.	Jiang Zhenghua		91/10
	Li Hongqui		94/02
	Liu Hanbin		91/10
	Peng Yu (f)		85/09
	Yang Kuifu		91/02

Nationalities Affairs

Chairman	Ismail Amat	CCm	86/01
V.-Chm.	Chen Hong		93/07
	Jiang Jiafu		86/07
	Li Jinyou		93/05
	Tudao Doje		91/10
	Wen Jing		90/06

Physical Culture and Sports

Chairman	Wu Shaozu	CCm	88/12
V.-Chm.	Xu Yinsheng		77/03
	Yuan Weimin	CCm	84/11
	Zhang Faqiang		94/05

Planning

Chairman	Chen Jinhua	CCm	93/03
V.-Chm.	Chen Tonghai		94/02
	Chen Yaobang		93/05
	Gan Ziyu		78/11
	Gui Shiyong	CCa	89/12
	Guo Shuyan	CCa	93/01
	Hao Jianxiu (f)	CCm	87/10
	Luo Zhiling		93/05
	She Jianming		93/05
	Wang Chunzheng		90/11
	Yao Zhenyan		91/10
	Ye Qing	CCa	88/05
	Zeng Peiyan	CCa	93/01

continued...

LEADERSHIP OF THE PRC, 1995 (continued)

Restructuring Economy

Chairman	Li Tieying	PBm	93/03
V.-Chm.	He Guanghui		84/02
	Hong Hu		91/02
	Liu Zhifeng		92/09
	Ma Kai		93/06
	Wang Shiyuan		93/06
	Wu Jie		93/05

Science and Technology

Chairman	Song Jian	CCm	84/09
V.-Chm.	Deng Nan (f)		91/10
	Duan Ruichun		91/04
	Han Deqian		93/09
	Huang Qitao		93/04
	Hui Yongzheng		90/11
	Zhu Lilan (f/exec.)	CCa	86/07

Science, Technology and Industry for National Defence

Chairman	Ding Henggao	CCm	85/06
V.-Chm.	Huai Guomo		88/05
	Nie Li (f)		89/10
	Shen Chunnian		93/06
	Shen Rongjun		85/04
	Xie Guang		85/04
Pol.Com.	Dai Xuejiang		92/12

MINISTRIES

Agriculture

Minister	Liu Jiang		93/03
V.-Min.	Hong Fuzeng		89/03
	Liu Chengguo		93/09
	Wan Baorui		93/04
	Wu Yixia		93/04
	Zhang Yanxi		92/05

Chemical Industry

Minister	Gu Xiulian (f)	CCm	89/07
V.-Min.	Cheng Siwei		94/05
	He Guoqiang	CCa	91/02
	Li Zibin		91/12
	Li Shizhong		93/04
	Tan Zhuzhou		84/02

Civil Affairs

Minister	Doje Cering	CCm	93/03
V.-Min.	Fan Baojun		87/09
	Yan Mingfu		91/05
	Yang Yanyin (f)		93/07

Coal Industry

Minister	Wang Senhao	CCm	93/03
V.-Min.	Fan Weitang		93/05
	Han Ying		93/05
	Pu Hongjiu		93/05
	Zhang Baoming		93/05

Communications

Minister	Huang Zhendong	CCm	91/03
V.-Min.	Li Juchang		92/09
	Liu E		93/03
	Liu Songjin		91/10
	Zheng Guangdi (f)		82/10

Construction

Minister	Hou Jie	CCm	91/03
V.-Min.	Li Zhendong		92/09
	Mao Rubo		93/05
	Tan Qinglian		88/11
	Ye Rutang		88/05
	Zou Yuchuan		93/10

Culture

Minister	Liu Zhongde	CCm	93/03
V.-Min.	Chen Changben		90/05
	Gao Zhanxiang (exec.)		86/03
	Liu Deyou		86/04
	Xu Wenbo		90/05

Electronics Industry

Minister	Hu Qili	CCm	93/03
V.-Min.	Liu Jianfeng	CCm	93/05
	Lü Xinkui		93/05
	Qu Weizhi (f)		93/05
	Zhang Jinqiang		93/05

Finance

Minister	Liu Zhongli	CCm	92/09
V.-Min.	Jin Renqing		91/11
	Li Yanling		93/07
	Liu Jibin		88/06
	Zhang Youcai		89/12

Foreign Affairs

Minister	Qian Qichen	PBm	88/04
V.-Min.	Dai Bingguo		94/02
	Jiang Enzhu		91/12
	Liu Huaqiu	CCa	89/10
	Tang Jiaxuan		93/03
	Tian Zengpei	CCm	88/05

Foreign Trade and Economic Cooperation

Minister	Wu Yi (f)	CCm	93/03
V.-Min.	Gu Yongjiang		90/08
	Li Guohua (f)		94/03
	Liu Shanzai		94/03
	Shi Guangsheng		93/05
	Zheng Silin	CCa	93/07

Forestry

Minister	Xu Youfang		93/03
V.-Min.	Liu Yuhe		94/05
	Shen Maocheng		88/05
	Wang Zhibao		92/09
	Zhu Guangyao		93/07

Geology and Mineral Resources

Minister	Song Ruixiang		94/05
V.-Min.	Zhang Hongren		86/09
	Zhang Wenju		85/11
	Zhang Wenyue		90/07

Internal Trade

Minister	Zhang Haoruo		93/03
V.-Min.	Bai Meiqing		93/07
	He Jihai		93/07
	Lu Jiang		93/07
	Ma Lisheng		93/07
	Ma Yimin		93/07

Justice

Minister	Xiao Yang		93/03
V.-Min.	Wang Julu		93/06
	Xiao Jianzhang		92/12
	Zhang Geng		93/06
	Zhang Xiufu		91/04

Labor

Minister	Li Boyong	CCm	93/02
V.-Min.	Liu Yazhi (f)		94/08
	Zhang Zuoji		93/02
	Zhu Jiazhen		91/10

Machine-Building Industry

Minister	He Guangyuan	CCm	93/03
V.-Min.	Bao Xuding		93/05
	Lü Fuyuan		94/05
	Shao Qihui	CCm	94/08
	Sun Changji		93/05
	Zhang Delin		93/05

Metallurgical Industry

Minister	Liu Qi	CCa	93/03
V.-Min.	Bi Qun		93/08
	Wu Xichun		93/08
	Xu Daquan		86/02
	Yin Ruiyu		89/03

National Defence

Minister	Chi Haotian	CCm	93/03

Personnel

Minister	Song Defu	CCm	93/03
V.-Min.	Cheng Lianchang		88/05
	Jiang Guanzhuang		89/03
	Zhang Hanfu		88/05
	Zhang Zhijian		88/05
	Zhao Zongnai		89/12

Posts and Telecommunications

Minister	Wu Jichuan	CCa	93/03
V.-Min.	Lin Jinquan		93/11
	Liu Pingyuan		91/05
	Yang Xianzu		90/08
	Zhu Gaofeng		82/05

Power Industry

Minister	Shi Dazhen	CCa	93/03
V.-Min.	Lu Yanchang		93/04
	Wang Shucheng		93/04
	Zha Keming		93/04
	Zhao Xizheng		93/04

Public Health

Minister	Chen Minzhang	CCm	87/04
V.-Min.	Gu Yingqi		84/10
	He Jiesheng (f)		86/03
	Hu Ximing		85/01
	Sun Longchun		90/09
	Yin Dakui		93/02
	Zhang Wenkang		93/02

Public Security

Minister	Tao Siju	CCm	90/12
V.-Min.	Bai Jingfu		91/10
	Hu Zhiguang		85/01
	Jiang Xianjin		91/11
	Mou Xinsheng		93/04
	Tian Qiyu		92/05

Radio, Film and Television

Minister	Sun Jiazheng	CCa	94/05
V.-Min.	He Dongcai		93/02
	Liu Xiliang		91/05
	Tian Congming		90/12
	Tong Xiangrong		93/02
	Yang Weiguang		94/08

Railways

Minister	Han Zhubin	CCm	92/09
V.-Min.	Fu Zhihuan		90/12
	Guo Lin		93/05
	Sun Yongfu		85/01
	Tu Yourui (exec.)		88/06

State Security

Minister	Jia Chunwang	CCm	85/09

Supervision

Minister	Cao Qingze		93/03
V.-Min.	Feng Tiyun		88/02
	He Yong		87/06
	Li Zhilun		92/03

Water Resources

Minister	Niu Maosheng		93/03
V.-Min.	He Jing (f)		93/05
	Yan Keqiang		90/11
	Zhang Chunyuan		88/09
	Zhou Wenzhi		91/04

ORGANS AT MINISTERIAL LEVEL

People's Bank of China

Governor	Zhu Rongji	PBm	93/07
V.-Gov.	Bai Wenqing		89/09
	Chen Yuan		88/05
	Dai Xianglong	CCa	93/07
	Wang Qishan		93/07
	Yin Jieyan		94/02
	Zhou Zhengqing (exec.)		86/11
	Zhu Xiaohua		93/07

Auditing Administration

Auditor-General	Guo Zhenqian	CCm	94/05
Deputy Auditors-General	Cui Jianmin?		85/04
	Jin Jipeng		92/12
	Li Jinhua		85/09
	Liu Hezhang		90/09
	Zheng Li (f)		87/07

Civil Aviation Administration of China

Director	Chen Guangyi	CCm	93/12
Dep.Dir.	Bao Peide		93/12
	Jiang Zhuping	CCm	93/12
	Li Zhao		88/10
	Shen Yuankang		93/12
	Yan Zhixiang		73/11

State General Bureau of Taxation

Director	Liu Zhongli	CCm	94/02
Dep.Dir.	Chen Jingxin		89/02
	Jin Xin		94/02
	Li Yongrui		92/09
	Lu Renfa		94/08
	Xiang Huaicheng		94/08
	Yang Chongchun		91/01
	Zhang Xianghai		92/04

WORKING BODIES UNDER THE STATE COUNCIL

Special Economic Zones Office

Director	Hu Ping	CCm	93/05
Dep.Dir.	Chen Shunheng		91/06
	Ge Hongsheng	CCm	94/01
	Ji Jusheng		93/10
	Zhao Guanghua		93/07
	Zhao Yundong		88/07

State Council Research Office

Director	Yuan Mu		88/09
Dep.Dir.	Jiang Yunbao		94/01
	Wang Mengkui	CCa	90/07
	Yang Yongzhe		90/06

continued…

LEADERSHIP OF THE PRC, 1995 (continued)

Hong Kong and Macao Affairs Office

Director	Lu Ping	CCm	90/11
Dep.Dir.	Chen Ziying		91/02
	Wang Fengchao		94/02

Office of Overseas Chinese Affairs

Director	Liao Hui	CCm	84/04
Dep.Dir.	Chen Baigao		86/04
	Li Xinghao		86/04
	Liu Zepeng		92/06

Office of Foreign Affairs

Director	Qi Huaiyuan	CCm	91/08
Dep.Dir.	Cheng Zhensheng		92/04
	Lü Congmin		94/08
	Xia Daosheng		92/04

Information Office

Director	Zeng Jianhui	92/12
Dep.Dir.	Li Bing	94/02
	Li Yuanchao	93/05
	Yang Zhengquan	93/05

Taiwan Affairs Office

Director	Wang Zhaoguo	CCm	90/11
Dep.Dir.	Chen Yunlin	CCa	94/02
	Deng Chaocong		91/03
	Sun Xiaoyu		88/09

ORGANIZATIONS DIRECTLY UNDER THE STATE COUNCIL

General Administration of Customs

Director	Qian Guanlin	93/01
Dep.Dir.	Huang Rufeng	93/04
	Liu Wenjie	91/11
	Wu Naiwen	88/03

State Bureau of Environmental Protection

Director	Xie Zhenhua	93/06
Dep.Dir.	Jin Jianming	88/11
	Wang Yangzu	89/09
	Ye Ruqiu	91/09
	Zhang Kunmin	89/02

State Administration Bureau for Industry and Commerce

Director	Liu Minxue	89/12
Dep.Dir.	Bai Dahua	91/09
	Bian Yaowu	91/06
	Cao Tiandian	90/07
	Gan Guoping	85/12
	Yang Peiqing	93/09

State Land Administration Bureau

Director	Zou Yuchuan	93/10
Dep.Dir.	Liu Wenjia	91/09
	Ma Kewei	94/04

Bureau of Legislative Affairs

Director	Yang Jingyu	91/07
Dep.Dir.	Cao Kangtai	91/12
	Huang Shuhai?	87/03
	Li Peichuan	87/01
	Wang Shirong?	89/02
	Xu Yulin	92/06

State Press and Publications Administration

Director	Yu Youxian	93/06
Dep.Dir.	Liang Heng	94/02
	Liu Gao	89/11
	Lu Yuyi	89/04
	Wang Qianghua	87/09
	Xie Hong	94/04
	Yang Zhengyan	87/09
	Yu Yongzhan	91/12

Bureau of Religious Affairs

Director	Zhang Shengzuo	92/09
Dep.Dir.	Cao Jinru?	89/02
	Chile?	90/08
	Luosang Chinai?	89/02
	Wan Yaobin	89/02
	Yang Tongxiang	91/08

State Bureau of Statistics

Director	Zhang Sai	84/08
Dep.Dir.	Lu Chunheng	93/11
	Qiu Xiaohua	92/06
	Shao Zongming?	89/04
	Sun Jingxin?	88/01
	Yu Guangpei?	87/09
	Zheng Jiaheng	87/03

State Bureau of Tourism

Director	Liu Yi	CCa	88/05
Dep.Dir.	Cheng Wendong		89/04
	He Guangwei		86/07
	Sun Gang		93/12

Councillors' Office

Director	Chang Jie	90/09
Dep.Dir.	Lü Derun	90/08
	Wang Chuguang	92/09
	Wang Hairong? (f)	87/01

Government Offices Administration Bureau

Director	Guo Ji	90/09
Dep.Dir.	Bao Xianguang	92/04
	Cao Jianfeng	92/04
	Jiao Huancheng	94/08
	Zhao Wenhai	94/08

INSTITUTIONS UNDER THE STATE COUNCIL

Academy of Sciences

President	Zhou Guangzhao	CCm	87/01
V.-Pres.	Hu Qiheng (f)		88/09
	Lu Yongxiang	CCm	94/01
	Wang Fosong		88/09
	Xu Zhihong		92/10
	Yan Yixun		92/10

Academy of Engineering

President	Zhu Guangya	CCm	94/06
V.-Pres.	Lu Liangshu		94/06
	Pan Jiazheng		94/06
	Shi Changxu		94/06
	Zhu Gaofeng		94/06

Academy of Social Sciences

President	Hu Sheng		85/09
V.-Pres.	Liu Ji		93/06
	Long Yongshu		93/11
	Ru Xin	CCa	82/11
	Teng Teng		93/05
	Wang Luolin	CCa	93/07
	Wang Renzhi (first)		92/12

Xinhua News Agency

Director	Guo Chaoren	CCm	92/12
Dep.Dir.	Nan Zhenzhong		93/04
	Pang Bing'an		86/04
	Xia Zanzhong		93/04
	Zhang Baoshun		93/04

Editor-in-Chief

	Nan Zhenzhong	85/12

Development Research Center

Director	Sun Shangqing		93/04
Dep.Dir.	Ji Chongwei		90/10
	Liu Zhongyi	CCm	93/04
	Lu Baifu		93/07
	Wang Huijiong		90/06
	Wang Jixuan		89/12

China Bureau of Meteorology

Director	Zou Jingmeng	CCa	82/11
Dep.Dir.	Li Huang		91/05
	Luo Jibin		85/03
	Ma Henian		90/04
	Wen Kegang		89/02
	Zhang Jijia		83/02

Patent Office of China

Director	Gao Lulin	89/09
Dep.Dir.	Jiang Ying?	89/10
	Ming Tinghua	90/11

China National Light Industry Council

Director	Yu Zhen	93/05
Dep.Dir.	Fu Limin	93/07
	Pan Beilei (f)	93/05
	Xu Rongkai	93/05

China National Textile Council

Director	Wu Wenying (f)	CCm	93/05
Dep.Dir.	Du Yuzhou		93/05
	Liu Heng		93/05
	Ren Chuanjun		94/05
	Xu Kunyuan		94/08

NON-STANDING BODIES UNDER THE STATE COUNCIL

Leading Group for the Detachment of Party and Government Departments from Economic Entities

Head	Chen Qingtai	93/11

Leading Group for Reforming the Banking System

		PBm 93/07

Anti-Smuggling Leading Group

Head	Li Lanqing	PBm 93/07

Leading Group for Helping the Poor Through Development

Chairman	Chen Junsheng	CCm 86/06

Leading Group for Nuclear Power Plants

Chairman	Zou Jiahua	PBm 88/05

Leading Group for the Reform of the Housing System

Head	Li Tieying	PBm 93/11

National Leading Group for the Work of Supporting the Army, Giving Preferential Treatment to the Families of Armymen and Martyrs, Supporting the Government and Cherishing the People

Head	Luo Gan	CCm 93/07

National Leading Group for Anti-Disaster and Relief Work

Head	?

State Leading Group for Disaster Relief and Disease Control

Head	Li Tieying	PBm 91/07

China Committee for International Decade for National Disaster Reduction

Chairman	Li Guixian	CCm 93/12

National Working Group for Screening of Publications and AV Market

Head	Liu Zhongde	CCm 89/09

State Forest Fire Prevention Headquarters

Head	?

State Flood-Control and Drought Relief Headquarters

Head	Chen Junsheng	CCm 93/05

National Greening Committee

Chairman	Chen Junsheng	CCm 93/12

National Narcotics Control Commission

Chairman	Tao Siju	CCm 93/07

National Production Safety Committee

Chairman	Zhu Rongji	PBm 91/06

National Committee for the Patriotic Public Health Campaign

Chairwoman	Peng Peiyun (f)	CCm 94/02

Coordination Committee for Women and Children's Work

Chairman	Li Tieying	PBm 90/02

Coordination Committee for the Handicapped

Chairwoman	Peng Peiyun (f)	CCm 93/10

Academic Degrees Committee

Chairman	He Dongchang	88/10

Environmental Protection Committee

Chairman	Song Jian	CCm 88/06

Distribution System Reform Committee

Chairman	Zou Jiahua	PBm 91/10

Securities Committee

Chairman	Zhu Rongji	PBm 92/10

China Securities Regulatory Committee

Chairman	Liu Hongru	92/10

State Organization Committee

Chairman	Li Peng	PBm 88/05

State Radio Regulatory Committee

Chairman	Zou Jiahua	PBm 94/06

Sanxia(Three Gorges)-Project Committee

Chairman	Li Peng	PBm 93/04

continued...

LEADERSHIP OF THE PRC, 1995 (continued)

ECONOMIC ORGANIZATIONS UNDER THE STATE COUNCIL

Aviation Industries of China
President   Zhu Yuli   93/04
V.-Pres.   Liu Gaozhuo   94/08
      Wang Ang   93/05
      Zhang Hongbiao   93/05
      Zhang Yanzhong CCa 93/05

China Aerospace Industry Corporation
(State Aerospace Bureau)
President (Director)
      Liu Jiyuan   CCm 93/04
V.-Pres. (Dep.Dir.)
      Bai Bai'er   93/05
      Luan Enjie   CCa 93/05
      Wang Liheng   93/05
      Xia Guohong   93/05

China National Nuclear Corporation
President Jiang Xinxiong CCm 88/05

China Armament Industry General Corporation
General Manager
      Zhang Junjiu CCa 93/04

China North Industries Group
President Lai Jinlie   90/05

State Agriculture Investment Corporation
President Tu Fengjun   88/07

State Communications Investment Corporation
President Xu Rongchu   93/08

State Energy Investment Corporation
President Wang Wenze   92/08

State Forestry Investment Corporation
President Xiao Chengjun   89/09

State Machine-Building, Electronics, Light and Textile Industries Investment Corporation
President Xiao Yongding   91/07

State Raw and Processed Materials Investment Corporation
President Kuang Yemei   88/07

China International Trust and Investment Corporation (CITIC)
Chairman Wei Mingyi   93/04
President Wang Jun   93/04

China International Engineering Consulting Corporation (CITIC)
President Shi Qirong   85/11

China National Coal Mine Corporation
President Wang Senhao   92/08

China National Nonferrous Metals Industry Corporation
President Fei Ziwen?   83/04

China Oil and Natural Gas Corporation
President Wang Tao CCm 88/05

China National Offshore Oil Corporation
President Wang Yan   92/12

China National Petro-Chemical Corporation
President Sheng Huaren   90/09

China National Tobacco Corporation
President Xun Xinghua   91/01

China Electronics Industry Corporation
President Zhang Xuedong   91/04

China State Shipbuilding Corporation
President Wang Rongsheng   93/11

China State Construction Engineering Corporation
President Ma Tinggui?   86/04

China Yangtze Three Gorges Project Development Company
General Manager
      Lu Youmei   93/09

Bank of China
Hon.Chm. Chen Muhua (f) CCm 85/11
Chairman Wang Qiren   93/12
President Wang Xuebing   93/12

Industrial and Commercial Bank of China
Chairman Gu Shifan   87/10
President Zhang Xiao (f) CCa 85/08

Agricultural Bank of China
President Ma Yongwei   85/07

People's Construction Bank of China
President Wang Qishan   94/08

State Development Bank
President: Yao Zhenyan   94/04

Import and Export Bank of China
Chairman Tong Zhiguang   94/04
President Lei Zuhua   94/04

People's Insurance Company of China
Chairman Li Yumin   91/01
President Li Yumin   90/08

PRC CENTRAL MILITARY COMMISSION

Chairman Jiang Zemin PBm 90/04
V.-Chm. Liu Huaqing PBm 90/04
      Zhang Zhen CCm 93/03

Members Chi Haotian CCm 88/04
      Fu Quanyou CCm 93/03
      Yu Yongbo CCm 93/03
      Zhang Wannian CCm 93/03

SUPREME PEOPLE'S COURT

President Ren Jianxin CCSm 88/04
V.-Pres. Duanmu Zheng   90/09
      Gao Changli CCa 93/07
      Liu Jiachen   93/07
      Ma Yuan (f)   85/06
      Tang Dehua   93/07
      Wang Jingrong   93/07
      Xie Anshan   92/09
      Zhu Mingshan   83/09

SUPREME PEOPLE'S PROCURATORATE

Procurator General
      Zhang Siqing CCm 93/03
Deputy Procurators General
      Chen Mingshu   91/10
      Liang Guoqing   86/06
      Wang Wenyuan   92/03
      Zhao Dengju   93/07
      Zhao Hong   93/09

CHINESE COMMUNIST PARTY

CCP CC General Secretary
      Jiang Zemin   89/06

POLITBURO
Standing Committee Members
      Jiang Zemin   89/06
      Li Peng   87/11
      Qiao Shi   87/11
      Li Ruihuan   89/06
      Zhu Rongji   92/10
      Liu Huaqing   92/10
      Hu Jintao CCSm 92/10

Other Politburo Members
      Chen Xitong   92/10
      Ding Guan'gen CCSm 92/10
      Jiang Chunyun   92/10
      Li Lanqing   92/10
      Li Tieying   87/11
      Qian Qichen   92/10
      Tian Jiyun   87/11
      Wei Jianxing CCSm 92/10
      Wu Bangguo   92/10
      Xie Fei   92/10
      Yang Baibing   92/10
      Zou Jiahua   92/10

Alternate Members
      Wang Hanbin   92/10
      Wen Jiabao CCSm 92/10

CCP CC Secretariat
Gen.Sec. Jiang Zemin PBm 89/06
Members Ding Guan'gen PBm 89/06
      Hu Jintao PBm 92/10
      Ren Jianxin CCm 92/10
      Wei Jianxing PBm 92/10
      Wen Jiabao PBa 92/10

CCP CC Military Commission
Chairman Jiang Zemin PBm 89/11
V.-Chm. Liu Huaqing PBm 89/11
      Zhang Zhen CCm 92/10
Members Chi Haotian CCm 89/11
      Fu Quanyou CCm 92/10
      Yu Yongbo CCm 92/10
      Zhang Wannian CCm 92/10

Commission for Inspecting Discipline
Secretary Wei Jianxing PBm CCSm 92/10
Dep.Sec. Cao Qingze   92/10
      Chen Zuolin   87/11
      Hou Zongbin CCm 92/10
      Wang Deying   90/12
      Xu Qing   92/10
Sec.-Gen. Wang Guang   94/04

General Office
Director Zeng Qinghong   93/03
Dep.Dir. Chen Fujin   93/09
      Hu Guangbao   93/07
      Xu Ruixin   88/02
      Yang Dezhong (first) CCm 80/10

Organization Department
Director Lü Feng CCm 90/01
Dep.Dir. Li Tielin   93/04
      Meng Liankun   87/09
      Song Defu CCm 93/08
      Wang Xudong   93/08
      Wu Lianyuan   92/08
      Zhang Quanjing (exec.)   91/06
      Zhao Zongnai   88/03
Sec.-Gen. Jiang Zhenyun   91/06

Propaganda Department
Director Ding Guan'gen PBm CCSm 92/12
Dep.Dir. Bai Keming   93/06
      Gong Xinhan   93/04
      Liu Yunshan CCa 93/08
      Liu Zhongde? CCm 90/08
      Nie Dajiang   90/09
      Xu Weicheng (exec.)   89/09
      Zeng Jianhui   88/10
      Zhai Taifeng (exec.)   91/11
      Zheng Bijian (exec.) CCm 92/10
Sec.-Gen. Shen Yizhi   87/07

United Front Department
Director Wang Zhaoguo CCm 92/12
Dep.Dir. Jiang Minkuan (exec.) CCm 90/12
      Li Dezhu CCm 92/11
      Liu Jidong   93/04
      Liu Yandong (f)   91/10
      Wan Shaofen (f)   88/11
      Zheng Wantong   93/08
Sec.-Gen. Zhang Mengna (f)   93/03

International Liaison Department
Director Li Shuzheng (f)   93/03
Dep.Dir. Huan Guoying   93/09
      Jiang Guanghua   82/11
      Li Beihai   93/08
      Li Chengren   88/07
      Zhu Shanqing   85/02
Sec.-Gen. Li Beihai   91/02

Commission for Politics and Law
Secretary Ren Jianxin CCSm 92/12
Dep.Sec. Luo Gan CCm 93/06

Commission for Comprehensive Management of Social Security
Chairman Ren Jianxin CCSm 92/12
V.-Chm. Cao Zhi   93/07
      Luo Gan CCm 93/07
      Zhang Siqing CCm 93/07

Commission for Protection of Party Secrets
Chairman Qiao Shi PBm 92/05

Central Organization Committee
Chairman Li Peng PBm 91/08
V.-Chm. Hu Jintao PBm CCSm 93/07
      Luo Gan CCm 93/07

Policy Research Office
Director Wang Weicheng CCm 89/09
Dep.Dir. Teng Wensheng   90/03
      Wei Jianlin   89/12
      Xiao Wanjun   93/07
      Zheng Keyang   90/01

continued…

LEADERSHIP OF THE PRC, 1995 (continued)

Work Committee for Organs under Central Committee

Chairman	Zeng Qinghong		93/03
V.-Chm.	Gu Yunfei (exec.)		88/06
	Li Dengzhu		94/05
	Li Yan		86/10
	Wang Jingmao		91/01

Work Committee for Central Government Organs

Chairman	Luo Gan	CCm	89/09
V.-Chm.	Jia Jun		88/12
	Li Mingyu		91/03
	Liu Zhengwei	CCm	93/07
	Qu Shouqing		88/12
	Wang Chuguang		88/06
	Zhang Jingyuan (exec.)		88/02

Party History Research Office

Director	Wang Weicheng	CCm	90/07
Dep.Dir.	Fan Shouxin		89/08
	Ma Shijiang		88/08
	Sha Jiansun	CCa	88/08
	Zheng Hui		87/06

Documents Research Office

Director	Pang Xianzhi		91/11
Dep.Dir.	Jin Chongji		84/00

CC Party School

President	Hu Jintao	PBm CCSm	93/10
V.-Pres.	Gong Yuzhi		94/05
	Liu Shengyu		93/07
	Su Xing		88/04
	Wang Jialiu (f) (exec.)	CCm	93/11
	Xing Bensi		89/07
	Xue Ju		89/08
	Yang Chungui		94/05
Sec.-Gen.	Yang Peixian		90/11

People's Daily

Director	Shao Huaze	CCm	92/11
Dep.Dir.	Zheng Mengxiong		90/04
Editor-in-Chief	Fan Jingyi		94/05
Dep.Eds.-in-Chief	Bao Yujun		88/10
	Tang Jiyu		90/04
	Wu Chunhe		93/09
	Zhang Yunsheng (exec.)		89/11
	Zheng Mengxiong		91/04
	Zhou Ruijin		93/04

Guangming Daily

Editor-in-Chief	Zhang Changhai		89/08
Dep.Eds.-in-Chief	Chen Tanqiang		91/06
	Fang Gongwen		87/06
	Jiang Dianming		89/00
	Lu Zhun		85/06
	Qi Zhiwen		91/01
	Wang Chen		86/08
	Xu Guangchun		91/11
	Zhou Longbin		91/11

Qiushi Bimonthly

Editor-in-Chief	You Lin		89/10
Dep.Eds.-in-Chief	Liu Yili		89/05
	Ma Yingbo		92/10
	Su Shuangbi		89/09
	Wu Jianguo		90/08

Leading Group for Agriculture

Head	Zhu Rongji	PBm	93/04
Dep.Heads	Chen Junsheng	CCm	93/04
	Wen Jiabao	PBa CCSm	93/04

Financial and Economic Leading Group

Head	Jiang Zemin	PBm	92/11
Dep.Heads	Li Peng	PBm	92/11
	Zhu Rongji	PBm	92/11
Sec.-Gen.	Wen Jiabao	PBa CCSm	93/03

Party Building Group

Head	Song Ping		89/09
Dep.Heads	Bo Yibo		90/03
	Deng Liqun		90/08

Leading Group for Party History Work

Head	Yang Shangkun?		84/12

Leading Group for Thought and Propaganda

Head	?		
Dep.Head	Ai Zhisheng	CCm	94/05

Foreign Affairs Leading Group

Head	Li Peng	PBm	89/12
Dep.Heads	Qian Qichen	PBm	89/12
	Wu Xueqian		89/12

Taiwan Affairs Leading Group

Head	Jiang Zemin	PBm	93/05
Dep.Head	Qian Qichen	PBm	93/05
Sec.-Gen.	Wang Zhaoguo	CCm	93/05

Leading Group for Taiwan Economic and Trade Coordination

Head	Li Lanqing	PBm	94/04
Dep.Head	Wang Zhaoguo	CCm	94/04

Overseas Publicity Group

Head	Zeng Jianhui		92/12
Dep.Head	Zhou Jue		91/03

Taiwan Affairs Office

Director	Wang Zhaoguo	CCm	91/06
Dep.Dir.	Li Qingzhou		91/02
	Sun Xiaoyu		93/04
	Tang Shubei		91/06

NATIONAL MILITARY LEADERSHIP

CCP CC Military Commission See under CCP

PRC Central Military Commission See separate entry above

General Staff

Chief	Zhang Wannian	CCm	92/11
Dep.Ch.	Cao Gangchuan		92/11
	Li Jing	CCm	92/11
	Xu Huizi (exec.)	CCm	85/04

General Political Department

Director	Yu Yongbo	CCm	92/11
Dep.Dir.	Du Tiehuan		94/01
	Wang Ruilin	CCm	92/12
	Xu Caihou		94/01
	Zhou Ziyu		93/06

General Logistics Department

Director	Fu Quanyou	CCm	92/11
Dep.Dir.	Liu Mingpu		85/04
	Wang Tailan		92/00
	Zhang Bin		85/08
	Zhou Youliang		94/01

PLA Navy

Commander	Zhang Lianzhong	CCm	88/01
Dep.Cdr.	Chen Mingshan		88/07
	He Pengfei		92/12
	Shi Tianding		90/10
	Xu Zhenzhong		90/10
Pol.Commissar	Zhou Kunren		94/01
Dep.P.C.	Li Shitian		90/07
	Tong Guorong		93/09

North China Sea Fleet

Commander	Wang Jiying		93/10
Dep.Cdr.	Shi Tianding		93/08
Pol.Commissar	Zhang Haiyun		90/07
Dep.P.C.	Jiang Zhaozhi		93/08

East China Sea Fleet

Commander	Yang Yushu		94/02
Dep.Cdr.	An Liqun		87/11
	Chen Qingji		94/04
	Liu Jipan		94/04
	Wang Yongguo		93/01
Pol.Commissar	Lian Yaoting		90/08
Dep.P.C.	Huang Huang		93/06
	Liu Shuyuan		93/01
	Wei Boliang		92/09

South China Sea Fleet

Commander	Gao Zhenjia		88/08
Dep.Cdr.	Liu Xizhong		87/03
Pol.Commissar	Kang Fuquan		93/06
Dep.P.C.	Xie Dazhong		93/04
	Zhao Yingfu		94/05

PLA Air Force

Commander	Cao Shuangming	CCm	92/11
Dep.Cdr.	Lin Hu		86/12
	Liu Zhitian		88/12
	Yang Zhenyu		94/03
	Yu Zhenwu		85/07
Pol.Commissar	Ding Wenchang	CCm	92/11
Dep.P.C.	?		

PLA Second Artillery

Commander	Yang Guoliang	CCm	92/11
Dep.Cdr.	Fu Guanghui		90/04
	Li Qianming		93/10
	Qian Gui		91/08
Pol.Commissar	Sui Yongju		92/12
Dep.P.C.	?		

National Defence University

President	Zhu Dunfa	CCm	92/11

Academy of Military Sciences

President	Zhao Nanqi	CCm	92/11

PLA Military Court

President	Quan Zengde		93/09

PLA Military Procuratorate

Chief Procurator	Liu Baochen		92/11

Liberation Army Daily

Director	Xu Caihou		93/06
Editor-in-Chief	Sun Zhongtong		93/06

Headquarters of Chinese People's Armed Police Force

Commander	Ba Zhongtan		93/01
Dep.Cdr.	An Jiaoju		93/09
	Wang Wenli		90/02
	Zuo Yinsheng		90/02
1st Pol.Commissar	Tao Siju	CCm	91/04
Pol.Com.	Zhang Shutian		93/01
Dep.P.C.	Lü Shouyan		90/02
	Xu Guibao		90/02

MILITARY REGIONS

Beijing

Commander	Li Laizhu	CCm	94/01
Dep.Cdr.	Guo Boxiong		94/07
	He Daoquan		94/07
	Jiang Hongquan		92/12
	Yao Xian		90/10
Pol.Com.	Gu Shanqing	CCm	92/12
Dep.P.C.	Wang Fuyi		90/07

Chengdu

Commander	Li Jiulong	CCm	92/11
Dep.Cdr.	Chi Yunxiu		92/12
	Huang Hengmei		94/01
	Liao Xilong		85/06
	Ma Bingchen		86/07
	Xie Decai		91/12
	Zhu Chengyou		94/01
Pol.Com.	Zhang Zhijian		94/01
Dep.P.C.	Jiang Futang		94/01
	Shao Nong		90/05
	Wu Runzhong		94/01
	Zhang Shaosong		92/12
	Zheng Xianbin	CCa	94/01

Guangzhou

Commander	Li Xilin	CCm	92/10
Dep.Cdr.	Liu Heqiao		87/10
	Tao Bojun		94/01
	Wang Shen		92/12
	Zhou Yushu	CCm	92/12
Pol.Com.	Shi Yuxiao	CCm	92/10
Dep.P.C.	Gao Tianzheng	CCm	90/05
	Liu Xinzeng		90/05

Ji'nan

Commander	Zhang Taiheng		92/10
Dep.Cdr.	Lin Jigui		87/12
	Yang Guoping		94/01
Pol.Com.	Song Qingwei	CCm	87/12
Dep.P.C.	Cai Renshan		90/05
	Qu Jining		90/05
	Zhang Wentai		94/03

Lanzhou

Commander	Liu Jingsong	CCm	92/12
Dep.Cdr.	Chen Chao		90/07
	Fu Bingyao		93/04
	Tang Guangcai		94/02
	Wang Lizhong		88/05
	Xing Shizhong		93/11
	Zou Yuqi		
Pol.Com.	Cao Pengsheng	CCm	90/06
Dep.P.C.	Gong Yongfeng		90/08
	Pan Zhaomin		92/12
	Qian Shugen	CCa	94/05
	Wang Maorun		90/07
	Xu Shouzeng		94/04

continued…

LEADERSHIP OF THE PRC, 1995 (continued)

Nanjing

Commander	Gu Hui	CCm	90/05
Dep.Cdr.	Guo Xizhang		90/05
	He Qizong	CCa	93/01
	Liu Lunxian		92/11
	Qu Zhenmou		93/03
	Yan Zhuo		94/01
Pol.Com.	Fang Zuqi		94/01
Dep.P.C.	Lan Baojing	CCa	94/01
	Pei Jiuzhou		90/05
	Wang Yongming		90/06

Shenyang

Commander	Wang Ke	CCm	92/12
Dep.Cdr.	Qi Lianyun		93/06
	Shi Baoyuan		85/08
	Tong Baocun	CCm	90/07
Pol.Com.	Li Xinliang		94/01
Dep.P.C.	Ai Weiren		91/02
	Huang Jianhong		93/03
	Zhou Wenyuan	CCm	93/03

CHINESE PEOPLE'S POLITICAL CONSULTATIVE CONFERENCE

Chairman	Li Ruihuan	PBm	93/03
V.-Chm.	An Zijie		93/03
	Ba Jin		83/06
	Deng Zhaoxiang		88/04
	Ding Guangxun		89/03
	Dong Yinchu		93/03
	Hong Xuezhi		90/03
	Hou Jingru		89/03
	Hu Sheng		88/04
	Huo Yingdong		93/03
	Liu Jingji		84/05
	Ma Wanqi		93/03
	Ngapoi Ngawang Jigme		93/03
	Qian Weichang		87/04
	Qian Xuesen		86/04
	Qian Zhengying (f)	CCm	88/04
	Seypidin Aze		93/03
	Su Buqing		88/04
	Sun Fuling		93/03
	Wan Guoquan		94/03
	Wang Zhaoguo	CCm	93/03
	Wu Xueqian		93/03
	Yang Jingren		88/04
	Yang Rudai		93/03
	Ye Xuanping	CCm	91/04
	Zhao Puchu		83/06
	Zhu Guangya	CCm	94/03
Sec.-Gen.	Zhu Xun	CCm	94/03

MASS ORGANIZATIONS

Communist Youth League

First Secretary
	Li Keqiang	93/05

Secretaries
	Bayinqolu	93/05
	Ji Bingxuan	93/05
	Jiang Daming	93/05
	Liu Peng (exec.)	93/05
	Yuan Chunqing	92/12
	Zhao Shi (f)	93/05

Federation of Trade Unions

President	Wei Jianxing	PBm CCSm	93/10
V.-Pres.	Fang Jiade		91/04
	Jiang Jiafu		93/10
	Li Qisheng	CCa	93/10
	Liu Heng		93/10
	Teng Yilong		93/10
	Xue Zhaoyun (f)		93/10
	Yang Xingfu		89/12
	Zhang Dinghua (exec.)	CCm	91/12
	Zhang Guoxiang		93/10

First Secretary
	Zhang Dinghua	CCm	91/12

Women's Federation

President	Chen Muhua	CCm	88/09
V.-Pres.	Hao Yichun		88/09
	He Luli		93/09
	Huang Qizao	CCm	88/09
	Kong Lingren		93/09
	Lin Liyun	CCm	78/09
	Liu Hairong		93/09
	Mahinur Kasim		78/09
	Ngapoi Cedain Zhoigar		78/09

	Nie Li		88/09
	Wang Shuxian		93/09
	Wei Yu		88/09
	Zhang Guoying (first)	CCm	83/09
	Zhao Di		90/12

First Secretary
	Huang Qizao	CCm	90/02

Youth Federation

President	Liu Peng	93/12
V.-Pres.	Bayingolu (exec.)	93/12
	Comoiling Dandzimchilai	90/08
	Guan Mucun (f)	90/08
	Huo Zhenhuan	90/08
	Li Keqiang	86/07
	Locong (exec.)	86/07
	Ni Yuan (f)	90/08
	Qin Dahe	90/08
	Sheng Chengfa	90/08
	Wu Yingfu	83/08
	Yang Yue	90/08
	Yu Guilin	93/12
	Yuan Chunqing	93/12
	Zhang Rongfang (f)	90/08
	Zhao Shi (f)	93/12
Sec.-Gen.	Yu Guilin	91/03

Students' Federation

President	Yang Yue	90/12

Chinese People's Association for Friendship with Foreign Countries

President	Qi Huaiyuan	CCm	94/05
V.-Pres.	Chen Haosu		90/03
	Wang Xiaoxian (f)		88/12
	Xu Qun		92/09

NON-COMMUNIST PARTIES

Revolutionary Committee of the Chinese Guomindang

Hon.Chm.	Hou Jingru	92/12
	Sun Yueqi	92/12
	Zhu Xuefan	92/12
H.V.-Ch.	Jia Yibin	92/12
	Zhao Zukang	88/11
Chairman	Li Peiyao	92/12
V.-Chm.	Cheng Zhiqing (f)	92/12
	He Luli (f)	88/11
	Hu Min	92/12
	Li Ganliu	83/12
	Peng Qingyuan	83/12
	Shen Qiwwo	91/12
	Tong Fu	92/12
	Xu Qichao	83/12
	Zhou Tienong	92/12
Sec.-Gen.	Zhu Peikang	92/12

China Democratic League

Hon.Chm.		
Chairman	Fei Xiaotong	87/01
V.-Chm.	Ding Shilin (exec.)	88/10
	Feng Zhijun	87/01
	Kang Zhenhuang	88/10
	Kong Lingren (f)	88/10
	Luo Hanxian	87/01
	Ma Dayou	87/01
	Qian Weichang	83/12
	Tan Jiazhen	83/12
	Tao Dayong	83/12
	Wu Xiuping	92/12
	Xie Songkai	88/10
	Zhang Yumao	92/12
Sec.-Gen.	Yu Zeyou	92/12

China Democratic National Construction Association

Chairman	Sun Qimeng	87/12
V.-Chm.	Bai Dahua	88/06
	Chen Mingshan	83/11
	Chen Suiheng	83/11
	Feng Kexu	92/11
	Feng Tiyun	83/11
	Huang Daneng	83/11
	Li Chonghuai	88/06
	Liu Heng	92/11
	Lu Ming	92/11
	Wan Guoquan (exec.)	83/11
	Zhu Yuancheng	92/11
Sec.-Gen.	Feng Kexu	88/06

China Association for Promoting Democracy

Hon.Chm.	Xie Bingxin (f)	88/11
	Zhao Puchu	92/12
Chairman	Lei Jieqiong (f)	87/06
V.-Chm.	Chen Nanxian	88/11
	Chen Shunli	83/11
	Chu Zhuang	84/12
	Deng Weizhi	88/11
	Feng Jicai	88/11
	Ge Zhicheng	84/12
	Mei Xiangming	88/11
	Xu Jialu	92/12
	Ye Zhishan	87/06
Sec.-Gen.	Chen Yiqun	89/03

Chinese Peasants' and Workers' Democratic Party

Hon.Chm.	Zhou Gucheng	88/11
Chairman	Lu Jiaxi	88/11
V.-Chm.	Chen Haozhu	88/11
	Fang Rongxin (exec.)	83/12
	Jian Tiancong	88/11
	Jiang Zhenghua	92/12
	Song Jinsheng	92/12
	Tian Guangtao	87/01
	Yan Hongchen	92/12
	Yao Jun	87/01
	Zhang Shiming	87/01
Sec.-Gen.	Song Jinsheng	92/12

China Zhi Gong Dang (Party for Public Interests)

Hon.Chm.	Huang Dingchen	88/04
H.V.-Ch.	Wu Juetian	92/12
Chairman	Dong Yinchu	88/12
V.-Chm.	Lu Rongshu	83/07
	Luo Haocai	92/12
	Wang Songda	88/12
	Yang Jike (exec.)	88/12
	Zheng Shouyi (f)	83/12
Sec.-Gen.	Wang Songda	88/12

Jiusan (September 3) Society

Hon.Chm.	Jin Shanbao	89/01
	Yan Jici	89/01
Chairman	Wu Jieping	92/12
V.-Chm.	An Zhendong	83/12
	Chen Mingshao	89/01
	Chen Xuejun	89/01
	Hao Yichun (f)	83/12
	Hong Fuzeng	92/12
	Jin Kaicheng	92/12
	Wang Wenyuan	89/01
	Xu Caidong (exec.)	83/12
	Yang You	89/01
	Zhao Weizhi	90/12
Sec.-Gen.	Liu Ronghan	92/12

Taiwan Democratic Self-Government League

Hon.Chm.	Su Ziheng	87/12
Chairman	Cai Zimin	88/12
V.-Chm.	Chen Zhongyi	87/12
	Zhang Kehui	92/11
Sec.-Gen.	Pan Yuanjing	87/12

All-China Federation of Industry and Commerce

Chairman	Jing Shuping		93/10
V.-Chm.	Chen Jingxin		93/10
	Guo Xiuzhen (f)		88/12
	He Fengzu		93/10
	He Houhua		93/10
	Hu Deping		93/10
	Huan Yushan		93/10
	Huang Changxi		79/10
	Jiang Minkuan	CCm	93/10
	Jiang Peilu		79/10
	Li Hongchang		93/10
	Liang Shangli		79/10
	Liu Minxue		93/10
	Liu Yimin		93/10
	Liu Yonghao		93/10
	Qi Jingfa		93/10
	Wang Zhiguo		93/10
	Zeng Xianzi		93/10
	Zhang Xuwu		88/12
	Zheng Yutong		93/10
	Zhu Wenju		93/10
Sec.-Gen.	Huan Yushan		93/10

continued...

LEADERSHIP OF THE PRC, 1995 (continued)

The Main Provincial Leadership of the PRC

(Changes are underlined)

Liu Jen-Kai

Anhui Province

CCP Sec.	Lu Rongjing	CCm	88/04
Dep.Sec.	Fang Zhaoxiang		93/09
	Fu Xishou	CCm	87/11
	Meng Fulin (exec.)		88/01
	Wang Taihua	CCa	92/10
	Yang Yongliang	CCa	89/04
Governor	Fu Xishou	CCm	89/04
V.-Gov.	Du Yijin		88/02
	Wang Xiuzhi		93/02
	Wang Yang		93/02
	Wang Zhaoyao		93/02
	Yang Duoliang		93/02
	Zhang Runxia (f)		88/02
PPC Chm.	Meng Fulin		93/02
PLA Cdr.	Shen Shanwen		90/07
Dep.Cdr.	He Yanran		90/07
	Liu Zhengzong		90/07
Pol.Com.	Chen Peisen		93/01
Dep.P.C.	Hu Daoren		93/06
	Lu Guangyan		90/07
	Zhang Honggui		93/06

Beijing Municipality

CCP Sec.	Chen Xitong	PBm	92/12
Dep.Sec.	Chen Guangwen		92/12
	Li Qiyan	CCm	87/12
	Li Zhijian		92/12
	Wang Jialiu? (f)	CCm	88/10
Mayor	Li Qiyan	CCm	92/12
Vice-M.	Duan Qiang		93/02
	He Luli (f)		88/01
	Hu Zhaoguang		93/02
	Li Runwu		93/02
	Lu Yucheng		88/01
	Meng Xuenong		93/02
	Wang Baosen (exec.)		91/06
	Zhang Baifa (exec.)		82/03
PPC Chm.	Zhang Jianmin	CCa	93/02
PLA Cdr.	He Daoquan		94/01
Dep.Cdr.	Gao Yunjiang		90/10
	Qin Tao		90/09
	Wang Pengtang		93/06
Pol.Com.	Zhang Baokang		91/02
Dep.P.C.	Huang Xiangchu		91/06

Fujian Province

CCP Sec.	Jia Qinglin	CCm	93/12
Dep.Sec.	Chen Mingyi	CCa	93/09
	Lin Kaiqin		92/04
	Yuan Qitong		90/02
Governor	Chen Mingyi	CCa	94/04
V.-Gov.	Shi Xingmou		88/01
	Tong Wanheng		93/01
	Wang Jianshuang		93/09
	Wang Liangpu		93/01
	Zhang Jiakun		92/04
PPC Chm.	Jia Qinglin	CCm	94/04
PLA Cdr.	Ren Yonggui		93/04
Dep.Cdr.	Chen Mingduan		90/10
	Wang Zhenyong		93/06
Pol.Com.	Sui Shengwu		94/06
Dep.P.C.	Zhang Lizhi		90/12

Gansu Province

CCP Sec.	Yan Haiwang	CCa	93/10
Dep.Sec.	Sun Ying		92/07
	Yang Zhenjie		93/04
	Zhang Wule		93/04
Governor	Zhang Wule		93/09
V.-Gov.	Chen Qiling		92/03
	Cui Zhenghua		93/01
	Guo Kun		93/01
	Lu Ming		85/12
	Yang Huaixiao		92/03
PPC Chm.	Lu Kejian		93/01
PLA Cdr.	Liang Peizhen		93/09
Dep.Cdr.	Lan Zhongjie		90/09
Pol.Com.	Li Zhong		90/10
Dep.P.C.	Du Hua		90/10

Guangdong Province

CCP Sec.	Xie Fei	PBm	91/01
Dep.Sec.	Huang Huahua		93/05
	Zhang Guoying (f)	CCm	90/01
	Zhu Senlin	CCm	91/05
Governor	Zhu Senlin	CCm	92/01
V.-Gov.	Gong Rongchang		93/04
	Li Lanfang (f)		91/07
	Liu Weiming		88/01
	Lu Ruihua (exec.)	CCa	91/07
	Lu Zhonghe		88/01
	Ou Guangyuan	CCa	93/02
	Zhang Gaoli		88/01
	Zhong Qiquan		94/04
PPC Chm.	Lin Ruo		90/05
PLA Com.	Wen Yuzhu		92/11
Dep.Cdr.	Yu Lusheng		92/10
	Zhou Jinxi		94/06
Pol.Com.	Liu Yuanjie		94/06
Dep.P.C.	Xie Youmin		91/12

Guangxi Autonomous Region

CCP Sec.	Zhao Fulin	CCm	90/10
Dep.Sec.	Cheng Kejie	CCm	89/12
	Ding Tingmo		90/10
Chairman*	Cheng Kejie	CCm	90/01
V.-Chm.	Lei Yu		92/04
	Li Zhenqian		89/01
	Lu Bing		93/01
	Xu Bingsong		93/01
	Yuan Fengjan (f)		93/01
	Yuan Zhengzhong		90/08
PPC Chm.	Liu Mingzu	CCa	93/01
PLA Cdr.	Wen Guoqing		90/09
Dep.Cdr.	Hu Jun		90/10
	Jia Fukun		90/01
	Liu Wenliang		94/06
Pol.Com.	Gong Pingqiu		94/06
Dep.P.C.	Zhan Kexun		90/10

Guizhou Province

CCP Sec.	Liu Fangren	CCa	93/07
Dep.Sec.	Chen Shineng		93/11
	Wang Siqi	CCa	92/12
Governor	Chen Shineng		93/01
V.-Gov.	Gong Xianyong		88/01
	Hu Xiansheng		93/09
	Mo Shiren		93/09
	Wang Guangdian	CCa	93/12
	Yao Jiyuan		93/01
	Yuan Ronggui		93/01
	Zhang Shukui (exec.)		85/05
	Zhang Yuqin (f)		80/01
PPC Chm.	Wang Chaowen	CCm	94/01
PLA Cdr.	Zhu Qi		90/07
Dep.Cdr.	Zhong Liming		90/07
Pol.Com.	Yu Zhonggui		90/07
Dep.P.C.	Deng Guoyong		90/07

Hainan Province

CCP Sec.	Ruan Chongwu	CCm	93/01
Dep.Sec.	Chen Yuyi		93/07
	Du Qinglin	CCa	92/05
	Wang Xiaofeng	CCa	93/01
Governor	Ruan Chongwu	CCm	93/02
V.-Gov.	Chen Suhou		90/02
	Liu Mingqi		93/02
	Mao Zhijun		91/05
	Wang Xiaofeng	CCa	93/02
	Wang Xueping	CCa	91/05
PPC Chm.	Du Qinglin	CCa	93/02
PLA Cdr.	Zhang Zhiqing		92/11
Dep.Cdr.	Chen Zuocai		94/05
	Liu Chengbao		90/12
Pol.Com.	Zhou Chuantong		94/05
Dep.P.C.	Ding Yucai		90/04

Hebei Province

CCP Sec.	Cheng Weigao	CCm	93/01
Dep.Sec.	Chen Yujie (f)	CCa	94/03
	Li Bingliang		90/07
	Lü Chuanzan		86/10
	Xu Yongyue		94/03
	Ye Liansong	CCm	93/04
Governor	Ye Liansong	CCm	93/05
V.-Gov.	Chen Liyou (exec.)		91/04
	Gu Erxiong		91/03
	Guo Hongqi		90/04
	Guo Shichang		93/05
	Li Haifeng (f)		92/12
	Liu Zuotian		93/05
	Wang Youhui		91/04
PPC Chm.	Lü Chuanzan		93/05
PLA Cdr.	Han Shiqian		90/12
Dep.Cdr.	?		
Pol.Com.	Wang Chaohai		94/05
Dep.P.C.	?		

Heilongjiang Province

CCP Sec.	Yue Qifeng	CCm	94/04
Dep.Sec.	Ma Guoliang		92/06
	Shan Rongfan		93/02
	Tian Fengshan	CCa	92/10
Governor	Tian Fengshan (act.)	CCa	94/05
V.-Gov.	Cong Fukui		90/08
	Ma Shujie		93/01
	Sun Kuiwen		90/08
	Tian Fengshan	CCa	94/05
	Wang Zongzhang		93/01
	Yang Zhihai		92/10
	Zhou Tienong		91/10
PPC Chm.	Sun Weiben	CCm	88/01
PLA Cdr.	Wang Guiqin		93/08
Dep.Cdr.	Yu Dianchen		88/08
Pol.Com.	Yu Jingchang		93/03
Dep.P.C.	?		

He'nan Province

CCP Sec.	Li Changchun	CCm	92/12
Dep.Sec.	Lin Yinghai		90/11
	Ma Zhongchen	CCa	92/12
	Ren Keli		93/03
	Song Zhaosu		93/06
Governor	Ma Zhongchen	CCa	92/12
V.-Gov.	Fan Qinchen (exec.)	CCa	91/03
	Li Chengyu		93/02
	Yao Zhongmin		93/04
	Yu Jiahua		93/04
	Zhang Honghua		93/04
	Zhang Shiying		93/04
PPC Chm.	Li Changchun	CCa	93/04
PLA Cdr.	Zhu Chao		90/07
Dep.Cdr.	Huang Qiugui		89/04
Pol.Com.	Wu Guangxian		90/07
Dep.P.C.	Zhang Sijing		90/07
	Xia Guangyao		93/07

continued…

LEADERSHIP OF THE PRC, 1995 (continued)

Hubei Province

Office	Name		
CCP Sec.	Guan Guangfu	CCm	83/03
Dep.Sec.	Hui Liangyu	CCa	92/10
	Jia Zhijie	CCm	93/02
	Qian Yunlu	CCa	83/03
	Zhong Shuqiao		92/09
Governor	Jia Zhijie	CCm	93/02
V.-Gov.	Chen Shuiwen		93/05
	Han Nanpeng		86/05
	Li Daqiang (exec.)		90/05
	Meng Qingping		93/05
	Su Xiaoyun		93/05
	Wang Shengtie		93/05
	Zhao Baojiang		93/05
PPC Chm.	Guan Guangfu	CCm	93/05
PLA Cdr.	Liu Guoyu		92/07
Dep.Cdr.	?		
Pol.Com.	Xu Shiqiao		93/06
Dep.P.C.	?		

Hu'nan Province

Office	Name		
CCP Sec.	Wang Maolin	CCm	93/09
Dep.Sec.	Chen Bangzhu	CCm	89/02
	Chu Bo		94/02
	Yang Zhengwu	CCm	90/06
Governor	Chen Bangzhu	CCm	89/05
V.-Gov.	Pan Guiyu (f)		93/01
	Tang Zhixiang		93/01
	Wang Keying		91/05
	Zheng Peimin		93/01
	Zhou Bohua		93/01
	Zhou Shichang		93/01
PPC Chm.	Liu Fusheng		88/01
PLA Cdr.	Pang Weiqiang		90/06
Dep.Cdr.	Deng Miaoquan		92/07
Pol.Com.	Deng Hanmin		93/04
Dep.P.C.	Huang Zuzong		90/06

Inner Mongolia Autonomous Region

Office	Name		
CCP Sec.	Liu Mingzu	CCa	94/07
Dep.Sec.	Bai Enpei	CCa	92/04
	Qian Fenyong?		83/03
	Wang Zhan	CCa	93/08
	Wu Liji	CCm	92/04
Chairman*	Wu Liji	CCm	93/05
V.-Chm.	Bao Wenfa		93/05
	Lin Yongsan		91/12
	Shen Shuji (f)		93/05
	Song Zhimin		92/04
	Yun Bulong		92/04
	Zhang Tingwu		93/05
	Zhao Zhihong		83/04
	Zhou Weide		93/05
PPC Chm.	Wang Qun	CCm	93/05
PLA Cdr.	Diao Congzhou		90/06
Dep.Cdr.	Baya Ertu		91/01
Pol.Com.	Yang Enbo		88/08
Dep.P.C.	Zhaori Getu		90/06

Jiangsu Province

Office	Name		
CCP Sec.	Chen Huanyou	CCm	93/09
Dep.Sec.	Cao Hongming		89/05
	Cao Keming		91/03
Governor	Chen Huanyou	CCm	89/04
V.-Gov.	Ji Yunshi		89/06
	Jiang Yongrong	CCa	93/04
	Wang Rongbing		93/04
	Yang Xiaotang		92/03
	Yu Xingde		92/03
	Zhang Huaixi		93/04
PPC Chm.	Shen Daren	CCm	93/04
PLA Cdr.	Zheng Bingqing		92/10
Dep.Cdr.	Chen Kehou		90/10
	Li Dekun		91/02
	Liu Boxing		93/01
	Xu Mingao		94/02
Pol.Com.	Wei Chang'an		90/07
Dep.P.C.	?		

Jiangxi Province

Office	Name		
CCP Sec.	Mao Zhiyong	CCm	88/04
Dep.Sec.	Lu Xiuzhen		93/04
	Wu Guanzheng	CCm	86/10
	Zhu Zhihong		91/06
Governor	Wu Guanzheng	CCm	86/10
V.-Gov.	Huang Maoheng (f)		93/02
	Huang Zhiquan		93/02
	Shu Huiguo		91/03
	Shu Shengyou (exec.)		91/03
	Zhang Yunchuan		93/02
	Zheng Liangyu		92/10
	Zhou Zhiping		91/03
PPC Chm.	Mao Zhiyong	CCm	93/02
PLA Cdr.	Feng Jinmao		93/04
Dep.Cdr.	Zhong Qingsheng		93/09
Pol.Com.	Zheng Shichao		93/04
Dep.P.C.	Lou Zhongnan		90/03

Jilin Province

Office	Name		
CCP Sec.	He Zhukang	CCm	88/04
Dep.Sec.	Gao Yan	CCm	93/04
	Wang Jinshan		93/02
	Zhang Dejiang	CCa	91/04
Governor	Gao Yan	CCm	92/03
V.-Gov.	Liu Shuying (f)		94/02
	Liu Xilin		83/04
	Quan Zhezhu		93/01
	Sang Fengwen		94/02
	Wang Guofa		93/01
	Wei Minxue		93/01
	Zhang Yueqi		90/08
PPC Chm.	He Zhukang	CCm	93/01
PLA Cdr.	Zhou Zaikang		90/07
Dep.Cdr.	Qian Bo		90/07
	Zhang Tizhen		93/03
Pol.Com.	Shi Zhaoping		92/08
Dep.P.C.	?		

Liaoning Province

Office	Name		
CCP Sec.	Gu Jinchi	CCm	93/10
Dep.Sec.	Cao Bochun	CCa	92/07
	Shang Wen		90/08
	Sun Qi		86/06
	Wang Huaiyuan		93/10
	Wen Shizhen		94/05
	Zhang Guoguang		93/10
Governor	Wen Shizhen (act.)		94/05
V.-Gov.	Cong Zhenglong		92/03
	Gao Guozhu		93/03
	Guo Tingbiao (exec.)		92/03
	Xiao Zuofu		88/01
	Zhang Rongmao		92/01
	Zhang Rongming (f)		93/03
PPC Chm.	Quan Shuren	CCm	93/03
PLA Cdr.	Xiang Jingyuan		90/08
Dep.Cdr.	Hou Xueyuan		93/06
	Liu Zhanying?		90/08
	Yuan Genshuan		86/08
	Zhu Chunfa		90/02
Pol.Com.	Gao Dianwu		93/05
Dep.P.C.	Ye Zhaohong		93/06

Ningxia Autonomous Region

Office	Name		
CCP Sec.	Huang Huang	CCm	90/01
Dep.Sec.	Bai Lichen	CCm	88/07
	Kang Yi		93/04
	Ma Qizhi	CCa	93/04
	Yao Minxue		93/04
Chairman*	Bai Lichen	CCm	87/04
V.-Chm.	Cheng Faguang		88/05
	Liu Zhong		93/05
	Ma Wenxue		93/05
	Ren Qixing		88/05
	Zhou Shengxian		93/05
PPC Chm.	Ma Sizhong		88/05
PLA Cdr.	Li Lianghui		93/12
Dep.Cdr.	Li Tiansheng		92/11
Pol.Com.	Wang Yongzheng		94/05
Dep.P.C.	Huang Jiuli		91/12

Qinghai Province

Office	Name		
CCP Sec.	Yin Kesheng	CCm	85/07
Dep.Sec.	Cai Zhulin		92/12
	Sang Jiejia	CCa	88/05
	Tian Chengping	CCa	88/02
Governor	Tian Chengping	CCa	92/12
V.-Gov.	Bainma Dandzin		81/11
	Labingli		89/06
	Liu Guanghe		93/01
	Ma Yuanbiao		88/02
	Wang Hanmin (exec.)		92/06
	Zhao Leiji?		94/07
PPC Chm.	Huanjue Cenam		88/02
PLA Cdr.	Zhang Meiyuan	CCm	93/11
Dep.Cdr.	Liu Dengyun		94/06
	Wang Yuyuan		90/09
Pol.Com.	Li Tianrong		94/03
Dep.P.C.	?		

Shaanxi Province

Office	Name		
CCP Sec.	Zhang Boxing	CCm	87/09
Dep.Sec.	Bai Qingcai	CCm	90/03
	Liu Ronghui		92/12
	Zhi Yimin		93/05
Governor	Bai Qingcai	CCm	90/04
V.-Gov.	Fan Xiaomei		93/04
	Jiang Xinzhen		91/01
	Liu Chunmao		88/12
	Sun Daren?		83/05
	Wang Shuangxi		88/05
	Xu Shanlin (exec.)		82/11
PPC Chm.	Zhang Boxing	CCm	93/04
PLA Cdr.	Wang Zhicheng		90/06
Dep.Cdr.	Qiu Guangcan		90/11
Pol.Com.	Zhao Lianchen		93/04
Dep.P.C.	Li Qilu		94/03

Shandong Province

Office	Name		
CCP Sec.	Jiang Chunyun	PBm	88/12
Dep.Sec.	Han Xikai		93/11
	Li Chunting	CCa	92/03
	Li Wenquan		93/11
	Zhao Zhihao	CCm	88/12
Governor	Zhao Zhihao	CCm	89/03
V.-Gov.	Chen Jianguo		93/04
	Li Chunting	CCa	88/02
	Song Fatang		89/06
	Wang Jiangong		91/03
	Wang Yuxi		93/04
	Wu Aiying (f)	CCa	93/04
	Zhang Ruifeng		89/04
PPC Chm.	Li Zhen		85/06
PLA Cdr.	Yi Yuanqiu		90/07
Dep.Cdr.	Huang Yonglu		91/06
	Wang Baoshu		93/10
Pol.Com.	Liu Guofu		92/01
Dep.P.C.	Yang Juqing		92/10

Shanghai Municipality

Office	Name		
CCP Sec.	Wu Bangguo	PBm	91/04
Dep.Sec.	Chen Liangyu		92/12
	Chen Zhili (f)	CCa	89/08
	Huang Ju	CCm	85/07
	Wang Liping		92/08
Mayor	Huang Ju	CCm	91/04
Vice-M.	Gong Xueping		93/02
	Jiang Yiren		93/02
	Meng Jianzhu		93/02
	Sha Lin		93/02
	Xia Keqiang		92/08
	Xie Lijuan (f)		85/07
	Xu Kuangdi (exec.)	CCa	92/08
	Zhao Qizheng		91/06
PPC Chm.	Ye Gongqi		88/04
PLA Cdr.	Xu Wenyi		90/07
Dep.Cdr.	Xiang Shourong		90/10
Pol.Com.	Wang Chuanyou		94/04
Dep.P.C.	Jiang Zhizhong		93/06

China Monthly, Apr 1995.

PARTY BUILDING TASKS, 1995

Six Major Industry Party Committee Secretaries Discuss Basic-Level Party Organization Building

"Vigorously Improve Leadership Quality and Raise Leadership Level of Rural Party Branch Secretaries," by Du Deyou, secretary of the Agricultural and Industrial Committee, Beijing Municipal CPC Committee

First, get a good grip on theoretical study and carry forward the emancipation of the mind. Closely integrate the current reform and opening up in rural areas with the reality of modernization and organize party branch secretaries to conscientiously study Comrade Deng Xiaoping's theory on building socialism with Chinese characteristics. At the same time there must be conscientious study of the series of the party's principles and policies for the rural areas. Through the study of theory and other effective measures, continue to carry forward the emancipation of the minds of party members and cadres, with the focus on overcoming the conservative thinking and narrow outlook of the small-scale peasant economy and on strengthening the spirit of daring and confidence in industry's great cause and in effecting modernization; and overcome the traditional concepts formed under the natural economy system and the planned economy system, strengthen market concepts, and understand the laws of the market economy.

Second, augment the training dynamic and study cultural knowledge. We must integrate short-term training with systemic training, and in particular put systemic standardized training in an important position. All fairly young party branch secretaries and party committee members who have a primary or middle-school education or higher, and important leading cadres and reserve cadres of other organizations at the village level must gradually receive a polytechnic school or college education. In 1993, at the Beijing Agricultural School, the Agricultural and Industrial Commission of the municipal party committee started a "rural economic management special course" geared to village-level cadres. After three years of study while not being relieved from their regular duties, the village-level cadres obtained a formal record of polytechnic school education recognized by the State Education Commission. In this way the difficult problem of village-level cadres receiving standardized education without being relieved from their regular duties has been solved, something that has been universally welcomed by the broad masses of rural cadres. In 1993, a total of 600 rural cadres passed school entrance examinations, and in 1994 another 600 village cadres entered school. This year good recruitment work must be continued among the rural party branch secretary and village-level reserve cadre ranks. At the same time, the municipality's counties must vigorously create conditions for selecting from among the students who have completed the course a number of comrades who will receive a college education.

Third, improve the cadre structure by selecting young cadres. With regard to those party branch secretaries and committee members whom practice has already proved to have difficulties in being competent at their posts, we must be determined to adjust them as quickly as possible and to make appropriate arrangements for their work and lives. At the same time we must boldly select to assume leading posts a number of party members whose ideological quality is good, whose educational level is high, who are young, and who have outstanding skills. Now, on the one hand, in many villages there are no better candidates for the post of party branch secreary; on the other hand, organizations from township and town level to county level are overstaffed, and the abilities of many young cadres cannot be fully displayed. Selecting and encouraging outstanding party members and organizations to return to their ancestral homes in the rural areas to become party branch secretaries or other cadres—this is an effective measure for strengthening the building of rural basic-level party branches, particularly the reorganization of reserve branches.

Fourth, strengthen ideological work and perfect the exciting mechanisms for it. A prominent problem now is that the ideological work of basic-level rural party branch secretaries and party members is weak and exciting mechanisms are not perfected—this is a problem that party committees at all levels must conscientiously study. We must, in line with the principle of integrating spiritual encouragement with material encouragement, set up an organically linked,

continued...

PARTY BUILDING TASKS, 1995 (continued)

unified complete set of exciting mechanisms that encourage belief in ideals, responsibility for objectives, advanced models, political honors, material remuneration, social insurance, as well as market competition. We must vigorously deepen the spirit of emancipating the mind and blazing new trails in reform; the spirit of valuing science and truly doing solid work; the spirit of taking the interest of the whole into account and coordinating in unity; and the spirit of struggling arduously and selflessly "offering tribute." We must make the expanded rural basic-level cadres fully understand the major responsibilities they shoulder, be worthy of the party's expectations and the trust of the rural masses, constantly advance toward higher goals, and strive to make new contributions to the building of the new socialist rural areas.

"Strengthen the Building of Basic-Level Party Organizations, With Stress on Doing Truly Solid Work," by Li Shen, deputy secretary of the Commerce, Trade, and Industry Commission, Beijing Municipal CPC Committee
Building the party's basic-level organizations is a solidly based engineering project. For 12 years our commercial and trade system has done solid work, and in this solidly based engineering project it has taken six measures, obtaining certain results and also accumulating Some experiences.

The six measures are:

1. Constantly improve ideological understanding. This includes both the understanding by party and government leaders and by the members of the basic-level party branches and all party members. Only when a common understanding by the entire party from top to bottom is obtained on the importance of basic-level party branch building can the branch's role as a fighting bastion be fully displayed and can the party member vanguard exemplary role be displayed.

2. Foster and set up advanced models. Over the past two years the commercial and trade system has set up many advanced models. So that their calls will be clear and they will be planted solidly, and thus have a mass foundation, we adopted ways and means for selecting them through public appraisal at all levels for conscientious examination and final determination to publicize their deeds, and prevented a situation in which, after being appraised and commended, the advanced models no longer "bore interest." On the other hand, we adopted the method of tracking and examining, at regular intervals finding out their performance, being concerned about their maturation, and helping them to solve real problems. This is a way of encouraging and supervising advanced models and prevents them from running their course.

3. In organization, create conditions for party branches to play their role. Like the Xidan Market, in all commodity departments there is a party branch secretary and also a first assistant manager, and they have both responsibility and authority. When the manager is absent, the branch secretary handles everything; when the manager is present, the secretary is also a main player, and it is his prerogative to take part in economic activities. This is advantageous to closely integrating party work with the department's professional work and is advantageous to understanding situations; it also helps in clearly doing ideological Work with regard to party members and the masses in order to solve real problems.

4. Enhance the management education of party members. Building a party branch well is absolutely not just a matter for members of the party branch, Only if all party members play their vanguard exemplary roles can the party branch become a strong fighting bastion. Therefore, we must conscientiously, regularly, and in a focused manner, conduct well party member management education. The party branch of the Management Office of the Beijing Tobacco Monopoly Bureau, focusing on the trade characteristics of tobacco management, constantly enhances the management education of party members. It successfully educates party members in observing discipline and obeying the law, and in "sounding the alarm bell for a long period of time." For several years there has not occurred a single case of using the power of office to seek private gain and of engaging in favoritism and fraudulent practices.

5. Conscientiously get a good grip on the work of rectifying backward party branches. At the end of every year, we analyze and rank all the branches and make the backward branches at

continued...

PARTY BUILDING TASKS, 1995 (continued)

the end of the line the key objects of the next year's rectification. At the beginning of 1994, the main leaders of the Commerce, Trade, and Industry Commission led a team that carried out a thorough investigation and study of eight backward party branches. The team interviewed more than 100 cadres, staff, and workers, and took timely effective measures. It not only promoted changes in these eight backward party branches, but also promoted the work of rectifying backward party branches by the entire system.

6. Get a good grip on building the ranks of party branch secretaries. Over the past two years we have successfully trained a number of young party members to move, one after another, into the post of branch secretary, thereby replenishing the branch secretary ranks. In line with the demands of the "three-year program outline" for enhancing party building, which was formulated by the fifth plenary session of the Seventh Municipal CPC Committee, we will continue to do this work well. Those who are assuming the post of branch secretary for the first time must undergo training first; those who have already assumed the post but who have not yet undergone the training must make up the training within one year.

"Get a Good Grip on Transforming Ordinary Party Branches," by Zhu Quanjun, deputy secretary of the Education Work Department, Beijing Municipal CPC Committee

I think the focus of effort in transforming ordinary party branches should be put on the following aspects: First, we must further clarify the guiding ideology for building basic-level party branches in higher schools and improve the content of activities and the methods of doing this work. The work of basic-level party branches in higher schools definitely centers closely on the fundamental tasks and central work of higher schools—this is the guiding ideology for enhancing the basic-level party branches in them. Specifically, we must comprehensively implement the party's basic line and education policy, closely center on cultivating talented persons—this being a basic task—and, in completing teaching, research, and other central work of schools, strengthen party building, by focusing on achieving reform and promoting development and stability in order to comprehensively promote branch building. Proceeding from this guiding ideology, we must strive to improve party branch activity content and work style. The experiences of some party branches prove that, with regard to the branch role as political nucleus and fighting bastion, only through ensuring, supervising, and taking part in administrative work on technological and scientific research will policy decisions be made on major issues. In the ordinary party branches, it is precisely on this fundamental issue that deviations and errors have appeared. Some of them only take charge of political studies and student activities, and very few of them take part in administrative and professional work; and some of them cannot integrate the new situation with the core work for students and vigorously initiate this work. Therefore, to change the state of ordinary branches we must, starting with changes in the guiding ideology, conscientiously improve the activity content and the work style. This is the fundamental point in changing ordinary branches.

Next, we must strive to build branch leading groups well, and in particular we must select and cultivate people who can take the lead as branch secretaries. We must select comrades whose political quality is good, whose professional level is high, whose work style is upright, who love party work, who have the spirit of "offering tribute," and who have the trust of the masses, and have them assume posts as branch secretaries. We must unremittingly grasp well the training of branch secretaries, and every year have at least one period of rotational training and provide on-site training for newly appointed party branch secretaries. At present we must make improving the political quality of basic-level party branch secretaries the focus of training. If the political quality of branch secretaries is not improved, and if their ideas and concepts are not replaced, it will be difficult to change ordinary branches. We must adjust the secretaries of party branches to work which has for a long time been ordinary. We must make the building of basic-level party branches and of administrative basic-level organizations tasks to perform as a whole, solve well the problem of joint branch installation of trans-administrative and trans-professional units, set up party branches as fast as possible in line with administrative and

continued...

PARTY BUILDING TASKS, 1995 (continued)

professional units, and build party branches in teaching and research sections as fast as possible.

Third, we must set up an evaluation system for basic-level party branches and perfect exciting mechanisms. With regard to innovation in the leadership system in basic-level party branches, a very important point is to apply management methods, changing soft restraint to hard restraint, changing elasticity to steeliness, and changing empty accomplishments to solid work. The setting up of an evaluation system for party branches is to be made part of the reform of the internal management system of higher schools. We must make the actual results of educational reform and scientific research on teaching the main criteria for evaluating the work of party branches. Evaluation criteria must be finely drawn, The inspection and evaluation system must be operable, and as much as possible quantified, and it must have features that enhance party building. In December 1989, the Education Work Commission formulated "trial regulations on the work of higher school basic-level party organizations," and it recently revised them into "detailed rules and regulations on the work of Beijing higher school basic-level party organizations." Among these rules are specific stipulations on the duties and responsibilities of higher school party branches which lay a foundation for setting up an evaluation system for party branches. Only by stipulating the goals and objective criteria of branch work can we make this work standardized, systematic, and scientific, and make the branch leading groups clearly discern their own position and play an encouraging role.

"During the Deepening of Enterprise Reform Give Play to the Political Nucleus Role of Party Organizations," by Wu Yingui, secretary of the Economic and Trade Work Commission, Beijing Municipal CPC Committee

Through practice we feel that for the party organizations to fully play their role as political nuclei in the process of promoting enterprise reform, stress must be laid on doing good work in five areas:

1. Guide public opinion, thought, and policy. Efforts must be concentrated on the three words "explain, dredge, stimulate." "Explain" means the vigorous, comprehensive, and accurate publicizing of party and state principles and policies on deepening enterprise reform and establishing a modern enterprise system and the publicizing of the goals and important measures in the reform of economic and trade enterprises, so that the cadres, staff, and workers better understand enterprise reform appearance of new problems, analysis of contradictions, resolving of contradictions, and adoption of many forms to resolve contradictions, and the maintaining of the stability of the ranks. [sentence as published] "Stimulate" means, through discussing the situation and tasks, publishing achievements, and setting examples, to arouse the enthusiasm and creativity of the cadres, staff, and workers. Through explaining, dredging, and stimulating, the "six new" concepts will be established: getting a clear understanding of the new situation, adapting to the new environment, solving new problems, grasping new opportunities, exploring new ways, and learning new methods.

2. Get a grip on the adjustment of organizational standards and the selection of leading groups. To uphold the principle of the party managing the cadres, first, the enterprise leading group must be designed well, and, based on the reality of the enterprise, the scope of the functions and powers of its board of directors, board of supervisors, and administrative groups must be defined by law, with good coordination of the relationships among the three, so that the enterprises leadership system truly reflects the party Central Committee demands in its "three sentences" concerning enterprise leadership. Second, we must select well the leading group and optimize its structures, particularly selecting its party and government members, so that leading groups at all levels truly have a fairly strong capability for leadership and a fairly high level of skills in leadership.

3. Get a grip on the role of party organizations in guaranteeing supervision. First, we must, in accordance with the demand for establishing a socialist market economy system, ensure the smooth supervision of changing enterprise operating mechanisms, check on the fixing of the

continued...

PARTY BUILDING TASKS, 1995 (continued)

changing mechanisms plan, check on choice of ways of operating, check on the evaluation of state-owned assets, check on the appointment of middle-level cadres, etc. Second, we must, in line with state laws, decrees, principles, and policies, supervise the direction of enterprise operations to prevent irregular or illegal operations. Third, in line with the demand for establishing a modern enterprise system, we must ensure the healthy, orderly movement of enterprise leadership. Fourth, in accordance with the characteristics of all types of enterprises, we must supervise thorough implementation of all systems of rules and regulations. Fifth, we must supervise and guarantee the macroeconomic regulation and control measures of the government and the high-level department in charge.

4. Get a grip on party organization participation in decision making on important issues. The participation by enterprise party organizations in decision making on important enterprise issues is an important duty bestowed upon party organizations by the party charter. Enterprise party organizations must vigorously take part in decision making on enterprise determination of the plan for changing mechanisms and operation, determination of the goals of development and the development of operations, determination of significant items of technological transformation and items of investment, appointment of enterprise deputies and middle-level cadres, distribution of enterprise interests and the welfare and remuneration of staff and workers, and other issues. We must strive to open wide the ways of and means for participating in decision making and must not rigidly adhere to a certain method or a certain pattern. Staff and workers should by many forms participate in decision making, constantly opening means and channels.

5. Get a grip on the building of party affairs contingents. During the establishment of a modern enterprise system, we must enhance and improve the leadership of the party affairs contingents, and, in line with the principle of being highly trained and highly effective, ensure the synchronous establishment of party organizations, the synchronous selection of party and government cadres, and the synchronous setting up of work organizations. We must enhance the management education of party affairs cadres, and adopt many forms to give them a free hand to be tempered in the practice of establishing a modern enterprise system, thus constantly improving the political and professional quality of party affairs cadres.

Xuexi Yu Yanjiu (Study and Research) No. 3, 5 Mar 1995.

NPC STANDING COMMITTEE REPORTS, 1995

The 16th Session of the Eighth National People's Congress [NPC] Standing Committee holds its second plenum today to hear a report made by Public Security Minister Tao Siju on the current situation of public security and a report made by Vice Chairman Li Peiyao on the enforcement of antidrug laws.

Chairman Qiao Shi attended the meeting. Vice Chairman Tomur Dawamat presided over the meeting.

Tao Siju said: It is fair to say the public security situation is basically stable and normal at a time of overwhelming socio-economic changes and development. The annual incidence of criminal cases over the past five years has dropped by 3.6 percent, as compared with the figure of five years ago. Initial success has been achieved in harnessing the rising trend of criminal cases.

Li Peiyao said: Yunnan, Guangxi, and Sichuan—areas in the proximity of the drug-producing "Golden Triangle"—have taken severe measures in recent years to crack down on Chinese and foreign criminal elements and to strengthen the work of helping drug addicts get rid of their bad habit. However, narcotic resources outside of the country still pose severe threats, drug trafficking is rampant, and the number of drug addicts also is on the rise.

He said: Our efforts to crack down on drug trafficking are handicapped by such problems as failing to enforce the law strictly, a poor contingent of antidrug personnel, and an insufficient budget. These problems are urgently requiring solutions.

continued...

NPC STANDING COMMITTEE REPORTS, 1995 (continued)

At today's meeting, Xue Ju, chairman of the Law Committee; Gu Linfang, vice chairman of the Internal and Judicial Affairs Committee; and Zhao Dongwan, chairman of the Education, Science, Culture, and Public Health Committee also respectively made reports concerning the results of examining the motions put forward by deputies. The examining work was assigned previously by the Presidium of the Third Session of the Eighth NPC. The meeting also examined an already-printed report by the NPC delegation to the 94th Congress of the Inter-Parliamentary Union.

According to the reports presented by these three special committees, China is prepared to enact a legislation law, antibribery law, administrative supervision law, juvenile crime prevention law, endemic disease prevention law, and a law prohibiting smoking in public places.

Attending the meeting were Vice Chairmen Tian Jiyun, Wang Hanbin, Ni Zhifu, Chen Muhua, Fei Xiaotong, Sun Qimeng, Lei Jieqiong, Li Ximing, Wang Guangying, Cheng Siyuan, Lu Jiaxi, Buhe, and Li Peiyao. Cao Zhi, secretary general of the NPC Standing Committee, also attended the meeting. State Councilor Li Guixian, President Ren Jianxin of the Supreme People's Court, and Procurator General Zhang Siqing of the Supreme People's Procuratorate attended the meeting as an auditor.

X, 28 Oct 1995.

DE-DENGIFICATION MOVEMENT, 1995

It's a terrible tongue-twister, but de-Dengification is set to dominate Chinese politics in the near future. The revisionism over the meaning and legacy of Deng Xiaoping's reforms has come much earlier than China watchers had expected, considering the fact that the patriarch did not begin to knock Mao Zedong down from his pedestal until 1981, five years after his death.

While President Jiang Zemin owes his rise to the "chief architect of reform", he is not expected to emulate Mr. Deng by treating his predecessor with kid gloves. The feidenghua (de-Dengification) movement will probably be more thorough and brutal than the de-Maoification exercise, bringing with it awesome implications for China and the world

While Mr. Jiang's legitimacy has rested upon his being an heir to Dengism, he needs to turn the table on Mr. Deng to buy support among the legions of Chinese who think they have been short-changed by the 16-year-old reform effort. In just a few months, Mr. Jiang has put together the underpinnings of a feidenghua crusade. At the moment the revisionism is largely underground warfare: it is couched in innuendo and circumlocution, but the target is clear.

—**Corruption:** Mr. Deng was never much of a graft buster. For the patriarch's go-go reformers, corruption was the accepted pace for a faster pace of "progress". An excessively squeamish and puritanical approach to probity would dampen a reformer's zeal. Numerous leftist ideologues, including those now allied to Mr. Jiang, have alleged that such Deng lieutenants as ousted party chief Zhao Ziyang had condoned if not coined the "corruption is inevitable" slogan. The anti-corruption campaign that Mr. Jiang is waging serves to enhance the president's prestige by letting on that the post-Deng leadership uphold the traditional, moralistic approach to curbing graft.

—**Egalitarianism and the Status of the Proletariat:** Mr. Deng's well-known formula for speedy development is to "let one group of people get rich ahead of the others." The scales are tipped in favor of the "gold coast", urban intellectuals and the entrepreneurs.

According to his handlers, the president has kicked off the most extensive fupin ("save the poor") movement in Chinese history to redress the imbalance. During the May Day festivities, he pulled out the stops to pacify China's 140 million workers calling them "masters" of the nation and the factories. While Mr. Deng and Mr. Zhao are best known for quasi-privatization—which led to the rise of a class of big-spending cowboy capitalists—Mr. Jiang is priding himself on being the progenitor of the country's first job and social insurance programs.

continued...

DE-DENGIFICATION MOVEMENT, 1995 (continued)

—**Spiritual Civilization:** Soon after the June 4, 1989, fiasco Mr. Deng admitted that his major shortcoming in the past 10 years had been the neglect of "education", meaning ideological and political work or indoctrination in Marxist norms. Since the winter, Mr. Jiang and the resurgent ideologues have revived the campaign against bourgeois liberalization. During study sessions last weekend on the "lessons" of disgraced Beijing party boss Chen Xitong, the emphasis was on "preventing the infiltration of corrupt capitalistic thoughts".

In addition to extolling what he calls the leitmotifs of the times, meaning "patriotism, socialism and collectivism", Mr. Jiang has sponsored an elaborate revival of Confucianism and traditional Chinese ethos. Apart from Confucius, propagandists have paid homage to such historical figures as the legendary emperor Da Yu, China's most successful flood controller. By contrast, Mr. Deng's younger followers had long traded their Confucian Analects for Adam Smith and Milton Friedman.

—**Foreign Policy and Nationalism:** The Dengists have been criticized for being "pro-West" and "pro-Japan". The theory goes that the radical reformers were so enamored of funds and technology from capitalistic countries that they were more ready to make foreign-policy compromises and were less vigilant about repelling the creeping influence of neo-imperialism.

The Jiang administration, however, wants to be seen as "standing up to the Americans and the Japanese". Earlier this year, Mr. Jiang's foreign trade team made much of the fact that they had put up a fight before succumbing to American demands of market access and intellectual property rights. In the past week, Beijing for the first time gave the green light to "people's, organizations" to seek wartime reparations from Japan.

With the erosion of Communist faith, "nationalism" is perhaps the only card Mr. Jiang can play to buttress the legitimacy of his regime and promote cohesiveness among Chinese. Recent policies on the Spratly Islands, Tibet, Taiwan and Hong Kong have indicated that the president's approach is more Maoist than Dengist.

—**Reform and Open-Door Policy:** The Dengists' single-minded quest for economic integration with the west will be fine-tuned by ideological and practical imperatives. Mr. Jiang said last weekend that the socialist market economy must not depart from the "basic system of socialism", meaning public ownership as the mainstay. Reforms will also be constrained by domestic factors such as the need to pacify peasants and workers.

Recent changes in trade and investment policies Indicate that the post-Deng leadership is much more concerned about protecting domestic markets and nascent industries. Now guidelines have been spelt out to attract only those kinds of investments that dovetail with local priorities.

These contrast with the Dengists' less discriminatory strategy of "suck them in first"—even though many "foreign investors" turn out to be speculators in the stocks or property market. Dengist reformers were receptive to the Western plea that the country adopt quasi-capitalistic trappings by the end of the decade. The post-Deng administration will bide its time, going by the body clock of the Middle Kingdom.

As the semi-official China News Service [ZHONGGUO XINWEN SHE] put it: "China will go about the open-door policy by sticking to its own time-table." Or as Premier Li Peng reportedly said in the early 1990s: "Moscow may want to do it (shock therapy) in 50 days; in China, we'll do it in l0 years or more."

The catalyst for de-Dengification will be a revaluation of Mr. Deng's worst mistake: the Tiananmen Square massacre. Intellectuals in Beijing see in the disgrace of Chen Xitong a plot by Mr. Jiang to gain points by selectively overturning elements of the June 4 verdict. Mr. Chen played a key role in persuading Mr. Deng to take "tough measures" against the student demonstrators.

Hong Kong papers have reported that while on an inspection trip of Jiangxi province in late March. Mr. Jiang paid a visit to the graveyard of the late party chief Hu Yaobang. There the president, a beneficiary of June 4, heaped praise on the "lofty character" of Mr. Hu, a hero among "bourgeois liberals". It was Mr. Hu's death on April l5, 1989, that ignited fiery demands for a head-long march into the future. Mr. Jiang wants Mr. Deng's demise to be no less of a watershed for himself and his agenda.

continued...

DE-DENGIFICATION MOVEMENT, 1995 (continued)

In 1989, the radical modernizers were brandishing the vista of a "Westernized China of the future". While it might be conducive to short-term stability and balance, Mr. Jiang's blueprint smacks of the ghosts of the past.

South China Morning Post, 3 May 1995.

JIANG ZEMIN ADDRESSES PARTY SECRETARIES, 1995

Comrades,

On the 74th founding anniversary of the CPC, the Organization Department of the CPC Central Committee is holding a meeting here to commend 100 outstanding county (city) party secretaries. Comrades from the CPC Central Committee Political Bureau and Secretariat are attending today's meeting to call on commended comrades, celebrate the party's birthday with all of you, and take this opportunity to extend holiday greetings to party organizations at all levels and CPC members on all fronts across the country!

The CPC is a well-organized Marxist political party. In the party's organizational structure, county (city) party committees, directly facing the grass-roots units and people and situated in an important position, are shouldering important responsibility. The leading members of county (city) party committees constitute a force full of vigor among the ranks of party cadres. A number of outstanding cadres have been trained in posts at this level, and group after group of middle and senior-ranking leading personnel have sprouted here. The comrades being commended today are representatives of numerous outstanding county (city) party secretaries over the past few years. You and members of the party committees have led party organizations and the broad masses of cadres and people in your respective counties (cities) in conscientiously following the party's line, principles, and policies with conspicuous achievements. Today's commendation meeting has confirmed these comrades' work performance as well as set forth stricter requirements on them. I hope you will remain free from arrogance and impetuosity, continue to make progress, and make new contributions to the cause of socialist modernization.

Comrades, the CPC's history of the past 74 years is the history of firmly integrating the fundamental tenets of Marxism-Leninism with actual conditions in China, the history of the establishment of a relationship as close as flesh and blood between the party and people after undergoing hardships and tests together, the history of turning a semi-colonial and semi-feudal old China into a socialist New China, and the history of turning a weak country subject to bullying and humiliation into one standing on its own feet among other nations in the world and marching toward modernization. We have always combined our goal of struggle at the present stage with lofty ideals and based ourselves on the present, while facing, grasping, and creating the future, our achievements in the new democratic revolution and socialist revolution and construction, made under the leadership of the first-generation central leading collective with Comrade Mao Zedong as the core, and achievements in reform, opening up, and socialist modernization drive, made under the leadership of the second-generation central leading collective with Comrade Deng Xiaoping as the core, have brought about and are continuing to bring about tremendous and profound changes in China. Now, we have started drawing up the "Ninth Five-Year Plan" for China's national economic and social development and long-range objectives by 2010. This is the first medium and long-term plan under the circumstances of developing a socialist market economy and a trans-century blueprint for economic and social development. We will begin implementing this plan next year. In the coming 12 years, we will continue to uphold the central task of economic construction; further develop and improve the socialist market economy, socialist democracy and legal system, and socialist spiritual civilization; accomplish the second-step strategic objective in an all-around way; and lay a firm foundation for accom-plishment of the third-step strategic objective.

History has proved that the unity of the Chinese nation, the national and social liberation of the Chinese people, the state's independence and sovereignty, and, after achieving these

continued...

JIANG ZEMIN ADDRESSES PARTY SECRETARIES, 1995 (continued)

three, the continuous liberation and development of productive forces as well as overall social progress can only be realized by relying on the leadership of the CPC and the joint struggle of all nationalities across the country. This leading position of the CPC is formed by history and is generally acknowledged by people nationwide. The reform, opening up, and socialist modernization drive, which we are pushing forward, constitute a new great revolution. To allow the party leadership to play its nuclear role even better, the party must constantly improve itself under the new circumstances, and strive to improve its ruling and leading levels.

The Fourth Plenary Session of the 14th CPC Central Committee placed the job of building a stronger party before the whole party as a great project, emphasizing especially the need to improve the overall proficiency of those in leading positions, and to train and temper tens of thousands of senior leading cadres. The session required that senior cadres not only must strive to become knowledgeable and competent professionals who are familiar with their jobs, but also statesmen who are loyal to Marxism, who insist in adhering to the socialist path with Chinese characteristics and who know how to manage party and state affairs well. This requirement was presented in accordance with the needs of the new situation and the new missions, as well as the actual state of the contingents of leading cadres. County- and higher-level leading comrades must temper and improve themselves in light of the requirement set by the plenary session and work hard to become qualified leading cadres in the new period. They must in particular, make a big stride forward with respect to adhering to the correct political course, being more aware of the interests of the whole, intensifying theoretical study, and serving the people wholeheartedly.

Always remaining sober-minded and firm politically is the most important requirement of becoming qualified cadres of intermediate and senior echelons. One whose political standing is ambiguous can hardly shoulder any important responsibilities or undertake any big assignments. Comrade Deng Xiaoping said: "Adhering to the socialist course during reform is an important issue." He wanted us to become familiar with the basic Marxist tenets, pointing out that "only by doing this can our party firmly adhere to the socialist course, building and developing socialism with Chinese characteristics, and reaching our final goal, namely achieving communism." The correct political course to which we must adhere today is the course of building socialism with Chinese characteristics. Our work at present is to uphold the main roles played by socialist public and state economies, and at the same time permit and encourage the development of non-public economies so they can give play to their beneficial, complementary roles. While we should encourage some people in some areas to become rich first through honest labor and legal operations, we must also encourage those who have already become rich to guide and help those who have yet to become rich so that eventually everybody will be affluent. While promoting material construction, we must also promote socialist ethics. We must be firm in both areas. At no time and under no circumstances should we try to seek economic development at the expense of ethics. While we must uphold the basic national policy of opening up to the outside world and work with daring to assimilate, emulate, and exploit all foreign things which are useful to us, we must firmly safeguard our national sovereignty and interests and firmly resist the inroads and infiltration of decadent capitalist ideas. We must make a clear-cut stand on major issues of principle. We must bravely support anything which is correct, commend advanced personnel and advanced deeds, and encourage people to explore and create along the correct course. We must he able to distinguish and firmly stop all ideas and acts which endanger the interests of the state and the people. Absolutely by no means should we disregard them, much less should we drift along with them. We must correct the phenomena of immersing ourselves in day-to-day affairs and being indifferent about political affairs, or paying no attention to ideological and political trends in society. We should be more politically sensitive and perceptive, be good at understanding and handling problems from a political angle, and remain sober-minded and firm while handling issues concerning political orientation and principles. These are the most important qualities a competent statesman must possess.

continued...

JIANG ZEMIN ADDRESSES PARTY SECRETARIES, 1995 (continued)

Anyone who is indifferent to the interests of the whole is not qualified to be in leading office. When one has been assigned to take charge of the work of any department at any level, he must always bear in mind the interests of the whole party and the whole country, and attach the greatest importance to the interests of the whole. One basic requirement of the party for leading cadres at various levels is that each of them must consider working hard to accomplish the assignments in their respective departments and regions as an essential step to achieving the party's general line and general mission. Seizing opportunities to deepen reform, open wider to the outside world, expedite development, and maintain stability are the general requirements for the whole party and the whole country and where the fundamental interests of 12 billion people lie. All localities and departments must be subordinate to and serve this general mission of overall interests. And the cause of our party will continue to thrive when we accomplish our respective assignments under the guidance of this mission of overall interests. We must safeguard this general mission of overall interests by voluntarily subjecting ourselves to party discipline. If we are indifferent to this general mission of overall interests, not only will the mission itself be damaged, but local authorities and departments will also be unable to protect their own interests. If our party is lax in discipline, weak, and demoralized, and party organizations go their own ways, our party will have no coherence in fighting power, and our country will be as incoherent as a pool of loose sand. Leading cadres at all levels must firmly implement the party's basic lines and all general and specific policies; correctly handle the relationship between central, overall interests and local, partial interests; and proceed in doing their work creatively in light of their actual situations.

Cadres in leading positions must study harder and perform better than other comrades. They cannot exercise effective leadership unless they are more knowledgeable and more capable. Since many things are new and strange to us today when we are confronted with the great project of achieving socialist modernization, and the situation keeps changing and new problems keep emerging, we must study hard to increase our leading capabilities. What should we study? We should study our society. We should study it and scientifically sum up the experiences the masses have gained from their work. We must also read books about science and other useful subjects. The most important thing we must do is to study Marxism-Leninism-Mao Zedong Thought, especially Comrade Deng Xiaoping's theory of building socialism with Chinese characteristics. We must also study the socialist market economy, modern science and technology, management, and other knowledge which we must know to do our jobs well. Today, we all are very busy with our heavy workloads. But if we shun unnecessary socializing activities and plan our work and life rationally, each of us will still have a lot of time for study. The key requirement is that we must have the sense of responsibility to do our jobs well, and the sense of urgency to improve our leadership.

Leading cadres must take the lead in setting an example in upholding the party's objective of serving the people wholeheartedly. Building socialism with Chinese characteristics is a common cause which Chinese people of all nationalities are undertaking for their own interests and to create a better life. The party must count on the people and trust them in exercising leadership and accomplishing all its work. The party must learn from the people's wisdom, respect their creativity, and accept their supervision, which all embody communists' world outlook and their concepts of life and values, as well as their methods of work. This is why we have urged leading cadres at all levels to think what the masses think, care about what the masses care about, do what the masses want to do, and work wholeheartedly for the interests of the masses. Whenever we have accomplished something, we should first of all give the credit to the people and the party. Today there are many problems we must resolve in our endeavor to expedite reform and construction. Where will good solutions to these problems come from? Solutions will never drop from the sky, nor are they inherent in our minds. In the final analysis, they come from the rich and colorful experiences the masses have accumulated from creating history. Thus, those who have taken root among the people and integrated themselves with the masses have strength, wisdom, and ways; and they can withstand tests, triumph over diffi-culties, and achieve remarkable success. The people, and the people alone, are the supreme

continued...

JIANG ZEMIN ADDRESSES PARTY SECRETARIES, 1995 (continued)

judge of the value of our work. Leading cadres at all levels must regularly go down to the masses at grass-roots units, especially in areas where life is hard and difficult, to conduct earnest investigation and studies, listen to the masses' views, and improve their methods of work so they will have the people's support while leading them in reforms and construction, and so they can forge closer ties to the masses. As for certain essential projects which the masses have yet to understand, we should conduct meticulous ideological and political work among them so we can properly handle the problems among the people and patiently guide them to move forward. Applying simplistic and rigid guidance is something we must resolutely avoid. As reform and opening up continue to proceed, it has become even more necessary for party members to improve their conduct, do their jobs honestly, and fight corruption. Leading cadres, in particular, must set an example in this regard by performing their duties honestly, exercising self-discipline, and abiding by party discipline and state laws.

While our party's priorities and specific assignments have been changing according to changes in the situation in different historical periods, the party's nature as the vanguard of the working class, its objective of serving the people wholeheartedly and the goal it is striving to reach will never change. Our party has had the people's support and respect because we have been upholding this principle for the past several decades. The Central Committee has time and again stressed that Communist Party members must firmly uphold the Marxist world outlook and concepts of life and values. A Communist Party member cannot possibly address this issue overnight, and this issue cannot possibly be taken care of once and for all. This issue can only be addressed naturally as he grows older and as he moves to higher positions. Our comrades must make constant efforts to temper their party spirit, strictly abide by party regulations and laws, lead a healthy party life, be brave in making criticism and self-criticism, remold their subjective world while remolding the objective world, and work hard all their lives for the interests of the people. The party's unity and the unity between the party and people of all nationalities are the prerequisites for the victory of our cause. Building socialism with Chinese characteristics is an unprecedented creative project, and it is an arduous but great project. Since the current reform and construction assignments are heavy, it is particularly necessary for comrades within the party to unite more closely on the basis of the party's basic theory and basic lines. We used to sing a song called "Unity Is Strength" quite often, and in recent years we have also repeatedly stressed that unity can generate coherence, fighting power, and productivity. These are historical experiences and a truth that have been proven time and again by objective facts. All the victories which our party has won during the past seven decades and more; and the great, world-renowned successes which China has achieved in reform, opening up, and modernization during the last 17 years are the results of the hard work and unity of the party and the people of all nationalities in the country. Our party is a united party, the party and the people are united, and people of all nationalities in the country are united. This constitutes an enormous spiritual asset and material strength. All comrades in the party, and especially leading cadres at all levels, must cherish and safeguard this unity. We all have the conviction of Marxism-Leninism-Mao Zedong Thought and Comrade Deng Xiaoping's theory of building socialism with Chinese characteristics, and we all consider achieving the party's basic lines our responsibility. When this foundation is strong, and when our stands, viewpoints, and methods of dealing with issues are the same, we will make concerted, positive efforts with one heart and one mind. And when each and every leading member takes the interests of the whole into consideration, upholds principles, thinks of the party's interests first in doing everything, upholds democratic centralism and accomplishes his assignments according to the party's rules, greater unity among them will have the support of party spirit and party institutions. Members of leading groups must trust, support, and understand each other. When our views differ, we should discuss the differences frankly and sincerely, disregard personal gains or losses, and give first priority to the cause of the party and the people. By doing this we can prevent the occurrence of problems that can affect unity, or deal with these problems promptly even if they do occur.

continued...

JIANG ZEMIN ADDRESSES PARTY SECRETARIES, 1995 (continued)

Comrades, we will usher in the 21st century in only five years. We deeply feel that the successes we have achieved in reform, opening up, and modernization did not come easily; and we must work even harder in the future, which is very bright. Let us, under the leadership of the Central Committee and the guidance of Comrade Deng Xiaoping's theory of building socialism with Chinese characteristics and that of the party's basic lines, work hard with one heart and one mind to build a stronger country in a down-to-earth manner, and strive to achieve the second- and third-step strategic objectives of China's modernization!

X, 30 Jun 1995.

VI MILITARY

POLITICAL-MILITARY OUTLOOK, 1995

In a new era, Jiang Zemin proposes new standards for military management and, upgrading in stages of the three commands of People's Liberation Army [PLA]. Liu Huaqing calls for stability in border environment, strengthening of defense research and development [R&D], and improved organizational structure. The military faces three major issues today, with higher echelons focusing on diplomacy of military exchanges.

Four Main Directions for Future Development of the Military
In the post-Deng era, it goes without saying that the Chinese military, the "great wall of iron and steel," which ensures stability for the Chinese Communist authorities, will play a very important role.

Latest information from military sources suggest that in the period to come, the Chinese military will develop in at least the following four directions:

1. Maintaining the authority of "Jiang as the core," giving priority to ideological training;
2. Anticipating crisis while at peace, vigorously modernizing national defense;
3. Stabilizing the environment along the borders, increasing exchanges with foreign military;
4. Emphasizing that the military and people are one family, strengthening implementation of projects to promote military-civilian unity.

Military as "Stabilizing Instrument" in Post-Deng Era
At various forums of the Chinese People's Political Consultative Conference [CPPCC] this spring, Jiang Zemin appeared very relaxed; showing up at meetings of some of the delegations, Jiang not only spoke warmly to the delegates, but even found time to read and to write personal replies to some of the delegates during this "the busiest of season."

On the Political Stage, Jiang Zemin Already Scored "Five Victories"
Observers believe that the reason Jiang Zemin showed such a seldom-seen relaxed demeanor was because he has already scored "five victories" on the political stage:

First, "Jiang as the core" is recognized and accepted by CPC elder statesmen; as a third-generation CPC leader, he has served nearly six years as general secretary; in that role, he takes charge of ideological and major political directions and is not burdened by specific day-to-day operational tasks; this is a "political victory."

Second, as head of state and of government, Jiang's signature is required for any major political directive to take effect; with his important position in the CPC and as chairman of the Central Military Commission [CMC], Jiang controls the nation's "great wall of iron and steel." This is a "victory of power."

Third, with Deng Xiaoping letting go of power completely because of age and health, Jiang Zemin is able to exercise all powers; on the world stage, advantages China enjoys outweigh

continued...

POLITICAL-MILITARY OUTLOOK, 1995 (continued)

disadvantages; domestically, the political scene is basically stable, and in terms of social and economic developments, notwithstanding certain difficulties, progress is still rapid and internationally recognized. This is a "victory of luck."

Fourth, Jiang understands that the key to establishing his leadership position is the extent to which he can contribute on issues which affect China and the Chinese as a nation and a people. After taking a firm stance in the interests of the Chinese people in last year's "GATT" negotiations, he came out in February with his "eight points" for solving the Taiwan question. It is said that Jiang in the coming days will take other steps on the issue of reunification that will gain even greater popular support. Further, the fiftieth anniversary of the War of Resistance against Japan this summer and the firm attitude he has displayed toward Philippine provocation over the Spratly Islands will help to further consolidate Jiang's position as the nation's leader. This is a "victory of doctrine."

Fifth, Jiang has initiated a series of steps on military management. On the eve of convocation of the "two congresses" in March, Jiang carried out a public relations campaign aimed at the commanders of the three services of the PLA by personally "calling" on the military delegates to the CPPCC at their guest houses and meeting the delegates individually in separate rooms. These military delegates were united in the view that in line with directives of the CMC and the tri-service command, they will maintain a high degree unity with the party Central Committee politically, ideologically and in their action. Before the opening of National People's Congress [NPC], CMC Vice Chairman Liu Huaqing mobilized members of the military NPC delegation to give firm political support to party central authority with Jiang Zemin as the core. When political reports were discussed at the "two congresses," CMC Vice Chairman Zhang Zhen [1728 7201]; Defense Minister Chi Haotian; Zhang Wannian, chief of the General Staff; Yu Yongbo, chief of the CMC General Political Department; and Fu Quanyou [0265 0356 2589], chief of the CMC General Reserves Department, all pledged to adhere to a "unified concept:" Namely, "to resolutely obey the command of the party Central Committee and CMC with Jiang Zemin as the core." That Jiang has won the support of the three services is crucial to ensuring a smooth transition in the post-Deng era. This is a "victory in prestige."

In China, the military and politics have always been inseparable, and the party commanding the gun is a "fact of life" in China. The military is a "stabilizing instrument" in China's socialist politics, and the basis for achieving all victories. Mao Zedong considered the soldier-peasant as the basis for victory; Deng Xiaoping has always emphasized the importance of military-civilian unity; and Jiang Zemin recently has proposed to carry on that tradition, to more effectively operate the military as one big educational institution in order to further consolidate political authority and stabilize the society. The most basic condition for Jiang to achieve the above-cited "five victories" is his ability to ensure stability of the military. As long as Jiang is able to continue to effectively sustain his "five victories," even though in the post-Deng era a certain amount of turbulence may be unavoidable, his position as the core of political power will be fully protected.

Political-Ideological Indoctrination as Priority Task

Because it is necessary to manage the military as a "stabilizing instrument," when Jiang Zemin addressed the PLA delegation to the NPC on 10 March, he proposed that the military operating as one big educational institution must seek to effectively educate and nurture all its personnel, beginning by vigorously strengthening ideological-political training and indoctrination.

In his remarks to the NPC military delegation on 9 March, CMC Vice Chairman Liu Huaqing quoted Jiang's guidance in stating that: "We must give great emphasis in the military to ideological and political indoctrination and training, and of all the projects the military undertakes, this should be given the highest priority." Liu Huaqing continued by emphasizing to the NPC military delegates that they "must earnestly carry out" this guidance from Jiang Zemin.

Jiang Zemin Calls For "Effectively Operating the Military as Major Educational Institution"

Continuing to "operate the military effectively as an educational institution" in the new era represents Jiang Zemin's thinking after he assumed control of the military. This thinking has

continued...

POLITICAL-MILITARY OUTLOOK, 1995 (continued)

provided the main framework for ideological and political training which the military will carry out henceforth. According to Jiang, the party Central Committee's thinking on managing the military has the following contents

Criteria for Military Management in Post-Deng Era

1. Origin of thinking. Jiang Zemin said that Mao Zedong had pointed out that "the PLA should be run like a big school." In a later period, Deng Xiaoping also emphasized that the military should be operated like a big school. Jiang Zemin has indicated he intends to follow the line of Mao's and Deng's thinking by keeping up the tradition, taking into consideration the new, and changing circumstances and effectively managing the military.

2. Goals to be achieved. The goals are: A) To enable all officers and men in the military to study politics, military affairs, the sciences and culture; B) to turn them into high-quality personnel with sound ideology, military skills, specialized knowledge, and correct behavior; and C) to ensure that they are resolute revolutionary fighters while in the military, conscientious workers in society after they are discharged and, in both cases, fulfill the important functions on both battle lines of defending and developing the motherland.

3. Training content. Of the highest priority is strengthening political and ideological training and indoctrination, particularly in carrying out effective programs to teach the value of struggle and perseverance, love of and sacrifice for the country, a revolutionary outlook on life, respect for cadres (soldiers showing respect for their officers), and love of soldiers (officers caring for and protecting their men).

4. Educational methods. In ideological and political education, Jiang pointed out there are several key issues today that need to be emphasized: To understand the current concerns of the officers and men and educate them at different levels keyed to these issues; to guide them to correctly understand the issues on money, fame and privilege, suffering and joy; to clearly draw the line between right and wrong, glory and shame, beauty and ugliness in order to strengthen ideological defenses against "corruption;" and to develop democracy and mobilize all officers and men to take part in education.

5. Jiang called upon those who are responsible for educating others to first educate themselves. Cadres themselves must first clarify their thinking. Officers must set good examples themselves before they try to educate or influence soldiers. As Jiang Zemin said, education by examples is more important than by words, for how can one teach others unless one himself is educated and upright.

6. Jiang also said that to build a good foundation for political and ideological education, officers and men must be guided to concretely probe and analyze military tactics and strategies.

Jiang Zemin's thinking on military management described above very quickly received the endorsement of the military high echelon. The PLA delegation to the 3rd Plenum of 8th NPC, at a delegation meeting on 16 March, focused discussion on Jiang's important remarks concerning operating the military effectively as an educational institution. Li Huaqing, Zhang Zhen, Chi Haotian, Zhang Wannian, Fu Quanyou, and others attended the meeting chaired by Yu Yongbo; nine delegates rose to address the gathering and offered significant comments and suggestions for implementing Jiang's proposals.

On 17 March, Liu Huaqing called the key cadres of the PLA delegation to the 8th NPC to a meeting and pointed out that Jiang's thinking and important proposals on military management provide extremely important guidance for the future in terms of strengthening the military across the board and raising its combat effectiveness. Liu Huaqing named several projects which should be given priority in building the military, and ranked the project to strengthen political and ideological training and indoctrination ahead of all others.

CMC Political Department Took the Lead to "Circularize" the Troops

On 18 March, the CMC General Political Department, in a circular calling on all troops to study and emulate the spirit of the 3rd Plenum of the 8th NPC, stressed that in carrying out Jiang Zemin's guidance, the military must vigorously strengthen ideological and political training,

continued...

POLITICAL-MILITARY OUTLOOK, 1995 (continued)

particularly programs to teach the rank and file the importance of patriotism and service to country, a revolutionary outlook of life, respect for cadres and love of the troops, struggle and perseverance; to guide officers and men to develop a correct outlook on life and concept of values; to insulate them against the corrupting influence of "wine, women and song"; and to ensure steadfastness and ideological and moral purity among the rank and file.

"Awareness of Hardship" Necessary for Raising Quality of Rank and File
In his government work report, Li Peng emphasized that the military must concentrate on building quality. In discussing this issue, the military high echelon called particular attention to the need of increasing awareness of suffering and hardship. Heightening the degree of such awareness while developing quality in the military will show the sense of urgency in the Chinese military for the modernization of national defense.

Observers conclude from this that the Chinese military, laboring under an inadequate military budget, but with perseverance and patience, will strive to develop itself and modernize national defense, and that this will be the direction of development of the Chinese military for a long period time to come.

Three Difficult Issues Confronting Chinese Military
The Chinese military is confronted by three major issues today: Inadequacy of military expenditures, weaknesses of weapons and equipment, and low pay and benefits for the troops. The obstacles posed by the three major issues must be overcome if China is to modernize its national defense. Of the three, inadequacy in military expenditures is the most serious. China is a developing country and at present has to devote significant resources and efforts to economic development, which necessarily limits the amount spent for national defense; the concern of some people abroad about "the Chinese threat" is, therefore, unfounded.

In 1994, China budgeted 55.062 billion yuan for military expenditures and, despite the constant calls of the higher echelons of the military for "persevering against hardship," actual expenditures were 105.8 percent of the budget, or 58.255 billion yuan. This year, the government defense budget estimate is 62.807 billion yuan, only 4.551 billion yuan more than last year's actual expenditures. If adjusted for inflation, this national defense budget is low and tight.

Even early on, in the era when Deng Xiaoping was running the military, officers and men were admonished to "persevere and be patient" and defer to the priority of overall national development. At the 3rd Plenum of the 8th NPC in March this year, the military again echoed the call of "striving to develop while persevering against difficulties." This is Jiang Zemin's "overall concept" for managing the military. From the concept of "developing by persevering," one can see in Jiang's military management style the new emphasis that it is people who control events and that everything depends on human effort. In terms of "military internal management," Fu Quanyou pointed out on 7 March that the military needs to deal with "four type of relationships," as follows:

First, in the relationship between national defense and economic development, to firmly adhere to the concept of overall needs.

Second, in the relationship between need and feasibility, to strictly go by available resources, not coveting maximum gains or seeking things foreign. The rank and file and all units must establish firm standards of self-reliance, develop the concept of maintenance and get the most use out of the money available, not leaving any gaps nor running into red ink.

Third, in the relationship between what is centrally important and what is of general utility, to concentrate resources and efforts on matters of central importance, and use the limited military budget on the most crucial projects where the money will do the most good.

Fourth, in the relationship between building up the military and supporting local development, to effectively manage both. While concentrating on training and building up equipment for war, the military must also positively participate in regional or local key construction projects, and shoulder important responsibilities for disaster relief and emergency assistance in the local areas.

continued...

POLITICAL-MILITARY OUTLOOK, 1995 (continued)

Zhang Zeng Calls for Development of Sideline Enterprises, Strengthening Self-Sufficiency
CMC Vice Chairman Zhang Zeng recently pointed out that when Jiang Zemin on several occasions elaborated on the political significance of the military developing a spirit of struggle and perseverance against hardship, that did not mean any lack of concern for the military livelihood. The military should concentrate on the details of implementation, give priority to what is urgent and important, strictly control military expenditures, increase effective utilization of the military budget and, at the same time, develop agricultural sideline products and strengthen its capacity for self-sufficiency.

Liu Huaqing Calls for Strengthening National Defense R&D, Improved Organizational Structure
Recently in talking about strengthening and building quality in the military, Liu Huaqing made the following points:

In line with Deng Xiaoping's thinking of developing the military in the new era and the overall requirement of Jiang Zemin's "five remarks," further develop political advantages unique to the military.

Emphasize the nurturing and training personnel in all fields, strengthen scientific R&D in national defense, improve military weapons and equipment and raise the standard of modernization.

Take further steps to improve organizational structure and make the military more scientifically and professionally oriented.

Strengthen the building of quality, focus on effective results, differentiate among the various levels, and strongly guard against empty talk and pretension.

Chi Haotian, talking about strengthening national defense modernization, noted that this year is the 50th anniversary of victory in the world war against fascism and also the 50th anniversary of victory in the anti-Japanese war. He said we must therefore always remember the painful lessons of history and that while working hard to develop economically, we must also develop national defense for never again can we allow that historic tragedy of the Chinese people to be repeated.

Zhang Wannian recently pointed out that China cannot begin to do anything if it does not have a stable and secure environment, both domestically and abroad. The military must therefore develop a strong awareness of possible threats, keep national security constantly in mind, be prepared to protect the country's stability and security, and, on a moment's notice, lead the troops to satisfactorily fulfill any tasks assigned by the Central Committee and CMC.

The Military Actively Carries Out Foreign Exchanges in Search of Comprehensive Benefits
Exchanges with foreign military are an important channel for gaining comprehensive benefits. Defense Ministry officials in charge of exchanges with foreign military recently indicated that this year the military is prepared to carry out an active program of friendly exchanges with the military of other countries.

What are the comprehensive benefits the Chinese military seeks to gain through foreign exchanges? Military sources reveal the following:

First, stability in the border environment.

Second, resumption of military exchanges with the West.

Third, strengthening of military technology exchange and cooperation.

Fourth, peaceful resolution of dispute over the Spratlys.

At the beginning of this year, General Fu Quanyou visited Pakistan, Bangladesh, and Thailand. Watthanachai Wutthisiri, commander of the Thai armed forces, and Belarus Defense Minister Kastenka also visited China in January. More recently, a Chinese military delegation visited Kazakhstan and Belarus. Chinese military leaders led a delegation to visit Vietnam, Laos, and Indonesia. In February, military delegations from such countries as Pakistan, India, Korea, Burma, Turkey, Kuwait, Nigeria, etc. visited China, while Chinese military delegations visited Australia, Chile, etc.

Last year, China's military achieved significant breakthroughs in developing relationships with the US and other Western militaries. The US visit of Deputy Chief of Staff General Xu Huizi

continued...

POLITICAL-MILITARY OUTLOOK, 1995 (continued)

[1776 1920 3320] and the China visit by US Defense Secretary Perry were the first exchange visits of high-level military leadership since 1989, and they mark the gradual normalization of Sino-US military exchanges.

In January and March of this year, Admiral Larson, former commander in chief, Pacific Fleet, and former Defense Secretary Cheney visited China in succession; at the same time, General Zhu Dunfa [2612 2415 3127], president of PLA National Defense University, and Lt. Gen. Xiong Guangjie [3574 0342 2818], assistant to the chief of the General Staff, also made official friendship visits to the United States.

In February of this year, the visit to China by General Nishimoto Tetsuya, chairman of the Japan Defense Agency Joint Staff and Japan's highest-ranking military leader, was a major event in Sino-Japanese military exchanges. The visit helped promote the overall development of the military relationship of the two countries.

Rear Admiral Lynne Mason, Canada's vice chief of the Defense Staff, visited China on 14 March, the first visit in recent years by a Canadian military leader.

Sources reveal that high-level military delegations from such countries as Spain, Portugal, Austria, Italy, etc., will be visiting China.

On 17 March, Jacques Langsade, chief of staff of France's armed forces, paid an eight-day visit to China in response to an invitation. This is another noteworthy event in exchanges between the Chinese military and the military in the West, for it is the first China visit since the 1989 incident by an important military leader of a major Western European nation. This visit will have a positive effect on the normalization and development of the Sino-French military relationship and in promoting exchanges between the military of Western European nations and the Chinese military.

An important aspect of the Chinese military's foreign exchange program are exchanges in specialized technical areas. It is said that the Chinese military this year will take steps to expand the proportion of specialized technical exchanges and cooperation with foreign military forces in the areas of education, training, scientific R&D, equipment, and facilities.

Questions of "the Chinese Threat" and Increase in Military Expenditures

Whenever Chinese military leaders meet with military leaders from abroad, they often have to explain the reason for the relatively large size of the Chinese armed forces and to point out that the Western view of the so-called "Chinese threat" shows a lack of understanding of realities in China. In his 23 March meeting with France's chief of staff, General Langsade, General Liu Huaqing again repeated the explanation he gave other foreign military leaders: The reason China has a 3-million men army today is because of the long coastal and border line of defense and the relative lack of mobility on the part of the military. As the quality of the military is raised, the numerical size will be reduced. Nevertheless, a long period of time will still be required for the Chinese military to truly modernize its national defense.

Kuang-Chiao Ching, 16 Apr 1995.

CHINA'S CHIEF OFFICERS OF THE SEVEN MILITARY REGIONS, 1994

New Post	Name	Explanation
Beijing Military Region Commander	Lt. Gen. Li Laizhu	Former Beijing Military
Region Deputy Commander Political Commissar	Lt. Gen. Gu Shanqing	Former Chendu Military Regional Political Commissar
Shenyang Military Region Commander	Lt. Gen. Wang Ke	Former Lanzhou Military Region Commander

CHINA'S CHIEF OFFICERS OF THE SEVEN MILITARY REGIONS, 1994 (continued)

New Post	Name	Explanation
Political Commissar	Lt. Gen. Li Xinliang	Former Guangzhou Military Region Deputy Political Commissar
Jinan Military Region Commander	Lt. Gen. Zhang Taiheng	Former Nanjing Military Region Deputy Commander
Political Commissar	Lt. Gen. Song Qingwei	Former Jinan Military Region Deputy Political Commissar
Nanjing Military Region Commander	Lt. Gen. Gu Hui	Former Jinan Military Region Deputy Commander
Political Commissar	Lt. Gen. Fang Zhuqi	Former Beijing Military Region Political Department Director
Guangzhou Military Region Commander	Lt. Gen. Li Xilin	Former Guangzhou Military Region Deputy Commander
Political Commissar	Lt. Gen. Shi Yuxiao	Former Nanjing Military Region Political Commissar
Chengdu Military Region Commander	Lt. Gen. Li Jiulong	Former Jinan Military Region Commander
Political Commissar	Lt. Gen. Zhang Zhijian	Former Beijing Garrison Commander
Lanzhou Military Region Commander	Lt. Gen. Liu Jingsong	Former Shenyang Military Region Commander
Political Commissar	Lt. Gen. Cao Fansheng	Former Jinan Military Region Deputy Political Commissar
PLA Navy Commander	Adm. Zhang Lianzhong	As Before
Political Commissar	V. Adm. Zhou Kunren	Former South China Sea Fleet Political Commissar
PLA Air Force Commander	Gen. Cao Shuangming	Former Shenyang Military Region Air Force Commander
Political Commissar	Lt. Gen. Ding Wenchang	Former PLA Air Force Political Department Director
PLA National Defense University Commandant	Gen. Zhu Dunfa	
Political Commissar	Lt. Gen. Li Wenqing	
Academy of Military Sciences President	Gen. Zhao Nanqi	
Political Commissar	Lt. Gen. Zhang Gong	(Zhang Xusan removed from office)
PLA Second Artillery Corps Commander	Lt. Gen. Yang Guoliang	
Political Commissar	Lt. Gen. Sui Yongju	
Commission of Science, Technology and Industry for National Defense Minister	Lt. Gen. Ding Henggao	
Political Commissar	Lt. Gen. Dai Xuejiang	

•   Most of the responsible persons in the table above have been in their present posts for more than two years.

China Daily, 17 Feb 1994.

CHINESE MILITARY REGIONS AND DISTRICTS MAP

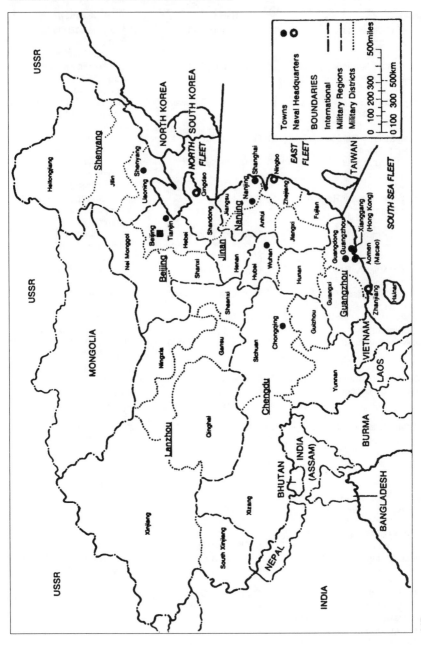

MB.

CHINA'S DEFENSE SPENDING, 1985–1994 (mn US$)

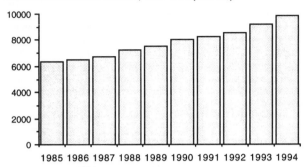

1985 1986 1987 1988 1989 1990 1991 1992 1993 1994

China Facts & Figures Annual, 1995

PLA CHIEF VIEWS MILITARY DISTRICT ROLE, 1995

[Article by Liu Guoyu (0491 0948 5940): "The Provincial Military District System Must Actively Assist Localities in Properly Handling Social Stability Work, Study Deng Xiaoping's Thinking on National Defense"]

Maintaining social stability is a complex systems engineering problem. In conducting this type of work, it is necessary to give full play to all the forces of society at one's disposal. As the provincial military district system engages in this work, five key conditions must be grasped:

First, it is necessary to establish a network for reporting on the situation in society. In assisting localities to properly handle the maintenance of public stability, the provincial military districts must thoroughly grasp developments occurring in society. If they do not know at when, where, or what is happening, they will also become like the deaf and the blind, and will inevitably make mistakes. At the opportune moment, they should accurately grasp circumstances and the social background, and the provincial military districts must form a system in conjunction with the provincial public security offices, state security offices, and locally quartered military organizations, educational institutions, and troops. They should establish a system for reporting on the social situation and exchanging information, for clearing intelligence channels, and for expanding the scope for grasping the situation; each unit must take the initiative in maintaining relations with the local government, public security, and People's Armed Police [PAP] units, and pay close attention to social developments. It is necessary to use existing peoples' militia organizations and reserve duty troops to establish a social situation liaison center, liaison groups, and liaison posts, etc., assign liaison personnel, and establish a reporting system, to form a top down reporting and notification network.

Second, it is necessary to formulate various types of contingency plans. This is a key link in ensuring the rapid reaction of the peoples' militia and reserve duty forces. Regardless of whether or not they are located in a key area where social order is comparatively chaotic, the peoples' armed forces of each military region and county (city, district) must all integrate their own real situations and the characteristics of the area under their jurisdiction, and pay close attention to drafting, examining, correcting, and perfecting plans for assisting localities in maintaining social stability, and plans for coping with suddenly occurring events. It is also necessary, in accordance with the missions that it could potentially shoulder, to revise and perfect advance operational and security plans for command, movement, communications, and safeguarding important targets. When drafting and perfecting various types of contingency plans, it is necessary to carefully plan based on complex situations, to anticipate various emergency measures, to organize a personnel familiarization plan, to implement various safeguard measures, and to conduct the necessary exercises for existing conditions in accordance with the plan, so that in a very short period at the required time it will be possible to master implementation according to the plan.

continued...

PLA CHIEF VIEWS MILITARY DISTRICT ROLE, 1995 (continued)

Third, it is necessary to properly handle the establishment of contingency forces. Peoples' militia contingency elements must strengthen their own development in accordance with the "three implementations" [organizational, political, and military] and "be ready to assemble at the first call" standards. We must integrate peoples' militia training with properly grasping the "four unities," and conduct a one-time organizational adjustment, replenish personnel, and bring the organizational readiness rate to over 80 percent. We must also conduct a one-time political examination and organize around principles and methods involving item by item examination to discern the real from the fake, and progressively become familiar with operational preplans by studying PLA regulations and mastering how to cope with situations that arise. In addition, we must conduct combat readiness exercises, and increase reaction speeds and organizational ability to handle various emergency missions. Finally, we must actively consult with relevant local departments, determine the required equipment and material for peoples' militia contingency elements when they are shouldering missions, work hard to improve command and communication conditions and methods, have contingency vehicles, properly handle safeguarding, and really turn the people's militia contingency elements into the "fists" of the people's militia forces working in our province to maintain social stability. We must ensure that for any situations that are encountered it will be possible to dispatch forces, gain the initiative, and have an effect.

Fourth, it is necessary to handle peacetime maintenance of public security work aptly. The people's militia assist localities in maintaining social stability, and frequent and large missions also involve maintaining the public security and normal order of their own units and their local region. For this reason, each unit must continue to organize the peoples' militia in factory, mine, store, village, and road protection in order to protect the normal production and livelihood of the masses; each unit must actively participate in local public security joint defense and attack all types of economic and criminal activity; and hard working peoples' militia units shouldering the mission of defending railroads and other important targets must enhance their sense of responsibility, and really protect important targets well. When organizing peoples' militia assistance to localities in maintaining public security it is necessary to note that peoples' militia organizations are not law enforcement departments, and do not have the legal authority of public security and judicial departments, hence they cannot independently conduct arrests, detentions, and interrogations, and cannot supersede the functions of public security departments. Therefore, when it comes to judicial matters that arise during the conduct of missions or criminal cases, it is necessary to handle these along with public security and judicial departments and not make decisions without authorization.

Five, it is necessary to take the initiative in allocating public security department and PAP forces to handle suddenly occurring events. Provincial military regions, and provincial subdistricts must prepare for organizing peoples' militia contingency elements to properly handle allocating public security and PAP forces to handle suddenly occurring events. First, it is necessary to establish sound command organs. All levels must establish contingency command posts or command groups, and command personnel must makes things clear to people and not leave gaps. Second, we must strengthen liaison between the militia, PAP, and military; especially important are sound liaison organizations and implementing enhanced leadership on political principles, political orientation, and major policy decisions for the peoples' militia and reserve duty troops in maintaining social stability, in order to ensure that the guns always heed the Party's command. Leadership at all levels must frequently analyze the situation, pay close attention to developments in society, and in a timely manner discover problems, take measures early on, and do work involving the maintenance of social stability in a down-to-earth and practical manner.

National Defense, 15 Dec 1994.

CHINA'S MILITARY PERSONNEL, 1982–1994 (mn)

Year	Total Personnel	Conscripts In Total (est.)	Para-Military	Reserves With Service Within Past Five Years
1982	4.74		12	
1983	4.0		12	
1984	4.1		12	
1985	4.0		12	5.0
1986	3.9	2.3	12	5.4
1987	3.2	1.4	12	4.4
1988	3.2	1.4	12	1.2
1991	3.0	1.4	12	
1992	3.0	1.3	12	1.2
1993	3.0	1.3	12	
1994	3.0	1.3	12	1.2

China Facts & Figures Annual, 1995

MILITARY MANPOWER, 1983–1994

	Total Manpower Available	Number Fit for Military	Number Reaching Age for Military (18 yrs.)
1983	279,548,000	156,416,000	13,423,000
1984	277,707,000	155,464,000	13,159,000
1985	285,513,000	159,299,000	13,080,000
1986	291,558,000	162,738,000	13,270,000
1987	31,258,000	173,945,000	13,317,000
1988	318,179,000	178,210,000	12,860,000
1989	325,073,000	181,047,000	10,968,000
1990	335,382,000	187,047,000	10,968,000
1991	335,382,000	187,047,000	10,968,000
1992	339,555,000	188,996,000	11,692,000
1993	341,635,000	189,704,000	12,712,000
1994	344,590,000	191,304,000	13,412,000

China Facts and Figures Annual, 1995

CHINA'S ARMY STRENGTH, 1982–1994

Year	Personnel	Artillery	Anti-Aircraft	Tanks
1982	3,900,000			11,000
1983	3,150,000	11,800	10,300	10,500
1984	3,250,000	12,800	10,000	11,450
1985	3,160,000	12,800	15,000	11,450
1986	2,973,000	12,800	15,000	11,800
1987	2,300,000	14,500	15,000	11,800
1988	2,300,000	14,500	15,000	15,700
1989	2,300,000	14,500	15,000	15,700
1991	2,300,000	14,500	15,000	15,700
1993	2,300,000	14,500	15,000	9,400
1994	2,405,000	14,500	15,000	10,300

China Facts & Figures Annual, 1995

CHINESE NAVAL STRENGTH, 1982–1994

	1982	1985	1989	1993	1994
Total personnel (th)	360	350	300	260	260
Coastal defense (th)	38	38	38	27	33
Marines (th)	87	5	6	8	
Naval air (th)	38	38	30	25	27
Aircraft	800	800	900	880	900
Major combat ships	32	36	53	54	54
Submarines	104	102	115	46 55	

China Facts & Figures, 1995

CHINA'S AIR FORCE STRENGTH, 1982–1994

	1982	1985	1989	1993	1994
Total personnel (th)	490	490	470	470	470
Strategic missile forces(th)			90	90	90
Air defense personnel(th)	220	220	220	220	220
Combat aircraft(th)	5.3	5.3	6.0	4.9	4.9

China Facts & Figures Annual, 1995

DESIGNATIONS OF CHINESE AIRCRAFT, 1995

Type	Name/ Designation	Origin	Maker
A-5	Fantan	China	Nanchnag
CJ-5	Yak-18	China	
F-5T	JJ-5	China	Shenyang
FT-5	JJ-5	China	CAC
H-5	Il-28	China	Harbin
H-6	Tu-16	China	Xian
J-2	MiG-15	China	
J-5	MiG-17F	China	Shenyang
J-6	MiG-19	China	Shenyang
J-7	MiG-21	China	Xian
J-8	Sov Ye-142	China	Shenyang
Y-5	An-2	China	Hua Bei
Y-7	An-24	China	Xian
Y-8	An-12	China	Shaanxi
Y-12	An-12	China	Harbin
Z-5	Mi-4	China	Harbin
Z-6	Z-5	China	Harbin
Z-8	SA-321	China	Changhe
Z-9	SA-365	China	Harbin

China Facts & Figures Annual, 1995

CHINA'S NUCLEAR-CAPABLE DELIVERY VEHICLES, 1993

	Year Deployed	Range (km)[a]	Throw-weight[b]	CEP (m)[c]	Launcher Total	Munition/ Warhead	Yield Per Warhead[d]	Remarks
LAND-BASED								
Strategic								
ICBM								
CSS-4 (DF-5)	1981	15,000	4.4	n.k.	2	single RV	5MT	
CSS-3 (DF-4)	1978/9	7,000	4.4	n.k.	6	single RV	3MT	
IRBM								
CSS-2 (DF-3)	1970	2,700	4.4	n.k.	60	single RV	2MT	
SEA-BASED								
Strategic								
SLBM								
CSS-N-3 (JL-1)	1983/4	2,200-3,000	n.k.	n.k.	12	—	ε2MT	Installed in 1 SSBN
		Radius of Action (km)[a]	Max Speed (mach)	Weapon Load (000 kg)		Maximum Ordnance Load		
AIR								
Strategic[e]								
Medium-range bombers								
H-6	1968/9	2,180	0.91	9	up to 120	ε2 bombs	n.k.	

• Chinese *tactical* nuclear weapons have been reported, but no details are available.

a. Ranges and aircraft radii of action in km; for nautical miles, multiply by 0.54. A missile's range may be reduced by up to 25% if max payload is carried. Radii of action for ac are in normal configuration, at optimum altitude, with a standard warload, without in-flight refueling. When two values are given, the first refers to a low-low-low mission profile and the high-low-high profile.

b. Throw-weight is the weight of post-boost vehicle (warhead(s), guidance systems; penetration aids and decoys), which can be delivered over a particular range in a stated trajectory. Weights are the max for the weapons system in question and are not necessarily for the range cited.

c. CEP (circular error probable) = the radius of a circle around a target within which there is a 50% probability that a weapon aimed at that target will fall.

d. Yields vary greatly; figures given are estimated maxima. KT range = under IMT; MT range = over IMT. Yield, shown as 1-10KT means the yield is between these limits; if shown as 1-10KT it means that yields between these limits can be selected. Yields shown as 1 or 10KT mean that either yield can be selected.

e. It is not possible to give launcher numbers as the vertical launch system (VLS) can mount a variety of missiles in any of its tubes.

Renmin Ribao, 18 Jul 1993.

DEPLOYMENT AND BASES, 1994

North Sea Fleet: Coastal defense from Korean border (Yalu River) to south of Lianyungang (approximately 35°10′N); equates to Shenyang, Beijing and Jinan Military Regions, and to seaward.
Bases: Qingdao (HQ), Dalian (Luda), Huludao, Weihai, Chengshan. Nine coastal defense districts.
Forces: 2 submarine, 3 escort, 1 mine warfare, 1 amph sqn; plus Bohai Gulf trg flotillas. About 325 patrol and coastal combatants.

East Sea Fleet: Coastal defense from south of Lianyungang to Dongshan (35°10′N to 23°30′N approximately); equates to Nanjing Military Region, and to seaward.
Bases: Shanghai (HQ), Wusong, Dinghai, Hangzhou. Seven coastal defense districts.
Forces: 2 submarine, 2 escort, 1 mine warfare, 1 amph sqn. About 270 patrol and coastal combatants. Marines: 1 cadre div. Coastal Regional Defense Forces: Nanjing Coastal District.

South Sea Fleet: Coastal defense from Dongshan (approximately 23°30′N) to Vietnam border; equates to Guangzhou Military Region, and to seaward (including Paracel and Spratly Islands).
Bases: Zhanjiang (HQ), Shantou, Guangzhou, Haikou, Yulin, Beihai, Huangpu; plus outposts on Paracel and Spratly Islands. Nine coastal defense districts.
Forces: 2 submarine, 2 escort, 1 mine warfare, 1 amph sqn. About 320 patrol and coastal combatants. Marines: 1 bde.

AIR FORCE: 470,000, including strategic forces and 220,000 AD personnel (160,000 conscripts); some 4,970 cbt ac, few armed hel. Seven Military Air Regions, HQ Beijing. Combat elm org in armies of varying numbers of air div (each with 3 regt of 3 sqn of 3 flt of 4-5 ac, 1 maint unit, some tpt and trg ac). Tpt ac in regt only.
Bombers:
  Medium: 120 H-6 (some may be nuclear-capable). Some carry C-601 ASM.
  Light: Some 350 H-5 (some with C-801 ASM).
FGA: 500 Q-5.
Fighter: ε4,000, including 400 J-5, some 60 regt with about 3,000 J-6/B/D/E, 500 J-7, 100 J-8.
Recce: ε40 HZ-5, 150 JZ-5, 100 JZ-6 ac.
Transport: some 600, including 18 BAe *Trident* 1E/2E, 30 Il-14, 10 Il-18, 50 Li-2, 300 Y-5, 25 Y-7, 25 Y-8, 15 Y-11, 2 Y-12.
Helicopters: some 400: including 6 AS-332, 4 Bell 214, 30 Mi-8, 250 Z-5, 100 Z-6, 15 Z-8.
Training: including CJ-5/-6, HJ-5, J-2, JJ-2, JJ-4/-5/-6.
Missiles:
  AAM: PL-2/-2A, PL-5B *Atoll-type,* PL-7.
  ASM: HOT: C-601 subsonic ALCM (anti-ship, perhaps HY-2 SSM derivative); C-801 surface skimmer.
AD ARTY: 16 div: 16,000 35mm, 57mm, 85mm and 100mm guns; 28 indep AD regts (100 SAM units with HQ-2/-2B, -2J (CSA-1), -61 SAM).

FORCES ABROAD: UN AND PEACE-KEEPING:
Middle East (UNTSO): 5 Observers.
Iraq/Kuwait (UNIKOM): 20 Observers.

PARAMILITARY: some 12,000,000, Ministry of Public Security: People's Armed Police: (750,000). 29 div, 1,029 bn border/mtn/internal defense.

Military Balance, 1993–1994

ASSESSMENT OF CHINA'S MILITARY, 1995

Article by Ikuo Kayahara, chief of the Asian Region Research Office of the National Institute for Defense Studies: "Thorough Analysis of the Chinese Military Power"

continued...

ASSESSMENT OF CHINA'S MILITARY, 1995 (continued)

In connection with the recent PRC effort to strengthen its naval force and the increase in its national defense expenditure, talks of the PRC's menace are gaining ground in the United States and Southeast Asian countries. In Japan, also, apprehension is being voiced about the PRC. For example, Professor Shigeo Hiramatsu of Kyorin University has long expressed worries about the PRC's strengthening its naval force and its advance into the open sea. Against this, Shunji Taoka, editorial staff member of ASAHI SHIMBUN, retorted in his article titled "Talks of the PRC Expansion of Military Power Is a Downright Lie" in the June 1994 issue of monthly magazine SHOKUN, by pointing out the reality of the national defense expenditure under inflationary economy and backwardness of weapons and equipment. Prof. Hiramatsu made another refutation in the August 1994 issue of SHOKUN in the article: "The PRC Military Power Is Being Strengthened." As of now, they are representative views about the PRC menace.

Although Beijing has been refuting the "talk of the PRC menace," the reality of the PRC with its gigantic size and peculiar character poses a potential threat because it is proceeding with a policy to enrich and strengthen the nation. In fact, the PRC conducted its 41st nuclear test in the autumn of 1994 in the face of world opinion and carried out a large-scale Army, Navy, and Air Force exercise under the code name of "East Sea 4," with landing operations on islands in mind. In addition, it is forecast in the United States that the PRC's economic power may exceed that of Japan in the beginning of the 21st century.

The PRC's military situation is not clear and is full of suspicions. Therefore an objective and comprehensive analysis may become necessary, without indulging in an ideological discussion of the menace. In order to bring about and enhance trust in the Asian region, it is not constructive at all to either exaggerate or underestimate the reality of the PRC military might that is expanding influence in the area.

Then, what are the realities of the PRC's menace? And what part of the PRC's military is blocking the enhancement of the effort to bring about trust in the Asian region? This article attempts rather hesitantly to throw light on the realities of the menace by summarizing five viewpoints about military factors presumed to be the source of the talk about the PRC menace.

Before going into military studies, peculiar characteristics of the PRC's military might must be summarized first of all. The PRC's military might is a colossal armed power that possesses even a military nuclear capability, and a combination of three groups: the Peoples Liberation Army [PLA], the main field army with a major duty of national defense; the local army in charge of border defense like armed police troops: and the militia that is mobilized when an emergency arises but the members are engaged in daily routines in peace time. The PLA was instrumental in the success of the revolution, as was said "political power grows out the barrel of a gun," and has engaged in extensive functions and roles as a power structure of the powerful nation due to its meritorious contribution in founding the nation, In addition to be a powerful armed force to function for the defense of the nation, the PLA has the following two characteristics: The first is that it is an assembly of indispensable party troops in support of the dictatorial regime of the CPC. It can be said that the PLA fulfills the function of maintaining public peace against anti-revolutionary activities and at the same time is an element to enforce political dictates of the Communist Party. The second is that it has the duty of production that it is engaged in traditional economic activities and that it has its own financial resources and partial ability to support itself.

In the process of carrying out the reform and open-door policy, the PRC may confront all kinds of trials at home and abroad and the military might with the PLA in the core is considered to shoulder increasingly important roles.

The PRC's Assessment of Post-Cold War Situation and National Defense Policy
The PRC has the following understanding of international situation: The post-Cold War world will become multipolar from the bipolar structure of the past and during that transition the United States, a superpower, will play a leading role in forming a new world order. As a result of the breakup of the bipolar order, the possibility of a third world war is gone and instead various contradictions that have been suppressed will erupt, and the world will see a multitude of local

continued...

ASSESSMENT OF CHINA'S MILITARY, 1995 (continued)

conflicts involving nations, territories, and regions. The frequent occurrence of local conflicts will pose a threat in the future, and the post-Cold War security will transit from "stability in tension" maintained by the nuclear fear to "turbulence in tension."

The PRC sees the situation in the post-Cold War Asia-Pacific region as the new military balance in the making as the military might of the United States and the Soviet Union recede and that the region is comparatively stable due to brisk economic activities. However, the PRC cannot get rid of alertness against the colossal military might of the United States and Russia and finds that some unstable factors still remain in the Asian region, in spite of lack of urgent threat.

With such strategic understanding, the PRC with its domestic stability and its realistic line of policy taking root now pursues a national strategy with the economic construction in the core. It has pursued the national defense policy in accordance with "a large view on the general situation" that puts priority on economic construction, and the PRC reduced to 3 million at present the strength of the PLA that had grown to nearly 5 million in the 1980's. In 1985, the PRC made a drastic change of its traditional understanding of war prospects from "a world war is inevitable" to "it can be avoided," and at the same time has proceeded with the modernization policy to shift the PLA under control of the CPC to a regular national defense army. Since the latter half of the 1970's in particular, relations between the United Slates and the PRC have improved, and the PLA to a certain degree succeeded in modernizing itself by introducing military techniques and weaponry from the West, including the United States. Its modernization program in weaponry and equipment has gained momentum after the Cold War, because it witnessed the power of high technology weapons demonstrated during the Persian Gulf War.

On the other hand, the Tiananmen Square incident and the collapse of the Soviet Union revealed the existence of serious domestic problems. The PRC is exposed to nonmilitary attacks of "war without the smoke of powder," such as human rights offensive from the United States, as a result of the Tiananmen Square incident. Because factors of domestic instability are envisaged after Deng Xiaoping's demise on top of external military threats, the PRC was compelled to adopt a comprehensive policy to safeguard its security. The present situation of the national defense modernization policy is that the PRC is compelled to take double standards that the arms are modernized and at the same time heightening ideological and political character of the PLA as the Army under the control of the CPC are sought.

Five Viewpoints of the PRC's Military
1. Viewpoint in Connection With the PRC's Huge Military Might

The core of the military might in charge of the PRC's defense is the regular army, the PLA of course, with a strength of approximately 3 million men. The PLA consists of four branches of the services—Army, Navy, Air Force, and the second artillery force that is the strategic nuclear missile unit. According to the annual report "Military Balance" of the Institute of Strategic Studies of the United Kingdom, the PRC's military power can be summarized as in Chart 1 [chart omitted].

The PRC is traditionally an Army-oriented nation, with a strength of 2.2 million men, 76 percent of the whole strength; its Army exceeds that of the United States or Russia as the largest Army in the world. This is more than six times that of the Vietnamese Army that fought against the PRC in 1979.

The main body of the Navy consists of three fleets and possesses approximately more than 2,000 warships with total displacement of about 1 million tons. It ranks the third largest in the world after the United States and Russia.

The Air Force consists of units with about 5,000 combat aircraft and antiair and airborne units. The PRC emphasizes that its Air Force has become "the world's third largest military power, capable of carrying out nearly all kinds of air combat operations including air attacks, support, transport, reconnaissance, and antiair defense."

The PRC, however, has a vast territorial land of 9.6 million square km, 26 times that of Japan, and a population of 1.17 billion and 23,000 km-long border with 14 countries. Therefore, in spite

continued...

ASSESSMENT OF CHINA'S MILITARY, 1995 (continued)

of the large Army, the land a soldier has to defend is about four square km, larger than that of Japan or India. The soldier's ratio against the population is 0.27 percent, higher than that of Japan but lower than that of India.

On top of it, the PRC's Armed Forces face the problem of backwardness of weapons, a military quality factor, that has to be taken into consideration in the analysis of military power. After witnessing the power of high technological weapons during the Gulf war, PRC military leaders did not conceal their shock by saying, "The PRC's weapons and military technology are 20 years behind." The Navy, for example, has only 55 principal vessels, including destroyers that can operate in open seas. Their average size is 485 tons, smaller than one-tenth that of Russia's Pacific Fleet, and a majority of naval vessels are for coast guards. The Air Force's latest model combat aircraft are remodeled MiG 21's and most of the remaining aircraft are two to three generation older than the MiG 21's.

It seems to be difficult to carry out in short time modernization of the PRC's weapons which remain at a considerably low level compared to high technology weapons due to limited investment in national defense and limit of military science and technology. In particular, the "quick response units" the PRC hopes to deploy in case of local wars it anticipates to "occur frequently" are not sufficiently organized in quality and quantity.

Furthermore, there are signs that metaphysical military power including that of soldiers' morale, an important foundation of war potential of the PLA, is declining. The decline of soldiers' morale, discipline, and solidarity due to poor treatment amidst the social trends stressing the importance of economy is a factor that cannot be overlooked in evaluation of military power.

For that reason, the PRC's present military power in quality is not at a level capable to stand against the modernized armed forces of the United States or Russia. Suppose that the PRC launches an armed liberation scheme against the Republic of China, such a modern transoceanic operation will suffer a great difficulty due to a shortage of air power.

However, the PRC's military has such overwhelming war potential in Asia that neighboring countries on the continent feel relatively heavy pressure. The Vietnamese and Philippine navies do not have the military potential to independently confront the PRC Navy in the South China Sea. The PRC also possesses Asia's only nuclear war capability deployed ready for actual warfare and it has to be noted that the neighboring countries, including Japan, are within range of the PRC's missiles and all of their means of delivery. The PRC's nuclear war capability will be dealt with later.

2. Viewpoint About National Defense Expenditure Expanding by Double-Digit Percentage
As for the PRC's national defense expenditure, Shanbogu [as published], researcher at UK's London University, made public his strong caution this spring that its actual national defense expenditure amounts to $42 billion, about seven times what has been announced publicly. The PRC's national defense budget since 1989 has been expanding for six consecutive years by double-digit percentages against that of each previous year. As a result, the fiscal 1994 national defense budget is more than double that of fiscal 1989.

Although the PRC's national defense expenditure increased during the 1980's, its percentage of total financial outlays fell from about 16 percent in the early 1980's to about eight percent in 1986 and has been maintained at a slightly higher level, nine percent, thereafter.

The "national defense expenditure" as publicly announced is comprised mainly of expenditures for the maintenance and management of the armed forces, such as wages, food expenses, and training costs of soldiers. Because the percentage increase of the "national defense expenditure" from the previous year is considered somewhat related to inflation, the PRC's claim that the increase in the "national defense expenditure" is appropriated to guarantee the soldiers' living is somewhat understandable. However, it is an accepted theory that the publicly announced "national defense expenditure" of the PRC does not include production and procurement expenditures for weapons and equipment. in Japan, the development, manufacturing, and procurement of weapons and equipment occupy about 30 percent of the national

continued...

ASSESSMENT OF CHINA'S MILITARY, 1995 (continued)

defense expenditure. It is necessary to note, however, that in the PRC, such expenditures are separately appropriated in the form of the expenditure for economic construction.

In addition, in the case of the PRC, the armed forces have vast fixed assets of their own and manage to raise money through traditional production activities. Those activities range from agriculture for the frontline troops to raise food, hogs and poultry at farms for their own consumption, to a wide variety of business activities, including the management of coal mines and pharmaceutical plants, forwarding businesses utilizing military trucks, rentals of harbor and airport facilities, and lately even hotel management. In recent days, actual combat troops, including group armies, devote themselves to training and are restricted from participating in production activities. But economic activities by enterprises in the military have been expanded and developed to supplement the "national defense expenditures" through the massive amount of funds created by the armed forces themselves. It has also been said that foreign exchange earned through the export of weapons and so on has been reinvested in national defense modernization programs.

It is needless to say that the total investment disbursed for the PRC's national defense must include the unpublicized sources of income noted above. It is construed that the total amount is at least two to three times the amount publicly announced. But the realities have not been made public at all. Unless they are publicized and the transparency of the national defense expenditure is maintained, it is impossible to erase the underlying fear of the PRC.

3. Viewpoint on Open Sea Advance and Strengthening of the PRC's Naval Power

The PRC's advance into the open sea in recent years has been viewed with alarm as the reappearance of the traditional expansion of the Chinese sphere of influence. As a matter of fact, the PRC claims that "the oceanic territory is an inseparable part of the PRC's territory and a space indispensable for the survival and development of the Chinese people. It is the place where the PRC's strategic interests lie." The "territorial waters law" enacted in February 1992 clearly stated the territorial possession of the Spratly Islands in the South China Sea. In May 1993, the PRC installed a signpost in the Daraku [as published] Atoll, seen as a noteworthy, forceful measure demonstrating territorial possession of the South China Sea.

In addition to the PRC, four nations, including Vietnam and the ROC, lay territorial claim to the Spratly Islands and about 30 island atolls are at present actually controlled by these countries, raising territorial disputes in the South China Sea.

As the economic construction efforts currently underway are being accelerated, the PRC confronted its shortage of energy resources, thus at last becoming an oil importing country in 1993. In the background of the PRC's advance into open seas are the tasks of developing marine resources in order to carry on economic development.

In relation to the maritime advance, the PRC has given the PLA an additional duty of defending "maritime rights and interests," by defining the duty as: the PLA "must strive to shoulder more excellently than before the defense of the sovereignty of territorial land, air space, and sea of the country and maritime rights and interests."

Therefore, the PRC's navy is being strengthened as an important part of the national defense modernization program and it attempts to contribute to the expansion of the nation's maritime rights and interests as a modern navy.

In this regard, the PRC's moves to possess aircraft carriers were widely reported in the mass media, and there were also various signs that the PRC was carrying forward armaments-strengthening programs in the 1980's to break away from a coast-guard-type navy to a navy controlling adjacent seas. In recent years, it was reported that a few larger vessels were built, and the number of vessels for amphibious operations such on supply, refueling, and personnel transport ships is increasing, in addition to the production of helicopter-bearing vessels. It is an indication that the PRC's capability of carrying out operations on the open sea and of amphibious operations with an eye on the South China Sea is being partially strengthened.

The PRC Navy's capability, however, to carry out operations on the open sea has not yet reached a full level, in terms of quantity or quality, in the 3 million square kilometers that the PRC

continued...

ASSESSMENT OF CHINA'S MILITARY, 1995 (continued)

claims as its exclusive economic zone. In particular, its anti-air defense capability on the open sea is insufficient, and the PRC's operations on the open sea remain at a limited level, indicating no immediate possibility that it can project great military power in the oceans. However, there is a historical precedent that the former Soviet navy had grown into a naval power threatening the US Navy by efforts pursued for long years through the initiative of Admiral Gorshkov. Likewise, in case the PRC follows through with emphasis on further strengthening its naval power, it is possible that it will be expanded and strengthened to the level of a powerful ocean navy in the medium-to-long term.

In that case, the PRC's advance into the open sea with its strengthened naval power will not only promote conflicts over territorial water claims and a strong offensive push toward the development of marine resources, but there is also a strong possibility that it will affect the Japanese security problem involving sea lanes. It cannot be overlooked that Southeast Asian nations think that "the PRC is aiming to put under its control not only oil resources but also the sea routes by advancing into the ocean."

4. Viewpoint on the PRC's Nuclear War Capability

The PRC's nuclear war capability consists of three delivery means—missiles, bombers, and nuclear submarines. Although they fall short of the overwhelming nuclear war capabilities of the United States and Russia, a few intercontinental ballistic missiles have major US and Russian cities within their range. In addition, according to the assessment of the British Strategic Institute, the PRC drastically increased its number of deployed ICBM's since 1993.

Japan has not considered the PRC's nuclear war capability an actual threat with Japan being effectively covered by the US nuclear umbrella, and friendly relations between Japan and the PRC in political and economic fields have improved. But the PRC's nuclear war capability was not clear because it remained out of international control following the end of the Cold War era. Today, after the end of the Cold War, when the negotiations on nuclear disarmament and so on continue between the United States and Russia, the nuclear war capabilities of those nations with mid-level nuclear arms capacities have drawn attention and have become an important pending issue of nuclear control. But the PRC has not made any positive response.

After the end of the Cold War, the PRC conducted its 41st in a series of nuclear tests in October immediately following the test in June 1994, despite the fact that both the United States and Russia continued their moratorium on nuclear tests. The United States indicated its strong concern over the report that the test was intended to develop a light-weight warhead capable of being mounted on mobile missiles. It can be used as a warhead for a mid-range missile of 2,500 km which has Asian countries within its range. It is ominous that the PRC continues to improve and strengthen this sort of nuclear war capability.

The PRC declares that it has conducted the least number of nuclear tests among the nuclear powers and "its nuclear war capability is totally intended for self-defense." But the fact that the PRC continues its nuclear tests in such an international situation, with post-Cold War nuclear control being centrally managed by the US and Russia, throws doubt on the reliability of that declaration.

The PRC's attitude toward the non-proliferation of nuclear arms has been a cause for concern. Although the PRC is opposed to nuclear proliferation by officially signing the "nuclear Nonproliferation Treaty" in the spring of 1992, Defense Minister Chi Haotian defended mounting suspicion about the DPRK's development of nuclear weapons by saying, "such reports highly exaggerate the facts." The PRC's announcement that "it will not interfere with the DPRK's domestic affairs" leaves doubt about its enthusiasm for nuclear nonproliferation.

5. Viewpoint on the PRC's Arms Transfer and Military Exchanges

In the 1980's, the PRC sought Western sources for procuring military technology; because the West imposed sanctions against the PRC following the Tiananmen Square incident, the PRC sought out non-western sources. Thus, the PRC purchased the latest long-range Su-27 fighters from Russia; this drew attention because of indications that the PRC, which wanted to acquire advanced military technology, switched its source of procurement to Russia from the

continued...

ASSESSMENT OF CHINA'S MILITARY, 1995 (continued)

West. Following the end of the Cold War, Russia dumped the weapons of the former Soviet Union on the international market in order to earn foreign exchange. According to reports, the PRC procured MiG-31 fighters, 400 T-72M tanks with 120-ram cannons, and a variety of electronic instruments, and even employed 1,000 nuclear-related specialists.

It is a very disquieting tendency for neighboring countries that the PRC is improving the quality of its military power and is proceeding with a policy of having a close military relationship with Russia. For instance, the PRC's introduction of 150 Su-27 Flanker fighter planes led the United States to supply 150 F-16 Eagle fighter planes and anti-air "Patriot" missiles to Taiwan, inviting a kind of cycle of armaments expansion. In relation to the PRC's advance into the South China Sea, Southeast Asian countries are being compelled to strengthen their armaments; for example, MiG-29 Fulcrum fighter planes for Malaysia, Scud missiles for Indonesia, and a helicopter-bearing aircraft carrier for Thailand.

Not only arms procurement but also military exchanges between the PRC and Russia have become so active that it is even felt that they may develop into a system of military cooperation. Recent Sino-Russian military exchanges have been active, illustrated by the signing of two military pacts negotiated during Yeltsin's visit to the PRC in 1993 and exchange of mutual visits by the two nations' fleets, in addition to the progress in the negotiations to pull their troops back from the border between the PRC and Russia. In September 1994, PRC President Jiang Zemin, who concurrently holds the post of chairman of the CPC Central Military Commission, visited Russia and declared in his joint statement on the detargeting of nuclear missiles. This sort of movement may serve the cause of improving mutual trust, but on the other hand, other Asian countries feel uneasy about the active and multidimensional military cooperation of the two giant military nations of the Eurasian continent.

Meanwhile, PRC arms exports were steadily expanding in scale during the last half of 1980's. According to data from the US Arms Control and Disarmament Agency, the PRC accounted for five percent of the total amount of global arms transactions in 1988, ranking the third after the United States and Russia. After the Gulf War, the PRC's arms exports decreased drastically, but the PRC remains the largest arms supplier in Asia, with deep-rooted demand among developing nations. Because it publicly pledged to participate in the "restriction of technology transfers involving missiles," the PRC is subject to light restrictions, but it may continue the policy of actively proceeding with arms exports in the future, as seen in the export to Pakistan of M-11 ground-to-ground missiles with a range of 300 km.

Realities of Menace and Tasks Being Asked of the PRC
As seen in the five viewpoints on military trends related to the theory of the PRC menace, it is understood that they are based on certain realities that require firm countermeasures in order to safeguard regional security and to such things that the fear and worries can be relieved to a certain degree by boosting mutual trust through increased transparency.

In the first place, a large factor considered to be the base of menace of the PRC is its nuclear war capability, because it is the only country in Asia that has deployed nuclear weapons capability in readiness for actual war. Against the PRC's nuclear tests, Japan has expressed concerns with an eye on its economic assistance to the PRC, including the fourth, yen-based official development aid (ODA) loan to that country, but the PRC has gone ahead with nuclear tests with the aim of strengthening its nuclear war capability. In an atmosphere wherein security is guaranteed with the progress of nuclear disarmament talks between the United States and Russia, the PRC cannot wipe out the fear of the PRC menace among its neighboring countries if it maintains a policy of strengthening its nuclear war capability.

In relation to nuclear nonproliferation, the PRC gives out such an impression that nuclear development-related technical knowhow is exported without interruption and its response that requires an urgency is ambiguous toward the DPRK to prevent it from developing nuclear weapons. With the transition period of the nuclear Nonproliferation Treaty system is up in 1995, the PRC menace will not be relieved unless it demonstrates an active attitude of cooperation

continued...

ASSESSMENT OF CHINA'S MILITARY, 1995 (continued)

on nuclear control by putting such actions immediately into effect, including the immediate suspension of nuclear testing.

The second factor involving fears against the PRC derives from its external military exchanges, including weapons transfers from the PRC. The PRC's procurement of the latest weapons from Russia will improve the quality of PRC military power and stimulate the military balance in the process of being newly formed in the Asian region. In reality, weapons transfer is actively taking place in Asian countries, giving rise to a kind of arms race in the region. The recent expansion of military exchanges between the PRC and Russia has touched off lively military relations between the United States and the PRC. This evokes an uneasy feeling among neighboring countries that new conflicts of interest may arise among the military powers of the United States, the PRC, and Russia in the post-Cold War Northeast Asian region.

Thirdly, the PRC's advance into open seas and related strengthening of its naval power are pointed out as the factor of increased menace from the PRC in parallel with its military trend. The PRC resorted to naval battles, though small in scale, against the Vietnamese Navy on two occasions in 1974 and 1988, revolving around claims on territory and territorial waters. The historical fact is not forgotten that the PRC dares to take stern action, including use of force, in settling disputes over territory and sovereignty.

The PRC has a strong economic motive in making advances into the ocean, and recent reports held that the PRC Navy had been mobilized to guard exploration efforts involving sea-bottom oil fields. Until now, the modernization of the PRC Navy has been progressing at a slow pace. At the recent centennial marking the Sino-Japanese War, Gen. Liu Huaqing, vice chairman of the CPC Central Military Commission, reemphasized by citing war events in the history of war 100 years ago that the Navy had to be strengthened. Should the strengthening of the PRC Navy and its comprehensive mobility in the outer oceans, including the procurement of aircraft carriers, be emphatically carried out in the future, a situation requiring acute alertness will be brought about.

In addition, the future trend of increase in the PRC's expenditure for national defense may be viewed with strong apprehension. As previously explained, there are unpublished, concealed investments in the PRC's national defense expenditure, and such apprehension cannot be cleared if the realities remain concealed. It must be pointed out that the national defense expenditure continues to increase at a far greater rate than the increases in outlays in such important fields as agriculture, and the total amount of deficit financing continues to rise by large amounts. Such facts have to be noted, because they go against the tendency for many nations to control their post-Cold War outlays for national defense. Without making public the purpose of strengthening its national defense, the PRC continues to increase the national defense budget without setting any ceiling for the future in consideration of the military. It is certainly a worrisome trend.

As for the assessment of the PRC's present military power, its present status remains unclear except that all military branches possess immense military power, leading to an undeniable uneasiness. If the realities of the military power and situation of military exercises are made public, misunderstandings may be cleared. The present PLA is mostly composed of personnel with versatile duties, and it is necessary to take into consideration the backwardness of qualitative military power and such geographical conditions that the country encompasses a wide area of territory. Therefore, as long as the US military continues to be maintained in the Asian region, the present level of PRC military power, though it is overwhelming to neighboring countries, cannot be directly construed to constitute a menace in terms of its external aggression capabilities. This article attempted to summarize factors relating to the menace theory of the PRC, and it can be concluded that the PRC in general embraces still unstable factors against post-Cold War Asian security.

The post-Cold War situation in Asia is considered relatively stable, such an aftereffect of the Cold War as the Korean peninsula continues to exist as an unstable factor on top of the fact that a framework of security be constructed. The first thing the PRC is required to do in order

continued...

ASSESSMENT OF CHINA'S MILITARY, 1995 (continued)

to foster trust in the Asian region is to make its military open and transparent. Next comes the PRC's awareness of the breadth of influenceary power plays in the security of the Asian region. The PRC is asked to play the role of proceeding with mutual cooperation in regionally coordinating with the Asian regional countries as it expands economic mutual reliance with the Asian region. Irrespective of whatever system the PRC will adopt in the 21st century, it is unmistakable that it will remain a potential giant in the Asian region, and it is essential to remain a substantial military menace. For that purpose, it is important to make an objective analysis of the PRC's military power and respond in a composed manner based on that analysis. They will constitute an important effort in confidence building in the Asian region.

Chou Koron, Feb 1995.

FIRST BOOK ON MILITARY SCIENCES PUBLISHED, 1995

China's first book to systematically expound an outline and basic knowledge of military sciences was published by the Military Sciences Publishing House.

The book, a key project under the state philosophy and social sciences plan, was written over five years by a dozen experts of the Academy of Military Sciences with Zehng Wenhan, former commandant of the Academy serving as chief editor. It covers theories of military thinking, military sciences and armed forces building as well as theories of military history, military geography, military technology, new frontier branches of learning and other relevant branches of learning.

X, 15 Jan 1995.

CHINESE ARMS SALES TO THE MIDDLE EAST, 1985–1992

FEER, 18 Sep 1994.

CHINA PURCHASED AIR TRANSPORTS FROM UZBEKISTAN, 1995
The Chinese Army contracted to purchase 15 IL-76M military transport planes manufactured at the Tashkent Aircraft Manufacturing Plant in Uzbekistan and by February 1995 had taken shipment of 10 such planes. The IL-76M is the Chinese Air Force's largest transport with a capacity of 40 tons and until late 1994 had been provided by Russian factories. China turned to weapons sources outside Russia because of concerns over Russia's abilities to provide on-time delivery and to provide parts in light of Russian economic problems. Military authorities believed that the new IL-76Ms would be deployed to China's 15th Airborne which will be the main body of a enlarged interceptor force used to rush a counter attack deep into enemy territory.

China Facts & Figures Annual, 1995

FIRST RUSSIAN PURCHASED SUBMARINE TRANSITS, 1995

The first of four Russian purchased submarines passed through the Strait of Malacca (sic) on its way to the North China Sea Fleet. China's purchase of four Russian-built K-Class diesel submarines attracted considerable attention from the world and the concern of peripheral countries. A high ranking Taiwan naval officer said, "Recent intelligence shows that the deal was for four K-Class submarines two of which are 877 EKM types for export purposes and the other two were the new 636 type, which have never before been sold to any other country."

Lien Ho Pao, 20 Feb 1995.

CHINA MASSES TROOPS NEAR RUSSIAN BORDER, 1995

According to information from officials of the Counterespionage Department and Police Department of the Maritime Kray in the Russian Far East, the Chinese Armed Forces massed troops near the China-Russian Border along the Maritime Kray, and have started military exercises in the area. Chinese troops from the Shenyang Military Region assembled on 28 January 1995. This was the first time since 1985 that Chinese Armed Forces conducted exercises along the Russian border. In response Russia mobilized 500,000 soldiers and made preparations to conduct exercises at the border as a countermeasure.

Since Russia started its transition to a market economy in 1992, there had been an influx of Chinese nationals to the Maritime Kray. As a result, Governor Nazdratenko of the Maritime Kray advocated restrictions on Chinese entry to Russia. The governor also demanded that the Sino-Soviet border treaty be his opposition to the return of 600 hectares of land designated as Chinese territory. It was believed that the gathering of Chinese forces was meant to contain such moves by the local Maritime Kray government.

Tokyo Shimbun, 16 Feb 1995.

QUALITY OF TAIWAN'S DOMESTIC TANKS, 1995

Lieutenant General Chang Kuang-chin, the Taiwan Army's Deputy Commander-In-Chief said that 120 US M60A3 tanks the army ordered would arrive in April 1995. General Chang pointed out that the domestically-produced M48H, Brave Tiger tank was less costly and 96.63 percent problem-free. The all weather Brave Tiger tanks were equipped with heat source image aiming equipment, laser distance-measuring device, trajectory computer, a stability system and a 105 mm cannon and had the ability to perform around the clock. An American expert, following testing, said the Brave Tiger tank outperformed the American-made M60A3 tank in fire-control and in stability. In addition, it was stated that its cross-country capability and fire-power were superior to the Communist China T-80 tanks.

Chung-Yang Jih-Pao, 25 Jan 1995.

VII INTERNATIONAL RELATIONS

CHINA'S VIEWS ON INTERNATIONAL ISSUES, 1995

[Interview by Feng Lidong (7458 4539 0392); place and date not given: "Prospects for World Situation in 1995—Director of International Studies Institute Yang Chengxu Answers Questions Raised by Staff Reporter"]

[Feng Lidong] Now, people generally believe that the post-Cold War world is turning into a multipolar one. What in your opinion are the features of a multipolar world? What type of relationships do you envisage evolving among the big powers?

continued...

CHINA'S VIEWS ON INTERNATIONAL ISSUES, 1995 (continued)

[Yang Chengxu] If we take 1994 as a year marked by continued and profound changes in the post-Cold War world, I believe that changes relating to the national strength of the big powers and major policy shifts among some of the big powers resulted in a more clearly defined global pattern.

The world is still undergoing a transition to multipolarization at the moment, while a relative balance of power has resulted in an effective check on all global forces. This transitional period will by and large come to an end early next century. The United States, as the sole superpower, is expected to continue to play a leading role in as wide a scope as possible, will continue to give economic interests primary consideration, and will compete more energetically for markets in developing countries. Besides, the United States is expected to follow less aggressive security policies, to concentrate on the resolution of more pressing and primary issues rather than non-urgent and secondary issues, and to try to tackle security issues in order of importance and urgency. Russia is expected to make redoubled efforts to build an integrated CIS economic and defense system with an eye on distancing CIS member countries from the western powers. Moreover, Russia is also expected to vehemently oppose central or east European countries becoming NATO members and will try to regain its superpower status. Germany and Japan have already explicitly demanded permanent membership of the UN Security Council. Germany has also enhanced its big power status by developing "leader-partnership relations" with the United States. Japan has for the first time vowed to become less dependent upon the US umbrella and has resolved to play a bigger role as regards regional security issues.

Following policy adjustments among the big powers, US policy has become less aggressive, while other big powers have started following more independent policies. This situation is definitely conducive to a multipolar global pattern and the status of small, medium-sized, and developing countries. One major feature of global politics in 1994 is that a growing number of big powers became bold enough to say "no" to the sole superpower, while a growing number of new-born and developing countries became bold enough to say "no" to the developed countries.

In an era marked by economic growth, trade frictions among the big powers are expected to multiply with each passing day. Due to different interests, big powers will inevitably have widely divergent views on regional conflicts and on major national security issues as well. For instance, they are expected to differ on such issues as whether or not it is desirable to institute a unitary social system and a unitary ideology or to build a multipolar world. Some big powers are maintaining alliances which are not as strong as the ones they maintained in the Cold War era, while other big powers are sometimes adversaries and sometimes partners with each other. The big powers are still contending with and trying to contain each other. They are allied and divided on certain global issues. They are sometimes adversaries and sometimes friends. They sometimes develop acute contradictions and sometimes make compromises or mitigate contradictions among themselves. People cannot but acknowledge that hegemonism and power politics still exist. A few big powers are still trying to expand their spheres of influence, seek global domination, and practice hegemonism. Should such a tendency develop unchecked and result in an imbalance of power, global peace and stability would certainly be jeopardized to a great extent.

[Feng] There are constant armed conflicts and a growing number of hot spots in a volatile world. In your opinion, how will these hot spots of conflicts change and develop this year?

[Yang] There are a growing number of hot spots and conflicts in the post-Cold War period. Statistics show that there were a total of 38 old and new conflicts and regional wars in 1994, much more than in 1992, and an increase of four conflicts and regional wars over 1993. It seems that we will still live in a volatile world in 1995. In the post-Cold War period, the former Soviet Union and Eastern Europe have been plagued by intensifying ethnic contradictions. As a result, there are now 27 countries in Eastern Europe compared with nine countries in the Cold War period. National independence, separatist, or irredentist movements have also come to a temporary conclusion. Lashed at by a "tide of democracy," quite a few African countries have basically brought an end to separatist or tribal wars after experiencing a period of turbulence

continued...

CHINA'S VIEWS ON INTERNATIONAL ISSUES, 1995 (continued)

and instability. Having experienced a most volatile period, the world will, I believe, continue to be volatile this year. Now, new breakthroughs have been made in the Arab-Israeli peace process, the United States and the DPRK have reached a nuclear agreement, South Africa has found a political solution to its problems, and the Angolan civil war has come to an end, while the world is less likely to witness new regional conflicts in future. The resolution of the above-mentioned conflicts attests to the fact that only through political dialogue and consultations and mutual compromise and concessions will the parties involved be able to attain the desired results. Measures like forcing others to accept what is given, applying sanctions against others, or bringing pressure to bear upon others will definitely not work.

A lot of armed conflicts still exist, most of which are civil wars. The chairman of the 29th UN General Assembly stated: A total of 83 armed conflicts have taken place over the past three years, 79 of which are civil wars. These conflicts have been factors of regional instability. However, due to their limited scale, they have not gotten out of control.

There are continuous and uninterrupted regional conflicts as well as intensifying national, ethnic, religious, political, and social contradictions in the world. As a result, armed conflict and civil wars are likely to break out at any time. Many African countries have been plagued by continuous political turmoil. The former Soviet Union and Eastern Europe face a host of ethnic problems. The war raging in Bosnia-Herzegovina is still going on. Due to complex internal and external factors, the country still has a long way to go before realizing reconciliation. Due to different interests, the EU, the United States, and Russia have failed to see eye to eye with each other on the Bosnia-Herzegovina question. Within the EU, Britain, France, and Germany often hold different views on the Bosnia-Herzegovina conflict, thereby further complicating the issue. In spite of fresh breakthroughs in the Middle East peace process, Palestine still remains in an awkward predicament and is still plagued by factors of instability. The Syrian-Israeli peace talks are likely to take a tortuous path full of stumbles due to growing differences of opinion within Israel on the issue of troop withdrawals from the Golan Heights.

[Feng] Now that economic competition has replaced military confrontation on the world stage, what do you think are the major manifestations of global competition at the moment?

[Yang] The most important feature of the world situation in 1994 was the overall economic recovery among the western countries. The world is expected to enter a period of sustained economic growth in the future. Some people have predicted that the upcoming economic boom will be the third global economic upsurge since the Second World War. In the second half of the 1990's, the world is expected to witness its fastest economic growth since the oil crisis of 1973, and to enjoy annual economic growth of 4 percent. This rapid economic growth is likely to last for one or two decades.

In accordance with an agreement signed at the GATT Uruguay Round, the World Trade Organization will be officially established on 1 January 1995, thus enhancing the mechanisms of the existing multilateral trade structure. Now, the world economy is rapidly undergoing regionalization. The North America Free Trade Agreement has also come into force and is being extended to Latin America at the moment. Having expanded to the north, the EU will soon extend to the Middle East and Mediterranean regions. The Asia-Pacific Economic Cooperation organization has also agreed to liberalize trade and investment on or before 2020.

The United States, Europe, and Japan have been locked in fierce competition for markets in developing countries through regional grouping. While the United States has been energetically systemizing Asia-Pacific Economic Cooperation organization and rapidly building a free trade zone in the western hemisphere, the EU has been formulating a long-term strategy aimed at thrusting into Asia and has upgraded relations with the four Mercosur countries, including Argentina, Brazil, and others. Japan has also been energetically forging closer economic ties with other Asian countries, working hard to set up a regional trade conglomerate and a Japanese Yen zone, rapidly expanding trade contacts with Mexico and other Latin American countries, and increasing investment in Latin American countries. Moreover, the United States and Europe have also been locked in a fierce contest for the Middle East and North African markets.

continued...

CHINA'S VIEWS ON INTERNATIONAL ISSUES, 1995 (continued)

The industrialized countries have attached great importance to markets in developing countries for various reasons. First, developing countries have registered much faster economic growth than developed countries. A few years ago, while western countries were bogged down in economic recession, the major developing countries in East Asia and other regions continued to maintain high rates of economic growth. As a matter of fact, it is the faster economic growth sustained by the developing countries which has given a powerful impetus to the current global economic recovery to a certain extent. Second, rising per capita income among the developing countries has created an excellent opportunity for absorbing exports from developed countries. Over the past few years, US, European, and Japanese industrial products have found large markets in Asia, East Asia in particular. In the 1988-1990 period, US exports to developing countries grew at an average annual rate of 12 percent, while US exports to developed countries grew at an average annual rate of 2 percent. Third, rapid industrialization in developing countries has sent large quantities of low-priced, good-quality labor-intensive products into industrialized countries, thus lowering commodity prices in developed countries.

Along with the industrialization of developing countries, more and more developing countries have not only become suppliers of raw materials and primary products but also producers of labor-intensive products. Some developing countries are also producing technology-intensive or capital-intensive products. Thanks to a high rate of economic growth and expanding markets, a batch of developing countries have been proven to possess great development potential. Although they possess adequate capital and advanced technology, industrialized countries will still have to open up new markets in developing countries in order to maintain sustained and steady economic growth. Only by complementing each other will developing countries and industrialized countries be able to bring about common development.

[Feng] Finally, would you please say something about China's international status and diplomacy?

[Yang Chengxu] The world reassessed China in 1993. In 1994, China moved further into the world with countless diplomatic successes. In 1995, China is expected to engage more in active diplomacy and make new diplomatic breakthroughs. In addition, China will continue to develop relations and forge more common interests with developing countries. China's good-neighbor relations with surrounding countries are expected to enter a new stage of overall growth. China will be recognized by a growing number of countries as an important factor of peace and stability in the Asia-Pacific region as well as in the world. The Asian market, especially the China market, is expected to become a popular market for all developed countries in the world. As China's pragmatic proposals and actions regarding Asia-Pacific and global security issues have been highly appraised by an increasing number of countries, more and more countries now hope to see China play a bigger role. China has made and will continue to make whatever positive contributions she can to regional as well as global peace and development.

Ban Yun Tan No. 1, 10 Jan 1995.

THE SPRATLY ISLANDS ISSUE, 1995

The Spratly Islands were an on-going point of contention among several Asian nations not the least of which was China. China had been unwilling to discuss the legal basis of its sovereignty claim in the Spratly Islands during a meeting of Asian Regional Forum (ARF) which included the Philippines, Vietnam, Malaysia and Indonesia. The Philippines Under-Secretary of Foreign Affairs Rodolfo Severino said China had not defined the "regime under which they claim the waters." All they say, according to Severino, is they have sovereignty over the entire area. Severino said that claim is not true if you consult the Law of the Sea but China is a military power. China used that power to maximum effect in the Spratly Islands issue and managed to keep the other claimants at bay while continuing to build a military force in the islands.

continued...

THE SPRATLY ISLANDS ISSUE, 1995 (continued)

Indonesia made a proposal to discuss ownership according to what was called the doughnut formula. Under that proposal only the hole in the doughnut, the middle of South China Sea, including the main islands of the disputed Spratly chain, would be discussed by competing claimants as an area for potential joint economic development.

No matter which direction discussions were to take no one in Asia or the rest of the world wanted to see or be dragged into a bilateral territorial dispute pitting China against Vietnam, Malaysia and the Philippines.

China Facts & Figures Annual, 1995.

MAP OF THE SPRATLY ISLANDS, 1994

FEER, 11 Aug 1994.

CHINA URGES VIETNAM AND RUSSIA TO STOP SPRATLY SURVEYS, 1995

A Chinese Foreign Ministry Spokesman urged Vietnam to stop its geological surveys on the Nansha (Spratly) Islands and further stated that he hoped other nations would not take part in such actions. The spokesman, Shen Guofang commented on reports in Vietnamese newspapers that Vietnam in collaboration with Russia carried out two geological surveys on the Nansha Islands in 1993 and 1994 and planned to conduct a third one in the summer 1995.

Shen said that the Nansha Islands had been part of the Chinese territory since ancient times and that China had indisputable sovereignty over the Nansha islands and their adjacent waters.

According to Shen the actions by Vietnam and Russia constituted an encroachment upon China's territorial sovereignty and maritime rights and interest and were illegal.

X, 21 Jan 1995.

PHILIPPINES PROTEST CHINA'S SPRATLY PRESENCE, 1995

Manila protested the presence of Chinese troops on a Philippine-claimed reef in the Spratly island chain. Chinese foreign ministry spokesman Chen Jian said , using the Chinese name for the Spratly chain, "The Chinese government has always proposed that disputes over Nansha island should be settled through consultations." In response to Philippine accusations that the island was being used as Chinese naval facility, Chen said it was being used as a shelter by Chinese fishermen. Philippine President Fidel Ramos said he had ordered Philippine forces in the Spratlys be strengthened.

AFP, 16 Feb 1995.

CHINA-US TALKS BREAKDOWN, 1995

Before lunch on 15 December 1994, the Chinese delegation to the Sino-US talks on intellectual property rights [IPR] made a phone call to the US embassy in China to inform their US counterparts that they would continue the talks with the US side on pending issues at 1500 on the same day.

At that moment, the Chinese representatives had a new, revised offer in hand, which was a product of what they had worked intensively on for the whole morning. The "Outline of the Program on Intensifying Inspection, Supervision, and Guidance Regarding the Enforcement of Laws Related to Intellectual Property Rights," which was drafted by the office of the IPR working group under the State Council, truly incorporated many features of the US version.

US Representative Left Without Even Saying Goodbye

The US embassy's reply on the telephone was simply a shock to the Chinese delegation.

The Chinese were told that the chief US representative, Lee Sands, was on his way to Beijing airport; he had left for the airport to catch a flight to Hong Kong scheduled for 1130 in transit to Geneva because he had received no message from the Chinese side that morning, and the talks originally scheduled to be held in China from 12 to 18 December had been called off because he had other important affairs to attend to at the ongoing Geneva meeting of the working group in charge of China's application to reenter the GATT.

"At least he should have notified us, but he did not. This is simply unreasonable!" The members of the Chinese delegation, who were psychologically unprepared for this, were all indignant.

That afternoon, the Ministry of Foreign Trade and Economic Cooperation and the Chinese delegation met an economic counselor from the US Embassy to China by appointment to express their regret at the US representative's departure from Beijing without notification, pointing out that the action showed a lack of sincerity and was rude.

The next afternoon the economic counselor from the US Embassy to China called on our negotiators and told them that Lee Sands was still in Hong Kong and, if the talks were likely to make progress, he would rush back to Beijing right away.

In reply, the Chinese delegation expressly told the counselor that it was up to Lee Sands himself to decide whether to return to Beijing to resume talks or not; he was welcome to come back for the talks, but the Chinese side did not mind reopening the talks later.

In fact, however, Lee Sands made public comments on the case to French reporters immediately after he emerged from the plane in Hong Kong. He made a unilateral announcement: "The Chinese and US sides suspended talks on intellectual property rights on 14 December." By now, the talks between the Chinese and US sides had been going on for 18 months and it was "now time to come to a decision," he added. His remarks were strongly threatening. "Now we have only two weeks left before the Sino-US talks on intellectual property rights end. If China refuses to take strong action to curb infringements of intellectual property rights, it will face trade sanctions imposed by the United States and the prospects for China's reentry to the GATT will be spoiled." He also disclosed that US Trade Representative Kantor would make a decision by 31 December on whether to impose trade sanctions on China for massive infringements of US intellectual property rights.

continued...

CHINA-US TALKS BREAKDOWN, 1995 (continued)

Spon after that Lee Sands flew directly to Geneva.

Value Involved in Sanctions Is Higher Than Predicted

His action meant a complete breakdown of the seventh round of 1994 Sino-US talks on intellectual property rights.

The Americans did not mean to merely threaten their negotiating counterparts but to really take action this time.

As expected, China's attempt to regain its GATT membership failed, again under US pressure.

As was expected, on the last day of 1994, US Trade Representative Kantor made a unilateral announcement: If China cannot fulfill by 4 February next year the requirements set by the US side regarding the protection of US intellectual property rights, the United States will impose trade sanctions on China. Kantor also released a list of Chinese commodities subject to sanctions, which may involve a total value of about $2.8 billion. And this figure is nearly $1.8 billion more than general estimates.

The Chinese Government, for its part, reacted with extraordinary strength to this. The Ministry of Foreign Trade and Economic Cooperation issued a statement: counter-retaliation will be launched against the United States in accordance with the "PRC Foreign Trade Law," and seven counter-retaliatory measures have been formulated.

The news of "retaliation" and "counter-retaliation" between China and the United States, which was announced on the first day of the new year, has drawn the attention of the whole country. To the Chinese public who have opened their country to the outside world, this news appears to be more important than any other at the beginning of the year. People are keeping their eyes wide open to closely watch what is going to happen by the deadline for "opinion solicitation" set in the statement.

The Chinese public cannot help asking: Actually, what are the Sino-US intellectual property rights talks all about? Why did the talks break down? And what do the talks imply for China in the future?

Therefore, at 2000 on the last day of 1994, I managed to contacted by phone the deputy director of the Copyright Department of the State Copyright Bureau, Gao Unghan, who had just returned to Beijing from Hainan.

It Is the US Side and Nobody Else Who Should Be Blamed for the Breakdown of the Talks

Gao, who has had experience in diplomatic and cultural work, was involved in the whole process of the formulation, enactment, and implementation of China's Copyright Law: From 1993 onward, as an expert in copyrights, he has been engaged in the Sino-US negotiations on intellectual property rights, and he personally took part in the whole process of the seventh round of Sino-US talks on intellectual property rights this year.

"In the past, on the Chinese side, we generally seldom talked to the public about the progress of the Sino-US talks on intellectual property rights, as we did not want to affect the process of negotiations. However, we noticed that the Americans did not follow the same rules.

Every time they passed through Hong Kong, they always aired their opinions, and the Hong Kong press reported their remarks without exception. Now that the Sino-US talks on intellectual property rights have broken down, if we continue to keep silent, then people will have the wrong impression that the Chinese side bears the responsibility. Therefore, we need to present the facts to the public to tell them: it is the US side and nobody else which should be blamed for the lack of progress in the talks between China and the United States."

At 1030 on 3 January 1995, I met Mr. Gao on the seventh floor of the State Press and Publications Administration Building, as the first reporter to hear the inside story of the breakdown of the Sino-US talks on intellectual property rights.

Lee Sands left without even saying goodbye, but when he came he was well prepared.

On 30 June 1994, the United States put our country on its list of "priority target countries" under "Special Section 301," so that a so-called six-month "investigation" could be carried out against China.

continued...

CHINA-US TALKS BREAKDOWN, 1995 (continued)

In 1993, the United States included China in the list of countries to be watched closely according to Special 301.

What is Special 301? It is Article 301 of the US trade act. The main point of this article is that the US trade representative should consider the adoption of retaliation measures against those who violate the intellectual property rights of the United States by first asking the other side to improve the situation, and if no improvement is made, the United States should take tougher trade retaliation measures.

Intellectual Property Rights Became a New Pretext

The article specifies a set of procedures. All of those having problems in protecting the US intellectual property fights will be included in a list, which is divided into several category. Observation will first be made; and this is followed by intensive observation; and the third category is key targets. Many developed countries, such as Germany and Japan, are included in the observation category; also in this category are some developing countries where there is rapid economic growth.

The United States put China in the top category and took China as one of the priority targets. India and Argentina are also in the same category.

Usually, April was a crucial month. According to the regulations, normally, the United States announced the list of countries being included in the key-target list.

However, in April last year, the US authorities only announced the "plan" for including three countries in the list of key targets, namely, China, India, and Argentina. The official announcement was postponed to late June. This was because in early June, the issue of China's most-favored-nation [MFN] trading status would have to be solved. Clinton openly announced that the MFN issue would no longer be linked with the human rights issue. After that, the United States would lose a lever to constrain China. The intellectual property issue could then be taken as a good pretext.

The contents of the unofficial documents shown by the United States continued to increase. In late 1993, the unofficial document they gave us had only five pages; but in late 1994, the document increased to 20 pages.

It Is Expected That the US Side Will Make Further Escalation

In April 1994, our delegation was in Washington. The then atmosphere made us feel that no matter what great efforts we make, there would not be a smooth sailing in the coming year; by the end of the year, the Americans would not announce the end of the investigation and would certainly come up with a retaliation list.

As we expected, when the year almost moved to the end and at the critical moment of the talks on our country's reentry to GATT, the United States linked the issue of intellectual property rights with the GATT issue and threatened to carry out trade retaliations. It tried by every possible means to set obstacles, used both hard and soft tactics, and exerted full pressure on China.

The two sides in the talks did not proceed from the same starting point, held different grounds, and looked forward to different aims. They did not stand on a completely equal footing.

The US Side Proceeded From the US Laws

According to the approach of the US side, the talks on the intellectual property rights should be based on Special 301 of the US trade act. However, the Chinese side held that talks should be based on the Sino-US Memorandum of Understanding on Intellectual Property Rights they signed on 17 January 1992, because the US trade act is only an internal law rather than an international law and it is unreasonable to take one's internal law as the grounds for negotiating with another country.

In more than two years after the memorandum of understanding came into force, China satisfied most of the requirements prescribed by the document: We revised the Patent Law and the Trademark Law; and expanded the scope of protection for those who have the rights. In just one year after the Copyright Law and the appended regulations came into force, China joined

continued...

CHINA-US TALKS BREAKDOWN, 1995 (continued)

the Bern Convention, the World Copyright Treaty, and the Audio Recording Products Convention. In a short period of several years, we completed the process that many countries, including the United States, had traversed for over 100 years. When did the United States join the Bern Convention? In 1988. That is to say, it took 104 years or more than one century to complete the process. However, according to its own interests, it was too impatient to wait and demanded that China join the international copyright protection organization as soon as China promulgated its own copyright law. It also demanded that China immediately take action to enforce the law. What the United States did was too unfair!

Figures Quoted by US Side Were Based on Guesswork

On 28 December 1994, THE WASHINGTON POST published an article by two researchers in the US Economic Strategy Institute. It said that in the past year, the violations of intellectual property rights in China caused nearly $1 billion of losses to the United States. The 30 compact disc factories in China produced 75 million pirate discs every year. Nobody knew where such figures came from, and the authors could not clearly say where they got such figures. Last year, the US representatives to the negotiations announced a figure of losses, which was $827 million, but they could not offer any explicit and convincing grounds. The fact was that each product line of compact disc in our country could not produce more than 2 million discs a year; if they produced in full capacity, the 30 production lines could at most produce 60 million discs a year, including the discs with legal copyrights. How come there be another tens of millions of discs?

It is said that the figures were calculated by an international intellectual property right alliance in the United States according to its conjecture. It estimated a loss of over $300 million caused by the pirate discs in China to the US music producers. This was absolutely impossible. The amount is converted to 2.4 billion yuan of Renminbi according to the exchange rate of 1 to 8. How could that be the case? The gross output value of the whole trade in China was just that amount. The pirate discs first caused losses to our domestic audio-video producers. Chinese people mostly like to listen to Chinese songs both created inside and outside the mainland, and very few people in China like to listen to songs by Jackson and Madonna. The market of the American record companies in China was actually very small. According to a survey of China's audio-video market, the sales of American music products accounted for less than 5 percent. Even the statistics kept by the US side showed that the figure was rather modest.

The piracy of computer software also mainly caused losses to China's domestic enterprises. Why? Because computers in the Chinese market need to have the capacity of processing Chinese language. There is little use if American software is directly pirated, and the market for such goods is very limited. Therefore, the figures offered by the US side were mainly based on their own guesswork, and they also frequently changed such unreliable figures.

The year-end talks focused on the copyright issue, which was related to many other issues as well. In addition to publication copyright in general terms, the issue also covered computer software and audio-video products, especially compact discs and laser discs, which have appeared in large quantities in the last few years.

Lee Sands, who had the authorization, came to Beijing without bringing any sincerity for the talks, and simply tried to take punitive action. The US side brought with them a "draft agreement," in which there were many harsh and unreasonable demands.

The Unreasonable Demands of the US Side

—Demanding that China revise its civil procedural law and intellectual property right law, shorten the time of handling and winding up of cases, lower legal costs, and abolish its existing trademark registration system.

—Demanding that the Supreme People's Court of China announce the judicial interpretation on the criminal punishments to those who encroach upon other people's copyrights according to the terms set out by the US side as of 1 January 1995.

continued...

CHINA-US TALKS BREAKDOWN, 1995 (continued)

—Demanding that China take measures to stop piracy and to establish an effective system for this purpose, and turning what has been done and will be done by the Chinese Government into a commitment to the United States.

They also demanded that a "coordinated suppression force" be organized, according to their requirements, to search main shopping centers twice a week and other areas once a week.

The Chinese Government must submit the statistical data about the results of the searches to the US Government on a quarterly basis, and the data should be classified according to regions and to categories of intellectual property rights [IPR].

They not only set out various unreasonable demands in the legislative, judicial, and judicial procedural system aspects, but also particularly mentioned the issue of market access. They demanded that China fully open its market to US-made audio and video products. The United States explicitly demanded that there be no restriction on the production and sale of audio-video products by US companies in China. This went beyond the scope of protecting intellectual property rights, and also went beyond the functions of the government because this was, in fact, an issue of expanding and fully opening the market to the United States. Our basic stance was that we need some US audio-video products, and as long as normal formalities are passed, such products can be produced and distributed in China. However, the US side was not willing to accept this, and simply insisted on having the right to do such business independently by themselves.

They blamed the Chinese side for being not effective in cracking down on piracy, and said that this was because the government had no intention of doing so.

We reiterated China's basic position on protecting intellectual property rights, and stressed that the relevant legal system was gradually being perfected and that the condition of law enforcement in this field was being continuously improved. We stated that there must be a severe crackdown on piracy.

In view of the serious pirating of compact discs in the coastal areas over the past few years, in April 1994 the State Copyright Administration and other six institutions jointly issued an Urgent Circular on Intensifying Control Over the Copying of Compact Discs and Laser Video Discs. Throughout the country, more than 2 million pirated discs were confiscated. The government also directly issued an order to halt the operations of four CD production lines in Guangdong. As of 1 October 1994, the Rules on Management of Audio and Video Products, which had been promulgated by the State Council, came into force. All CD production lines in the country had to renew their registrations, and were required to adopt by the end of 1994 the SIR patent technology offered by Phillips. In order to intensify administration in this field, the State Council began to pursue the IPR work conference system in July 1994.

The Chinese Government made great efforts to crack down on piracy, but this did not mean that all problems would be thoroughly solved overnight. However, an American said: "I have no patience, and I am only concerned about the result." I also wanted to ask: Did the US Government have any intention of cracking down on drug trafficking? Why does drug trafficking still continue in your country?

The Chinese Side Set Out Its Draft Declaration

A US representative to the talks said recklessly and with an arrogant attitude: "Aren't the enterprises engaged in piracy your state-owned enterprises? Why didn't your government issue an order to close down such enterprises?" There must be good legal grounds for closing down an enterprise, and there must be evidence; otherwise, the factory has the right to demand compensation. The US representatives also rudely criticized our country's judicial system, saying that "your judicial system is unreliable," "your market is out of control, laws are not enforced effectively, and there is no unified law enforcement authority."

The Chinese delegation certainly refuted such unreasonable arguments.

On 13 December 1994, in order to express the sincerity of the Chinese side, we delivered our draft of the Joint Declaration to the US side, and the document was drafted according to the spirit of the State Council's IPR work conference.

continued...

CHINA-US TALKS BREAKDOWN, 1995 (continued)

In accordance with Article 5 of the Memorandum of Understanding—which reads: "the two governments will adopt effective measures in their own territories to prevent and check the encroachment of intellectual property rights, and to curb any further encroachment"—the draft statement summed up the main facts concerning what the Chinese side had done to implement the Memorandum of Understanding, as well as the Chinese side's promise to take new important measures to protect intellectual property rights. At the same time, according to the principle of keeping one's rights on a par with one's duties, we also required that the US side promise to revise its patent law and other laws according to the requirements of TRIRS [acronym printed in English—expansion unknown]. According to its demands on China, the US side itself should promise to set up the copyright confirmation system in its own country, and adopt customs measures for IPR protection (at present, the US customs handles only imported products and does nothing to examine the IPR aspects of export commodities).

The Chinese Side Accepted the US Legislative Proposal
That same evening, Lee Sands met with the Chinese negotiation representative, saying that he could not accept the document, which demanded changes in existing US systems, as "the Chinese version may irritate Representative Kantor and all social circles in the United States."

Our representative refuted his peremptory arguments, and insisted that a bilateral agreement should make both sides enjoy rights and undertake commitments at the same time, and that the Chinese side would never accept an "agreement" based on the instructions of one side to another.

After the talks were bogged down in an impasse, Lee Sands again proposed that some demands of the US side be added to the "Implementation Guidelines" formulated by the State Council's IPR Work Conference, and then that the talks be concluded in the form of an exchange of documents.

Our side expressed agreement, and also proposed that the issue of market access not be included in the discussion on the IPR issue, indicating that the Chinese side would handle the legislative issue by giving consideration to the US proposals.

Lee Sands expressed agreement in principle, and showed a positive attitude, while indicating willingness to give consideration to this.

The next day, when the representatives of the two sides met, the US side gave its draft of the points to be added to China's "Implementation Guidelines." As expected, they included all the harsh demands in their original draft of the agreement, and showed an attitude completely different from that on the previous evening by insisting that agreement on market access must be reached in the IPR talks.

We said that we would do our utmost and would work out our own revised draft not later than the morning of 16 December.

That day, shortly after noon, while our representatives were too busy with their work to have lunch, Lee Sands stalked off and left Beijing without giving us any notice.

Two Signal Flares Were Shot to the Sky
The two signal flares of "retaliation" and "counter-retaliation" already have been shot to the sky by the United States and China. The two sides are still discussing the resumption of the talks. It is always difficult to predict the final result, but there will be only two possibilities. The Chinese Government is always willing to reach agreement, as long as the proposals raised by the United States are reasonable, and will give consideration to the US side's opinion when taking actions. Whether the coming talks will achieve a good result and whether the two sides will call off their reciprocal trade retaliations will depend entirely on the attitude of the US side.

X, 17 Jan 1995.

CHINA, RUSSIA, US TO DEVELOP USSURI RIVER, 1995

The first meeting of representatives from China, Russia and the US concerning a program to develop the Ussuri River basin ended 25 February 1995. Representatives from the three countries put forward proposals on the sustained use of land along the river. The meeting meant that the three-nation program had entered a period of practical operation. The program's purpose was to formulate economic plans guaranteeing production and ecological balance, to improve living conditions along the basin. Expected to be completed in 1996, the program would also restore the biological diversity and environmental conditions of the region. The three countries were scheduled meet in Russia in early 1996.

China Facts & Figures Annual, 1995

TAIWAN-PRC TRADE RELATIONS, 1995

This year has seen some new changes in the development of economic and trade relations between the two sides of the Taiwan Strait. On one hand, the growth of the entrepot trade between the two sides has slowed down, and Taiwan investment in the mainland has declined by a big margin in terms of both the number of investment projects and the amount agreed upon through negotiations. On the other hand, there has been a change in Taiwan investment patterns in the mainland plus a breakthrough in the bilateral economic and trade relations between the two sides. Taiwan has begun introducing mainland technology as well as scientific and technical personnel into the island. The two sides have also made relatively big strides in developing cooperation in the economic as well as the scientific and technological fields. This shows that the fast-growth stage has basically ended for trade between the two sides and for Taiwan investment in the mainland. Now, the cross-strait economic and trade relations have entered a new phase of relatively stable development in breadth and depth.

A Drop in the Growth Rate of Entrepot Trade Between the Two Sides

While the entrepot trade between the two sides has continued to grow quickly, the growth rate has declined compared with the previous years. Mainland customs statistics show that Taiwan-mainland indirect trade in the first half of this year was $6.94 billion, up 23.7 percent from last year's corresponding period. Of this amount, mainland exports to Taiwan accounted for $880 million, and imports from Taiwan, $6.06 billion. These were, respectively, 60 percent and 20 percent higher than the same period last year. However, the increases were way below the 108.6-percent and 119.9-percent growth rates registered in 1993. According to figures published by Taiwan's "Board of Foreign Trade," the total trade volume between the two sides from January to June 1994 reached $7.435 billion, surpassing the same period last year by 10.53 percent. Taiwan's exports to the mainland amounted to $6.83 billion, a growth of 9.62 percent, while imports from the mainland were $605 million, a growth of 16.88 percent. Both of these growth rates show a drop from last year. According to Hong Kong customs statistics, the growth rate of Taiwan-mainland entrepot trade began to shrink considerably in 1993, and what is more, that year, mainland exports to Taiwan showed negative growth. From January to June this year, Taiwan exports to the mainland with transshipment in Hong Kong amounted to $4 billion, an increase of 10 percent over last year's corresponding period, while Taiwan imports from the mainland through transshipment were $600 million, an increase of 17 percent. These yielded a total entrepot trade of $4.6 billion, up 11 percent from the same period last year.

The relatively low growth rate of entrepot trade between the two sides is related to the decline in Taiwan investments in the mainland and the mainland's macroeconomic regulation. This is not an accidental phenomenon, but represents a natural process of development. In the past, the cross-strait entrepot trade, though full of fluctuations, scored an average growth rate as high as more than 40 percent. This means that the entrepot trade between the two sides has already reached a fairly big volume, and with such a high base figure, there could hardly be any further sustained high growth. However, there will still be ample room for developing trade between the two sides in the future. Up to present, Taiwan authorities have allowed about 2,000 products to be imported from the mainland (1,935 products in early September). In the future,

continued...

TAIWAN-PRC TRADE RELATIONS, 1995 (continued)

Taiwan will continue to ease restrictions on imports of mainland products. Accordingly, the trade volume between the two sides will continue to rise.

Taiwan Investment on the Mainland Declined
This year, Taiwan investment on the mainland has declined in both the number of investment projects and the total negotiated amount. According to mainland statistics, Taiwan businesses launched 3,218 investment projects on the mainland in the first half of 1994 with a total negotiated investment amount of $2.55 billion. The number of projects and the amount were down 34 percent and 45 percent, respectively, compared with last year's corresponding period. Statistics compiled by Taiwan's "Investment Commission" show that from January to June 1994, Taiwan investment on the mainland was $430 million, 35.8 percent less than the $670 million registered a year ago. But in the first quarter of the year, Taiwan investment projects and investment amount on the mainland both increased to a great extent, growing by 4.6 times and 2.3 times respectively.

The preceding is mainly attributable to the following: First, it was due to mainland macroeconomic regulation and control plus the change in the overall economic environment. The decline in Taiwan investment on the mainland in the first half of this year was consistent with the big drop in the total foreign investment received by the mainland. The second reason was policy adjustment by Taiwan. After the Qiandao Lake incident, Taiwan authorities adopted boycotting and restrictive measures with regard to investment in the mainland and cross-strait economic and trade exchange. As a result, investment on the mainland changed from the first quarter's big increase to a big drop (based on Taiwan statistics). Third, though total Taiwan investment overseas rose 54 percent in the first half of this year compared with the same period last year, its investments in Indonesia, the Philippines, and Vietnam all declined (from January to May. Investments in these three countries declined by 59, 82, and 0.52 percent respectively). That is, the mainland was not the only place where Taiwan made less investment.

In-Depth and In-Breadth Development of Taiwan Investment in the Mainland
The in-depth and in-breadth development of Taiwan investment in the mainland can be seen from the following:

It has become a basic trend for listed Taiwan companies to make investment in the mainland. Statistics compiled by Taiwan's Security and Exchange Commission show that, as of 1993, a total of 94 stock-issuing companies (including those whose stocks are listed or placed on the counter) had invested on the mainland, and the investment funds they remitted from Taiwan to the mainland amounted to NT$7.388 billion [New Taiwan dollars]. Of this amount, the investment made in 1993 alone was NT$3.886. Among the enterprises approved this year to make investment in the mainland, many are listed companies and big enterprises.

The investment scale has been expanded. In August this year, for example, the Taiwan authorities approved 147 projects of investment in the mainland, totaling $250 million. This gives an average investment amount of $1.7 million per project, as against $610,000 per project registered for the same period last year. Now, among Taiwan investment projects on the mainland, the number of big projects—each in the amount of millions and even tens of millions of US dollars—has greatly exceeded that in the past. In the first half of this year, the percentage decrease in the number of Taiwan investment projects in the mainland surpassed to a great extent the percentage of reduction in the amount of investment. This means an increase in the average scale of the investment project. As noted by the French press when commenting on Taiwan investment in the mainland, "small and medium-sized investors have given way to multinational companies."

Taiwan investment in the mainland has "changed from relocating export-processing sites to exploring local markets." Now, Taiwan investment in the mainland is no longer limited to manufacturing products for export. Rather, it is targeted at exploring mainland markets

Taiwan investment in the interior of the mainland has also become a current trend. With the change of investment target from the promotion of exports to the exploitation of mainland markets and resources, and because of rising production costs in coastal areas, Taiwan

continued...

TAIWAN-PRC TRADE RELATIONS, 1995 (continued)

businesses have begun to locate their manufacturing projects in the interior of the mainland rather than coastal areas.

More Cooperation in Economy, Trade, Science, and Technology
Cooperation in economic and scientific and technological fields and bilateral economic and trade exchanges between the two sides have become a new development trend. The past two years have seen more and more major economic cooperation projects between the two sides. One is their joint investment in the Asia-Pacific optical-fiber communications network. This project, the first of its kind between the two sides, marks the beginning of their joint investment. Another example is a man-made satellite launching project, the first case of cooperation in science and technology between the two sides. In this project, the Juntat Group and the KMT [Kuomintang]-owned China Development Corporation in Taiwan and the mainland's APT [expansion unknown] Satellite Company jointly invested in launching the telecommunications satellite Aptstar-1. This is the first instance of concrete cooperation between the two sides in the field of space science. Third, early this year Taiwan's Chinese Petroleum Corporation submitted to the "Mainland Affairs Council" a proposal for cooperation with the mainland's China International Offshore Oil Corporation in exploiting oil deposits in the East China Sea. Although so far no progress has been made with this proposal, such cooperation is believed to have great possibilities and development potentials. Fourth, cooperation has been conducted in establishing joint ventures overseas. For example, the Taiwan International Securities Corporation and the Shanghai International Securities Corporation, together with the Tachung [1129 5883] Investment Company of Hong Kong, purchased a listed Hong Kong company and formed a new enterprise in Hong Kong. Fifth, cooperation in the financial field has relatively great potential for development. Joint loan business and financial cooperation started long ago between financial institutions on the two sides. On 9 August this year, Taiwan's "Ministry of Finance" gave approval for 26 overseas branches of four Taiwan banks to do overseas business directly with mainland bank overseas branches and banks belonging to China-funded organizations. This will greatly facilitate financial cooperation and economic exchange between the two sides.

Besides the considerable development of cross-strait bilateral economic and trade exchanges, Taiwan will introduce more mainland technology and personnel on the island. On 29 August, the Taiwan authorities approved two such projects: One is the transfer of production technology from the Shanghai pharmaceutical Industrial Research Institute to the Yunghsin Pharmaceutical Corporation of Taiwan. The other is the acquisition of production technology and recruitment of technical personnel from the mainland by the Taichuan Electrical Machinery Corporation. Increases in such projects will promote the bilateral economic, technology, and science exchanges between the two sides.

Increasing Competition for Overseas Market Between the Two Sides
The United States is the biggest export market for Taiwan and the mainland alike. The US market shares enjoyed by Taiwan and the mainland have undergone a remarkable change during the past decade or so. The market share enjoyed by Taiwan's products increased from 4.37 percent in 1983 to 6.12 percent in 1987. Since then, it has declined continuously to 4.35 percent in 1993. Mainland products, on the other hand, have enjoyed an ever-growing share of the American market—from 0.88 percent in 1983 to 5.47 percent in 1993 (CHUNG KUO SHIH PAO [CHINA TIMES], 20 August 1994). According to US statistics, the amount of mainland exports to the United States exceeded the amount of Taiwan's exports to that country for the first time in 1992, and since then the gap between the two amounts has widened quickly. In 1993, US imports from the mainland amounted to $31.42 billion, while its imports from Taiwan were $24.98 billion. As far as US market shares are concerned, the mainland outstrips Taiwan mainly in labor-intensive products, including leather products, textiles, and footwear, while Taiwan remains in a favorable position to compete with the mainland in technology-intensive products, such as machines and electrical appliances. However, technology-intensive products made in the mainland are showing a tendency to increase rapidly in the US market.

continued...

TAIWAN-PRC TRADE RELATIONS, 1995 (continued)

Such a change is especially noticeable in the Japanese market. Since the 1980's, Taiwan's exports to Japan have been less than the mainland's. The gap has widened further since the end of 1990. In 1993, Japan's imports from Taiwan and the mainland were $9.67 billion and $20.56 billion, respectively. The market shares enjoyed by Taiwan and mainland products in Japan were 4.02 percent and 8.54 percent respectively. In the first half of this year, the market share of Taiwan product in Japan further declined to 4 percent, while the mainland share rose to 9.2 percent.

A study by an economic research institute in Taiwan predicts that Taiwan products replaced by mainland products in the future export markets will be equivalent in value to 20.56 percent of the total export volume registered by Taiwan last year. Even for those Taiwan products that are relatively competitive and are constantly upgraded in quality, 40 percent of their export value will be under the threat of the products from the mainland.

Cross-Strait Division of Labor in Industry Is in the Making
Under circumstances where trade between the two sides and Taiwan investment in the mainland are continuously developing and relations across the strait are becoming increasingly close, a system of division of industrial labor between the two sides is in the making. Since the late-1980's, Taiwan has lost its relatively favorable conditions for developing labor-intensive industries. Accordingly, many labor-intensive product manufacturers have gradually moved their plants to the mainland, where they have scored new business achievements. This has not only stimulated the mainland's economic development, but also spurred on a change or an upgrading, of Taiwan's export makeup and even its production structure due to the large quantities of machinery, equipment, and raw materials purchased from Taiwan by Taiwan-funded enterprises on the mainland. A mutually beneficial pattern of division of labor has thus come into being between the two sides. In the footwear industry, for instance, Taiwan-funded enterprises on the mainland and the mainland's own enterprises are principally making shoes of medium and low grades, where the main products turned out by manufacturers on Taiwan are high-grade shoes. In the electronics industry, the mainland is the production site for PC's, monitors, and electronic accessories and parts, while the work of development and design is carried out in Taiwan.

However, this simple division-of-labor pattern is undergoing a new change. Now, Taiwan enterprises are paying more attention to industrial integration between the two sides and the development of the mainland market in planning their cross-strait investment. Meanwhile, in line with the division of industrial labor between the two sides, the Taiwan authorities have announced a list of projects for Taiwan investment in the mainland. This year Taiwan has enlarged the list based mainly on the evaluation of such a division of labor. On 29 August 1994, Taiwan's "Ministry of Economic Affairs" announced that an additional 285 projects were added to the list, and in September and October, another 220 and 132 projects were added, respectively. These add up to a total of 637 new projects. As of now, there are altogether some 4,400 projects on the list, and nearly one-half of the types of industries in Taiwan are involved. With the development of their economic and trade relations, it is expected that the two sides of the Taiwan Strait will further strengthen their economic cooperation, improve their division of industrial labor, and enhance their economic ties and mutual reliance.

Economic Reporter No. 43, 31 Oct 1995.

CHINA REBUKES OTHER NUCLEAR NATIONS, 1995

In a major policy statement on arms control, China rebuked the United States, Russia, Britain and France for continuing to develop nuclear weapons and outer space weapons while denying developing nations the right to peaceful use of nuclear technology. The statement said, "they resort to discriminatory anti-proliferation and arms control measures directing the spear head of arms control at the developing countries."

continued...

CHINA REBUKES OTHER NUCLEAR NATIONS, 1995 (continued)

China's policy statement may have been timed to blunt the international criticism that was expected to resume when Beijing detonates its third underground nuclear warhead in 1995, part of a series of tests which would conclude in 1996.

China Facts & Figures Annual, 1995

BEIJING WARNS US AND OTHERS ABOUT "2 CHINAS POLICY," 1995

Chinese government and communist party officials warned the United States and all other nations that their diplomatic stance must be one that supports but one China. Speaking to the US, General Deng Xiaoping said that recognition of Taiwan as an independent state would be viewed by the Chinese government as an insult which could result in an explosive situation. Even though relations between China and western nations have improved in 1993 and 1994 the issue of one China could bring a chasm between that nation and western nations and the US in particular.

Following a visit by Taiwan President Lee to Cornell University China withdrew its ambassador from Washington for five months and canceled exchanges on military trade and human rights issues.

In a show of support for China's "one China policy" Australian officials would not let representatives from Taiwan visit an Australian university.

In 1994 China conducted military training exercises near Taiwan on several occasions. Officials of other governments believe those exercises were intended to intimidate Taiwan.

China Facts & Figures Annual, 1995.

SCHOLARS VIEW WEST-WEST RELATIONS, 1994

[Editor's note] On 13 December 1994, the editorial board of this publication held a workshop on West-West relations. Experts and scholars from the American Research Institute, the Western Europe Research Institute, and the Japan Research Institute of the Chinese Academy of Social Sciences, XINHUA's International Department, the Economic Research Center of the National Planning Commission, the International Politics Department of Beijing University, the Department of Affairs of the Americas and Oceania of the Ministry of Foreign Affairs, and the Chinese Contemporary International Relations Institute attended or provided written statements. The delegates engaged in a lively and thorough examination of the conflicts, compatibility, and the competition and cooperation among developed Western nations. Their remarks are provided below in four sections. [end editor's note]

On Western Big Power Relations
Li Changjiu [2621 7022 0036] (Research fellow and director of the Research Office of the International Department of XINHUA):
    First, I will talk about America's, Japan's, and Europe's rapid readjustment of policies and the problems in relations among them.
    Since the end of the Cold War, the international situation has eased overall. The intense turmoil that the end of the Cold War engendered has gradually abated. The big Western powers have gone from idealism to pragmatism, and they are now in the process of rapidly readjusting their foreign strategies and policies in terms of their separate future status, roles, and mutual relations. Economic factors have become the key factor in international relations. Following dissolution of their common adversary, the USSR, the major western powers have devoted more attention to the maintenance of their own economic and trade interests, status, and role. Conflicts, frictions, and competition have increased markedly in the economic and trade realm among the United States, Japan, and western European nations.
    The United States is bending every effort to maintain its superpower position and "world leadership role," but it has encountered numerous difficulties and problems. On 21 September

continued...

SCHOLARS VIEW WEST-WEST RELATIONS, 1994 (continued)

1993, the American president's national security advisor, Anthony Lake, proposed for the first time an "expansion strategy" as America's basic foreign strategy in the post-Cold War era. Lake declared: "As a follow-on to the containment strategy, the United States must adopt an expansion strategy, expanding the large free family of the world's market and democratic nations." On 21 July 1994, President Clinton emphasized in his "National Security Strategy Report" that the United States will promote global "participation in an expansion strategy." Despite a lowering of the tone, he continues to reiterate that "America's long-term goal is establishment of a world in which every large country is a democracy, with many other countries also entering the large family of the market democracy system as well." On 28 November of the same year, the United States Information Office published an article by the chairman of the Joint Chiefs of Staff, John Shalikashvili entitled. "Diplomacy and Power in the 21st Century." Shalikashvili believes that the United States "is facing two challenges," or one might say that the United States "must deal with two problems, namely "redefining the correlation between post-Cold War-era diplomacy and power, directing, using, and balancing these two elements of our national power to attain a common goal. Particularly as we enter the 21st century," we must "learn how to deal with steadily increasing military actions short of war." Shalikashvili feels that without the use of military force, the United States will be unable to maintain its world leadership position. Unless it is willing to spare no sacrifice to protect interests that are crucial to America's security, it will have to be circumspect, not becoming excessively involved. These different points of view show that the United States is in the process of readjusting its foreign policy and strategy.

Since the end of 38 consecutive years of Liberal Democratic Party rule in Japan on 18 June 1993, political factions have constantly split and recombined. Today, a Socialist Party and Liberal Democratic Party coalition rules. In December 1994, nine opposition parties formed the "New Progressive Party," with former Prime Minister Toshiki Kaifu becoming the first leader of the party. No matter how the various political forces in Japan continue to change and combine, and no matter whether they form a two-party political system or have one party rule, Japan's strategic goals have already been largely defined. Japan has already begun its third major readjustment since the Meiji restoration: It is moving from big economic power status to big political power status, and setting up a political system to go with the change. Economically it continues to catch up with and surpass the United States. On 7 October 1994, the government of Japan decided to invest 630 trillion yen in public works between 1995 and 2005. Japan's development potential should not be underestimated. Japan's use of the United States to become a major political power, and its use of American technology and markets to compete with the United States have aroused disquiet in the United States. Economic and trade frictions between the United States and Japan are increasing daily. Even while maintaining its leadership position in NATO, the United States intends to gain a dominant position in the Asia-Pacific Economic Cooperation Organization [APEC] in order to restrain Japan, and Japan will use investment, assistance, and trade to define its dominant position in Asia.

Germany has become the third economic power in the world and the first in western Europe. Since the early 1990s, Germany has infused more than 643 billion marks into Germany's eastern zone. The economic difficulties of the eastern zone during the early period of the changeover have been transcended. Now, exports have increased, investment is brisk, and entrepreneurs have full confidence in Germany's economic prospects. Germany's role as the "nucleus" in the European Union [EU], and its dominant position are increasing. Its economic and political influence in eastern Europe is also expanding rapidly. At the same time, Germany is actively developing economic and trade relations with Asian nations, and quickening its pace in becoming a major world political power. Germany's rapid resuscitation has changed the power balance among major European powers, thereby setting off concerns among the other nations of Europe. During a visit to Germany in July 1994, President Clinton announced that Germany is "the cornerstone of America's European policy," and that he looked forward to Germany "playing a greater leadership role" with the United States in international affairs. This change in America's relations with the western European powers aroused displeasure in the

continued...

SCHOLARS VIEW WEST-WEST RELATIONS, 1994 (continued)

UK and France, the traditional "special relationship" between the United States and the UK was weakened, core contradictions between France and Germany increased, and France and the UK began to draw closer together, even going so far as to join Russia in expressing opposition to NATO's eastward expansion. The French "Liberation" published an article that declared that the era of distrust between Europe and the United States has begun. On 2 December 1994, the British newspaper "The Guardian" said that during a period of increasing splits within NATO, Russia's proposal for increasing security cooperation with the EU has the isolation of the United States as its goal.

In short, 1994 was the most important year since the end of the Cold War for the adjustment of the foreign strategy and policies of big Western powers. The policies of every country have become more pragmatic, and the contradictions and frictions among these nations have also increased further. Nevertheless, for a long time to come, coordination will remain the most important element of relations between the big Western powers and the former Soviet Union and eastern European nations with regard to regional hot spots and global issues. Jockeying for advantage among the big Western powers, economic and trade conflicts, competition, and friction will intensify, but they will be settled when they hurt the common interests of these nations. The United States will play a dominant role in international affairs, but it will need the cooperation of other big Western powers. The big Western powers are becoming more independent, but they lack strength, and they are also unlikely to unite in opposition to the United States. In short, conflicts, struggles, and friction, as well as coordination, compromise, and cooperation will coexist in big Western power relations.

Zhou Yong [0719 0516] (assistant researcher at the China Research Institute of Modern International Relations): A currently popular description may be applied to relations among the big Western powers, namely "the co-existence of competition and cooperation, and mutual restriction and interdependence." However, the truth is that cooperation is waning and competition is increasing in the present situation. A battle of control and countercontrol is developing.

Relations among the big Western powers have been in the readjustment stage since the end of the Cold War. Among the five big world powers, China is "hiding its capacity and biding its time," and Russia is weaker than during the USSR era; consequently, relations among the big Western powers have come to the fore. Actually, these relations consist of three major Western forces carving out spheres of influence. The spheres of interest on which this division impinges is, first the former USSR sphere of influence, followed by markets that the United States formerly occupied. This division is bound to bring about clashes among the three major powers. Events suggest that the major Western nations speak with one voice to the United States. Today, Japan and Europe both dare to say "no" clearly. Economically, Japan says "no," and on the Bosnia-Herzegovina problem, Europe says "no," and Europe has also raised the slogan of many years ago of "Europe for the Europeans." This shows that contradictions and clashes are developing among the big Western powers.

Since the end of the Cold War, geoeconomics and both national and ethnic interests have replaced geopolitics and East-West relations, their escalation becoming a basic factor affecting the world situation and relations among the big Western powers. Despite the mutual interest and complementary nature of Western big power economic relations, I personally feel that economic clashes will occur first among adversaries among whom competition is most intense. Extreme competition cannot occur between the United States and the Third World because the strength of the United States is overwhelming. By comparison, the strength of the three Western power groups is relatively even; there are no marked differences in the products they sell or their level of science and technology. Consequently, mutual frictions are more likely to erupt among them and become more intense. Therefore, I feel there is both competition and cooperation among the three main Western power groups, but that competition is on the rise.

Zhang Yebai [1728 0048 4101] (research fellow, American Institute, Chinese Academy of Social Sciences): First, I will talk about how to evaluate "West-West contradictions."

continued...

SCHOLARS VIEW WEST-WEST RELATIONS, 1994 (continued)

Following the end of the Cold War, the cohesiveness of the Western alliance declined, and "West-West contradictions" developed; nevertheless, "to regard the West-West contradiction as the main contradiction in the modern world is wrong." Main contradictions always play a guiding and decisive role. They determine or influence the existence and development of other contradictions. However, the problems that the world faces in the wake of the Cold War are extremely complex and varied. Every country in the world is considering this problem today, but they have yet to find a "main contradiction" that can determine and influence other contradictions in the way that the confrontation between the United States and the Soviet Union did during the Cold War era. The United States feels at sea about the loss of its "main enemy," and it is preoccupied with setting up a new one. Iraq and North Korea are regarded as nations antagonistic to the United States, but they are only regional powers. Some would like to pin the main enemy label on China, but China poses no threat to the United States. The "cultural clash theory" that Huntington put forward reflects the American frame of mind in finding a "main contradiction." Strictly speaking, this frame of mind is a manifestation of "Cold-War thinking." Some people are still accustomed to regarding events in terms of the Cold War era. To regard "West-West contradictions" as a main contradiction is an exaggeration. This is because they are, after all, contradictions when there is agreement about basic interests. Even in the economic realm, because interdependence among the Western nations has deepened to the point that there is something of each in the other, and one cannot part from the others, cooperation and compromise among them is bound to be paramount.

Wan Shuyu [8001 2885 3768] (researcher, Chinese Modern International Relations Institute: I will make two points: The first is an examination of the basis for Western interdependence; and the second is changes in America's position.

Despite the contradictions and frictions in West-West relations of recent years, and their rather general occurrence, interdependence and assistance remain the main current and the dominant theme; contradictions and frictions are a lesser current and a minor theme. At the present time, West-West contradictions and frictions are not conflicts and clashes of basic interests and basic points of view. Formerly, common opposition to the Soviet threat was the main basis for the alliance of the Western powers, but dissolution of the Soviet Union has far from become a solvent or separator. Not only do two basic foundations exist for their continued adhesion, but two new foundations have formed under the new conditions and circumstances as a result of their common basic interests and basic points of view. Their two basic foundations are: 1) A common socio-political system and values. Despite the various unjust and irrational social problems that exist, and despite their inglorious human rights record, the Western powers have never attacked or undercut each other on this account, but rather have directed their attacks against non-Western nations. On the so-called human rights issue, they point the finger at other countries, boss them around, and even trump up charges in an effort to find fault. 2) Economically, they are deeply involved with each other and interdependent. Although they seize markets from each other everywhere, they are still each other's main objects for trade and investment. This is the reason they have become so intertwined in adverse trade balances, market access, commodity dumping and antidumping, exchange and interest rates, and farm-product price policies, and why they maintain and increase economic and trade contacts. The two new foundations are: I) Joint global promotion of "Westernization," making this their new strategic objective. Before the Cold War, their main strategic goals were containment of the Soviet threat and of communism. Their spears were directed against the socialist countries. Today, the scope of Westernization is broader. It is directed at three levels: At the first level are the countries of the former Soviet Union and eastern Europe; at the second level are socialist countries elsewhere; and at the third level are other non-western democracies, including the far-flung developing nations. The emphasis today is on the former Soviet Union and eastern Europe, where the Western powers are trying to move ahead across the board in the economic, political, and defense fields. In pursuit of the "Westernization" goal, this or that difference of

continued...

SCHOLARS VIEW WEST-WEST RELATIONS, 1994 (continued)

opinion may occur about whether to use a soft or a hard or an open or secret approach, about the emphasis, the choice of methods, and the timing, but these do not affect the overall goal. They do not get in the way of the Western powers pursuit of the overall goal of "Westernization." 2) Joint elimination of regional disturbances and hot spots. Since the end of the Cold War, the Western powers have felt that the real threat to their security and economic interests comes from regional disturbances. Even though their individual specific interests are not the same, the degree of their concern and depth of involvement differs or has a different emphasis, and although their methods differ too, they have formed a fairly uniform standard and common point of view that is based on the Western political outlook and values, which is basic. Because of these four foundations in West-West relations, their interdependence is bound to be greater than their mutual contradictions. Their differences and frictions may also be resolved or even overcome through compromise.

2.[numbering as published] Who is the dominant force in West-West relations? Have there been any changes, and if so, what changes? The United States still has the most power in West-West relations; the United States is still the dominant force. Economically, the EU is a worthy adversary overall, but militarily it cannot match the United States. Much less is the EU a fully and highly integrated complete entity. It also goes without saying that Japan still ranks second to the United States in overall power. Therefore, it is not difficult to understand that no matter how hard Japan contests dominion in the Asia-Pacific region with the United States, in the end it has no choice but to follow America's course. Although some EU nations seek ways to wrest the leading position in European security matters from the United States, as time has gone on, an increasing number of nations have acknowledged the EU's limitations in resolving local conflicts. European security still cannot do without the "existence" and the "support" of the United States. In recent years, however, the role and status of the United States has also undergone some fairly marked changes: A) Its paramount position has met strong challenge from the EU, and it is weaker than formerly. For the first time, Japanese leaders, who once bowed and scraped to the United States, have openly said "no" to the United States. Where formerly individual EU nations talked back to the United States, now there is multiple nation or even mass resistance to the United States. For example, when the United States announced its unilateral decision to stop enforcing the UN arms embargo against Bosnia-Herzegovina, not only did the EU nations not respond, but some issued communiqués terming America's action "regrettable." B) Because of the weakening of its dominant position, America's posture toward the EU has declined, and its tendency toward conciliation has increased. In recent years, the United States has become reconciled to a lowering of its status. It has proposed to Japan the "sharing" of world "leadership responsibilities," and it has proposed to Germany the establishment of a "leadership partnership" between the two countries. America's increased requests to Japan and the EU have also widened the basis for interdependence.

US-Japan Relations

Zhang Yebai—I will now express some thoughts about US-Japan relations and the China factor:

1. Major changes have occurred in the basis for US-Japan relations and the character of the US-Japan alliance as a result of the end of the Cold War and the dissolution of the USSR. Nevertheless, US-Japan relations hold paramount importance among the foreign relations of the two countries. Japan continues to rely on the United States both for its security, and politically and economically as well. Despite the tilt toward Asia in Japan's foreign relations, Japan's relations with the United States are paramount. For the United States, Japan is its major ally in Asia; thus, US-Japan relations are the cornerstone of United States policy in the Asia-Pacific region. Japan holds a particularly important position in US foreign relations. Some say that America's Asia-Pacific policy is facing a choice between US-Japan relations and US-China relations as a basis. Such a formulation is inaccurate because, in America's view, Japan is the largest democratic nation in Asia except for India, and Japan is its ally, while China is still a socialist country. Even though America's relations with both Japan and China are both very

continued...

SCHOLARS VIEW WEST-WEST RELATIONS, 1994 (continued)

important, they differ in character. Particularly now that the Cold War is over, America's Asia-Pacific policy cannot be based on US-China relations.

2. Some people suppose that conflicts between the United States and Japan are bound to escalate because of the collapse of the original basis for the US-Japan alliance. This view is also somewhat skewed. US-Japan relations do indeed face new problems and new challenges, but the common interests of the two nations transcend the differences and clashes between them. On security matters, Japan's dependence on the United States has decreased; nevertheless, security issues remain the center of the US-Japan alliance. The United States maintains a cautious attitude about the strengthening of Japan's military might, and it may be vigilant about Japan's development of nuclear weapons. Nevertheless, while continuing responsibility for Japan's security, the United States wants Japan to play a more active role in Asia-Pacific security matters. Because of increased apprehensions in recent years about Asia-Pacific security matters, the United States needs Japan even more to take the lead in maintaining the stability of the Asia-Pacific region, playing a role in US-Japan relations. Politically, US-Japan relations are becoming an equal partnership. Japan wants to become a major political power, and increasingly it dares say "no" to the United States. On major international issues, however, it still coordinates fully with the United States, and there are no fundamental differences between the two nations on these issues. The United States also supports Japan's quest for major political power status. It supports Japan's bid to become a permanent member of the UN Security Council. Economically, competition between the United States and Japan has become more intense. America's trade imbalance with Japan continues to widen, and the attitude of both sides has become tougher on the handling of trade frictions. Nevertheless, the common interests of the two nations have also increased, and the interdependence and intertwining of interests are also increasing. This forces both parties to reach a compromise at the negotiating table at crucial times. With the upturn in the American economic situation in recent years, American apprehensions about Japan's economic threat have abated.

3. The China factor in US-Japan relations. In recent years, people in other countries have repeatedly emphasized the importance of a "triangular" relationship to Chinese researchers. This makes a certain amount of sense. This is because even though the world is making a transition to multi-polarity in the wake of the Cold War, big power politics remains extremely important during the present stage. When people observe international issues, they are always interested, first of all, in the role of big powers and big power relations. Some people propose multi-polarity around the United States, Japan, and Europe, or around the United States, Europe, Japan, Russia, and China, and in Asia around the United States China and Japan, or the United States, China, Japan, and Russia. I do not approve use of the term "triangular relationship," because it is an outgrowth of the big power politics of the Cold-War era. Continued use of this term may easily give rise to misunderstandings. After all today's triangular relationships do differ from the past. During the Cold-War era, strategic security was the focus of the triangular relationship. Mutual checks and balances were fairly strict, and the state of relations between two countries frequently had an important effect on the third country. Nowadays, security issues are not that overriding. Big power relations have become more diversified, and mutual checks and balances have become more limited and looser. The "zero sum" rule of the past in which one side's gain was another side's loss has been replaced by relationships of common benefit or common loss. The China factor still has a certain importance to US-Japan relations, but for most Americans, use of a communist party country to restrain a democratic country and an ally runs contrary to American moral values. There are indeed some people in the United States who feel that, over the long run, China is important to America as a counterweight to Japan, but few are willing to say so.

Tao Jian [7118 1017] (assistant research fellow, Chinese Contemporary International Relations Institute): 1. Since the end of the Cold War, both the United States and Japan have pursued their own national interests. Their strategic focus has shifted to improving their own economic foundations, increasing aggregate national power, and improving their international

continued...

competitiveness. Foreign relations focus more on protecting the economic interests of the home country. Economic relations and trade override politics and security, becoming the priority topic of the US government. The Clinton administration made the National Economic Council the hub for administering trade with Japan and for promoting economic policy. Consequently, discord between the United States and Japan, which has long pursued economic interests as its external goal, have increasingly occurred over the division of foreign interests. This shows up prominently in trade friction. When the United States entered into rivalry over economic interests in the Asia-Pacific region, a confrontation between US and Japanese "economic diplomacy" ensued. "Economic diplomacy" is now paramount in US-Japan relations.

2. "Sharing responsibilities" and "ceding authority." These phrases refer to cooperation and conflict in US-Japan relations. Increasingly, the United States wants wealthy Japan to share some global responsibilities. At the same time, it is unwilling to cede some international authority to Japan. For example, even though Japan is second only to the United States in payment of UN operating expenses, it "can only wait outside the door to hear announcements about the results of discussions." Therefore, Japan is increasingly seeking a new position of equality. It wants to become a permanent member of the Security Council. Japan feels that given its position and power in the world economy, continuation of the post-World War II pattern of the five victorious powers being members of the Security Council is no longer in tune with the times. In the wake of the Cold War, Japan's demand to develop from an economic power into a political power has become more urgent, and the pace is also picking up.

3. "The red sun is in the ascendant," and "Uncle Sam is resurgent." These phrases refer to the change in the contrasting states of Japanese and American strength. In 1985, Japan supplanted the United States as the world's number one creditor nation. The reaction to this of the American government and public was mixed. Quite a few people felt that Japan posed a mortal threat to the American economy, and some power groups even advocated listing Japan as an "enemy nation." Others felt differently. Now, America's domestic economy has improved markedly; the painful readjustments of its domestic economy during the past several years have begun to show results, and budget deficit-inflation momentum has been contained. Once again, the United States has become the world's largest exporting nation, its exports accounting for more than 13 percent of GNP, an amount higher than Japan's 9 percent. In addition, it has wrested from Japan's hands the international competition championship that it had lost for 8 years, etc., hence the saying in recent years that "Uncle Sam is resurgent." The United States has made progress in espousing the liberalization of global trade, and the liberalization of Asia-Pacific region trade. The United States and a large number of developing nations have a greater advantage in practicing regional cooperation than Japan. "America First" great power consciousness has begun to grow again. This has already generated, and will continue to generate, an effect on both competition and cooperation in US-Japan relations.

Luo Zhaohui [5012 3564 6540] (second secretary, Department of Affairs of the Americas and Oceania, Ministry of Foreign Affairs): I will talk mostly about cooperation in US-Japan relations.

Despite the constant conflicts and frictions between the United States and Japan since the end of the Cold War, both sides continue to increase cooperation on political and security support. Even on economic matters, coordination and cooperation between the United States and Japan continues to outweigh competition. First of all, when Prime Minister Morohiro Hosokawa visited the United States, although the two sides did not reach agreement on solving America's adverse balance of trade with Japan, and although discussion of a host of economic issues was suspended for a time, the American trade representative and the Japanese foreign minister continued reciprocal visits later on, both sides showing that they wanted to continue discussions. Not long afterward, Japan compromised on the issue of the Motorola Corporation's entry into the Japanese market. The United States also relented, not insisting on solution to all problems, but switching instead to gradual advance, first solving the problems that can be

continued...

solved. Next, Japan and the United States reached an agreement on Japan's opening up of government procurement of telecommunications equipment and medical equipment and its plate-glass market, thereby temporarily averting, once again, initiation by the United States of unilateral trade sanctions against Japan that might lead to a trade war. Second was the East Asia Economic Conference (EAEC) that Malaysia proposed. Even though Malaysia still wanted American capital and technology, it also expressed its independence and its struggle to become a first-rate nation in East Asia; thus, it excluded the United States, Australia, and New Zealand from the EAEC. At first, Japan favored the EAEC and quietly expressed support for Malaysia. Reportedly, however, as a result of the intervention of the trade representative that the United States dispatched to Japan, Japan backed off from its position. Out of concern for the United States, it did not explicitly support Malaysia. Third was the handling of the APEC issue. On the timetable for the liberalization of Asia and Pacific trade and investment, Japan agreed to go along with the United States on this crucial issue. The United States was rather pleased.

Zhao Jieqi [6392 7132 3823] (deputy director and research fellow, Japan Institute, Chinese Academy of Social Sciences): US-Japan relations in recent years may be capsulized in the following two sentences: Since the end of the Cold War, the two nations have continued to maintain close political, security, and diplomatic relations, but the Japan-US security system has taken on new meaning, with Japan's independence and autonomy increasing. Economic frictions between the two nations have intensified and are adversely affecting the political basis for bilateral relations; however, these frictions can still be controlled and will not lead to a worsening of mutual relations in the near term.

1. Maintenance and strengthening of bilateral relations remains the basic foreign policy of both nations. During the past more than a year, despite the number of cabinet changes in Japan, the Hosokawa, Hata, and Murayama cabinet, the last with the head of the Socialist Party as prime minister, have all announced that adherence to the Japan-US security treaty is basic to Japan's foreign policy. It is particularly noteworthy that following the installation of the Murayama cabinet, the Socialist Party thoroughly changed its attitude toward the Japan-US security treaty. As is generally known, the Socialist Party's original policy opposed it and advocated the scrapping of this security treaty. After Murayama took office, however, not only did he change the policy, but repeatedly stated that there was no change from previous cabinets in the Murayama cabinet's realization of the importance of the Japan-US security treaty. Japan would continue to "uphold the Japan-US security treaty." In the United States, after Clinton took office even though he had adopted a tough attitude about solving Japan-US economic frictions, and brandished the "super 301 provisions" to put pressure on Japan, thereby forcing Japan to give way, he also declared repeatedly that America's adoption of "retaliatory measures" economically could threaten bilateral political and security relationships, and that strengthening continuation of the Japan-US alliance system is the "cornerstone" of US Asia-Pacific policy.

Nevertheless, one must realize that the meaning of, or the strategic basis for, the Japan-US alliance system has changed since the Cold War. It is generally realized that during the Cold-War era, joint opposition to Soviet expansion and the Soviet threat was the foundation for maintenance of the Japan-US alliance system. Following the end of the Cold War, because of the dissolution of the USSR, the role of the Japan-US alliance changed from the former joint opposition to the USSR to joint containment of regional clashes, and from "protecting Japan" to "watching Japan." America's policy toward Japan today is as follows: It contains both a hope that Japan will work with the United States to play a political role both globally and in the Asia-Pacific region, and trepidations about Japan becoming a political power and going on to become a military power. The United States wants Japan both to increase its military strength and financial responsibility for US forces stationed in Japan, and to limit the scale of Japan's armed forces expansion. It also intends to prevent Japan from developing "a capacity to deploy combat forces (abroad)," and to "research and develop (like the United States) noncomplementary weapons systems (i.e., strategic weapons)" in order to prevent Japan from becoming a major

continued...

military power. The United States has said it wants to "maintain bases and forward deployments in Japan for a long time" so that American forces can "play a bottle-cap role (in preventing the militarization of Japan)." Following the end of the Cold War, Japan has also ascribed new meaning to the Japan-US alliance system. In addition to continuing to emphasize the role of the Japan-US alliance system in the "nuclear containment" of nuclear nations, and having the system serve as a "backstop" for Japan's conduct of diplomatic activities, it also believes that upholding the Japan-US security treaty and maintaining American garrison forces in Japan and the Asia-Pacific region helps contain the outbreak of regional clashes in the Asia-Pacific region and maintains the prosperity and stability of the region. In addition, it feels that because of events in World War II, the countries of Asia have become wary of Japan becoming a big political and military power. Japan's maintenance of the Japan-US security treaty helps eliminate apprehension in these countries. It "enables each country to accept Japan's greater political and economic role in Asia." It is noteworthy that not long ago the Japanese prime minister's private consulting organization, the "Forum on Defense Affairs" proposed that the scope of the Japan-US security treaty should be "limited not just to Japanese-American defense matters, but made one of the hubs of an Asia and Pacific region security support system." This is to say an expansion of the role of the Japan-US security treaty to the Asia-Pacific region.

Yet another noteworthy issue is that in the process of transition from bipolarity to multi-polarity in international relations, and with a steady narrowing of the gap between Japanese and American economic strength, Japan's independence from the United States and autonomy have increased further. Japan strongly hopes to play a role as "equal partner" with the United States on the international stage. As long ago as May 1990, the administrative vice-minister of foreign affairs at the time, Naoichi Kuriyama, wrote that today when the economic gap between Japan and the United States is steadily narrowing, "the age of Japan's sole reliance on the United States has passed. Japan and the United states—two advanced democratic coun-tries—are in a position, along with the EU, of being jointly responsible for world peace and prosperity." This is to say that Japan wants to become an equal partner with the United States and Europe. During his visit to Japan in early 1992 President George Bush's statement that Japan and the United States are "equal partners" showed that Japan had begun to be in an equal position with the United States. Militarily, ranking leaders in the Self-Defense Force [SDF] justifiably called for "independent" expansion of the armed forces. In May 1993, SDF Chief-of-Staff Maichi Saku proposed that Japan establish a "functionally complete self-defense force." By "functionally complete self-defense force" is meant "getting away from the current situation in which it exists as an auxiliary to the American armed forces, enabling it to become a 'national military force' that stands shoulder to shoulder with those of advanced countries." Maritime SDF Chief-of-Staff Chiaki Hayashizaki wrote in February 1994: "The Maritime SDF's equipment is unbalanced today. One hundred percent of its mobile strike force comes from the American Seventh Fleet." "Continuing in this way is not necessarily good." Naturally, his meaning was that Japan must develop its own mobile strike force in the future. Incumbent high-level SDF leaders' continuous expression of such views was a rarity in the past. Yet another conspicuous manifestation of Japan's quest for independence and autonomy occurred when Japanese Prime Minister Morohiro Hosokawa visited the United States in February 1992. During nego-tiation of a new economic agreement between the United States and Japan, Japan said "no" for the first time in opposition to America's demand that Japan set a "numerical quota" for American products, thereby precipitating a rupture in Japan-US negotiations.

2. Increasing economic frictions between Japan and the United States cannot be easily solved. The rupture of negotiations during Hosokawa's visit to the United States produced tension for a time in relations between Japan and the United States. First, the United States announced that Japan had not lived up to the agreement between Japan and the United States on the importation of American mobile telephones, so it was going to issue "sanctions" against Japan (a solution being found later only after Japan yielded). Next, Clinton declared intention

continued...

SCHOLARS VIEW WEST-WEST RELATIONS, 1994 (continued)

to invoke the "super 301 provisions" against Japan. He warned that unless Japan yielded on a new economic agreement, he would take "retaliatory measures" against Japan. At the same time, in order to improve the Asia-Pacific environment, the United States readjusted its Asia-Pacific policy, including softening its tough stand against Japan. Japan yielded correspondingly; thus, on 2 October 1994, the two nations reached an agreement on Japanese government procurement, insurance, and plate-glass issues for a temporary easing of the tension in relations between Japan and the United States. Nevertheless, economic frictions between Japan and the United States were not resolved. One of the fundamental reasons leading to an intensification of economic friction was the continued rise in the adverse balance of trade with Japan, which reached $59.4 billion in 1993, up $9.7 billion from 1992 for an all-time high. It will remain high during 1994. This set off new conflicts. Second was failure to reach agreement about the importation of American automobiles and spare parts. Automobiles and spare parts account for two-thirds of America's deficit with Japan. The United States cannot relent, and Japan is unwilling to yield further. It appears that negotiations will continue to be very difficult. If agreement cannot be reached, the United States will institute sanctions, thereby intensifying conflicts even more.

3. Outlook for Japan-US relations. For both Japan and the United States, the joint benefits from maintenance of mutually close relations outweigh the mutual conflicts. In addition, the intertwined economies of the two countries makes separation difficult. Therefore, there will be no worsening of relations between the two countries in the foreseeable future. Relations between the two will be maintained and develop through cooperation and competition and through battle for control and counter-control.

Huang Fanzhang [7806 5400 4545] (deputy director and research fellow, Economic Research Institute, State Planning Commission): The Asia-Pacific Region is the main battleground in which the United States and Japan contend for foreign investment.

1. Following the end of the Cold War, when economic cooperation is moving ahead in the Asia-Pacific region, China is facing a new situation of three large, medium, and small "triangular relationships." The big triangular relationship is among China, the United States, and Japan, the medium-sized relationship is China, the four small dragons, and ASEAN, and the small triangle is the mainland, Hong Kong, and Taiwan. I have already written an article proposing a strategic approach of "using the small triangle as a foothold, winning a position in the medium-sized triangle, and moving about in the big triangle."

I have termed relations among China, the United States, and Japan a "big triangle" not only because the United States and Japan are world economic powers and because China is both a "political power" and the developing country that has greatest economic development potential, but also because any change in bilateral relations among these three countries (whether good or bad) will have an effect on the region's overall situation. This means that the governments of the three countries must adopt highly responsible and prudent attitudes in handling bilateral relations among them. Naturally, changes in bilateral relations among them can cause serious concern for the governments and people of all countries in the region. This is particularly true of relations between Japan and the United States.

2. The Asia-Pacific region remains the main battle ground for economic conflicts and clashes between the United States and Japan. With the development of economic regionalization and the establishment of common markets, with establishment of the North American Free Trade Area [NAFTA] and the decision to establish a Pan-American Free Trade Area before 2005 only the Asia-Pacific region, particularly East Asia, is not only permeated with vitality, but its economic regionalization is fairly low. It provides substantial room for contention.

For a long time, Japan has steadily widened its economic and trade contacts with Asia, particularly East Asia, through industry transfers and the import-export trade that has occurred in conjunction with its own restructuring and industrial upgrading. By contrast, Europe has always been the strategic focus of the United States to the neglect of Asia. Pressured by events in recent years, America has expanded its stake in Asia and has also actively expanded

continued...

SCHOLARS VIEW WEST-WEST RELATIONS, 1994 (continued)

economic and trade relations with Asia. In recent years, America's sales to Asia have increased an average of 10 percent per year, which is higher than its sales to any other region. Reportedly, America's present volume of trade with Asia totals more than $374 billion per year, or almost 40 percent of America's merchandise trade with the world. America's direct investment in Asia stands at $92 billion. Clearly for both the United States and Japan, Asia, and particularly East Asia, is an area of crucial economic interest. It is an area in which the United States and Japan are bound to be future rivals.

3. In order to penetrate East Asia economically, during the 1980s Japan proposed and put into effect a "flying wild goose column" strategy in which Japan is the "head goose," and the four small dragons and ASEAN are the two columns with Japan's translational corporations making industry transfers. During the Cold-War era, Japan had to rely on the United States for trade and technology; militarily and politically, it had to shelter even more under America's nuclear umbrella; consequently, it resorted to a strategy of concealing its capabilities and biding its time, moving ahead quietly.

At that time, America's attention was focused mostly on Europe. America adopted a "bilateral policy" or promoted NAFTA to deal with exclusionary blocs. In the Asia-Pacific region, the United States also relied heavily on "bilateral" tactics, working from its bilateral relationship with Japan and using US-Japan, US-South Korea, and US-Australia bilateral relations as a nucleus and a framework in an effort to promote a so-called "fan-shaped" strategy in East Asia.

4. Circumstances changed somewhat following the end of the Cold War. Although Japan continued quietly to push its "flying goose column" strategy as before, because of its diminished need to rely on America's nuclear umbrella, not only did it cause more economic friction with the United States, but it also raised the cry of "a Japan that dares to say 'no'," and openly sought "political big power" status.

Faced with a booming East Asian economy, the United States also adjusted its Asia-Pacific strategy somewhat, namely increasing Asia's share in its strategy. Tactically, it switched from "bilateralism," to "multilateralism." Preaching "open regionalism," it actively used APEC to promote regional economic cooperation, hoping to establish an "Asian Economic Community" headed by the United States. It was under these circumstances that the United States linked "most-favored-nation treatment" with "human rights issues" in US-China bilateral dealings. Under impetus from the United States, the "Bogor Declaration," which was passed in Indonesia in 1994, announced a timetable for Asia-Pacific region developed nations and developing nations to promote trade liberalization in 2010 and 2020 respectively.

Naturally Japan had misgivings about America's active promotion of "Asia-Pacific coopera- tion" under American aegis, but it did not want to come out openly against the United States. Although Japan secretly favored Malaysian Prime Minister Datuk Seri Mahathir Mohamad's open clash with the United States, it did not openly say so. It did not dare support Mahathir's proposal for founding of an East Asian Economy Nuclear Forum that includes Japan, China, South Korea, and ASEAN, but not the United States. Mahathir showed open dissatisfaction at Japan's "softness." This was the tactic of "hiding capabilities and biding time" that Japan wanted to maintain.

5. What is the trend of US-Japan contradictions? Let me present the following several views: 1) Both the United States and Japan want to expand overseas markets and investment arenas. The main battleground in their rivalry for overseas markets and investment areas is the Asia- Pacific region or East Asia. 2) Japan will continue its "hiding capabilities and biding its time" tactic. Even though the Cold War is over, Japan not only needs the American market and technology, but it also needs full US support on a series of major issues (such as permanent UN Security Council membership, its northern territories problem, and security problems).

The United States will continue to use APEC to realize its preeminence in economic cooperation in that region. In particular, it will use "eminent persons groups" (EPG) to design and promote various plans. So long as Japan does not use multilateral organizations in an open collision with the United States, the United States will value "cooperation" between itself and

continued...

SCHOLARS VIEW WEST-WEST RELATIONS, 1994 (continued)

Japan. Predictably, the United States and Japan will either openly or secretly link hands in the Asian Regional Forum to get rid of the so-called "territorial sovereignty issue," the "collective security" issue, and even the "China threat theory." They want to both restrain China and "deter" East Asia. The thing that perplexes the United States and Japan most is seemingly clear evidence that Russia will expand once it gets out of its economic difficulties. In short, economic conflicts and clashes between the United States and Japan are fundamental and enduring, their "alliance" will be temporary. Should another threat of Russian expansionism occur, that will be another story.

Jiang Xiaoyan [1203 2556 3601] (assistant research fellow, Chinese Contemporary International Relations Research Institute): In continuing, I will express some views about the rivalry between Japan and the United States in the Asia-Pacific region.

1. The world economy has entered an era of unprecedented competition in which the Asia-Pacific region will be the main battle ground for rivalry between the United States and Japan.

Because of the reduced danger of a major war following the end of the Cold War, the developed nations began an all-out quest for economic returns. The nations that formerly operated centrally planned economies also became market economies through a series of reforms. Developing nations are vying with each other to bring in capital and technology to make an economic take-off. The obstacles that often existed between one country and another are crumbling rapidly. One might say that the world economy is entering a period of global competition. The Asia-Pacific region is bound up with the interests of the United States and Japan. In this competition on an unprecedented scale, the Asia-Pacific region has become the main arena for struggle between the two economic powers, the United States and Japan.

A) The Asia-Pacific region is the world economic growth center. The United States and Japan must draw support from the harnessing of economic growth in the Asia-Pacific region to give impetus to their own economic growth. A Japanese economic research center predicts that Asia will maintain 8.6 percent economic growth during the 1990s, the highest in the world, but America's and Japan's growth rate will be only 2.2 and 2.7 percent respectively.

B) Tremendous growth markets exist in Asia. The United States and Japan must improve their economic relations with this region and expand exports to increase domestic employment and ease their increasingly serious unemployment problems. The countries in Asia that formerly pursued a planned economy system and a closed economy system have a population of 2.5 billion that offers an enormous potential market. With the changed approach of these country's planned economy systems and the change from a closed to an open economy, these potential markets are becoming "enormous growth markets."

2. The United States and Japan have begun to compete in the Asia-Pacific region.

A) Competition centers around preeminence in APEC. With the shift in America's economy toward the Asia-Pacific region, the United States has begun to show interest in Asia-Pacific regional economic cooperation. In July 1993, American President Clinton proposed a "Pacific Ocean Commonwealth," and actively encouraged and supported the convening of the first information conference of APEC heads of state. His goal was to gain preeminence in APEC for the fashioning of an economic, political, and military order headed by the United States in the Asia-Pacific region.

America's active involvement in APEC makes Japan feel threatened. Japan has always regarded East Asia as where its own fundamental interests lie. It is here that it has actively sought to build a regional economic bloc based on the "wild goose model" with Japan at its center, later expanding toward a wider Pacific Rim region, and finally establishing an East Asia Economic Commonwealth in which Japan plays the leading role. America's active participation in APEC made Japan feel that the fruits that had begun to be gained from Asia-Pacific cooperation centering around Japan might be taken from Japan's hands. Thus, Japan emphasized that the APEC should be purely an economic organization. It should not become a regional political and security organization. Moreover, in response to the demands of developing countries in the Asia-Pacific region, Japan said that APEC should do some things,

continued...

SCHOLARS VIEW WEST-WEST RELATIONS, 1994 (continued)

particularly those pertaining to developing economy members, developing cooperation in the fields of manpower resources, medium-sized and small enterprises, and infrastructure. Japan also used the apprehensions of countries such as China and ASEAN about America's leading Asia-Pacific economic cooperation to launch an active diplomatic offensive. It constantly adopted a posture of serious concern for Asia in the hope of winning the support of China and ASEAN in APEC to maintain its own dominant position in APEC.

B) Vying to improve relations with all the countries of Asia. The Clinton administration gradually realized that its high pressure policies on human rights and trade negotiations evoked only resentment from Asian countries, and that it was not in keeping with America's fundamental interests. Consequently, America's Asia-Pacific policy began to change from "idealism" to "realism." It adopted "conciliatory" tactics toward Asian countries, developing relations with each country. By decoupling human-rights issues from most-favored-nation treatment in trade, American improved its relations with China. It took the initiative in approaching Myanmar [Burma], proposing that if Myanmar would adopt economic deregulation policies, it would consider canceling sanctions against it. It canceled sanctions against Vietnam, repaired relations with India, and actively supported the ASEAN Regional Security Forum. By readjusting its foreign relations with the Asia-Pacific region, the United States paved the way for the entry of American business into the region for an expansion of America's economic presence, and the winning of economic benefits.

Japan improved its relations with the ASEAN countries in a counter move. In 1993, US Secretary of Treasury Lloyd Bensen engaged in shuttle diplomacy in Asia. After he visited Indonesia, Thailand, and China, Japan immediately sent government officials to Indonesia Malaysia, and Thailand to discuss greater economic cooperation. Right after taking office, Japanese Prime Minister Murayama set off on a visit to four countries in Southeast Asia in the course of which he explicitly adopted a posture of war responsibility in an effort to court goodwill in each country. Japan's diplomacy with Southeast Asia, which centers around economic cooperation and civilian investment, is improving dialogue and cultural exchanges for the building of more broadly based relations. The goal is to seize opportunities for improving "all-around cooperation" with each country in Southeast Asia during the "new era in Southeast Asia" in order to build "a partnership in preparation for another take-off," to sweep away obstacles to Japan's becoming a new political power and to win the support of ASEAN in all regards.

3. Active efforts made to gain new and developing markets in the Asia-Pacific Region. In 1992, America's trade with 10 countries of Asia other than Japan and Taiwan amounted to $186.6 billion, surpassing the volume of trade between the United States and Canada ($185.8 billion). America's annual volume of trade with the Asia-Pacific region is 50 percent greater than its volume of trade with Europe. Exports to the Asia-Pacific region created 2.5 million employment opportunities for America. United States statistics show that by 2010, America's exports to Asia will reach $248 billion; therefore, the United States will shift its focus to encourage exports to the new and developing nations of the Asia-Pacific region and to urge these countries to reduce their trade barriers. As part of its urging American firms to expand exports, the United States government has begun commercial diplomacy, taking the initiative to build bridges for business concerns. The Import-Export Bank has increased financial assistance to Asian exporting firms. "Japan Incorporated's" experiences with the use of state power to serve business has begun to be used by the American government.

Japan's trade with Asia has also developed by leaps and bounds. In 1983, Japan's exports to the United States were one-third more than to Asia, but in 1991, Asia surpassed the United States to become Japan's largest export area. Trade between Japan and Asia totaled $185 billion in 1992 exceeding the volume of trade between the United States and Japan ($148 billion). In 1993, for the first time, Japan's favorable balance of trade with Asia exceeded its favorable balance of trade with the United States.

The United States used to hold the lead in direct investment in Asia, but since the 1980s, Japan has used the rise in value of the yen to expand its investment in this region steadily.

continued...

SCHOLARS VIEW WEST-WEST RELATIONS, 1994 (continued)

Economic Cooperation Organization [ECO] statistics show that between 1980 and 1985, American and Japanese direct investment in Hong Kong, South Korea, Malaysia, Singapore, Taiwan, and Thailand accounted for a respective 35 and 20 percent, 49 and 30 percent, 10 and 23 percent, 50 and 14 percent, 40 and 26 percent, and 31 and 27 percent of the direct investment that these countries and territories received. Except for Malaysia, America's investment was vastly greater than Japan's. However, between 1986 and 1990, these percentages changed to a respective 25 and 46 percent, 31 and 46 percent, 5 and 26 percent, 39 and 37 percent, 21 and 33 percent, and 11 and 44 percent. Except for investment in Singapore, where the United States was somewhat higher than Japan, the United States lagged far behind Japan in investment elsewhere. A Japanese Ministry of International Trade and Industry [MITI] survey shows that Japan's direct investment in Asia increased 87.5 percent in 1993. At this rate, by the end of the present century, Asia will become the largest recipient of direct investment from Japan. In order to turn this unfavorable direct investment situation around, American businesses have begun hot pursuit, steadily expanding their investment in the Asia-Pacific region, particularly in fields such as finance and banking, telecommunications equipment, and power generating machinery in which the United States holds an advantage. It is rapidly catching up with Japan. The two nations are engaged in a new rivalry.

3. [numbering as published] Despite the contradictions and steadily deepening rivalry between the United States and Japan, the two countries still have numerous common interests based on a common viewpoint, values, and a joint-security strategy. While engaging in rivalry, they will continue to cooperate.

For Japan, the Cold War has not ended in Asia. Russia still has 320,000 troops in the Far East, and nuclear submarines carrying nuclear weapons still patrol the Sea of Okhotsk. Japan also regards China's modernization of its navy as a threat to the security structure in East Asia. Since Japan needs to maintain a political and military presence in the Asia-Pacific region, the US-Japan alliance will not change. The two sides will continue further strengthening of coordination and cooperation in the military realm. For the United States, American trade with the Asia-Pacific region is one and one-half times its trade with Europe. America's trade strategy is tilted more toward the Asia-Pacific region than in the past. While improving cooperation with the Asia-Pacific region, the United States also needs to cooperate with Japan. America's active participation in Asia-Pacific affairs can restrain the Asia economy from tilting in the direction of exclusionary regionalism, and it is also consistent with Japan's interests. Therefore, both sides will contain both rivalry and cooperation in the Asia-Pacific region.

US-Europe Relations
Chen Chaogao [7115 2600 7559] (assistant research fellow, Chinese Contemporary International Relations Institute): Since the end of the Cold War, differences have steadily increased between Europe and the United States on economic, security, and foreign relations matters, with their alliance weakening commensurably, but their interdependence still dominates. Thus, mutual competition and frictions have also increased at the same time.

1. Continued development of interdependence between Europe and the United States
A) Western Europe and the United States are the world's largest traders. They are major export and import partners. Statistics show that between 1990 and 1992, European (including the European nations in the ECO and Turkey) imports from the United States climbed from more than $124.16 billion to $127.66 billion in a 2.8 percent increase. Europe's exports to the United States declined slightly from $113.65 billion to $111.06 in a 0.3 percent decrease. During these two years, Western Europe's exports to the United States accounted for a respective 7.3 and 6.9 percent of its total world trade. During this same period, US imports from Western Europe rose from $108.14 billion to $110.2 billion, up 1.9 percent, and its exports to Western Europe rose from $112.22 billion to $116.42 billion, up 3.7 percent. During these two years, America's trade with Western Europe accounted for a respective 21.5 and 21.8 percent of its total world trade. Relatively speaking, America's dependence on Western European markets

continued...

SCHOLARS VIEW WEST-WEST RELATIONS, 1994 (continued)

is much greater that Western Europe's dependence on American markets. At the same time, however, the United States is Western Europe's largest export market.

B) Europe and the United States remain the largest investment arena. Despite changes in Europe's and America's foreign investment patterns since the beginning of the 1990s, the two remain the largest arena for mutual investment. Statistics show a rise in cumulative direct Western European investment in the United States from $241.5 billion in 1990 to $270.77 billion in 1993, a 12.1 percent rise. Nevertheless, this investment has slowed in comparison with the more than 16 percent annual increase during the late 1980s. During the same period, US cumulative investment in Western Europe increased from $228.52 billion to $269.16 billion, up 9.3 percent. The general trend is greater American reliance on Western European capital than European reliance on American capital. However, Europe and the United States are each other's largest areas for direct investment and profits.

It was with this in mind that during his visit to Europe in 1994, American President Clinton constantly reiterated that Europe is where America's main interests lie. America holds the advantage in European-American trade relations, such as its tremendous favorable balance of trade and its attraction of more European capital. At the same time, however, America's dependence on Western European markets is increasing steadily. Furthermore, Western Europe is also obtaining greater market share, large quantities of capital, and much sophisticated technology and equipment from the United States. Clearly, economic and trade relations between Europe and the United States remain important to both. It is anticipated that for a long time to come, economic and trade relations between Europe and the United States will continue and develop.

C) In the political and security fields, Europe and the United States still have common interests. In the wake of the Cold War, Europe and the United States are pondering ways to consolidate and develop political and security benefits stemming from the dramatic changes in eastern Europe and the dissolution of the USSR, so that these countries will continue to develop in the direction that the West desires. They are also trying to find ways to exert further pressures on socialist countries in order to advance their "Westernization" strategy. During the past several years, Europe and the United States have exerted various pressures on developing nations, including promotion of so-called Western human rights value concepts and the Western political system. Despite certain differences and contradictions between Europe and the United States in their handling of developing nations, their overall strategy and policy is the same. Following the end of the Cold War, long-term disturbances in areas of the former Soviet Union and the Balkans have troubled Europe's political and security situation. This chaotic situation directly threatens the security and stability of Western Europe; thus, it strikes at America's and Europe's fundamental interests. Western Europe has long regarded the United States as the protector of its political and security interests, and the United States, in turn, regards Europe as a base and backstop for the maintenance of its leading position in Europe and the world. With the gradual revival of nationalism in Russia, its policies and attitude toward the West have toughened, increasing European and American apprehensions and concerns. Consequently, relations between Europe and the United States, which turned chilly for a time following the Cold War, have eased. Clinton has visited Western Europe three times for the purpose of repairing and strengthening relations between Europe and the United States in order to deal with the emergence of a situation that might be detrimental to Europe.

2. Sharpened clashes of trade and security interests between Europe and the United States.

A) The battle for export markets has intensified. The battle between Europe and the United States to get export markets has become increasingly clear and open in recent years. Instances of attacks on each other have been common. European nations generally use soft loans to promote the export of electric power and high technology equipment, which puts American firms at a disadvantage. One American survey report condemned Germany for "not living up to its international responsibilities," and "violating international agreements" in using soft loans to help its companies enter the China market. It condemned the governments of European

continued...

SCHOLARS VIEW WEST-WEST RELATIONS, 1994 (continued)

countries for frequently violating the Helsinki Agreement under the terms of which ECO-member nations are to reduce the use of soft loans to assist exports. The US Department of Commerce emphasized that rivalry for large world projects is currently mostly between the United States and Europe; consequently, it demanded that the US government "must revive with all possible speed" the Trade and Development Board, and the Import-Export Bank should provide "more liberal assistance" to counter the "soft loan competition" coming from Europe. However, the European nations did not take this lying down. They pointed out that the United States "uses export subsidies to shut Europe out of the world wheat market." France condemned the Americans for having "locked" the main gate to the European wheat market; consequently, Europe "cannot meet" the continued challenge from the United States.

B) In the financial and monetary realm, frictions occur repeatedly between Europe and the United States, and clashes of interests are increasingly apparent. Germany's Minister of Economics condemned the United States saying that the American government lacks a coherent policy for supporting the dollar. Germany's central bank noted further that the United States has relied on the influx of foreign money to make up for its low savings rate. The slide in American exchange rates is attributable to the large outflow from the United States of long-term capital, particularly the outflow of Japanese capital. This shows that "deep-rooted structural problems" exist in the United States.

C) A battle for markets is unfolding everywhere. Europe is trying to improve economic relations and trade cooperation with developing countries and regions to improve its competitiveness with the United States. During 1995, the EU. has continued to propose the establishment of a free trade zone with North African and Middle Eastern countries on the south coast of the Mediterranean, the signing of free trade agreements with Arab-Magreb countries and South Africa, and the mapping of a strategy to improve trade and investment with Asia-Pacific countries, particularly ASEAN and China. It is particularly noteworthy that the EU has decided, in principle, to increase economic and government financial assistance to central and eastern European countries, to liberalize trade conditions further, and to open eastern European markets. It is also considering bringing central and eastern European countries into the EU by the end of the present century. The EU is doing this in preparation for the battle for markets primarily with the United States and secondarily with Japan and the newly emerging industrializing nations and territories of Asia.

D) Differences over European security problems have deepened further. An example is solution to the Bosnia-Herzegovina warfare problem. The EU has done all possible, including the use of peace-keeping forces in the areas concerned and weapons embargoes, in an attempt to separate the combatants, and it has held political negotiations in a quest for peace. After the Serbs refused to accept the Western peace plan, the Clinton administration unilaterally announced cancellation of its arms embargo against the Muslim government of Bosnia-Herzegovina. Fearing a worsening of the Bosnia-Herzegovina war situation, and that the lives of the members of their peacekeeping forces might be endangered, the European countries condemned this action of the United States as creating an "extremely grave crisis," and as "having a serious effect on relations between both sides of the Atlantic Ocean." Another example involves Europe's defense. The United States seeks to continue its NATO leadership role, but the EU's intention is that it will gradually supplant NATO with EU defense. The NATO crisis is turning into a crisis in relations between the two sides of the Atlantic.

Li Juan (Politics Department, Beijing University): I would like to state some views on new post-Cold War-era relations between the United States and Europe, particularly structural trade differences:

With the end of the Cold War, the need for joint US-European resistance to the Soviet threat ceased to exist, and cohesion diminished sharply. As Europe's security situation improved markedly, economic factors and economic competition came to the fore. The United States sought to establish a new world order under its leadership and to play the leading role in relations between the two sides of the Atlantic and in NATO. However, western European

continued...

SCHOLARS VIEW WEST-WEST RELATIONS, 1994 (continued)

nations clamored to "fight for an equal partnership." In recent years, some voters and interest groups have appeared in European countries who do not value relations between the two sides of the Atlantic. They have gained substantial rights to speak out on behalf of each nation deciding its own policy regarding trans-Atlantic relations. The result of all this has been that relations between the United States and the EU have entered a new phase of development. As one British publication said, "relations between the United States and Europe consist of competition and cooperation,'" rather than a "harmonious partnership." The two sides depend on each other and compete with each other. Conflicts are rampant and coordination difficulties have increased. Not only have the conflicts and friction ramified into the future of NATO, European security arrangements, tactics for dealing with regional issues such as Bosnia-Herzegovina, and disagreements over approaches, but they are also expressed strongly in economic relations and trade. In the economic and trade realm, not only are their battles over policy and activities such as protection and antiprotection, limitations and counterlimitations, dumping and antidumping, and sanctions and countersanctions, but also differences about the ingrained organizational structure.

According to the analysis of a Western publication the major American and European differences over the economic relations and trade system are three: 1) Regarding economic strategy and macroeconomics, the United States mostly feels that economic growth and economic operation are more important than stable exchange rates, while the European view is largely that the stability of exchange rates is a precondition for the maintenance of steady economic growth and the avoidance of currency inflation. 2) The EU's policy regarding trade and investment is founded largely on mutual recognition and sovereign countries' exercising control. This is the way the unified European market works. In the United States, trade and investment is founded broadly on the national treatment principle. On the basis of this principle, foreign suppliers, foreign service trades, and foreign investors may enjoy the same treatment as home country suppliers. However, these two principles conflict and contradict each other in many crucial areas of domestic American and European laws and regulations and in multilateral system contacts under GATT. The national treatment principle contains clear-cut provisions and is easy to apply, but it also means that each government is able to draft national laws and regulations that may restrict trade. Unlike the unified European market, the method founded on national treatment limits the effect of global economic integration. 3) Differences also exist between Europe and North America on a market economy model. Europe has numerous forms of capitalism. Among the distinctive ones that play a substantial role, one is called Rheinland capitalism, which is founded on a long-term relationship among investors, suppliers, and customers, which places less emphasis on capital markets, a series of clear-cut rules and regulations, and wide-ranging consensus among interest groups. An Anglo-Saxon market economy is founded on the following: short-term financial behavior; large, open capital markets; non-regulation; and competition among individuals and interest groups with no unanimity of views. Japan's market economy is closer to the European Rheinland type rather than the Anglo-Saxon type. In short, structural differences in trade existed between the United States and Japan even during the Cold War period, but they were not evident. With the end of the Cold War, they have come out into the open.

Li Baowen [2621 0202 2429]: (assistant research fellow, Chinese Contemporary International Relations Research Institute): I will focus on how cooperation between the United States and Europe is greater than the differences between them. With the end of the Cold War and the steady political and economic rise of the Asia-Pacific region, the center of United States foreign policy has tended to shift eastward, but overall, Europe remains its strategic focus. Cooperation between the United States and Europe is greater than their differences, and coordination is greater than conflict, particularly on major issues of common interest on which unanimous agreement can still be attained. The main reasons are as follows:

1) The United States and Europe have a similar culture and values, and they also have a long relationship as allies. America's 1994 "National Security Strategy Report" emphasized that

continued...

SCHOLARS VIEW WEST-WEST RELATIONS, 1994 (continued)

"the long-term goal of the United States is establishment of a world in which every major country is a democracy," and strengthening of relations with Europe is an important link in the realization of this goal.

2) Following the dissolution of the USSR, the United States became the world's only superpower, and conflicts between the United States and Europe over control and countercontrol also intensified. However, the United States believes that "a unified Europe not only poses no threat to America's security, but rather is in keeping with America's interests."

A) The three mainstays of the Clinton administration's domestic and foreign policy are economic security, military strength, and global democratization, and the key one is economic security. A unified and prosperous Europe can carry more responsibility in the world, thereby reducing the burden on the United States. In addition, America's investment in Europe is still greater than elsewhere. The development of economic relations and trade is a need of both the United States and Europe.

B) Under present circumstances, Europe's unification helps harmonize relations among Europe's big powers—Germany, France, and the UK. Following unification, Germany's political influence steadily increased, arousing alarm in other countries. Incorporating a unified Germany into a unified Europe and improving European big power relations helps eliminate elements for instability in that region.

C) Following the evolution of eastern Europe and the dissolution of the USSR, both the "democratic system" and the "market economy" of these transitional nations remained very fragile. Preventing a reversal in these countries, and making these nations a part of the "big democratic family" is a common strategic goal of the United States and the EU. Nationalist forces have risen in Russia, and it is demanding revival of its big power status. The United States feels that a unified Europe will not only help develop relations with Russia, but also restrain the development of Russian chauvinism.

3. Following the American mid-term elections, the Republican Party controls both houses of Congress; consequently, the Clinton administration's foreign policy will be somewhat restricted. Nevertheless, it will not change fundamentally. America's policy toward Europe, which will still be premised on maintenance of America's leading role, doing all possible to permit Europe to assume greater political, military, and economic responsibility to enable the United States to concentrate its energies on invigorating its economy and maintaining its status as the world's only superpower.

On European Big Power Relations

Yang Zugong [2799 4371 0501] (research fellow, Europe Research Institute, Chinese Social Sciences Academy): I will focus on a discussion of the triangular relationship among Germany, the UK, and France, and related problems. The factors having a substantial bearing on the landscape of Europe are the dissolution of the Soviet Union and dramatic changes in eastern Europe, unification of the two Germanys, and Europe-US relations. The changes that these three factors have wrought are now discernible, and will develop in the future.

The main change is the marked rise in Germany's position in Europe following unification. Germany has the greatest economic strength in Europe, and plays a role as a "locomotive" in the development of Europe's economy. The monetary crisis that occurred in 1993 shows that the Deutschmark can control development of Europe's economy. Another factor is Germany's position. Following unification, Germany became the center of Europe. However, this also causes certain problems for Germany. Today, many of Europe's contradictions focus on Germany. Despite amelioration of economic problems, internal contradictions and contradictions between Germany and other countries are gradually coming to the fore. The Germans themselves repeatedly emphasize that Germany is powerful, but it is not so strong that it is able to deal with an alliance of neighboring countries. Both German officialdom and the public realize this. They both know that neighboring countries are very frightened of Germany's power. Related to this is another change, namely readjustment of the triangular relationship among Germany, France, and the UK. Following World War II, relations among Germany, France, and

continued...

SCHOLARS VIEW WEST-WEST RELATIONS, 1994 (continued)

the UK played a decisive role on the direction that Europe would take. Nevertheless, this "small triangle" was never able to form an equilateral triangular relationship. The "Franco-German axis" provided the power and support for the European alliance. Following the end of the Cold War, even though France and Germany continue to be each other's principal ally the "Franco-German axis" has loosened. On numerous important issues, France and Germany used to coordinate their position and act in concert in foreign affairs through discussions and exchanges at annual heads of state conferences. Today, however, Germany frequently acts first on some issues, and France sometimes does not bother to talk with Germany and the UK. The position of France and the UK on European security issues has become closer recently, and they have increased cooperation. Both France and the UK were extremely upset about President Clinton's open endorsement of Germany as the leader of Europe, and his removal of the embargo on weapons to the Bosnia-Herzegovina Muslims. Major disagreements occurred between France and Germany over expansion of the EU into eastern Europe, on the European Currency Union, and on the Uruguay round of GATT talks. However, the UK had a clash of interests with France on the EC's fiscal subsidy policy, its position being close to that of Germany. It is still too early to say that the "Franco-German axis" cannot be revived or that is completely broken, but the direction in which an equilateral triangular relationship among Germany, France, and the UK is moving will bear watching.

To a very large extent, geopolitical rules are a power contest among big powers. In the final analysis, the structure of Europe will be determined by the relative strength of Germany, France, and the UK, and by the changes in their domestic situation. Germany has now become the political and strategic center of Europe. Sooner or later, Germany, which is economically strong, and whose currency, in particular, plays a decisive role in Europe will play a greater role in Europe and internationally.

West-West contradictions are one of several basic contradictions in the modern world. They are real. The recent changes in the triangular relationship among Germany, France, and the UK, and in relations between Europe and the United States demonstrate that with the end of the Cold War pattern of East-West confrontation differences and clashes of interests among the Western nations have truly become more evident. Nevertheless, one cannot suggest on this basis that the rise in west-west contradictions has become the major contradiction in the contemporary world. Clashes of economic interests, disagreements over strategy or tactics, and national or cultural differences exist among them, but after a period of wrangling, they are always able to devise ways of finding a temporary compromise. At crucial moments, they remain united against the outside, maintaining their alliance relationship.

Recent changes in the triangular relationship among Germany, France, and the UK and between Europe and the United States also show that despite the trend toward international economic integration, regional political cooperation, and establishment of a collective security system, and despite Europe's marked achievements since the end of World War II, under most circumstances, each country still puts the principle of "ethnic and national interests first." The countries of Europe are numerous, their peoples varied, and some nation states remain in a state of turmoil and constant reorganization. Different interest relationships and historical origins exist among nation states. Among Germany, France, and the UK and between Europe and the United States contradictions and conflicts exist in the economic, political, military, and cultural fields. All do everything possible to protect the rights and interests of their own nation state. They can compromise and come to terms, take united action, and adjust home country policies only on issues on which their individual national interests are the same or when their basic interests do not suffer. The intricate and complex contradictions and interest relationships among the nations of Europe and between Europe and the United States illustrate this point. In addition, in order to safeguard their own interests, they bend every effort to maintain the impetus of European unity and safeguard the alliance between Europe and the United States and to increase economic, political, and military cooperation or coordinate mutual action.

continued...

SCHOLARS VIEW WEST-WEST RELATIONS, 1994 (continued)

Fang Zhongxia [2455 0022 7209] (researcher, Chinese Contemporary International Relations Research Institute: I will talk about some contradictions in relations among Germany, France, and the UK, the reasons for them, and prospects.

1. Principal manifestations of changes in relations among the three powers and their contradictions:

A) In the economic realm, Britain and France are unhappy about Germany's high interest rates. A financial crisis occurred in Western Europe during the autumn of 1992 and the summer of 1993, the British pound sustained grievous losses and withdrew from the European monetary system. The French franc also suffered serious damage. The reason was Germany's maintenance of a high interest rate policy. Although German interest rates have declined gradually, an EU finance ministers conference has been set, and the various currencies in the European exchange rate mechanism fluctuate 15 percent above and below the central exchange rate, the UK is still unwilling to return to the European monetary system. This causes complaints from both Germany and France. On trade, particularly the subsidization of farm products, British and German conflicts with France are rather glaring. Both Britain and Germany practice a free trade policy, but France pursues protectionism. France derives most benefit from the EC's agricultural subsidies. Agricultural subsidies account for a substantial portion of the EU's budget. This puts a fiscal strain on the EU. Furthermore, Germany and the UK contribute most to the EC, so both countries want France to reform its agricultural policy.

B) On building the EU, Germany advocates simultaneous broadening and deepening, but France advocates broadening after deepening. Britain, however, approves broadening but does not want deepening. Germany and the countries of eastern Europe have traditional economic interests, and Germany has invested greatly in that region since the end of the Cold War. If the EU expands eastward, Germany will be in the center of the EU, thus its security position will be enhanced. France fears that once the EU expands the balance of power will favor Germany to the detriment of France's dominant position in the EU. Therefore, France advocates further building of the EU first, with broadening coming later. Britain hopes that the EU will become a loose free trade zone, so it favors broadening. On the ultimate goal for building the EU, both France and Germany originally proposed the unified founding of a federal-style "Republic of Europe." France hoped that integration would tether Germany. Recently, however, France has begun to worry that if Europe institutes a federal system, Germany will restrain France, so it has backed off somewhat. Recently, Francois Mitterand said there is no need for haste on this issue. Britain has all along opposed the establishment of a federal Europe, fearing loss of its sovereignty and its big power status.

C) In the diplomatic field, the extent to which each of the three powers pursues its own course has increased markedly. Germany rushed to recognize the independence of Croatia and Slovenia without consulting the EC. When the conflict in Bosnia-Herzegovina escalated recently, and the United States announced a halt to the weapons embargo on Bosnia-Herzegovina, the British and French reaction was strong, only Germany expressing approval. In addition, Germany has done all possible to expand its influence in central and eastern Europe and in Russia. This has also aroused British and French apprehensions.

D) In the security and defense field, conflicts have always existed among Germany, France, and the UK. France and Germany emphasize establishment of an independent defense system for Western Europe, but the UK argues that NATO should not be affected on this account. Recently, because of the dilution of the "special relationship" between the UK and the United States and out of a desire to splinter the Franco-German axis Britain has improved relations and defense cooperation with France. The two nations signed an agreement on a "British-French European Military Team." Germany was somewhat displeased about the UK and France drawing together. On the eastward expansion of NATO, France maintains a negative attitude. The views of Britain and France are close with only Germany favoring

2. The changes and conflicts in relations among the three powers have a deeply rooted international and domestic background.

continued...

SCHOLARS VIEW WEST-WEST RELATIONS, 1994 (continued)

A) Changed international situation. The Franco-German axis began during the early 1960s. France used it as a counterweight to the United States and the USSR to establish big power status. Germany used it to improve its defeated-nation image. Faced with the powerful USSR, the alliance between Germany and France became closer during the Cold War era. Following the dramatic changes in eastern Europe and the dissolution of the USSR, France's and Germany's powerful adversary no longer existed. The strength of the only remaining super-power, America, was relatively weak and consequently, relations between France and Germany underwent corresponding adjustments.

B) Dominant status waxed and waned. During the Cold War era. France's dominant political and military position put it in a dominant position in the EU. Not only did post-unification Germany's economic strength increase, but its political and strategic position also improved greatly. By comparison, France's dominance gradually declined. These changes were bound to find reflection in relations between the two powers. Germany's rise and its quest for big power status created new challenges for the status and role of France.

C) In the handling of international affairs, every country paid closer attention to economic interests. Because of the decline in the rule of military factors in the wake of the Cold War, the role of economic factors rose. The three powers emphasized their own interests more. In addition, because of the economic slump in Western countries for the last two years and an increase in internal conflicts, not only did competition increase among the big western European powers, but relations among them also changed correspondingly.

D) Britain gradually changed its attitude, drawing closer to the EC. After John Majors took office, he made substantial changes in Margaret Thatcher's former policy toward Europe, played an active role in western Europe's integration, announced that the UK wanted to "return to Europe's central position," and sought to expand Britain's right to speak out on European affairs. Consequently, Britain's relations with Germany and France improved. At the same time, the UK was also rather concerned about Germany's steadily growing strength in Europe. The rapprochement of Britain and France was also aimed at countering Germany.

3. Although political and economic conflicts and frictions among Germany, France, and the UK increased, and relations among the three tended to slacken, for a long time to come the three powers will maintain both mutual rivalry and mutual dependence, a need for each other. This is for the following reasons:

A) Europe's unification and integration are irreversible; building of the EU is in the interest of all parties. Although Germany's power is increasing, it cannot play a dominant role by itself; it still requires the support and cooperation of France and the UK. Each of the three powers has its own individual strengths and weaknesses and this provides a basis for their interdependence and mutual support. Britain is fairly weak, and with the dilution of its "special relationship" with the United States, it needs the support of France and Germany all the more. Nevertheless, the UK is still a permanent member of the UN Security Council, and it is also a major world military power. It also has strong scientific, technical, and industrial strength. It must still be regarded as a major European power; therefore, both France and Germany must enlist the support of the UK.

B) The three nations have a common interest in protecting the overall interests of western European nations, in jointly fending off competition from the United States and Japan, and in guarding against Russia as well as the policies of the Third World. They have a real need to stick together and cooperate with each other.

C) The three powers share tremendous economic interests. Germany, France, and the UK are important mutual targets of investment and trade. Germany's direct investment in France totals 22.7 billion marks. It is the second largest foreign investor in France. France's investment in Germany also totals 12.7 billion francs holding sixth place in foreign investment in Germany. More than 60 percent of Britain's trade is with nations on the European continent, and Germany is the UK's most important trading partner. ECO statistics for July 1994 show that trade between the UK and Germany in 1992 totaled $61.236 billion, leading trade between the UK and Western European nations.

continued...

SCHOLARS VIEW WEST-WEST RELATIONS, 1994 (continued)

Today, Germany wants to direct Europe's affairs, France wants to maintain its position as leader of the EU, and the UK is also striving to enter Europe's power center. Each of the three powers is having trouble realizing its individual goals. The Franco-German axis will continue to operate. but its center is shifting toward Germany. Relations between the UK and France will develop, but within certain limits. It appears that on different issues, the three powers will be able to form a different combination of interests.

The world is in the process of changing from bipolarism to multipolarism today during which relations among all major powers are undergoing readjustment. Relations among Germany, France, and the UK will be subject to changes in the world situation. Nevertheless, the small triangular relationship will likewise produce an effect on other big power relationships. These changes will have an effect on Europe, particularly on the EU, making relations among the EU nations more complex.

Liu Hairu [0491 3189 1172] (research fellow, Chinese contemporary International Relations Research Institute): I will concentrate on several views of relations between France and German.

1. Differences and frictions between France and Germany have increased since the end of the Cold War; bilateral relations have cooled, and the former friendliness has disappeared. This is demonstrated concretely in the following: I) An increase in national consciousness in both France and Germany, and a rise in the importance of economic factors, which occasion more clashes of real interests. Following the unification of Germany, the United States sought to form a "leadership partnership." Following the dilution of the "special partnership" between Britain and the United States, Britain bent efforts to draw closer to France to great effect. "Third-party intervention" in the relationship between France and Germany is increasingly frequent. Maintenance of the former situation is very difficult. 2) Differences in policy trends of the two countries have widened. On foreign policy matters, Germany looks increasingly eastward, not only because eastern Europe and the Balkan peninsula are traditional sphere of German influence but because they are of crucial importance to Germany's security. Consequently, Germany actively espoused the eastward extension of NATO and the EC, and it uses its economic clout to steal the march in the development of relations with its neighboring countries. It assists former small pro-German countries in the Danube basin and in the Adriatic Sea area. France looks elsewhere. Because of the development of the power of Islam since the end of the Cold War, it increasingly shifts its attention to the south, i.e., along the Mediterranean Sea and in African areas such as Algeria. It also demands that the EC develop relations with southern nations. In eastern Europe, however, France has gained a foothold only in Romania. As a German big power foreign policy offensive unfolds, such differences between France and Germany will increase. 3) Both countries are striving for big power status. Their mutual jealousies and mutual suspicious have increased markedly. England frets and France is also unhappy about America's courting of a partnership with Germany. France used to be western Europe's big brother, the rise in status and power of Germany following unification poses a challenge to France's status in both the UN and Europe. France's fears of Germany have re-emerged. It has two main fears: Its first fear is of the pre-eminent position of Germany in building the EU, consequently, its attitude is not as positive as previously about deepening the sphere of matters within the purview of the EU. Its second fear is that once Germany becomes a permanent member of the UN Security Council, its own position will be weakened.

2. Increase in the variables in the Franco-German relationship. The Franco-German axis dates back to its founding 31 years ago when French President Charles de Gaulle signed a treaty with German Prime Minister Konrad Adenauer. The most important consideration in this agreement was to change centuries of hatred into good-neighborliness, gradually realizing reconciliation between France and Germany. Today, relations between France and Germany are affected by all major post-Cold War European problems and even world problems, such as the Bosnia-Herzegovina problem, the NATO eastward expansion problem, and world trade problems. A public opinion survey of French attitudes toward the EU problem shows a "steady

continued...

SCHOLARS VIEW WEST-WEST RELATIONS, 1994 (continued)

decline in the support rate." Jacques Chirac rejects "federalism," and Edouard Balladur has more interest in the economic community than in the political community. Reduced joint support from France and Germany on the building of Europe is bound to weaken the efficiency of this engine of the Franco-German axis, and have a detrimental affect on relations between the two countries. Edouard Balladur has secretly asked that two small circles be drawn in the EU namely a "military circle," and a "monetary circle," meaning that in involving the United States as a counterweight to Germany, he is not prepared to put all his eggs once again in the Franco-German axis basket. Shaude of the Germany Foreign Policy Association said recently: "Both countries will substitute a new regime for the old. When looking at relations between Germany and France, the new generation will be less swayed by emotions; they will pay closer attention to the interests of their own country." Whoever comes to power in the French presidential election of May 1995 will have a direct effect on the development of relations between France and Germany.

3. During the near term, the main current of Franco-German relations will remain mutual cooperation. 1) In terms of national power, both Germany and France are currently medium-sized nations. Neither has the strength to counter and deal independently with the increasingly complex European problems that have appeared in the wake of the Cold War. Klaus Kinkel [German foreign minister] said recently that like all industrial societies, European society has gone though a profound structural change. "The production-style society is giving way to a services society and an information society;" consequently, we are facing brand new and difficult problems that sole reliance on the techniques that European nation states possess cannot solve. 2) Both France and Germany believe that only if the two nations cooperate more closely, promote progress in European unification, and apply Europe's overall strength will it be possible to deal with the increasing number of world challenges and ensure the position and influence of both countries in the world. 3) After long development following World War II, Franco-German relations have put down deep roots. The foundation is quite solid. Contacts among people in the economic, political, and military spheres and among young people in both countries are very numbers, and unity is close. Although Germany has great power ambitions, many factors stand in the way just now. Germany has learned the lessons of history; its actions are fairly cautious. Its present policy toward France enjoys substantial support from both the German government and the public. Therefore, Germany will continue to forge good relations with France. Although interest in forming a European Union has declined in France, and France's enthusiasm for the Franco-German axis has diminished formation of a European union will continue, and the relationship between France and Germany will continue to be protected.

Xiandai Gouji Guanxi, No. 1, 20 Jan 1995.

VIII FOREIGN TRADE

CHINA'S TRADE WITH SELECTED COUNTRIES, 1991–1994 (mn$, monthly averages)

	Jan-Dec 1991	Jan-Dec 1992	Jan-Dec 1993	Jan-Mar 1993	Jan-Mar 1994
Imports from China					
Industrial countries					
Hong Kong	3,146.4	3,815.4	4,332.3	3,570.3	4,241.0[a]
USA[b]	1,581.3	2,139.6	2,627.9	2,046.8	2,479.6
Japan	1,184.7	1,412.7	1,714.2	1,410.4	1,802.8
Germany[c]	582.2	623.9	693.8	676.5	na

continued...

CHINA'S TRADE WITH SELECTED COUNTRIES, 1991–1994 (mn$, monthly averages) (continued)

	Jan-Dec 1991	Jan-Dec 1992	Jan-Dec 1993	Jan-Mar 1993	Jan-Mar 1994
France	250.6	293.3	313.4	289.1	342.3
Italy	197.6	231.1	215.7	241.1	262.5[a]
Canada[b]	134.9	169.8	199.1	175.4	204.2
UK	103.8	139.1	165.9	137.9	199.4
Australia[b]	112.3	141.3	165.3	150.1	176.3
Netherlands	86.2	77.9	122.1	119.9	166.1[d]
Spain	95.4	135.0	111.6	109.9	122.5
Sweden	47.2	62.0	68.8	68.2	79.6
Switzerland	41.3	51.9	61.1	55.8	70.6
Austria	38.4	45.6	55.8	52.5	63.0
Belgium-Luxembourg	28.7	33.2	35.9[e]	33.9	na
Denmark	41.6	46.5	18.2[f]	13.3[f]	16.0[af]
Total	**7,672.6**	**9,418.3**	**10,901.1**	**9,151.1**	**10,225.9**
Others					
Singapore	185.6	186.1[f]	200.3	162.7	134.0[af]
Malaysia	66.8	81.3	91.3	77.7	67.7[af]
Thailand	65.9	101.6	75.4	90.3	43.3[af]
Indonesia	69.6	43.3[f]	77.9[g]	57.7	40.0[af]
Saudi Arabia	52.2	40.7[f]	53.1[f]	39.3[f]	31.0[af]
Macao[f]	43.8	44.0	43.7	29.4	23.9[a]
Pakistan	29.8	35.1	35.2	32.5	36.3[a]
New Zealand	13.3	20.2	24.3	21.9	26.7
Philippines	20.2	20.5[f]	17.4[g]	12.2	18.5[af]
Total	**547.2**	**572.8**	**618.6**	**521.7**	**421.4**
Exports to China					
Industrial countries					
Hong Kong	2,228.1	2,950.9	3,640.4	3,114.3	3,421.0[a]
Japan	716.1	995.8	1,440.1	1,131.2	1,463.7
USA	523.9	622.5	730.6	643.9	737.2
Germany[c]	204.3	307.9	482.9	458.0	n/a
Italy	108.8	124.5	205.6	162.0	142.4[a]
France	114.6	116.1	134.0	108.3	112.9
Australia	96.7	112.6	128.0	116.8	145.9
Canada	137.4	157.6	108.5	110.2	97.5
UK	47.3	62.7	92.4	78.8	94.7
Belgium-Luxembourg	41.1	36.6	53.7[e]	45.3	na
Netherlands	25.0	36.1	57.9	48.8	31.8[d]
Switzerland	27.4	36.8	53.2	51.2	45.5
Spain	26.8	22.5	53.1	28.7	56.6
Sweden	22.1	35.9	51.4	38.5	64.0
Austria	23.9	19.8	26.2	18.6	24.8
Finland	19.2	22.3	21.4	20.4	23.1
Total	**4,362.7**	**5,660.6**	**7,279.4**	**6,175.0**	**6,461.1**
Others					
Singapore	71.5	93.7[f]	158.8	119.3	116.0[af]
Indonesia	99.3	117.6[f]	104.2[g]	109.0	79.0[af]
Malaysia	53.3	64.3	100.3	71.9	59.4[af]
Brazil	18.8	38.4	64.9[g]	46.3[g]	13.0[af]
Thailand	28.9	32.1	35.8	41.3	42.0[af]
Chile	6.6	22.4	15.3	19.7	8.0[af]
New Zealand	13.2	16.0	17.7	14.6	27.1
Macao[f]	14.3	13.8	12.8	9.5	6.4[a]

continued...

CHINA'S TRADE WITH SELECTED COUNTRIES, 1991–1994 (mn$, monthly averages) (continued)

	Jan-Dec 1991	Jan-Dec 1992	Jan-Dec 1993	Jan-Mar 1993	Jan-Mar 1994
Philippines	10.7	12.4[g]	18.5[g]	16.3	12.6[af]
Total	**316.6**	**410.7**	**528.3**	**447.9**	**363.5**

a. January only; b. Imports fob; c. Includes former East Germany from July 1990; d. January-February; e. January-September; f. Derived; g. DOTS estimate.

EIU Country Report, 3rd Quarter 1994.

CHINA'S TRADE WITH EAST EUROPEAN COUNTRIES, 1989–1993 (mn$)

	Jan-Dec 1989	Jan-Dec 1990	Jan-Dec 1991	Jan-Dec 1992	Jan-Dec 1993
Chinese Exports fob					
Former USSR	1,849	2,048	1,860	2,690	2,692[a]
Poland	383	71	56	119	248
Hungary	84	24	20	45	165
Romania	306	189	84	78	120
Czechoslovakia	376	305	27	38	58[b]
Bulgaria	61	36	24	20	36
Total	**3,405**	**2,673**	**2,071**	**2,990**	**3,319**
Chinese Imports cif					
Former USSR	2,147	2,213	2,109	3,889	4,986[a]
Romania	473	214	200	211	379
Czechoslovakia	522	275	154	176	210[b]
Poland	365	253	88	90	224
Bulgaria	111	101	95	58	137
Hungary	143	113	36	19	62
Total	**4,124**	**3,169**	**2,682**	**4,443**	**5,998**

a. Russia.
b. January-September.

EIU Country Report, 3rd Quarter 1994.

CHINA'S DIRECT FOREIGN INVESTMENT, 1988–1994 (bn US$)

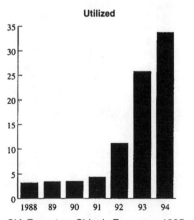

Utilized

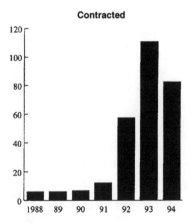

Contracted

CIA Report on China's Economy, 1995.

ANNUAL INDICATORS OF ECONOMIC ACTIVITY IN CHINA, 1984–1993

		1984	1985	1986	1987	1988	1989	1990	1991	1992	1993
Monthly Production	**Average**										
Industrial	1990=100	44.4	53.9	60.2	70.8	85.5	92.8	100.0	114.5	na	na
Agricultural	1990=100	76.7	79.3	82.0	86.7	90.1	92.9	100.0	103.7	na	na
Prices											
Consumer prices:	1990=100	54.0	60.4	64.6	70.2	84.8	98.6	100.0	105.1	114.1	133.5
Change year-on-year	percent	2.8	11.9	7.0	8.7	20.8	16.3	1.4	5.1	8.6	17.0
Agricultural goods	1990=100	56.1	60.9	64.8	72.6	89.3	102.7	100.0	98.0	na	na
Money[a]	**Year-end**										
M1, seasonally adj.[b]	Rmb bn	230.1	276.1	368.9	438.1[b]	526.1	561.0	674.6	866.7	1,128.6	1,372.3
Change year-on-year	percent	41.8	20.0	33.6	na	20.0	6.6	20.2	28.5	30.2	21.6
Foreign Trade	**Annual Totals**										
Exports fob	Rmb bn	58.0	80.9	108.6	147.2	177.0	195.3	293.1	375.0	444.0	524.2
Imports cif	Rmb bn	61.4	126.0	149.9	161.5	205.8	220.0	251.2	333.1	421.1	594.0
Exchange Holdings	**Year-end**										
Gold[c]	mn$	3,179	3,089	3,848	4,506	3,958	3,712	3,618	3,429	3,222	3,517[de]
Foreign exchange[f]	mn$	16,705	11,913	10,514	15,236	17,548	17,022	28,594	42,664	19,443[f]	20,860[dg]
Exchange Rate											
Official rate	Rmb:$	2.796	3.202	3.722	3.722	3.722	4.722	5.222	5.434	5.752	5.800[h]

a. Consolidated accounts of the People's Bank of China, domestic branches of the Bank of China and the Bank of Agriculture.
b. Revised from 1987.
c. End year holdings at year's average of London daily prices less 25%.
d. End-November.
e. End-April 1994, 3,594.
f. From 1992, excluding foreign exchange holdings of the Bank of China.
g. End-April 1994, 30,142.
h. End-May 1994, 8,660.

EIU Country Report, 3rd Quarter 1994.

CHINA'S TRADE WITH MAJOR TRADING PARTNERS, 1991–1993 (th $, monthly averages)

Imports from China cif	Total Exports Jan-Dec 1991	Total Exports Jan-Dec 1992	Hong Kong Jan-Dec 1992	Hong Kong Jan-Dec 1993	USA Jan-Dec 1992	USA Jan-Dec 1993	Japan Jan-Dec 1991	Japan Jan-Dec 1992	Germany Jan-Dec 1991	Germany Jan-Dec 1992
Food	615,632	690,753	153,733	133,356	57,806	52,465	199,768	227,470	24,359	26,516
Of which:										
Live animals	36,596	38,257	35,307	32,670	38	64	219	229	30	62
Fish and preparations	98,430	129,886	24,346	19,931	36,665	26,865	74,421	83,892	1,773	2,065
Fruit and vegetables	162,176	175,269	48,668	40,790	11,193	13,412	61,497	75,604	18,779	18,120
Beverages and tobacco	44,084	60,003	30,691	34,568	2,331	3,653	2,409	2,722	810	1,440
Textile fibers and waste	93,786	74,989	16,006	14,789	703	1,293	27,866	18,393	4,463	4,766
Crude animal and vegetable materials	58,310	65,932	23,705	20,013	10,188	9,811	18,428	21,775	8,741	12,011
Petroleum and products	325,651	320,217	15,468	13,556	47,487	21,118	180,656	172,231	557	1,063
Chemicals	320,741	359,054	101,179	97,000	45,579	52,583	52,841	50,421	28,028	30,193
Paper, etc. and manufactures	26,796	36,363	20,866	23,290	8,364	11,597	1,875	2,351	1,914	2,252
Textile yarn, cloth and manufactures	667,843	723,397	399,945	381,581	81,822	89,484	82,742	86,213	28,482	29,272
Non-metallic mineral manufactures	139,027	142,402	52,944	53,573	32,165	41,830	12,805	18,165	6,052	7,018
Iron and steel	139,094	120,380	15,755	15,262	5,390	6,092	40,897	23,842	2,105	1,532
Non-ferrous metals	46,718	60,953	30,097	28,632	7,784	7,021	11,904	10,533	1,248	3,471
Metal manufactures	141,973	191,513	72,785	89,216	57,808	71,589	10,264	12,736	21,870	24,045
Machinery, incl. electric	706,255	928,945	758,704	927,966	373,012	501,009	58,391	76,859	75,163	95,560
Road vehicles	423,814	96,744	38,320	48,379	14,767	22,924	1,512	2,477	5,318	5,325
Heating and lighting fixtures, etc.	15,414	34,580	34,256	48,729	22,532	40,035	828	1,362	4,417	6,105
Furniture	38,741	68,779	32,897	40,611	33,100	48,012	8,139	11,697	4,914	5,025
Travel goods	41,031	123,053	170,687	195,648	98,288	118,124	17,374	25,837	30,313	31,043
Clothing	1,020,391	1,394,597	777,253	889,279	452,879	546,490	271,021	404,761	190,938	174,876
Footwear	239,623	340,374	295,948	395,926	300,064	397,906	26,111	42,155	20,056	29,933
Scientific instruments, etc.	127,516	176,818	161,108	191,895	44,224	63,141	8,483	12,306	11,416	13,865
Toys, etc.	204,538	290,601	295,444	342,557	347,792	402,160	20,660	37,153	48,977	55,093
Total, incl. others	5,986,878	7,078,339	3,816,278	4,333,895	2,287,520	2,806,101	1,184,655	1,410,494	582,201	623,941

EIU Country Report, 3rd Quarter 1994.

CHINA/US IMPORTS/EXPORTS, 1993–1995

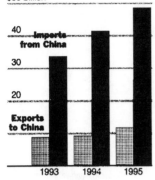

NYT, 16 May 1996.

US IMPORTS FROM CHINA, 1995

	Imports (mn US$)	Percent
Electrical and electronic goods	8,188.1	16.9
Toys, games and sporting goods	6,721.2	13.9
Footwear	6,147.4	12.7
Apparel	4,912.8	10.1
Machinery and mechanical goods	3,783.3	7.8
Leather and leather goods	2,680.7	5.5
Furniture, bedding and lighting	2,197.1	4.5
Textiles	939.3	1.9
Agricultural products and foods	860.8	1.8
All other goods	12,084.5	25.0
Total (bn US$)	48.5	

NYT, 16 May 1996.

US EXPORTS TO CHINA, 1995

	Exports (mn US$)	Percent
Machinery and mechanical goods	2,190.2	18.6
Electrical and electronic goods	1,270.1	10.8
Fertilizers and pharmaceuticals	1,235.5	10.5
Aircraft and parts	1,175.8	10.0
Cereals and grains	1,144.8	9.7
Cotton, cotton fabric and yarn	833.6	7.1
Cameras and film	456.8	3.9
Animal and vegetable fats	396.4	3.4
Other agricultural goods, food and drinks	264.5	2.3
Vehicles and parts	171.5	1.5
Toys, games and sporting goods	70.6	0.6
All other goods	2,538.7	21.6
Total (bn US$)	11.7	

NYT, 16 May 1996.

CHINA-US TRADE, 1991–1994/CHINA'S TRADE IN GRAIN, 1984–1995 (mn metric tn)

CHINA-US TRADE, 1991–1994

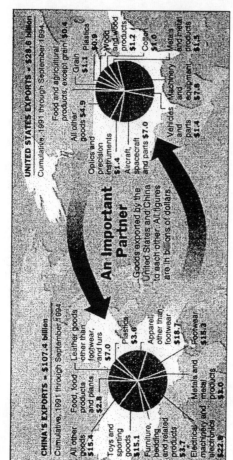

NYT, 14 Oct 1995.

CHINA'S TRADE IN GRAIN, 1984–1995 (mn metric tn)

CIA Report on China's Economy, 1995.

CHINA'S EXPORTS TO THE US, 1980–1990 (th US$)

COMMODITY	1980	1981	1982	1983	1984	1985	1986	1987	1988	1989	1990
MINERAL MANUFACTURES	19731.	32514.	41383.	48093.	60398.	54536.	67197.	109041.	154429.	170424.	197001.
GLASS	18251.	30877.	39246.	46185.	58439.	52462.	63814.	101517.	139361.	146239.	172027.
CONSTRUCTION MINERAL	1480.	1637.	2137.	1908.	1959.	2074.	3383.	7524.	15068.	24185.	24974.
OTHER SEMI-FINISHED	7925.	12367.	11909.	14222.	20984.	23169.	28547.	49123.	86389.	116482.	150246.
LEATHER MFRS	906.	2568.	1954.	3206.	5888.	3249.	4921.	8554.	18672.	31505.	38373.
RUBBER MFRS	146.	693.	679.	562.	2376.	2498.	2474.	4606.	9460.	4897.	6739.
PLYWOOD MFRS	5103.	6388.	6384.	7502.	8352.	10347.	10816.	16149.	25484.	30338.	47786.
PAPER	1770.	2718.	2892.	2952.	4368.	7075.	10336.	19814.	32773.	49742.	57348.
MACHINERY	6204.	41333.	45836.	35405.	44464.	48329.	77031.	225515.	534832.	789999.	1144291.
ENGINES	141.	723.	944.	1099.	1627.	2616.	6347.	7202.	8947.	12091.	12029.
AUTO ENGINES	109.	636.	425.	592.	502.	470.	737.	695.	1561.	1950.	2975.
AIRCRAFT ENGINES	0.	6.	11.	94.	1096.	1126.	2367.	2707.	3950.	5528.	3729.
GAS TURBINES(N-ACFT)	0.	0.	2.	18.	15.	227.	2505.	1173.	1875.	3015.	3471.
STEAM ENGINE,BOILERS	0.	73.	230.	227.	0.	4.	129.	262.	87.	183.	10.
ENGINES N.E.S.	32.	8.	276.	168.	14.	789.	609.	2365.	1474.	1415.	1844.
FARM MACHINES	122.	97.	1666.	3309.	3526.	2926.	3208.	6249.	6601.	3676.	4372.
TRACTORS	9.	16.	246.	217.	244.	121.	84.	426.	623.	455.	1073.
AGR MACH	113.	81.	1420.	3092.	3282.	2805.	3124.	5823.	5978.	3221.	3299.
ELECTRICAL MACHINERY	1765.	3979.	5331.	4103.	10460.	14731.	35624.	130945.	300198.	472157.	684858.
EL MACH & SWITCHGEAR	107.	1331.	2005.	426.	1600.	2301.	3602.	10015.	41074.	64137.	130720.
TELECOM EQUIP	32.	287.	508.	1481.	4773.	5596.	19851.	75545.	145191.	308884.	427923.
TRANSISTORS	135.	271.	364.	417.	997.	611.	1176.	1130.	2301.	4077.	4840.
BATTERIES,ACMULATORS	458.	834.	361.	766.	446.	395.	1328.	1799.	4553.	3910.	5112.
ELECTRON ACCELERATOR	0.	0.	0.	0.	0.	0.	0.	0.	0.	0.	0.
OTH ELECTRIC MACH	1033.	1256.	2093.	1013.	2644.	5828.	9667.	42456.	107079.	91150.	116264.
HEAVY INDUSTRIAL MCH	1915.	5717.	11340.	11093.	9065.	9829.	10989.	19199.	43245.	72229.	104018.
TEXTILE MACH	5.	15.	43.	8.	38.	155.	543.	1340.	2833.	6091.	10949.
CNSTRCT, MINING MACH	2.	3.	779.	157.	130.	203.	43.	1866.	1092.	610.	2236.
PAPER, PULP MILL MCH	0.	0.	149.	46.	45.	260.	285.	493.	207.	1163.	2097.
FOOD PROCESSING MACH	11.	7.	20.	25.	86.	31.	115.	54.	156.	133.	178.
MINERAL, GLASS MACH	0.	194.	852.	654.	418.	96.	702.	2403.	3766.	3464.	4918.
OTH IND MACH	8.	568.	1503.	3267.	2529.	3938.	1456.	2607.	10017.	9575.	16579.

continued....

CHINA'S EXPORTS TO THE US, 1980–1990 (th US$) (continued)

COMMODITY	1980	1981	1982	1983	1984	1985	1986	1987	1988	1989	1990
INDUST MCHNRY & TOOL	1889.	4930.	7994.	6936.	5819.	5146.	7845.	10436.	25174.	51193.	67061.
METALWK MACH	0.	0.	34.	0.	0.	0.	7.	55.	248.	264.	335.
MACH. TOOLS, METALS	1807.	4466.	4960.	4561.	2501.	1943.	3775.	4452.	8933.	17350.	27408.
OTH MACHINE TOOLS	22.	247.	631.	598.	1087.	1327.	2475.	2855.	4748.	7632.	9022.
BALL,ROLLER BEARINGS	60.	217.	2369.	1777.	2231.	1876.	1588.	3074.	11245.	25947.	30296.
BUSINESS MACHINES	27.	16.	854.	961.	1905.	1877.	3115.	8134.	33890.	70858.	120780.
OFFICE MACH	26.	15.	721.	115.	654.	645.	2028.	3154.	14521.	10152.	24294.
COMPUTERS	1.	1.	133.	846.	1251.	1232.	1087.	4980.	19369.	60706.	96486.
SCIENTIFIC INSTRUMEN	498.	1206.	2236.	2484.	4692.	4174.	6505.	16245.	40324.	74636.	113684.
ELECTRIC MEDICAL APP	4.	16.	28.	22.	105.	60.	126.	141.	1005.	501.	1765.
ELECTRIC MEASURING	10.	276.	362.	94.	261.	276.	2088.	1684.	2887.	2804.	10077.
OPTICAL INSTRUMENTS	3.	46.	224.	494.	344.	1092.	808.	3816.	11390.	23699.	42298.
MEDICAL INSTRUMENTS	275.	659.	516.	332.	809.	358.	522.	3262.	12422.	23604.	15692.
METERS AND COUNTERS	1.	0.	0.	5.	1.	18.	18.	2857.	2982.	1479.	5648.
SCNTIFIC INSTRMS NES	205.	209.	1106.	1537.	3172.	2370.	2943.	4485.	9638.	22549.	38204.
OTHER MACHINERY	1736.	29595.	23465.	12356.	13189.	12176.	11243.	37541.	101628.	84352.	104551.
HEAT/COOL EQ	0.	12.	0.	52.	27.	44.	37.	201.	653.	294.	398.
PUMPS	655.	23318.	12383.	1799.	5473.	5175.	5925.	24935.	72519.	26757.	31403.
FORK LIFTS	1043.	5131.	6541.	7848.	5953.	5109.	3478.	7606.	16878.	38699.	47379.
NUCLEAR REACTORS	0.	0.	0.	0.	0.	0.	0.	0.	0.	0.	0.
MACHINE PARTS	38.	1134.	4541.	2657.	1736.	1848.	1803.	4799.	11578.	18602.	25371.

continued...

CHINA'S EXPORTS TO THE US, 1980–1990 (th US$) (continued)

COMMODITY	1980	1981	1982	1983	1984	1985	1986	1987	1988	1989	1990
TRANSPORT	35.	746.	4531.	4636.	4113.	11013.	8469.	13407.	24284.	53370.	99794.
ROAD VEHICLES	35.	489.	3147.	2082.	911.	2518.	2490.	7242.	15271.	39945.	78675.
CARS	0.	0.	0.	0.	0.	0.	0.	4.	46.	28.	0.
TRUCKS	0.	0.	0.	0.	1.	281.	12.	63.	177.	32.	41.
AUTO ELECTRIC EQUIP	0.	0.	163.	79.	162.	174.	602.	1139.	1436.	5660.	12138.
RMV PARTS	6.	264.	780.	773.	525.	1526.	1236.	2680.	5344.	8857.	21620.
MOTORCYCLES	0.	3.	0.	0.	0.	0.	4.	807.	58.	42.	140.
TRAILERS	29.	222.	2204.	1230.	223.	537.	636.	2549.	8210.	25326.	44736.
TRAINS	0.	1.	925.	1107.	1305.	3434.	1142.	114.	262.	1022.	1164.
AIRCRAFT & PARTS	0.	182.	372.	912.	966.	2444.	3006.	3934.	5201.	11179.	18606.
SHIPS(NON-WAR)	0.	74.	87.	535.	931.	2617.	1831.	2117.	3550.	1224.	1349.
CONSUMER GOODS	418752.	680053.	948768.	1141354.	1579882.	1897798.	3051678.	4371031.	5796000.	8798054.	11357628.
CONSUMER ELECTRONICS	376.	3227.	5122.	8399.	24036.	30020.	39870.	174009.	383376.	779004.	771710.
TELEVISION	0.	1.	0.	4.	2.	346.	452.	13058.	14744.	105086.	72397.
RADIO	376.	2970.	4395.	6940.	21809.	27350.	32414.	119780.	235761.	492518.	516632.
SOUND RECORDERS	0.	256.	727.	1455.	2225.	2324.	7004.	41171.	132871.	181400.	182681.
APPAREL	299880.	496979.	724335.	878907.	1048452.	1112977.	1958921.	2350050.	2579698.	3879873.	5263453.
CLOTHING	278029.	457833.	681462.	840687.	1000120.	1051726.	1875148.	2193350.	2215608.	3134903.	3724446.
FOOTWEAR	21851.	39146.	42873.	38220.	48332.	61251.	83773.	156700.	364090.	744970.	1539007.
LEISURE PRODUCTS	3755.	7729.	22023.	23042.	131695.	290126.	414927.	805144.	1204393.	1974362.	2447710.
CAMERAS	18.	59.	17.	144.	156.	1170.	1088.	14341.	27730.	47907.	47473.
FILM	25.	293.	744.	149.	503.	328.	199.	654.	403.	221.	507.
BOOKS	957.	722.	680.	394.	879.	1222.	1429.	2766.	8202.	13020.	15437.
TOYS,SPORTING GOODS	2755.	6628.	20543.	21632.	128882.	286225.	407620.	772920.	1147715.	1895798.	2378475.
HUNTING,SPORT GUNS	0.	27.	39.	328.	1224.	1090.	3929.	9775.	19181.	12809.	3149.
SPORTS AMMUNITION	0.	0.	0.	395.	51.	92.	663.	4688.	1162.	4607.	2669.
ART AND JEWELRY	47115.	37032.	29216.	34629.	63358.	60795.	114984.	139561.	126395.	54571.	85143.
PRECIOUS STONES	1097.	1455.	1397.	1598.	4346.	3943.	6374.	2317.	1896.	1960.	2549.
AUTHENTIC JEWELRY	5738.	6815.	3267.	3273.	3882.	2464.	2260.	2798.	3509.	6885.	12253.
IMITATION JEWELRY	1186.	2003.	2554.	1761.	2301.	2231.	2874.	7776.	23791.	30187.	51056.
WORKS OF ART	39094.	26759.	21998.	27997.	52829.	52157.	103476.	126670.	97199.	15539.	19285.
OTHER CONSUMER GOODS	67627.	135087.	168073.	196378.	312342.	403880.	522976.	902269.	1502141.	2110252.	2789621.

continued...

CHINA'S EXPORTS TO THE US, 1980–1990 (th US$) (continued)

COMMODITY	1980	1981	1982	1983	1984	1985	1986	1987	1988	1989	1990
FURNITURE	9641.	18837.	28645.	33670.	37576.	44031.	50186.	78684.	104297.	123362.	167986.
ELECTRIC DOMESTIC EQ	114.	303.	533.	660.	3074.	11697.	33377.	102209.	318168.	520885.	621914.
RECORDED MEDIA	11.	100.	28.	170.	566.	1366.	1744.	2362.	4768.	20371.	42488.
MUSICAL INSTRUMENTS	571.	1578.	2051.	1583.	1702.	1525.	1521.	5363.	15061.	23563.	35123.
WATCHES & CLOCKS	513.	1722.	1057.	2044.	4033.	6053.	12671.	28124.	56564.	38158.	123681.
MISC CONSMR	56777.	112547.	135759.	158251.	265391.	339208.	423477.	685527.	1003284.	1383913.	1798429.
OTHER	3383.	6317.	7532.	10390.	22466.	43477.	87925.	82401.	136853.	98452.	132838.
TOTAL TRADE	1161102.	2062314.	2502385.	2476773.	3381133.	4221960.	5243179.	6910417.	9268640.	12838800.	16260808.
FOODSTUFFS	69355.	304585.	142175.	138278.	167557.	185903.	228544.	309645.	531748.	538143.	591252.
GRAINS	272.	194681.	2156.	7652.	2943.	3233.	1749.	1258.	3593.	2728.	2082.
WHEAT	0.	0.	0.	0.	0.	0.	7.	1.	0.	0.	0.
RICE	0.	147.	365.	24.	4.	5.	36.	29.	38.	5.	19.
CORN	0.	0.	0.	0.	0.	0.	0.	0.	0.	3.	0.
FEED	63.	46.	4.	2.	19.	3.	97.	35.	1875.	119.	64.
SOYBEANS	147.	194341.	1661.	7450.	2633.	2847.	1424.	971.	1619.	2503.	1940.
OTH CEREALS	62.	147.	126.	176.	287.	378.	185.	222.	61.	98.	59.
MEAT & FISH	8152.	25929.	20012.	13520.	22076.	32895.	76714.	144862.	331576.	317325.	418419.
MEAT	1240.	1096.	1271.	1362.	1357.	1176.	105.	1519.	524.	393.	235.
FISH	6912.	24833.	18741.	12158.	20719.	31719.	76609.	143343.	331052.	316932.	418184.
FRUIT & VEGETABLES	27679.	45317.	57780.	57543.	77132.	75064.	69579.	94381.	108316.	129306.	80204.
FRUIT	4241.	5754.	9141.	13596.	14902.	12900.	12269.	16370.	19252.	22251.	16482.
VEGETABLES	23438.	39563.	48639.	43947.	62230.	62164.	57310.	78011.	89064.	107055.	63722.
DAIRY	316.	313.	500.	661.	1149.	905.	1336.	1332.	1284.	1872.	3341.
COFFEE & COCOA	15458.	19000.	39649.	34396.	40384.	47085.	43002.	34148.	47072.	47856.	47656.
COFFEE	33.	37.	7031.	7844.	1858.	306.	390.	2.	158.	159.	99.
COCOA/TEA/SPICES	15425.	18963.	32618.	26552.	38526.	46779.	42612.	34146.	46914.	47697.	47557.
SUGAR	7783.	8942.	8337.	9030.	6047.	8295.	14156.	8010.	8713.	10989.	12044.
ANIMAL & VEG. OILS	2157.	373.	709.	1675.	2964.	1475.	2734.	3587.	4583.	2621.	1572.
OTHER FOODS	7538.	10031.	13032.	13801.	14862.	16951.	19274.	22068.	26612.	25447.	25936.

continued...

CHINA'S EXPORTS TO THE US, 1980–1990 (th US$) (continued)

COMMODITY	1980	1981	1982	1983	1984	1985	1986	1987	1988	1989	1990
FURNITURE	9641.	18837.	28645.	33670.	37576.	44031.	50186.	78684.	104297.	123362.	167986.
ELECTRIC DOMESTIC EQ	114.	303.	533.	660.	3074.	11697.	33377.	102209.	318168.	520885.	621914.
RECORDED MEDIA	11.	100.	28.	170.	566.	1366.	1744.	2362.	4768.	20371.	42488.
MUSICAL INSTRUMENTS	571.	1578.	2051.	1583.	1702.	1525.	1521.	5363.	15061.	23563.	35123.
WATCHES & CLOCKS	513.	1722.	1057.	2044.	4033.	6053.	12671.	28124.	55564.	38158.	123681.
MISC CONSMR	56777.	112547.	135759.	158251.	265391.	339208.	423477.	685527.	1003284.	1383913.	1798429.
OTHER	3383.	6317.	7532.	10390.	22466.	43477.	87925.	82401.	136853.	98452.	132838.
TOTAL TRADE	1161102.	2062314.	2502385.	2476773.	3381133.	4221960.	5243179.	6910417.	9268640.	12838800.	16260808.
FOODSTUFFS	69355.	304585.	142175.	138278.	167557.	185903.	228544.	309645.	531748.	538143.	591252.
GRAINS	272.	194681.	2156.	7652.	2943.	3233.	1749.	1258.	3593.	2728.	2082.
WHEAT	0.	0.	0.	0.	0.	0.	7.	1.	0.	0.	0.
RICE	0.	147.	365.	24.	4.	5.	36.	29.	38.	5.	19.
CORN	0.	0.	0.	0.	0.	0.	0.	0.	0.	3.	0.
FEED	63.	46.	4.	2.	19.	3.	97.	35.	1875.	119.	64.
SOYBEANS	147.	194341.	1661.	7450.	2633.	2847.	1424.	971.	1619.	2503.	1940.
OTH CEREALS	62.	147.	126.	176.	287.	378.	185.	222.	61.	98.	59.
MEAT & FISH	8152.	25929.	20012.	13520.	22076.	32895.	76714.	144862.	331576.	317325.	418419.
MEAT	1240.	1096.	1271.	1362.	1357.	1176.	105.	1519.	524.	393.	235.
FISH	6912.	24833.	18741.	12158.	20719.	31719.	76609.	143343.	331052.	316932.	418184.
FRUIT & VEGETABLES	27679.	45317.	57780.	57543.	77132.	75064.	69579.	94381.	108316.	129306.	80204.
FRUIT	4241.	5754.	9141.	13596.	14902.	12900.	12269.	16370.	19252.	22251.	16482.
VEGETABLES	23438.	39563.	48639.	43947.	62230.	62164.	57310.	78011.	89064.	107055.	63722.
DAIRY	316.	313.	500.	661.	1149.	905.	1336.	1332.	1284.	1872.	3341.
COFFEE & COCOA	15458.	19000.	39649.	34396.	40384.	47085.	43002.	34148.	47072.	47856.	47656.
COFFEE	33.	37.	7031.	7844.	1858.	306.	390.	2.	158.	159.	99.
COCOA/TEA/SPICES	15425.	18963.	32618.	26552.	38526.	46779.	42612.	34146.	46914.	47697.	47557.
SUGAR	7783.	8942.	8337.	9030.	6047.	8295.	14156.	8010.	8713.	10989.	12044.
ANIMAL & VEG. OILS	2157.	373.	709.	1675.	2964.	1475.	2734.	3587.	4583.	2621.	1572.
OTHER FOODS	7538.	10031.	13032.	13801.	14862.	16951.	19274.	22068.	26612.	25447.	25936.

continued…

CHINA'S EXPORTS TO THE US, 1980–1990 (th US$) (continued)

COMMODITY	1980	1981	1982	1983	1984	1985	1986	1987	1988	1989	1990
CRUDE VEGETABLE MTRL	16630.	9904.	19469.	13336.	11701.	13067.	12501.	18845.	20786.	37363.	45798.
FIBRES	12981.	19032.	16258.	14328.	17086.	15792.	12176.	16375.	16438.	22258.	12884.
COTTON FIBRE	881.	554.	483.	423.	1575.	23.	261.	2540.	91.	7.	9.
OTH TEXTILE FIBRES	12100.	18478.	15775.	13905.	15511.	15769.	11915.	13835.	16347.	22251.	12875.
FUELS	151243.	319484.	643577.	468502.	655908.	1052676.	718837.	530138.	499029.	567722.	723718.
CRUDE PETROLEUM	20148.	0.	212113.	84969.	249017.	758086.	528516.	385047.	437684.	517906.	686313.
PETRO PRODUCTS	131095.	319484.	431464.	383517.	406876.	293903.	190315.	145090.	59032.	40786.	37405.
COAL	0.	0.	0.	16.	15.	2.	6.	1.	2038.	9031.	0.
GAS, ELECTRICITY	0.	0.	0.	0.	0.	686.	0.	0.	275.	0.	0.
MANUFACTURES	772997.	1224320.	1518161.	1722181.	2380649.	2727195.	4054472.	5732085.	7807742.	11272121.	11498289.
CHEMICALS	114755.	134381.	148173.	144593.	171224.	177121.	191939.	215817.	252423.	295423.	364440.
INDUSTRIAL CHEMICALS	69277.	75666.	82896.	67220.	94652.	92661.	97540.	107911.	141902.	155144.	222181.
ORGANIC CHEMICALS	20285.	24995.	26248.	33180.	44253.	33536.	41411.	41292.	48880.	64137.	74890.
INORGANIC CHEMICALS	33657.	38801.	41707.	16122.	32881.	40402.	33949.	43412.	61802.	59338.	69191.
RADIOACTIVE MATERLS	1.	0.	73.	455.	281.	359.	2253.	1005.	1630.	4177.	40222.
SYNTHETIC DYESTUFFS	301.	832.	1428.	2643.	1798.	3601.	5007.	6265.	6701.	10148.	18012.
SYNT. TANNING MATRL	0.	0.	0.	0.	0.	0.	0.	0.	0.	0.	0.
COLOURING MTRL. NES	36.	32.	83.	140.	283.	563.	296.	427.	478.	2584.	2133.
OILS AND PERFUME	14997.	11006.	13357.	14680.	15156.	14200.	14624.	15510.	22411.	14760.	17733.
FARM CHEMICALS	5.	566.	2599.	3767.	2537.	1969.	3649.	4189.	4546.	2978.	1829.
FERTILIZERS	2.	0.	1.	2.	3.	147.	95.	711.	0.	2070.	273.
INSECTICIDES	3.	566.	2598.	3765.	2534.	1822.	3554.	3478.	4546.	908.	1556.
MEDICINES	11354.	20066.	20350.	26962.	24253.	29280.	30186.	33785.	36098.	51380.	48701.
PHARMACEUTICAL GOODS	33.	206.	206.	16.	55.	203.	32.	81.	354.	4565.	7603.
MEDICINAL PRODUCTS	11321.	19860.	20144.	26946.	24198.	29077.	30154.	33704.	35744.	46815.	41098.
OTHER CHEMICALS	34119.	38083.	42328.	46644.	49782.	53211.	60564.	69932.	69877.	85921.	91729.
COSMETICS	342.	1192.	875.	954.	1126.	925.	1680.	1815.	3033.	5859.	6387.
PLASTICS	18.	10.	119.	2715.	5251.	1946.	4107.	4529.	9362.	10843.	15127.
EXPLOSIVES	25760.	27759.	35493.	33414.	35399.	42179.	48169.	51175.	45933.	58798.	56030.
CRUDE CHEMICALS	0.	0.	0.	0.	0.	3.	4.	0.	19.	0.	0.

continued...

CHINA'S EXPORTS TO THE US, 1980–1990 (th US$) (continued)

COMMODITY	1980	1981	1982	1983	1984	1985	1986	1987	1988	1989	1990
OTH DYE MATERIALS	1.	0.	0.	3.	56.	35.	64.	445.	605.	1882.	2340.
OTH CHEMICALS N.E.S	7998.	9122.	5841.	9558.	7950.	8123.	6540.	11968.	10925.	8539.	11845.
SEMI-FINISHED GOODS	233251.	367807.	370854.	396193.	580967.	592935.	725355.	906317.	1200203.	1335277.	1532135.
TEXTILES	149372.	257139.	244914.	255362.	392253.	398933.	505955.	545609.	602375.	615384.	654690.
YARN OF SYN. FIBRES	48.	74.	151.	303.	125.	1993.	5217.	6813.	7561.	8540.	3279.
OTH YARN & THREAD	485.	286.	458.	1202.	1472.	5713.	20397.	6302.	14758.	9394.	5127.
TEXTILE FABRICS	58102.	113725.	101637.	107650.	173163.	143449.	216922.	183337.	160236.	205767.	220643.
OTH TEXTILE PROD.	90737.	143054.	142668.	146207.	217493.	247778.	263419.	349157.	419820.	391683.	425641.
SEMI-FIN NON-FERROUS	31884.	19121.	8231.	4127.	12910.	17086.	19178.	26389.	58318.	36134.	40581.
COPPER MANUFACTURES	21.	0.	10.	4.	25.	52.	54.	884.	1805.	1697.	1529.
ALUMINUM MANUFACTURE	13.	5.	0.	73.	785.	189.	25.	157.	1728.	502.	496.
NICKEL MANUFACTURES	0.	0.	0.	0.	0.	1.	5.	176.	103.	29.	76.
ZINC MANUFACTURES	0.	0.	28.	0.	0.	0.	0.	89.	0.	0.	28.
TIN MANUFACTURES	0.	0.	0.	0.	0.	0.	0.	9.	77.	0.	13.
OTH NON-FER MFGS	31850.	19116.	8193.	4050.	12100.	16844.	19094.	25074.	54605.	33906.	38439.
METAL MANUFACTURES	24339.	46667.	64417.	74390.	94422.	99211.	104479.	176156.	298693.	396854.	489618.
STEEL	33.	106.	2168.	2785.	3400.	2238.	9787.	16266.	33559.	61158.	80730.
STEEL CASTING	12.	0.	6.	0.	20.	0.	0.	9.	319.	13505.	15672.
INGOTS OF STEEL	6.	0.	20.	0.	0.	25.	0.	31.	140.	230.	20.
STEEL BARS & RODS	11.	2.	461.	1317.	777.	173.	3678.	2229.	1716.	2009.	3266.
STEEL SHEETS, PLATES	0.	0.	0.	0.	0.	1.	3.	168.	29.	284.	150.
STEEL TUBES AND PIPE	4.	89.	1654.	1309.	1431.	1319.	3832.	10096.	25820.	38025.	57050.
OTH STEEL MFGS	0.	0.	27.	159.	1172.	720.	2274.	3733.	5535.	7105.	4572.
CUTLERY	5840.	11688.	12654.	12408.	15225.	16139.	15842.	23616.	48154.	81525.	110404.
FARM HAND TOOLS	33.	401.	764.	1104.	2144.	2593.	1564.	2865.	4619.	4359.	4457.
OT HAND & MACH TOOLS	1618.	5008.	11903.	14492.	17914.	17976.	22014.	34510.	57758.	81889.	94663.
OTH METAL MFRS	16815.	29464.	36928.	43601.	55739.	60265.	55272.	98899.	154603.	167923.	199364.

continued...

CHINA'S EXPORTS TO THE US, 1980–1990 (th US$) (continued)

COMMODITY	1980	1981	1982	1983	1984	1985	1986	1987	1988	1989	1990
MINERAL MANUFACTURES	350.	951.	4010.	2343.	2383.	3113.	6937.	4179.	10333.	18081.	11854.
GLASS	184.	574.	488.	1407.	961.	1067.	1512.	1286.	2669.	5899.	4654.
CONSTRUCTION MINERAL	166.	377.	3522.	936.	1422.	2046.	5425.	2893.	7664.	12182.	7200.
OTHER SEMI-FINISHED	185466.	125548.	102036.	67604.	73868.	92370.	97805.	126756.	99929.	121195.	96536.
LEATHER MFRS	49131.	64242.	65123.	26044.	39473.	62708.	31402.	18347.	16743.	7348.	3917.
RUBBER MFRS	4521.	557.	741.	347.	1328.	1803.	1366.	1136.	3473.	2544.	4413.
PLYWOOD MFRS	1425.	66.	22.	46.	777.	524.	2836.	879.	981.	4555.	3721.
PAPER	130389.	60683.	36150.	41167.	32290.	27335.	62201.	106394.	78732.	106748.	84485.
MACHINERY	219390.	222044.	247491.	461848.	665414.	1371263.	1406992.	1126301.	1296014.	1535419.	1318988.
ENGINES	12882.	10259.	6512.	53932.	26663.	77572.	88754.	119541.	135532.	183840.	150390.
AUTO ENGINES	1096.	1876.	3377.	3101.	5838.	8426.	9336.	4122.	8052.	10716.	13663.
AIRCRAFT ENGINES	456.	246.	2201.	5464.	3331.	6204.	12565.	12514.	27919.	96497.	68063.
GAS TURBINES(N-ACFT)	6711.	4198.	212.	24802.	5598.	51247.	45166.	31042.	51778.	24043.	24331.
STEAM ENGINE,BOILERS	4618.	3784.	590.	20493.	11890.	11322.	17219.	71568.	46555.	47194.	41473.
ENGINES N.E.S.	1.	155.	132.	72.	6.	373.	4468.	295.	1228.	5390.	2860.
FARM MACHINES	9787.	2931.	4273.	1806.	18530.	11143.	16383.	11309.	10699.	17870.	10748.
TRACTORS	3634.	551.	3308.	807.	11436.	6776.	5224.	5019.	2913.	7217.	959.
AGR MACH	6153.	2380.	965.	999.	7094.	4367.	11159.	6290.	7786.	10653.	9789.
ELECTRICAL MACHINERY	19211.	24430.	28772.	44158.	54828.	136192.	187582.	158628.	183397.	217908.	240816.
EL MACH & SWITCHGEAR	3253.	3518.	4993.	6175.	8106.	30832.	42278.	24178.	19639.	45182.	76100.
TELECOM EQUIP	5284.	10260.	10284.	15209.	23167.	41759.	62346.	82575.	97622.	77011.	77771.
TRANSISTORS	1188.	2023.	2207.	3395.	3204.	8155.	10633.	7183.	8086.	26679.	33051.
BATTERIES,ACMULATORS	57.	263.	91.	225.	143.	753.	605.	724.	1965.	5790.	1152.
ELECTRON ACCELERATOR	88.	3759.	1635.	4183.	2900.	4747.	7071.	4764.	5969.	995.	710.
OTH ELECTRIC MACH	9341.	4607.	9562.	14971.	17308.	49946.	64649.	39204.	50116.	62251.	52032.
HEAVY INDUSTRIAL MCH	62589.	70219.	65175.	110368.	200866.	507734.	454549.	299237.	384137.	416021.	354811.
TEXTILE MACH	2042.	4806.	2661.	3303.	9147.	18164.	13909.	20344.	38911.	55995.	32585.
CNSTRCT, MINING MACH	42387.	31884.	47846.	51481.	135883.	325159.	137996.	59215.	79087.	73819.	78538.
PAPER, PULP MILL MCH	411.	11852.	275.	864.	2843.	2506.	2702.	2732.	7773.	10253.	9465.
FOOD PROCESSING MACH	845.	1310.	283.	1191.	1697.	5904.	10988.	10722.	8224.	7883.	2369.
MINERAL, GLASS MACH	864.	8238.	2046.	15379.	6565.	15899.	14262.	12218.	50704.	29266.	18922.

continued...

CHINA'S EXPORTS TO THE US, 1980–1990 (th US$) (continued)

COMMODITY	1980	1981	1982	1983	1984	1985	1986	1987	1988	1989	1990
OTH IND MACH	8174.	7099.	8389.	11118.	20157.	77835.	136157.	115846.	124844.	132809.	127495.
INDUST MCHNRY & TOOL	7866.	5030.	3675.	27032.	24574.	62268.	138535.	78160.	74594.	105996.	85437.
METALWK MACH	183.	261.	41.	4075.	4443.	17698.	66885.	17728.	17207.	25112.	22917.
MACH. TOOLS, METALS	6698.	1499.	2425.	17263.	13804.	28754.	52802.	40785.	37611.	40215.	35941.
OTH MACHINE TOOLS	724.	3133.	1131.	5466.	6082.	15267.	18438.	19228.	18874.	37144.	22579.
BALL,ROLLER BEARINGS	261.	137.	78.	228.	245.	549.	410.	419.	902.	3525.	4000.
BUSINESS MACHINES	30736.	21913.	36046.	50417.	101209.	190131.	243616.	188987.	199921.	152371.	137502.
OFFICE MACH	6541.	4038.	9375.	12650.	21258.	32675.	48506.	36324.	46357.	26510.	23746.
COMPUTERS	24195.	17875.	26671.	37767.	79951.	157456.	195110.	152663.	153564.	125861.	113756.
SCIENTIFIC INSTRUMEN	52731.	61031.	75739.	164182.	210555.	315781.	297039.	197997.	236962.	266031.	221794.
ELECTRIC MEDICAL APP	5889.	5189.	10032.	19220.	27836.	32674.	39582.	27627.	35319.	26063.	28786.
ELECTRIC MEASURING	40271.	48223.	55515.	127430.	154970.	184449.	175433.	119632.	149542.	73222.	69174.
OPTICAL INSTRUMENTS	162.	503.	648.	2505.	1965.	5512.	3033.	2946.	4171.	6551.	5936.
MEDICAL INSTRUMENTS	542.	1131.	826.	2841.	4342.	5375.	5578.	3135.	3624.	9161.	8325.
METERS AND COUNTERS	56.	15.	87.	89.	152.	729.	523.	77.	719.	1722.	469.
SCNTIFIC INSTRMS NES	5811.	5970.	8631.	12097.	21290.	87042.	72890.	44580.	43587.	149312.	109104.
OTHER MACHINERY	31454.	31261.	30974.	36986.	52763.	132711.	119070.	150603.	145367.	281380.	202928.
HEAT/COOL EQ	4267.	14593.	8608.	6442.	15273.	25254.	31207.	40886.	37046.	69346.	45750.
PUMPS	18844.	10126.	16933.	12491.	25662.	78058.	60788.	80815.	74598.	113686.	59885.
FORK LIFTS	6807.	2071.	3170.	13566.	6708.	23365.	14992.	17208.	20371.	68585.	63168.
NUCLEAR REACTORS	0.	0.	0.	0.	0.	6.	17.	0.	156.	1539.	992.
MACHINE PARTS	1536.	4471.	2263.	4487.	5120.	6028.	12066.	11694.	13196.	28224.	33133.
TRANSPORT	181364.	35369.	28497.	258493.	418817.	844125.	551913.	518253.	381208.	595973.	807204.
ROAD VEHICLES	17826.	6493.	9338.	22380.	62540.	98728.	86157.	23742.	40703.	55613.	52182.
CARS	112.	47.	100.	149.	1182.	1638.	1151.	662.	3010.	5513.	2035.
TRUCKS	13062.	3812.	5368.	12953.	50331.	80632.	63520.	4062.	24581.	30228.	33022.
AUTO ELECTRIC EQUIP	11.	12.	22.	238.	17.	215.	480.	272.	250.	1859.	1809.
RMV PARTS	3395.	2501.	3644.	8404.	10856.	15377.	19488.	18119.	12043.	17034.	14851.
MOTORCYCLES	1.	6.	71.	50.	0.	30.	0.	0.	2.	0.	4.
TRAILERS	1245.	115.	133.	586.	154.	836.	1518.	627.	817.	979.	461.
TRAINS	411.	25.	44.	136.	240898.	75672.	170662.	7285.	4861.	997.	5260.

continued....

CHINA'S EXPORTS TO THE US, 1980–1990 (th US$) (continued)

COMMODITY	1980	1981	1982	1983	1984	1985	1986	1987	1988	1989	1990
AIRCRAFT & PARTS	155058.	7756.	19017.	234696.	113584.	656983.	294957.	477640.	334017.	536086.	749010.
SHIPS(NON-WAR)	8069.	21095.	98.	1281.	1795.	12742.	137.	9586.	1627.	3277.	752.
CONSUMER GOODS	13975.	24144.	22528.	32300.	28254.	41750.	76771.	63224.	61861.	67860.	64318.
CONSUMER ELECTRONICS	3173.	6821.	1535.	3104.	2782.	2460.	3650.	2023.	2153.	5116.	3406.
TELEVISION	2046.	5372.	222.	355.	17.	266.	603.	55.	305.	3367.	1387.
RADIO	106.	33.	1.	0.	115.	89.	14.	65.	8.	449.	88.
SOUND RECORDERS	1021.	1416.	1312.	2749.	2650.	2105.	3033.	1903.	1840.	1300.	1931.
APPAREL	90.	289.	112.	69.	240.	324.	899.	1574.	1931.	3364.	5271.
CLOTHING	89.	286.	98.	63.	187.	195.	886.	1547.	1919.	3299.	4691.
FOOTWEAR	1.	3.	14.	6.	53.	129.	13.	27.	12.	65.	580.
LEISURE PRODUCTS	5860.	7670.	12534.	21555.	15120.	21664.	51949.	28376.	20936.	19027.	16417.
CAMERAS	908.	2220.	1851.	3530.	3223.	5444.	15256.	7069.	3171.	3294.	4372.
FILM	201.	234.	367.	808.	717.	1653.	4063.	6514.	3074.	1497.	923.
BOOKS	4504.	4097.	3988.	10405.	5772.	13072.	30867.	13290.	12562.	11940.	8064.
TOYS,SPORTING GOODS	247.	1117.	6327.	6803.	5386.	1483.	1753.	1404.	2124.	2292.	3050.
HUNTING,SPORT GUNS	0.	2.	1.	9.	1.	12.	2.	99.	0.	2.	0.
SPORTS AMMUNITION	0.	0.	0.	0.	21.	12.	8.	0.	5.	2.	8.
ART AND JEWELRY	1251.	971.	1091.	591.	1067.	1493.	2067.	1494.	5872.	4171.	1183.
PRECIOUS STONES	1190.	28.	611.	113.	818.	533.	755.	144.	440.	466.	375.
AUTHENTIC JEWELRY	1.	47.	156.	0.	10.	3.	115.	301.	1101.	2811.	395.
IMITATION JEWELRY	9.	21.	213.	4.	0.	41.	2.	5.	42.	43.	56.
WORKS OF ART	51.	875.	111.	474.	239.	916.	1195.	1044.	4289.	851.	357.
OTHER CONSUMER GOODS	3601.	8393.	7256.	6981.	9045.	15809.	18206.	29757.	30969.	36182.	38041.
FURNITURE	225.	1169.	711.	379.	1561.	1134.	1690.	3795.	5299.	2966.	5242.
ELECTRIC DOMESTIC EQ	72.	317.	608.	643.	359.	662.	607.	350.	3155.	5663.	2368.
RECORDED MEDIA	474.	1964.	1966.	3000.	3401.	9835.	8830.	11962.	9937.	11176.	14637.
MUSICAL INSTRUMENTS	5.	26.	95.	77.	35.	50.	51.	155.	78.	307.	247.
WATCHES & CLOCKS	1089.	2880.	1950.	1338.	481.	280.	1263.	43.	55.	160.	509.
MISC CONSMR	1736.	2037.	1926.	1544.	3208.	3848.	5765.	13452.	12445.	15910.	15038.
OTHER	2136.	2533.	2801.	5527.	10474.	39414.	30240.	38867.	58260.	30858.	50162.

Directorate of Intelligence, 1995.

CHINA'S IMPORTS FROM THE US, 1980–1990 (th US$)

COMMODITY	1980	1981	1982	1983	1984	1985	1986	1987	1988	1989	1990
TOTAL TRADE	3754352.	3602680.	2912071.	2173130.	3004029.	3851737.	3105402.	3488356.	4956691.	5806828.	4805546.
FOODSTUFFS	1494187.	1485075.	1308377.	541202.	587928.	116720.	49319.	351033.	716174.	1187392.	536015.
GRAINS	1419738.	1461245.	1299407.	535579.	577925.	109664.	30091.	320930.	698819.	1133349.	513240.
WHEAT	1039309.	1268976.	1046693.	377686.	575319.	97009.	379.	139202.	697838.	1092970.	497348.
RICE	0.	0.	0.	12.	1.	8.	0.	0.	0.	13.	3.
CORN	224540.	62470.	189358.	158140.	2489.	0.	4241.	94926.	0.	33537.	15044.
FEED	191.	59.	102.	136.	36.	73.	64.	907.	625.	6804.	810.
SOYBEANS	155681.	129740.	63255.	0.	59.	12574.	25407.	85895.	0.	6.	0.
OTH CEREALS	18.	0.	0.	6.	22.	0.	0.	0.	456.	19.	36.
MEAT & FISH	28.	435.	781.	4277.	979.	5442.	9173.	5366.	8228.	5714.	8961.
MEAT	28.	426.	313.	205.	295.	3578.	5499.	4343.	7695.	4819.	8032.
FISH	0.	9.	468.	4072.	684.	1864.	3674.	1023.	533.	895.	929.
FRUIT & VEGETABLES	283.	266.	347.	346.	261.	184.	395.	1569.	688.	2951.	1472.
FRUIT	266.	262.	326.	345.	254.	136.	348.	1463.	572.	2319.	632.
VEGETABLES	17.	4.	21.	1.	7.	48.	47.	106.	116.	632.	840.
DAIRY	326.	21.	26.	2.	33.	23.	61.	74.	157.	81.	348.
COFFEE & COCOA	20.	20.	29.	144.	1.	15.	28.	109.	218.	149.	149.
COFFEE	0.	0.	3.	11.	1.	0.	0.	51.	0.	0.	0.
COCOA/TEA/SPICES	20.	20.	26.	133.	0.	15.	28.	58.	218.	149.	149.
SUGAR	14.	0.	0.	0.	0.	24.	21.	15636.	281.	119.	121.
ANIMAL & VEG. OILS	73426.	21797.	6575.	1.	7458.	72.	2758.	555.	1928.	208.	1697.
OTHER FOODS	353.	1292.	1213.	453.	1271.	1296.	6792.	6795.	5756.	44822.	10027.
BEVERAGES	147.	432.	207.	144.	124.	20.	3.	79.	8.	197.	132.
TOBACCO	203.	703.	79.	274.	1143.	1216.	6483.	6381.	4340.	42599.	7831.
PREP FOODS	3.	157.	927.	35.	4.	60.	306.	335.	1408.	2026.	2064.
RAW MATERIAL	1045436.	981338.	548565.	390596.	489815.	599537.	341247.	357467.	759996.	738166.	740346.
CRUDE METALS	15073.	8168.	22494.	90545.	30592.	44157.	1145.	7589.	21928.	50983.	17866.
PIG IRON	179.	2.	4.	1.	606.	0.	27.	508.	60.	216.	86.
NON-FERROUS UNW META	14894.	8166.	22490.	90544.	29986.	44157.	1118.	7081.	21868.	50767.	17780.
UNWROUGHT COPPER	0.	0.	21786.	3730.	76.	9198.	0.	0.	9149.	32750.	9897.
UNWROUGHT ALUMINUM	14894.	8113.	0.	86560.	28726.	34266.	16.	619.	1089.	8987.	1829.

continued...

CHINA'S IMPORTS FROM THE US, 1980–1990 (th US$) (continued)

COMMODITY	1980	1981	1982	1983	1984	1985	1986	1987	1988	1989	1990
UNWROUGHT NICKEL	0.	0.	0.	0.	0.	0.	0.	0.	935.	27.	24.
UNWROUGHT ZINC	0.	0.	0.	0.	1.	0.	0.	0.	10.	0.	32.
UNWROUGHT TIN	0.	0.	0.	0.	0.	0.	2.	0.	0.	0.	13.
URANIUM THOR. ALLOYS	0.	0.	0.	1.	0.	0.	0.	0.	0.	7.	0.
OTH UNWROUGHT METALS	0.	53.	704.	253.	1183.	693.	1100.	6462.	10685.	8996.	5985.
ORES	5403.	412.	167.	267.	21212.	42814.	41777.	26605.	27522.	35582.	83519.
IRON ORE	0.	50.	109.	177.	21189.	32793.	28506.	23681.	5010.	11129.	11372.
NON-FERROUS ORES	5403.	362.	58.	90.	23.	10021.	13271.	2924.	22512.	24453.	72147.
ORES OF COPPER	5399.	0.	0.	0.	0.	9097.	11898.	2094.	19271.	8016.	49773.
ORES OF ALUMINUM	0.	0.	0.	0.	0.	0.	0.	0.	0.	47.	0.
ORES OF NICKEL	0.	0.	0.	0.	0.	0.	0.	0.	0.	78.	0.
ORES OF ZINC	0.	0.	0.	0.	0.	0.	0.	0.	0.	0.	0.
ORES OF TIN	0.	0.	0.	0.	0.	0.	0.	0.	0.	0.	0.
URANIUM THORIUM ORES	0.	0.	0.	0.	0.	0.	0.	0.	0.	0.	0.
OTH NON-FERROUS ORES	4.	362.	58.	90.	23.	924.	1373.	830.	3241.	16312.	22374.
CRUDE MATERIALS	129707.	181320.	253012.	266538.	338755.	390672.	244841.	258220.	566829.	295755.	254106.
HIDES	13354.	7594.	11033.	3668.	22225.	29959.	17213.	11715.	7018.	7400.	1917.
CRUDE RUBBER	4594.	5433.	3135.	5358.	9273.	8589.	13463.	3998.	4255.	6426.	5777.
WOOD	41460.	99178.	219362.	234342.	286981.	328355.	179712.	167379.	447104.	179100.	177975.
PULP	68328.	68625.	17980.	21389.	17884.	19476.	28015.	65262.	95283.	88053.	57510.
CRUDE MINERALS	1359.	88.	142.	269.	792.	1463.	2582.	2972.	2520.	5586.	4627.
CRUDE ANIMAL MATRLS	143.	90.	346.	249.	305.	684.	1975.	2562.	7000.	5079.	5189.
CRUDE VEGETABLE MTRL	469.	312.	1014.	1264.	1296.	2147.	1881.	4332.	3650.	4112.	1111.
FIBRES	895253.	791438.	272892.	33246.	99256.	121894.	53484.	65053.	143717.	355846.	384856.
COTTON FIBRE	701298.	463965.	177774.	4405.	3582.	1582.	294.	260.	25181.	258764.	277213.
OTH TEXTILE FIBRES	193955.	327473.	95118.	28841.	95674.	120312.	53190.	64793.	118536.	97082.	107643.

continued...

CHINA'S IMPORTS FROM THE US, 1980–1990 (th US$) (continued)

COMMODITY	1980	1981	1982	1983	1984	1985	1986	1987	1988	1989	1990
FUELS	1773.	3075.	3109.	495.	730.	2193.	7887.	6774.	12412.	14267.	2775.
CRUDE PETROLEUM	0.	0.	0.	0.	0.	0.	0.	0.	0.	0.	0.
PETRO PRODUCTS	1773.	421.	180.	409.	722.	2103.	7867.	6712.	12374.	14241.	2764.
COAL	0.	2651.	2923.	83.	0.	26.	6.	0.	0.	23.	3.
GAS, ELECTRICTY	0.	3.	6.	3.	8.	64.	14.	62.	38.	3.	8.
MANUFACTURES	1210832.	1130670.	1049231.	1235323.	1915095.	3093885.	2676722.	2734227.	3409932.	3836255.	3476298.
CHEMICALS	383094.	408706.	496727.	353799.	644309.	512817.	438310.	801036.	1379979.	1135375.	1053115.
INDUSTRIAL CHEMICALS	62127.	50435.	48154.	45730.	92616.	99742.	112710.	225074.	329711.	383317.	290906.
ORGANIC CHEMICALS	39685.	44398.	39460.	25464.	71422.	86510.	73839.	149860.	256712.	286579.	245296.
INORGANIC CHEMICALS	22186.	5789.	8176.	19813.	18945.	11329.	36543.	71917.	67627.	83615.	19822.
RADIOACTIVE MATERLS	9.	89.	336.	316.	653.	727.	402.	444.	975.	1115.	1137.
SYNTHETIC DYESTUFFS	16.	109.	101.	78.	746.	88.	938.	454.	776.	535.	837.
SYNT. TANNING MATRL	0.	4.	3.	2.	13.	0.	0.	0.	9.	197.	13.
COLOURING MTRL. NES	38.	27.	0.	0.	390.	0.	250.	223.	964.	7912.	17579.
OILS AND PERFUME	193.	19.	78.	57.	447.	1088.	738.	2176.	2649.	3365.	6222.
FARM CHEMICALS	180981.	159463.	175240.	204157.	303748.	163354.	108239.	283333.	427639.	494300.	548542.
FERTILIZERS	152575.	130954.	147034.	167701.	267294.	152167.	96138.	270004.	378711.	487422.	543854.
INSECTICIDES	28406.	28509.	28206.	36456.	36454.	11187.	12101.	13329.	48928.	6878.	4688.
MEDICINES	384.	658.	1671.	1520.	2278.	2060.	3237.	17431.	7108.	8439.	13945.
PHARMACEUTICAL GOODS	305.	260.	274.	418.	405.	704.	510.	306.	392.	1158.	179.
MEDICINAL PRODUCTS	79.	398.	1397.	1102.	1873.	1356.	2727.	17125.	6716.	7281.	13766.
OTHER CHEMICALS	139602.	198150.	271662.	102392.	245668.	247661.	214124.	275199.	615521.	249320.	199724.
COSMETICS	299.	400.	1466.	117.	534.	587.	1990.	1656.	2974.	3501.	6259.
PLASTICS	119608.	170068.	237271.	92116.	233878.	227985.	192220.	252032.	590364.	208903.	159088.
EXPLOSIVES	141.	62.	146.	115.	918.	1553.	831.	121.	358.	129.	252.
CRUDE CHEMICALS	0.	2.	0.	0.	0.	0.	0.	182.	32.	1382.	3281.
OTH DYE MATERIALS	442.	545.	227.	96.	522.	1180.	864.	1237.	4907.	6665.	3560.
OTH CHEMICALS N.E.S	19112.	27073.	32552.	9948.	9816.	16356.	18219.	19971.	16887.	28740.	27284.

continued...

CHINA'S IMPORTS FROM THE US, 1980–1990 (th US$) (continued)

COMMODITY	1980	1981	1982	1983	1984	1985	1986	1987	1988	1989	1990
SEMI-FINISHED GOODS	413011.	440408.	253990.	128884.	158302.	323931.	202737.	225414.	290870.	501627.	232673.
TEXTILES	133628.	283881.	128008.	17481.	46374.	141203.	62611.	50671.	75256.	62127.	57961.
YARN OF SYN. FIBRES	62553.	199005.	115278.	13377.	38837.	120681.	38105.	993.	24352.	13608.	8026.
OTH YARN & THREAD	4163.	5638.	6881.	99.	39.	90.	63.	785.	5204.	5540.	781.
TEXTILE FABRICS	64782.	77394.	5266.	3435.	5838.	17616.	23053.	46914.	40795.	22612.	19430.
OTH TEXTILE PROD.	2130.	1844.	583.	570.	1660.	2816.	1390.	1979.	4905.	20367.	29724.
SEMI-FIN NON-FERROUS	9285.	2147.	714.	4548.	4368.	10327.	9707.	13498.	15534.	27854.	19848.
COPPER MANUFACTURES	188.	193.	394.	260.	132.	352.	397.	603.	2373.	9076.	4687.
ALUMINUM MANUFACTURE	341.	162.	249.	104.	198.	743.	497.	4110.	8733.	13780.	11950.
NICKEL MANUFACTURES	0.	11.	0.	0.	5.	309.	102.	125.	380.	1406.	834.
ZINC MANUFACTURES	0.	0.	4.	0.	10.	20.	0.	0.	61.	16.	835.
TIN MANUFACTURES	20.	10.	7.	7.	11.	88.	24.	13.	114.	0.	208.
OTH NON-FER MFGS	8736.	1771.	60.	4177.	4012.	8815.	8687.	8647.	3873.	3576.	1334.
METAL MANUFACTURES	84282.	27882.	19222.	36908.	31309.	76918.	25677.	30310.	89818.	272371.	46474.
STEEL	42218.	7042.	10596.	6776.	3467.	11971.	10319.	7304.	61721.	245987.	23027.
STEEL CASTING	0.	0.	0.	0.	0.	155.	153.	376.	1311.	1849.	926.
INGOTS OF STEEL	0.	0.	0.	0.	0.	157.	0.	0.	11.	0.	2210.
STEEL BARS & RODS	28663.	5724.	29.	27.	255.	210.	489.	32.	388.	2254.	2036.
STEEL SHEETS, PLATES	5275.	758.	266.	2954.	1510.	4893.	5654.	4557.	51842.	151512.	1841.
STEEL TUBES AND PIPE	7986.	556.	10296.	3757.	1667.	3957.	3962.	2146.	2991.	87403.	15798.
OTH STEEL MFGS	294.	4.	5.	38.	25.	2599.	61.	193.	5178.	19.	216.
CUTLERY	14.	615.	367.	239.	183.	268.	170.	360.	782.	137.	887.
FARM HAND TOOLS	87.	1.	1.	1.	7.	21.	25.	794.	1026.	12.	10.
OT HAND & MACH TOOLS	29090.	16009.	4570.	26386.	14448.	55052.	8045.	5167.	9374.	10799.	8749.
OTH METAL MFRS	12873.	4215.	3688.	3506.	13204.	9606.	7118.	16685.	16915.	15436.	13801.

Directorate of Intelligence, 1995.

STRUCTURE OF SINO-US TRADE, 1993–1994

China: Top 10 Imports From the United States
By Value

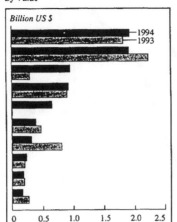

As a Share of US Exports by Category

China: Top 10 Exports to the United States
By Value

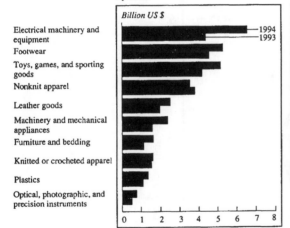

As a Share of US Imports by Category

[a]Products are ranked on 1994 data. Data in these charts are based on HSN two-digit-level product classification and are not comparable to the SITC series used in previous years.

US Department of Commerce, 1995.

CHINA, HONG KONG AND TAIWAN TRADE WITH US, 1985–1994 (bn US$)

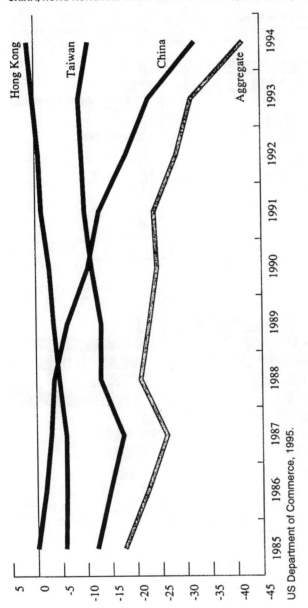

US Department of Commerce, 1995.

ANHEUSER-BUSCH CEO VISITS WITH VICE-PREMIER, 1995

Chinese Vice-Premier Li Lanqing met with August Busch III, Chairman and chief executive officer of Anheuser-Busch of the United States. Li commenting on the China and the US signing of an agreement on intellectual property rights said that since China is the largest developing country in the world and the US the largest developed one, enhancing cooperative ties between the two is beneficial to both, and that a trade dispute would damage the interests of the two countries and their citizens. It was revealed that Anheuser-Busch, one of the largest breweries in the world, had established joint-ventures with China's Qingdao Brewing Company and Changjiang Brewing Company in central China's Wuhan City, in Hubei province.

China Facts & Figures Annual, 1995

EXPORT OF MAJOR COMMODITIES, 1995 (th US$)

Item	Quantity	Value
Pig (10,000 head)	20	22,083
Poultry (10,000 birds)	436	10,009
Frozen beef (10,000 tn)	0	3,061
Frozen pork (10,000 tn)	1	17,998
Frozen chicken (tn)	17,057	38,531
Rabbit meat (tn)	1,459	3,732
Aquatics (10,000 tn)	.4	143,602
Live fish (tn)	5,339	16,605
Frozen fish (tn)	14,200	32,547
Prawn (tn)	396	2,545
Shrimp meat (tn)	2,904	15,787
Fresh eggs (mn)	25	1,141
Cereals (10,000 tn)	2	5,489
Rice (10,000 tn)	0	69
Maize (10,000 tn)	0	4
Vegetables (10,000 tn)	14	118,788
Dry soybean (10,000 tn)	8	44,672
Dry cassava (10,000 tn)	—	—
Dry sweet potato (10,000 tn)	0	206
Fruits (10,000 tn)	5	52,128
Orange (tn)	2,917	1,355
Apple (tn)	14,876	6,785
Walnut kernel (tn)	176	483
Chestnut (tn)	9,918	20,813
Ginkgo (tn)	1,533	7,419
Pine nut kernel (tn)	314	1,416
Oil seeds (10,000 tn)	3	18,857
Of which:		
Soybean (10,000 tn)	1	1,641
Peanut (10,000 tn)	1	8,404
Edible oil (tn)	12,959	9,904
Baked peanut (tn)	4,518	4,615
Sugar (tn)	60,213	23,769
Natural honey (tn)	6,258	7,223
Tea (tn)	12,137	19,786
Dry hot pepper (tn)	1,079	1,692
Canned pork (tn)	5,143	8,852
Canned mushroom (tn)	5,508	7,245
Beer (10,000 liter)	752	3,497

continued...

EXPORT OF MAJOR COMMODITIES, 1995 (th US$) (continued)

Item	Quantity	Value
Leftovers of pressed plant (10,000 tn)	2	2,978
Bristle (tn)	764	4,863
Casing (tn)	2,991	18,169
Goose/duck feather (tn)	1,637	14,065
Medicinal materials (tn)	11,797	25,940
Tobacco (tn)	3,689	5,559
Cigarettes (10,000 cartons)	4,220	124,596
Goatskin (tn)	—	—
Rough fur (tn)	2	176
Mink (tn)	0	1,951
Raw silk (tn)	725	16,478
Cashmere (tn)	87	7,146
Rabbit hair (tn)	429	7,205
Raw cotton (tn)	0	0
Ramie (tn)	342	1,170
Natural graphite (tn)	15,261	3,820
Fluorspar (10,000 tn)	10	9,889
Barytes (10,000 tn)	17	5,343
Natural magnesite and magnesia (10,000 tn)	16	23,948
Talc (10,000 tn)	18	8,771
Aluminum ore (10,000 tn)	2	2,514
Aluminum oxide (10,000 tn)	6	2,955
Tungsten ore (tn)	—	—
Coal (10,000 tn)	161	59,024
Coke/semicoke (10,000 tn)	89	71,667
Crude benzene (10,000 tn)	—	—
Crude oil (10,000 tn)	191	218,004
Oil products (10,000 tn)	19	43,072
Paraffin (10,000 tn)	2	9,3904*
Ammonium paratungstate (tn)	1,408	9,443
Zinc oxide (tn)	2,801	2,490
Radioactive elements/isotope and compounds (kg)	30	41
Furfural (tn)	1,195	1,873
Synthetic organic dyestuffs (tn)	6,441	27,778
Lithopone (tn)	10,515	4,314
Medicines	11,815	114,206
Antibiotics (tn)	1,508	37,449
Chinese patent medicine	1,814	9,932
Medical dressings	3,570	18,008
Perfume (tn)	45	232
Cosmetics (tn)	1,099	4,583
Oral cleanser (tn)	1,783	3,064
Washing powder (tn)	4,684	2,191
Firecrackers (tn)	16,129	20,006
Rosin/resin acid (tn)	13,139	8,429
Primary polyethylene chloride (tn)	4,001	3,015

continued…

EXPORT OF MAJOR COMMODITIES, 1995 (th US$) (continued)

Item	Quantity	Value
Tyre (10,000)	364	35,952
Woodworks (tn)	20,546	34,345
Paper/paperboard (10,000 tn)	2	20,563
Textile yarn/fabrics	—	1,010,892
Including:		
Cotton yarn (tn)	12,266	39,158
Linen/ramie yarn (tn)	2,187	9,058
Yarn with synthetic short fiber		
above 85 percent (tn)	4,147	12,130
Synthetic short fiber/cotton		
blended yarn (tn)	1,734	5,428
Yarn with artificial short fiber		
above 85 percent (tn)	2,698	7,216
Silk (10,000 m)	1,250	40,475
Machine woolen fabrics		
(10,000 m)	1,114	36,040
Machine cotton fabrics		
(10,000 m)	27,927	256,107
Machine linen/ramie fabrics		
(10,000 m)	7,641	52,107
Synthetic/cotton blended		
machine fabrics		
(10,000 m)	18,159	191,904
Artificial short fiber machine		
fabrics (10,000 m)	1,754	28,532
Carpets (10,000 sq m)	118	29,158
Blankets (10,000 pcs)	2	568
Cotton towel (10,000 pcs)	1,407	15,548
Table cloth (10,000 pcs)	266	2,763
Gunny sacks (10,000 pcs)	175	784
Plastic bags (10,000 pcs)	8,600	14,247
Cement (10,000 tn)	67	25,433
Plate glass (10,000 sq m)	475	14,990
Glass products	—	20,286
Household ceramics (tn)	53,036	42,604
Decorative ceramics (tn)	24,521	36,055
Pearl/gem (kg)	128,897	14,875
Pig iron (10,000 tn)	38	58,810
Silicon iron (10,000 tn)	3	16,742
Steel billets (10,000 tn)	29	75,928
Rolled steel (10,000 tn)	43	177,865
Rod (10,000 tn)	8	28,646
Iglers (as received)/forged		
steel (10,000 tn)	4	11,270
Plate/sheet (10,000 tn)	25	94,580
Wire (10,000 tn)	1	7,209
Pipe fitting (10,000 tn)	2	18,412
Copper (tn)	9,057	30,041
Unforged copper/copper		
alloys (tn)	1,336	2,496
Copper products (tn)	7,721	27,545

continued...

EXPORT OF MAJOR COMMODITIES, 1995 (th US$) (continued)

Item	Quantity	Value
Aluminum (tn)	18,107	26,786
Unforged aluminum/alumi- num alloys (tn)	7,259	11,959
Aluminum products (tn),	10,848	14,827
Unforged zinc/zinc alloys (tn)	7,232	6,772
Unforged tin/tin alloys (tn)	3,318	19,124
Unforged stibium (tn)	3,500	10,768
Unforged magnesium (tn)	3,480	5,793
Steel/copper fasteners (10,000 tn)	2	26,802
Enamel ware (tn)	4,587	6,853
Tools	27,416	60,746
Locks (tn)	8,635	23,207
Electric fans (10,000 sets)	553	44,591
Textile machinery	—	8,608
Common sewing machine (10,000 sets)	28	8,213
Industrial sewing machine (10,000 sets)	5	7,367
Metal processing Machine tool (10,000 sets)	18	17,746
Including:		
Lathe (sets)	3,176	5,404
Miller (sets)	414	1,090
Electronic calculator (10,000 sets)	2,607	24,405
Bearing (10,000 sets)	5,028	26,134
Electric motor/generator (10,000 sets)	17,390	73,997
Static inverter (10,000 sets)	1,048	39,817
Galvanic cell (10,000 sets)	62,063	26,749
Accumulator (10,000 sets)	2,036	19,854
Flashlight (10,000 sets)	2,720	8,754
Telephone (10,000 sets)	643	74,036
Loudspeaker (10,000 sets)	6,188	31,602
Recorder, radio, cassette/- Hi-Fi (10,000 sets)	1,647	256,671
Radio (10,000 sets)	1,382	37,683
TV Set (10,000 sets)	105	76,970
Including:		
Color (10,000 sets)	63	62,371
Black/white (10,000 sets)	43	14,600
Wireless telecom accessories	3,755	53,910
Capacitor (tn)	1,457	24,212
On-off/protection circuit installation	13,648	69,939
Diode, transistor/radio parts (10,000 sets)	158,895	26,031
Wire/cable (tn)	18,640	45,589
Container	68,039	194,411
Auto/chassis (set)	1,087	17,975

continued...

EXPORT OF MAJOR COMMODITIES, 1995 (th US$) (continued)

Item	Quantity	Value
Auto parts	—	32,301
Bicycle (10,000 sets)	138	57,099
Motorcycle/bicycle parts	—	23,871
Ship	1,345	30,227
Camera (10,000 sets)	612	53,799
Medical apparatus	—	18,705
Watch (10,000 pcs)	6,790	103,307
Mechanical (10,000 pcs)	321	7,922
Electronic(10,000 pcs)	6,469	95,385
Watch movement (10,000 pcs)	3,009	19,939
Clock (10,000 pcs)	1,956	27,048
Furniture	—	89,799
Bed ware	—	50,919
Lamp/similar products (tn)	45,762	111,197
Travel goods/bags	—	202,871
Garment/accessories	—	2,110,504
Footwear	—	534,957
Shoes (10,000 pairs)	18,956	499,627
Footwear accessories (tn)	5,092	35,330
Plastics (tn)	141,105	210,814
Toy	—	363,279
Football/basketball/volleyball		
(10,000 balls)	391	7,510
Pencil (10,000 pcs)	1,941	4,811
Crafts/antiques	—	4,426
Precious metals	—	80,777
Umbrella (10,000 pcs)	3,199	32,440
Bamboo woven goods (tn)	10,906	10,660
Cane woven goods (tn)	1,839	4,920
Straw woven goods (tn)	1,714	4,112
Willow woven goods (tn)	4,858	10,697
Bristle brush (10,000 pcs)	2,338	3,237
Man-made flower (tn)	10,652	34,914
Thermos (10,000 pcs)	404	8,126

*   As received.

CEI Database, 5 Dec 1995.

CHINESE AND CUBAN TRADE MINISTERS PRESIDE OVER TRADE TALKS, 1995

The Chinese Minister of foreign Trade and Economic Cooperation Wu Yi and her Cuban counterpart Ricardo Cabrisas Ruiz presided over the 7th session of the China-Cuba Ministerial Economic and Trade Mixed Committee. According to sources, China registered a bilateral trade volume of 580 million US$ with Cuba in 1990, and among Latin American countries, Cuba was second only to Brazil in terms of volume of trade with China. However, Sino-Cuba trade declined in 1993 and 1994. Among China's major exports to Cuba were rice, beans, medicine, chemical products, machinery and electrical products and light industry products while raw sugar and medicine are China's main imports from Cuba.

X, 16 Feb 1995.

PRC TRADE WITH TAIWAN, 1979–1993

Table 1. Taiwan's Indirect Trade with Mainland China in Value and Dependency (in millions of dollars)

Year	Total Trade			Entrepot Trade via Hong Kong						Trade Surplus/ Deficit
				Taiwan Exports to Mainland			Taiwan Imports from Mainland			
	Value	Difference (%)	Dependency	Value	Difference (%)	Dependency	Value	Difference (%)	Dependency (%)	
1979	77.76		0.25	21.47		0.13	56.29		0.38	-34.82
1980	311.18	300.18	0.79	234.97	994.41	1.19	76.21	35.39	0.39	158.76
1981	459.33	47.61	1.05	384.15	63.49	1.70	75.18	-1350.35	308.97	
1982	278.47	-39.37	0.68	194.45	-49.38	0.88	84.02	11.76	0.44	110.43
1983	247.69	-11.05	0.55	157.84	-18.83	0.63	89.85	6.94	0.44	67.99
1984	553.20	123.34	1.06	425.45	169.55	1.40	127.75	42.18	0.58	297.70
1985	1102.73	99.34	2.17	986.83	131.95	3.21	115.90	-9.28	0.58	870.93
1986	955.55	-13.35	1.49	811.23	-17.78	2.04	144.22	24.43	0.60	667.11
1987	1515.47	58.60	1.38	1226.53	51.18	2.29	288.94	100.35	0.83	937.59
1988	2720.91	79.54	2.47	2242.22	82.81	3.70	478.69	65.67	0.96	1763.53
1989	3483.39	28.02	2.94	2896.49	29.18	4.38	386.90	22.61	1.22	2309.59
1990	4043.62	16.08	3.32	3278.26	13.18	4.38	768.36	30.41	1.40	2512.90
1991	5793.11	43.26	4.16	4667.15	42.35	6.12	1125.95	47.11	1.79	3541.20
1992	7406.90	27.86	4.83	6287.93	34.73	7.72	1118.97	-0.62	1.55	5168.96
1993	8588.98	17.31	5.36	7585.42	20.63	8.93	1103.56	-1.38	1.43	6481.86

Notes: 1) Source: Statistics on the dollar value of trade come from the Office of Statistics, Government of Hong Kong. 2) "Difference (percent)" refers to percentage increase or decrease compared with corresponding period a year earlier. 3) Dependency is expressed as percentage of Taiwan's total foreign trade.

The official Taiwan policy at the present stage is to encourage Taiwan companies to ease up on investment on the mainland to strengthen the government's political hand in future negotiations with the mainland. However, the mainland market is a pie contested by corporations around the world. Giving up the mainland market not only will deprive Taiwan businesses of the opportunity for expansion, but will also affect survival chances in the future. For Taiwan business, therefore, faced with an once-in-a-lifetime opportunity, the toughest challenge in the days ahead is probably to make the optimal choice regarding mainland investment at a time when they have come under dual pressure—political pressure and survival. The most important mission on either side of the strait today is to develop the economy to raise the population's living standards. The biggest challenge confronting the leaders of both the mainland and Taiwan in the future is figuring out a way to engage in constructive economic competition with each other on the basis of mutual respect and full communication and then moving onto their historic mission of reunification.

Chinese Government Statistics, 6 Apr 1995.

GATT TALKS, 1994

According to reports from Geneva on 20 December 1994, the 19th meeting of the China Working Group of the General Agreement on Tariffs and Trade (GATT) failed to reach an agreement on bringing an end to substantive talks on China's reentry into GATT.

Since July 1986, when China official submitted an application for reentry into GATT, eight years have passed. Why did the talks in which China wanted to reenter GATT by the end of 1994 and to become a founding member of the World Trade Organization in its capacity as a signatory to GATT fail in the end? Will this affect the pace of China's opening up to the outside world?

continued…

GATT TALKS, 1994 (continued)

Why Does China Want To Reenter GATT?

GATT is a provisional multilateral agreement for readjusting and standardizing tariff levels and trade relations among signatory states. GATT, the World Bank, and the International Monetary Fund are called "the three mainstays of the international economic system" as well as the "economic united nations." On 30 October 1947, when 23 countries first signed GATT concerning the reduction and concession of tariffs in Geneva, China was among them. Therefore, China is a founding signatory to GATT. In March 1950, Taiwan's Kuomintang authority announced its withdrawal from GATT. Since then, China has been excluded from GATT.

There are currently more than 120 signatory states in GATT. They include major developed countries and two-thirds of the developing countries. Signatory states of GATT have laid down many principles conducive to their development, such as free competition based on the market economy, the principle of mutual benefit in bilateral trade, unconditional most favored nation treatment and national treatment for one another, the consideration of tariffs as the only protective measure for domestic national industries, the prohibition of non-tariff barriers, the reduction of tariffs to promote international trade, a commitment to fair trade, and the opposition to dumping and export subsidies. Since GATT was established in 1947, the average tariffs of finished products of industrialized and developed countries have dropped from 40 percent to about 5 percent. This has greatly promoted trade among the signatory states as well as throughout the world.

China has applied to restore its signatory status in GATT because it is required for reform and opening up. China needs GATT, and, likewise, GATT needs China.

The volume of trade between China and GATT signatory states accounts for 80 percent of China's total volume of foreign trade. China's reentry into GATT undoubtedly will be conducive to China's commodity exports to the outside world and will also provide more equal opportunities for products of various other countries to be imported into China. This is helpful for China's effort to form an open multilateral trading system to participate in the international division of labor and competition.

On the other hand, since the beginning of reform and opening up, China's economy has developed vigorously. China's position in international trade has risen from the 32nd place in 1978 to the 11th place in 1994. This has provided opportunities for foreign enterprises to enter the vast market of China. Beside, if China, which has a population of 1,200 million and which occupies such an important position in international trade, is excluded from this global trade structure for a long period, the world trade organization will remain incomplete. In this sense, China's reentry into GATT is the inevitable demand of the development of international trade.

China has not waited passively. Since it submitted its application for reentry into GATT, China has unremittingly made efforts toward this end:

—The establishment of the new structure of the socialist market economy in China at the 14th CPC National Congress conforms with the basic prerequisite of GATT;

—Since 1992, China has abolished all import regulation taxes and export subsidies, has drastically shortened the list of commodities managed with quotas and permits, has abolished mandatory plans for import and export, and has abolished over two-thirds of import permits in two years;

—In the two years from 1992 to 1993, the tariff rates of 6,269 kinds of imported commodities have been reduced on three occasions so that the general tariff level has been lowered by a large margin;

—From the end of 1993 to the beginning of 1994, China completed the convergence of foreign exchange rates in three months, which China had originally planned to complete in five years;

—In May 1994, China promulgated the "Foreign Trade Law" and thus increased the transparency of foreign trade policies and regulations;

—Striving to reenter GATT in 1994, China exerted its utmost to meet the demands of the signatory side and made many substantive promises, including setting the general upper limit of tariffs at a level of 35 percent (which it would further lower to 30 percent within five years after

continued...

GATT TALKS, 1994 (continued)

its reentry into GATT), gradually abolishing 90 percent of non-tariff measures, and submitting to GATT lists of future concessions in the areas of improved tariffs, agricultural products, and the service trade.

These measures have enabled China to satisfy all its conditions for reentry into GATT.

Resistance Has Come From the Other Side of the Pacific
In a bid to restore its GATT signatory status, China has taken a series of reformative measures. This is clear to people throughout the world. In eight years, China has answered or explained more than 4,500 questions raised by various other countries. This shows its greatest sincerity and patience and is appreciated by the overwhelming majority of the GATT signatory slates.

However, the United States, a country on the other side of the Pacific, has made use of its special position in GATT to consistently create obstacles to China's reentry into GATT.

GATT makes certain allowances for tariffs and the protection of national industries in developing countries. China is a developing country, and should naturally reenter GATT, undertake obligations as a signatory state, and enjoy relevant rights in its capacity as a developing country. However, the United States is demanding that China reenter GATT in the capacity of a developed country and has forbidden China from quoting the relevant provisions of GATT concerning the position of the developing countries. This is the crux of the matter.

The United States has made demands of China which are higher than those asked of the developing countries and which cannot be borne by China's economy. For example, it has demanded that China abolish all non-tariff barriers on the day of its reentry into GATT and that China immediately practice free conversion of foreign exchange, among others.

The United States is demanding that China reenter GATT in the capacity of a developed country in order to seek commercial interests by asking an exorbitant price for China's reentry into GATT and to make China undertake the obligations of a GATT signatory state while being deprived of rights it is entitled to in GATT. Such a move of proceeding only from its own interests, ignoring the stance of the overwhelming majority of other countries, and obstructing China's reentry into GATT completely contradicts the spirit of fair competition and free trade advocated by GATT.

China's two basic principles for reentry into GATT are: First, China must not be deprived of any right which GATT and the World Trade Organization gives to the signatory states or to the developing countries. Second, the balance between the rights and obligations after China reenters GATT must be ensured, and the obligations undertaken by China should not exceed in principle those of the developing countries. The purpose of China's reentry into GATT is to further converge its economy with the international economy and to speed up its economic development. If China reenters GATT simply for the sake of reentering it without striving for the rights it is entitled to—thus resulting in a certain impact on China's production and damaging its social stability and economic development—it will go against the original goals behind its bid to reenter GATT. This is something we cannot accept.

Being Obstructed From Reentering GATT Will Not Affect Reform and Opening Up
We have worked arduously for eight years to reenter GATT. During these eight years, tremendous changes have taken place in the economic structure of China, and we have been unswervingly carrying out reform and opening up and moving toward the outside world. To reenter GATT, China has improved its foreign trade structure step by step and has also made efforts to introduce to the world its achievements in reform and opening up. This has narrowed the gap between China and the outside world. This itself represents a great success. Before China reenters GATT or becomes a founding member of the World Trade Organization, we are not entitled to the rights of member states of that organization. Therefore, we cannot undertake any obligation which we have promised during talks on reentry into GATT and in the agreement of the Uruguay Round of talks.

However, this will never affect the progress of China's reform and opening up. The tremendous achievements made by China in the 16 years since reform and opening up began has proved an indisputable truth: Without reform and opening up, it would be impossible to have

continued...

GATT TALKS, 1994 (continued)

the vigorous economic development seen in China today. China's economy can no longer be separated from the international economy, and they will become even closer in the future. Therefore, in further carrying out its reforms at a deeper level in the future, China will not waver in strengthening economic cooperation with various other countries of the world. From a long-term perspective, China's entry into the World Trade Organization is just a matter of time.

As a spokesman of the Ministry of Foreign Trade and Economic Cooperation put it: China wants to reenter GATT and become a founding member of the World Trade Organization because it is a requirement of practicing reform and opening up in China. No matter when China enters the World Trade Organization, China will uphold the policy of reform and opening up, will continue to expand its trade and economic cooperation with various other countries of the world on the basis of equality and mutual benefit, and will contribute to the development of the global economy and international trade.

Ban Yue No. 1, 10 Jan 1995.

HONG KONG COUNCIL OPENS MORE OFFICES IN CHINA, 1995

The Hong Kong Trade Development Council, the region's major trade promotion organization, plans eight more offices on the mainland in 1995–1996.

The focus will be on inland cities such as Xi'an, Chengdu and Wuhan in line with shifting investment emphasis of Hong Kong businesses from coastal areas to inland provinces, said Stephen Mak, chief representative of the council's Beijing office.

By the end of 1996, the organization will have 60 offices worldwide, of which five will be located on the mainland.

As of early 1995, the council has established offices in Beijing, Dalian, Guangzhou, Shanghai, Shenzhen and Tianjin.

China Daily (Business Weekly), 4 Feb 1995.

VOLKSWAGEN OFFICIAL VISITS LI PENG, 1995

Chinese Premier Li Peng said here today that China wishes to strengthen the friendly relations of cooperation with the German economic circles on the basis of equality and mutual benefit.

Li made the remark during his meeting with Ferdinand Piech, president of the German Volkswagen Automobile Corporation.

Piech led a German Volkswagen delegation to Shanghai to mark the tenth anniversary of the founding of the Shanghai Volkswagen Automobile Company.

Li expressed appreciation of the successful cooperation between Volkswagen and China's automobile producers. He hoped the German Volkswagen will continue to make efforts in helping with local production of automobile parts. This will be beneficial to both sides, he added.

Piech thanked the Chinese premier for his support to Volkswagen's development in China.

X, 21 Apr 1995.

FOREIGN FIRM'S ARCHIVES REGULATIONS, 1995

Article 1. These regulations are hereby formulated in accordance with the "PRC Archive Law" and other state laws, ordinances, and regulations concerning foreign-funded enterprises, with a view to strengthening the control of archives related to foreign-funded enterprises (including Sino-foreign equity joint ventures, Sino-foreign contractual joint ventures, and wholly foreign-owned enterprises), effectively protecting and using archives, and safeguarding the enterprise's legitimate rights and interests.

continued...

FOREIGN FIRM'S ARCHIVES REGULATIONS, 1995 (continued)

Article 2. Archives of foreign-funded enterprises denote all documents (stored in various carriers) arising from all kinds of activities since the founding of the enterprise which are useful and of value to the enterprise, the state, and the society.

Article 3. Archives of foreign-funded enterprises belong to the enterprises. They are protected by state laws. And the enterprise is responsible for protecting the archives.

Article 4. Archive management in a foreign-funded enterprise is part of the enterprise's basic management work; a task aimed at preserving the economic interests and other legitimate rights and interests of the enterprise, as well as historical facts and data about its development; and a part of the state's archive control as a whole. This task mainly involves implementation of the laws, ordinances, and regulations related to the state's archive control, the establishment and improvement of the enterprise's own archive control regulations and system, the unified management of the enterprise's archives, and the supervision and guidance for archive control in the enterprise's subordinate units.

Article 5. A foreign-funded enterprise should strengthen leadership over its own archive work, make the enterprise archive work a part of the enterprise management plan, and designate specific departments and personnel to take care of the enterprise's archives.

Personnel in charge of archive management should be equipped with professional knowledge and techniques of archive management as well as knowledge of enterprise management.

Archive administrative departments of governments at all levels and their superior departments have the right to supervise and inspect the archive management work of foreign-funded enterprises operating within their administrative divisions, systems, or trades; on the other hand, they are also required to render supporting services in this regard.

Article 6. Documents related to foreign-funded enterprises that need to be kept in the archives include the following main categories:

1. Documents concerning the project application, examination, approval, and registration process for the establishment or change of status of foreign-funded enterprises, and the termination and liquidation of such enterprises (including deeds of association of foreign-invested enterprises, and contracts signed between partners of equity joint ventures and contractual joint ventures):

2. Documents concluded within the board of directors or joint management organization;

3. Financial, accounting, and related managerial documents;

4. Documents concerning salaries and wages, personnel, and legal affairs management;

5. Documents concerning enterprise operation and management;

6. Documents concerning production technological control;

7. Documents concerning production;

8. Documents concerning instruments and equipment;

9. Documents concerning capital construction;

10. Documents concerning scientific and technological research, introduction of technology, and technological transfer;

11. Documents concerning education and training;

12. Documents concerning business intelligence and information;

13. Documents concerning CPC and trade union organizations in the enterprise;

14. Other documents that are of value and worth keeping in archives.

Article 7. Documents prepared by a department of a foreign-funded enterprise are in principle gathered and kept in archives by the department itself. Such documents, according to the specific enterprise's regulations, shall be regularly handed over to the archive administration or any designated department, and no individual person shall keep them as his personal effects.

Article 8. Archives prepared by foreign-funded enterprises shall be classified and sorted out in a scientific manner, with reference to national standards and regulations and to advanced international practices.

continued...

FOREIGN FIRM'S ARCHIVES REGULATIONS, 1995 (continued)

Article 9. Foreign-funded enterprises shall set up a storeroom and install other necessary facilities and protective equipment to house their archives and make sure that they are securely maintained. Those enterprises temporarily unable to store their archives securely may entrust storage to their supervisory departments or local state archive offices. The entrusted parties shall ensure the security of the archives and render good services to the owners of archives with regard to use of the archives.

Article 10. Foreign-funded enterprises shall list out specific retention periods for different types of archives, in accordance with the real value of individual archives and the relevant regulations of the state. The length of archive retention period is set in three classes: permanent, long-term, and short-term. Archives that prove useful as reference or research materials over a long period in the future shall be retained permanently, while those that prove useful as reference or research materials for only a certain period of time can be retained on a long-term or short-term basis. Archives that can be defined for either a longer or shorter period shall take the longer retention period.

Article 11. An archive kept by a foreign-funded enterprise shall be examined upon the maturity of its retention period. An archive examination group formed by persons in charge of the enterprise, professional personnel, and archive control personnel will carry out direct examination of the archives in question. A list of archives that no longer need to be retained will be prepared, and such archives will be destroyed with the permission of the board of directors, whereas the list itself will be kept forever. The disposal of accounting archives is subject to relevant provisions of the "PRC Accounting Law."

Article 12. Both Chinese and foreign partners of a foreign- funded enterprise have the right to use the enterprise's archives. A system governing the use of archives shall be established, perfected, and strictly enforced, with a view to preventing loss and leakage of secrets.

The enterprise shall cooperate with any relevant Chinese Government department that needs to search the enterprise's archives while performing official duties according to law.

Article 13. When a foreign-funded enterprise ceases to operate or is disbanded, the archives of the enterprise, whether it be an equity joint venture or contractual joint venture, shall be handed over to the Chinese partner, who shall in turn properly keep the archives or turn them over to the local state archive office. Foreign-funded enterprise archives shall be disposed of according to different cases as prescribed below:

1. In case of extension of the joint venture contract, separation of a subsidiary from its parent company, merger of enterprises, or other change in the enterprise's status, the archives of the foreign-funded enterprise in question shall be handed over to the new enterprise.

2. In case of expiry of the joint venture contract or declaration of bankruptcy according to law, the archives of the foreign-funded enterprise shall be disposed of according to the provisions of Article 11.

3. In case a foreign-funded enterprise is ordered to close down for violating laws or administrative ordinances and regulations, its archives shall be disposed of according to the decision of the relevant government department.

4. The enterprise may keep duplicate copies of their archives if it needs to do so.

Article 14. An enterprise involved in any of the following circumstances is liable to receive administrative action or punishment, in accordance with the seriousness of the specific case; it shall be ordered to compensate for any loss of archives in accordance with the value and quantity of archives; and the party concerned shall be held responsible for his legal responsibility if the offense is of a criminal nature:

1. Damaging, losing, or destroying without permission any documents or archives that should have been kept in archives;

2. Altering or forging archives;

3. Selling or reselling archives in private;

4. Holding archives without authorization, or illegally carrying archives out of the country;

continued...

FOREIGN FIRM'S ARCHIVES REGULATIONS, 1995 (continued)

5. Losses caused as a result of dereliction of duty on the part of the archive keeper.

Article 15. An enterprise established on the Chinese mainland by a company, enterprise, or other economic organization or individual in Hong Kong Macao, and Taiwan shall handle its archives with reference to these regulations.

Article 16. The State Bureau of Archives is responsible for interpreting these regulations.

Article 17. These regulations shall enter into force from the date of promulgation.

Guoji Shangbao, 14 Feb 1995.

MINISTRY OF FOREIGN TRADE AND ECONOMIC COOPERATION CIRCULAR, 1995

[Circular of the Ministry of Foreign Trade and Economic Cooperation and State Administration for Industry and Commerce: "Regulations and Procedures Relating to the Adjustment of the Total Investment and Registered Capital of Foreign-Funded Enterprises"]

Table of Contents
1. Circular of MOFTEC and the State Administration for Industry and Commerce [SAIC] on Regulations and Procedures Relating to the Adjustment of the Total Investment and Registered Capital of Foreign-Funded Enterprises

2. Circular of MOFTEC and SAIC on the Publication and Distribution of the "Regulations on Trademark Management in Foreign Trade"

3. Circular of MOFTEC on Matters Relating to Foreign-Funded Enterprises Making Tenders With Charge for Export Commodity Quotas

4. General Customs Administration Circular on Amending Regulations on Tax Reimbursement for Exports Stored in Warehouses for Exports Supervision and Control

Circular of the Ministry of Foreign Trade and Economic Cooperation and the State Administration for Industry and Commerce on Regulations and Procedures Relating to the Adjustment of the Total Investment and Registered Capital of Foreign-Funded Enterprises

No. 366 (1995)

To: Foreign economic relations and trade commissions (departments, bureaus) and bureaus of administration of industry and commerce of all provinces, autonomous regions, municipalities directly administered by the central government, and cities with province-level economic decision-making authority; and the foreign economic relations and trade commissions of Harbin, Changchun, Shenyang, Nanjing, Wuhan, Chengdu, Xian, Guangzhou, and Shantou:

On 3 November 1994 the State Administration for Industry and Commerce [SAIC] and MOFTEC jointly issued the Circular on Matters Relating to Further Strengthening the Examination and Approval and Registration of Foreign-Funded Enterprises." According to Article 11 of that circular, during its period of operation, a foreign-funded enterprise may apply to the original examination-and-approval department to reduce its scale of production and adjust its total investment and registered capital provided that it has a legitimate reason, its regular operations would not be affected, and the interests of its creditors would not be infringed upon. With the approval of the original examination and approval department and that of the original registration department, the enterprise may register anew and shall report to the SAIC for the record. Below are the rules and procedures governing the application by a foreign-funded enterprise thereafter abbreviated as enterprise) to adjust its total investment and registered capital based on relevant laws and regulations, such as the "Company Law" and the provision of the circular mentioned above.

1. An enterprise may not apply to adjust its total investment and registered capital where any one of the following conditions applies:

continued...

MINISTRY OF FOREIGN TRADE AND ECONOMIC COOPERATION CIRCULAR, 1995 (continued)

1) The amount of registered capital after adjustment would be lower than the minimum stipulated in existing statute or regulation.

2) The enterprise is involved in an economic dispute and has entered judicial or arbitration proceedings.

3) The amount of total investment after adjustment would fall short of the minimum scale of production or operations set by the enterprise in its contract or articles of incorporation.

4) The enterprise is a Sino-foreign cooperative venture whose contract stipulates that the foreign partner may recoup its investment first and has done so in full.

2. Detailed procedures for applying for an adjustment of total investment and registered capital:

1) The enterprise which finds it necessary to adjust it's total investment and registered capital shall submit to the examination-and-approval department a resolution adopted unanimously by its board of directors and an application signed by its board chairman. The application shall explain in detail why the reduction in the scale of operations and production is being sought and specify the total investment and registered capital after adjustment. It shall be accompanied by copies of the enterprise's assets to liabilities statement, assets statement, list of creditors, and business license, all examined and verified by a Chinese-licensed public accountant.

2) The original examination-and-approval department shall make a preliminary reply in writing within 30 days after receiving the above-mentioned documents, indicating its approval or otherwise of the application. Within 10 days after the original examination-and-approval department tentatively approves its application to adjust the total investment and registered capital, the enterprise shall notify its creditors accordingly and, within 30 days, put an announcement at least three times in a newspaper above the provincial level. Within 30 days after receiving notification, a creditor may demand that the enterprise pay off its debt or provide appropriate guarantees. The creditor who has not been notified may demand the same within 90 days after the public announcement first appears in, the newspaper

3) After the announcement is published three times, the enterprise shall submit to the original examination-and-approval department evidence that a newspaper has published three times its announcement on its application to lower its registered capital. It shall also submit information on debt repayment or debt guarantees. Within 30 days alter receiving the above-mentioned evidentiary documents. The original examination-and-approval department shall decide whether or not to approve the application. Where approval is granted, the original examination-and-approval department shall have copies made and sent to the bureau of industry and commerce administration, The tax department, customs, and other departments concerned.

4) Within 30 days after its application to adjust the total investment and registered capital is approved by the original examination-and-approval department. the enterprise shall submit the adjusted numbers to the original examination-and-approval department and report to the SAIC for the record. Where the value of the equipment and raw materials already imported tariff-free based on the amount of the original total investment exceeds the total investment after adjustment, the General Customs Administration shall be asked to determine if the enterprise owes any taxes on those imports.

All examination-and-approval departments and registration departments are requested to do a good careful job in the adjustment of total investment and registered capital and promptly report any problems they come across to MOFTEC and SAIC.

Ministry of Foreign Trade and Economic Cooperation State Administration for Industry and Commerce 25 May 1995.

MOFTEC Gazette, Serial No. 77, No. 25, 16 Aug 1995.

IX ECONOMY

MAJOR ECONOMIC INDICATORS, 1988–1995

Real GDP Growth

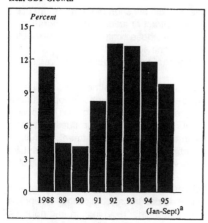

Nominal Growth in Investment in Fixed Assets

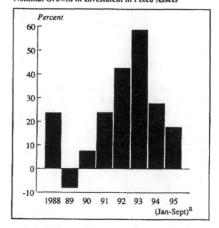

Industrial Output Growth[b]

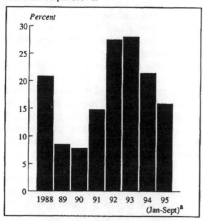

Inflation[c]

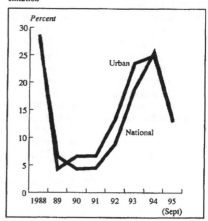

a. Compared with the same period in 1994.
b. Gross value of industrial output (GVIO) calculated using constant prices.
c. Consumer price indexes for December of each year compared with December of preceding year. Urban inflation is based on the consumer price index for workers and staff in 35 large cities.

CIA Report on China's Economy, 1995.

CHINA'S GROWING ECONOMY SLOWS, 1995

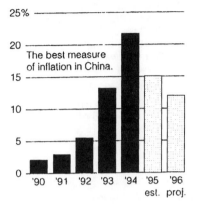

REAL G.D.P. GROWTH

CHANGE IN THE RETAIL PRICE INDEX

The best measure
of inflation in China.

NYT, 19 Mar 1995.

NATIONAL BANK CREDIT RECEIPTS AND PAYMENTS, 1995 (100 mn yuan)

Particulars	Balance at End of Third Quarter 1995
All deposits	36,629.93
Enterprise deposits	13,785.79
Government deposits	1,301.55
Government organization and group deposits	831.34
City and town savings deposits	20,366.75
Agricultural deposits	185.43
Other deposits	159.07
Bonds	1,394.22
Obligations to international financial institutions	382.36
Currency in circulation	7,368.94
Bank funds	2,272.21
Interbank running accounts	4,037.17
Other	-2,444.92
Total funds provided	49,639.91
All loans	36,397.22
Industrial production enterprise loans	8,176.01
Materials supply and marketing enterprise loans	1,024.93
Commercial enterprise loans	10,847.96
Construction enterprise loans	889.66
City and town collective enterprise loans	1,024.54
Individual industrial and commercial business loans	30.44
Agricultural loans	1,839.69
Fixed assets loans	9,012.76
Three kinds of partially or wholly foreign-owned enterprises loans	807.77
Other loans	2,243.56
Bond purchases	2,633.28
Money committed to gold	12.04
Money committed to foreign exchange	3,112.36

National Bank Statistics, 26 Dec 1995.

ECONOMIC POLL, 1995

An influential Chinese research center recently conducted an opinion survey on China's economy in 1994 and the projections for development in 1995. Respondents were professionals and experts from the State Commission for Restructuring the Economy; State Council's Research Center for Development of the Economy, Technology and Society; the State Planning Commission; the State Economic and Trade Commission; the Ministry of Finance; and the People's Bank of China, as well as economists from the Chinese Academy of Social Sciences and the People's University of China. Therefore, the survey carries much weight.

1. Economic Growth: Rising or Falling?

	Proportion of Respondents		Proportion of Respondents
1994 GDP growth rate		Estimates for higher 1995	
Unduly high	20%	GDP growth rate	
A bit high	30%	Maintaining same level	10
Moderate	50%	Slight fall	90

Some 50 percent of those responding to the survey agreed that last year's growth rate of 11.8 percent was a moderate rate for China. Had the growth rate been lower, revenue might have failed to meet the needs of key national construction projects and resources might not have been fully used.

However, some proponents of this view noted that growth was underlined with serious hidden structural contradictions, characterized by excessive numbers of inefficient enterprises and an imbalance between various industries.

Another 50 percent of the experts considered the 11.8 percent growth rate as either slightly high or excessive. They held that this growth rate has caused overexpansion of consumption and a drastic increase of labor cost, thereby resulting in a 20-odd percent price rise. On the other hand, the added value of industry rose by 18 percent, while that for agriculture grew by just 3.5 percent, with the ratio between the two standing at 5:1. The industrial growth rate was much higher than others, leading to an imbalance in the development of various trades. The low level of economic operations has added impetus to the decline of the marketing rate of industrial products, overstocking of finished products and payment default between enterprises.

More than 90 percent of respondents predicted that the Chinese economic growth rate will slow to some extent this year, but said it could retain a rate as high as 10 percent.

They held that the successful carrying out of various restructuring policies will create more favorable conditions for economic development. In addition, various key construction projects have successively been launched over recent years, forming increased productive capacity and lifting the strain on the supply of energy and raw materials. The strong desire of various localities for more rapid development coupled with the growth of non-state economies will contribute to retaining a fairly high economic growth rate in 1995. Moreover, growing savings deposits will spur rapid growth, and increased purchasing power will greatly stimulate production.

Macro-control policies will slow economic growth, however. This year, the state will implement a moderately tight fiscal and monetary policy, with the result that restraints on economic, development caused by capital shortages will become greater. The strain on the supply of major agricultural products will also handicap economic growth. Moreover, the amount of foreign capital input and China's net export volume is estimated to be lower than last year.

continued...

ECONOMIC POLL, 1995 (continued)

2. Prices: Increasing or Decreasing?

	Proportion of Respondents		Proportion of Respondents
Inflation rate in 1994		Estimates for inflation	
Excessively high	80%	rate in 1995	
A bit high	20%	Rising	
Reasonable	—	Maintaining same level	—
		Falling	100%

Some respondents believed that the overheated demand in 1993 was a key factor causing price hikes, which hit 24.2 percent last year. Another factor was the increase of production costs. In 1993, the price of capital goods rose by 38 percent, and the labor cost also grew rapidly. Other factors were the increase in foreign exchange reserves and structural factors brought about by reform of the pricing, taxation and foreign exchange systems. Some experts believed that last year's skyrocketing prices were partly caused by increases in the prices of farm produce and labor.

Respondents agreed that the rate of price increases in 1995 will be lower than last year, with the growth rate remaining high in the first half of the year and falling in the latter half.

Some experts based their estimates of the decline in price hikes on the state's fairly tight fiscal and monetary policy and curbs on investment in fixed assets for this year. In particular, new projects will be strictly controlled and, generally speaking, the state will avoid new price readjustment schemes during the year. However, soaring prices in 1994 will continue to produce a considerable lingering influence on price increases in 1995. The strain on the supply of grain, oil, sugar, meat and vegetables will by no means improve in the short term, and the price of agricultural capital goods will escalate. Both factors will combine to further boost the price of foodstuffs. At present, domestic industrial enterprises are still weak in absorbing growing costs. Therefore, the effects caused by the excessive issuance of banknotes, price readjustment and cost increases over past years will continue to hold sway.

Other experts noted that controlling inflation in 1995 will not be easy. The lag in agricultural development might possibly witness a turn for the better only through a long-term effort. Meanwhile, increasing imports of high-grade agricultural products will be limited by both the international market supply and prices, as well as by domestic ability to bear added costs. Some localities are seeking solutions to losses incurred from poor management of enterprises and the shortage of construction funds through raising prices. Current price control measures adopted by the central government are comparatively weak, which makes it difficult to arrest the interest-prompted actions in diverting burdens.

Some experts surveyed believed that although current inflation was caused by the excessive issuance of banknotes, it is also related to the reform of pricing, foreign exchange, the fiscal and taxation systems, problems in circulation management, growing stocks of unmarketable products and farmers' desire for higher income. Thus, lowering inflation requires time.

3. Scale of investment in Fixed Assets: Expanding, Shrinking?

	Proportion of Respondents		Proportion of Respondents
1994 investment in fixed assets		Estimates for 1995 actual increase rate of invest-	
High	80%	ment	
Moderate	20%	Up 20%	10%
Low	—	Up 10-15%	80%
		Zero increase	10%

continued...

ECONOMIC POLL, 1995 (continued)

Although the country reaped fruits in curbing investment in fixed assets in 1994, the year still saw an actual increase of about 18 percent. Some 80 percent of the respondents considered investment as remaining on the high side, especially the scale of projects under construction. The pressure on investment this year has not been removed due to the existence of the expansionism in enterprises and local governments. Whenever there is a slight slacking in macro-control, investment demands rebound.

Most experts held that the reason for the excessive scale of investment in fixed assets lies in the difficulties in control. In one sense, no one is responsible for the risk of investment by state-owned units, which has not only fostered the indiscriminate expansion of investment, but has also resulted in an irrational investment structure and inefficiency. In another sense, it is difficult to subject the investment of non-state units to macro-control policies. The sustained growth of investment by non-state units has been chiefly fueled by foreign financing.

Experts predicted that, thanks to the lingering influence of the macro-control policy last year, the investment growth rate this year will remain under control. The nominal investment, in fixed assets throughout the year will reach 1,800-1,900 billion yuan, up 25 percent over last year, with a slight decline in the growth rate.

4. Consumer Goods Market: Brisk or Sluggish?

	Proportion of Respondents
Growth of consumer goods retail sales in 1994	
Excessively high	10
Moderate	70
A bit low	20
Estimates for consumer goods market in 1995	
Tending brisk	10
Stable	80
Sluggish	10

Some 70 percent of the respondents agreed that market sales roughly matched economic growth in 1994. Except for the short supply of certain farm produce and a small number of industrial products, balance was attained between supply and demand of most goods, with supply of some exceeding demand.

Some 80 percent of the experts believed that China's market will remain brisk this year, ruling out the possibility of both sluggish sales and panic purchasing. In the meantime, sales of capital goods will remain stable with a slight increase.

Some respondents predicted that the country's consumer goods market will flourish this year. Their viewpoint was based on the fact that those who waited for price reductions may make purchases in 1995. Income of urban residents will grow rapidly, and their predetermination of price rises and changes in buying habits will guide a considerable sum of their income into real consumption. Alongside the increase of farmers' earnings, demand in the rural market will further expand.

Other experts held that sluggishness may appear in the consumer goods market this year. The state will strengthen macro-control, income will fall, and consumption will decline correspondingly. In addition, the state's emphasis on the importance of state-owned enterprises is bound to produce a certain negative impact on non-state enterprises, thereby resulting in drops in both investment and consumption.

5. Renminbi: Appreciating or Depreciating?

	Proportion of Respondents
Balance of international payments in 1994	
Very good	30%
Good	70%

continued...

ECONOMIC POLL, 1995 (continued)

	Proportion of Respondents
Poor	—
Tendency of Renminbi exchange rate in 1995	
Appreciate	50%
Unchanged	40%
Depreciate	10%

Some experts said that the favorable balance of international payments last year featured significant increases in exports—estimated to have grown by 30 percent, up 22 percentage points over 1993—plus the successful merger of exchange rates, the drastic rise in foreign trade balance and the growth of actual direct foreign investment, expected to have reached US$35 billion, a rise of 35 percent. Under the circumstances which saw domestic prices rise by 24.2 percent last year, the conversion rate of Renminbi against US dollars remained fairly stable, with a slight increase. This year, the experts predict that due to the increase of costs in terms of foreign exchange and the gradual diminishing of stimulus to exports brought about by the merger of exchange rates, the growth rate of exports will be lower than 1994. On the other hand, imports will climb at a faster rate, leading to the reduction of foreign exchange reserves. The growth rate of direct foreign investment will also be lower than last year.

Other experts held that the appreciation in the Renminbi exchange rate was brought about by abnormal factors. Taking advantage of the country's reform of foreign exchange and foreign trade systems, some overseas businesses have injected huge amounts of foreign exchange into China to obtain higher interest rates or to profit from the high interest loans. This forced the Chinese central bank to issue a great amount of Renminbi to stabilize exchange rates. Some experts noted that the significant increase of foreign exchange reserves in 1994 was good, but it in turn created pressures on curbing inflation. In 1995, they said, the Renminbi exchange rate will remain basically stable because its appreciation may be influenced by the reduction of exports, whereas its depreciation may cause inflation. Some experts suggested that the country appropriately reduce its foreign exchange reserves in 1995 and expand imports so as to effectively increase supplies of consumer goods.

Beijing Review, 19 Mar 1995.

ECONOMIST FORECAST, 1995

[By Rowena Tsang and Dusty Clayton]

One of China's top number crunchers says the country's economic boom has peaked and that inflation will decrease later this year.

State Statistical Bureau [SSB] director-general Zhang Sai said yesterday the Chinese economy was still on a fast-growth track, but at a later stage of the boom cycle. He expected a slowing down in economic development this year. Mr. Zhang said it was likely China would maintain inflation at 15 per cent this year as planned in the government report by Premier Li Peng.

He said there would be some difficulty in meeting the target.

Beijing set the mainland's economic growth rate at eight to nine per cent this year. Last year, the economy expanded by 11.8 per cent. Mr. Zhang said it was more appropriate for China to maintain an annual gross domestic product (GDP) growth at eight to 10 per cent in the 1990s.

"If the rate is under eight, social resources will not be fully utilized," he said. "However, if it is above 10, prices will soar, leading to an overhearing economy."

The fight against inflation is topping the government's agenda this year. Last year, the consumer price index increased 24.1 per cent and retail prices, excluding the service sector, jumped 21.7 per cent, the highest since the introduction of economic reforms during the past 16 years. [passage omitted]

continued...

ECONOMIST FORECAST, 1995 (continued)

Supplies of agricultural produce was a major factor affecting price rises, and Mr. Zhang said the government should, for example, import more rice in a bid to increase supply. He said it should strengthen price controls and controls on investment in fixed assets.

Jing Ribao, 18 Jan 1995.

RURAL CREDIT COOPERATIVE SAVINGS AND LOANS, 1995 (mn yuan)

Particulars	Balance as of End of Third Quarter 1995
All deposits	6,782.83
Collective demand deposits	808.47
Collective fixed deposits	85.87
Peasant household savings deposits	5,888.49
All loans	5,019.69
Agricultural loans	1,107.58
Township and town enterprise loans	2,595.86
Other loans	1,316.25

National Bank Statistics, 26 Dec 1995.

URBAN CREDIT COOPERATIVE CREDIT RECEIPTS AND PAYMENTS, 1995 (100 mn yuan)

Particulars	Balance as of End of Third Quarter 1995
All deposits	2,953.54
Collective enterprise deposits	789.57
Other enterprise deposits	789.57
Individual industrial and commercial account deposits	122.15
Residents' savings deposits	1,091.79
Other deposits	448.37
Loans to People's Bank	28.57
Inter-financial institution running accounts	263.16

National Bank Statistics, 26 Dec 1995.

FOREIGN RESERVES GROWTH AND RMB APPRECIATION, 1995

The national economy is developing very well. First quarter GDP shows a 22.3 percent increase, and industrial value added is 14.4 percent, both showing a downturn in growth rate from the end of 1994. The second quarter saw further steadying, GDP for the first half of the year, figured at comparable prices, increased 10.3 percent over the same period in 1994. The degree to which prices rose also showed a downturn; the retail price index at the end of the first half of the year being 7.21 percentage points lower than at the end of 1994. National bank loans for the first half of the year did not exceed the plan, and central bank loans were recovered according to schedule. As of the end of June, a cumulative net 28.5 billion RMB was recovered. This was the most currency removed from circulation during the first half of any year since the founding of the People's Republic. Thanks to such an improved macroeconomy and financial situation, the continued increase in foreign exchange reserves and the sustained firmness of the RMB exchange rate were spectacular, attracting attention both inside and outside China.

In 1993, the country's foreign exchange reserves totaled $21.2 billion, reaching $51.5 billion by the end of 1994. During the first quarter of 1995, they increased another $6.4 billion. Foreign

continued…

FOREIGN RESERVES GROWTH AND RMB APPRECIATION, 1995 (continued)

exchange reserves as of the end of the quarter totaled $58 billion. China now ranks fifth after Japan, Taiwan, the United States, and Germany in foreign exchange reserves.

Associated with the increase in foreign exchange reserves has been a sustained rise in the RMB exchange rate since the first quarter of 1994. When the Shanghai foreign exchange market began operation on 1 April 1994, the exchange rate was $1.00 to 8.70 RMB. By year's end, it was $1.00 to 8.45 RMB for a three percent appreciation of the RMB. As of the end of June 1995, the RMB exchange rate reached $1.00 to 8.30 RMB in a 1.8 percent appreciation since the beginning of the year.

The climb in foreign exchange reserves and in the RMB exchange rate showed virtually the same characteristics, namely a substantial rise during 1994 followed by a weakening of momentum during 1995. At the end of the first quarter of 1994, foreign exchange reserves stood at $28.4 billion, but by the end of the year, they increased an average $2.57 billion per month for nine months. During the first quarter of 1995, the rate of increase declined to an average $2.13 billion per month, a 17 percent fall in the rate of increase. During the second quarter, the rate of increase declined further. Since the first quarter of 1994, the RMB exchange rate has climbed an average 0.027 RMB per month. During the first quarter of 1995, it climbed an average of 0.01 RMB per month, and during the second quarter, it climbed an average 0.005 per month. The gentle, straight line slide in the RMB exchange rate since 1994 has changed to moderate fluctuations.

People regard this situation with a combination of joy and worry. Their joy is at the increase in foreign exchange reserves. They regard the firmness of the RMB exchange rate as an important indicator of, and a strong testament to a turn for the better in the macroeconomic situation. Their worry is that such large foreign exchange reserves and so much RMB tied up in foreign exchange causes problems with the domestic and foreign balance of macroeconomic finance. On the one hand, the high foreign exchange reserves have not been put to effective use for the time being, in addition to which foreign debt and the use of foreign capital have also reached a fairly high level, so a substantial contrast exists between the total amount of foreign exchange and returns from it. At the same time, rises in the RMB exchange rate hurt exports. Foreign trade swap costs are close to (or higher than) the exchange rate. On the other hand, from the angle of the Chinese People's Bank's monetary policy, a continuing rise in foreign exchange reserves has forced the issuance of large quantities of RMB, causing a tremendous amount of basic money to be put into circulation. This is also bound to have a certain adverse effect on domestic inflation that is seemingly at odds with the country's anti-inflation efforts.

The steady climb in the RMB exchange rate during a trend toward devaluation of the US dollar is understandable, but its steady climb in the face of a steady rise in domestic inflation is puzzling and worrisome. The puzzlement lies in why the exchange rate remains steady when domestic inflation is running at more than 20 percent. The worry is that it is impossible to say when inflationary pressure driving down the exchange rate will suddenly burst forth forcing a sudden and tremendous slide in the RMB exchange rate.

This both heartening and worrisome trend also has a negative effect on analysis of the future direction of foreign exchange reserves and RMB exchange rates. Those who see the trend as heartening feel that although foreign exchange reserves may be a little high, they are not too high, or that 50 billion in foreign exchange reserves is basically normal. They feel that foreign exchange reserves will increase in the future with the inflow of foreign capital resulting from a favorable balance of trade, but the mechanism being what it is, there is nothing wrong with this (or nothing can be done about it). Since foreign exchange market supply of foreign exchange may continue greater than demand, the RMB exchange rate is likely to remain stable. At the same time, however, its possible effect on foreign trade will likely be relatively slight. In other words, no good way exists to make matters fine in both regards. Those who see the trend as worrisome feel that in view of the assimilation and disappearance of the various factors causing the increase in foreign exchange reserves in 1995, and in view of the central bank's moderate tight monetary policy, the inflow of foreign money will also decrease, thereby causing a slowing

continued...

FOREIGN RESERVES GROWTH AND RMB APPRECIATION, 1995 (continued)

in the growth of foreign exchange reserves. Thus, the RMB exchange rate will gradually become less firm, the RMB foreign exchange rate possibly being forced down out of concern for foreign trade exports and to meet the rise in foreign exchange costs.

Cause and Effect of the "Twin Rise," and Its Remedies

First of all, in international balance of payments terms, a favorable balance of trade and invisibles can be the only source of accumulated foreign exchange reserves, and a net inflow of capital. People used to put much stock in analyzing the effect of capital inflow on foreign exchange reserves growth. One view even held that the inflow of foreign capital was the primary influencing factor when, actually, the balance of trade—particularly a great increase in exports—is the main factor influencing foreign exchange reserves growth. Please see the following table:

	1992	1993	1994	First Quarter 1995
Foreign trade exports ($100 million)	849	918	1,210	309.5
Foreign trade exports (percent increase)	(18.3)	(8)	(31.9)	(62)
Foreign trade imports ($100 million)	806	1,039	1,157	238

Finance and Trade Economics No. 10, 11 Oct 1995.

SCALE OF INVESTMENT AND INFLATION, 1981–1994

	Investment Rate	Currency Inflation Rate		Investment Rate	Currency Inflation Rate
1981	20.1	2.4	1988	25.9	18.5
1982	23.7	4.9	1989	25.2	17.8
1983	24.7	4.5	1990	27.3	3.1
1984	26.5	2.8	1991	32.2	2.9
1985	29.8	8.8	1992	37.7	5.4
1986	31.2	6.0	1993	37.1	13.2
1987	32.0	7.3	1994*		19.5

*   The 1994 figures are estimated.

X, 23 Mar 1995.

FINANCE, CREDIT AND INVESTMENT INSTITUTION CREDIT RECEIPTS AND EXPENDITURES, 1995
(100 mn yuan)

Particulars	Balance as of End of Third Quarter 1995
All deposits	2,570.32
Consignment deposits	1,799.43
Trust deposits	592.66
Security deposits	21.67
Other deposits	156.56
Bond issues	17.97

National Bank Statistics, 26 Dec 1995.

continued...

OTHER BANK CREDIT RECEIPTS AND EXPENDITURES, 1995 (100 mn yuan)

Funds Provided	Balance as of End of Third Quarter 1995
All deposits	1,338.89
Enterprise deposits	914.18
City and town savings deposits	214.15
Rural deposits	2.30
Trust deposits	173.12
Other deposits	35.14
Finance bonds	0.23
Security business funds	18.23

National Bank Statistics, 26 Dec 1995.

IMPACT OF EXCHANGE REFORM ON BANKS, 1994

I. Since 1 January 1994, China's foreign exchange system has been significantly reformed, the immediate aim of which was to achieve conditional renminbi convertibility for current accounts. This has had an enormous impact on the growth of China's financial firms, particularly bringing a series of changes to the development of foreign exchange financial services and to the operation and management of financial assets.

1. It has provided the terms for the fair competition and equal development of China's financial firms.

Foreign exchange reform will forcefully promote the formation of an order of equal competition among banks, eliminating past factors such as an irrational division of labor and policy inequality among banks, and making it possible for all banks to develop their advantages in fair competition to grow together. Before foreign exchange reform, the Bank of China's [BOC] foreign exchange assets had the absolute advantage, with abundant might, because the BOC had been in operation longer, had rich experience and a very quick and convenient foreign exchange settlement system, while all other foreign exchange banks had been in operation for a shorter period of time, and lacked experience, so that their foreign exchange settlement generally had to be handled by the BOC, which had a certain negative impact on their settlement speed. But since foreign exchange reform, foreign exchange settlement is organized by the foreign exchange management sector, so that all designated foreign exchange banks can handle foreign exchange settlement and sales services, as well as local-foreign currency fund transaction services through the exchange transaction market. Local-foreign currency fund conversion is more convenient and faster, while foreign exchange funds are obviously less advantageous, with enterprise import exchange purchases, export earnings, and exchange settlements all inseparable from renminbi funds and services. In this sense, renminbi funds obviously are particularly crucial in foreign exchange dealings. This enables all designated foreign exchange banks to try to expand their business and raise their efficiency in a climate of fair competition and equal development.

2. As to our banking asset structure, local and foreign currency assets will be inherently consolidated and more mutually complementary, with foreign exchange assets better diversified and internationalized.

Since foreign exchange management reform, our exchange transaction market has increasingly improved, which has changed the mandated separation of local and foreign currency assets. Banks can act in line with their real business development needs and operating and management objectives, adjusting their order of local and foreign currency business, and rationally deploying their local and foreign currency fund positions. Since we went to an exchange system of conversion and sale by banks, the foreign exchange fund-source structure of banks has changed, with existing deposits by state enterprises and institutions down, while banks retain their foreign exchange capital, individual foreign currency savings deposits, and

continued...

IMPACT OF EXCHANGE REFORM ON BANKS, 1994 (continued)

FIE [expansion unknown] foreign exchange deposits. In a certain sense, the possession of large amounts of foreign exchange funds is certainly not a good thing, As domestic cash lending shrinks, with enterprises shifting from loans to exchange purchases, banks should consider shifting part of their foreign exchange funds from domestic to international markets, and shifting their asset form from an overemphasis on credit to an equal emphasis on interbank lending and financial investment along with credit, to diversify their foreign exchange asset operations. In the long run, these changes in foreign exchange asset structure and operating form will spur banks to internationalize their foreign exchange operations, thus raising their foreign exchange asset operation and management level.

3. Renminbi funds needed by banks to cover foreign exchange holdings will increase, directly affecting the operation of renminbi assets.

In early 1994, in support of the exchange rate merger, the central bank was forced to put into circulation in January and February net amounts of respectively 79.423 billion yuan and 44.049 billion yuan. While all designated foreign exchange banks have handled their own renminbi funds needed for exchange settlement since 1 April, with the central bank withdrawing currency from circulation better from March through June, this was still not enough to make up the enormous demand for domestic currency formed by the sharp increase over 1993 in the first half of 182.527 billion yuan in foreign exchange holdings. So the central bank could only use the domestic enterprise funding source of savings deposits, which was bound to make the existing fund shortages of domestic enterprises even worse, thus having an enormous impact on the next round of financial deficits and even expansion of the money supply. The real causes of China's sharp increases in money supply in 1992 and 1993 were financial deficits and hard fiscal deficits, while the biggest factor affecting our money supply in the first half of 1994 was the sharp increase in our foreign exchange holdings. If our renminbi exchange rate stays at its low price-position of the first half, the net inflow of China's foreign exchange assets in the second half will not be lower than in the first half, with the monetary demand so formed being hardly sustainable by the current Chinese economy, which will undoubtedly add to the difficulties of bank asset operations, putting renminbi funds in even shorter supply.

4. As to profits and exchange rate changes, there is a certain degree of risk.

In a floating exchange rate system, with foreign exchange operations highly marketized, whether banks, when conducting market foreign exchange transactions and handling exchange settlement and sales services, can effectively avoid and prevent exchange rate risks, will affect bank profits. If banks incorrectly manipulate their local and foreign currency positions in self-run exchange settlement and sales, this will create a certain degree of interest losses. With the renminbi funds needed for exchange settlement having to be handled by banks—in which to handle enterprise exchange settlement, banks must take out renminbi revolving funds to buy foreign currency for enterprises, with enterprises buying exchange from banks, and banks having to use their own foreign exchange revolving funds to sell—then how the designated foreign exchange banks handle the foreign currency ratio of their exchange settlement and sale revolving funds is a very crucial matter. With the current terms of the interest rate difference between local and foreign currency being as high as 4 percent, a foreign currency long position of $1 million would mean that banks could lose 340,000 renminbi in interest. Meanwhile, when the designated foreign exchange banks handle enterprise exchange settlement and sales, if they buy more of a foreign currency than they sell, such foreign currency is called long foreign currency. When such long currency is later sold, there may be profits or losses due to exchange rate changes, posing loss risks. So in the course of partially adjusting foreign exchange assets, due to the relatively high risk, with a higher percentage of lower return-rate interbank lending and financial investment, short-term book foreign exchange surpluses may be down somewhat.

II. The above analysis shows that foreign exchange reform has had a far-reaching impact on our financial businesses. So all foreign exchange banks need to take relevant contingency steps to adjust their local-to-foreign currency fund operations and asset structures, as well as to ensure sound internal mechanisms.

continued...

IMPACT OF EXCHANGE REFORM ON BANKS, 1994 (continued)

1. The foreign exchange market should be closely coordinated with the renminbi fund market.

Merging our local and foreign currency funds hinges mainly on the degree of coordination between our foreign exchange and renminbi fund markets. As it is only on these terms that the local and foreign currency funds of all banks can be quickly converted, the central bank needs to conduct further system reform, better merging our foreign exchange and renminbi fund markets, to form a standard money market combining local and foreign currency funds. Such a market can handle not only lending in foreign currency and renminbi funds, but also local-foreign currency transactions and spot and futures transactions between foreign currencies, to ensure that both local and foreign currencies operate smoothly in one market system.

2. We need to establish mechanisms for the organic combination and coordinated development of local and foreign currency operations.

We need to study ways to draw up a realistic and operable system in areas such as organizational setup, personnel disposition, work coordination, and fund allocation. As to form, this should generally be head offices being responsible for fund management and planning, with qualified, mature branches being granted a certain degree of autonomy to facilitate adjustment in line with market conditions, increase flexibility, and raise fund operating efficiency.

3. We need to set the most rational ratio of local-to-foreign-currency revolving funds.

Setting the best ratio of local-to-foreign-currency funds is a key method in the scientific use of funds. It hinges mainly on the following points: 1) If the Shanghai Exchange Transaction Center's operations are normal, if foreign exchange can be bought and sold conveniently and quickly, and if transactions are convenient, designated foreign exchange banks can force their turnover down to the minimum; 2) exchange rate trends need to be accurately forecast; 3) foreign currency exchange rates need to be kept abreast of in a timely fashion, to tighten capital management. If these points can be achieved, we can ensure that funds meet exchange settlement and sale needs, while using our capital to the maximum to reap the greatest profits. In addition, prevention of exchange rate risk in exchange settlement and sale is very crucial. Since we began to practice self-run exchange settlement and sale by banks on 1 April 1994, the renminbi to US dollar exchange rate has quietly risen daily within a narrow range, with the exchange rate of the US dollar to the renminbi down 461 points from the end of April 10 the end of June, so that any bank that overbought without balancing would have sustained sharp exchange rate losses.

Intertrade No. 11, 20 Nov 1994.

EXCHANGE RATES, GOLD AND FOREIGN EXCHANGE RESERVES, 1995

Exchange Rates	July	August	September
Special drawing rights units conversions into renminbi (end of period figure)	12.9185	12.4081	12.5021
US dollar conversions into renminbi (end of period figure)	8.3003	8.3198	8.3185
US dollar conversions into renminbi (average figure)	8.3007	8.3075	8.3188
Gold reserves (10,000 ounces)	1,267	1,267	1,267
National foreign exchange reserves ($100 mn)	655.94	675.19	698.00

National Bank Statistics, 26 Dec 1995.

SUPPLY OF FORMS OF MONEY, 1995

Particulars	End of Quarter Balance	Balance as Percent of Same Period in 1994
Money and quasi-money (M_2)	56,813.2	30.6
Money (M_1)	22,493.8	18.3
Cash in circulation (M_0)	7,368.9	14.9
Demand deposits	15,124.8	20.1
Quasi-money	34,319.4	40.1
Fixed deposits	3,095.7	73.2
Savings deposits	27,569.7	38.1
Other deposits	3,654.0	33.1

National Bank Statistics, 26 Dec 1995.

GOVERNMENT TO CONTROL PRICES, 1995

What is the trend of commodity prices at the beginning of the year? Are prices going up or down? Whether or not inflation can be capped at 15 percent is an issue people are most concerned about. With this key issue of public concern in mind, we interviewed the people concerned at the market and price regulation and control department of the State Planning Commission.

Overall Level of Commodity Prices At the Beginning of the Year
Since the central and local governments at various levels adopted diverse regulatory and control measures to contain spiraling commodity prices in November last year, the rise of commodity prices has slowed down and has begun to decrease. In November and December, the retail commodity prices were up 25 percent and 23.8 percent respectively over the same period of the previous year, a successive drop of 1-2 percentage points.

In January this year, even though demand for commodities was relatively high and purchasing power was strong as a result of the New Year and the Spring Festival, the rate of increase in commodity prices continued to decline over the corresponding period of last year.

The statistics for January released by the State Statistics Bureau showed that the monthly chain index for January this year rose while the index of comparable items dropped. The index of retail commodity prices in January rose 21.2 percent, representing a drop of 2 percentage points over December 1994. The indices of comparable items in February and March are expected to continue to fall.

An Urgent Task Is To Stabilize the Prices of Chemical Fertilizers and Other Means of Agricultural Production
The commodity prices frequently discussed at the beginning of the year focus on two main points: First, grain prices still rose in some localities in the spring. Moreover, with the arrival of the spring plowing season, chemical fertilizer prices surged sharply. The rise in grain prices was effected by the reduction of grain yields. The main reasons for the increasing prices of chemical fertilizer are: First, in the past two years, the state has substantially raised the prices of oil, natural gas, coal, railway transportation, power and other commodities, thereby boosting the production cost of chemical fertilizers. Second, increase in grain prices last year has raised peasants' enthusiasm to grow grain and a rapid increase in demand for chemical fertilizers has caused supply to fall short of demand. Third, in the last few months, chemical fertilizer prices in the international market have also surged significantly and the order price for bulk urea has risen to more than $245 [per ton]. Prices for the means of agricultural production such as farm chemicals, plastic sheeting, and small farm machinery have also increased to various extent. This issue has drawn the close attention of the relevant department which is taking appropriate measures.

This year, agriculture should be developed to a new stage and governments at all levels will also increase inputs in agriculture. This will enhance demand for the means of agricultural

continued...

GOVERNMENT TO CONTROL PRICES, 1995 (continued)

production. If the supply of chemical fertilizers cannot be guaranteed, we shall lose the foundation for achieving a bumper harvest for the whole year. If chemical fertilizer prices rise too sharply, it will considerably offset the material benefits the peasants gain from the raised prices of grain and cotton, dampening the enthusiasm of peasants for production and adversely affecting their inputs into agriculture as well as the production and supply of grain and cotton. As a result, it will directly boost the prices of grain and cotton and make it more difficult to combat inflation. For this reason, governments at all levels will take vigorous measures:

1. Increase production, carry out measures for imports, and balance overall volume well. Early this year, the State Council set aside 2.5 billion yuan in reserve funds for enterprises engaged in production of chemical fertilizers and farm chemicals. It calls on all the production enterprises to first complete their production tasks for the first half of the year. The import volume of chemical fertilizer set by the state should also be accomplished. Railway departments and agricultural means of production companies at various levels should actively take orders and make adjustments to ensure that chemical fertilizers can be delivered to the peasants in good time.

2. Implement state pricing policies and stabilize chemical fertilizer prices. The general requirement is that chemical fertilizer prices should remain relatively stable and that the prices of chemical fertilizers to be actually bought by the peasants should be prevented by all possible means from further increasing. Efforts should be made to reduce excessively high prices in some localities. It should be clearly stipulated that: the ex-factory price of produced urea under the production plan of large chemical fertilizer enterprises managed by the central government should not exceed 1150 yuan per ton; the price of imported chemical fertilizers should be set on the agency basis with foreign trade commissions charged in accordance with the relevant state regulation. The standard of dispatching charges should be rigidly formulated so that no excessive profits can be made from it.

3. The retail prices of chemical fertilizer should be strictly managed and rationally set by various provinces.

The general requirement is to maintain relatively stable prices. Retail prices should not be badly managed, still less should they be changed every day. The operational departments should use profits to make up for losses, but they should not incline toward setting high prices.

In terms of agricultural production, our country uses a large quantity of chemical fertilizers mainly in the spring. From April 10 June is the peak season in terms of demand for chemical fertilizers, which accounts for 70 percent of the chemical fertilizers used for the whole year. Thus, an urgent task at present is to achieve stability in chemical fertilizer prices and other means of agricultural production in order to maintain the enthusiasm of the peasants to grow grain, ensure stable production of grains, cotton and other agricultural products, and stabilize commodity prices.

Analysis of the Price Trend for the Whole Year
First of all, the central government has taken curbing inflation as the main task for this year. Many localities have implemented a "leadership responsibility system" toward price work under which the ability to control runaway inflation is used to evaluate leaders' achievements.

Second, in light of the upward movement of commodity prices last year, the state is to continue adopting a moderately tightened financial and monetary policy designed to strictly control the size of investment and credit. Since all macroeconomic targets are set on the basis of the core task of curbing inflation, they have created a good macro-environment for stabilizing commodity prices.

Furthermore, the role of policy-related price adjustment in boosting prices will be greatly reduced. To ease inflationary pressure, the state requires governments at all levels not to introduce price-adjustment measures in the first half of this year. This will have a positive effect on combating the upward movement of commodity prices.

Judging from agricultural production, the scarce supply of the main agricultural products is likely to improve. With regard to a significant increase in agricultural commodity prices and the

continued...

GOVERNMENT TO CONTROL PRICES, 1995 (continued)

problems arising from the weak foundation of agricultural production, the State Council and all local governments have increased inputs in agriculture and adopted a series of measures to increase agricultural production and income since the second half of last year. This year, the sowing areas for grains, cotton and oil- bearing crops will be larger than last year. If no relatively big natural disasters occur output of the main agricultural products will increase, thereby improving market supply.

In addition, the main factors putting upward pressure on commodity price such as tax reform, wage reform, foreign exchange and foreign trade structural reforms, are to ease this year.

Meanwhile, in economic operations, there are also some factors adversely affecting a drop in commodity prices such as: the rising commodity prices last year had a relatively great impact on prices this year. It is estimated that this will boost prices by about 10 percentage points while prices of principal commodities that need to be imported have soared substantially in the international market. The upward pressure exerted by costs on commodity prices will continue to be released rapidly. Therefore, it is still very difficult to fulfill the target controlling the overall level of commodity prices. In short, the central and governments at all levels are confident about fulfilling their target in controlling commodity prices, namely, "strive to achieve a remarkable drop in the index of retail commodity prices and control it within 15 percent."

Liaowang Nò. 13, 27 Mar 1995.

WU BANGGUO ON ECONOMY, 1995

[By RENMIN RIBAO reporter Mo Xinyuan (5459 2450 0337) and XINHUA reporter Jiao Ran (3542 3544)]

Wu Bangguo, CPC Central Committee Political Bureau member and State Council vice premier, spoke at a national work conference on the economy and trade, which ended today. He said: As far as next year's work on the economy and trade is concerned, we should enhance our confidence in reform, opening up, and economic development and fully recognize the significant achievements of this year and the favorable conditions of next year. Meanwhile, we should pay close attention to new circumstances of enterprises and problems that are existing or that may crop up in economic activity, make a correct assessment of the circumstances, and advance in a pioneering spirit. We should actively push ahead economic restructuring, transform the economic growth mode, and deepen the reform of enterprises so as to strengthen all-round coordination in economic operations and to solve contradictions and problems in the course of advance, thereby promoting a sustained, rapid, and healthy development of the national economy.

Wu Bangguo said: Since the beginning of this year, localities and departments have conscientiously implemented the basic principles of "seizing the opportunity, deepening reform, opening up wider, promoting development, and maintaining stability" as well as the guidelines laid by the Central Economic Work conference in strengthening macroeconomic regulation and control and all-round coordination of economic operation to promote a sustained, rapid, and healthy development trend in the national economy. As a result, the economy as a whole is heading toward the targets of macroeconomic regulation and control. Industry in general has also witnessed a sound situation, with industrial and transport production maintaining a stable increase while its growth rates have dropped steadily. During the January-October period, the accumulated value-added output turned out by industrial enterprises run by units at and above the township level nationwide amounted to 1,432.5 billion yuan, up 13.3 percent from the same period last year. New headway has also been made in the reform of state enterprises, and they are (1) the thought of reforms has been further unified and a broad consensus has taken shape; (2) experiments in state enterprise reforms have been made in an all-round way; and (3) breakthroughs have been achieved in enterprises merger and bankruptcy. However, the vice premier noted, low economic efficiency as a whole is the major problem facing the industries;

continued...

CHINA FACTS & FIGURES ANNUAL 173

WU BANGGUO ON ECONOMY, 1995 (continued)

and it is manifested mainly in the fact that enterprises have increased their output but not their revenues. During the first 10 months of this year, the value-added output of industrial enterprises covered by the state budget rose 7.9 percent, but their profits dropped 22.6 percent. The number of loss-making enterprises and their deficits rose; the prices of raw and semi-finished materials and fuels increased, especially in the textile industry; and financial expenditures increased sharply, thus triggering the cost hike.

Wu Bangguo emphasized: To ensure a good job in economy and trade next year, we should actively push ahead economic restructuring and transform the economic growth mode, making the improvement of economic efficiency the central task of economic work. Through more than four decades of construction, China now has a fairly large-scale national economy. However, due to historical, economic structural, and other factors, the national economy as a whole has basically developed on an extensive mode, characterized by high input and high consumption, but low yield and low quality. With such growth mode. we overextended construction scale, made a big increase in the input of production elements, neglected technological advancement and scientific management, and failed to raise the efficiency of utilizing production elements and the quality of economic operations. In 1996 and throughout the Ninth Five-Year Plan period, we should make economic restructuring an important link in the transformation of economic growth mode, promote economic efficiency, and pay keen attention to the work in the following aspects: (1) we should bring into full play local resources, make the best use of the advantage and avoid the disadvantage, and adhere to the principle of doing things within the limit of capabilities in mapping out economic adjustment programs suited to local conditions; (2) in restructuring the economy, priorities should be given to promising enterprises and sectors with greater potential for development; and (3) funds should be concentrated on and channeled to key projects so as to raise the efficiency of capital. The vice premier emphasized: The 18 pilot cities designated for "optimizing the structure of capital," the six old industrial bases in particular, should organically combine the reform of enterprises with economic restructuring and promote the optimization of stock assets for developing a rational, intensive, and export-oriented economy and for nurturing new economic growth areas, thereby raising the overall market competitiveness of the industrial cities as well as the quality and efficiency of their economic growth. As far as the technological advancement of enterprises in 1996 are concerned, particular emphasis should be placed on upgrading the quality of commodities, adopting advanced techniques, and improving economic efficiency of enterprises. We should make better use of funds for the technical transformation of enterprises and concentrate funds on promising enterprises and sectors with greater potential of development so as to help them boost product quality, expand production scale, and scale new heights.

Wu Bangguo pointed out: The central authorities have decided to accelerate the strategic reorganization of state enterprises by invigorating the big ones and adopting flexible measures with regard to the small ones. Of the 1,000 enterprises selected by the Economic and Trade Commission for guidance in different categories, next year we should focus attention on 300 enterprises and pay particular attention to the work in the following areas: (l) We should ensure a good job in the "separation" work of enterprises; (2) We should step by step solve the problems related to accumulation and development of enterprises, improve their mechanisms for self-accumulation and self-development, and explore ways for enterprises to raise funds; (3) We should encourage large enterprises to set up technology development centers and step up efforts to combine production with research so as to build up enterprises' capabilities to up-date and assimilate new technology; and (4) We should deepen reform and strengthen internal management in line with the requirements of the modern enterprise system. We should set up various rules and regulations for the internal management of enterprises in keeping with the market mechanisms and do well in the reforms of labor, distribution, and personnel systems. Where conditions permit, enterprise groups should be established. Discussing flexible measures with regard to small enterprises, Wu Bangguo stressed: We should strengthen the leadership. As the conditions of small enterprises vary, we should give guidance of different

continued...

WU BANGGUO ON ECONOMY, 1995 (continued)

categories and by no means regard the adoption of flexible measures as the end of a task. We must guard against the loss of state-owned enterprises because the purpose of adopting flexible measures is to further enliven small enterprises and it does not simply mean selling out small enterprises. We should appraise the value of state-owned assets to ensure that the value of assets is preserved and increased Stock assets should not be transferred to individuals, much less be misappropriated. In the process of adjustment, workers' daily necessities and jobs should be taken care of.

Wu Bangguo said: To do next year's economic and trade work well, we must strive to improve the quality of economic operations and go all out to reduce the deficit. Currently a large number of Chinese enterprises are running in the red and their deficits have increased year after year, which is seriously hindering the healthy development of the national economy and is becoming a major problem in economic operations. If this problem remains unsolved, it can lead us to a passive situation and affect the overall interests of reform, development, and stability. Next year, we should make energetic efforts to tackle the deficit problem, which remains a formidable task. There are many causes for the deficits of enterprises. All in all, however, poor management should be the root cause. The overwhelming majority of deficit-ridden enterprises are small enterprises. To enable enterprises to stop the deficits, start making profits, and improve the quality of economic operations particular emphasis should be placed, first, on strengthening the internal management of enterprises and tapping their internal potential; and second, using the mechanism of survival of the fittest to strengthen the effort at enterprises merger and bankruptcy. The fundamental solution lies in the deepening of reforms in state-owned enterprises.

In conclusion, Wu Bangguo emphasized: We should correctly handle the relationship between reform, development, and stability; show concern for the daily necessities of enterprise workers in financial straits; and solve practical problems for them. In solving problems for enterprises caught in financial straits, we should not merely give subsidies and relief funds, but should help them develop productive forces and solve production problems. We should deepen reform and strengthen management to help enterprises tide over difficulties. The state's assistance is essential, however, the solution to problems ultimately will depend on the enterprises' own efforts. Wu Bangguo urged all localities to strengthen the leadership over next year's industrial and transport work, step up study, build up the quality of enterprise leading bodies, strengthen and improve ideological and political work in enterprises, foster the thinking of relying wholeheartedly on the working class, improve work methods, and transform the work style. Responsibilities in the reform of state enterprises and industrial and transport production should be clearly assigned in various localities, as in the case of governors being responsible for grain production and mayors being responsible for vegetable production, striving to make a good start next year.

X, 10 Dec 1995.

FIVE YEAR PLAN ECONOMIC ELEMENTS, 1995

Beijing is set to continue state control over the prices of essential products and services, according to the Ninth Five-Year Plan.

The blueprint for the years 1996 to 2000, which is expected to be endorsed by the fifth plenum of the party's Central Committee this week, points out price reform in the Chinese context does not mean "the comprehensive 'decontrol' of prices".

One of the major goals of the plan is keeping inflation below 10 per cent—ideally maintaining it at just eight percent. "The Government will continue to regulate the prices of commodities vital to the state plan and to the people's livelihood," a draft of the plan reportedly says.

These categories include essential raw materials, grain, cotton, electricity and water supply as well as major services such as transport. Instead of letting the marketplace set prices, the plan says they will be determined through "a system of trial and error" administered by the State

continued...

FIVE YEAR PLAN ECONOMIC ELEMENTS, 1995 (continued)

Planning Commission and the price regulators. "A system of comparative pricing based on production costs will he set up, so the profits and salaries of production units in different departments and trades will be more or less on the same level," the document says.

It adds this will do away with the phenomena of certain departments and trades enjoying an unfair advantage owing to a stilted pricing system. "China is resolutely opposed to the shock therapy of blindly opening up prices," the draft reportedly says. According to Beijing economists familiar with the plan, the prices of about two dozen essential commodities and services which were frozen in early 1994, will remain under tight government regulation.

The state planners will raise the prices of those goods and services which are in scarce supply or which dovetail with the national production strategy. But the prices of non-essential consumer products ranging from cosmetics to mobile telephones will continue to be determined by market forces. The plan encourages the establishment of a "brand-name concept" so that the prices of products of different qualities and sophistication will he spread over a larger range.

The five-year blueprint will extend state control over a large range of commodities and products to abolish the so-called "double-track pricing system". For example, the prices of basic industrial and agricultural raw materials, as well as raw materials "produced in a near-monopoly environment", will be put under state control. The double-track system whereby the same product has a "state-plan price" and a market price, is regarded as a source of corruption

The Beijing economists said the cautious agenda reflected the views of "neo-conservative" leaders such as Vice-Premier Zhu Rongji, who had scolded unnamed cadres for their "blind worship" of Western economic textbooks. Mr. Zhu, who has played a key role in drafting the plan, has also recommended the Government take over or regulate the distribution and sale of essential raw materials and commodities such as fertilizers, grain and cotton.

The five-year plan, in addition to a supplementary economic blueprint up to the year 2010, sets no target for the abolition of regulation on pricing or distribution.

Foreign economists have cast doubt on Mr. Zhu's strategy, saying it perpetuates Soviet-style planning and cripples the development of the market economy.

Beijing's bill for price subsidies, mainly on grain and other agricultural produce, is expected to go up by about 80 per cent this year compared with 1994.

Chemical Industry Projects
China is set to produce a number of international chemical giants during the course of next five-year plan period. Those domestic enterprises will be leaders in the chemical industrial sector and will become prime earners of foreign exchange. They will also play a role in the international economic system, according to the Minister of Chemical Industry Gu Xiulian.

Ms. Gu said that the nation's chemical industry had forged a sound industrial base over the last 40 years. However, no individual domestic enterprise had earned a name as renowned as that of either Du Pont of the United States, Germany's Bayer or Shell of Britain [as received] in the international chemical industrial arena.

The Minister said that at the beginning of the current five-year plan, the ministry had put forward targets based on international economic development. One of the desired targets was that, by the year 2000, China's chemical industry had to earn foreign exchange of US$ 10 billion annually. Introduction of foreign capital would total US$ 10 billion while 100 export-oriented chemical industrial groups would be in operation by the turn of the century.

To date there are some 3,000 chemical industrial enterprises whose products grace the international market. About 57 of these each earn foreign exchange of over US$ 10 million annually in exports. These targets for the chemical industry will be further promoted in the next five-year plan.

Train of Thought for Economic Development Under China's Ninth 5-Year Plan Has Been Fixed
Authoritative advice from Beijing notes that during the period of the Ninth Five-Year Plan (1996-2000), the Chinese Communists will put stress on resolving problems in eight areas including establishing a market economy, enterprise reform, and establishing a new mechanism. In

continued...

FIVE YEAR PLAN ECONOMIC ELEMENTS, 1995 (continued)

terms of industrial development, they will rely on scientific and technological progress, optimizing the industrial structure, and alleviating the "bottleneck" restraints in basic industries, so as to realize economic invigoration for the push into the next century.

There Are Disparities Between Local Demands and Central Demands
According to the sources, the state planning, investment, and market aspects of the Ninth Five-Year Plan have already been drafted. Seen from the situations reported by the various localities, their economic planning growth will be in excess of 15 percent. However, this is greatly different from the central authorities' goal of containing growth to about 10 percent. Further, the localities' enthusiasm for invigorating the economy is quite high. The momentum is very powerful in seven areas, including vehicles, real estate, and light industry, and investment enthusiasm is growing. Not only is this much higher than under the national plans, but if the investment is carried out poorly, the results will be negative.

The Fifth Plenary Session of the CPC Will Fix Arrangements for the Ninth Five-Year Plan
This summer in Beidaihe, the CPC will hold a meeting to discuss problems such as holding down inflation, enterprise reform, and carrying out macroeconomic regulation and control. They will also deliberate on the major arrangements under the Ninth Five-Year Plan. At the subsequently convened Fifth Plenary Session of the CPC, the plans will be fixed and will be transmitted to the Fourth Session of the Eighth NPC for a decision. Finally they will be promulgated and implemented throughout the country.

Zhang Haoruo [1728 4110 5387], deputy head of the State Commission for Restructuring the Economic System, has said that the Ninth Five-Year Plan is very crucial for China's reform and development. In accordance with the demands of the central authorities, the Commission is now centralizing its forces in studying the problems of deepening reform and establishing a new structure during the Ninth Five-Year Plan, and it has stressed resolving eight major problems.

CPC Will Stress Resolving Eight Major Problems
First, they aim to achieve coordinated progress between strengthening the market mechanism and perfecting the macroeconomic regulation and control mechanisms. On the one hand, they will relax controls and let the market mechanism play its basic role, and as far as possible create conditions for fostering the market. On the other hand, they will strengthen the government's macroeconomic regulation and control functions.

Second, they will actively promote the development of the public-ownership economy while continuing to encourage the development of individual, private, and foreign-funded operations. State-owned capital will be mainly centered in banking, railways, civil aviation, highways, ports, water conservancy, posts, telecommunications, military weapons, aerospace, major mechatronic equipment, and cutting-edge electronics. The state will assist and develop 500 to 1,000 major enterprises or enterprise groups which are essential for national development and the people's livelihood, which tap into the arteries of the economy, and which have international competitiveness. They will seriously clean up the existing systems and policies, and will set down various boundaries based on ownership systems. They will further make clear the principle that the state will create equal environments for all types of enterprises and will actively eliminate the various types of non-unified and non-standardized practices.

Third, the reform of state-owned enterprises will start by resolving practical problems, and the building of a modern enterprise system will be accelerated. During the Ninth Five-Year Plan, the relationships among the governments, financial administrations, banks, and state-owned enterprises will be basically put in order, and the assets-liabilities problems left over by history will be properly handled, so that state-owned enterprises truly become independent corporate bodies. The reform of government organs will basically abolish the specialized management departments and will strengthen macroeconomic regulation and control, and economic supervisory departments.

continued...

FIVE YEAR PLAN ECONOMIC ELEMENTS, 1995 (continued)

Fourth, centering around enterprise reform, the establishment of new-type social security systems will be accelerated. During the period of the Ninth Five-Year Plan, the focus of reform of the social security system will be on establishing new-type social security systems with old-age, medical, and unemployment insurance as the main elements. At the same time, great efforts will be put into promoting reform of the housing system.

Fifth, in accordance with the principle of giving priority to efficiency while concurrently considering fairness, social income distribution relation will be put in order. While continuing to uphold the basic distribution system which has distribution according to work as the main part and diverse distribution forms coexisting, and while respecting the principle of giving priority to efficiency while concurrently considering fairness, the market mechanism and drive mechanism will be drawn in. Thus will be established a growth mechanism for individual income which is determined by market supply and demand and efficiency, and an individual income regulation and control mechanism which has taxation as its main part.

Promoting Reform of the Central and Western Regions, and Accelerating the Development of Backward Regions

Sixth, the reform and opening up of the central and western regions will be promoted and the development of the backward regions will be accelerated. It will be necessary to consider the establishment of a transferred payments system on a rational scale, as the focus of state investment will be on developing basic educational, health, science and technology, energy, transportation, and communications facilities in the backward areas. The state will also create similar systems environments throughout the country, so as to gradually remove policy differences and systems disparities between areas, promote mutual assistance and economic cooperation between regions, and through its policies promote the opening up to the outside of the central and western regions.

Seventh, rural reform will be deepened and agriculture which is in accord with the market economy will be promoted. Rural reform during the Ninth Five-Year Plan period will, in accordance with the demands of the commercialization of agriculture, the diversification of the rural economy, and the development of rural urbanization, further strengthen the agricultural base and promote the degree of integration of the urban and rural economies.

Eighth, the complementarity of the domestic economy and the international economy will be further promoted. During the period of the Ninth Five-Year Plan, there will be initially established an operational mechanism which is in accord with the general principles of the international market and a new-type economic and trade management system which is in accord with the demands of a socialist market economy system.

Establishing New Market Relationships

According to sources, one of the goals during the period of the Ninth Five-Year Plan is to establish a unified national open market system. This is aimed at achieving a situation where the urban markets are closely combined, and where domestic and international markets are mutually linked, so as to create new-type market relationships, promote the optimal deployment of resources, and ensure that under state macroeconomic regulation and control the market plays a basic role in resource deployment.

In realizing the goals of market construction under the Ninth Five-Year Plan, the basic indicator will be the establishment of a mechanism by which prices are formed by the market. In particular, major progress should be achieved in the marketization of prices of major production factors. The commodity market system will move toward maturity and a new-type circulation system for a small number of important commodities will be initially established; a financial market with bank financing as the main part will see improvement; a labor market will be basically formed; the real estate market will move toward standardization; there will be commercialization and marketization of technology and information; a quite complete legal framework which will standardize trading activities and guarantee market order will be established; an effective market monitoring, supervision, and macroeconomic regulation and control mechanism will be formed; and a major market and circulation structure under which domestic

continued...

FIVE YEAR PLAN ECONOMIC ELEMENTS, 1995 (continued)

and international elements are combined and under which domestic and international markets are linked will be basically formed.

According to the sources, the relevant state departments have formulated some work focuses in the circulation sphere during the Ninth Five-Year Plan.

New Focal Points in the Circulation Sphere

1. The circulation system for major commodities which affect the national economy and the people's livelihood will be reformed and improved, and the commodity market will be further developed. First, in key production, sales, and distribution areas, they will establish wholesale markets for major agricultural and sideline products, including grain, cotton, edible oil, sugar, pigs, major daily-use industrial consumer products, and major means of production.

Second, state-owned circulation enterprises will further change their operational mechanisms and continually raise their market competitiveness, and with respect to major commodity operations, they will actively bring into play their guiding role. At the same time, a commercial market network will be formed in which large, medium, and small are combined, in which all sorts of economic forms and operational forms coexist, where facilities are advanced, where functions are complete, where service is first-class and where the regional deployment and organizational levels are relatively rational.

2. There will be active exploration, research, and propagation of various new-type circulation organizational forms and operational modes which are in accord with China's national situation. This will include implementation of an agency system and trial-point distribution systems, the development of chain operations, supermarkets, warehouse-type commerce, large circulation industrial enterprises (comprehensive commercial agencies), and so on. As new industrial and commercial relationships will be created in an overall way, and with new operational concepts and advanced operational modes, it will be possible to promote the fine development of circulation itself and of the national economy.

3. In recent year, the Shanghai Non-Ferrous Metals Wholesale Market, the Qinhuangdao Coal Wholesale Trading Market, the Zhengzhou Rural Wholesale Market and Agricultural Machinery Market, the Wuhan Vehicle Trading Market, and the Guangzhou Rubber Wholesale Market have been established. In addition, three non-ferrous metals markets have been established in Wuhan, Shanghai, and in the northeast region. The fostering and building of production factor markets including financial markets, labor markets, real estate markets technology markets, and information markets has been accelerated, their level has been raised, and the various trading activities have been standardized. This has resulted in the production factor markets, the commodity markets, and the overall national economy pushing each other to higher levels while still remaining in accord with each other.

4. In the circulation sphere, while continuing to uphold opening to the outside and drawing in foreign funds, the work focus will as quickly as possible be shifted to drawing in advanced technology and managerial experience from abroad. The overall operational and management levels of China's circulation enterprises will be continually raised as will their domestic and international competitiveness, so that they can as quickly as possible come into line with international practices, actively participate in multilateral economic activities around the globe, and further expand and raise the scale and level of China's foreign trade.

5. Establishing a complete national macroeconomic regulation and control market system. Apart from appropriately and effectively implementing indirect economic regulatory measures such as fiscal and monetary measures and necessary administrative and legal measures, this will also involve effective regulatory measures governing state purchasing and storage of major commodities, risk funds, and imports and exports.

How China Will Enter the 21st Century

The Ninth Five-Year Plan will be a crucial period in China's economic and social development. China intends during these five years to initially establish a new market economy structure and to lay down a fine base for realizing the third-phase strategic goal.

continued...

FIVE YEAR PLAN ECONOMIC ELEMENTS, 1995 (continued)

In order to change the economic growth mode and promote a fine cycle, the upper levels of the CPC have stressed that it is necessary to put great efforts into promoting the advance of industrial technology, to promote the economic and comprehensive use of new technology, and to accelerate the reorganization and transfer of traditional industry. Centering on raising the quality of labor, great efforts will be put into popularizing nine-year compulsory education, developing professional and technical education and adult education, and establishing multi-level, multi-channel technological training systems. The integration of the economy and science and technology will be promoted, the development of scientific and technological achievements in the direction of productive forces will be accelerated, and efforts will be put into ensuring that enterprises become the main elements in scientific and technological progress and scientific and technological investment. The establishment of an enterprise technological progress mechanism which combines markets, science and technology, experimentation, and production will be accelerated. The combination of the reforms for implementing a modern enterprise system, for structural readjustment of enterprise organization, and for technological transformation will be supported, and a number of enterprise groups which combine technology, industry, and trade will be fostered. In accordance with the requirement to promote the technological progress of domestic industry and achieve structural upgrading, China will continue to do well in technological imports and technological cooperation with the outside world, guaranteeing a stable increase in the income of the peasants.

The State Planning Commission has pointed out that in strengthening readjustment of the industrial structure, it is necessary to strengthen the building of basic facilities for water conservancy, transportation, communications, energy, and major goods and materials, so as to further alleviate the "bottleneck" restrictions on economic development in these sectors. In terms of communications and transport, the stress will be on developing a comprehensive transport system and strengthening the building of railways, highways, water transport, airlines, and conduit transport. Particular stress will be placed on accelerating railway construction. A number of airports, ports, and high-grade highways will be built. With the construction of the "eight vertical and eight horizontal" optical fiber trunk line as the focal point, a modern communications network will be gradually established. Energy construction will concurrently stress resource development and economizing on energy. In the near term, saving energy will be placed in a prominent position. Oil exploration and development both on shore and offshore will be accelerated. There will also be appropriate increases in the scale of construction in the electricity and coal sectors. The development of nuclear energy will be placed in a primary position.

In terms of optimizing the industrial structure, the State Planning Commission has decided to investigate the machine-building, electronics, petrochemical, vehicle manufacturing, and construction industries, so that they become pillar industries of the national economy. The machine-building industry will have as its main orientation the building of basic machine parts and major complete sets of technological equipment. The electronics Industry will take micro-electronics as its focal point and will greatly develop large-scale integrated circuits, so as to make information provision an integral part of the national economy. The "vehicle industry policy" will be implemented and the focal point will be on developing key parts for sedans, economy cars, large passenger vehicles, and specialized vehicles, so as to satisfy the demands of the domestic market. The petrochemical industry will take the transformation and expansion of existing enterprises as its main task, while the construction of some appropriate new projects will be arranged so as to deepen processing. The construction industry will see great development and the focal point will be on accommodation for urban and rural residents. The state will stress engineering projects and basic public facilities in urban areas, while new-type construction material industries and interior decorating industries will be developed.

South China Morning Post, 25 Sep 1995.

ENTERPRISE REFORM CLASSES, 1995

In front of the Yuyuan Building in the Central Party School, the flowers are in full bloom in the genial spring sunlight. It was the morning of 31 March.

"How are you doing? I think you all look well and are in high spirits. You have learned something from the study, have you not?" asked Wu Bangguo, CPC Central Committee Political Bureau member, secretary of the Secretariat, and vice premier of the State Council, in an amiable manner on meeting the students from the study class in the courtyard of the above building where he had just issued certificates to them. "Yes, we have learned a lot. We are full of confidence now that we have a clear direction," answered the students one after another.

This scene took place immediately after the conclusion of the "State-Owned Enterprise Reform" study class which lasted one month. It was jointly sponsored by the State Economic and Trade Commission, the Central Organization Department, and the Central Party School on behalf of the party's Central Committee and participated in by leading cadres at the provincial and ministerial levels. The study class is of extraordinary significance. The central authorities gathered the leading cadres from some provinces and cities in charge of the industrial work, comrades responsible for pertinent ministries and commissions, and representatives of the "bosses" from large and medium state enterprises in Beijing to attend the study class and discuss matters of vital importance.

In the spring of 1995, there are voices calling for deepening state-owned enterprise reform and re-portraying the "eldest son of the republic." During the study course students affectionately called the state-owned enterprises the "eldest son of the republic." They said: "Let the eldest son have more vigor and strength."

Strengthen the Faith: Party Leadership Is the Fundamental Guarantee for Appropriately Carrying Out State Enterprise Reform

How to regard the state-owned enterprises has become a focus of discussion at home and abroad.

The students maintained that the party central committee always takes state-owned enterprise reform seriously. Looking back at history, there are three stages regarding the reform: 1. During the Third Plenary Session of the 11th CPC Central Committee in 1978, the party Central Committee made a decision on delegating power to lower levels and letting them retain a proportion of profits as well as increasing the decision making power of enterprises. 2. The central authorities proposed practicing a contract responsibility system under which enterprise ownership is separated from the management rights at the Third Plenary Session of the 12th CPC Central Committee. 3. Since Deng Xiaoping's south China tour in 1992, enterprise reform has entered a new stage of transforming mechanisms and establishing structures. Practice of the exploration and development of state-owned enterprise reform for 16 years has proved that the party's principles and policies concerning state-owned enterprise reform are correct and the development of state-owned enterprises is healthy, as they have increased actual strength and enhanced economic results. Since 1992, the gross output value of state-owned industrial enterprises has grown at an average annual rate of 8.2 percent and their profits and taxes turned over to the state have increased by an average 29.5 percent a year. Guo Shichang, vice governor of Hebei Province, and Liang Guoying, deputy secretary of Shanxi Provincial CPC Committee, shared the same view: "Whom will foreign investors talk about investment projects with when they come here? They will talk with none except the large and medium-sized state enterprises because they value the strength and quality of these enterprises." As regards the difficulties that exist in the state-owned enterprises, the students did not evade the question: They include heavy burdens, staff redundancies, outmoded equipment, and inadequate funds. After making analyses, the students pointed out that this is a concentrated expression of the deep contradiction generated from the transition of the national economy as a whole from a planned structure to a market structure. Jin Lianshu from the Ministry of Finance said: "It is necessary to regard the reform of state-owned enterprises from a long-term and dynamic point of view. As long as we maintain the steady growth momentum in the macroeconomic situation, it is not difficult to resolve the problems. The

continued...

ENTERPRISE REFORM CLASSES, 1995 (continued)

economic results of state-owned enterprises further improved in 1994, with a 10.6 percent growth in profits, which exceeded the 5.7 percent growth in production."

The students firmly believed the following truth: Thanks to the leadership of the party, remarkable achievements have been attained in the reform of state-owned enterprises over the past 16 years and, by continuously relying on the party's leadership, we will certainly overcome the current difficulties confronting the state-owned enterprises. Comrade Jiang Zemin's opinion that the "crux of the issue lies in separating government functions from those of enterprises, exercising proper internal management, and gradually establishing a social insurance system" has hit home the crucial point of in-depth reform in state-owned enterprises, charted the course for furthering the reform, and strengthened our confidence.

Clarify the Focus of Attention: Revitalizing the Public Economy as a Whole, Rather Than Each Individual Enterprise

In his speech at the study class, Comrade Wu Bangguo pointed out: "Reform of state-owned enterprises should be aimed at revitalizing the national economy as a whole rather than revitalizing each individual enterprise." This new concept was greatly appreciated by the students.

The goal of China's socialist economic structural reform is to establish the socialist market economy, which is governed by the universal law that the superior wins while the inferior is eliminated, so that some will survive and others will cease to exist. Hence, it is unnecessary as well as impossible for all enterprises to be revitalized without exception. Under the planned economy, enterprises were appendages of the government Since the government had unlimited liability for enterprises, its burden became increasingly heavier.

In recent years, the Shanghai Municipal CPC Committee and Government have tightened macroeconomic control over enterprises and vigorously made adjustments to industrial structure. They did not evaluate their work by the success or failure of an individual enterprise; instead, they evaluated it by judging whether or not the quality of a trade or even the city's economy as a whole had been enhanced and the actual strength augmented. They put forward the "tertiary-secondary-primary" principle of readjusting structure and developing industries that hold a predominant position: Vigorously boosting the tertiary industry, positively readjusting the secondary industry, and steadily upgrading the primary industry. As a result, pillar industries including automobile, communications, petrochemistry, household electrical appliances, iron and steel, power plant equipment, and so on sprang up one after another. While inspecting work in Shanghai last year, Li Peng said: "I have watched the above mentioned principle for three years, and it has been proved to be correct."

Efforts were concentrated on changing the concept of operators. This is another "play involving much singing and action" which was put on by the Shanghai Municipal CPC Committee and Government in exercising leadership over economic work. Since 1991, they have led and organized enterprises to hold mass discussions on economics once a year. For instance, they organized the mass discussion on the development strategy of Shanghai's industrial products in 1991 and the discussion on raising the level of Shanghai's industrial economy in 1992. Through these mass discussions, enterprises' market awareness was enhanced and the concept that the superior wins while the inferior is eliminated was fostered. In this way, they have smashed the old practices whereby the superior were unable to win and the inferior could not be discarded. Specifically speaking, enterprises with poor performance records could not be closed down and dissolved. It is natural that some should cease to exist while others should survive or be brought back to life after death.

Over the past few years, 257 enterprises have been closed down, suspended, merged, or transferred, and 254,000 staff and workers have been assigned jobs in the merged enterprises. The reorganization of stock structure has optimized the allocation of social resources, invigorated asset stock, and ensured the value preservation and increase of state-owned assets. The Sanqiang [Three Guns] Group, which was said to "have produced economic results through

continued...

ENTERPRISE REFORM CLASSES, 1995 (continued)

merger" by Comrade Zhu Rongji, has formed into an enterprise group with good economic results through the process of repeated merger and digestion on six occasions.

The reorganization of enterprises has created conditions and opportunities for transforming mechanisms to increase results. Taking assets as key links and purchases and mergers as basic means, the municipal party committee and government proposed the necessity of integrating the internal functions of enterprises through diversifying investment structure. As a result, Shanghai's industrial growth rate between 1991 and 1994 registered 17.1, 21.4, 18.3, and 17.1 percent respectively.

A Path Was Discovered, Which Is the Only Way for Appropriately Carrying Out Current Reform of State-Owned Enterprises

The path comprises the meanings of restructure, reorganization, transformation, and intensification of enterprise's internal management. In their speeches at the study class, both Comrade Wu Bangguo and Comrade Wang Zhongyu, minister of the State Economic and Trade Commission, stressed that the above four aspects should be integrated. Here, restructure means transforming mechanisms and establishing new structures, reorganization means readjusting the product mix, and transformation means increasing the intensity of technological transformation. They cover the contents of the regulations on transforming operational mechanisms in state-owned industrial enterprises and the institution of a modern enterprise system. On the other hand, they are aimed at summarizing the previous tendency of slackened enterprise management. Hence, they are a summary of experience from various localities over the past few years.

The students were of the opinion that the above mentioned restructure, reorganization, transformation, and intensification are not in conflict with the institution of a modern enterprise system. On the contrary, they will contribute to the institution of the system. This reflects comprehensive coordination and overall advance. To carry out the in-depth enterprise reform we should not, under any circumstances, engage ourselves "in the battle with only a single weapon" but march as a "combined fleet," or even advance with the escort of "aircraft carriers."

Beijing's vice mayor, Li Runwu, told this reporter: "In 1994, we disseminated the experience of No. I Beijing Municipal Light Industrial Corporation regarding the institution of a modern enterprise system and practiced the authorized management of state-owned assets in some industrial corporations which were no longer under government control, to lay down the foundation for further realizing the separation of government functions from those of enterprises and the separation of administration from assets [zheng zi fen kai 2398 6327 0433 7030]."

Gao Shuping, deputy secretary of the party committee and concurrently chairman of the board of supervisors of No. I Beijing Municipal Light Industrial Corporation, said in a briefing that their conditions of raising economic results and reform experience in the areas of "increasing asset value, transferring industries, transforming mechanisms, changing functions, and diverting staff and workers" have demonstrated the prowess of experiments in establishing a modern enterprise system.

Zhang Ruimin, president of Qingdao Haier Company Group, and Ma Yue, general manager of Dongfeng Automobile Group, passed on their experience to the students regarding the implementation of "applying the daily clearing up and daily upgrading management method and taking the road of producing profitable products with famous brands" as well as "practicing a quality and cost responsibility system with eyes set on the vast domestic markets." This has proved that scientific management is a part and parcel of instituting a modern management system. Many academics said that intensification of management should be an eternal theme in whatever society and whatever era.

Beijing Yanhua Company's project to increase its output of ethylene from 300,000 to 450,000 tons—is said by Comrade Zhu Rongji to "have made breakthroughs in building ideology, building model, and building methods." Liu Haiyan, manager of the above mentioned company and general director of the project, also briefed the students on his experience in technical transformation. The general response of the students is a single word—"realistic."

continued...

ENTERPRISE REFORM CLASSES, 1995 (continued)

How should enterprises in underdeveloped areas carry out in-depth reform? Shen Shuji, vice chairman of Inner Mongolia Autonomous Region, said at the discussion that the answer to the question is to readjust product mix and develop industries which hold a predominant position, meaning: Resource predominance plus supporting policies plus modern science and technology plus strict management equals industries holding a predominant position equals products of famous brands. Under the policy of exploiting everyone's advantages, Eldos, King Deer's cashmere sweaters, Ski Western clothes, and Crown cashmere products have dashed out of Asia and hold their market shares in the world. Similarly, the Yili milk product series has become popular throughout the entire country.

Keep This Guiding Ideology Firmly in Mind: Arm Our Minds With Deng Xiaoping's Theory Or Building Socialism With Chinese Characteristics
All this has indicated the concern shown and attention paid by the central leading comrades to the study class.

In their speeches, many central leaders stressed the necessity of taking Deng Xiaoping's theory of building socialism with Chinese characteristics as a guide to study new conditions and resolve new problems in carrying out the in-depth reform in state-owned enterprises. The students maintained that the essence of the theory of building socialism with Chinese characteristics lies in emancipating the mind and seeking truth from facts. Our party adhered to this principle in guiding agricultural reform and scored a breakthrough success 16 years ago; 16 years afterward, we are marching on the road which has never been taken by anyone before in storming the heavily fortified position—the in-depth reform of state-owned enterprises. Since there is no ready-made experience to learn from, we must change our concepts and be bold in exploration and practice.

We should stick to the orientation of state enterprise reform. Comrade Deng Xiaoping said: "We always adhere to two fundamental principles in reform: One is taking the socialist public economy as a main body and the other is achieving common prosperity." The students believe that Western politicians welcome China's reform in the hope of seeing privatization practiced in China. That is why we must maintain a sober mind.

We should stick to the criteria of "three beneficial's." Comrade Deng Xiaoping said: "Our criteria for judging everything should mainly cover whether it is beneficial to promoting the productive forces, beneficial to reinforcing the comprehensive national strength of our socialist country, and beneficial to enhancing the living standards of the people." The students thought it necessary to judge the success or failure of the state enterprise reform with these "three beneficial's." We must be bold in practice, refrain from hesitating, rely on our own strength, and pay respect to the pioneering spirit of the masses.

We should stick to the principle of proceeding from actual conditions in doing everything. The students felt that conditions differed in various enterprises, trades, and regions. In making experiments of instituting a modern enterprise system and optimizing the capital structure in 18 cities, and in performing our work in the entire area, we must always be realistic in accordance with the varying conditions in enterprises and avoid the practice of rigidly clinging to a single pattern.

We should correctly handle the relations between the in-depth reform in state-owned enterprises and the development of multiple economic sectors as well as the relations between reform development, and stability. The students held that the development of non-public economic sectors will reduce the burdens of state-owned enterprises. Although we take the public economy as the main body, we should still develop other economic sectors so that they will supplement each other. Maintaining social stability is the precondition of reform and development and deepening enterprise reform is an arduous and meticulous task, so we must have the overall situation in mind and fully consider the tolerance of the state, society, and staff and workers.

The students believed that armed with Comrade Xiaoping's theory and led by the party's central committee, with Jiang Zemin at the core, with one heart and one mind, our state-owned

continued...

ENTERPRISE REFORM CLASSES, 1995 (continued)

enterprises will certainly display their powerful strength and hold a favorable position in international competition in the 21st century.

With the breath of spring infiltrating the atmosphere of the metropolis fruits are growing in close clusters and hanging heavy on the trees. When the study class concluded, Chen Qingtai, vice minister of the State Economic and Trade Commission and secretary of the party branch of the class encouraged the 60 students to bring home the fruits of their study, just like 60 seeds that will take roots, sprout, blossom, and yield fruits in the course of state enterprise reform.

Renmin Ribao, 14 Apr 1995.

COTTON MARKET REFORM, 1995

I. Current Cotton Circulation System and Framework for Reform

A) Existing Cotton Circulation System and Policy

China's existing cotton circulation system is characterized by direct state regulation and control, complete with planned management and government-set prices. The supply and marketing cooperative monopolizes the procurement and trading of cotton. The cotton market is not open and dual pricing has no place in the cotton market. The current system, in existence for more than 40 years, has been supplemented by a string of government measures designed to encourage peasants to grow cotton. This management model has been instrumental in protecting peasant interests, ensuring that state textile enterprise demand for raw materials is met and the availability of cotton for civilian use and promoting industrial and agricultural production. But there is no doubt that this circulation system rests on the state monopoly of procurement of agricultural products and the purchase and marketing of textile products and China's chronic cotton undersupply. To date, with the national economy booming, reform and the open policy deepening continuously, and the economic structure and enterprises both undergoing profound changes, the shortcomings of a management model and price system based on command planning and direct government distribution have become increasingly evident. Reform has become imperative.

1. Centralized management has not been adept at closing the cotton supply-demand gap, which results when there is too much or too little cotton vis-a-vis demand. Owing to ineffectual macroeconomic regulation and control by the state, the government cannot get its hands on the entire crop when there is a cotton shortage. Nor does it do a good job buying up all cotton when there is too much of the commodity around. As a result, the command allocation, transfer, and supply plan is often not implemented and official prices are disregarded. In time of cotton shortages, the functional departments in charge and local administrative departments put up obstacles level after level. Their obstruction, coupled with local protectionism, prevents allocation and transfer plans from being implemented successfully. Consequently, cotton is not shipped out in accordance with the plan and the normal production of some textile enterprises is disrupted. Certain textile mills outside the state plan are quick to scramble for cotton anywhere they can, offering to buy up cotton at inflated prices, thus driving a large quantity of high-priced but inferior cotton onto the market. This not only severs the continuity between the plan and prices, causing loss of resources on an enormous scale, but also upsets the balance between aggregate supply and demand nationwide. When the shortage of cotton eases off or is replaced by an oversupply, some textile enterprises fail to purchase cotton as required under the plan or to stock their warehouses in accordance with the rules. As a result, a large amount of cotton just sits idle in cotton-producing areas, dampening the latter's production enthusiasm.

2. Allocation in accordance with the plan does not bring about fair competition or the intelligent allocation of resources. The purview of the state plan for the use of cotton is limited to enterprises within the plan, not those outside it. Sheltered by the planned economy, state textile enterprises lack the drive to compete or develop. As for textile plants outside the plan, they have to live with the uncertainty surrounding raw materials supplies. Consequently, China's textile industry is slow to make technological advances or improve product quality.

continued...

COTTON MARKET REFORM, 1995 (continued)

Other consequences are contradictions within the textile industry, conflicts between producing areas and consuming areas, and competition between the Ministry of Finance and its local counterparts.

3. The total centralization of the buying and selling of cotton is easier said than done. Officially, there is no open cotton market. In reality, there has always been a cotton market.

4. The existing price system lacks the flexibility that the law of value demands or the initiative to regulate the market. Cotton procurement and marketing prices cannot be adjusted in a timely way in response to changes in the supply-demand situation. This adversely affects the effort to increase cotton output and exacerbates the imbalance between supply and demand.

5. A fragmented and everybody-on-his-own cotton trading system does nothing to help bring out the collective strength of cotton and flax mills. The buying and selling of cotton is monopolized by the supply and marketing cooperative, a massive top-down system. Within this enormous system, there are multiple levels, made up of provincial, municipal or prefectural, and county cooperatives, each of them an economic entity that practices independent accounting and is held accountable for its own profits and losses. Out of self-interest, each unit jockeys for business and scrambles for profits at one another's expense. It is not uncommon for them to compete against one another. Some localities have even introduced preferential policies and marginal measures in violation of national policy, undermining to varying degrees peasant enthusiasm to sell cotton in accordance with their contracts and causing cotton to be shipped back and forth, which severely disrupts normal cotton procurement Some localities have imposed protectionist measures, artificially obstructing implementation of the state plan. They ship out either more or less than required under the plan and pass along the losses, in the process taking away from the central government its ability to balance cotton supply and demand overall.

6. Cotton production development does not have enough staying power. There is an exclusive emphasis on the quantity of output while ignoring market demand.

In recent years the growing of cereals, vegetables, fruit, and aquatic products has all been deregulated. Practice proves that instead of ushering in chaos, deregulation has energized markets for those products. Why is it that only cotton remains under government control, some comrades ask? Should cotton be decontrolled? Or should it remain regulated for the time being? At stake here is a major macroeconomic regulatory and control policy. We must consider this issue with reality as our starting point. In 1993, unfavorable climatic conditions conspired with ineffectual boll worm control, the mismanagement of cotton fields, local natural disasters, and the fact that not enough cotton fields were set aside to drive down cotton output. Even to date cotton production remains highly unstable. Peasants have little interest in growing cotton. Just as unenthusiastic are the localities. Meanwhile government cotton reserves have dropped significantly and the government has very limited macroeconomic regulatory and control ability. If we do not regulate or control the market these days, it may be thrown into chaos, leading to a string of adverse consequences. So it would be premature to deregulate cotton at this point. The national cotton work conference convened by the State Council in March 1993 decided that while we should proceed systematically step by step, in general, we must actively experiment to build up our experience.

In September 1994, the State Council reiterated the basic policy in cotton procurement and selling: "Do not deregulate cotton trading. Do not open up the cotton market. Do not decontrol cotton prices." In addition, a number of new decisions were taken, as follows:

—"Raise the procurement price of standard-grade lap waste cotton to 500 yuan per 50 kilograms, starting with the 1994 cotton year. Offer peasants extra incentives. In the past, cotton mills were given 44.62 yuan, all of it coming from the central treasury, for every 50 kilograms of ginned cotton they bought, including 14 yuan to offset the difference between the official and negotiated prices and 30.62 yuan in government subsidy. Now 44 yuan of this sum is to be awarded to cotton growers by the procurement department (regardless of the grade of the cotton or the length of the fiber) instead of giving it to the cotton-consuming enterprises. The

continued...

COTTON MARKET REFORM, 1995 (continued)

remaining 0.62 yuan goes to the Ministry of Agriculture to be spent exclusively on developing new and improved cotton varieties that are high-yield, good-quality, and highly resistant to plant diseases and insect pests."

—"In good-variety breeding areas, factories that process good varieties and state farms are allowed to procure and process only cotton produced locally. All cotton processed shall be included in the state plan to be available for allocation and transfer by supply and marketing cooperatives at or above the county level in accordance with the state plan.... No cotton procurers shall take cotton to cotton mills on their own for processing into yarn."

—"The policy of giving a 30-yuan incentive to a province for every 50 kilograms of cotton it ships out shall continue. The incentive shall be borne by the finance department of the province which purchases the cotton in question."

Our search for new cotton management methods proves that we must proceed from national interests and think about the long and medium term. We must explore ways of reforming the cotton circulation system with the criterion that they promote productive forces.

B. Reform: Basic Direction and Guiding Thought

We should consider the following basic factors in an overall context when we design a plan to reform the cotton circulation system:

1. Cotton production takes a long time and is at the mercy of Mother Nature in that it is highly vulnerable to natural and climatic conditions. Bumper harvests may alternate with crop failures, which has a vast impact on normal national economic development. Cotton production is disorganized. On their own individual peasants cannot solve the problems they encounter in production.

2. The reform of the cotton circulation system is not just a question of distributing interests among the various sectors. Also at stake are relations between the state and peasants and among industry, agriculture, and commerce, which are even more important.

3. There is a trend for the price scissors between industrial and agricultural products to continue to widen. Cotton-growing income has been on a downward slide even in normal years. When cotton prices sag, cotton production inevitably falls. When cotton prices go up, on the other hand, they necessarily drive up the costs of industrial production. As a result, industry suffers losses and consumers are adversely affected. This contradiction cannot be resolved without government intervention.

4. The current structure of the textile industry must be adjusted to meet the needs of developing a market economy, an adjustment that will take a period of time.

5. It will also take time to work out a string of major issues related to reform of the cotton circulation system, such as price formation, quality management, production planning, financial support, macroeconomic regulation and control, market development, and circulation management.

6. Relations within the supply and marketing cooperative need to be straightened out.

7. We must move in unison on the reform front. It would not be right for the provinces to launch pilot projects across the board separately. That would cause unnecessary confusion.

To sum up, the reform of the cotton circulation system must be preceded by careful verification. Our approach must be one of smooth transition, not one of making hasty moves. Tentatively we think the basic direction in cotton reform should be as follows: Develop official regulatory and control methods by sorting out policies and formulating laws and regulations, culminating in a full-fledged market system under which the state relies mainly on regulating the reserves as a means of controlling market supply and demand.

This is the basic guiding thought behind the reform of the cotton circulation system: Through hard work in the last two years of the Eighth Five-Year Plan and throughout the Ninth Five-Year Plan, we should set up a socialist cotton circulation system, complete with a new operating mechanism, that is compatible with the state of the Chinese nation. Under the guidance of the national plan and within the framework of macroeconomic regulation and control, we should gradually broaden the role of market mechanisms and continuously increase market-regulated cotton circulation. The production, supply, and marketing of cotton should become part of the

continued...

COTTON MARKET REFORM, 1995 (continued)

socialist market economy, using market regulation as the main tool. We should guide cotton production and consumption through an efficient, orderly, and smooth-flowing market where domestic and foreign trade are joined.

—Gradually roll back command planned management and replace it with cotton production, procurement, and marketing plans of a guiding nature, the ultimate goal being market regulation.

—Introduce price reform in stages. To protect cotton and textile production and meet the needs of international trade, the state should emulate the practice of most cotton-producing nations in the world by giving financial support to cotton production. This kind of support must be flexible, however, so that it will not become an onerous burden on the treasury. Specifically, financial subsidies currently shelled out by the treasury should be replaced in part by a policy of price supports so that the opening of the cotton market and the free buying and selling of cotton will not come about at the expense of cotton growers.

—Establish a diversified circulation system. Cotton should be able to circulate through multiple channels. Operating units must undergo necessary examination to verify their credentials. An integrated circulation entity bringing together agriculture, industry, commerce, and trade under one roof should be created in the course of time on the principles of equality, voluntary participation, and mutual benefit in order to encourage the balanced and simultaneous development of cotton production, supply, and marketing and to ensure that each gets its fair share.

—Establish a national unified cotton market under state guidance and management. Gradually set up a modern market whose core is the national cotton exchange, whose backbone is the regional markets, and whose base is the primary markets. Develop cotton spot trading and futures contract trading in accordance with a plan, forming a cotton market system that is multi-level and standardized. Organize production and circulation in accordance with the principles of the market economy through open, fair, and regularized market competition within a legal framework. Government regulation of cotton prices should be effected through the formulation of cotton procurement prices and the determination of the range within which prices may float, which are of a guiding nature and maintained through buying up or selling cotton on the cotton exchange and wholesale market.

—Establish and perfect a system in which direct and indirect government regulation of cotton production, supply, and marketing is integrated and which features regulation and control at two levels—central and local (provincial)—with indirect, central regulation and control playing the dominant role in order to ensure the stability of the cotton market and cotton prices. Central regulation and control consists mainly of formulating a national cotton production and financial support plan, offering credit on preferential terms, and establishing a reserve system. Local regulation and control consists mainly of formulating a local cotton production and financial support plan and ensuring local reserves. Furthermore, a national cotton regulation and control system should be created, including a cotton quality assurance and testing program. Perfect a cotton exchange management system.

—Reform the cotton production structure. Gradually bring about the regional and scale planting of improved cotton varieties to meet the needs of domestic and international markets.

II. Feasibility of Reform

In its commodity state as an industrial raw material, cotton is traded on the market as bales of ginned cotton. The production base of cotton currently consists of myriad fragmented small peasant households. To drive hundreds of thousands of these households onto a cotton market that is still taking shape will produce uncertain adverse consequences. As for cotton enterprises, if they are not organized and remain on their own, they will not be as competitive on the market as they should be. Thus one of the goals of the reform of the cotton circulation system is to develop new market players and spur the formation of good cotton circulation organizations. Toward that end, we may closely integrate producers and enterprises using a particular form of organization and management and a particular interest distribution relationship. For

continued...

COTTON MARKET REFORM, 1995 (continued)

instance, procurement contracts may be signed with cotton growers based on market demand, and peasants may be provided with information, science and technology, and material services so that they do not have to worry about the future. That way we can build a unified entity within a particular geographical area, a unified entity in which the various components complement one another's strengths and each component is a member of the market. After state planned regulation of the cotton market is gradually lifted, a forum is needed where buyers and sellers can trade to regulate cotton surpluses or shortages. Clearly the cotton procurement station is not up to this task. What is also needed are cotton exchanges, both nationwide and in the principal cotton-producing areas, so that fair, open competition can take place in cotton trading in a legal environment. To expedite the standardization and modernization of the cotton market within a legal framework and the improvement of the cotton market system, we should stipulate that cotton enterprises must be examined to see if they meet set criteria before they can enter the market. An enterprise must seek permission before it is allowed to enter the market. Provided all participants in the market unite as one and make the most of their edge in resources, funding, and technology, and provided we rely on market regulation and the law of value, we can create a new, highly efficient, and smooth-flowing cotton circulation system that brings production, supply, and marketing under one roof and combines domestic with foreign trade. Not only will cotton enterprises be able to fulfill their regulatory and control function better, which will facilitate the organization of cotton supply, but it will resolve some of the problems encountered by cotton growers in the course of production, such as difficulties in securing materials, lack of technology, and not being able to find buyers. This, in turn, will mobilize peasant cotton-production enthusiasm and ensure the steady expansion of cotton production.

We should set up a cotton futures market in accordance with a plan under state guidance. Such a development will help stabilize supply-demand relations within the nation and prices, reduce market risk, help promote foreign trade by easing our entry into the international market, and help earn foreign exchange.

We must proceed cautiously with reform of the cotton circulation system, carrying it out step by step. Such caution is necessary given the characteristics of this particular commodity. It is an economic crop grown by tens of thousands of peasant households. Cotton growers sell 90 percent of their crop, so cotton is a major source of earnings for them. Cotton grown in a particular locality is consumed nationwide. What is produced in one season is used year-round. Cotton goods are a leading commodity in world trade. Given all these constraints, we must be extremely cautious and not try to accomplish our goals overnight. Right now we are still in the stage of relying on government policies to protect cotton production. We should not try to skip this stage by adjusting the policy too radically. We must maintain peasant incomes from cotton growing at the present level; otherwise they may lose interest in the crop, with unthinkable consequences. Precisely because cotton is unique, we can neither remain in a closed system of command planning nor deregulate the market completely and allow free trade. In the long haul, cotton circulation must assume a brand-new look. It must go the route of market regulation and futures trading, with the market guiding enterprises. But that is not possible at the moment.

Cotton circulation reform must proceed vigorously but cautiously so that it boosts cotton production, stabilizes cotton buying and selling, raises the quality of cotton, and spurs development of the textile industry. Given the present situation, the reform of cotton procurement and selling should take the approach of stabilizing procurement while deregulating selling. Only when the procurement end is secured will growers feel confident. Deregulating the market indiscriminately will only throw production into chaos, leading to a steady decline in output. As for the supply and marketing ends, we must gradually energize them under state planned guidance by holding "goods ordering gatherings" and using other methods. That way the market can optimize resource allocation.

A gradual approach should also be the rule when it comes to reforming cotton price management. Specifically, state-fixed prices should progressively be replaced by state guiding prices. Also, floating limits should be established to regulate production and supply. A gradual transition to market-guided production and marketing should be effected.

continued...

COTTON MARKET REFORM, 1995 (continued)

Given the unique nature of cotton, it is imperative that we step up macroeconomic regulation and control over cotton production and trading. At a time when cotton resources are in short supply and there is a wide gap between cotton supply and demand, planned guidance, centralized management, administrative intervention and other measures are still necessary in the production and circulation stages to help bring about a recovery in cotton production and development. Such measures are also essential to our success in reforming the cotton circulation system smoothly.

III. Impact of Reform on Interests of All Parties Involved
We should steer the buying and selling of cotton onto the market in accordance with the law of value so that it realizes its own true value. Such a development will not only help straighten out the interest relations among the various parties involved in the production, supply, and marketing of cotton, but will also help protect the interests of cotton growers.

After cotton enters the market and prices are deregulated, cotton growers will not be selling cotton to the state at one fixed price. Instead, the buyer and seller will negotiate a price depending on the supply-demand situation at the time. The peasants—the seller—will have as much right as the buyer to set prices. Since the prices arrived at will essentially be determined by market supply-demand relations, it is clear cotton selling prices will simply be market prices. Reform, the opening of China, and China's accession to GATT all require that the domestic market be ultimately realigned with the international market. Moreover, the effective trading prices of cotton on the domestic market will inevitably tend to match the international level. Therefore, when we consider the effects of cotton deregulation on the interests of cotton growers, we should use the difference between the price level set by cotton-growing nations and the price level actually reached on the international market as a bench mark. In 1994, cotton was traded at 67 cents a pound on the international market in January, 79 cents in March, and 84 cents in June. With that trend, in mind along with the cotton supply-demand situation on the world market, the price of cotton on the world market could not be expected to drop below 75 cents per pound for all of 1994. Even in the absence of a major surge, it should hold steady between 75 and 80 cents. Assuming a FOB [free on board] of 79 cents per pound and an exchange rate of $1:8.75 yuan, and adding five or six cents in shipping costs, tariff free and with a refund of value-added tax, the CIF [cost insurance, and freight] should be about 820 yuan per dan. In contrast, the standard supply price, tax included, at a grade 2 station was a mere 613.49 yuan per dan during the 1994 procurement year and only 742.32 yuan for the highest grade cotton as determined by state regulations, 206.51 yuan and 77.68 yuan lower than the CIF on the international market, respectively. It can thus be seen that a switch from the existing cotton management system to a market system will inevitably boost cotton prices, enhancing the incomes of cotton growers and correspondingly raising the costs for textile enterprises.

The fair formation of cotton prices through market supply and demand helps promote fair competition among the various parties in market trading. Their interest relations are straightened out through adaptation to the market and by adjusting the structure. Since the market for textile products, including cotton yarns, as well as their prices have been deregulated, and particularly because of the drop in cotton output, cotton prices set by the state have often been pushed higher in reality.

In effect, therefore, the production of textile products such as cotton yarns is already based to varying degrees on high-priced raw materials. As far as industry is concerned, an across-the-board increase in the prices of raw materials would be passed onto the market (consumers), so pressure on industry would be neutralized. For this reason, cotton deregulation would not affect the interests of the textile industry in a significant way. On the contrary, the early deregulation of cotton will only accelerate technological transformation in the textile industry, strengthen its management, raise its efficiency, and trim its costs. In particular, it would consolidate its processing capacity, adjust the production structure and distribution system, and increase product varieties that are sought-after on the market, as well as multiple processed products.

continued...

COTTON MARKET REFORM, 1995 (continued)

When cotton is deregulated and prices are formed by the market, the state can recover about 4 billion yuan each year that would otherwise be used to subsidize cotton procurement prices. Instead this sum of money can be put into the cotton risk regulation fund to support prices. That would help shape up the government's financial support system for agriculture.

Zhongguo Wujia, No. 2, Feb 1995.

MOFTEC OUTLINE FOREIGN AID POLICY, 1995

On 15 June, the Ministry of Foreign Trade and Economic Cooperation [MOFTEC] convened a meeting to relay a State Council directive to put into effect as quickly as possible the State Council directive on reform of foreign aid work. Minister Wu Yi made an important speech at the meeting in which she cited the need for diligent study, resolute implementation, and earliest possible action.

In her speech, Minister Wu Yi noted that the State Council directive underscores basic policy and basic principles regarding foreign assistance. She summarized accomplishments in foreign aid work during the past 45 years, and set forth the guiding policy for further reform of foreign aid work under new circumstances. She said that continued good foreign aid work holds important significance for the enhancement of friendly relations and for economic and trade cooperation between China and developing countries.

In this regard, Wu Yi said that greater understanding of the significance of reform of foreign aid work, and a unified approach are the main tasks in carrying out the State Council directives.

Wu Yi said that during the past several years leading comrades in the central government have issued numerous important instructions on reform of foreign aid work. These directives have elaborated on important issues such as reform of foreign aid methods, readjustment of the aid mix, and the use of government discounted soft loans.

Reform is necessary for development of the situation at home and abroad, and it is also a new stage in the development of foreign aid work.

Wu Yi stressed that the key to implementation of the State Council directive lies in action. Thus, she set forth several concrete measures and requirements.

(1) Adherence to the basic policy for foreign aid work, i.e., both carrying forward the fine tradition of foreign aid work, and reforming and innovating under the new circumstances. The foreign aid goals are to assist the development of the indigenous economy of recipient countries, and to promote friendly relations and economic and trade cooperation between China and far-flung developing countries. Foreign aid is an important part of China's work abroad. During the past 45 years, China has provided aid to developing countries in Asia, Africa, Latin America, and the south Pacific. Aid projects helped recipient nations complete 1,426 projects. It provided large amounts of material and technical assistance. Personnel made nearly 500,000 visits abroad to help aid recipient nations train a large number of technicians. Under the new circumstances, aid work must both carry on the fine tradition, continue to abide by the eight principles, and make the most of China's political advantages. It must also reform and innovate, and borrow effective aid methods currently in use internationally so that limited aid funds can play a greater role and bring better results.

(2) Energetic spread of government-discounted soft loans for foreign assistance. This assistance method is widely used internationally. China's banks provide soft loans of a government aid character with the difference in interest between the preferential interest rate and the standard bank interest rate being subsidized as a government aid cost. This way of doing things not only combines government foreign aid funds with bank funds to expand the scale of foreign assistance, but also permits banks, in their role as institutions administering the soft loans, to improve returns from the use of aid funds. At the same time, it also promotes cooperative investment by enterprises in both countries, which stimulates exports of Chinese equipment, processed materials, and technology.

continued...

MOFTEC OUTLINE FOREIGN AID POLICY, 1995 (continued)

Discounted loans are a new method in which new problems may appear in the process of their implementation. Agencies concerned must: 1) publicize them well, and 2) make a major effort to spread this method. They must study and solve problems that arise in a timely fashion so that discounted loans will begin to be used with all possible speed and produce good results.

(3) Active promotion of foreign aid project joint ventures and cooperative ventures. Aid project joint ventures and cooperative ventures are a new form of aid that combines aid with investment, and trade with other forms of mutual cooperation. The advantages of this way of doing things are as follows: First, they tie together government aid funds and enterprise funds, thereby enlarging sources of funds and project size. Second, long-term cooperation on management and technology by enterprises of both countries, and the linking of returns from projects with the interests of enterprises, can solidify project accomplishments, thereby increasing returns from assistance. Third, recipient countries can increase investment and employment with enterprises in both countries benefiting. Foreign aid expresses direct cooperation between Chinese enterprises and enterprises in recipient countries.

(4) Proper readjustment of the make-up of aid means greater future use of government discounted soft loans. Generally speaking, interest-free loans will no longer he provided. In addition, insofar as China's financial resources permit, nonrepayable aid will be provided to developing countries that are in dire economic straits. Some nonrepayable aid funds may be combined with funds from UN development agencies for technical co-operation among developing countries. In the selection of aid projects, emphasis will be on medium and small projects that produce goods to help recipient countries develop their economy. More aid will also be provided in the form of technology, human talent, and intellect. In addition to projects that produce goods, some social welfare projects that the recipient country urgently needs such as hospitals, schools, and low construction cost housing may be undertaken as the recipient country requires.

Finally, Wu Yi emphasized that as the agency in charge of foreign aid work, MOFTEC has the responsibility for administering foreign aid work. Therefore, it must improve administration and direction of foreign aid work, improve administration of all aid projects, and particularly improve macroeconomic regulation and control of foreign aid work. It must formulate and perfect various administrative systems actively in conjunction with foreign aid reform for the gradual shaping of a more uniform, and more scientific foreign aid administrative system that is consistent with the development of events at home and abroad.

Guoji Shangbao, 17 Jun 1995.

X BUDGET AND FINANCE

STATE ENTERPRISE DEBT RESTRUCTURING IN NINTH PLAN, 1995

To solve the debt problem between state enterprises and banks, we must work with specific targets and do a quantitative analysis. Only then can we have a fairly clear idea of how to proceed. Moreover, the solution may take several forms, which then raises the issue of their numerical proportions. Here we would like to present some general ideas on debt restructuring during the Ninth Five-Year Plan.

1. Debt Restructuring: Targets and Numbers

These days a high debt ratio is eroding the enterprises' margin of profit. The latter, in turn, has saddled banks with bad assets. This is the reason we must lower enterprises' debt ratio progressively over a period of time.

continued...

STATE ENTERPRISE DEBT RESTRUCTURING IN NINTH PLAN, 1995 (continued)

1) Systematic Targets for Debt Ratio, Interest Rate, and Earnings Rate

Pointing to the capital structure of state or public enterprises in the United States, France, Germany, Britain, Switzerland, Singapore, and Malaysia, which are significantly more profitable than their Chinese counterparts, some experts suggest that the assets to liabilities ratio of state enterprises should be lower than 50 percent. In fact, what the assets to liabilities ratio of a state enterprise should be depends on its profitability and interest rate. 1) In view of the fact that currently state enterprises' assets to earnings ratio is about 6 percent and the annual interest rate is 12 percent or so, even if the enterprises' assets to liabilities ratio is trimmed to 50 percent, they will merely be breaking even and not making a profit. Hence these two crucial assumptions. One, enterprise profitability is bound to improve with a drop in the assets to liabilities ratio. Two, other reforms are also necessary if profitability is to improve. Otherwise, state enterprises as a whole will not operate normally even if the assets to liabilities ratio drops to 50 percent. 2) Interest rates charged by banks must be lowered year by year. Given an assets to earnings ratio of 6 percent, the annual interest rate must be reduced to 8.6 percent just to prevent the state economy from losing money, never mind making a profit. Therefore, we must gradually put an end to the current situation in which a substantial number of enterprises pay interest on their loans at a rate higher than their assets to earnings ratio. Some are even unable to balance their books after making interest payments. The assets to earnings ratio must gradually match the average interest rate. By the year 2001, the assets to earnings ratio of the entire state economy must top the interest rate on loans.

Accordingly, the targets for debt restructuring must be determined by taking into consideration the expected improvement in the state enterprises' assets to earnings ratio and changes in interest rates. See Table 1 below.

Table 1. Systematic Targets for Debt Restructuring During the Ninth Five-Year Plan (bn yuan)

Item	Debt Restructuring for Each Year in Ninth Five-Year Plan						Debt Restructuring in 1996
	1995	1996	1997	1998	1999	2000	1996
Total state assets at year end	3,105.0	3,570.7	4,106.3	4,722.3	5,430.6	20,934.9	3,570.7
Assets to liabilities ratio	80	76	71	65	60	55	55
Loans to liabilities ratio	70	67	63	58	54	50	50
Assets to earnings ratio	6	6.5	7	7.5	8	8.5	6.5
Interest rate	12	11	10	9	8	8	11
Profits/losses	-74.5	-31.0	28.7	107.6	199.8	249.8	35.7

• Assets increases are calculated using 1994 real prices and assuming an average increase of 15 percent, unadjusted for inflation. The last item refers to losses and profits after paying taxes and interest.

If the numbers in Table 1 are adjusted for inflation, then losses would be somewhat smaller and profits a little higher.

If debt restructuring is to be spread out through the Ninth Five-Year Plan, then this would be our target: lower the average debt ratio of state enterprises to 55 percent or so and the loans to liabilities ratio to 50 percent by the year 2000. As the enterprises transform their operating mechanism, investment reform is fully implemented, and inflation slows its pace, the excessively robust demand for funds will be reined in structurally and the average annual interest rate will drop below 8 percent. When that comes to pass, the performance of state enterprises will improve strongly and their average assets to earnings ratio will rise over time from the current 6 percent to 8.5 percent, tying the interest rate on loans. By 2000, the entire state economy is projected to rake in 250 billion yuan (in real 1994 prices) in real earnings after paying taxes and interest (not owing any interest).

Suppose debt restructuring is to be completed within 1996. Then the targets are as follows: lower the state enterprises' average assets to liabilities ratio to 55 percent or so and the loans to liabilities ratio to 50 percent within just one year, with the interest rate on loans possibly dipping to 11 percent.

continued…

STATE ENTERPRISE DEBT RESTRUCTURING IN NINTH PLAN, 1995 (continued)

There will be a slight improvement in the performance of state enterprises, their average assets to earnings ratio rising from the existing 6 percent to 6.5 percent. However, both the feasibility and probability of completing debt restructuring in just one year are rather slim, the main obstacles being the pace of enterprise structural reform, investment reform, and banking reform, and the tolerance of all social quarters for such a restructuring. It is also highly risky to try to accomplish debt restructuring within a single year.

2) Amount of State Enterprise Debt That Needs To Be Restructured Each Year

One-year debt restructuring offers the following advantages: The bad debt problem between banks and state enterprises can be solved across the nation at the same time and enterprises can compete on a level playing field as far as their debt ratio is concerned. In theory, as soon as the debt problem is solved, the state economy can operate profitably on a sustained basis. On the other hand, one-year debt restructuring is constrained by the following: the adaptability of the systems; the validity of the assumption that profitability would go up after debt restructuring; and the tolerance of the finance departments, banks, and society for debt restructuring. For all practical purposes, therefore, debt restructuring must be phased in systematically. For one thing, the financial ability of all quarters to cope with debt restructuring is limited. For another, it is less risky to spread out debt restructuring over several years. Table 2 presents the debt restructuring targets for each of the years in the Ninth Five-Year Plan. If our aim is to restructure the enterprises' excessive debt within one year, only 714.1 billion yuan worth of excessive loans (89 percent of conservative estimates of the banks' current uncollectible loans) and 178.5 billion yuan worth of excessive nonloan debt (also about 89 percent of the current estimates of uncollectible debt) need to be restructured to lower the state enterprises' average assets to liabilities ratio and the loans to liabilities ratio to 55 percent and 50 percent, respectively. If debt restructuring is to be confined to large and mid-sized state enterprises, the amount of excessive loans and nonloan liabilities to be restructured will be 142.8 billion yuan and 571.3 billion yuan [as published], respectively.

Table 2. Phasing In Debt Restructuring During Ninth Five-Year Plan (bn yuan, percent)

Item	Annual Debt Restructuring					Ninth Five-year Plan Total	Debt Restructuring in 1996
	1996	1997	1998	1999	2000	Plan Total	1996
Total state assets at year-end	3,570.7	4,106.3	4,722.3	5,430.6	6,245.2	—	3,570.7
Assets to liabilities ratio	76	71	65	60	55	—	55
Loans to liabilities ratio	67	63	58	54	50	—	50
Non-loan restructuring	35.7	41.0	47.2	54.3	62.4	240.6	178.5
Including large and mid-sized enterprises	28.5	32.8	37.7	43.4	49.9	192.3	142.8
Loan debt restructuring	107.1	164.2	236.1	217.2	249.8	974.4	714.1
Including large and mid-sized enter-prises	85.7	131.4	188.8	173.8	199.8	779.5	571.3

• Figures not adjusted for inflation.

As noted above, one-year debt restructuring is impractical because of various constraints. Enterprise debt restructuring is a dynamic process. If debt restructuring cannot be completed within one year, the dynamic process in effect becomes a soft-landing process for enterprises' high debt ratio. In other words, since enterprises cannot bring about debt restructuring in one fell swoop due to various reasons such as their operating mechanism, the need for accumulation, and inefficiency even as their production continues and expands, there will be new uncollectible loans on top of old

continued...

ones. For this reason, debt restructuring means the restructuring not only of the existing 714.1 billion yuan worth of excessive uncollectible loans and 142.8 billion yuan worth of nonloan bad accounts, but also of the new excessive liabilities that will be incurred in the next five years. Hopefully by the year 2001, there will be by and large no more new excessive liabilities as the enterprises' debt ratio approaches what is considered a normal level.

We can see that we need to restructure a total of about 1,215 billion yuan worth of debts (including 972 billion yuan incurred by large and mid-sized state enterprises), of which nonloan liabilities amount to 240.6 billion yuan and loan liabilities amount to 974.4 billion yuan (including 779.5 billion incurred by large and mid-sized enterprises) in order to solve the enterprises' high debt ratio and the banks' bad loans in stages during the Ninth Five-Year Plan so that by the year 2000 the enterprises' debt ratio would drop below 55 percent and the loans to liabilities ratio would be less than 50 percent. On average 243 billion yuan worth of debts need to be restructured each year (including 194.4 billion incurred by large and mid-sized enterprises), including 38.9 billion yuan in nonloan liabilities (of which the share of large and mid-sized enterprises is 31.1 billion) and 194.8 billion in loan liabilities (of which the share of large and mid-sized enterprises is 155.9 billion).

2. Proposed Mix of Debt Restructuring Forms

As noted above, debt restructuring can take a variety of forms and must proceed hand in hand with assets restructuring.

1) Convert government loans, which themselves have replaced government grants earlier, into government capital funds and invest the latter in enterprises. Loans obtained by enterprises from capital construction funds, both central and provincial, also should be replaced by government capital funds. Some enterprises have fallen behind in their payments to the "two funds," namely the energy and transportation fund and the capital construction fund. Central ministries in charge of specific industries as well as their provincial counterparts have been setting aside some of their own budgetary funds to make special investment loans to enterprises. Both enterprise contributions to the "two funds" and special investment loans to enterprises should be converted into enterprise capital funds as investment. First of all, convert into state capital funds for investment in enterprises those loans owed by enterprises to the state as a result of the loans-in-lieu-of-grants policy change, depending on the type of loan in debt restructuring. The sum of money involved here is about 66.6 billion yuan, 5 percent or so of the total debts slated for restructuring in the Ninth Five-Year Plan. Since this is a relatively easy task, perhaps we should spend the second half of 1995 sorting out these loans, stopping interest payments, and converting them into state capital funds and invest them in the enterprises in the first half of next year. After the loans-in-lieu-of-grants system is replaced by the investment-in-lieu-of-loans system, the loan liabilities ratio of state enterprises will drop 1.1 percentage points. It is estimated that between them, loans by the capital construction funds, money owed the "two funds," and special loans by the various central ministries to enterprises underneath them amount to more than the loans replacing grants earlier. A moratorium also should be imposed on these loans in the second half of 1995 in preparation for their conversion into capital funds in the first half of 1996. All told, the conversion of grants into loans into investment, the conversion of capital construction fund loans into investment, the conversion of the unpaid contributions to the two funds into investment, and the conversion of special loans to enterprises by central ministries and their provincial counterparts are expected to lower the enterprises' assets to liabilities ratio 3 percentage points.

2) Loans borrowed from the Ministry of Finance and its provincial and municipal counterparts should all be converted into government capital funds for investment in state enterprises provided the loans were originally financed by funds allocated in a budget. However, there are some exceptions: loans financed by proceeds from the sale of bonds issued by the treasury, loans borrowed from a bank by a finance department, and funds borrowed by a finance department from other financial and non financial institutions. It is estimated that converting

continued...

STATE ENTERPRISE DEBT RESTRUCTURING IN NINTH PLAN, 1995 (continued)

loans funded by budgetary outlays into investment can lower the enterprises' assets to liabilities ratio 0.2 percentage point.

3) Converting bank loans into enterprise stock. Not all bank loans are candidates for conversion into enterprise stock. This is why. About 70 percent of bank deposits these days consist of household savings. If an enterprise loses money or is barely profitable, it will not be possible to turn stock into principal so converting all bank loans into enterprise stock is very risky. However, we are not proposing that a bank turn the money owed it by every debt-ridden enterprise into shares across the board. Instead, we suggest that banks select those enterprises which are fairly profitable even though they have mountains of debt and buy a stake in them to the tune of 5 to 10 percent of the enterprises' net assets. Under Japanese law, a bank's stake in an enterprise may not exceed 10 percent of the latter's net assets.

One possibility is to hive off branches of the People's Bank and turn them into a China state enterprise investment bank staffed with existing personnel. The various commercial banks should make loans to it. The latter, in turn should buy up the excessive loans held by the commercial banks and use them to buy stock in the enterprises.

Table 3. Turning Bank Loans Into Enterprise Stock During Ninth Five-Year Plan (bn yuan, percent)

Item	1996	1997	1998	1999	2000
Total state assets at year-end	3,560.7	4,106.3	4,722.3	5,430.6	6,245.2
Net enterprise assets	821.8	1,190.8	1,652.8	2,172.2	2,810.3
Bank capital stock ratio	2	4	6	8	10
Loans converted into stock for the year	16.4	23.8	33.0	43.5	56.2
Bank shares	16.4	40.2	73.2	116.7	172.9
Drop in debt ratio	0.46	0.98	1.55	2.15	2.77

If we go about converting bank loans into enterprise shares in accordance with Table 3, the amount converted would be smaller in the first years and gradually increase as time goes by. By the year 2000, this approach will have taken care of 14 percent of the debt restructuring problem of all state enterprises.

4) The central government and local authorities may share the costs of enterprise debt restructuring. Each year both may set aside a predetermined portion of their revenue to finance debt restructuring. At the same time, each year they may use some of the profits from the issue of money (such profits are split between the central government and banks at the rate of 62 percent to 38 percent, in effect forming part of the revenue of the central government) to write off enterprises' bad debts. Based on my calculations, the central government should allocate 10 billion yuan from its profits from the issue of currency each year starting in 1996, increasing the amount by 30 percent each year for the next four years for the purpose of canceling the bad debts of state enterprises under the central government. Similarly, local governments should set aside 15 billion yuan each year starting in 1996 and increase it by 30 percent each year for the next four years. Half of that sum should be used to finance the conversion into government stock of the debts of state enterprises under local governments. The other half should be used to write off outright the bad debts of these enterprises. See Table 4.

When profits from the issue of money and local revenue are used for loan write-off purposes, the loans should be limited to those that the enterprises have borrowed from banks. This would ensure the safety of depositors' money in the banks and avoid any financial unrest. Using local revenue to convert debts into stock means that a local finance department purchases an enterprise's excessive bank loans, in effect repaying the loans on behalf of the enterprise. The local outlay on the enterprise thus becomes the state's capital stock in the enterprise. A local finance department may dip into its local income tax revenue or resort to other ways to raise the necessary funds.

continued...

STATE ENTERPRISE DEBT RESTRUCTURING IN NINTH PLAN, 1995 (continued)

Table 4. Using Revenue and Profits From Issue of Currency to Restructure Debt During Ninth Five-Year Plan (bn yuan, percent)

Item	1996	1997	1998	1999	2000	Ninth Five-Year Plan Total
Total state assets at year end	3,570.7	4,106.3	4,722.3	5,430.6	6,245.2	—
Profits from issue used to write off debts	10.0	13.0	16.9	1.9	28.5	90.3
Local revenue used to write off debts	7.5	9.8	12.7	16.5	21.4	67.9
Local revenue used to convert loans into stock	7.5	9.8	12.7	16.5	21.4	67.9
Drop in debt ratio	0.7	0.79	0.89	1.01	1.14	3.62

5) The state enterprise investment bank may issue priority shares to be used for purchasing the loans owed by an enterprise to a commercial bank, thereby converting such loans into an investment in the enterprise. The advantage of issuing priority shares to members of the public is that there is no need to return the principal to the shareholders and shareholders have no voting right.

Thus the state remains in control over the state enterprise investment bank. The disadvantage is that the state enterprise is required to pay fairly high dividends to the shareholders on a prolonged basis. After their debts are converted into investment, enterprises must be required to become more profitable while lowering risk.

Table 5. Debt Restructuring Through the Issue of Priority Shares During Ninth Five-Year Plan (bn yuan, percent)

Item	1996	1997	1998	1999	2000	Ninth Five-Year Plan Total
Total state assets at year-end	3,570.7	4,106.3	4,722.3	5,430.6	6,245.2	—
Priority shares issued by investment bank	20.0	24.0	28.6	34.6	41.4	148.8
Drop in debt ratio	0.55	0.58	0.61	0.63	0.66	2.38

The issue of priority shares must be limited to those enterprises which are both profitable and promising. After lowering their debt ratio, these enterprises have a chance of raising their earnings rate to a level higher than the interest rate. This will make it possible in the future for the state enterprise investment bank to earn dividends from its investment in the enterprises, which, in turn, will enable it to pay dividends properly to the shareholders.

6) Select a number of enterprises which have bright prospects and are fairly profitable, but are so saddled with debt that they are not capable of sustained development. Impose a moratorium on their interest payments. Meanwhile the treasury should step in to subsidize their interest rate for five years to give the enterprises a breathing spell, but only if they meet one ironclad condition, which is that the principal must be repaid after five years. After the five-year breather, or at any time during the five years, the enterprises must pay off the principal. Suppose the amount of debt to be restructured using this approach is 50 billion yuan nationwide and interest subsidies amount to 5.5 billion yuan each year, then the total outlay for the entire Ninth

continued...

STATE ENTERPRISE DEBT RESTRUCTURING IN NINTH PLAN, 1995 (continued)

Five-Year Plan will be 27.5 billion yuan. By the end of five years, enterprises pay off their principal and the debt ratio will drop 0.8 percentage points.

7) Use acquisitions and bankruptcy to lower the level of debt of state enterprises. Enterprises with substantial economic resources may buy up other enterprises, thereby lowering the debt ratio overall. For that to happen, the well-heeled enterprises must also take over the liabilities of the acquired enterprises at the time of acquisition. After they are bought up, the enterprises may find themselves in a better position with more advanced equipment and bigger plants. Their market prospects may also look brighter with reorganization. As for those enterprises whose liabilities exceed their assets and which are beyond salvage, they should take the bankruptcy route with the help of funds from the reserve fund for unpaid and uncollectible bank loans. Their debts should be written off using money from the reserve fund.

Table 6. Debt Restructuring Through Acquisitions During the Ninth Five-Year Plan (bn yuan, percent)

Item	1996	1997	1998	1999	2000	Ninth Five-Year Plan
Total state assets at year-end	3,570.7	4,106.3	4,722.3	5,430.6	6,245.2	—
Liabilities assumed at acquisition	15.0	18.0	21.6	26.0	31.1	111.7
Debts written off at bankruptcy	7.0	8.4	10.1	12.1	14.5	52.1
Drop in debt ratio	0.62	0.64	0.67	0.70	7.30	2.62

If acquisitions are to play the role in debt restructuring described above, there must be many more enterprise acquisitions in the Ninth Five-Year Plan. On average 22 billion yuan worth of liabilities should be taken over as a result of acquisitions each year. When it comes to enterprise bankruptcy, we must be extremely careful in order to avoid a bankruptcy fever, which will put great pressure on banks as enterprises seek to dodge their creditors. Consider also the distribution of enterprises whose liabilities exceed their assets and which are deemed unsalvageable. It seems that the proportion of such enterprises should be a little higher in the northeast.

8) Find overseas buyers to assume the claims of some enterprises, particularly those of a number of small enterprises. The proceeds from such sales may then be used to repay the banks, thus reviving a portion of their assets which have gone sour. Depending on the circumstances, some of the claims of a number of small state enterprises may be taken over by their employees. When the employees of a small state enterprise assume its liabilities, its assets should also be allocated among the employees in proportion to the liabilities assumed. This approach enables the state to concentrate its financial resources on the debt restructuring of large and mid-sized state enterprises, at the same time unburdening it of numerous unprofitable outfits and turning a substantial portion of the inactive assets of banks into normal active assets again. This protects the interests of whose who have deposited their savings in banks.

Table 7. Debt Restructuring by Selling Off Claims During Ninth Five-Year Plan (bn yuan, percent)

Item	1996	1997	1998	1999	2000	Ninth Five-Year Plan Total
Total state assets at year end	3,570.7	4,106.3	4,722.3	5,430.6	6,245.2	—
Claims sold at home and abroad	20.0	24.0	28.8	34.6	41.4	148.8

continued…

STATE ENTERPRISE DEBT RESTRUCTURING IN NINTH PLAN, 1995 (continued)

Item	1996	1997	1998	1999	2000	Ninth Five-Year Plan Total
Loans converted into assets through sale to employees	20.0	24.0	28.8	34.6	41.4	148.8
Drop in debt ratio	1.12	1.17	1.22	1.27	1.33	4.77

Reform No. 5, 20 Sep 1995.

TAX INCREASE FOR STATE ENTERPRISES AFTER REFORM, 1995

On 25 November 1994, the three major papers in the capital all carried a report on a special survey of 1,809 Chinese-funded enterprises in 30 provinces and municipalities across the country (hereafter referred to as "sample survey") conducted by the China Entrepreneur Investigative Group and the Policy and Regulation Department of the State Administration of Taxation. The conclusion presented in the report is: With the implementation of the new tax system, enterprise turnover tax rates have come down, resulting in a decline in their total tax burden.

The above conclusion, however, is not in line with the feeling of most enterprises, nor does it agree with the comprehensive official statistics published by the relevant departments of the state. Moreover, it is diametrically contrary to the findings we have obtained through constant follow-up studies. To apprise our readers and the policy-making departments of the true situation with respect to enterprise tax burdens, we elucidate below the results of our investigations and studies.

I. Before Tax Reform, State-Owned Enterprises Already Had an Excessive Tax Burden
Whether the tax burden on state-owned enterprises is too heavy has long been a disputed issue. Most people are not very clear about the actual tax burden borne by our state-owned enterprises. As a first step to probe into this issue, let us make a comparison of the tax burdens among different types of enterprises at home and between enterprises in China and in foreign countries.

Within our country, of all types of enterprises, state-owned enterprises have the heaviest tax burden. If the turnover tax burden borne by state-owned enterprises during the period from January to September 1993 is taken as 100 percent, then the burden is 58.7 percent for collective enterprises, 53.7 percent for township enterprises, and 62.9 percent for other enterprises, including the "three kinds of foreign-funded" enterprises. As turnover taxes are principal taxes, the above data are indicative of the excessive total tax burden on state-owned enterprises. To reduce the difference in tax burden, we do not believe that we should raise the taxes on non-state owned enterprises, because their tax burden is by no means lighter compared with enterprises in foreign countries. Instead, we should reduce the overly heavy tax burden on state-owned enterprises so that they may compete with others on a parity basis.

The following table shows a comparison of enterprise tax burdens in China and in other countries.

continued...

TAX INCREASE FOR STATE ENTERPRISES AFTER REFORM, 1995 (continued)

Table 1. Comparison of Enterprise Tax Burdens in United States, Japan, and China (%)

	3.7 million enterprises in U.S. (1992-1993)	430,000 manu-facturing enterprises in Japan (1988)	70,000 state-owned indus-trial enterprises in China (1992)
Taxes to sales	3.5	3.4	10.9
Retained enterprise profits to sales	7.4	2.2	1.6
Taxes to total earnings	31.8	61.0	87.4
Retained enterprise profits to total earnings	68.2	39.0	12.6

II. Tax Burden Is Heavier, Not Lighter, After the Tax Reform

The following is a comparison between the results derived from the "sample survey" and the data of practical operations based on the government statistics. Also given is an explanation of the comparison.

1. Table 2 shows the results of the "sample survey."

Table 2. Turnover Tax Burden Before and After Tax Reform

Types of Enterprises Surveyed	Number	Actual Tax Burden % Jan-Jun 1994	Nominal Tax Burden % Under Old Tax System	Actual Tax Burden % Under Old Tax System	Increase/Decrease in Tax Burden Before and After Tax Reform
Industrial Enterprises with Independent Accounting System	1809	6.99	8.81	7.51	-0.52
Including State-Owned Enterprises	1268	7.44	9.31	7.84	-0.40
Collective Enterprises	68	4.49	5.16	4.96	-0.47
Township Enterprises	95	3.71	5.32	4.53	-0.82
Other Enterprises	378	5.30	6.96	6.32	-1.02

• Data obtained from RENMIN RIBAO, JINGJI RIBAO, and ZHONGHUA GONGSHANG SHIBAO [CHINA INDUSTRIAL AND COMMERCIAL TIMES], 25 Nov. 1994, pp. 1-2.

• The turnover tax burden is the ratio of turnover taxes to sales. Increases and decreases are expressed in percentage points.

Table 2 shows an apparent decline in the enterprise turnover tax burden after the implementation of the new tax system.

2. Table 3 gives the results of government statistics based on data provided by the State Statistical Bureau, the Ministry of Finance, and Beijing Municipality.

continued...

TAX INCREASE FOR STATE ENTERPRISES AFTER REFORM, 1995 (continued)

Table 3. Turnover Tax Burden Before and After Tax Reform (percent)

Table 3. Turnover Tax Burden Before and After Tax Reform %

Types of Enterprises	Number	Turnover Tax Burden Before Tax Reform		Turnover Tax Burden After Tax Reform		Increase/Decrease Before and After Tax Reform
		Jan-Jun 1993	Jan-Sep 1993	Jan-Jun 1994	Jan-Sep 1994	Jan-Sep 1993—Jan-Sep 1994
Industrial Enterprises with Independent Accounting System	370,000		7.10		8.20	-1.10
Including: State-Owned Enterprises	70,000		8.42		9.92	-1.50
Collective Enterprises	300,000		4.94		6.03	-1.09
Including: Township Enterprises	190,000		4.52		5.53	-1.01
Other Enterprises	20,000		5.30		6.04	-0.74
Industrial Enterprises Included in Budget	36,000	8.83	8.84	11.33	10.52	-1.68
Including: Enterprises in Beijing	400	8.55	8.66	9.44	10.24	-1.50

Economic Management No. 2, 5 Feb 1995.

FINANCIAL STRUCTURE REFORMS, 1995

[Editor's note] This article was supplied by Zhonghua Institute for Comprehensive Development, an academic institution registered with the state of California. Most of its researchers are scattered among professional and academic organizations all over China. This article is a research report submitted to the government by a think tank in Beijing. It was written by a researcher with the Zhonghua Institute and is published here under the writer's pen-name. The article does a good job in explaining the current state of China's financial system, the thinking behind reform, as well as the resistance and difficulties it has encountered. The article is published in two parts. The first part discusses the importance of the central bank and the monetary policy. The second part looks at the commercialization of financial institutions and the establishment of a financial market. [End editor's note]

The bank is merely the government's accountant and cashier. The three episodes in which we lost control of the economy were all triggered by the modest easing of funds which had been very rigidly controlled by the financial system.

The most salient feature of economic reform is the shift from direct control to indirect control. It should be the central bank's job to implement monetary policy. Special banks should operate in accordance with market principles.

Chapter 1. Thorough Financial Reform Brooks No Delay

Back in October 1979 Deng Xiaoping told a national symposium for provincial, municipal, and autonomous regional CPC secretaries: "Banks should tackle the economy. These days, however, banks just do the books. They are like mere cashiers. They are not doing the things banks really should do." He instructed that "banks are the lever for economic development and technological innovation. We must turn banks into bona fide banks." As one of the three major pillars (the other two being the commodity market and the market for qualified personnel), the financial market has not kept up with reform comprehensively and in a coordinated way because the economy as a whole has been hamstrung by politics and ideology. Like state enterprises, financial institutions display the three characteristics inherent in and unique to the non-private economy: muddled property rights relationships, mismanagement, and inefficiency. After several rounds of major reform, banking is stuck in the same old mold. The central bank is not working the way a central bank should. Nor have special banks been able to shake off intervention by local governments.

continued...

FINANCIAL STRUCTURE REFORMS, 1995 (continued)

What is Fundamentally Wrong with the Financial System
That the financial system is woefully backward and corrupt has caused the national economy to go through cycles of losing control and balance, giving rise to destructive inflation and frenzies of speculation, which have had disastrous effects on the economic climate as a whole. In the 15 years since reform got under way and the opening policy was introduced, there have been three major economic crises, in 1984, 1988, and 1993, the last one still going on today. All three crises were caused by a slight easing of funds which had hitherto been controlled to death by a backward financial system.

Despite the substantial achievements of reform in recent years, the current financial system as a whole is still essentially a vertical structure, at most a collection of several vertical structures.

As far as the relationship between the financial system and the government is concerned, banks are still under the control of the State Council (and before that the State Planning Commission). On the surface they now have nothing to do with the national budget deficit. However, local authorities can exercise their administrative power and order banks to extend loans to units and construction projects which will not be able to repay them. Localities frequently overdraw their bank accounts and demand that hundreds of billions of yuan worth of bad loans be written off each year.

Turning to macroeconomic financial regulation and control, there has been no basic shift from the use of administrative management tools. Although documents now explicitly stipulate that the People's Bank is in charge of overseeing and managing all financial undertakings in the nation and that special banks are to be commercialized, the central bank continues to use the battery of administrative tools, including planning and targets, of the past in its dealings with the special banks. So do the head offices of special banks in their dealings with units beneath them.

Turning to the microeconomic level, banks lend to enterprises regardless of the latter's economic performance. Consequently, an excess of funds is tied up in loans which are often uncollectible. Local authorities, various sectors, and enterprises are only interested in expanding the scale of fixed assets investment and could not care less how working funds are used or where they come from. Few enterprises tap after-tax production development funds to supplement their own working funds. Some enterprises simply have no self-retained working funds, which does not help the effort to limit the scale of fixed assets investment or the drive to rationalize the enterprise production structure.

Needless to say, the absence of conditions for macroeconomic control has spawned a string of problems which must be resolved in the course of time through further reform: an underdeveloped financial market, lack of diversity in the forms of credit, the dearth of financial service outlets, the poor quality of their services, the dire shortage of qualified financial personnel, the poor caliber of financial workers, and imperfections in financial laws.

Chapter 2. Clarifying the Central Bank's Role and Policies
A developed commodity economy is necessarily a monetary and a credit economy. Hence the need to develop the banking industry broadly, put together financial institutions of all forms and shapes, and create many different forms of credit. To do that, we must have a strong central bank in charge of the issuance of money, management of credit, and stabilization of banking. Years of practice prove that when financial institutions proliferate without leadership, "the four dragons will release the water." In that kind of situation, banks will scramble to make loans, and there will be a credit explosion.

The most salient feature of economic restructuring today should be the shift from direct control to indirect regulation and from in-kind control to value control. A mere government body with no currency or funds at its disposal is not in a position to use economic tools to control the fund movements of special banks effectively, and therefore is powerless to bring about indirect regulation. Thus the foremost function of a sound central bank is to regulate the economy indirectly, manage it through value, limit aggregate social demand by controlling the money

continued...

FINANCIAL STRUCTURE REFORMS, 1995 (continued)

supply, provide credit selectively, steer the flow of funds into those sectors of society which need them most, and adjust the economic structure.

Necessary Conditions for a Monetary Policy

A central bank typically has two paramount objectives;

1. Formulating monetary policy and organizing its implementation. The objective of the existing monetary policy of the People's Bank of China is to develop the economy and stabilize the currency. In practice, though, this objective lacks a body of intermediate objectives, which is confusing to the public.

2. Protecting and nurturing the development of the banking industry. The social and economic impact of the banking industry is deep and wide. Even after the banking industry has come to life, we must ensure its stability and reliability and preserve and enhance its reputation.

Implementing the central bank's monetary policy remains an uphill battle in China today. The reason is that a number of conditions must be met before the monetary policy can be implemented.

1. The central bank must be independent and free to formulate a monetary policy independently and implement it flexibly. It must be free from external interference so that the issue of money will not be determined solely by the amount of funds the government and enterprises want. Instead, the central bank must be free to take measures expeditiously in light of economic conditions to ensure stable economic growth.

2. To operate thoroughly like an enterprise, the special bank must comply with market laws in business operations. Under China's current banking system, loans are distributed in accordance with an established credit plan, so in-kind distribution is still very much alive. The inter-sector circulation of money is reactive and does not play any role in regulating the economy. The bank is nothing more than the State Planning Commission's currency management arm. Special banks must improve the quality of their operations, be sensitive to interest rates, and watch economic conditions and market demand closely. It must absorb and use funds independently and assume the risks of accepting deposits and making loans.

3. Industrial and commercial enterprises must be bona fide enterprises. They must practice independent accounting and enjoy decision-making authority in their operations. They must modify their operations, production, and investment promptly in response to changes in interest rates. They must assume the risks of borrowing, calculate production costs most meticulously, and be super-sensitive to market changes.

4. Monetary policy must be closely coordinated with the financial and foreign exchange policies.

5. A strong research arm and information system is needed. When the central bank achieves a fair measure of independence, the principal basis for its decision making process would no longer be the government, but market monitoring, economic research, and up-to-the-minute economic information.

Transition to Indirect Regulation

At present, China still does not meet the preconditions described above. Direct control methods, including credit planning, setting credit ceilings, and restrictions on interest rates, must therefore be retained for some time to come. In the future we must work to meet these prerequisites to bring about the transition to full-fledged indirect regulation.

In China today there is only one macroeconomic financial control instrument, namely comprehensive credit planning, which may take the form of either the deposits to reserve funds ratio or interest rates. However, interest rates are set so low that they bear no relationship to reality. Circumscribed by the comprehensive credit plan, the deposit to reserve funds ratio simply cannot change in a way that could influence the total money supply. Thus these two instruments exist in name only.

The transition to indirect control is necessary not only for financial reform but also for economic restructuring as a whole. For this reason, the central bank should implement monetary

continued...

FINANCIAL STRUCTURE REFORMS, 1995 (continued)

policy on three levels. On the first level, control the deposits to reserve funds ratio. On the second level, control rediscount and relending interest rates. On the third level, conduct open market operations (the buying and selling of securities). All three levels are necessary if we are to control and regulate the total money supply, regulate aggregate social demand, and achieve monetary policy goals. Certainly, utilization of all three methods to regulate the economy is still a very remote prospect in China. In the foreseeable future, the central bank should use a mix of direct and indirect controls while striving for the exclusive use of indirect control over time. Accordingly, the central bank should work out the total money supply needed based on the projected GNP growth rate for the year in question, the projected inflation rate, international economic conditions, and other factors. Next, it should examine the relationship between the total money supply and the overall scale of lending in the past and figure out the necessary overall scale of lending for the whole nation. In actual practice, the central bank also needs to consider a string of indicators, including the rate of monetary circulation, the retail price index on the market, capital goods price index, and interest rates on the money market. Through adjustment of a mix of indicators, including the amount of re-lending by the central bank, rediscount volume, basic interest rates, and the deposits to reserve funds ratio, the central bank regulates the money supply in society in order to realize set policy goals.

Chapter 3. Tightening Credit Control
There are objective limits to the money supply necessary for a given scale of production and commodity circulation. Having a money supply that is too much or too little is not good for production. As the scale of social expanded reproduction increases, so should the money supply needed. The increase in the money supply comes from additional loans made by banks. In the past we did not pay much attention to limiting the total amount of lending. Judging from the situation in the last few years, we still have some problems in controlling the scale of lending and the total money supply.

Causes of Credit Explosion
First, there is not a body of intermediate targets to control the overall scale of credit and the total money supply.

1. We only emphasize the amount of cash that goes into the money supply, not the amount of loans. We have not yet found a method to calculate the total money supply that is universally recognized to be effective.

2. There is absolutely no agreement on how big a money supply is needed in the market and its rate of circulation. Currently one can count as many as 15 formulas for calculating the former and nine for working out the latter. The head office of the People's Bank of China alone uses four formulas to figure out the rate at which money circulates on the market. (Xie Ping [6200 1627], "A Brief Introduction to the Methods Currently Used To Calculate the Volume of Currency in Circulation," in JINGJI YANJIU CANKAO ZILIAO)

3. Banks have never made limiting the scale of fixed assets investment a major objective in macroeconomic financial control. As a result, the expansion of the scale of fixed-assets investment has fueled an increase in the scale of working-fund loans and overall credit.

4. Although balancing China's international payments is recognized as essential to achieving an overall balance in the national economy, our foreign exchange and exchange rate policies are not well defined.

5. There must be a comprehensive balance between public finance and credit. This is a basic principle recognized by all. Nevertheless the principle has become more fiction than fact in recent years as finance departments continue to take advantage of banks. Each year the budget deficit each year is still covered by overdrawing one's bank accounts. Increased government appropriations in recent years notwithstanding, funds are not actually made available.

Second, the credit explosion may come about in the following ways:

continued...

FINANCIAL STRUCTURE REFORMS, 1995 (continued)

1. The practice of controlling the planned credit target based on the increase/decrease differences prompts a stampede for lending base figures, a serious situation in which lending can get out of hand (as in 1984).

2. The adoption of "differential contracting" at a time when the basic money supply has not been brought under control using the multiplier effect may make us lose control of the volume of credit. (Witness the credit and monetary chaos of 1988.)

3. The method of "linking the amount of lending to the actual amount of deposits on hand," adopted in 1985, has proved to have a powerful effect in controlling the scale of credit and the total money supply. However, when this method, which requires both "gain coupons" (credit target) and "money" (self-raised funding sources), is strictly enforced in conjunction with the fragmented management of special banks, the result is over-regulation; funds cannot be deployed flexibly, the horizontal circulation of funds is impeded, and the enthusiasm of grass-roots bank branches is not put to use (as exemplified by the effort to impose a single policy across the board in 1989).

Credit Control Procedures

All these problems urgently await solution as we continue reform. To control the scale of credit, we should take the following reform steps beginning now:

1. Instead of concentrating on controlling the flow of cash, we should shift to control of the total money supply as soon as possible (at the same time bearing in mind changes in the rate of circulation), and then work on limiting the total volume of credit in light of the money supply. We should make the balance between aggregate social supply and aggregate social demand a leading target of macroeconomic financial control.

2. Promptly set an optimal size for the money supply and use it as the basis for China's monetary policy. There should be a most stable relationship between the total money supply and the aggregate demand for currency (the maximum gross output capacity). It should be able to provide statistics quickly and is something the central bank can control directly. In actual practice, it should be put in the hands of a relatively independent commission charged with formulating a monetary policy based on market parameters.

3. In China, an enterprise is allowed to open an account with only one bank, and a bank may operate in only one jurisdiction or sector. Hence the need to examine the monetary-multiplier effect under these conditions so that the central bank can use the multiplier to control the basic money supply and hence the specified total money supply.

4. Before we start controlling the basic money supply based on the monetary-multiplier effect, we may adopt the following transitional measure, which is to allow savings and fixed deposits of enterprises and institutional units to be linked to credit even as the scale of credit is brought under control. We should make sure, however, that deposits are used to expand the scale of capital construction.

5. To ensure the stability of the money supply and reduce buck-passing, it is that proposed deposits of a fiscal nature (except for deposits in the treasury) be set aside as a source of funds for special banks. We should raise the deposits to reserve funds ratio too.

Chapter 4. Perfect the Family of Interest Rates; Gradually Use Interest Rates To Regulate the Economy

There are currently two major problems with interest-rate management by banks. One, the interest-rate management system is too rigid. Two, interest rates are too low. The power to set interest rates is highly centralized in the hands of the head office of the People's Bank. The branches and grass-roots banks can only vary the rates within a pathetically narrow range. In a majority of cases, banks simply have no wriggle room at all. Besides, once interest rates are set, they remain unchanged for years. Banks and society at large are not used to the idea of adjusting interest rates regularly; some bank regulations actually work against frequent interest rate adjustments. The one-size-fits-all attitude toward interest rates along with regulations meant to be applied universally mean that the localities are powerless to modify interest rates

continued...

FINANCIAL STRUCTURE REFORMS, 1995 (continued)

flexibly. Inevitably interest rates are the same from industry to industry with no regard for their individual economic performance.

The fact that they are set too low is an important reason interest rates are not effective as an economic lever. Following the adjustments of the last few years, interest rates paid by banks have gone up slightly. If we factor in inflation, however, the effective interest rates are still significantly lower than the cost of funds. Low interest rates frustrate the effort to attract savings deposits broadly and also decrease enterprise interest expenditures relative to total production costs, which works against the drive to improve the bottom line. Needless to say, the fact that there are too few levels of interest rates, which means limited variability, also presents a problem.

Objectives of Interest Rate Reform

The ultimate objective of interest rate reform is to have the central bank set re-lending and rediscount rates for special banks and adjust them as changes in economic conditions warrant. Interest rates charged by special banks should be completely deregulated. Banks should be free to set their own interest rates after considering returns, mobility, and safety in an overall context. Certainly, this can be realized only after special banks are fully commercialized in their conduct, that is, after they have adopted a full-fledged shareholding system. For a considerable period of time before this goal is achieved, there is a need for the central bank to continue to determine directly the upper and lower limits of interest rates charged by special banks on major types of loans or payable by them on major types of deposits. Over time the ranges of such interest rates should be eliminated. Meanwhile the money market and capital market should be used to accustomize and sensitize banks and enterprises to interest rate changes.

Even as the central bank directly sets rediscount and re-lending rates as well as the upper and lower limits of interest rates charged by special banks, it must do so based on what is happening in the economy. First, a key point of reference is whether there is a balance between aggregate social demand and aggregate social supply and if not, the size of the imbalance. Second, it must take into account national social and economic development objectives such as the GNP growth rate and the unemployment rate. Third, also to be considered is the average margin of profit of industrial and commercial enterprises so that interest rates do not go up so much that they undermine the enthusiasm of industrial enterprises or drop so low that they fuel a round of consumption explosion. Fourth, the social commodity retail price index and other price indexes must be taken into account too. When interest rates are too high, they diminish supply and drive up the costs of a variety of products, triggering inflation and rampant speculation. If interest rates are too low, on the other hand, they could become ineffective in checking the growth of the total money supply, leading to price increases and other problems. Fifth, interest rates must be set in conjunction with the supply and demand of funds. To keep the total money supply from rising above the projected level, we must regulate interest rates to a point of balance (or let interest rates float freely). Sixth, the costs to banks of accepting deposits and doing business must be taken into consideration. Seventh, consideration must also be given to interest and exchange rates on the international financial market. Needless to say, even as they make loans to industrial and commercial enterprises charging interest rates within officially set limits, special banks must comprehensively look at the specifics of the case in question, including the location, the borrower, the duration, and the time period.

Banks should reform themselves by becoming enterprise-like operations and gradually evolving into economic entities that practice independent accounting. To that end, they should adopt the shareholding system, but not immediately.

Regarding reform of the financial market, a socialism versus capitalism debate is now going on in the top echelons in China. Yet perfecting the financial market not only meets social and economic needs but is also consistent with the deepening of economic reform.

Part one of this article discussed the importance of the central bank and monetary policy. This part looks at the commercialization of financial institutions and the establishment of a financial market.

continued...

FINANCIAL STRUCTURE REFORMS, 1995 (continued)

Chapter 5. Spurring Reform of Financial Institutions Through Commercialization

Everybody knows that financial institutions in China are inefficiently run and offer poor services. Their operations have the following problems:

1. Banks are treated as administrative budgetary units. They are underfunded and understaffed. Their workers are grossly undertrained. The result is that banks at the grass roots spontaneously resist business growth.

2. The vertical management system within banks and the practice of "eating from the treasury's big rice pot" have dampened the enthusiasm of banks at all levels to do business.

3. There is no competition among banks. They don't care about efficiency and are very inefficient in their operations.

4. The responsibilities, rights, and interests of grass-roots banks are not well defined or specified. It makes no difference how much business a bank does or how well or poorly it performs. It has no incentive and is under no pressure to do well.

For these reasons, Zhao Ziyang made this exhortation back in the Seventh Five-Year Plan (1986-1990) report: "All special banks should adhere to the reform direction of commercialization and gradually evolve into economic entities that practice independent accounting."

Banks Should Turn to the Shareholding System

Although the idea of bank commercialization has been around for some time, the public still does not understand what "commercialization" really means, so the objectives of bank reform through commercialization remain fuzzy. As some people see it, at its core bank commercialization means establishing a level of profit a bank should strive for, making the bank itself assume the risk of doing business, and holding the bank and its employees accountable for the bottom line. A host of models have been put forward, including the "head office-branch profit center system," "multiple-level majority shareholder system," and "hybrid system." (See Hu Jingyan [5170 4544 3508], "Ideas on the Commercialization of Special Banks in China," in SHANGHAI JINRONG, No 10, 1989). In this writer's opinion, however, special banks cannot achieve bona fide commercialization if they try to commercialize without changing their ownership system. This is why:

First, the single ownership system in banking is incompatible with the development of a commodity economy.

1. The lack of varied ownership in the financial system is incompatible with the diversified economic structure that has emerged in the national economy and hinders the development of many new-born economic formats.

2. Under a single ownership system, funds are under a highly centralized vertical form of management, which is at odds with the ever-broadening horizontal cooperation and all-round development taking place today.

3. Monopolism has restricted competition and encouraged bureaucratic practices in banking. Banks come under no outside pressure and have no driving force inside. As a result, they are not motivated to improve their banking operations or update their information service technology.

4. Outdated and rigid financial management tools, lack of diversity in the forms of credit available and the methods of raising short-term loans, and the crudity of credit tools all are not congruent with the development of a commodity economy which is diversified and multilevel.

Second, the fusion of ownership and management powers in the hands of the state is the root cause of the "supply system" and the practice of "eating from one big rice pot." Since the state owns bank funds and capital, it is only logical that it has the power to formulate the credit plan and adopt a highly centralized form of management. Banks have no choice but to carry out these orders. Profits are submitted to the higher levels in their entirety. Loans that have gone bad are written off by the state (the bank at a higher level) and fund losses are also borne by the state.

Third, since banks do not practice the shareholding system, responsibilities, rights, and profits bear no relationship to one another. This tends to give rise to the unbridled pursuit of the

continued...

FINANCIAL STRUCTURE REFORMS, 1995 (continued)

maximization of short-term profits, which has a disruptive effect on the entire economy and society. Also because of the absence of the shareholding system from banking, banks have no genuine decision-making authority in their operations; nor do they have financial autonomy or control over personnel.

It Is Inadvisable To Adopt the Shareholding System Immediately
Are the current conditions fight for the immediate adoption by banks of the shareholding system? In other words, should banks take up shareholding right away? In our opinion, there are still some problems remaining today which make it inadvisable for banks to adopt the shareholding system at this point.

1. The entire price system is irrational. It neither reflects value accurately nor mirrors supply-demand relationships properly. Thrusting the shareholding system on special banks prematurely under these circumstances may exacerbate imbalances in the industrial and product structures. At a time when prices are still distorted, moreover, it is impossible to put a correct price tag on the net assets of existing special banks, something that must be done to convert them into state shares and absorb capital from collectives and private individuals.

2. As yet the central bank is incapable of deploying economic tools to control the total money supply, total credit, and the direction of investment skillfully. If banks adopt the shareholding system sooner than is justified, we may end up with too much or too little money supply and funds may be channeled in directions that do not meet social needs, resulting in a serious imbalance between aggregate supply and aggregate demand.

3. There is still an acute desire for investment on the part of production enterprises during the economic transitional period. The consumption fever, too, remains very much alive among members of the public. The premature adoption of the shareholding system by banks under these conditions will bring together the profit-maximizing behavior of banks which have adopted the shareholding system and investment and consumption fever, which may send the aggregate effective demand soaring in a pernicious way.

4. The masses do not have much income at present, which means they do not have enough funds to buy shares. The same is true for collective units. This problem can be solved only after fiscal reform and the formulation of a national income distribution policy. As of now, finance departments still control the bulk of the national income, only a very small portion of which is distributed through state enterprises and an even tinier share through collective enterprises. The share of the national income distributed through individuals is downright negligible.

5. The public has precious little knowledge of finance and investment. Besides, workers in the financial industry are generally of poor quality. The premature adoption of the shareholding system in banking will make it easier for speculators and criminals to exploit loopholes and create financial disorder, causing losses to the national economy.

Reform: Where Do We Start?
As far as special banks are concerned, therefore, a prerequisite for the shareholding system is commercialized management. Special banks should accustom themselves to doing things in accordance with economic principles, pursue profit maximization within limits, and assume the risk of lending. Starting now, the following reform measures should be introduced:

1. Promote competition among special banks.'Competition is a characteristic of a commodity economy. As the most essential component of a commodity economy, banks cannot stay outside the reach of competition either. As we demand that banks assume responsibility for their own operations, the overlapping of financial activities, which accompanies the growth of lateral ties in a commodity economy, will inevitably lead to competition. Interbank competition is good for society. It breaks up old monopolies and blockades; prompts banks to exercise more rigorous supervision over enterprises, which in turn will force enterprises to increase the returns on fund use and elevate their management standard; and enhances the banks' own vitality, upgrades their operations, compels them to consider whether funds are safe, and makes them more eager to increase their value. Competition must not be limited to improving the quality of services. Competition should also involve making interest rates more competitive within certain

continued...

FINANCIAL STRUCTURE REFORMS, 1995 (continued)

limits. The inflation factor must be taken into account when setting the interest rates on loans. Banks should go about lending money following this basic formula:

Bank profit equals amount of loans times the interest rate on loans minus the sum of interest rate on deposits plus the inflation rate.

Right now there is high inflation in China. In contrast, interest rates charged by banks are very low. Even when calculated using actual purchasing power, bank profits are on the low side and often fall into negative territory. To ensure competition, we must get rid of rules which enable one bank to monopolize an industry or jurisdiction. Instead, all special banks should be allowed to operate freely in any industry or jurisdiction.

2. Even as we endorse small collective banks, small shareholding banks, and other financial institutions, we should gradually regularize newly established collective and shareholding financial institutions and increase their share of the entire banking industry over time so they become a supplement to society's credit overall. By doing business with collective and private enterprises and individual and special households in both urban and rural areas, these new banks have become familiar with those niches of the economy that large banks shy away from. They have a flexible way of doing business and offer good services. The fact of the matter is that the nascent collective and shareholding financial institutions played a major role in revitalizing the urban and rural economies and put additional competitive pressure on large special banks to nudge them to improve management and operational standards. Their growth and business activities provide a lesson that special banks can learn from as they take up the shareholding system in the future. They also can familiarize the public with shareholding financial institutions and make them more knowledgeable about finance and investment, paving the way for the adoption of the shareholding system by special banks in the days ahead. For the moment, however, we must perfect the legal system, eradicate disorder, and prevent a loss of control.

3. Right now in special banks there are three levels of management for each level of operations. This must be brought to an end. The head offices of special banks should be abolished by turning them into nationwide clearing houses. All other special banks should practice independent accounting. The various levels may borrow from one another and deposit funds with one another. People's Bank offices at the Grade 1 provincial level (except for economically developed municipalities) should be abolished. The jurisdiction in question should be directed to set up a special bank to be its agent in order to prevent local separatism.

4. In strict accordance with regulations on the expansion of the power of large and mid-sized state enterprises, we should formulate a reform plan for special banks and reform outdated and restrictive policies and regulations pertaining to the finances, costs, and fees of special banks. Using the tax separation provisions of large and mid-sized state enterprises as a guide, a profits distribution plan for special banks should be decided upon. What is the proportion to be turned over to government as income tax? What is the percentage to be set aside to supplement the credit fund? What is the percentage to go to the welfare, risk readiness, development, and education funds, and so on? A special bank should have a board of directors at each level armed with independent power over personnel.

Chapter 6. Establishing a Financial Market

The expansion of a commodity market and development of a trade center necessarily entail the circulation and active deployment of funds among all trades, industries, and regions, leading to the creation of a financial market and the formation of a financial center. A financial market is not unique to capitalism; rather, it belongs in the commodity economy. In a socialized commodity economy, the market as a whole is comprised of the commodity, financial, and labor markets. These three markets are the three pillars of a socialized commodity economy.

Debate at the Highest Level Over Financial Reform

The financial market is an inevitable product of the flourishing of a commodity economy and credit system. Not only is it a major bridge forging horizontal linkages between regions, enterprises, investors, and savers, but it also makes it possible for the state to regulate the

continued...

FINANCIAL STRUCTURE REFORMS, 1995 (continued)

supply and demand and steer the flow of funds, and hence control the macroeconomy. In the wake of the rapid development of a planned commodity economy and credit system, the creation and deregulation of the financial market has become inevitable.

Right now a heated debate is under way at the highest levels in China over reform of the financial market. A minority of people are opposed to it. Proceeding from Marxist tenets, they argue that the establishment of a financial market is bound to undermine the social economy at its very foundation, namely the system of public ownership by the whole people, which will lead to China embarking on the road toward wholesale capitalism. The majority refute this viewpoint, arguing that since the credit system, a product of the capitalist era, has been used in the socialist economy without leading to capitalism, the financial market, another product of the advanced form of capitalism, can also be employed in the socialist market economy without necessarily converting China to capitalism. They insist that one must not decide whether a thing is good or bad based on the kind of society which has given rise to it. Instead we need to determine whether or not the thing is good for an economic society, to be more precise, a commodity economic society, and whether or not it complies with the law of commodity value.

Financial Market Helps Determine Enterprise Vitality

Perfecting the financial market has beneficial results in the following ways:

1. It will stimulate enterprises by vitalizing them. The hundreds of thousands of enterprises (including 462,300 industrial enterprises) in the nation are the cells of the Chinese economy. Their revitalization lies at the heart of economic reform. Today, almost 12 years after economic restructuring was first launched, enterprises remain far from brimming with energy. A key reason is that although they no longer rely on the treasury as paymaster, they still depend on low-interest bank loans as the sole source of their funds. With the creation of a sound financial market, both enterprises and individuals can choose between depositing money in a bank to earn interest and buying stock and bonds. Also, when there are choices and competition, banks will make loans to enterprises based on fund relationships and on how well the enterprise is being managed. It is also certain that interest rates on loans will be higher than the current rates as a way of putting funds to the best possible use. That way enterprises will become more careful and shrewd when it comes to the use of funds and strive to improve their own operations and management in order to get the right interest rates. Banks, for their part, will also step up the monitoring and auditing of enterprises in order to minimize bad loans.

The establishment of a financial market will give a strong boost to development of the nascent shareholding system. The development of a shareholding economy can bring together the interests of all three parties: the state, the collective, and the individual. Under a shareholding economy, the ownership of an enterprise resides in its shareholders (real human beings, not the so-called controlling shareholder of the state). Shareholders take an interest in the enterprise's investments and how it is being run. They select the managers who try in each and every way to improve management. The enterprise automatically goes after long-term profits, pays attention to the returns on investment, and distributes after-tax net profits fairly. In the process the current tendency to "spend everything and distribute everything"—handing out bonuses and material objects—will be checked and the chronic enterprise malady—"investment fever"—will also be eliminated once and for all.

Channeling the Flow of Funds

2. Financial market reform will lead to pooling of idle social funds and increase returns on social funds utilization. In recent years both urban and rural savings deposits have risen sharply, and many commercial organizations, both large and small, insurance companies, and administrative units are also flush with funds. Although the bulk of these funds are deposited in banks and serve as the primary source of credit funds, in most cases they are held in current accounts, preventing banks from knowing precisely how much depositors withdraw and the putting of these funds to full use. If depositors and money-holders are given a choice between putting money in banks and purchasing marketable securities, funds will be put to much better use.

continued...

FINANCIAL STRUCTURE REFORMS, 1995 (continued)

3. Reform will steer social funds into those production sectors where social need is the greatest and which have the highest economic returns, thereby enhancing social economic benefits overall. Perfecting the financial market and allowing enterprises to issue stock and bonds under a specified set of conditions will give investors a range of choices in the form and terms of investment and provide fund-raisers with alternatives in sources of funds, methods, and terms. The buying and selling of the stock and shares of various companies on the securities market (a component of the financial market), with their prices clearly marked, reflects society's demand for the companies' products. Social information and public assessments also reflect the performance of a company or industry and its future prospects. If an enterprise has a high level of profitability and bright prospects and its products are sought after on the market, the prices of its stock and bonds on the market will go up. And when it issues additional securities to raise funds for expanded reproduction, it will easily achieve its purpose. That way the financial market succeeds in its purpose of channeling social resources (human resources, natural resources, and surplus social productive capacity) into the most important and profitable factories and industries in society, thereby maximizing the well-being of society as a whole.

Regulate the Economy; Attract Foreign Capital

4. Perfecting the financial market will facilitate macroeconomic regulation by the state and coordinate the state's fiscal policy. The issue of bonds and treasury bonds on the financial market can raise large sums of money for the national treasury and local financial departments to meet spending needs. Even more importantly, it makes it possible for the central bank to enter the open market to regulate the total money supply and hence control the aggregate demand, thus striking an essential balance between aggregate supply and aggregate demand. It is particularly worth mentioning that the issue of public, treasury, and capital construction bonds can divert some of the swollen consumption funds into the "bottlenecks" of the national economy, such as the energy, transportation, communications, and raw materials industries. Of course, funds would flow into those sectors only if there is a reasonable return and full convertibility. Otherwise, people would still shy away from them in the same way they steer clear of state treasury bonds today.

5. The financial market attracts foreign capital. At present, many foreign companies want to invest in China with hopes, needless to say, of netting a return higher than the interest rates they get by lending to the government or banks. Wholly foreign-funded enterprises are still excluded from a handful of industries. That aside however, foreign investment typically takes the form of a Sino-foreign joint venture. When foreign investors invest in China by setting up the three kinds of enterprises either wholly or partially foreign-funded, namely joint ventures, cooperative ventures, and wholly foreign-owned enterprises, they are hemmed in by restrictions which regulate the prices and supply of raw materials, stipulate where their goods can be sold, and determine other aspects of their operations. They demand that the areas open to investment be broadened. Foreign companies also hope to invest in China by purchasing stocks and bonds on the financial market as a way of minimizing losses. In particular, foreign investors who don't have enough funds to build plants, along with middle-income people, also would like to try investing in China. Accordingly, in conjunction with a fair tax code, a financial market will be able to dispel the worries of foreign investors and attract foreign funds on a large scale. Of course, the state may consider limiting investors to just the preferred stock or to the purchase of a fixed amount of ordinary stock. It may also stipulate that foreign investors invest in specific industries.

Procedures in Reforming the Financial Market

Improving and perfecting China's financial market can only be a gradual process. For starters, we should regularize the short-term funds market and then proceed to set up a long-term capital market. This is why; For one thing, the Credit system is fairly chaotic right now; for another, there is a widespread shortage of working funds; third, the scale of fixed assets investment is already

continued...

FINANCIAL STRUCTURE REFORMS, 1995 (continued)

over-extended; and fourth, enterprises can retain only a very small amount of profits. The specific reform steps should be as follows:

1. Improve the short-term re-lending market between banks and financial institutions. The main objective is to meet the short-term funding needs of banks and financial institutions at reasonable interest rates and stimulate horizontal economic cooperation. The current deposits-based lending system seeks to control credit on two fronts. One, the head office of the People's Bank divides up the credit quota for distribution to each special bank. The special banks, in turn, break them up and distribute them to their branches at different levels. Two, the head office of the People's Bank breaks up the total target and hands it down to its branches at all levels. It will then be up to the branch banks to engage in interbank borrowing depending on the scale of credit of the various special banks and whether there is a shortage or surplus of funds within the plan, and then make loans in accordance with the credit policy. Laws should be written to further strengthen the short- term re-lending market. The methods, duration, and interest rates of re-lending may be agreed upon through negotiation between the two parties involved within statutory limits. The limits may be gradually liberalized over time.

2. Next, establish a bill-discounting market dominated by the acceptance and discounting of trade bills. At present enterprises owe each other a lot of money and have fallen behind in their repayments. This does nothing to speed up the circulation of funds among enterprises; nor does it contribute to controlling the money supply. We should turn commercial credit into bills and develop the acceptance and discounting of bills and rediscounting by the central bank. That way we can accelerate horizontal fund circulation and turn bank credit into bills. In addition, the central bank may be able to control and regulate the money supply through rediscounting.

3. Expand the short-term bond market. One should be able to buy and sell short-term bonds through financial institutions. Popularize the use of money orders and cashier's checks. Also consider increasing the large-volume transferable fixed deposits of banks.

4. The final step: Gradually establish a long-term financial market. First of all, improve the discount and transfer markets for state treasury and financial bonds in the near future, as soon as possible. Mind you, we must not overdo it in issuing state treasury bonds in order to avoid a serious "squeeze" effect, that is, siphoning off too much funds which otherwise would have gone to profitable enterprises. Nor should we issue an excessive amount of financial bonds to avoid a reduction in direct finance. Second, perfect the issue and transfer markets for company bonds. Allow enterprises to issue bonds to raise working funds and finance projects in the plan. Third, put the issue and transfer markets for enterprise stocks on a sound footing. Encourage individuals and enterprises to purchase and resell shares freely. For the moment we should begin by improving stock issue and transfer market legislation. Rely mainly on the variety of trust and investment companies and allow trust companies to rely on banks. Trust companies know the financial business well and have a good understanding of the way enterprises are run. A prerequisite for all the developments mentioned above is freedom from administrative interference.

Needless to say, there is still a string of problems to be resolved in succession in the course of perfecting the financial market. For instance, a quarterly price index and key resources price index need to be put together, a host of laws and regulations (including interbank borrowing regulations, discount regulations, and modern enterprise, bankruptcy, and securities trading laws) need to be formulated, a tax policy consistent with the financial market must be developed, and a financial market management commission made up of competent, efficient, fair-minded, and selfless people should be set up.

In short, we should go about creating a financial market right now and gradually improve it so as to keep up with the deepening of the reform of the financial and economic systems. There certainly will be numerous difficulties, but with the rank-and-file financial workers and people in the economic community working jointly and cooperatively hard, success is a foregone conclusion.

The Nineties No. 10, 1 Oct 1994; No. 11, 1 Nov 1994.

FOREIGN BANKS ESTABLISH PRESENCE, 1995

By the end of 1994, a total of 109 foreign banks had set up branches in Shanghai, Shenzhen, Guangzhou, Tianjin and nine other cities, according to the People's Bank of China.

By late November 1994, 100 foreign banks, including finance companies had gone into operation in China, with combined assets of US$12.45 billion. They offered US$7.28 billion in loans and had a deposit balance of US$2.699 billion, bringing in net profits of US$89.45 million for the year. Net cash flow from abroad totaled US$5.8 billion. Ninety percent of foreign bank loans were in China, with about 50 percent being offered to foreign-funded enterprises. In terms of savings deposits, 55 percent came from foreign-funded enterprises.

By the end of December 1994, foreign financial institutions had numbered 118, including 109 foreign-funded banks, five jointly-funded and wholly foreign-funded finance companies and four branches of foreign insurance companies. Among the 109 foreign-funded banks, 99 are branches of foreign banks, five wholly foreign-funded banks and five jointly-funded banks. There are now 393 foreign financial agencies in 18 Chinese cities.

Among them, 70 are insurance companies, 250 banks, 40 stock companies, 11 finance companies, 4 credit companies and 18 other financial institutions.

Distribution of 118 Foreign Financial Institutions in China

City	Branches of Foreign Banks	Wholly Foreign Funded Banks	Jointly Funded Banks	Wholly Foreign Funded Finance Companies	Jointly Funded Finance Companies	Branches of Foreign Insurance Companies
Shanghai	27		1	1	2	2
Shenzhen	21		1		1	1
Guangzhou	12		1			
Xiamen	8	1				
Tianjin	9					
Dalian	8					
Zhuhai	3	1				
Shantou	3	1				
Haikou	2			1	1	
Fuzhou	2		1			
Qingdao	3					
Ningbo		2	1			
Nanjing	1					

China Daily Express, 4 Feb 1995.

"B" SHARE QUOTA ALLOTTED BY SHENZHEN STOCK EXCHANGE, 1995

Shenzhen Securities Regulatory Office allotted the quota for B shares to companies dealing in warehousing, petroleum, timber processing and airport services. Companies in these business sectors had never been listed on the stock exchange. Companies expected to issue B shares in 1995 included Shenzhen Sungang Industrial Company Ltd., Shenzhen Shiwan Company Ltd., Shenzhen Airport, Shenzhen International Group and Northern Industrial Group.

Hong Kong AFP, 18 Jan 1995.

STATE TREASURY REVENUE, 1995

China's treasury reaped some 102.7 billion yuan in revenue during the first three months of this year, up 15.7 percent over the corresponding period of 1994.

The figure represents 18 percent of the year's budgeted total, according to the Ministry of Finance.

Yet the country's expenditure from January to March amounted to 102.9 billion yuan, a jump of 27 percent over last year's same period.

Vice Finance Minister Jin Renqing called the budgetary implementation "smooth" and the fiscal situation "normal".

He said the treasury income kept climbing steadily in the first three months, with the consumption tax growing by 77.8 percent, the value-added tax up by 15 percent and the business tax rising by 26.9 percent.

The fiscal input into agriculture rose by 45.7 percent during the January-March period, and that for technical upgrading and new product research was up 18.1 and 30.6 percent, respectively.

Jin said that 24.92 billion yuan-worth of unregistered treasury bonds for 1995, which had been underwritten by primary dealers, had been sold by the end of March. The certificated bonds sold so far amounted to 73.22 billion yuan-worth.

"The active purchasing of the bond promises a smooth issuance for this year," said Jin.

Jin said the ministry will ensure the implementation of this year's budget. "Government departments and local officials will not be allowed to give revenue cuts or expand expenditure scales without the ministry's permission," he added.

He called for a tightened crackdown on fraud in export refunding. The ministry will tackle tax defaults by "economic and legal" means, said the vice minister.

X, 20 Apr 1995.

GOVERNMENT ENFORCES INDIVIDUAL INCOME TAX, 1995

According to the latest statistics, Guangzhou city in south China's Guangdong Province received more than 900 million yuan in such taxes last year.

In the past, individual income taxes were mostly paid by private entrepreneurs and businessmen since most people did not earn a monthly salary of more than 800 yuan, which is the baseline for paying individual income tax.

As common people's salary and other income have risen in recent years, more people are obligated to pay taxes. Because people are unaware of the necessity of paying taxes, with some deliberately avoiding paying them, individual taxes for the country last year only accounted for 1.17 percent of the total amount of tax revenues, according to government sources.

Tax evasion is especially common among some actors, artists, or self-employed persons with much higher incomes than other people.

Another reason is that there are not enough tax officers. At present, there is one tax collector for every 200-some enterprises, making it difficult to collect taxes.

As the market economy develops, the Chinese people have more ways of earning money. But, there has been no effective method of finding out the extent of people's actual income.

continued...

GOVERNMENT ENFORCES INDIVIDUAL INCOME TAX, 1995 (continued)

Some avenues of preventing people from avoiding paying individual income taxes are being explored. In Shenyang City in northeast China's Liaoning Province, a system requiring residents to accurately report their monthly income to tax bureaus is now being implemented and its methods might spread to the rest of the country.

X, 20 Apr 1995.

ROLE OF HONG KONG FINANCE, 1995

[Article by Chen Yuan [7115 0337], vice governor of the People's Bank of China: "Hong Kong and the Mainland Make Joint Efforts To Promote Development of Financial Markets"]

Development and Utilization of Capital Markets in the Two Places

Since the beginning of reform and opening up, Hong Kong's securities market has made positive contributions to the development of the mainland economy. Of the companies listed in Hong Kong, about 40 percent have invested in close to 1,000 projects in the mainland, involving total investment of about HK$500 billion. As to the red counters directly controlled by China-funded enterprises, including those China-funded Hong Kong-based listed companies, those shells bought and listed by mainland companies, and state-owned enterprise H shares, the total market value is close to HK$100 billion. Their proportion in the stock market is now about 5 percent.

As far as the mainland is concerned, the increase in the China component of the Hong Kong stock market provides a large amount of funds for economic development. At the same time, by the share holding transformation of mainland-funded enterprises through their listing on the exchange, experiences are provided for the reform of the mainland enterprise system. As far as Hong Kong is concerned, in the Hong Kong stock market the proportion of basic industries and manufacturing industries is increasing, which means that the industrial mix in the stock market is becoming more rational. In addition, Hong Kong and foreign investors can enjoy the benefits of the growth in China's economic strength through the increasing number of holders of Hong Kong shares. At present, the development of the mainland securities market is still at a primary stage, and the Hong Kong securities market not only can provide opportunities for raising capital, but through contacts and cooperation between the securities administrators of the two places, it will be possible to promote stable development of the mainland market. Since the signing of the memorandum on supervisory and management cooperation among the five securities organs in the mainland and Hong Kong, a fine relationship of cooperation has been developed. This has played a positive promotional role in developing the markets in the two places. We hope that this cooperative relationship can continue.

Development and Management of a Foreign Exchange Market

The Hong Kong foreign exchange market is the sixth largest in the world, and it holds a position of decisive importance in the Asian market. At present, the cooperative relationship between the two places in terms of the foreign exchange market is mainly manifested in three respects: 1) Because they are situated in the same time zone, quite a proportion of state foreign exchange reserve management is carried out through the Hong Kong market. 2) The foreign exchange needs of the two places generated by investment and trade activities are mainly supplied by the Hong Kong market. 3) In supervision and development of the foreign exchange market, the supervisory authorities and those engaged in the foreign exchange market business have already established an initial cooperative relationship. As the history of the development of the mainland foreign exchange market is not long and has been restrained by the non-convertibility of the renminbi, the scale of the market and trading products are limited and management experience is insufficient. In this respect, contacts and exchanges with the Hong Kong foreign exchange supervisory and management departments and specialized personnel provide beneficial experiences for developing and perfecting the mainland foreign exchange market. We need to continue to promote such contacts.

continued...

ROLE OF HONG KONG FINANCE, 1995 (continued)

Bond Markets and Liability Relations

Although China has gained some experience in utilizing the Hong Kong stock market, it has learned very little about the Hong Kong debt market. This is mainly because, as compared to other markets, the Hong Kong Dollar debt market was, in the past, not very developed. In recent years, the Hong Kong Monetary Authority has made positive progress in developing a debt market and through various measures has developed a Hong Kong Dollar debt market. I believe that following the future increase in demand for funds in Asia and the whole world, the appeal of the Hong Kong debt market will become increasingly great, and the Chinese mainland will increasingly utilize the Hong Kong debt market to raise funds. This will further promote the development of the Hong Kong debt market.

I wish to stress one point, and that is, following 1997, the creditor and debtor relationship between the mainland and Hong Kong will still be seen as a foreign creditor and debtor relationship. That is to say, on the one hand we will continue to act as fund-raisers in an equal position with other participants in international and local markets, and will not enjoy any preferences. At the same time, we will continue to maintain our country's international prestige by fulfilling our debt liabilities to Hong Kong.

With respect to the various concerns which some circles in the international community feel over the 1997 factor in the Hong Kong market, I note that we were very happy to see that the 1997 factor seems to have not had ally negative effects on the first batch of three-year foreign exchange fund bonds to straddle 1997, issued by the Hong Kong Monetary Authority in July last year.

Relationship Between Hong Kong and Shanghai

Everyone knows that in history Shanghai was old China's financial center. Today, following the continued deepening of reform and opening up, Shanghai is increasingly showing its vigorous vitality, and it has various advantages, conditions, and prospects for becoming an international financial center. The Chinese Government certainly does not deny this. As to the idea that people from various circles frequently put forward on the possibility of Shanghai replacing Hong Kong in the future, I would like to put forward a few comments.

First, as an international financial center which has already been formed, Hong Kong has the advantage of having an international nature. Second, the "Basic Law" clearly notes that China will continue to "maintain Hong Kong's position as an international financial center," and to this end it has put forward a series of concrete stipulations making this a basic state policy. Third, in accordance with the "Basic Law," after 1997 Hong Kong will be a special administrative region of China enjoying a high degree of autonomy, and the SAR will be able to exercise sovereignty in all spheres except foreign affairs and national defense. This will assist Hong Kong in continuing to maintain its special effectiveness and vigor. Fourth, Hong Kong will maintain its capitalist system without change. This will help in continuing to promote and develop various economic links between Hong Kong and the major developed countries and regions. Fifth, Hong Kong's economic base and financial strength provide guarantees for maintaining and developing its position as an international financial center.

Thus, within the short term, prior to the renminbi becoming a freely convertible currency, Shanghai cannot become a complete international financial center, and it will be unable to replace Hong Kong. Seen from the medium to long term, after 1997 the relationship between Shanghai and Hong Kong will be a relationship between two financial cities within one sovereign state, with their own characteristics, supplementing each other, promoting each other, and seeing common development. I believe that viewed from the long term, while Hong Kong is promoted as an international financial center, Shanghai will certainly swiftly develop into a financial center which relies on the broad land of China and which has trading in renminbi as its main currency. At the same time, it will support the continual development of the international financial center of Hong Kong and on this basis will gradually develop into an international financial center. The two financial centers will be mutually complementary and neither will replace the other.

Renmin Ribao, 24 Jun 1995.

TAX ENFORCEMENT, 1995

[Interview with Xiang Huaicheng (7309 2037 6134), deputy director of the State Administration of Taxation, by ZHONGGUO SHUIWU BAO reporter; place and date of interview not given: "Tax Law Enforcement Inspection To Be Ongoing Effort"]

Editor's note: China overhauled its industrial and commercial tax system in 1994. The transition from the old system to the new has been a tentative success. However, consolidating and perfecting the new tax system remains an arduous task. To ensure the implementation of the new system and preserve the uniformity and consistency of the nation's tax law, the State Administration of Taxation launched a nation-wide inspection of the enforcement of the new tax system in the first part of this year. Problems in law enforcement by tax agencies were cleared up and corrected in order to further standardize such enforcement and put tax management on a legal footing. Deputy Director Xiang Huaicheng of the State Administration of Taxation was interviewed by this newspaper recently and asked about the latest inspection. [end editor's note]

[ZHONGGUO SHUIWU BAO] Director Xiang, could you tell us the reasons for launching the current tax law enforcement inspection?

[Xiang Huaicheng] Launching this inspection was an objective demand placed on us by the new tax system one year after it went into effect. It is an important measure taken by the tax community to consolidate and perfect the new tax system.

Following the reform of the industrial and commercial tax system in 1994, a new tax system that satisfies the needs of a developing socialist market economy has been put into effect, the government's ability to regulate and control revenue on a macro level has been enhanced markedly, and the tax law enforcement environment has improved. However, the new tax system is not yet well established and activities injurious to the new system occur frequently. Another problem that could not be ignored was that some tax agencies failed to enforce the law strictly. For instance, the leaders of some local governments and tax agencies did not fully appreciate the profound change wrought by tax reform and insisted on approving tax waivers and tax cuts. Touting their so-called "flexibility," they even ignored the uniform provisions in the nation's tax law and came up with their own tax policies without authorization. With their underdeveloped sense of legality, some tax cadres cut, exempted, or delayed taxes as they pleased in their tax collection work and even allowed people to owe the government taxes. They failed to collect taxes for reasons having to do with personal feelings and relations, which is a very serious matter. Departing from the uniform tax law, the Wuhan Tax Bureau formulated and issued on its own its "120 rules." The tax bureau of the Dinghu district in Zhaoqing Shi, Guangdong province, arbitrarily broadened the definition of ordinary taxpayers for the purpose of collecting the value-added tax [VAT] and issued special VAT receipts for nonexistent merchandise. These were some of the more typical cases. These problems have done serious damage to the uniformity and integrity of the tax code and disrupted the implementation of the new tax system. If left unchecked and allowed to proliferate, not only would they undo the achievements of tax reform, but they would also undermine social stability and economic development. Accordingly, we must take practical and effective steps, consolidate and perfect the new tax system, and preserve the consistency and dignity of the tax code. It is precisely this kind of consideration that prompted us to launch an inspection of the enforcement of the new tax law even as we work to improve the way it is enforced.

[ZHONGGUO SHUIWU BAO] Describe for us the basic situation in the inspection.

[Xiang Huaicheng] The inspection formally began in early February this year and has been under way for almost four months now. The scope of the inspection includes all enforcement behavior by tax agencies. Also covered are local tax rules and regulations formulated by the localities and standardization documents. The inspection has seven emphases, including changes to official tax rates and tax bases, particularly those relating to the VAT and consumption tax; violations of special VAT receipt management regulations; overissue of receipts for nonexisting goods, and the purchase of forged receipts. The principal method of inspection is self-inspection. Branches of the State Administration of Taxation in the provinces, autonomous regions, municipalities directly administered by the central government, and municipalities with

continued...

TAX ENFORCEMENT, 1995 (continued)

provincial-level decision making authority as well as local tax agencies are required to inspect in depth at least two municipalities or districts directly administered by a province.

Tax agencies everywhere have done a good deal of meticulous work in accordance with the plan developed by the State Administration of Taxation. First of all, they have self-inspected the standardization documents issued by their own locality's tax community. Second, they have submitted reports to the higher authorities on regulations formulated by the locality that were inconsistent with the unified tax code and put forward suggestions for improvement. Third, they have corrected documents formulated by the lower levels that violated the tax policy and reported the results to the higher level. Fourth, they have corrected the actual problems in tax collection and management, such as the application of a wrong tax system, under-collection of taxes, and overissue of receipts.

[ZHONGGUO SHUIWU BAO] What we have in this inspection is self-inspection by the tax agencies. That being the case, how do you ensure its quality and results?

[Xiang Huaicheng] "Don't wash your dirty linen in public," so goes a common saying. It hurts to pull the scab off one's sore. The first thing the latest inspection tackled had to do with understanding and concepts. The position of the leaders of the State Administration of Taxation in this matter is clear. The inspection of the enforcement of the new tax system must be carried out and conduct in violation of the tax code must be corrected. Under no circumstances would the intents and wishes of a locality or department be allowed to supersede the nation's tax code. We must be the protector and defender of the new tax system. The reason we wash dirty linen in public is to get rid of the dirty linen, and to make sure there will be no more dirty linen.

To prevent the inspection from becoming a mere formality, we took pains to step up publicity about the inspection and organize its leadership. We expended a lot of effort on the measures and methods. We demanded that the entire nation's tax community unify its thinking and enhance its understanding. It must summon the courage to examine itself and expose its own weaknesses. Taking advantage of the opportunity presented by the inspection, we have standardized tax collection behavior and raised its standard. Our earlier studies had identified the more outstanding problems in the implementation of the new tax system, so we decided to concentrate on these problems in our inspection to make it more focused and practical. Even as the inspection was launched, we reported to the whole nation the erroneous ways of Wuhan Shi's Tax Bureau and the Dinghu case and dealt with them strictly, both as a warning to tax agencies everywhere and as a lesson to them. This move was a boost to inspection work on all fronts. During the inspection, the State Administration of Taxation formulated and issued the "Notice on Launching an Inspection of the Enforcement of the New Tax System," convened a telephone conference among tax bureau chiefs nation-wide, and dispatched three working groups to seven provinces to supervise the inspection. I myself visited the office of the State Administration of Taxation in Beijing's Huadian District as well as a local tax bureau to familiarize myself with the situation.

Although the latest inspection is one of self-policing, it has been quite successful because the leadership made it a priority and took effective measures. It has created an atmosphere, and at the same time laid bare some problems.

[ZHONGGUO SHUIWU BAO] What are the major achievements of the inspection of the enforcement of the new tax law? What is its significance for improving the tax law enforcement climate and accelerating the legal construction in taxation?

[Xiang Huaicheng] The tax law enforcement inspection is now coming to an end. On the whole, tax agencies everywhere have done serious inspection work and the results have been outstanding. Among some of the more serious problems uncovered during the inspection are the following. In issuing special VAT receipts to small-time taxpayers, a number of provincial tax agencies collected the tax at 6 percent but indicated 17 percent on the receipts, which caused the state to lose tax revenue. Some local governments, particularly those at the prefectural and county levels, introduced tax policies as they pleased, cutting or waiving taxes at random. Some tax agencies allowed enterprises to write special VAT receipts on behalf of

continued...

TAX ENFORCEMENT, 1995 (continued)

other taxpayers. Others altered the character of a tax and the level at which revenue went into the treasury without authorization. Yet others approved deferred tax payment willfully.

The latest inspection not only has uncovered conduct in tax work that violated the law but has also taught the rank-and-file tax cadres a lively lesson in the legal system. In this sense, it has enormous significance for and lasting impact on strengthening tax legal construction. Tax agencies everywhere have identified some problems during the inspection. An overwhelming majority of these problems have been promptly rectified, while a few are being tackled, which no doubt will help improve the climate for implementing the tax code. In the past, as soon as the term "tax inspection" was mentioned, a number of tax agencies and tax cadres thought of "inspecting the taxpayers and enterprises." This tax law enforcement inspection has made them realize that their own conduct likewise must be subject to inspection and supervision. Tax agencies are the administrative and law enforcement organs of the state and tax cadres the administrative and law enforcement personnel of the state. In tax administration and management, they must operate in accordance with the law and collect taxes in accordance with the tax rates. Under no circumstances are they to act as they think fit or do things their way. The inspection would help create an effective self-supervision and self-restraint mechanism within the tax agencies, warding off possible trouble. In this sense, it has contributed to the goal of educating and protecting the cadres.

[ZHONGGUO SHUIWU BAO] In what ways has the latest inspection fallen short?

[Xiang Huaicheng] This is the first large-scale inspection of law enforcement in the tax field since the PRC was founded. Time was short and the task was arduous, so inevitably there were some weaknesses. One outstanding problem was that certain localities and comrades, especially leading cadres, did not fully appreciate the importance of this project. For instance, some comrades believed that the foremost duty of tax agencies should be to look for revenue and considered the inspection irrelevant and insignificant. Others were worried that the inspection would affect their relations with local governments. Since some policies have been set by the local governments or tacitly approved by local leaders, it was feared that any effort to change them would give offense. The existence of this kind of thinking has interfered with the inspection up to a point. In some localities, therefore, inspection work has been superficial, measures are half-hearted, some problems have yet to be identified, while those already brought to light have not been tackled in earnest.

[ZHONGGUO SHUIWU BAO] What are the tax agencies new plans to deepen law enforcement inspection?

[Xiang Huaicheng] Law enforcement inspection cannot win the war with just one battle. It must be an unremitting effort. Law enforcement inspection will become a regular job for tax agencies in the future. Currently, the legal organs within tax agencies are still underdeveloped and the quality of the personnel is not high enough to meet the demands of work. In both aspects we still don't have what it takes to accelerate tax legal construction. Accordingly, we must make organizational development and cadre training an important part of the push for law enforcement in the next several years. Legal offices must be set up within tax agencies all the way down to the prefectural or municipal levels. Every provincial-level tax agency must have a legal department. A top priority at the moment is to train a number of professionals who are both well versed in taxation and familiar with the law.

Putting local tax rules and regulations and standardization documents on file for future reference is a basic piece of work in law enforcement inspection. We demand that all localities continue to tackle this job. The State Administration of Taxation last year introduced a system for the filing of standardization documents for future reference as a way of intensifying its day-to-day supervision of the abstract administrative conduct of tax agencies everywhere. So far this task has not been satisfactorily executed and awaits further improvement.

Another task that must be accomplished is writing and perfecting the rules and regulations of inspection. This is essential if law enforcement inspection is to be deepened. As a form of internal supervision within tax agencies, law enforcement inspection itself must have rules to follow. After wrapping up the latest inspection, we must review the experience carefully and

continued...

TAX ENFORCEMENT, 1995 (continued)

standardize its organization, methods, content, and procedures in order to make any law enforcement inspection as effective as possible.

We will convene a national tax law conference in the second half of the year to review and sum up legal: work in tax collection this year and make plans for next year. At that point a number of routine measures for law enforcement inspection will also be introduced.

Zhongguo Shuiwu Bao, 28 Jul 1995.

XI INDUSTRY

INDUSTRY OUTPUT, 1994 (100 mn yuan)

	Total		Percent Increase Over Same Period of 1993	
	Jan–Jun	Jun	Jan–Jun	Jun
Gross output value of industry				
(based on 1990 instant prices)	19,789.76	3,871.39	18.78	18.23
Light industry	9,373.80	1,807.72	20.08	19.36
Heavy industry	10,415.96	2,063.67	17.63	17.26
State-owned enterprise	9,000.12	1,689.38	5.26	7.91
Collective-owned enterprise	7,582.97	1,552.59	27.83	21.51
Township enterprise	5,089.56	1,031.28	41.94	28.78
Other ownership industry	3,206.67	629.42	43.73	41.45
Gross output value of industry				
(at current prices)	24,162.87	4,814.31		
New product output value	875.97	176.57		
Light industry	10,238.18	2,053.19	32.06	
Heavy industry	13,924.69	2,761.12	26.70	
State-owned enterprise	12,532.75	2,418.14	19.97	
Collective-owned enterprise	8,010.63	1,667.55	34.10	
Township enterprise	5,338.92	1,116.24	50.44	
Other ownership industry	3,619.49	728.62	58.92	

China Monthly Statistics, Jun 1995.

INDUSTRY OUTPUT BY REGION, 1994 (100 mn yuan)

Region	Gross Output Value of Industry	Percent Increase Over the Same Period of 1993	Gross Output Value of Light Industry	Percent Increase Over the Same Period of 1993
National total	3,871.39	18.2	1,807.72	19.4
Beijing	121.26	26.6	47.99	35.3
Tianjin	88.03	13.7	38.11	18.9
Hebei	139.70	16.4	56.50	17.7
Shanxi	68.51	12.1	14.32	13.3
Inner Mongolia	34.04	5.1	12.69	8.6

continued...

INDUSTRY OUTPUT BY REGION, 1994 (100 mn yuan) (continued)

Region	Gross Output Value of Industry	Percent Increase Over the Same Period of 1993	Gross Output Value of Light Industry	Percent Increase Over the Same Period of 1993
Liaoning	215.20	12.2	62.48	24.9
Jilin	86.37	22.5	27.26	17.6
Heilongjiang	97.12	12.0	32.87	22.2
Shanghai	264.60	18.7	121.17	19.0
Jiangsu	553.58	17.1	261.04	9.9
Zhejiang	274.37	23.0	177.09	23.8
Anhui	108.46	23.4	55.73	24.9
Fujian	100.64	26.1	62.48	26.7
Jiangxi	75.67	24.6	33.94	26.7
Shandong	360.82	18.8	182.72	20.0
Henan	141.62	23.5	63.82	30.8
Hubei	170.01	24.0	73.30	26.8
Hunan	105.63	15.9	42.72	21.3
Guangdong	385.73	20.4	256.47	19.1
Guangxi	57.22	12.4	26.84	16.2
Hainan	6.78	0.6	4.35	0.7
Sichuan	201.54	15.8	77.81	17.3
Guizhou	27.89	6.2	9.18	20.5
Yunnan	44.94	13.0	21.93	13.5
Tibet	0.40	21.2	0.16	33.3
Shaanxi	61.08	10.6	21.79	10.7
Gansu	39.57	12.0	9.58	18.3
Qinghai	7.03	9.8	1.80	8.4
Ningxia	8.94	4.4	1.73	-17.6
Xinjiang	24.64	6.4	9.85	2.9

China Monthly Statistics, Jun 1995.

SALE OUTPUT VALUE OF INDUSTRY, 1994 (100 mn yuan)

	Total		Percent Increase Over Same Period of 1993	
	Jan–Jun	Jun	Jan–Jun	Jun
Sale output value of industry (at 1990 year prices)	18,147.49	3,566.66	16.80	15.71
Light industry	8,591.93	1,673.17	18.04	17.33
Heavy industry	9,555.56	1,893.49	15.71	14.33
State-owned enterprise	8,449.90	1,589.37	2.96	4.56
Collective-owned enterprise	6,707.60	1,386.70	27.37	20.49
Township enterprise	4,511.23	932.15	44.27	30.66
Other ownership industry	2,989.99	590.59	42.03	39.74
Sale output value of industry (at current prices)	22,352.81	4,470.89	26.45	
Light industry	9,437.20	1,891.78	29.67	
Heavy industry	12,915.61	2,579.11	24.19	
State-owned enterprise	11,832.51	2,280.70	17.02	

continued…

SALE OUTPUT VALUE OF INDUSTRY, 1994 (100 mn yuan) (continued)

	Total		Percent Increase Over Same Period of 1993	
	Jan-Jun	Jun	Jan-Jun	Jun
Collective-owned enterprise	7,140.95	1,504.92	33.39	
Township enterprise	4,734.05	1,000.53	51.76	
Other ownership industry	3,379.35	685.27	22.34	
Rate of sales output value (percent)	92.51	92.87	-1.81	

China Monthly Statistics, Jun 1995.

SALE OUTPUT OF INDUSTRY BY REGION, 1994 (100 mn yuan)

Region	Sale Output Value of Industry	Percent Increase Over the Same Period of 1993	Sale Output Value of Light Industry	Percent Increase Over the Same Period of 1993	Rate of Sale Output Value at Current Prices (percent)
National total	3,566.66	15.7	1,673.17	17.3	92.87
Beijing	111.86	25.5	40.74	29.7	90.06
Tianjin	85.37	13.3	38.74	25.7	95.67
Hebei	126.99	10.7	49.47	9.9	91.12
Shanxi	58.83	5.6	11.71	1.6	88.11
Inner Mongolia	30.64	3.4	10.39	1.7	92.15
Liaoning	188.46	8.2	53.32	16.9	89.63
Jilin	77.83	14.0	23.14	3.6	91.23
Heilongjiang	88.06	4.8	28.59	9.0	93.46
Shanghai	255.08	15.8	114.27	12.6	96.87
Jiangsu	505.29	16.4	253.11	15.6	94.03
Zhejiang	253.66	19.2	163.76	21.5	91.59
Anhui	98.44	20.6	50.30	20.7	92.90
Fujian	94.21	27.0	59.32	27.9	91.44
Jiangxi	69.81	26.7	31.47	29.2	93.61
Shandong	334.59	21.8	167.38	25.5	93.55
Henan	135.18	23.3	61.54	28.2	95.02
Hubei	155.86	21.3	65.36	23.9	91.59
Hunan	94.75	11.7	38.38	23.3	90.58
Guangdong	364.82	17.5	241.54	15.2	93.88
Guangxi	52.94	4.8	25.35	3.4	95.01
Hainan	6.27	-3.4	4.10	-2.1	98.85
Sichuan	180.32	11.8	70.18	13.8	91.03
Guizhou	24.60	6.0	7.92	16.6	87.62
Yunnan	43.29	8.1	22.01	6.5	95.72
Tibet	0.30	36.4	0.10	25.0	98.55
Shaanxi	54.51	6.3	19.63	8.5	90.10
Gansu	35.49	9.1	7.79	3.6	94.03
Qinghai	6.48	8.9	1.46		91.90
Ningxia	8.64	-3.5	1.68	-22.9	98.96
Xinjiang	24.09	-7.2	10.42	-21.0	94.93

China Monthly Statistics, Jun 1995.

CHINA'S TOP 250 INDUSTRIAL ENTERPRISES, 1994 (sales, mn RMB)

#	Enterprise	Sales	#	Enterprise	Sales
1	Shanghai Automobile Industry General Co.	30,703.25	48	Tianjin Steel Factory	4,233.90
2	Daqing Petroleum Administrative Bureau	26,952.32	49	Jinxi Oil Refinery & Chemical Industry General Factory	4,188.32
3	Anshan Iron & Steel Corp.	21,687.35	50	Ningbo Zhenhai Petrochemical Industry General Factory	3,968.70
4	No. 1 Automobile Group Corp.	21,611.35	51	Jinan Iron & Steel General Factory	3,838.91
5	Baoshan Iron & Steel Corp.	20,154.36	52	Shanghai Electrical Allied Co.	3,809.54
6	Dongfeng Automobile Corp.	20,043.73	53	Datong Mineral Administrative Bureau	3,651.64
7	Shoudu Iron & Steel General Corp.	17,519.12	54	Shanghai Cigarette Factory	3,601.15
8	Shengli Petroleum Administrative Bureau	14,627.03	55	Xinyu Iron & Steel General Factory	3,583.47
9	Wuhan Iron & Steel (Group) Corp.	14,008.58	56	Chengdu Steel Pipe Corp.	3,328.17
10	Beijing Yanshan Petrochemical Industry Corp.	11,410.99	57	Dagang Petroleum Administrative Bureau	3,325.48
11	Liaohe Petroleum Prospecting Bureau	10,162.94	58	Shenzhen Huaqiang Electronics Industry Corp.	3,311.30
12	Xinjiang Petroleum Administrative Bureau	9,697.82	59	Beijing Jeep Co.	3,306.19
13	Qilu Petrochemical Industry General Factory	9,550.12	60	Anqing Petrochemical Industry General Factory	3,285.77
14	Fushun Petrochemical Industry Corp.	9,465.65	61	Liaoyang Petroleum & Chemical Fibre Corp.	3,270.28
15	Shanghai Petrochemical Industry Joint-Stock Corp.	8,531.79	62	Shenzhen Yingda Group Joint-Stock Corp.	3,262.08
16	Panzhihua Iron & Steel (Group) Corp.	8,361.20	63	Jingzhou Petrochemical Industry Corp.	3,246.22
17	Daqing Petrochemical Industry General Factory	8,350.10	64	Jinbei Automobile Joint-Stock Corp.	3,101.00
18	Jilin Petrochemical Industry Group	8,269.36	65	Tonghua Iron & Steel Corp.	3,071.83
19	Maoming Petrochemical Industry Corp.	7,780.11	66	Northeast Power Transmission & Transformer Equipment Group Joint-Stock Corp.	3,037.68
20	Tianjin Automobile Industry General Co.	7,537.33	67	Jilin Oilfield Administrative Bureau	2,908.52
21	Baotao Iron, Steel & Rare-Earth Corp.	7,068.19	68	Changhong Machinery Factory	2,894.47
22	Jinling Petrochemical Industry Corp.	6,927.63	69	Lianyuan Iron & Steel Joint-Stock Corp.	2,887.06
23	China National Heavy-Duty Truck Corp.	6,689.33	70	Caihong Electronics Group Corp.	2,885.18
24	Shanghai Gaoqiao Petrochemical Industry Corp.	6,674.87	71	Nanjing Radio Factory	2,880.66
25	Yuxi Cigarette Factory	6,544.25	72	Sichuan Petroleum Administrative Bureau	2,867.80
26	Shanghai No. 1 Iron & Steel Factory	6,542.93	73	Shanghai Meishan Metallurgical Industry Corp.	2,848.02
27	Ma'anshan Iron & Steel Corp.	6,521.90	74	Jingmen Petrochemical Industry General Factory	2,845.40
28	Shanghai No. 3 Iron & Steel Factory	6,456.25	75	Chongqing Automobile Manufacturing Factory	2,827.00
29	Benxi Iron & Steel Corp.	6,392.51	76	Shanghai Bell Telephone Equipment Manufacturing Corp.	2,826.15
30	Taiyuan Iron & Steel Corp.	6,026.11	77	Nanjing Automobile Manufacturing Factory	2,810.27
31	Baling Petrochemical Industry Corp.	5,810.17	78	Xuanhua Iron & Steel Corp.	2,810.17
32	Tangshan Iron & Steel (Group) Corp.	5,742.47	79	Daye Steel Factory	2,806.99
33	Chongqing Iron & Steel (Group) Corp.	5,693.41	80	Gansu Machinery Group Corp.	2,805.58
34	Yizheng Chemical Fibre Industry Associated Group	5,502.51	81	Kunming Iron & Steel General Corp.	2,788.76
35	Yangtze Petrochemical Industry Corp.	5,272.46	82	Shenzhen 999 Group	2,677.50
36	Guangzhou Petrochemical Industry General Factory	5,253.24	83	Luoyang Petrochemical Industry General Factory	2,615.25
37	Dalian No. 7 Petrochemical Factory	5,178.46	84	Sichuan Construction Machine Tools Factory	2,578.62
38	Kunming Cigarette Factory	5,066.81	85	China Jialin Industrial Joint-Stock Corp.	2,572.83
39	China No. 1 Tractor Engineering Machinery Corp.	4,993.34	86	Guangzhou Peugeot Automobile Co.	2,558.32
40	Beijing Chemistry Industry Group Corp.	4,987.52	87	Xiangtan Iron & Steel Corp.	2,539.05
41	Tianjin Petrochemical Industry Corp.	4,727.71	88	Wuhan Petrochemical Industry Factory	2,520.62
42	Sichuan Jiuda Salt Industry (Group) Corp.	4,497.21	89	Tianjin Bohai Chemical Industry Group Corp.	2,482.90
43	Lanzhou Oil Refinery General Factory	4,367.13	90	Jiuquan Iron & Steel Corp.	2,416.52
44	Shanghai No. 5 Iron & Steel Factory	4,365.09	91	Jiangxi Isuzu Automobile Group Corp.	2,415.76
45	Shanghai Broadcast & TV Joint-Stock Corp.	4,356.48	92	Jiujiang Petrochemical Industry General Factory	2,413.61
46	Anyang Iron & Steel Corp.	4,298.33	93	Fushun Steel Factory	2,403.00
47	Handan Iron & Steel General Factory	4,260.59			

continued...

CHINA'S TOP 250 INDUSTRIAL ENTERPRISES, 1994 (sales, mn RMB) (continued)

94	Urumqi Petrochemical Industry General Factory	2,377.29	144	Fushun Mineral Administrative Bureau	1,778.38
95	Hangzhou Iron & Steel Factory	2,368.44	145	Guangdong Huabao Air-conditioner Factory	1,775.71
96	Huaibei Mineral Administrative Bureau	2,348.35	146	Changsha Cigarette Factory	1,773.09
97	Huangzhou Iron & Steel Corp.	2,343.20	147	Kelong Electrical Appliance Joint-Stock Corp.	1,761.17
98	Laiwu Iron & Steel General Factory	2,333.23	148	Chongqing Petroleum Prospecting Bureau	1,752.98
99	Foshan Electronics Industry Group Corp.	2,316.63	149	Huludao Zinc Factory	1,734.97
100	Guangdong Shaoguan Iron & Steel Group Corp.	2,310.03	150	Jixi Mineral Administrative Bureau	1,731.04
101	Pingdingshan Mineral Administrative Bureau	2,300.35	151	Jianlibao Group Corp.	1,719.39
102	Chunlan Group	2,296.14	152	Guangxi Iron & Steel (Group) Corp.	1,716.95
103	Tianjin Iron Factory	2,292.98	153	Xishan Mineral Administrative Bureau	1,716.63
104	Shenzhen Saige Group Corp.	2,292.49	154	Qujing Cigarette Factory	1,709.95
105	Harbin Power Station Equipment Group Corp.	2,231.99	155	Guangzhou Motorcycle Group Corp.	1,705.69
106	Great Wall Special Steel Corp.	2,223.92	156	Shanghai Pacific Chemical Industry (Group) Corp.	1,681.02
107	Shenzhen Konka Electronics (Group) Joint-Stock Co.	2,202.88	157	Jincheng Motorcycle Group Corp.	1,673.17
108	Xuzhou Engineering Machinery Group Corp.	2,140.92	158	Fuxin Mineral Administrative Bureau	1,662.47
109	Fujian Oil Refinery Factory	2,140.27	159	Linyuan Oil Refinery Factory	1,659.35
110	Wujiang Xinlian Silk Weaving Factory	2,136.20	160	Northeast Pharmaceuticals Manufacturing Group	1,656.29
111	Shenzhen Petrochemical Industry Group Joint-Stock Corp.	2,135.00	161	Jiangsu Shagang Steel Group Corp.	1,649.68
112	Guizhou Aviation Industry Group	2,133.54	162	Great Wall Computer Group Corp.	1,646.25
113	Jiangxi Copper Industry Corp.	2,122.22	163	Beijing Tongrentang Group Corp.	1,645.36
114	Nanjing Iron & Steel Factory	2,112.53	164	Echeng Iron & Steel Factory	1,631.00
115	China Offshore Oil Bohai Corp.	2,109.09	165	Shanghai General Machinery (Group) Corp.	1,629.10
116	Guangdong Tri-Star Enterprise (Group) Joint-Stock Corp.	2,098.47	166	Hefei Iron & Steel Corp.	1,629.01
117	Kailuan Mineral Administrative Bureau	2,090.96	167	Pigeon Bicycle Group Corp.	1,625.70
118	Huainan Mineral Administrative Bureau	2,082.44	168	Guizhou Aluminium Factory	1,604.18
119	Dalian Steel Factory	2,064.91	169	Dalian Chemical Industry Corp.	1,595.26
120	Chongqing Special Steel (Group) Corp.	2,064.01	170	Chengde Cigarette Factory	1,592.51
121	China Light-Duty Motorcycle Group General Corp.	2,023.03	171	Guizhou Shuicheng Iron & Steel Corp.	1,586.71
122	China Southern Aviation Power Machinery Corp.	2,209.91	172	Beijing Light-Duty Automobile Manufacturing Corp.	1,584.06
123	China Yaohua Glass Group	1,984.62	173	Chengde Iron & Steel Corp.	1,581.93
124	Beijing Internal-Combustion Engine Group	1,981.00	174	Jinchuan Non-ferrous Metal Corp.	1,580.39
125	Shanghai No. 2 Iron & Steel Factory	1,952.03	175	Jianghan Petroleum Administrative Bureau	1,577.96
126	Nanjing Chemical Industry (Group) Corp.	1,944.91	176	Shanghai Electrical Machinery (Group) Corp.	1,577.48
127	Shanghai Tyre & Rubber (Group) Joint-Stock Corp.	1,931.24	177	Sanming Iron & Steel Factory	1,573.68
128	Xuzhou Mineral Administrative Bureau	1,925.77	178	Chuxiong Cigarette Factory	1,564.16
129	Chang'an Machinery Manfacturing Factory	1,925.03	179	Shanghai Fenghuang Bicycle Joint-Stock Corp.	1,554.34
130	Yanzhou Mineral Administrative Bureau	1,923.02	180	China Great Wall Aluminium Industry Corp.	1,551.60
131	Guangzhou Baiyunshan Enterprise Group Corp.	1,902.81	181	Tianjin Communication & Broadcasting Corp.	1,539.62
132	Yumen Petroleum Administrative Bureau	1,902.09	182	Hangzhou Telecommunications Equipment Factory	1,536.59
133	China Eastern Electrical Group Corp.	1,887.76	183	Shandong Aluminium Industry Corp.	1,530.77
134	Hegang Mineral Administrative Bureau	1,886.98	184	China Zhenhua Electronics Group	1,527.67
135	Lanzhou Chemical Industry Corp.	1,881.98	185	Beigang Group Corp.	1,522.95
136	Shijiazhuang Oil Refinery Factory	1,860.53	186	Xinjiang Bayi Iron & Steel General Factory	1,518.26
137	Silver Non-ferrous Metal Corp.	1,858.15	187	Shenyang Electric Cable Factory	1,512.86
138	Wanbao Electrical Appliance Group Corp.	1,855.39	188	Xinwen Mineral Administrative Bureau	1,508.29
139	Tongling Non-ferrous Metal Corp.	1,840.65	189	Beijing Matsushita Colour Picture Tube Co.	1,503.54
140	Shaotong Cigarette Factory	1,835.01	190	Hebei Automobile Manufacturing (Group) Corp.	1,498.05
141	Beijing Construction Material Group General Corp.	1,818.40	191	Xining Steel Factory	1,490.08
142	Guangdong Foshan Ceramics Group Joint-Stock Corp.	1,795.19	192	Xi'an Electrical Machinery Manufacturing Corp.	1,484.19
143	Qingdao Iron & Steel Corp.	1,791.62	193	China New Construction Material Corp.	1,471.50

continued…

CHINA'S TOP 250 INDUSTRIAL ENTERPRISES, 1994 (sales, mn RMB) (continued)

194 Fushun Iron & Steel Corp.	1,466.49	
195 Shuangyashan Mineral Administrative Bureau	1,465.87	
196 Feng Feng Mineral Administrative Bureau	1,461.42	
197 Fujian Hitachi TV Set Co.	1,441.33	
198 Qitaihe Mineral Administrative Bureau	1,440.37	
199 Beijing Automobile & Motorcycle Associated Manufacturing Corp.	1,436.53	
200 Jinan Cigarette Factory	1,430.79	
201 Guiyang Cigarette Factory	1,422.27	
202 Shanghai Leather Co.	1,406.12	
203 Shanghai Chlorine & Aicali of Chemical Industry Joint-Stock Corp.	1,396.55	
204 Shanghai Electrical Appliance Joint-Stock Corp.	1,384.25	
205 Zhuhai Dongda Group Joint-Stock Corp.	1,337.89	
206 Yangquan Mineral Administrative Bureau	1,333.94	
207 Shanghai Mitsubishi Elevator Co.	1,329.24	
208 Guangzhou No. 2 Cigarette Factory	1,320.81	
209 Zhangjiakou Cigarette Factory	1,305.69	
210 Shanghai Xinhu Iron & Steel Factory	1,303.58	
211 Shantou Ocean (Group) Corp.	1,303.38	
212 Daye Non-ferrous Metal Corp.	1,302.96	
213 Zhuzhou Smelting Factory	1,291.83	
214 Bengbu Cigarette Factory	1,284.83	
215 Lanzhou Iron & Steel Group Corp.	1,279.44	
216 Linyuan Iron & Steel Corp.	1,276.92	
217 Shanghai Machine Tools General Corp.	1,274.00	
218 Qingdao Cigarette Factory	1,271.92	
219 Benxi Bentai Iron & Steel General Factory	1,270.73	
220 China Yangtze Group	1,268.99	
221 Harbin Oil Refinery Factory	1,262.38	
222 Wuyang Iron & Steel Corp.	1,255.46	
223 Jinan Oil Refinery Factory	1,246.24	
224 Qianguo Oil Refinery Factory	1,240.72	
225 Yunnan Smelting Factory	1,239.56	
226 Xiamen Huaxia Group	1,236.03	
227 Qiqiha'er Rolling Stock Plant	1,235.42	
228 Shanghai Non-ferrous Metal General Corp.	1,231.36	
229 Shanghai Paper Corp.	1,223.49	
230 Taiyuan Chemical Industry Group Corp.	1,219.03	
231 Jilin Ferro-alloy Factory	1,217.86	
232 Hudong Shipyard	1,214.81	
233 Beijing Mudan Electronics Group Corp.	1,213.52	
234 Shanghai Shangling Refrigerator General Factory	1,211.14	
235 Shenyang Smelting Factory	1,201.51	
236 Yibing Wuliangye Distillery	1,194.26	
237 Tiefa Mineral Administrative Bureau	1,191.49	
238 Fushun Aluminium Factory	1,191.05	
239 Shanghai Heavy-Duty Mining Machinery Corp.	1,176.26	
240 Jiacheng Machinery Factory	1,172.86	
241 Huhhot Oil Refinery Plant	1,165.11	
242 Changsha Sino-Italian Electrical Appliance Joint-Stock Corp.	1,163.76	
243 Luoyang Chundu Group Joint-Stock Corp.	1,158.59	
244 Hengyang Steel Pipe Factory	1,156.95	
245 Guangzhou Baojie Co.	1,154.94	
246 Luoyang Floating Glass Group	1,152.65	
247 Hangzhou Cigarette Factory	1,142.38	
248 Chengdu Iron & Steel Factory	1,128.47	
249 Hualin Group General Corp.	1,116.21	
250 Dalian Shipyard	1,116.06	

China Trade Report, Dec 1994.

MAP OF CHINA'S INDUSTRIAL OUTPUT, 1994

Top five producers
Second five producers

China Business, 22 Aug 1994.

REFORM OF STATE OWNED ENTERPRISES, 1995

[Article by staff reporter Wu Naitao: "95 Goals for Reform of State-Owned Enterprises"]

Reform of China's macroeconomic system was the subject of significant progress during 1994, and the reform effort for the coming year will focus on improving the management of large and medium-sized enterprises and the establishment of a modern enterprise system.

During a recent inspection tour of Shanghai, which emphasized the reform of large and medium-sized state-owned enterprises, Zhu Rongji, vice-premier of the State Council, presided over a discussion meeting attended by the directors and managers of 10-odd state-owned enterprises, and conducted an investigation of loss-making enterprises. According to Zhu, Shanghai's state-owned enterprises occupy a decisive position in the economic construction and social development of both Shanghai, and the country as a whole.

While state-owned enterprises are currently facing various difficulties, they will nonetheless be able to turn the corner so long as they effectively change their operational mechanisms and establish a modern enterprise system. In 1994, the government adopted a series of important reform and macro-control measures designed to create a sound macroenvironment for improving state-owned enterprises. However, the only way such enterprises can truly change their operational mechanisms is to establish a genuine market. Only then can reform of the macro-economic system be put into practice and yield expected results in terms of establishing macro-controls.

There is absolutely no doubt that China's over 400,000 state-owned enterprises play a decisive role in the national economy. Hence, if China's 14,400 large and medium-sized state-owned enterprises are operated effectively, well over 50 percent of the country's industrial economy will be operating on the right track.

According to statistics provided by the State Economic and Trade Commission, by the end of 1993, China had 71,600 state-owned industrial enterprises subject to independent accounting, a figure accounting for 17 percent of the country's total number of industrial enterprises, including those at or above the township level practicing independent accounting. The total number included 14,400 large and medium-sized state-owned enterprises, or 4 percent of the country's total number of industrial enterprises. The combined industrial output value of state-owned industrial enterprises represented 53 percent of the nation's total industrial output value, with that of large and medium-sized state-owned enterprises accounting for 44 percent of the national total. The net value of the fixed assets of state-owned enterprises accounted for 75 percent of the total for all industrial enterprises, with that of large and medium-sized state-owned enterprises accounting for 62 percent of the total. State-owned enterprises contributed 66 percent of the profit and tax payments of all industrial enterprises, with large and medium-sized state-owned enterprises contributing 59 percent of the total. In the first half of 1994 alone, the profits and taxes of state-owned enterprises accounted for 62 percent of the total for China's industrial enterprises, with taxes paid by the former accounting for 68 percent of total tax payments. The figures indicate that state-owned enterprises, especially large and medium-sized ones, continue to occupy a decisive position in the national economy.

However, difficulties and problems confronting state-owned enterprises have attracted special attention. With this in mind, the Chinese government has continuously considered strengthening the vitality of state-owned enterprises, particularly large and medium-sized ones, as the focal point of economic structural reform, and has extended great effort in this regard. The past 15-odd years of reform have basically resolved the numerous problems enterprises faced as a result of the traditional planned economic system. State-owned enterprises have been the subject of monumental changes, and most existing problems are the result of deep-rooted contradictions which are difficult to resolve. The State Council has outlined the deepening of enterprise reform as the focus of the economic structural reform for 1995, with major goals centering on resolving deep-rooted contradictions and creating new systems.

continued...

REFORM OF STATE OWNED ENTERPRISES, 1995 (continued)

Major Contributions

Since the introduction of reform, the strategic role of state-owned enterprises and the vigorous development of collective, township and foreign-funded enterprises have been complimentary, and have thus created a situation featuring the sustained and rapid growth of the national economy. In terms of constant prices, between 1979 and 1993, the gross national product (GNP) recorded an average annual growth of 9.3 percent. Non-state enterprises not only benefited from the availability of raw materials, adequate power, public utilities, technology and equipment provided by state-owned enterprises, but also enjoyed favorable conditions the state-owned sector created to ensure their rapid accumulation and development, and the progress all economic sectors gained through competition. State-owned enterprises bore greater responsibility for state financial income, mandatory planning arid public welfare, while at the same time supporting the state's efforts to offer differing degrees of preferential policies for collective, individual, private and foreign investment. The extensive contributions made by old industrial bases, based mainly on state-owned enterprises, have supported key state construction projects and the accelerated opening and development of new industrial areas. In particular, the transfer of a large number of managerial and technical personnel from state-owned enterprises to other enterprises through various channels has helped the latter to rapidly gain strength. Hence, the absence of the support of state-owned enterprises and the heavy burden they shouldered would have made it impossible for China to have achieved such high level reform and economic progress. Without a doubt, state-owned enterprises have and continue to play an irreplaceable role in providing effective channels for supply, assisting in agricultural development, readjusting social distribution, maintaining social stability, enhancing the quality of the national economy and ensuring the normal operation and development of the national economy.

Unequal Competition

Historically, old state-owned industrial enterprises have shouldered a heavy burden. For example, the Shanghai Corduroy Factory once enjoyed a ready market for its products both at home and abroad. Over the past 40-odd years, the factory has paid the state treasury more than 700 million yuan in profits and taxes, a figure several dozen times greater than state inputs. However, confronted with competition of newcomers to the market, particularly foreign-funded and township enterprises receiving preferential treatment from the government, the 65-year-old factory which operates with obsolete equipment is gradually losing its market. This in turn has forced the factory to reduce its output and declare one-half of its work force as redundant. Nevertheless, the factory continues to pay pensions to retirees numbering 1.3 times more than the current number of active employees. At the same time, unavoidable losses have placed the factory in a precarious position.

Many state-owned enterprises face similar problems. In many cases their rate of development has failed to match that of non-state enterprises, and a considerable number are barely surviving due to long-term losses. The plight of state-owned enterprises, revolving around the severe curtailment of the capacity for self development which has placed them in a position of unequal competition as they strive to gear themselves to a market economy, centers on the following reasons:

—Heavy long-term tax burden. On average, between 1980 and 1993, the profits, taxes and energy and transportation funds paid by budgeted state-owned industrial enterprises accounted for 86 percent of the national total, with actual profits retained representing only 14 percent of their total yield of profits and taxes. According to the report entitled Financial Statistics of State-Owned Enterprises compiled by the Ministry of Finance, the sales income of state-owned enterprises has jumped considerably over the past 15 years, with simultaneous steady increases in payments of sales taxes. Meanwhile, total profits have dropped, and the amount of profits actually retained has remained low. On the other hand, non-state enterprises had a light tax burden and enjoyed differing degrees of preferential policies. Along with implementation of the new tax system in 1994, state-owned enterprises finally enjoyed equal

continued...

REFORM OF STATE OWNED ENTERPRISES, 1995 (continued)

tax rates with non-state enterprises, and thereby acquired the opportunity to engage in equal competition.

—Heavy debt burden. Special conditions led to state-owned enterprises shouldering a heavy debt burden. According to the results of a recent investigation of state-owned enterprises in Shanghai, Tianjin and 16 other cities, the capital of state-owned enterprises available for production and management accounted for a mere 4.61 percent of their total circulating funds. Moreover, various latent losses such as credit sales and other inaccessible capital exceeded one-third of their total circulating funds. The idle capital of a considerable number of enterprises and unavailable channels of circulation resulted in mutual defaults and declining credit.

—Excessive redundancies. Problems surfaced in terms of redundant employees resulting from the economic structure, as well as various other lingering social factors. The former policy of "full employment" has been the major cause of redundancies which are now a major blockade hindering the development of enterprises and the focal point of enterprise reform.

—Public welfare services. From the very beginning, many state-owned enterprises shouldered the burden of providing their employees with various kinds of living services such as housing, hospitals, nurseries and schools, as well as community services such as police protection, savings banks and tax collection offices. Such services siphoned large amounts of productive capital, which in turn hampered the efforts of enterprises to improve production and management efficiency.

—Heavy burden for pension and medical expenses. All state-owned enterprises pay pensions to a considerable number of retirees and allocate a significant level of funding to ensure health care for their employees. However, over the long term, such enterprises have had little or no accumulation of insurance funds, a fact which has resulted in the current excessive load on pensions and medical expenses. This in turn has placed the enterprises in an unfavorable position in terms of market competition.

—Most state-owned enterprises, which operate with obsolete equipment and backward production technology, have a low-level capability for self-development and require long-term product development cycles.

While some problems formed and accumulated under the planned economic structure, new problems have emerged during the course of reform. Speaking at a 1995 meeting on economic reform, Minister Wang Zhongyu of the State Economic and Trade Commission called for a clear understanding of the grim situation facing state-owned enterprises. Under the current economic pattern with public ownership as the mainstay and the joint development of diversified economic sectors, township enterprises have rapidly emerged to the forefront as a new force, the urban collective economy has continued to expand, and the private and individual economic sectors have experienced sustained and rapid development. Solely foreign-funded enterprises, joint ventures and cooperative enterprises have experienced rapid development as the country has opened its doors ever wider to the outside world. Faced with acute market competition, state-owned enterprises face both internal and external challenges in terms of their existence and development. Wang noted that the on-going situation requires the government to further resolve the deep-rooted contradictions of state-owned enterprises, free and develop their productive forces, consolidate their competitive position as the mainstay of the national economy, and enable them to display their leading role in economic construction.

Short-Term Goals

Minister Wang Zhongyu of the State Economic and Trade Commission stressed that resolving deep-rooted contradictions requires changing the concepts, forms and measures in order to achieve new breakthroughs in enterprise reform. Firstly, the emphasis of enterprise reform should be shifted from expanding decision-making power and profits concessions to the establishment of new systems which will enable state-owned enterprises to enjoy equal competitive conditions with enterprises in other economic sectors. Secondly, main efforts should be shifted from individual reform items to comprehensive and coordinated reform, and combining overall progress with breakthroughs in certain primary areas. Thirdly, priorities

continued...

REFORM OF STATE OWNED ENTERPRISES, 1995 (continued)

should be shifted from improving the management of individual enterprises to upgrading the state-owned economic sector as a whole, effectively combining system reform with technological transformations and reorganization, optimizing the structure of state-owned assets, completing the strategic shift of state-owned assets, and enhancing the operational efficiency of state-owned assets. Finally, the emphasis of reform should also be shifted from resolving isolated historical problems of state-owned enterprises to coordinated reform of the financial, investment and social security systems, and resolving problems by establishing the enterprise capital system, a system of reserve funds for bad debts, and unemployment and old-age insurance systems.

Vice-Minister Chen Qingtai who is in charge of enterprise reform for the State Economic and Trade Commission noted that imminent tasks facing reform in 1995 will be arduous. However, he pointed out that the following series of reform measures have already been worked out.

—Selecting a batch of enterprises as experimental units for the establishment of a modern enterprise system. The list of 100 units has already been issued.

—Continuing to implement the Regulations on the Transfer of Operational Mechanisms and quickly putting the Regulations on the Supervision and Management of the Property of State-owned Enterprises into practice. The latter regulations, promulgated in July last year, chiefly delineate the property rights relationship of state-owned enterprises, ensure increases and guarantee the value of state-owned property, and consolidate and develop the state-owned economy. A list of about 1,000 enterprises subject to the supervision of supervisory organizations empowered by the State Council will be announced, and related coordination measures will be formulated. Supervisory committees will be sent to various enterprises step by step with the approval of the State Council.

—Using multiple channels to increase the production and management funds of enterprises and establishing related mechanisms. In line with the principle of relying chiefly on enterprises to raise supplemental funds and adopting government policies to encourage such activities, 15 percent of the enterprise income tax paid to the government will be returned to supplement production and management funds.

—Enhancing investments in technological transformations of enterprises. An earnest effort will be made to strengthen the activity by gradually raising the proportion of investments in technology upgrades to more than one-third of the country's total investments in fixed assets.

—Appropriately rearranging redundant employees and separating the public service functions of enterprises. Appropriately rearranging redundant employees requires mobilizing the initiative of the government, enterprises and individuals. The effort will include the adoption of measures such as encouraging the development of tertiary projects, encouraging redundant employees to seek new jobs and encouraging the early retirement of some employees. The method of relying on enterprises to rearrange redundant employees will gradually be replaced by the regulatory mechanisms of the labor market in order to achieve employment through competition, with the state providing guidance and assistance.

—Separating the public service functions of enterprises will include placing emphasis on separating auxiliary units from enterprises. Enterprises in cities or prefectures with appropriate conditions will be selected to transfer the management of existing public service units such as schools and hospitals to local governments, with the effort designed to explore new avenues for thorough separation.

—Implementing experimental trials with enterprise bankruptcy. In line with the Bankruptcy Law and the State Council's Circular on Issues Concerning the Trial Practice of the Bankruptcy of State-owned Enterprises in Selected Cities which will be promulgated in the near future, a batch of state-owned enterprises unable to repay due debts and have no hope of reversing their loss-making situation will be ordered to declare bankruptcy. Income earned from the sale of property and land-use rights must first be used to make arrangements for unemployed workers and staff. Methods to guarantee the welfare of the employees of bankrupt enterprises will be gradually improved and perfected.

continued...

REFORM OF STATE OWNED ENTERPRISES, 1995 (continued)

—Adopting various measures to resolve lingering historical problems plaguing state-owned enterprises, such as latent losses, credit sales and excessive debt burdens. Since numerous factors have led to the diversified debts of state-owned enterprises, such debts should not be and most likely will not be exempted or offset completely. Efforts to restructure assets and debts should be carried out in conjunction with the reform of the state-owned assets management and operation system, and the state investment and financing systems.

—Strengthening the internal management of enterprises, managing factories in strict accordance with the law and enhancing the quality of enterprises as a whole.

—Strengthening guidance for the strategic structural readjustment of state-owned enterprises.

—Continuing trial experiments with establishing enterprise groups.

Enterprise System

According to the design of the State Economic and Trade Commission, the strategic targets for enterprise reform between now and the turn of the century are to basically establish the framework and operational mechanisms of a modern enterprise system suited to the socialist market economic structure. Fulfillment of the targets will enable large and medium-sized state-owned enterprises to play the leading role in the socialist market economy.

The basic characteristics of the modern enterprise system to be established in China are as follows:

—Clearly defined property rights relationships. The proprietary rights for state-owned assets of enterprises belong to the state. Enterprises funded by the state and other investors with all property rights enjoyed by legal entities will shoulder specified civil rights and responsibilities.

—Enterprises, using property rights they are entitled to a legal entity, operate independently according to law, assume responsibility for their own profits and losses, pay stipulated taxes, and are responsible for guaranteeing and increasing the assets of investors. [sentence as received]

—Investors enjoy rights and interests in proportion to the amount of capital they have invested in enterprises, as well as proportional rights to enjoy financial benefits, participate in policy decision-making and select managers. In cases when an enterprise declares bankruptcy, investors bear limited liability for debt in accordance with the amount of invested capital.

—Enterprises organize production in line with market demand, and with the objective of enhancing labor productivity and economic returns. The government refrains from directly interfering in the production and management of enterprises. Superior enterprises will survive and the inferior will be eliminated through market competition. Those sustaining long-term losses and failing to offset debts will be forced to declare bankruptcy according to law.

—Scientific enterprise leadership and organizational management systems will be established to regulate the relationship between proprietors, managers and employees, and operational mechanisms combining encouragement and restraint will be formed.

Speaking of the aforementioned characteristics, Vice Premier Zou Jiahua noted that the most important aspects are to perfect the system to ensure that enterprises are treated as legal entities, institute the limited liability system and establish scientific enterprise leadership and organizational systems. Zou predicted that state-owned enterprises will face an arduous course in the transformation from simply being subordinates of government organizations under the planned economic system to becoming the main bodies of competition under a market economic structure. He pointed to the fact that China lacks mature system experience in this regard. Hence, pilot projects will be launched to accumulate experience for the establishment of a modern enterprise system. The effort to establish a modern system will place China's state-owned enterprises at the forefront of profound reform which will result in major changes in the relationship between the government and enterprises, as well as in the proprietary rights relationship, and the organizational structure and management system of enterprises.

continued...

REFORM OF STATE OWNED ENTERPRISES, 1995 (continued)

Coordinated Reform

Enterprise reform over the past 15 years proves the inadequacy of simply relying on the reform of enterprises themselves to change operational mechanisms and genuinely transform them into the main body of market competition. Hence, the necessity for the coordinated reform of relevant systems, such as expediting changes in government functions and organizational structural reform, expediting price reform and establishing a market system, expediting the establishment of a social security system and a unified social security management organization, and expediting and perfecting a social service system.

According to a spokesman for the State Commission for Restructuring Economic Systems, in 1995, reform of China's social security system will take a giant stride forward through the establishment and improvement of new unemployment, old-age and health care insurance mechanisms designed to facilitate the deepening of enterprise reform and the establishment of a modern enterprise system. The priority for reform of the social security system will be to ensure the continuous improvement and perfection of the unemployment insurance system. The unemployment insurance fund will be managed in a unified way in accordance with the principles of ensuring inputs on the basis of expenditures and maintaining an appropriate level of reserves. Enterprises currently pay unemployment premiums equivalent to 1 percent of their gross payroll. The major portion of the unemployment insurance fund should be used as a relief fund for the unemployed and paying medical expenses during the period the unemployed receives relief funds. Individuals who have worked for their units continuously for one year prior to being made redundant are eligible to receive unemployment relief funds for two months. The amount of unemployment relief paid is equivalent to 50 percent of the average per capita salary of the relevant locality, a standard which ensures the basic living costs of unemployed workers. Simultaneously, efforts will be made to extend unemployment insurance services from employees of state-owned enterprises to those working for state-owned urban collectives, as well as shareholding, private and foreign-funded enterprises.

In 1995, comprehensive reform of the old-age and health care insurance system will be carried out nationwide. In urban areas, unified old-age and health care insurance will be combined with personal accounts, and the system of spot income and expenditures will be replaced by a system based on contributing and accumulating funds in advance. The old-age insurance system will be formed by multi-level services, including basic old-age insurance, enterprise supplemented old-age insurance, social mutual-aid insurance and personal savings deposits for old-age insurance. Personal accounts will include old-age insurance premiums paid by employees and enterprises in proportion to gross payroll, and old-age insurance premiums enterprises credit the personal accounts of employees in proportion to the per-capita salary level in relevant localities.

The government will establish a special insurance fund to provide unemployment insurance to employees of enterprises which have suspended production, declared bankruptcy or have undergone reorganization, with capital to be raised from various channels.

Even though state-owned enterprises currently face numerous difficulties in production and management, favorable conditions still exceed unfavorable conditions whether viewed in terms of the background of reform, the opening effort and economic development, or the respective situation of state-owned enterprises themselves. Moreover, favorable conditions are constantly emerging. In general, major measures for reform of the fiscal, taxation, financial, foreign exchange and foreign trade systems undertaken in 1994 have operated normally. This in turn has not only further promoted the normalization and standardization of the macro-control system, but has also provided a basic guarantee for further improving the conditions of state-owned enterprises. The goal of the reform of state-owned enterprises is to establish a modern enterprise system which fits the needs of the socialist market economy and provides them with operational mechanisms approximating those of their counterparts abroad. State-owned enterprises will continue to extend great effort to fulfill the goal during the new year.

Beijing Review, 15 Jan 1995.

NUMBER OF STAFF AND WORKERS AND LABORERS, JULY 1993–JULY 1994 (th persons)

Year/-Month	Total	Subtotal	State Owned Units Permanent Employees	Contractual Employees	Urban Collective Owned Units	Other Ownership Units
1993						
Jul	146,977	108,187	74,204	21,592	35,623	3,167
Aug	147,355	108,452	74,297	21,769	35,707	3,196
Sep	147,373	108,576	74,064	22,048	35,506	3,291
Oct	147,533	108,679	74,014	22,202	35,528	3,326
Nov	147,716	108,833	74,070	22,306	35,524	3,359
Dec	150,400	110,940	74,330	23,300	36,030	3,430
1994						
Feb	147,857	108,789	98,622	24,095	34,952	4,116
Mar	147,449	108,564			33,897	4,988
Apr	147,408	108,692	100,053	25,632	33,692	5,024
May	147,530	108,726	100,234	25,622	33,639	5,165
Jun	147,447	108,674	101,459	25,298	33,431	5,342
Jul	147,577	108,747	101,344	25,423	33,446	5,384

• Other ownership units include units jointly owned by (1) State and Collectives, (2) State and Individuals, (3) Collective and Individuals, (4) Chinese and Foreign Investors and units singly owned by (1) Overseas Chinese or Chinese businessmen from Hong Kong and Macao, (2) Foreign investors.

China Monthly Statistics, Jun 1995.

NUMBER OF STAFF AND WORKERS BY REGION, 1995 (10,000 persons)

Region	Total	State-Owned	Collective-Owned of Township	Other
National total	14,744.7	10,867.4	3,343.1	534.2
Beijing	469.0	369.2	79.2	20.6
Tianjin	289.9	204.1	69.3	16.5
Hebei	701.4	539.5	147.0	14.9
Shanxi	459.2	359.9	95.1	4.2
Inner Mongolia	383.6	303.2	77.1	3.3
Liaoning	1,033.1	674.0	317.5	41.6
Jilin	525.1	382.5	131.4	11.2
Heilongjiang	863.2	643.2	208.9	11.1
Shanghai	482.1	351.4	85.8	44.9
Jiangsu	904.4	568.8	289.3	46.3
Zhejiang	491.0	295.2	170.2	25.6
Anhui	492.7	348.8	134.4	9.5
Fujin	337.4	215.7	71.3	50.4
Jiangxi	410.0	324.9	79.7	5.4
Shandong	858.8	617.3	214.3	27.2
Henan	766.1	596.6	160.1	9.4
Hubei	738.7	565.0	158.4	15.3
Hunan	588.1	453.2	125.8	9.1
Guangdong	875.3	559.3	200.5	115.5
Guangxi	330.9	273.9	48.5	8.5
Hainan	112.7	98.9	9.6	4.2
Sichuan	977.6	729.2	221.1	27.3

continued...

NUMBER OF STAFF AND WORKERS BY REGION, 1995 (10,000 persons) (continued)

Region	Total	State-Owned	Collective-Owned of Township	Other
Guizhou	233.5	193.3	38.6	1.6
Yunnan	304.0	257.1	44.6	2.3
Tibet	16.9	15.7	1.1	0.1
Shaanxi	394.1	325.7	63.6	4.8
Gansu	253.0	208.2	43.8	1.0
Qinghai	66.0	57.3	8.6	0.1
Ningxia	71.4	60.0	10.8	0.6
Xinjiang	315.5	276.3	37.5	1.7

China Monthly Statistics, Jun 1995.

COMPARISON RATES OF CHINA'S CONSTRUCTION INDUSTRY, 1991-1993

In 1990, China's construction industry's completed output value accounted for only 4.0 percent of the GDP, and in 1992, the industry's total employment only accounted for 1.95 percent of the nation's total labor force.

As the pace of China's construction accelerated in recent years, and especially after Deng Xiaoping's South China speech, China's economy has begun to take off, allowing the construction industry to temporarily escape the predicament of underdevelopment, and its real strength has actually increased somewhat (see Table 3.) In only a few years time, its added-value as a percentage of the GDP was able to surpass that in Singapore and India and others in 1988. Thus, the industry's development has laid a sound foundation for boosting its status in the national economy. But labor productivity in China's construction industry is still low. Tables 4 and 5 show the productivity rates in terms of per capita completed area per year in square meters [sq m] and in terms of volume of business, and from those figures, it is clear that we are still trailing far behind the developed countries.

Table 3: Chinese Construction Industry Added-Value as a Percentage of the GDP in the Last Two Years

Year	GDP (trillion yuan)	Added-Value (bn yuan)	Percentage
1992	2.3938	139.2	5.8
1993	3.1380	210.5	6.7

Table 4: Comparison of Per Capita Area Completed Per Year (sq m)

Country	Singapore	Japan	China	China
Year	1984	1985	1992	1993
Area	102	60.4	5.10	7.75

Table 5: Prime Contractor Per Capita Volume of Business ($10,000)

Country	US	Japan	Japan	Korea	China
Contractor	GRS	Dacheng	Dazhu	Hyundai	CSCEC
Volume of business	13.3	73.3	60.4	44.3	1.14

Obviously, if China's construction industry is to become a mainstay industry, external conditions must be improved, and the industry's internal quality must also be improved at the same time. In particular, we must increase substantially the industry's capacity to create wealth, that is, raise the in-kind labor productivity rate.

continued...

COMPARISON RATES OF CHINA'S CONSTRUCTION INDUSTRY, 1991-1993 (continued)

Main Problems Preventing the Construction Industry From Becoming a Mainstay Industry
Reform of the construction industry had a head start, but hampered by many obstacles, progress was slow. The main reason is that our understanding of the construction industry is, to a very large extent, still hamstrung by the planned economic system. First, since the founding of the PRC, we have basically followed the former Soviet Union's system and have never treated the construction industry as an independent material production sector but only as a intermediate link during the completion of a capital construction investment. Until the last few years, when leaders at all levels talked about the construction industry, their priority was to "fulfill social fixed asset investment" quotas rather than focusing on how the construction industry could create wealth for society. The construction industry was treated as a sector that provided services to capital construction, and, in turn, the industry's independence and the commodity attributes of its product were never recognized. Second, exactly because the construction industry was treated as an intermediate link, a low-price, low-profit policy was implemented in the industry according to the "fund idling" theory, which radically slowed the industry's development. Furthermore, enterprise reform and other necessary measures have not kept up; many problems are far from being resolved, and these also obstruct the industry's development.

Construction enterprises are put in a subordinate position.
As market entities, enterprises should have equal status in the market, but in China's construction projects, parties A and B have never been equals. Despite the diversification of investment entities, many government departments still stand at the side of the investors and zealously exercise administrative interventions. They stick to their biased interpretation of such viewpoints as "conserving investments for the state's sake," and no guarantees are given and no importance is attached to the construction enterprise profit. Second, in large government projects with huge state investments, the proprietors and departments in charge never act like independent legal persons in the market; they do not take any economic or legal responsibility. Some "chief engineers" make arbitrary demands and hand down orders without taking any responsibility. All responsibilities and risks are shoved onto the construction enterprises. Furthermore, before a project is started, the methods of the planned economy apply, and after it has begun, the practices of the market economy come into play. This leaves construction enterprises very little room to compete over prices during the construction period. In essence, enterprises have lost the legal person status they deserve. They not only are reduced to being appendages of the government but also of party A. Meanwhile, because construction units often are linked to administrative departments, when there are disputes, both party A and the arbitrator claim that they represent the state; party B is put in a disadvantaged position no matter what.

Construction product prices are grossly distorted.
For years, the construction industry simply followed the former Soviet Union's fixed quota pricing system. They calculated the project cost based on a previously fixed budget, combined all prices and fees, and used relatively static fixed quotas as the basis for figuring prices, and the government also set rigid regulations; prices were not calculated based on the necessary amount of labor. This neither reflected the value of the construction product nor supply-demand relations in the market. It seriously violated general price laws, and construction product prices had nothing to do with their value. This was the core problem in the reform of the construction industry.

In a socialist market economy, enterprises, as market entities, must maximize profit. The current low-price, low-profit policy the state implements in the construction industry leads to improper pricing, and it causes the surplus value created by that industry to be diverted to other industries, and as a result, the construction industry's profit level is far below society's average rate of profit, which greatly hampers the industry's development (see Tables 6 and 7.)

continued...

COMPARISON RATES OF CHINA'S CONSTRUCTION INDUSTRY, 1991-1993 (continued)

Table 6: Comparison of Rates of Enterprise Operating Profit in Different Industries

Year	CSCEC	Beijing People's Publishing	Beijing Travel and Passenger Cars	Shanghai Haixin	Jiangsu Chunlan	Hainan Chemical Fibers
1991	1.90	13.9	3.10	18.1	17.4	17.1
1992	1.50	9.90	4.20	20.0	13.7	9.92
1993	1.10	24.9	5.70	24.5	9.11	28.1

Table 7: Operating Profit Rates of Enterprises of Different Types Under CSCEC Jurisdiction (percent)

Year	Installation	Prospecting and Design	Industrial Services	Real Estate
1991	1.90	9.80	12.4	7.40
1992	1.50	14.1	17.2	8.90
1993	1.00	14.7	14.0	31.6

Chinese Government Statistics, 1995.

STATE ENTERPRISES CONTINUED LOSSES, 1995

[By Dede Nickerson in Beijing] Losses incurred by state-owned enterprises continue to grow, remaining a huge burden as China reforms fiscal policy.

At a press conference yesterday, Minister of the State Economic and Trade Commission Wang Zhongyu and Labor Minister Li Boyong gave a candid assessment of problems facing the state sector.

"With the deepening of reform, the contradictions resulting for the transformation of the management mechanism have been sharpened. These problems can only be solved by deepening reform," said Mr. Wang. He drew attention in particular to poor management and the inability of firms to adjust production to meet market demand.

Mr. Wang said: "Some money-losing enterprises are not very conscious of the needs of the market and their reputation in the market." He said these enterprises would be told to adjust accordingly in 1995.

China's loss-making state firms cost the country billions of yuan in 1994—the unsold product inventory increased by 100 billion yuan (HK$91.70 billion) compared with the 1994 value. More than 70 percent of bank loans currently go to state firms, according to official data. This is seen as a major obstacle to China's efforts to reform the banking system.

One of the proposed solutions is simply to allow unprofitable firms to go bankrupt and Prime Minister Li Peng acknowledged that very proposal in his annual address on Sunday. Mr. Li said all relevant parties were now working on development of job opportunities. However, analysts are skeptical about how far China will go with the bankruptcy experiment because maintaining social stability remains a top priority for the central authorities.

Despite the mooted bankruptcy law, analysts are not confident such a step will be enough or, indeed, that it will be implemented soon.

Executive director of Asia Infrastructure Fund Ted Rule said: "It's desirable that they should have a bankruptcy law, but we've been hearing about it for years and so far, nothing has been done.

"When the Government takes such a step, it's imperative that they allow foreign banks to access the assets of the bankrupt companies."

A gray area also exists in the bankruptcy arena when assessing who has control of assets.

Mr. Rule explained: "As it stands, you cannot distinguish between the assets of the company and those of the state.

South China Morning Post, 8 Mar 1995.

TOTAL WAGE BILL OF STAFF AND WORKERS, JULY 1993–JULY 1994 (mn yuan)

Year/Month	Total Wage Bill	State Owned Units Subtotal	State Owned Units Bonuses	Urban Collective Units	Other Ownership Units*
1993					
Jul	37,052	28,720	6,305	7,030	1,302
Aug	36,209	28,565	5,838	6,379	1,265
Sep	38,889	30,441	7,350	6,783	1,665
Oct	40,299	31,697	6,955	7,098	1,504
Nov	40,023	31,289	6,705	7,184	1,549
Dec	81,479	64,004		15,039	2,463
1994					
Jan-Feb	82,941.1	64,865.9	14,631.9	14,405	3,669.8
Mar	43,682.7	34,129.5		6,868.4	2,684.8
Apr	42,513.5	33,382.8		6,923.3	2,207.8
May	43,176.8	33,860.4		6,983.5	2,333.0
Jun	51,025.3	40,009.4		7,957.1	3,058.6
Jul	47,932.1	37,581.1		7,724.4	2,626.7

* Other ownership units include units jointly owned by (1) State and collectives, (2) State and individuals, (3) Collective and individuals, (4) Chinese and foreign investors and units singly owned by (1) Overseas Chinese or Chinese businessmen from Hong Kong and Macao, (2) Foreign investors.

China Monthly Statistics, Jun 1995.

WAGE BILL OF STAFF AND WORKERS BY REGION, 1995 (10,000 yuan)

Region	Total	State-Owned	Collective-Owned of Township	Other Ownership
National total	26,333,939.3	20,624,800.1	4,313,734.6	1,395,404.6
Beijing	1,267,540.4	1,042,819.3	157,423.4	67,297.7
Tianjin	606,005.7	465,875.5	94,314.9	45,815.3
Hebei	1,150,049.1	966,308.5	154,948.3	28,792.3
Shanxi	695,240.9	594,835.2	92,193.6	8,212.1
Inner Mongolia	543,456.8	454,905.0	83,997.9	4,553.9
Liaoning	1,792,394.9	1,319,625.0	386,263.5	86,506.4
Jilin	723,741.7	588,310.6	118,153.1	17,278.0
Heilongjiang	1,110,044.2	905,797.8	173,172.2	31,074.2
Shanghai	1,448,649.9	1,080,464.8	190,725.9	177,459.2
Jiangsu	1,761,269.6	1,215,971.2	434,502.7	110,795.7
Zhejiang	1,008,999.0	647,010.2	300,881.0	61,107.8
Anhui	711,363.9	552,801.6	128,005.3	30,557.0
Fujian	596,793.5	392,227.4	98,211.5	106,354.6
Jiangxi	564,789.6	485,815.9	70,407.7	8,566.0
Shandong	1,535,535.2	1,197,260.7	284,146.2	54,128.3
Henan	1,032,747.5	866,675.9	149,563.3	16,508.3
Hubei	1,182,793.2	972,347.2	180,578.3	29,867.7
Hunan	915,986.0	749,096.0	149,195.0	17,695.0
Guangdong	2,501,348.3	1,677,607.0	444,443.9	379,297.4
Guangxi	610,894.3	522,812.3	69,667.6	18,414.4
Hainan	191,842.9	163,379.6	15,230.0	13,233.3
Sichuan	1,528,428.8	1,226,877.8	243,341.8	58,209.2
Guizhou	343,707.9	303,267.8	37,750.4	2,689.7

continued...

WAGE BILL OF STAFF AND WORKERS BY REGION, 1995 (10,000 yuan) (continued)

Region	Total	State-Owned	Collective-Owned of Township	Other Ownership
Yunnan	581,371.5	509,083.3	66,735.0	5,553.2
Tibet	37,390.7	35,713.3	1,517.7	159.7
Shaanxi	576,563.9	506,568.5	60,312.4	9,683.0
Gansu	438,435.0	385,966.4	51,090.4	1,378.2
Qinghai	121,112.4	112,585.0	8,292.1	235.3
Ningxia	127,057.5	113,195.7	13,032.0	829.8
Xinjiang	628,385.0	569,595.6	55,637.5	3,151.9

• At current prices

China Monthly Statistics, Jun 1995.

TEXTILE OUTPUT IN FOURTH QUARTER, 1994

Beijing (CEIS)—Following is a list of the output of textiles in December 1994, released by the State Statistical Bureau:

Item	Unit	12/94	12/93
Yarn	10,000 tn	33.15	41.07
Yarn	10,000 pc	184.48	229
Cloth	100 mn m	17.21	17.06
Of pure cotton	100 mn m	9.55	10.71
Chemical fiber	100 mn m	5.10	4.44
Silk	10,000 tn	0.84	0.95
Silk fabric	100 mn m	3.50	2.59
Woolen fabric	10,000 m	3,059.41	3,249
Knitting wool	10,000 tn	4.49	3.48
Garment	100 mn pc	6.25	4.89

• tn=ton, pc=piece, mn m=million meters, mn pc=million piece.

CEI Database, 18 Jan 1995.

METAL INDUSTRY'S BAD YEAR, 1994

[By Xiao Yu] Cash-strapped metal producers struggled through 1994 the worst year on record for the industry, according to China's Metallurgical Industry Minister Liu Qi.

Speaking at the three-day national metallurgical working conference in Beijing this week, Mr. Liu said last year was marred by an increase in default payments by enterprises and a growing stockpile of locally produced metals resulting from too many imports.

Despite the industry problems, observers said Beijing offered no "preferential policies" to factory managers who voiced grievances at the meeting. Mr. Liu was the only senior official from either the Communist Party or the Government to attend.

"Enterprises suffered from difficulties in getting working capital, and there were more cases of default payments on loans. All of this has made 1994 the most difficult year for the industry," he said.

Official statistics showed metal production last year totaled 91.53 million tons, an increase of three percent on 1993 and slightly less than amount of metal in the marketplace—about 100 million tons. But industry sources have pointed out that large amounts of metal—including steel products—available domestically had instead been imported to China, and this had hurt local enterprises.

Some industry experts suggested this indicated a loss of control and "blindness" as China's foreign trade management system was restructured. They said serious bureaucratic problems

continued...

METAL INDUSTRY'S BAD YEAR, 1994 (continued)

and poor service provided by some local enterprises also forced clients to buy from overseas suppliers.

Mr. Liu wants cash-strapped enterprises to maintain "simple" production procedures using existing resources before pursuing more fixed-assets investment. He said these enterprises should shorten the period of capital circulation. Mr. Liu said those heading badly run enterprises whose debts had been growing for two consecutive years would have to step down.

It is understood that authorities have demanded that local metal producers further drop prices in a bid to increase sales and grab a bigger slice of the market. But industry sources said prices of domestic products were already lower than those for imported metal. Sources said some large enterprises planned to cut production this year to improve the situation.

Meanwhile, Beijing will lift the proportion of domestic metal usage in major enterprises from the present 85 percent to more than 90 percent as part of its five-year plan starting in 1996, sources say.

South China Morning Post, 21 Jan 1995.

METAL OUTPUT, 1992-1994 (th tn)

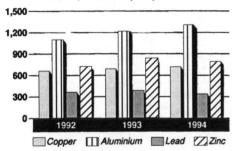

China Trade Report, Nov 1995.

THE PROBLEM OF PIRACY, 1995

"They are more afraid of their shareholders than they are of the court." Those words of Cheng Ching-ming, the Chinese representative for the association of music companies explains why piracy of intellectual property, music in particular, was a huge problem between China and its trading partners in 1995. In addition to manufacturer's fear of stockholders the government's stand against piracy was weak at best and corrupt at worst. Only a handful of intellectual property cases in China had ever been decided in favor of foreign companies. The first was the Walt Disney Company's victory in Beijing Intermediate Court in August 1995, when it won a US$77,000 judgment against Chinese companies that were producing children's books based on Disney's animated films. Many foreign companies would not take on pirates in court because it was both lengthy and costly and was seldom fruitful. Companies preferred to counter their product piracy problem quietly by administrative measures. That usually meant fines and sanctions which were ordered by officials known as the copyright police.

The US threatened China with trade sanctions but took little action, even though pirated films, music and software had already cost US corporations US$800 million, because it was feared this would widen the breach in relations between the two countries.

Even when Chinese companies engaged in piracy were brought to task for their illegal activities they did not stop but merely paused before beginning production again often producing even greater numbers of contraband items than before prosecution.

By the end of 1995 Chinese government officials began in earnest to battle piracy but were frustrated by fast paced economic growth and receding regulation which made controlling offenders much more difficult as companies became less accountable and harder to prosecute.

China Facts & Figures Annual, 1995

XII RESOURCES

CHINA'S ENERGY SOURCES, 1992–1993

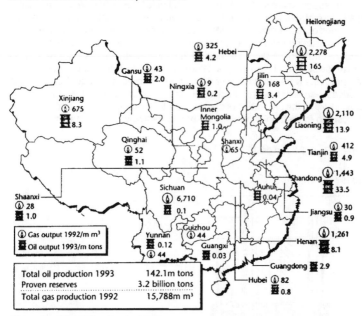

Total oil production 1993	142.1m tons
Proven reserves	3.2 billion tons
Total gas production 1992	15,788m m³

China Statistical Yearbook, 1994.

OUTPUT OF PRIMARY ENERGY, JULY 1993–JULY 1994

Year/Month	Total (mn tn, SCE)*	Coal (mn tn)	Crude Oil (th tn)	Natural Gas (bn cu m)	Hydro-Electric Power (bn kwh)	Nuclear Power (bn kwh)
1993						
Jul	94.76	96.42	12,409	1.42	15.53	0.19
Aug	101.44	106.16	12,096	1.41	15.99	0.15
Sep	91.66	93.93	11,860	1.35	14.42	0.14
Oct	93.98	95.74	12,601	1.46	14.00	0.17
Nov	96.45	101.34	12,076	1.36	12.38	0.17
Dec	107.00	116.46	12,272	1.43	10.83	0.21
1994						
Jan	83.65	86.16	13,261	1.49	9.67	0.20
Feb	65.76	65.00	11,554.10	1.31	8.72	0.08
Mar	91.21	98.44	12,374.9	1.43	10.71	0.21
Apr	94.21	103.37	11,892.9	1.38	12.66	1.11
May	100.93	110.83	12,582.6	1.41	15.60	1.53
Jun	101.45	112.11	12,231.1	1.37	16.85	1.49
Jul	92.86	99.09	12,555.8	1.42	18.34	0.95

* SCE refers to the standard coal equivalent.

World Resources, 1994-1995.

ELECTRICITY PRODUCTION, 1994

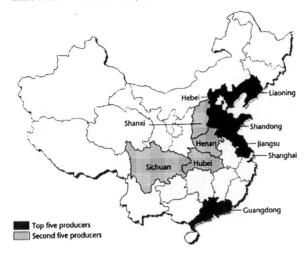

China Market Atlas, 1994.

ENERGY OUTLOOK TO 2010, 1995

Much has been made of China's infrastructural bottlenecks ever since it embarked on its policy of opening to the world 15 years ago. And for many firms trying to do business in the country they are a serious impediment—whether through unreliable power supplies or taking weeks rather than days to ship or receive goods. Nonetheless the shortcomings of the country's transport and power networks have apparently done little to hold back overall growth rates. That is so far. What of the next 15 years, up to around 2010? In particular, does China have the capabilities to tap its abundant natural resources and generate enough power to maintain its sprint towards economic superpower status?

Ever More Efficient
The simple answer is yes, probably. The simple reason for this is that China has treated energy generation extremely seriously and will continue to do so. Its Soviet-style emphasis on developing heavy industry up to the end of the 1970s led to the establishment of a reasonably sound energy infrastructure.

As a result, the light and export-oriented industrial growth of the 1980s and 1990s were able to increase the country's energy efficiency. According to the International Energy Agency (IEA)'s *World Energy Outlook,* while overall economic growth averaged 9.1% between 1981 and 1991, commercial energy intensity—the amount of energy required to produce a fixed amount of economic output—declined by around 4% over the same period.

This decline, calculated on a US dollar basis, is almost certainly exaggerated. But it does mean that China's energy output targets can be considerably below its overall economic growth targets. Thus the IEA estimates that over the next decade and a half China will only have to increase its energy output by around 4% a year, while overall economic growth should average double this.

Under-Oiled
This straightforward case for optimism, however, masks a number of problems that China will have to resolve, three of which stand out:

Distance between energy resources and energy users. As the maps opposite show, China's energy resources are heavily concentrated in the north of the country; its industrial output is concentrated along the eastern coast and in Guangdong.

continued...

ENERGY OUTLOOK TO 2010, 1995 (continued)

At the moment more than 40% of China's oil comes from the far north-eastern province of Heilongjiang. This is inconvenient, but nothing compared to the problems of having to move oil from Xinjiang in the far north-west, the only other oil-rich region in China. Before resources there can be realistically tapped—and first they have to be discovered—a pipeline with a cost of around US$10 billion will have to be built.

Dominance of coal. One worry China does not have is running out of coal. Its proven reserves could meet current demand levels for approaching 1,000 years. There are grounds for concern at this dominance, notably environmental issues. It is also worrying its share of total energy production has grown at the same rate as primary economic growth.

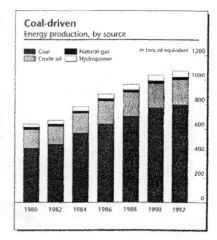

Coal-driven
Energy production, by source

Business China, 22 Aug 1995.

COAL PRODUCTION, 1994

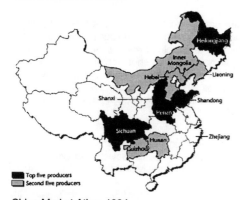

China Market Atlas, 1994.

CRUDE OIL PRODUCTION 1ST QUARTER, 1995

China produced more than 36 million tons of crude oil in the first quarter of this year, a slight increase from the same period of last year.

According to the China National Petroleum Corporation today, China's onshore oil production in the first three months stood at 34 million tons, 0.3 percent more than a year earlier.

Figures released by the China National Offshore Oil Corporation showed that the country's offshore crude output registered a 30-percent increase, to reach 2.14 million tons during the January-March period.

Oil experts said that the major oilfields in eastern China have continued to maintain stable production, while the newly developed oilfields in the western region, such as those in the Turpan-Hami and Tarim basins, hiked their output.

continued...

CRUDE OIL PRODUCTION 1ST QUARTER, 1995 (continued)

They said they believed that the country's crude oil yield for the whole year will exceed 145 million tons.

Meanwhile, during the first three months China produced more than four billion cubic meters of natural gas, up two percent from the corresponding period of last year. Of the total, the onshore output amounted to 3.98 billion cubic meters.

China is expected to produce about 16.5 billion cu m of natural gas this year, according to experts.

X, 26 Apr 1995.

OIL PRODUCTION, 1994

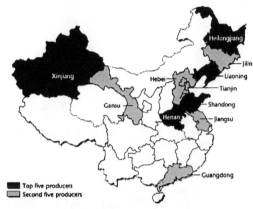

China Market Atlas, 1994.

CHINA'S OIL BALANCE SHEET, 1995

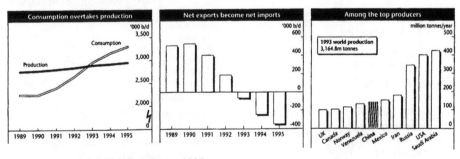

Jardine Fleming & British Petroleum, 1995.

FUEL SHARES IN CHINA'S INDUSTRIAL ENERGY DEMAND, 1990-2010

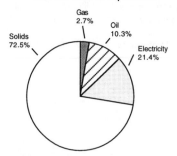

1990
312 mn tn of oil equivalent

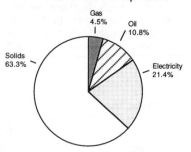

2010
616 mn tn of oil equivalent

International Energy Agency, 1995.

CHINA'S ENERGY IMPORTS UP, 1992–1993 (mn tn)

Crude oil

Exports   Imports   Balance

Refined products

Exports   Imports   Balance

☐ 1992   ■ 1993

FEER, 11 Sep 1995.

CHINA'S ENERGY SHORTFALL, 1982–1992

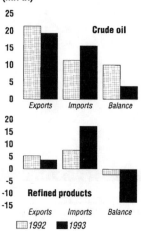

Indicators

China's energy
shortfall

% year-on-year

Supply

Demand

'82 '84 '86 '88 '90 '92

FEER, 23 Jul 1995.

INDUSTRIAL ENERGY DEMAND, 1991-2010 (mn tn of oil equivalent)

	1991	2000	2010	Percent Change, 1991–2010
China				
Solids	231	297	374	62
Oil	33	46	64	94
Gas	9	19	27	200
Electri-city	49	81	127	159
Total	322	440	592	84

	1991	2000	2010	Percent Change, 1991–2010
East/South-east Asia*				
Solids	45		67	49
Oil	48		84	75
Gas	8		30	275
Electricity	18		43	139
Total	119		224	88

* Excluding Japan.

International Energy Agency, 1995.

POWER PROJECTIONS, 1985-2010 (generating capacity, gigawatts)

	1985	1991	2000	2010
Thermal	60.7	113.3	176.0	294.0
Hydro	26.4	37.9	70.4	123.7
Nuclear	0	0.3	202	10.7
Total	87.1	151.5	248.6	428.4

International Energy Agency, 1995.

CHINA'S STANDING IN WORLD PETROLEUM PRODUCTION, 1973-1994 (th barrels per day)

	Total OPEC	Ecuador	Persian Gulf Nations	Canada	China	Mexico	United Kingdom	United States	Former U.S.S.R.	Other	World
1973 Average	30,779	209	20,668	1,798	1,090	465	2	9,208	8,324	R 3,804	55,679
1974 Average	30,552	177	21,282	1,551	1,315	571	2	8,774	8,912	R 3,862	55,716
1975 Average	26,994	161	18,934	1,430	1,490	705	12	8,375	9,523	R 4,139	52,828
1976 Average	30,549	188	21,514	1,314	1,670	831	245	8,132	10,060	R 4,355	57,344
1977 Average	31,115	183	21,725	1,321	1,874	981	768	8,245	10,603	R 4,616	59,707
1978 Average	29,673	202	20,606	1,316	2,082	1,209	1,082	8,707	11,105	R 4,782	60,158
1979 Average	30,734	214	21,066	1,500	2,122	1,461	1,568	8,552	11,384	R 5,089	62,674
1980 Average	26,761	204	17,961	1,435	2,114	1,936	1,622	8,597	11,706	R 5,204	59,599
1981 Average	22,632	211	15,245	1,285	2,012	2,313	1,811	8,572	11,850	R 5,390	56,076
1982 Average	18,934	211	12,156	1,271	2,045	2,748	2,065	8,649	11,912	R 5,846	53,481
1983 Average	17,654	237	11,081	1,356	2,120	2,689	2,291	8,688	11,972	R 6,248	53,255
1984 Average	17,599	258	10,784	1,438	2,296	2,780	2,480	8,879	11,861	R 6,897	54,488
1985 Average	16,353	281	9,630	1,471	2,505	2,745	2,530	8,971	11,585	R 7,540	53,981
1986 Average	18,441	283	11,596	1,474	2,620	2,435	2,539	8,680	11,895	R 7,850	56,227
1987 Average	18,672	174	12,103	1,535	2,690	2,548	2,406	8,349	11,985	R 8,242	56,601
1988 Average	20,483	302	13,457	1,616	2,730	2,512	2,232	8,140	11,978	R 8,869	58,662
1989 Average	22,279	279	14,837	1,560	2,757	2,520	1,802	7,613	11,625	R 9,338	59,773
1990 Average	23,465	285	15,278	1,553	2,774	2,553	1,820	7,355	10,880	R 9,785	60,471
1991 Average	23,569	299	14,741	1,548	2,835	2,680	1,797	7,417	9,887	R 10,074	60,105
1992 January	25,100	295	16,130	1,585	2,830	2,675	1,920	7,361	9,115	R 10,526	61,407
February	24,880	295	16,010	1,560	2,865	2,665	1,905	7,389	8,650	R 10,375	60,584
March	24,170	315	15,510	1,620	2,835	2,680	1,755	7,348	8,760	R 10,429	59,912
April	24,205	315	15,487	1,535	2,855	2,680	1,835	7,293	9,025	R 10,523	60,265
May	24,265	315	15,592	1,510	2,835	2,660	1,700	7,169	8,455	R 10,251	59,160
June	24,420	315	15,716	1,560	2,830	2,680	1,545	7,167	8,440	R 10,443	59,400
July	24,660	320	15,916	1,630	2,825	2,660	1,780	7,131	8,365	R 10,498	59,869
August	25,005	330	16,220	1,675	2,815	2,685	1,825	6,922	8,130	R 10,472	59,858
September	25,245	330	16,330	1,620	2,860	2,685	1,830	7,030	7,980	R 10,543	60,123
October	25,685	330	16,670	1,665	2,875	2,655	1,930	7,126	7,965	R 10,687	60,918
November	25,770	330	16,755	1,740	2,845	2,640	1,945	7,024	7,910	R 10,517	60,621
December	25,945	330	16,905	1,575	2,785	2,655	1,935	7,103	7,870	R 10,744	60,942
Average	24,947	318	16,104	1,598	2,838	2,668	1,825	7,171	8,388	R 10,501	60,255

continued...

CHINA'S STANDING IN WORLD PETROLEUM PRODUCTION, 1973-1994 (th barrels per day) (continued)/THE REPUBLIC OF KOREA AND CHINA COOPERATE IN OIL EXPLORATION, 1995

	Total OPEC	Ecuador	Persian Gulf Nations	Canada	China	Mexico	United Kingdom	United States	Former U.S.S.R.	Other	World
1993 January	26,145	330	17,105	1,570	2,885	2,605	1,815	6,961	7,800	R 10,406	60,517
February	26,250	330	17,325	1,610	2,875	2,610	1,925	6,943	7,785	R 10,547	60,874
March	25,585	330	16,855	1,635	2,885	2,635	1,710	6,974	7,685	R 10,714	60,154
April	25,010	330	16,350	1,605	2,900	2,674	1,695	8,881	7,665	R 10,679	59,439
May	25,238	345	16,548	1,660	2,925	2,673	1,745	6,847	7,495	R 10,703	59,630
June	25,400	350	16,740	1,725	2,960	2,675	1,675	6,795	7,400	R 10,381	59,361
July	25,795	350	17,135	1,710	2,930	2,650	1,930	6,688	7,120	R 10,795	59,968
August	25,775	350	17,045	1,770	2,855	2,650	1,940	6,758	7,025	R 10,671	59,794
September	25,875	350	17,135	1,740	2,895	2,700	1,945	6,712	6,915	R 10,685	59,817
October	25,795	360	17,085	1,725	2,975	2,700	2,080	6,839	6,910	R 10,909	60,273
November	25,495	360	16,795	1,675	2,945	2,730	2,195	6,912	6,915	R 11,100	60,327
December	25,835	360	16,955	1,710	2,898	2,745	2,270	6,858	6,885	R 11,158	60,718
Average	25,681	346	16,921	1,678	2,911	2,671	1,909	6,847	7,297	R 10,731	60,070
1994 January	25,865	360	16,895	R 1,665	2,900	2,745	2,280	E 6,777	6,885	R 11,071	R 60,548
February	25,820	360	16,850	R 1,720	2,920	2,710	2,280	E 6,745	6,615	R 11,227	R 60,397
March	25,895	360	16,955	R 1,705	2,920	2,685	2,315	E 6,719	6,560	R 11,147	R 60,306
April	R 25,715	360	R 16,845	R 1,660	2,940	R 2,700	2,340	E 6,634	R 6,385	R 11,118	R 59,852
May	25,845	360	16,915	1,680	2,940	2,700	2,345	E 6,658	6,495	11,076	60,099
5-Mo. Avg.	25,829	360	16,893	1,685	2,924	2,708	2,312	E 6,707	6,589	11,126	60,240

Energy Information Administration Monthly Energy Review, Aug 1995.

THE REPUBLIC OF KOREA AND CHINA COOPERATE IN OIL EXPLORATION, 1995

The Taeryuk Group Corporation, based in the Republic of Korea (ROK) signed a letter of intent with China's National Petroleum Corporation for co-operation in oil exploration and the petrochemicals industry. The company had already worked with China in a large scale agricultural project in Heilongjiang Province.

X, 13 Jan 1995.

THREE GORGES DAM MAP, 1995

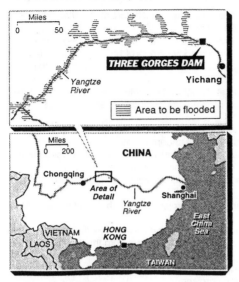

NYT, 15 Sep 1995.

THREE GORGES PROJECT, 1995

Construction of the Three Gorges Dam continued on schedule in 1995 despite setbacks caused by weather and at times a lack of construction materials. World environmentalists outside China made formal protests to Chinese government officials and called the stoppage along the free flowing Yangtze River "an insult to the environment and a detriment to the world at large because the river's abundant waters which flow into the sea would be slowed and contaminated." If all goes as planned the construction crews working around the clock will have breached the Yangtze River with a buffer dam or earthen berm by the end of 1997. The waters will then be diverted down a man-made channel and construction will begin on the permanent main dam and engineers will install the first 12 of 26 generators scheduled to produce energy by 2003.

China Facts & Figures Annual, 1995

THREE GORGES TO GET FOREIGN FUNDS, 1995
China will introduce overseas funds and technology to the Three Gorges Dam project "under the right circumstances," a senior governmental official told Business Weekly.

The bulk of the funds needed for the hydro-power station construction, however, should rely on domestic sources, said Wei Tingcheng, deputy director of the executive office of the Three Gorges Project Construction Committee.

The committee is a policy-making body for the on-going water project, and is affiliated with the State Council, China's cabinet.

"As long as there are appropriate opportunities and conditions, we will absorb overseas capital in various ways for the construction of the Three Gorges Project," Wei said.

Wei said that no form of overseas funds have been used so far for the dam construction.

He also noted that China could issue bonds overseas to take advantage of favorable international financial markets.

continued...

THREE GORGES TO GET FOREIGN FUNDS, 1995 (continued)

Convertible bonds have a "greater possibility" of being issued before the first batch of power generating units begin operation in 2003, Wei said.

From 1993 until the year 2005, when profits made by the dam can support its further construction, the Three Gorges project will need a total investment of 146.8 billion yuan ($17.48 billion). Of that, China will consider seeking $2 billion to $3 billion in overseas loans to import equipment.

He said around 12 of the 26 hydro turbogenerator units for the Three Gorges Dam may possibly be produced with the cooperation of overseas companies, and six units will be purchased from overseas.

Wei emphasized that, while the nation is still developing its power generating equipment industry, "China's existing technology should (not be) underestimated.

"The domestic technological standard can be upgraded in a short time if overseas equipment is introduced based on the country's current technology level."

He noted that opening the project to the outside world should be well-coordinated with the development of the national industry.

This year, total investment in the gigantic water project will reach 7 billion yuan ($833 million).

To raise the funds, the government levied an extra 0.4 fen (less than five-thousandth of one cent) for every kilowatt-hour of electricity consumed in the country from the beginning of this year. The figure last year was 0.3 fen.

In addition, all profits from the Gezhouba dam, currently China's biggest hydro-power station, will be channeled to the Three Gorges project.

Combined funds from the above two sources will inject more than 3 billion yuan ($3.57 billion) into the Three Gorges dam.

The State Development Bank will also provide over .3 billion in loans for the dam construction.

"So the fund gap is quite narrow," Wei said.

As a result, issuing bonds for the water project would likely only be considered in the second half of this year.

The Ministry of Finance had planned earlier this year to issue $100 million worth of bonds in overseas markets.

The Three Gorges Dam formally started construction last December. It will close the Yangtze's flow in 1997.

China Daily, 29 Apr 1995.

TUMEN RIVER PROJECT, 1995

The Tumen River Project to create a 10,000 square kilometer free trade zone in the Tumen River delta where the borders of China, Russia and North Korea meet faltered along in 1995. Most of the problems were caused by the immensity of the project which called for the cooperation of China, Russia, North Korea, South Korea and Japan. The problems between the governments were essentially political, and they worsened in 1995. Japan and South Korea were important to the project because they were the only countries with money to invest in the project. But Japan would not lend money to the Russians because of their dispute over the Kurile islands and it would not lend money to the North Koreans because of their nuclear ambitions. The Japanese did, however, make small amounts of money available to China to use on the project. The South Koreans although more agreeable with the other countries involved were no more willing to make funds available for the overall project. Russia's President Yeltsin expressed support for the project but inside Russia economists argued that the project would harm Russian national interest. Many Russians regarded the project as Chinese dominated and likely to develop Chinese territory rather than Russia's Vladivostock region.

continued...

TUMEN RIVER PROJECT, 1995 (continued)

North Korea had no money, few allies and little commitment to the project. Their only contribution toward the project was a promise to use any funds Japan may pay them in retribution for alleged "war crimes" for that purpose. Most foreign diplomats labeled such expectations as naive. China was the only country actively engaged in construction along the river and the Chinese even lent money to Russia to complete the link on the Russian side of the border. Meanwhile the United Nations committed US$5.5 million to the project despite the lack of agreement between the countries involved.

China Facts & Figures Annual, 1995

TUMEN RIVER PROJECT MAP, 1994

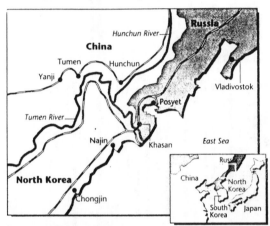

Business China, 22 Aug 1994.

HUANENG POWER'S BUILDING PLANS, 1994

	Capacity (mw)		Capacity (mw)
Shantou	600	Fuzhou (expansion)	700
Shangan (expansion)	600	Nantong (expansion)	700
Dalian (expansion)	700	Jinling	1,200
Dandong	700	Shantou (expansion)	700

FEER, 29 Sep 1994.

CHINA'S RESOURCES PRINCIPAL COMPANIES, 1994

Name	Established	Business	Agency arrangements
Ng Fung Hong	1951	Cereals, oils, foodstuffs, storage, transport, packaging, slaughtering	China National Cereals, Oils & Foodstuffs Import-Export Corp
Teck Soon Hong	1950	Tea, tobacco, medicines, rugs	China Native Produce & Animal By-products Import-Export Corp; China Tobacco Import-Export Corp; China Native Medicines & Health Products Import & Export Corp
China Hua	1964	Appliances, hospital products, toys, sportswear, metal wares	
Chinese Arts & Crafts	1959	Arts, crafts, ceramics, furniture, gems	China National Arts & Crafts Import-Export Corp; China National Native Produce and Animal By-products Import-Export Corp
China Resources Textiles	1980	Cloth, yarn, fibres and knitwears	China National Textiles Import-Export Corp
China Resources Metals & Minerals	1983	Metals	
China Resources Petroleum & Chemicals	1972	Petroleum and petroleum products, organic and inorganic chemicals, plastics, rubber, fertilizer, pharmaceutical, medical supplies	China National Chemicals Import-Export Corp
China Resources Machinery	1980	Machine tools, computers, precision instruments, packaging equipment, construction equipment, telecommunications equipment	China National Machinery Import-Export Corp, China National Instruments Import-Export Corp
China Resources Machinery & Equipment	1983	Machine tools, power machinery, printing machinery, food processing plants, textile machinery, agricultural machinery	China National Machinery & Equipment Import-Export Corp
China Resources Transportation & Godown	1984	Shipping, land/air/sea freight, forwarding and warehousing	
FARENCO	1949	Chartering and broking of ships, purchase and sale, operation and management	China National Foreign Trade Transportation Corp, China National Chartering Corp
China Resources Artland	1983	Interior design and trade of related materials	
Finarts Trading	1980	Textiles, leathers, furs, light industrial products, fertilizer	China Silk Import-Export Corp
Longdation Enterprises	1983	Building operation, management, services	
China Resources Silk	1933	Silk yarns, cloth and garments	China Export Bases Development Corp
Plymouth	1985	Investment and import, export financing	China National Packaging Import-Export Corp
Chungkuo Chung Fah	1958	Bedding, knitwears, embroidered clothing	
Wan Hsin	1962	Fashion garments, night-wear	
Callary	1975	Tanker chartering, management, bunkering, insurance	
China Resources Textile Materials	1985	Fibres, packing materials and textile equipment	Chinatex Raw Materials Import-Export Corp, Chinatex Cotton Import-Export Corp, Chinatex Garment Accessories Import-Export Corp
China Resources Development & Investment	1988	Identifying, studying and planning investments for the group	
China Products	1938	General merchandise	

Business China, 5 Sep 1994.

XIII AGRICULTURE

AGRICULTURAL PRODUCTS MARKET EXCHANGE PRICE CATEGORIES INDEX, 1995 (same month of 1994=100)

	August (percent)		August (percent)
National Agricultural Products	128.6	Meat, poultry and eggs	141.6
Market Exchange Index		Aquatic products	118.6
Grain	153.4	Fresh vegetables	125.4
Fining grain	160.4	Dried vegetables	107.3
Raw grain	124.2	Fresh fruits	126.2
Fat and oil	170.3	Dried fruits	114.0

China Facts & Figures Annual, 1995

ANALYZING AND PROJECTING COTTON DEMAND BY THE YEAR 2000, 1994

[Article by Dong Ying (5516 6601) of the Research Institute of the State Restructuring of the Economic System Commission, Zhang Yujun (1728 6276 6511) of the Planning and Development Office of the Federation of Textile Industry, and Ma Shuping (7456 3219 5493) of the Office of Agriculture of the Ministry of Agriculture: "Cotton Supply, Demand by Year 2000"]

Analyzing and Projecting China's Total Effective Cotton Demand by Year 2000

When people in real economic life talk about cotton demand, they frequently have in mind three different kinds of demand: 1) A processing demand commensurate with the production capacity of the cotton spinning industry; 2) a planned demand in line with cotton spinning resources; and 3) an actual demand that corresponds with cotton consumption. As we see it, only the actual demand represents society's effective demand and is relevant to our discussion of the total supply and demand of cotton. Our analysis, therefore, uses this definition of cotton demand exclusively.

The social demand of the cotton yarn industry accounts for the bulk of total cotton demand and influences such demand in complex ways. Centering on the social demand of the cotton yarn industry, we will do a preliminary analysis of the domestic and foreign markets and project total social demand for cotton yarn in 1995 and 2000. Next we will work backward to figure out the amount of cotton needed to produce the projected levels of cotton yarn. Finally we will add to this figure other social uses of cotton to come up with the total projected cotton demand.

1) Analyzing and projecting cotton yarn demand on the domestic market

The next few years represent an important stage in the quest of the Chinese people for a comfortable standard of living. They are also a critical time for the textile industry as it accelerates its reorganization and transformation and reaches a new standard. Accordingly, we need to analyze and estimate the demand on the domestic market by correctly presaging trends in the textile market.

An analysis of factors determining domestic textile demand.

1) Per capita fiber consumption level. The per capita fiber consumption level has a direct impact on the demand for textile goods. Currently per capita fiber consumption averages 7.5 kg worldwide, which approximately corresponds to a per capita GNP of between $800 and $1,000. In China, per capita fiber consumption has been rising briskly since the 1980's, reaching 4.1 kg in 1990, up from 2.8 kg in 1980, for an average annual growth rate of 3.9 percent. Right now per capita fiber consumption in China is 4.3-4.4 kg, still lower than the world's average. As the Chinese economy continues to grow rapidly and living standards keep climbing in the 1990's, per capita fiber consumption will also go up. In light of China's resource situation and actual consumption patterns, the textile industry development plan has set a per capita consumption level of 4.6 kg by 1995 and 5.2-5.3 kg by the year 2000. The average annual growth rate between 1995 and 2000 is projected to be 2.6 percent, lower than that in the 1980's.

continued...

ANALYZING AND PROJECTING COTTON DEMAND BY THE YEAR 2000, 1994 (continued)

2) Population increase. China's population reached 1.185 billion back in late 1993, having grown 15 million net each year on average. Based on the existing fiber consumption level, we figure that textile consumption in China must increase by 70,000 to 80,000 tons each year just to satisfy the textile demand of the net increase in population.

3) Consumption level. Let's take a look at the two consumption markets—urban and rural—in the 1980's. Clothing accounted for 14-15 percent of the living expenses of the average urban dweller. The corresponding figure in the countryside was 9-10 percent. In dollars and cents, what the rural dweller spent on clothing was a mere one-third or so of the clothing budget of his urban counterpart. In other words, it took far more in terms of quantity to satisfy the clothing needs of the urban population. Since 1990, clothing consumption by the urban population has become more quality-oriented and less geared toward quantity. A small number of urban residents now go after the upscale, the fashionable, and the comfortable, having entered the stage of selective consumption. The vast majority of the rural population, on the other hand, remain in the quantitative consumption stage. In overall terms, therefore, the growth rate of quantitative demand in rural China will be faster than that in the urban areas. We can also break down consumption by income level. At present the middle and low-income strata account for a much larger share of cotton consumption. As income levels rise across the country, swelling the ranks of the high-income people, quality-oriented demand will increase correspondingly and the demand for textile products will show much greater diversity as well.

4) Substitutes. Chemical fibers, the principal substitute for natural textile fibers, have experienced rapid development in recent years. In 1993, China's chemical fiber production capacity was 2.79 million tons and actual output 2.21 million tons. Already chemical fibers accounted for 36 percent of all fibers used in the textile processing industry, which nevertheless was still much lower than in that in developed nations. Chemical fiber products are a major growth sector within the textile industry in the 1990's. According to the plan, chemical fiber production capacity and output would reach 3 million and 2.5 million tons, respectively, by 1995, and 4 million and 3.5 million tons, respectively, by the year 2000. Chemical fibers are poised to make up 38 and 42 percent of all processed textile fibers in 1995 and 2000, respectively, thereby easing pressure on cotton demand. To put it differently, if China is to develop the textile industry in a healthy way even as it faces a cotton resource shortfall in the near term, a major way to satisfy an ever-rising textile demand is to accelerate the development of substitutes. This is a course we must follow; there is no other way. Meanwhile, in the wake of endless advances in science and technology, especially the development of differentiated fibers, the quality and properties of chemical fibers will improve steadily. It is less costly to use long-staple chemical fibers in apparel processing than it is to use cotton. Chemical fiber products are poised to capture a larger share of the market. For these reasons, the trend in the development of the textile industry both on the domestic market and around the world is to rely heavily on use of chemical fibers to raise the fiber consumption level.

5) Changes in the uses of textile products. Textile products are used in three broad areas: clothing, industry, and furnishings. In China, the current ratio among the three is 75:8:17. Generally speaking, textiles used in furnishings increase sharply when a nation's economy reaches a certain stage. As the Chinese people's living standards rise and their accommodations increases in size in the 1990's, demand will grow. By the year 2000, furnishings are expected to take up about 25 percent of all processed textile fibers. Owing to a number of major breakthroughs in textile materials and processing methods, the share of industrial textile products is projected to rise to 15 to 20 percent by the year 2000. With furnishings and industry taking up a growing share of all textile products, the latter will be used in an ever-widening area, which in turn will boost total demand and spur the improvement of the structure of the textile processing industry.

6) Processing capacity. China's textile spinning processing industry had 41.4 million spindles at the end of 1993, quantitatively more than enough to meet the demands of both the domestic and the international markets. But there is one mismatch: backward equipment and

continued...

ANALYZING AND PROJECTING COTTON DEMAND BY THE YEAR 2000, 1994 (continued)

the demand for better quality products. Of China's cotton spinning capacity today, about one-third of the equipment is of a fairly advanced level, one-third is mediocre, and one-third downright backward. The transformation and reorganization plans of the Eighth and Ninth Five-Year plans demanded that obsolete equipment be largely discarded and that mediocre equipment be modernized. If the plans are successfully implemented, we can expect product quality to improve across the board before the year 2000.

Apart from the several major elements described above that help determine cotton demand, there also exists in China a regional factor, including regional climatic variations, differences in level of economic development, and divergent consumption preferences. These will not be analyzed here one by one.

The synergistic effect of these elements interacting with one another is this: Domestic demand for textile products will increase steadily in the next few years with no sharp fluctuations. The growth rate will not be as high as in the 1980's.

Projecting domestic demand for textile products. We use three methods to project the domestic demand for textile products in order to come up with comprehensive and accurate estimates that can be readily verified against one another.

A) Making projections based on the growth rate of the consumption of textile products.

Calculations by the Federation of the Textile Industry show that domestic sales of textile products made of cotton yarn grew 3.9 percent each year on average between 1980 and 1990. Several authoritative bodies around the world have estimated the growth rate of global fiber consumption during the 1990's to be between 2.5 and 3.5 percent. Based on the above analysis, we figure that the growth of textile products in China in the 1990's may not be as strong as in the 1980's but will still stay within the world's average. Thus we can expect China's textile product consumption to grow 2.5 or 3 percent in the next few years. This figure is consistent with the goal in the industry's 10-year development plan to increase per capita fiber consumption in the country 2.6 percent annually in the 1990's.

We take the lower limit as the amount needed to satisfy basic domestic demand, the upper limit as the amount needed to meet a more rapidly growing demand.

Using the annual growth rate of 2.5 percent, we figure that domestic textile demand for cotton yarn will be 17.8 million pieces by 1995 and about 20.4 million pieces by the year 2000. If the 3 percent figure is used, the corresponding figures would be 18.25 million pieces in 1995 and 21.15 million pieces in 2000.

B) Projection based on per capita fiber consumption and population growth.

By using the data presented earlier on per capita fiber consumption and population growth, we can work out fiber consumption demand and then convert it into the amount of yarn needed. It has been projected that China's population will reach 1.21 billion and 1.28 billion by 1995 and 2000, respectively.

Based on the current per capita fiber consumption of 4.4 kg, total domestic fiber consumption will be 5.33 million tons or so by 1995. After eliminating wool, flax, and silk consumption of 600,000 tons and long-staple chemical fiber consumption of 1.3 million tons that year, we figure the consumption of fibers processed through the cotton spinning system to be 3.43 million tons, or 17.65 million pieces of cotton yarn. Assuming that the current per capita fiber consumption is 4.6 kg, on the other hand, we would project the total fiber consumption to be 5.57 million tons, converted into 18.89 million pieces of yarn, by the year 1995, after deducting the consumption of wool, flax, silk, and chemical fibers. The same method can be used to estimate total fiber consumption by the year 2000. If we use the lower limit of 5.2 kg as per capita fiber consumption by the year 2000, we arrive at these numbers: Total fiber consumption, 6.66 million tons, converted into 20.38 million pieces of cotton yarn after deducting wool, flax, silk, and long-staple chemical fiber consumption of 2.7 million tons. Taking the upper limit of 5.3 kg, the total fiber consumption converts into cotton yarn would be 21.04 million pieces.

C) Making projections based on the relationship between total apparel retail sales and the amount of textile products converted into cotton yarn.

continued...

ANALYZING AND PROJECTING COTTON DEMAND BY THE YEAR 2000, 1994 (continued)

We first use a linear regression equation to establish the relationship between total apparel retail sales and the amount of domestically sold textile products converted into cotton yarn for the period 1980-1990. Then we estimate the amount of textile products converted into cotton yarn based on apparel consumption projections for the years 1995 and 2000.

Apparel retail sales are estimated to be worth 165 billion yuan by 1995 and 190 billion yuan by 2000. It follows that domestic yarn consumption would therefore be 18.04 million pieces and 19.3 million pieces in 1995 and 2000, respectively. Add other uses of yarn, namely military industry, military consumption, and others (projected to reach 800,000 pieces in 1995 and 15 million pieces by 2000), and total domestic cotton yarn demand would be 18.84 million pieces and 20.8 million pieces by 1995 and 2000, respectively.

It needs to be explained here that the use of a mathematical model to establish a relationship between apparel retail sales and the amount of textile products converted into yarn presumes a fully linear relationship between them. In the real economic world, the relationship between the two is not fully linear because of a variety of factors: Changes in the price index, the growing consumer preference for finished products, textile products becoming more expensive as a result of improving quality and rising technological content, and changes in public consumption patterns all change the equation. Nevertheless, the overall development trend is basically consistent with a linear relationship. Considering that the increase in retail apparel sales typically outpaces that of textile products consumption, we adjust the outcome of our computations by reducing it by 2 percent. Thus we project textile products demand converted into cotton yarn to be 18.46 million pieces by 1995 and 20.4 million pieces by 2000.

2) Analyzing and estimating size of textile products for sale overseas converted into cotton yarn
Since reform and opening up began, China's textile industry has exported enough fibers, textile products, and apparel to earn over $160 billion in foreign exchange, while spending just $78 billion in foreign exchange on imports, earning a net $82 billion in foreign exchange and strongly supporting economic construction in the nation. Since 1990, textile exports and foreign exchange earnings derived from them have continued to increase briskly.

The next few years will be full of challenges as well as opportunities for China's textile export industry.

Analysis of factors influencing China's textile exports.

A) Domestic and international environments.

Domestic environment. The Chinese economy has been growing at a high 8-9 percent in the 1990's, up from the originally set rate of 6 percent. The textile industry has been expanding correspondingly, perhaps even a little faster. Further opening China to the outside world is bound to impose on the textile industry even more taxing export and foreign exchange-earning tasks and require it to continue to be a leading foreign exchange earner. On the other hand, we should realize that to steer the textile industry onto the course of healthy development, we need to successfully overcome the powerful disruptions caused by the transition from the old system to the new and by adjustment of the industrial structure.

International environment. According to the analyses of people in the textile industry, the global market for textile products and apparel will move from saturation to glut between now and the year 2000, and the growth of the textile trade would slacken off. One explanation is an excess of supply over demand. Western developed nations, which account for about 62 percent of worldwide fiber consumption, will see a moderation in textile demand growth once their per capita fiber consumption hits 17-20 kg. Second, a number of Western countries have been stagnating economically since the opening of this decade. Countries in Latin America and Africa are saddled with massive debts while the Commonwealth of Independent States and Eastern Europe are in the midst of economic upheaval, severely weakening the global textile market. On the other hand, bright prospects still loom ahead for China's textile and apparel trade, what with the world's population poised to increase 1.64 percent through the end of the century and the possibility that the Asia-Pacific region may replace industrial nations in the West as the world's largest textile market. But we should also note that competition on the

continued...

ANALYZING AND PROJECTING COTTON DEMAND BY THE YEAR 2000, 1994 (continued)

international market is becoming more ferocious and the commodity mix is evolving in a way that favors producers of finished, good-quality, and diversified products, which portends even more competition on quality and technology. Moreover, the textile exports of countries in south Asia and ASEAN and other peripheral nations have become markedly more competitive. Meanwhile, trade protectionism is constantly on the rise in developed nations. All of which will mean rough sailing for China's textile trade and production.

B) The overall standard of the textile industry.

After decades of development, China has created a textile industry which has always lived up to the demand of the domestic and international markets offering a full lineup of products and using essentially integrated processes. For a variety of reasons, however, there are a host of underlying and sharp contradictions in the textile industry, both in its system and in its structure, primarily the following: the low technical level of its equipment, a lopsided overall mix, poor product quality, and low labor productivity. As a result, the profitability of the industry has been slipping and its export competitiveness is lackluster. To increase its exports further and meet the needs of the international market, we must accelerate adjustment of the industry as well as its product mix, speed up technological advances, enhance the competitiveness of its output, and upgrade the standards of the industry as a whole to ensure that the textile industry will remain a backbone industry and a key earner of foreign exchange.

C) Foreign trade system.

The foreign trade management system has undergone extensive reform in recent years, which has been a boost to the textile industry as an exporter and foreign exchange earner. Be that as it may, the textile industry today essentially still practices the procurement system when it comes to foreign trade and therefore suffers from the same problem characteristic of the traditional foreign trade system—too many middlemen. Genuine industry-trade integration and a unified national market still elude the industry. Only the further deepening of the reform of the textile foreign trade system can meet the demand to expand textile exports.

D) Foreign exchange earnings per ton of fibers.

The level of foreign exchange earnings per ton of fibers is an all-round gauge, reflecting the quality of textile products, whether they are at the lower or upper end of the market or somewhere in between, and their technological content. In recent years China's textile exports have increased rapidly, but they remain essentially a resource and quantity-oriented type of export with a relatively low level of foreign exchange earnings per ton of fibers. According to statistics from the International Federation of Textile Manufacturers, Italy earned $17,200 in foreign exchange for every ton of fibers exported in 1989; Japan, $13,000; and the United States, $11,400. China, however, earned just $5,600. There have been substantial improvements in both the mix and quality of Chinese textile exports in the past two years, boosting foreign exchange earnings per ton of fibers to $8,700 in 1993, still a long way behind those of other textile-exporting nations and regions in the world. That same year Italy earned $22,000 in foreign exchange per ton of fibers. Overseas, since there is a limit to the capacity of the global textile market, it is no longer realistic to seek to increase textile exports by taking the quantitative approach. Domestically, the demand may keep rising, but given finite textile resources, quantitative expansion is not the trump card that it was in the past. For this reason, China's textile export strategy must shift from one based on quantity to one based on quality or performance. The industry must upgrade itself in quality and go after the upper end of the market. Based on this strategy, the foreign exchange earnings per ton of fibers should reach $10,000 by 1995 and exceed $14,000 by 2000.

E) The mix of textile exports. The sharp jump in textile industry exports and foreign exchange earnings in the last few years has been accompanied by some striking improvements in the exports mix. That the amount of foreign exchange earnings has risen faster than the volume of converted yarn exported indicates that China has made considerable progress in the areas of multiple processing, finishing, and high added value work. Back in the early 1980's, textile exports were dominated by raw material-type of products such as the two yarns and two fabrics. By 1987, however, finished products already made up 53.2 percent of all textile exports, and

continued...

ANALYZING AND PROJECTING COTTON DEMAND BY THE YEAR 2000, 1994 (continued)

by 1993, 63.4 percent. Apparel exports increased 28.18 percent annually on average between 1986 and 1993, significantly faster than textile exports overall. Provided multiple processed products like apparel continue to grow at a strong pace in the next few years, we can be sure the industry will be able to continue steadily to increase its export-derived foreign exchange earnings. Accordingly, we ask the industry to redouble its efforts to adjust its products mix and raise the share of exports consisting of apparel and other multiple processed goods to over 70 percent, approximating the level in developed nations.

Projecting textile exports converted into yarn.

Here, too, we use two methods of calculation.

1) Making projections based on the foreign exchange earned by textile exports.

Since 1990 Chinese textile exports have shot up, climbing from $13.8 billion that year to $27.1 billion in 1993, up 96 percent, or 25 percent annually on the average. Chinese textile exports are expected to increase at the average annual rate of 9-10 percent for the next few years, lower than the average rate of 14.3 percent recorded in the 1980's, but both feasible and consistent with what the development of the nation's economy requires of the textile industry on the exports front. Assuming that exports increase a little less rapidly than the average in the earlier period, the foreign exchange earnings of textile exports will reach $30-$32 billion by 1995. Export growth is expected is pick up slightly in the latter period, generating between $50 and $55 billion in foreign exchange earnings by 2000.

It needs to be pointed out here that China has made substantial headway in processing with materials provided in recent years. By 1995, that sector is expected to make up 15 percent or so of total textile exports. Processing with materials provided does not require domestic fiber resources and should be deducted from the amount of total textile exports converted into cotton yarn below.

Based on the projected foreign exchange earnings of textile exports, foreign exchange earnings per ton of fibers, and foreign exchange earnings of processing with materials provided for 1995 and 2000, we estimate the amount of textile exports converted into fibers to range between 2.55 million and 2.72 million tons by 1995 and between 2.85 million and 3.14 million tons by 2000. Calculations show that fibers processed through the cotton spinning system account for 70 percent of total fibers. With this figure, we can work out the textile exports converted into cotton yarn which have undergone processing through the spinning system as follows: Between 9.46 million and 10.09 million pieces by 1995 and between 10.6 million and 11.65 million pieces by 2000. The lower numbers—9.46 million by 1995 and 10.6 million by 2000—represent the amount needed to satisfy basic export demand for the year in question. The higher numbers—10.09 million by 1995 and 11.65 million by 2000—represent what is needed to satisfy a higher export demand.

2) Making projections based on the growth rate of textile exports converted into fibers.

In the 1980's, China was a winner as a textile exporter in quantitative terms. In the 1990's, the emphasis in textile exportation will shift to quality and profitability, while the rate of quantitative growth will trail that of the increase in value. Based on projections of the growth rate of fiber consumption on the international market and analyses and projections of domestic resources, it would be advisable for China's textile exports converted into fibers to make up one-third of all textile processed fibers, growing at a rate basically the same as textiles sold domestically, that is, between 2.5 and 3 percent. Accordingly textile exports converted into fibers should amount to anywhere between 257 and 265 tons [as published] by 1995, and between 2.9 million and 3 million tons by 2000. Based on these numbers, we can project the amount of converted fibers needed to satisfy the demand of the textile exports sector by 1995 to be 9.54 million pieces in case of slow growth and 9.83 million pieces if it is experiencing fast growth. Corresponding figures for the year 2000 would be 10.75 million pieces and 11.15 million pieces, respectively.

Combining the two sets of projections, we arrive at these figures: The amount of commercial yarn needed to satisfy the basic demands of the textile export sector would be 9.5 million and

continued...

ANALYZING AND PROJECTING COTTON DEMAND BY THE YEAR 2000, 1994 (continued)

10.7 million pieces by the years 1995 and 2000, respectively, and, in the event of a higher demand, 10 million pieces and 10.40 million pieces by 1995 and 2000, respectively.

3) Predicting China's total social cotton yarn demand by 1995, 2000
Projections on domestic and foreign-sale textile demand converted into yarn are presented in the paragraphs above. Combining the two sets of projections, we predict that we will need 27.5 million pieces of cotton yarn by 1995 and 31 million pieces by the year 2000 to satisfy the basic demand of both domestic and foreign markets. Should the market demand be higher, we will need 28.5 million pieces and 32 million pieces by 1995 and 2000, respectively. (See Table 1)

Table 1. Total Social Cotton Yarn Demand by 1995, 2000. unit: in 10,000 pieces

Scenario	Domestic-Sale Demand		Foreign-Sale Demand		Total Demand	
	1995	2000	1995	2000	1995	2000
Lower	1,800	2,050	950	1,070	2,750	3,120-3,100
Higher	1,850	2,100	1,000	1,140	2,850	3,240-3,200

4) Projecting total effective social demand for cotton
In China, total social cotton demand consists of four parts: First, cotton for use in the textile industry; second, other social uses; third, cotton reserves: and fourth, exports.

Owing to the special circumstances currently surrounding China's cotton exports, this particular use should be omitted from our demand projection. This is why: Although China is a major cotton-producing and consuming nation, it is not a major cotton importer and exporter, its cotton imports and exports accounting for a very modest share of international cotton trade. Since 1983, China has been a steadfast cotton exporter and accounts for a fair portion of the international market, particularly the regional market. This policy was prompted by a largely strategic consideration. History shows, and the principle of international competition tells us, that if China fails to be a cotton exporter of a decent size, it will be at the total mercy of the international market, which will ultimately affect its cotton imports. We will not discuss here whether or not such a strategy is appropriate. What we do know from export figures over the years is that for a number of reasons cotton exports tend to go up and down quite sharply in a way that is unrelated to the supply and demand of cotton resources at home. Since including cotton exports in demand projections tends to skew the outcome significantly, it is necessary for us to exclude it for the moment and limit our forecasting to the first three categories.

Table 2. Total Social Cotton Demand by 1995, 2000 (10,000 dan)

Category	Time 1995	2000
Textile industry	7,900-8,200	8,600-8,900
Other Uses of cotton	1,000	1,000
Cotton reserves	300	300
Total cotton demand	9,200-9,500	9,900-10,200
(in 10,000 tn)	(460-475)	(495-510)

Cotton demand of textile industry.
The cotton demand of the textile industry is calculated based on the social cotton yarn demand and the share of cotton in the cotton spinning system.

Products processed through the cotton spinning system constitute a very high proportion of the output of China's textile industry. Even as the share of substitutes increases steadily year after year in the wake of the development of the chemical fiber industry in recent years, cotton spinning will remain irreplaceable as the mainstay of the textile processing industry for a long time to come. By breaking down the actual cotton yarn output in China since 1986, we see that cotton accounts for between 76 and 81 percent of cotton yarn processing and has slowly been

continued...

ANALYZING AND PROJECTING COTTON DEMAND BY THE YEAR 2000, 1994 (continued)

on a downward trend in the last few years. In light of the situation concerning textile raw material resources and textile consumption trends and by analyzing the development of China's chemical fiber industry, it is clear that cotton will continue to decline as a share of the raw materials used in textile spinning and processing even though the absolute amount required will keep rising. In our projections, chemical fibers (including long-staple chemical fibers) will account for 25 percent or so of the cotton spinning system by 1995 and 28 percent by 2000. Based on these percentages and total social cotton yarn demand, we estimate the cotton demand of the textile industry to range between 79 million and 82 million dan (equivalent to 3.95-4.1 million tons) by 1995 and between 86 million and 89 million dan (4.3-4.45 million tons) by 2000.

Other social uses of cotton.

These uses refer to uses other than cotton spinning, including civilian wadding, the war industry, cotton for the military, medical uses, odds-and-ends-uses, and wastage.

Based on data collected over the years, other social uses of cotton range between 10 and 12 million tons annually. At present, because of advances in research and development as well as applications, a number of superior fibers can replace cotton in part to meet certain social needs. Wadded quilts made of hollow crimped polyester fibers, for instance, are as good as quilts made of cotton and stand out on account of their warmth, lightness, fluffiness, softness, and resistance to moisture. These chemical fibers, therefore, have a strong potential as a substitute for cotton. Accordingly we put cotton demand in this category at 10 million dan, a level we believe is high enough to meet social demand.

Cotton reserves.

Cotton is a daily necessity for the people. With its vast territory and enormous population, China must equip itself with an effective cotton reserve to meet emergency needs caused by disasters, man-made and natural. Furthermore, cotton is an essential raw material for the textile industry whose production is highly vulnerable to natural conditions. That being so, it is all but inevitable for the level of cotton output to fluctuate. To ensure the availability of a stable supply of cotton, the government must have a reserve that can be tapped to regulate the market and prop up or lower prices as necessary.

At present, China's cotton reserves consist of a mere 10 million dan, the minimum necessary to meet emergency needs, but insufficient to play a regulatory role. Hence the urgent need to supplement it. Given the reality of resource availability, we cannot expect to boost our reserve to a proper level in one fell swoop. Barring the emergence of special supplies in the next few years, we believe a more feasible approach would be to create a reserve enhancement mechanism of gradual accumulation. To bring the level of reserve up to a minimum level of 30 million dan by the year 2000, we need at least an additional 20 million dan. By spreading out the work over the next 7 years, this means we need to increase the reserve by a net 3 million dan annually on the average, which should be incorporated into the total demand.

II. Analyzing and Predicting China's Cotton Supply Trends By the Year 2000

Total cotton output is a function of two variables: Acreage under cotton and cotton yield per unit area. For this reason maintaining the cotton-cultivated area at a high level and working hard to raise the yield per unit area are the absolute prerequisites for increasing effective supply.

The potential of increasing acreage under cotton.

In China, deciding the size of the land set aside for cotton cultivation must start with resolving two contradictions in the real world: 1) The rising population, dwindling farmland; and 2) the fierce competition between grain and cotton for land. A fact of life in China is its huge population and limited cultivated land. Moreover, there is precious little additional land that can be made arable. Since the PRC was rounded, farmland has shrunk by more than 33 million mu as more and more land is being taken up by other uses. What is more, much of the land lost to non-agricultural purposes is high- or stable-yield farmland. Judging from the situation in recent years, farmland is disappearing at the annual rate of almost 8 million mu. At present per capita

continued...

ANALYZING AND PROJECTING COTTON DEMAND BY THE YEAR 2000, 1994 (continued)

farmland in China has dropped to 1.2 mu and may continue to decline in the future. Extrapolating from this trend, per capita farmland nationwide will fall below 1 mu by the year 2000. China accounts for 22 percent of the world's total population but a mere 7 percent of its farmland. What this state of affairs indicates is that China's cultivated land is overburdened and lacks development potential. Faced with the pressure of population growth, China's top priority is to ensure that its people do not go hungry. Accordingly, in considering how much land should be devoted to cotton cultivation, we must proceed from the need to ensure that enough land is planted with grain. When it comes to the farming system, a realistic option in China is to raise the multiple crop index.

Calculations based on empirical data indicate that the amount of land under grain must not be allowed to drop below 1.65 billion mu in the future, about 75 percent or so of all land sown with crops. After setting aside enough land for grain cultivation on a priority basis, cotton planting can take up only about 4 percent of all cultivated land. Push it above this level and one sets the stage for competition with grain for land. On that basis we can probably expect with some confidence that the acreage under cotton will range between 8.5 million and 9.1 million mu by the year 2000.

Distribution of cotton-growing regions.

China's major cotton-growing areas are concentrated in the Chang Jiang and Huang He valleys and Xinjiang.

The Chang Jiang valley is China's high-yield cotton-growing region, with 30 million mu under cotton in an average year. It consists of 3 major areas: 1) The cotton-growing area in the Sichuan basin in the upper reaches of Chang Jiang has achieved some degree of balance after a dozen years of adjustment. This area has been hovering at the level of 2 million mu in size in recent years and is not expected to expand significantly in the future. 2) The Shanghai, Zhejiang, and Jiangsu cotton-growing area in the Chang Jiang delta. The fact that this is an economically developed area has eroded the comparative advantage of cotton growing, with a subsequent reduction in the land devoted to that purpose. In 1994 about 9.36 million mu in the three jurisdictions were sown with cotton, almost 4 million mu and 2 million mu less than the early 1980's and 1990's, respectively. The cotton-growing acreage here is expected to stabilize at 9.2 million mu or so by 1995 and 2000. And 3) the cotton-growing area in the middle reaches of Chang Jiang. The acreage under cotton has held steady at 7.5 million mu in Hubei, but is poised for growth in the three provinces of Hunan, Anhui, and Jiangxi, totaling 11.6 million mu in all in 1994, 2.5 million mu more than the early 1980's. These three provinces are well endowed by nature to produce cotton; their cotton yield per unit area is high and the product is of a superior quality. The scarcity of alternative avenues to wealth in these provinces also enhances the comparative advantage of cotton-growing. Moreover, all three provinces produce enough grain to "export" some to the rest of the nation, which means that the grain needs of cotton growers in areas where cotton is the only crop can be met within the province. For all these reasons, the acreage under cotton is expected to increase each year to reach 15 million mu. The total acreage under cotton in the Chang Jiang basin is projected to be 31.5 million mu and 33.5 million mu by 1995 and 2000, respectively.

The cotton-growing region in the Huang He valley is represented by the three provinces of Hebei, Shandong, and Henan. Cotton-growing areas in these three provinces and their combined output accounted for 50 percent and 46 percent of the nation's total acreage under cotton and overall cotton output, respectively, in the early 1980's. Both acreage and output peaked in 1984, when 65 million mu were planted with cotton, 63 percent of the nation's total, and the region produced 3.85 million tons of cotton, 62 percent of China's overall cotton output. Since 1990, however, the quality of cotton fields has declined and there have been major outbreaks of cotton diseases and insect pests, severely undermining the enthusiasm of cotton growers. As a result of these and other reasons, the yield per unit area has fallen, along with a drop in the growers' profits. Acreage under cotton has decreased drastically and total output has slipped. According to statistics, 36.56 million mu were planted with cotton in this region in

continued...

ANALYZING AND PROJECTING COTTON DEMAND BY THE YEAR 2000, 1994 (continued)

1993, yielding an output of 1.36 million tons, 48 percent and 37 percent, respectively, of the nation's totals. Provided the comprehensive treatment of plant diseases and insect pests is stepped up and new cotton varieties are introduced in the next few years, cotton yield per unit area may rebound. However, do not expect major gains in the acreage under cotton, which will probably level off at 40 million mu or so in the years ahead.

Ecologically Xinjiang is very well placed to grow cotton. Southern Xinjiang, in particular, is the one area in China that is best suited for that crop, almost as good as any high-yield superior-quality cotton-growing area in an advanced cotton-growing nation in the world. It is also the production base of long-staple cotton in China. This region abounds with resources. Experts who study the area say that there are still 370 million mu of undeveloped land which can be turned into new oases, including, of course, new cotton fields. After coordinated irrigation works are put in place and transportation is improved, particularly after a water-saving irrigation system is installed, we can expect cotton fields in Xinjiang to increase 4 to 5 million mu within the next five to six years. With that in mind, cotton-growing areas in Xinjiang are expected to total 12 million and 16 million mu by 1995 and 2000, respectively.

In addition, there is an area in northeastern China that grows a specially early maturing variety of cotton. It is expected to stabilize at 800,000 mu or so.

The potential of increasing cotton yield per unit area.

Right now the average cotton yield per unit area in China is about 50 kg, but regional variations are substantial. So the potential exists for further improving output per unit area. It is estimated that it may reach 60 kg on the average by 2000 as a result of a host of measures designed to improve conditions of production. Among the major technical approaches are:

1) Transform low- and medium-yield cultivated land and increase output in a balanced way. About half of China's cotton fields are low- or medium-yield land whose yield per unit area falls below the nation's average. They are mainly concentrated in the cotton-growing region in the Huang He-Huai He valley. Take 1993, for instance, when 74.78 million mu were sown with cotton nationwide and the yield per unit area was 50 kg. Of these 74.78 million mu, 41.21 million mu had a yield of just 40 kg, below the national average. If we increase input and manage to increase the output per unit area of low- and medium-yield cotton fields by 10 percent, raising it to 44 kg, the nation's total cotton output will go up 165,000 tons, boosting China's average yield per unit area 3.6 percent.

2) Increase the acreage where advanced and applicable technologies are used. Cotton plastic film and seedling transplanting effectively raise cotton output, typically by 10-15 percent, and can improve crop quality. Right now these methods are being used on over 64 million mu of land, 70 percent of all areas under cotton cultivation. If the proportion can go up to 80 percent by 2000, that is, if their application is extended to an additional 10 million mu, then the nation's average yield per unit area would climb 1.6 percent or so. Popularizing chemical fertilizer deep application technology usually raises yields 10-20 percent, but must be accompanied by large-scale farming and a higher level of mechanization. At present the utilization rate of chemical fertilizer deep application technology is only 20-30 percent in China, a far cry from the 50-60 percent in developed nations. Raising that rate by creating the conditions necessary for popularizing the technology represents an effective means for China to boost its cotton yield per unit area. Beginning this year, this particular piece of technology is being popularized in one cotton-growing area after another and is projected to be applied on 30 million mu by 2000.

3) Introduce new superior varieties and make sure more such varieties are made available across the board. Using superior varieties is the most effective way to increase yield per unit area. Generally speaking, every time a new variety is introduced, output goes up 10-15 percent. Thus far China has changed varieties six times, reaping a notably more bountiful harvest each time. Under the Ninth Five-Year Plan, China is scheduled to overhaul existing varieties in a big way by 2000 through self-fertilization or by using varieties imported from abroad. Furthermore, China manages a unified seed supply rate of just 30 percent at the moment. Even as we build cotton-producing bases, nurture cotton counties, and undertake comprehensive regional development during the Ninth Five-Year Plan, we must take pains to establish an improved variety

continued...

ANALYZING AND PROJECTING COTTON DEMAND BY THE YEAR 2000, 1994 (continued)

propagation system and raise the unified seed supply rate to 80 percent. By changing cotton varieties and raising the unified seed supply rate, we hope to increase cotton yield per unit area nationwide by more than 10 percent.

4) Intensify the comprehensive treatment of plant diseases and insect pests to cut losses. The decline in yield per unit area in the cotton-growing area in the Huang He-Huai He valley over the last few years has been a drag on the nation's yield per unit area, causing the latter to stagnate. A major reason for the decline is the extensive outbreaks of plant diseases and insect pests and severe natural disasters. In response, the government has mobilized the agencies concerned to mount a joint attack. China won the first round of its battle against the cotton aphid in 1993. The "Project Bumper Harvest" of 1994 also includes prevention and treatment of the cotton aphid as one of its top popularization efforts. Already cotton aphid prevention and treatment demonstration zones have been set up in the three provinces of Hebei, Henan, and Shandong. Together with the successful effort to develop new pest-resistant varieties, this has given hope that cotton aphid will cease to pose a major hazard. Meanwhile, as more and more areas are planted with short-season cotton, losses caused by early frost in areas planted with both cotton and wheat will decrease.

In short, it is possible to raise cotton yield per unit area 15 to 20 percent through the implementation of the above-mentioned measures. In other words, cotton yield per unit area may reach 57.5-60 kg.

Projected output for 1995 and 2000.

To sum up, by 1995 the acreage under cotton will range between 85 and 86 million mu; yield per mu, 52-53 kg; total output, between 4.4 million and 4.55 million tons (88 million-91 million dan); by the year 2000, acreage under cotton will be 90-91 million mu; yield per mu, 57.5-60 kg; and total output, 5.2-5.4 million ton (104 million-108 million dan).

China's Rural Economy No. 11, 20 Nov 1994.

CHINA'S COTTON PRODUCTION, 1986–1994 (mn metric tn)

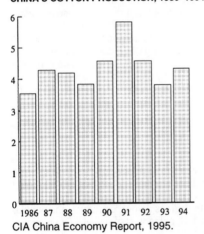

CIA China Economy Report, 1995.

GOVERNMENT CONCERNED ABOUT FARM LAND LOSS, 1995

Chinese agriculture officials expressed grave concern over the continuing loss of much needed farm lands. Although thousands of hectares of land were lost to natural disasters in 1994 many more hectares are converted to factory and housing use. General Secretary Jiang Zemin while passing through Zoumadi, Huian County in February 1994, lamented the loss of farms to

continued...

GOVERNMENT CONCERNED ABOUT FARM LAND LOSS, 1995 (continued)

factories and said, "Food is the foremost concern of the people, farmland is our rice bowl. It is true we need to build and develop but we cannot do it on an empty stomach...to permit our people to survive and develop we must act promptly to protect our lifeline."

China Facts & Figures Annual, 1995

GOVERNMENT TO FIGHT DESERTIFICATION, 1995

China is to intensify its desert-control efforts by promoting scientific and technological advances and integrate scientific research with desert-control projects.

At a conference on desert-control research, Minister of Forestry Xu Youfang said China will organize joint studies of some key technological issues concerning desert control and make optimal use of the existing technology.

Since 1991, the minister said, China has brought 2.2 mn ha (hectares) of desert and arid areas under control, and reclaimed about 100,000 ha of arable land from the desert.

However, about 1.5 mn sq km of land in China is still desert or badly eroded, equal to one-sixth of China's total land area. Worse still, such areas are expanding at 2,100 sq km annually, affecting the lives of 170 million people.

X, 17 Jan 1995.

AGRICULTURE WEAKEST LINK IN CHINA'S ECONOMY, 1995

Peasants deserted China's farmland by the thousands in 1995. Drought, skyrocketing prices for fertilizer, farm implements and gasoline and a lack of electricity to pump water for irrigation were some of the reasons why peasant farmers moved to towns and cities to take on factory jobs in record numbers. Exacerbating the farmers' problems was government takeover of private plots. According to one farmer, "a farmer without land can't be a farmer anymore. How will I feed my family? What will be my livelihood?" China's official stand was that the most important of all workers was the farmer. But little support was given to this avowed important member of society. With all the development that gave China an enviable record in the third world, the country's base of arable land was disappearing under the 200 cities that have sprung up since 1980. In a country of 900 million peasants, the last thing China could afford was mass migration to the cities. But until something could be done to improve the farmers plight the migration would continue. Though farm income increased by 5 percent, urban incomes rose twice that amount. The official feeling was that without the peasant farmer China would lose the battle for agricultural self sufficiency.

China Facts & Figures Annual, 1995

FARM WOES PLAGUE CHINA, 1995

Some 25 years ago, China's path-breaking agricultural reforms produced a 30 percent increase in grain output in just half a decade. But recently, a drastic runup in food prices exacerbated by natural disasters has exposed festering problems in the nation's agricultural sector.

Since 1990, annual growth rates of industrial output, gross domestic product, and population have averaged 22.8 percent, 11.4 percent, and 1.16 percent, respectively. Grain output, however, has edged up an average of only 0.1 percent.

continued...

FARM WOES PLAGUE CHINA, 1995 (continued)

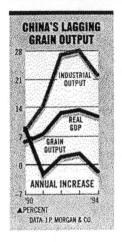

According to economist Guocang Huan of J.P. Morgan & Co., several factors are behind this dismal performance. Government investment in agriculture, mainly in infrastructure, has fallen sharply, from over 13 percent of total fixed investment in 1978 to 1.8 percent last year. Use of agricultural technology is lagging, and farmers have been squeezed by high input inflation (particularly for capital goods), rising taxes and consumer prices, and limits on grain prices.

Meanwhile, cultivated land has fallen by about 2.7 percent since 1985, in the wake of rapid urbanization, real estate development, deteriorating infrastructure, and natural disasters. And millions of farm workers are seeking better jobs in rural industries and coastal industrial areas.

Last year, China shifted from being a net grain exporter to being a net grain importer. It now plans to step up agricultural investment, limit local taxes on farmers, and cap prices on farm machinery. But unless it develops a comprehensive long-term strategy to boost grain output and farm productivity, warns Huan, its economic future may be threatened by chronic food shortages and high inflation.

Business Week, 10 Apr 1995.

GRAIN FUTURES PRICES, MARCH 1994–JANUARY 1995 (yuan/contract, 10 tn, Zhengzhou delivery)

	Previous	High	Low	Settle	Volume
Wheat					
Mar	16,360			16,360	
May	15,600			15,600	
Jul	14,860			14,860	
Sep	12,700			12,700	
Nov	13,860			13,860	
Jan	16,000			16,000	
Maize					
Mar	14,880	14,880	14,880	14,880	30
May	14,780			14,780	
Jul	15,600			15,600	
Sep	14,580			14,580	
Nov	14,200			14,200	
Jan	14,000			14,000	
Soybean					
Mar	22,000			22,000	
May	21,980			21,980	
Jul	20,000			20,000	
Sep	20,000			20,000	
Nov	22,000			22,000	
Jan	23,000			23,300	

Zhenjiang Ribao, 28 Jan 1995.

CHINA'S GRAIN PRODUCTION, 1986–1994 (mn metric tn)

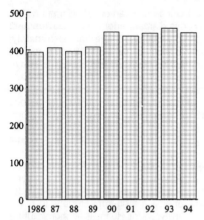

CIA China Economy Report, 1995.

HEILONGJIANG GRAIN PRODUCTION COSTS, 1994

To promote a sustained increase in grain output in Heilongjiang, develop a two-high and one-good agriculture, make the rural economy more productive overall sooner, and help realize the strategic goal of quadrupling agricultural output and bringing about a fairly comfortable standard of living, we recently conducted an input-output analysis of the cultivation of four cereals (wheat, rice, corn, and soybeans) at the 96 costs survey points in the province's 24 municipalities and counties in 1994. We feel strongly that despite the increases in agricultural output and peasant earnings in 1994, there is still much potential in the province that can be tapped. Provided we sort out our thinking, adopt the right policies, and preserve peasant enthusiasm, grain production throughout the province will rise even further from the level it has reached so far.

I. Production Costs and Profits of Four Cereals in Heilongjiang in 1994

1. Total output went up, as did per unit area yields. Province-wide, 112.499 million mu were sown to grain in 1994, basically the same as in 1993. Total grain output, however, may exceed 50 billion jin for all 1994, 5 billion or so more than the preceding year's output of 46.1 billion. The increase in total grain output can mainly be attributed to the following factors: A) More acres were sown to high-yield high-quality cereals, while fewer acres were planted with inferior low-yield crops. For instance, the acreage under corn, a high-yield cereal, went up 10.2 percent from 26.652 million mu in 1993 to 29.465 million mu in 1994, and that under rice increased 1.7 percent from 11.032 million mu to 11.215 million mu. In contrast, the acreage under soybeans and wheat, both low-yield cereals, fell 6.7 percent and 10.3 percent, respectively, from the levels a year ago. B) Per unit area yields increased. Rainfall, light, temperatures, and other natural conditions favored grain cultivation in much of the province in 1994. As a result, the per unit area yields of all four crops rose last year, from 355.85 jin to 370.79 jin per mu in the case of wheat, a gain of 14.94 jin, or 4.2 percent; rice, from 754.47 jin to 783.77 jin, up 29.30 jin, or 3.9 percent; corn, from 767.69 jin to 905.69 jin, up 137.95 jin, or 18 percent; and soybeans, from 223.92 jin to 310.18 jin, up 86.26 jin, or 38.5 percent.

2. Procurement prices have gone up, boosting the per mu output value substantially. Grain procurement prices were raised by the state in 1994. Meanwhile, per mu grain yields also went up. Consequently, per mu output value increased sharply for each of the four cereals in 1994. In the case of wheat, for instance, per mu output value rose 36.41 yuan (15 percent due to higher yield, 85 percent to higher prices), a gain of 25.4 percent. The per mu output value of rice

continued...

HEILONGJIANG GRAIN PRODUCTION COSTS, 1994 (continued)

climbed 152.96 yuan (8.5 percent due to higher yield, 91.5 percent due to higher prices) from 312.43 yuan in 1993 to 465.39 yuan in 1994, up 49 percent. The per mu output value of corn rose 130.59 yuan (27.8 percent due to higher yield, 72.2 percent to higher prices) from 211.39 yuan in 1993 to 341.98 yuan in 1994, up 61.8 percent. The per mu output value of soybeans rose 123.35 yuan (54 percent due to higher yield, 46 percent to higher prices) from 164.98 yuan in 1993 to 288.33 yuan in 1994, up 74 percent. It is clear that in terms of per mu output value, rice was the leader, followed by corn, soybeans, and wheat, in that order. In terms of percentage gain in per mu output value, soybeans was the pacesetter, followed in descending order by corn and rice, with wheat again bringing up the rear.

3. Production costs rose for all four cereals. First, material costs. The prices of capital goods have been soaring. For instance, the prices of chemical fertilizers and seeds jumped 47.8 percent and 23.6 percent, respectively, in 1994 compared with the previous year, thus jacking up the material costs of grain production 26.6 percent per mu on the average. Specifically, material costs went up 32.7 percent for the wheat grower; 11.5 percent for rice; 45.9 percent for corn; and 16.2 percent for soybeans. Next, let us look at labor costs. The province's unified daily wage increased 12 percent from 6.25 yuan in 1993 to 7 yuan in 1994, which also boosted the labor costs of grain production. In short, because of the increase in costs, both material and human, the costs of growing one mu of grain rose 23.1 percent in 1994 compared with 1993. Specifically, they rose from 92.82 yuan in 1993 to 126.96 yuan in 1994, up 126.96 yuan, or 36.6 percent, in wheat growing; from 195.48 yuan to 209.87 yuan, up 7.4 percent, in rice growing; from 111.44 yuan to 150.83 yuan, up 35.4 percent, in corn growing; and from 93.42 yuan to 105.77 yuan, up 13.2 percent, in soybean growing.

4. With output exceeding input, and also because of tax cuts, peasants were able to increase their net profits. Grain production costs may have gone up in 1994, but because of rising per mu output value, peasants managed to boost their net profits considerably. According to surveys, the net profits in grain cultivation in Heilongjiang averaged 162.75 yuan per mu, 82.92 yuan more than that in 1993, which was 79.83 yuan. Specifically, the net profit in rice cultivation was 247.42 yuan per mu; corn, 183.20 yuan; soybeans, 174.16 yuan; and wheat, 46.29 yuan.

II. Major Issues Concerning Costs and Profits of Producing the Four Cereals To Date

1. Low per unit area yields. By and large, per unit area grain yields are still very low because grain production remains in the extensive mode. Take wheat, for instance. Although wheat output per mu averaged a mere 370.79 jin province-wide in 1994, Huachuan County managed to produce 650 jin of wheat per mu, more than any other county in the province. In the case of corn, the provincial average was 905.64 jin per mu; in Shuangcheng, however, the corn yield per mu was a high 1,225 jin. Qin Yuhai, a peasant in Zhaodong, is a practitioner of scientific corn cultivation. By adhering strictly to intensive farming and using a mix of chemical fertilizers and farm manure, he has raised per mu output to a high 2,300 jin. It is clear that there is still much potential to be tapped in raising per unit area yields.

2. Wide gap between input and output. Let us do a material input-output comparison for each of the four cereals on a per mu basis: wheat, 1:1.8; rice, 1:3.47; corn, 1:3.48; and soybeans, 1:3.96. On the other hand, the ratio between material input and net profits in wheat farming, again on a per mu basis, was 1:0.8; rice, 1:1.84; corn, 1:1.87; and soybeans, 1:2.4. We can see that it was most profitable to grow soybeans in 1994, followed by rice and corn. The most "uneconomical" cereal was wheat.

3. Soaring agricultural capital goods prices have had a major impact on grain production costs. According to statistics, agricultural capital goods, whose prices have risen briskly, accounted for over 65 percent of the material input in the cultivation of wheat, rice, corn, and soybeans. As a result, grain production costs rose rapidly in 1994, which did nothing to encourage peasants to grow cereals.

4. The grain mix is still not balanced enough and needs to be further adjusted. We need to do far more multiple and deep grain processing. Because of the lack of such processing, the cereals are not converted into processed products with a high added value.

continued...

HEILONGJIANG GRAIN PRODUCTION COSTS, 1994 (continued)

III. Some Proposals To Promote Sustained Increases in Grain Output and Make Rural Economy More Profitable Overall

1. Adhere to the strategy of using science and technology to revitalize agriculture and go all out to popularize superior varieties and strains and advanced farming technology to raise the utilization rate of high-yield, good-quality varieties. In rice cultivation, for instance, we should work hard to widely introduce the proven new dry farming xizhi technology. In corn farming, we should popularize double cross seeds, disseminate close planting technology, improve field management, and increase the use of farm manure. In wheat farming, we should apply good-quality varieties. And in soybean farming, we should take pains to solve problems relating to crop rotation. Meanwhile, we should make a push for intensive farming and bring an end to backward extensive agriculture as soon as possible.

2. Make the mix of cereal crops more balanced based on the objective of low input, high output. In light of the current production cost and profits pattern for each of the four cereals, we should sow more acres with high-yield cereals like rice and corn and transform as much low-lying, flood-prone land into rice fields as possible. That way we can increase output and use rice to prevent flooding at the same time. Moreover, dry land should be turned into irrigated land or level-terraced fields by sinking electro-mechanical wells in an all-out drive to increase the acreage under rice. The input-output tables suggest that we should continue to increase the acres sown to soybeans. However, already 37 percent of all farmland in the province is devoted to that cereal. The quality of the soil, the short frost-free period, and other natural conditions in the northern pan of the province favor wheat-corn rotation. Therefore we should properly limit the acreage under soybeans for the time being and increase that under wheat to facilitate wheat-soybean rotation and prevent soybeans from interfering with the effort to raise output and improve quality. Needless to say, the acreage under wheat cannot be increased regardless of conditions. Instead, it should come about through the wider application of good varieties, by raising wheat prices properly, and by taking other non-price preferential measures designed to make wheat growing more profitable. This is the only way to mobilize peasant enthusiasm and achieve the goal of sowing more acres with wheat as appropriate.

3. Further control the soaring prices of agricultural capital goods, particularly chemical fertilizers, pesticides, and seeds. In accordance with the demands in the CPC Central Committee circular on rectifying the prices of agricultural capital goods and restoring circulation order, we should work earnestly to tighten management and do our best to prevent skyrocketing agricultural capital goods prices from pushing up grain production costs in order to preserve peasant enthusiasm for growing cereals.

4. Go all out to develop multiple and deep processing of cereals to add value to them and gradually end Heilongjiang's backward status as a seller of raw materials. Soybeans, for instance, can be processed into bean dregs, bean oil, bean products, bean dairy products, and protein meat, which all have a higher added value. Similarly, wheat and rice can be turned into name-brand flour which is sought after on the market to pull in additional income. Also, we should adopt the complex agriculture approach, which means combining farming with animal husbandry—using grain and straw to develop the latter industry. Corn and its straw, for example, can be processed into raw materials through over-warming. That way we can spur the development of animal husbandry, on the one hand, and generate more income, on the other, thereby hastening the achievement of a fairly comfortable standard of living.

5. Apply ourselves to farmland capital construction and enhance the ability of farmland to resist drought and prevent floods. In 1994, most flooding occurred in the basins of small rivers, while the western pan of the province was more vulnerable to drought. Accordingly, besides continuing to bring Songhua Jiang under control, we must step up our effort to tackle the problems of small river basins and increase irrigated land by sinking electro-mechanical wells. To that end, resources in all quarters must be mobilized and input in agriculture increased to ensure the sustained expansion of grain output.

Prices In China No. 2, Feb 1995.

REGIONAL PREDICTIONS FOR GRAIN INCREASE POTENTIAL, 1994

Region	Total Grain Output in 1993	Estimated New Increase of Grain Output	Estimated Total Grain Output (tn)
Northeast	1,197.5	250	1,447.5
North	2,513.2	300	2,813.2
Northwest	598.4	100	698.4
Southwest	1,525.5	100	1,625.5
Southeast	3,295.0	250	3,545.0
Total	9,129.6	1,000	10,129.6

Region	Estimated Population (100 mn people)	Grain Demand*	Difference Between Supply and Demand (tn)
Northeast	1.1314	905.1	+542.4
North	3.4491	2,759.3	+53.9
Northwest	0.9266	741.3	-42.9
Southwest	2.5514	2,041.1	-415.6
Southeast	4.9415	3,953.2	-408.2
Total	13.000	10,400.00	-270.4

* Standard grain demand is calculated at 800 jin per person.

Grain Increases in Five Regions in Four Stages (100 mn jin)

Region	1949– 1958	1958– 1978	1978– 1984	1984– 1992
Northeast	133.0	280.4	261.8	233.9
North	361.8	630.0	414.0	589.4
Northwest	99.1	138.8	88.4	135.4
Southwest	265.8	374.2	253.4	104.5
Southeast	552.9	1,053.0	867.9	-79.7

Beijing Liaowang No. 14, 3 Apr 1995.

LIAWANG STRESSES IMPORTANCE OF FARMING, 1995

Over the past few years, the central authorities held a series of rural work meetings, which all stressed the importance of agriculture and rural issue by issuing serious warnings. Why so? This is because there exists a certain striking contrast in our social life: On the one hand, in recent years, agricultural development and rural work in our country have encountered many new problems, which, if not properly solved, may have serious consequences for the overall situation; on the other hand, some localities and some comrades have not had the necessary understanding of this important point.

With regard to the understanding of the importance of agriculture and rural issues, it is indeed time to give a serious warning to some comrades. So far, they are still muddle-headed about agriculture and rural issues, saying that our reform started from the rural areas and achieved great results acknowledged by the whole world and questioning why it is being said in such an alarmist way that agriculture is facing a serious situation today.

Nothing in the world is constant. When the Third Plenary Session of the 11th CPC Central Committee was held, the main problems in our agriculture were primarily the damage caused by the "Gang of Four," the people's commune system shaped under the influence of the previous "leftist" ideology, and other "leftist" policies, such as the "big pot" practice. Such things seriously restrained the peasants' work initiative and led to the stagnation of agricultural production. Under the guidance of the spirit of the resolution of the Third Plenary Session of the

continued…

LIAWANG STRESSES IMPORTANCE OF FARMING, 1995 (continued)

11th CPC Central Committee, through the reform of the rural economic structure and the adoption of the contract responsibility system on a household basis linked to output, these problems were properly solved and rapid development was brought about in the rural economy for several consecutive years. However, in the middle and late 1980's, agricultural development encountered new problems. It failed to keep pace with the new situation in the development of the socialist market economy. While facing the new situation, peasants were at a loss for what to do, and the relevant administrative departments also could not work out effective countermeasures. Agriculture was bogged down in an extremely unfavorable condition. That was the root cause of the various problems that agriculture and the rural economy are currently facing. The party central leadership held a series of rural work meetings to study the new situation, unify people's thinking and understanding, and work out correct countermeasures.

With the in-depth development of economic structural reform and the market economy in our country, the people's living standards are being raised, and the market demand for farm produce is increasing. This undoubtedly provides a good opportunity for agricultural development. However, in the market economy, resources and production factors are distributed according to market needs, and this gives prominence to economic efficiency and to competition between various trades. This poses a serious challenge to agriculture. Agriculture is the foundation of the economy, the mother of all industries, but it is also a vulnerable trade. If no effective and strong support is given to agriculture, how can it withstand the winds and waves of the market economy?

The vulnerability of agriculture is caused by its own characteristics and always exists. Such vulnerability gets more prominent in the conditions of a market economy. In the past, peasants could get no other job but only engage themselves in farming. However, in the development of the market economy, they are attracted by the better economic results of other trades and shift to secondary and tertiary industries.

X, 3 Apr 1995.

CHINA IMPROVES EFFECTIVE MICROORGANISM TECHNOLOGY, 1995

Chinese scientists have made important progress in the study and use of EM (effective microorganism) biotechnology, according to a symposium held in February, 1995 in Jiangsu Province.

EM is a compound microbial reagent developed in Japan. Its applications include improvement of soil and water quality and the treatment of garbage. EM was introduced into China in 1991, and the first EM-producing lab was set up in Nanjing.

Tests done by Jiangsu Academy of Agriculture Sciences and Nanjing Agricultural Science University showed that EM can markedly improve the growth of plants and when used as an additive to fodder the quality of meat and eggs.

EM plus organic fertilizer can increase vegetable output by 13 percent when compared with chemical fertilizers. Chinese agriculture officials saw EM as a chemically free way to increase agricultural output and decrease food shortages in the country.

X, 7 Feb 1995.

CHINA'S ABILITY TO PRODUCE FOOD, 1995

[Article by Soft Science Committee Under Ministry of Agriculture: "Does China Have Ability To Feed Itself?."]

In September last year, Brown and others from the World Survey Research Institute in the United States issued a report entitled: "The Problem To Be Faced in 2030: Who Will Feed China." This report held that following the continuous reduction in China's cultivated land, from 1990 to 2030 China's grain output volume will decline by one-fifth, while population and demand

continued...

CHINA'S ABILITY TO PRODUCE FOOD, 1995 (continued)

for grain will continue to grow. The report noted that the prospect of a grain shortage in China will affect the world, and it asserted that "no one can feed China." Is the situation truly thus? Please read on...

The Chinese People Can Support Themselves

China's successful experience in feeding 22 percent of the world's population with only 7 percent of the world's cultivated land shows that the Chinese people can support themselves. People will probably remember that just before New China was established, some people predicted that the Chinese government would be unable to resolve the problem of feeding the people. However, in the 45 years since the establishment of New China, there has been a great increase in grain output volume. While per capita area of cultivated land has declined from 2.7 mu to 1.2 mu, the per capita output of grain has grown from 209 kilograms to 380 kilograms. Thereby the problem of providing people with enough to eat has been successfully resolved, and today people are moving toward a comfortably well-off life.

In the next few decades, the acceleration of the process of industrialization in China will face the pressures of increasing population and decreasing area of cultivated land. However, Brown and the others simply take as their basis of reference the reduction in grain output and the great volume of grain imports which occurred in the process of industrialization in Japan and Korea. From this they conclude that China will also see a great reduction in grain output and thus assert that "the Chinese people will be unable to support themselves." This is not in accord with China's actual situation and lacks a scientific basis. China's reserve cultivated land resources are quite great, there is great potential for utilizing them, and they can, to a certain degree, make up for the land being used up in industrial construction. Of China's cultivated land at present, two-thirds is medium- or low-yield fields. Following the improvement of agricultural production conditions and the progress of science and technology, they will see successive improvements in per-unit yield. The development potential of China's non-cultivated land resources is very great, and they provide broad prospects for increasing the output of animal and plant foodstuffs. We believe that after entering the 21st century, China will certainly be able to promote continuous growth in the production of grain and other agricultural products, and that China will have the capacity to feed itself.

The 378 Million Tons of Grain That Will Not Need To Be Imported

Chinese and foreign scholars generally agree that by the year 2030 China's population will be approaching or will have reached 1.6 billion. That is to say, in the 40 years from 1990 to 2030, China's population will grow by 490 million, or an annual average natural growth rate of 9.2 per 1,000. At that time, China's population will reach its peak.

Today, the per capita consumption of major foodstuffs in China has basically reached or surpassed world average levels. After entering the next century, following the sustained and rapid development of the Chinese economy and the raising of income levels, the levels of people's food consumption will be further increased and improved. Th general trend will be as follows: The per capita direct consumption of grain will continue to decline, while meat, fruits, vegetable oils, and sugar will see upward consumption trends. According to estimates, the per capita consumption of major foodstuffs by Chinese people in 2030 will approach or reach the level achieved by Japan, an advanced Asian country, at the beginning of the 1990s, and will see continuing stability. Calculating on the basis of Japanese foodstuff consumption at the beginning of the 1990s, the average consumption of grain will be about 450 kilograms. However, considering the characteristics of China's animal foodstuff production, whereby it can utilize broad non-cultivated land resources, at that time per capita grain consumption of about 400 kilograms will be sufficient.

In this way, when the population reaches 1.6 billion, to meet the per capita consumption demand for grain of 400 kilograms, the total demand for food grain in China in 2030 will be 640 million tons. Compared with the 1990 figure, this represents an increased demand for grain totaling 190 million tons, or an annual average increase of 4.75 million tons over the 40 years.

continued...

CHINA'S ABILITY TO PRODUCE FOOD, 1995 (continued)

Clearly the assertion by Brown and the others that China will need to import 378 million tons of grain is without foundation.

Could Grain Production Decline by One-Fifth?
Brown and the others hold that because China is changing from an agricultural society to an industrialized society at an astonishing rate, a large volume of agricultural fields is being taken over. At the same time, it is not possible for there to be a great increase in per-unit yield of grain. Thus, from 1990 to 2030, China's grain yield will decline by at least one-fifth.

Seen from the actual situation in China, while a large amount of cultivated land is being used for industrial production and other purposes, as China's reserve cultivated land resources are quite numerous, it will be possible to open up or restore these lands to add much cultivated land. To a certain degree, this will make up for the cultivated land which has been used up. For example, from 1990 to 1993, at the same time as there was a new decrease of 9.1 million mu of cultivated land annually, there was a further 7.02 million mu of new cultivated land added. This gave a net annual loss of cultivated land of only 2.08 million mu.

At present, China has 500 million mu of wasteland which is suitable for agriculture. According to government plans, every year during the period 1990 to 2000, five million mu will be opened up for cultivation. If this rate of opening up can be maintained until 2030, just this factor will provide a further 200 million mu of cultivated land. Thus, the reduction in China's cultivated land will not be as swift as estimated by Brown, and there will certainly not be a 20-percent reduction in output compared with 1990.

The Aim of Self-Sufficiency in Grain Can Be Achieved
Seen from the grain production potential in China, by 2030 there will be an increase of 190 million tons of grain, which will provide a per capita figure of 400 kilograms. Through major efforts this target can be achieved.

The goal of adding 190 million tons of grain between the years 1990 and 2030 will require an annual increase of 4.75 million tons of grain output, an average annual increase of less than 1 percent. This rate of growth is only one-quarter the average annual rate of growth in China's grain production for the 40 years prior to 1990. Of course, our determination to realize the goal of increased grain yields is not only based on historical experience but also on scientific analysis of potential for future increases in grain yield.

Through increasing the multiple cropping index, it will be possible to maintain the area sown to grain crops at 1.6 billion mu until 2030.

Through improving production conditions and promoting scientific and technological progress, it will be possible to greatly raise the per-unit yield of grain. This has been the main avenue for increasing grain production over the past several years in China and also where our hopes lie for realizing China's grain output increase figures for 2030. Over the period 1990 to 2030, if grain per-unit yield (yield per mu) is raised from 262 kilograms to 400 kilograms, it will mean an increase of 138 kilograms for every mu. This will allow the total grain yield to reach 640 million tons.

At present, China still has about 900 million mu of low- or medium-yield fields, where per-mu yield is 150-200 kilograms lower than high-yield fields in the same climate areas. Thus, the potential for increasing production is very great.

The role of agricultural science and technology is very great in increasing grain production. At present, every year 6,000 new achievements are realized in the fields of agricultural science and technology. By tightly grasping, spreading, and applying these achievements it will be possible to greatly increase grain yield. In addition, research in and application of modern biological engineering techniques, especially breakthroughs in crop breeding, will provide even better prospects for production of grain and other foodstuffs in the 21st century.

Renmin Ribao, 23 Jun 1995.

CHINA'S AGRICULTURAL IMPORTS FROM THE US, 1990–1994

TYPE	1990	1991	1992	1993	1994
Wheat	497.35	363.34	272.95	278.39	264.27
Soybeans	0	0	29.68	22.99	12.33
Cattle Hides	1.25	7.19	6.24	10.37	10.37
Soybean Oil	0	.85	7.88	.27	0
Cotton	272.21	318.79	185.94	.18	0
Corn	15.03	0	0	0	0
Tobacco	.94	0	0	0	0
Total agricultural imports from US	814	722	545	376	287

China Facts & Figures Annual, 1995

CHINA'S AGRICULTURAL OUTPUT, 1994

Agricultural production triumphed over serious natural disasters to bring in a fine harvest. Outputs of principle farm products showed a decline in grain output declined, revival of cotton output in the reversal of a declining trend, all-time high outputs of oil-bearing crops, and another bumper crop of vegetables and fruits. Outputs of sugar-bearing crops, hemp, and flue-cured tobacco fell. Sluggishness in the development of agricultural production contrasted sharply with rapid development of the national economy and steady rise in the people's standard of living.

Outputs of principal farm products were as follows:

	1994	Percent Increase Over 1993
Grain	444.5 million tons	-2.5
including: Cereal crops	393.97 million tons	-2.8
Oil-bearing crops	19.84 million tons	10.0
including: Peanuts	9.64 million tons	14.4
Rapeseed	7.46 million tons	7.5
Cotton	4.25 million tons	123.6
Jute and ambari hemp	380,000 tons	-44.1
Sugarcane	60.86 million tons	-5.2
Sugarbeets	12.53 million tons	4.0
Flue-cured tobacco	1.95 million tons	-35.2
Tea	580,000 tons	-2.9
Fruit	34.78 million tons	15.5

Forestry production and forest building moved ahead steadily, afforestation quality rising steadily. Afforestation of a total of 5.9 million hectares was completed, the pace of building key national forestry projects picking up. Forest fire prevention, disease and insect pest prevention and control, and resources management and protection work continued to improve, the forest cover rate rising to 13.9 percent.

The livestock industry showed all-around growth, with the output of meat, poultry, eggs, and dairy products increasing.

Outputs of principal livestock products and numbers of livestock in inventory were as follows:

	1994	Percent Increase Over 1993
Meat	43 million tons	11.9
including pork and mutton	36.7 million tons	13.8
Cow's milk	5.3 million tons	6.2
Sheep wool	260,000 tons	6.2
Silkworm cocoons	830,000 tons	10.2
Year-end number of hogs in inventory	412.18 million	4.9
Year-end number of sheep in inventory	239.59 million	10.2
Year-end number of cattle, horses, donkeys, mules, and camels	150.32 million	7.5

Fishing industry production continued to develop. Aquatic products output for the year totaled 20.98 million tons, up 15.1 percent from 1993. This included an output of 8.9 million tons of freshwater aquatic products, a 19.1 percent increase, and an output of 12.08 million tons of marine aquatic products, a 12.3-percent increase.

Agricultural production conditions continued to improve. Total agricultural machinery power stood at 336.85 million kilowatts at the end of the year. This was 5.9 percent more than at the end of 1993. Large and medium-sized tractors numbered 690,000, 4.6 percent fewer than in 1993. Small tractors, and hand tractors numbered 8.21 million, up 4.1 percent. Farm trucks totaled 760,000, up 9.9 percent. Chemical fertilizer (pure fertilizer) use totaled 33.13 million tons for a 5.1-percent increase. Rural electric power consumption totaled 151.1 billion kilowatt hours, up 21.4 percent. Farmland water conservancy construction increased further, the effectively irrigated farmland area increasing.

continued...

CHINA'S AGRICULTURAL OUTPUT, 1994 (continued)

2. Industry and the Construction Industry

Industrial production continued high-speed growth. Industrial added value for the year totaled 1.8359 trillion yuan in an 18-percent increase over 1993. In industry as a whole, state-owned enterprises increased 5.5 percent (if state-owned shareholding enterprises are included, they increased 6.8 percent): collective enterprises increased 21.4 percent, including a 27.3-percent increase in township-peraeted enterprises; and Sino-foreign joint venture, cooperative venture, and foreign-owned enterprises increased 28 percent. Large and medium-sized enterprises increased 12 percent for maintenance of steady growth momentum.

Light industry grew faster than heavy industry. The added value of light industry for the year was 766.8 billion yuan, 19.6 percent more than in 1993. The added value of heavy industry for the year was 1.0691 trillion yuan, up 16.5 percent. The output of some industrial products rose; others fell.

Outputs of principal industrial products were as follows:

	1994	Percentage Increase Over 1993
Chemical fibers	2.69 million tons	13.3
Cotton yarn	4.7 million tons	-6.3
Cotton cloth	20 billion meters	-1.5
Machine-made paper and cardboard	20 million tons	4.5
Sugar	5.819 million tons	-24.6
Crude salt	29.746 million tons	1.1
Cigarettes	34.213 million cases	1.4
Synthetic detergent	1.964 million tons	4.3
Color television sets	16.895 million units	17.7
Household washing machines	10.964 million units	22.4
Household refrigerators	7.645 million units	28.1
Aggregate energy output (in terms of standard fuel)	1.12 billion tons	4.7
Raw coal	1.21 billion tons	5.3
Crude oil	146 million tons	1.0
Electric power	920 billion kwh	9.6
Steel	91.532 million tons	2.2
Steel products	80.036 million tons	3.7

Ten non-ferrous metals	37.52 million tons	7.5
Cement	405 million tons	10.1
Timber	61 million cubic meters	-4.5
Sulfuric acid	14.947 million tons	11.8
Soda ash	5.684 million tons	6.3
Chemical fertilizer (100 % strength)	22.76 million tons	16.3
Chemical pesticides (100 % strength)	268,000 tons	4.4
Power generating equipment	17.069 million kw	15.9
Metal cutting machinery	192,000 units	-26.8
Motor vehicles	1.402 million vehicles	8.0
Tractors	46,000	21.8

Economic returns from industry rose. The composite economic returns index for industrial concerns for the year was 97.0, up 0.4 percentage points from 1993. Nevertheless, stocks on hand of industrial goods increased. A substantial number of concerns showed losses, and a large number of them owed each other money. Further improvement of the overall level of economic returns from industry is needed.

Production and business in the construction industry saw sustained and steady growth. Construction industry added value for society as a whole totaled 290 billion yuan for a 12-percent increase over 1993. State-owned construction firms began construction of 370 million square meters of housing, up 15.1 percent. Housing floor space completed totaled 120 million square meters, tieing the 1993 amount. The all-personnel labor productivity rate was 8,969 yuan, rising a real 21.5 percent. Per-capita profits and taxes exceeded 1660 yuan, but losses rose slightly.

Prospecting produced new findings. Main ore fields containing industrial mineral deposits were newly discovered or newly verified at 150 locations throughout the year, and major new advances were made at 58 mineral prospecting areas. Major geological reports of use for construction were provided, and new additions were made to proven reserves of 30 different mineral deposits. These included 8.2 billion tons of coal, 1.2 million tons of copper ore, 53.3 million tons of pyrite, and 90.61 million tons of phosphate. A total of 15.9 billion yuan was invested in geological prospecting work. A total of 3.84 million meters of rock core borings were machine-drilled in connection with prospecting.

3. Investment in Fixed Assets

Investment in fixed assets was brought under control to a certain extent. Investment in fixed assets for the year totaled 1.5926 trillion yuan, up 27.8 percent from 1993 (after deducting for price increases, the increase was 15.8

continued...

CHINA'S AGRICULTURAL OUTPUT, 1994 (continued)

percent), the extent of increase taking a 30.8 percentage point downturn from 1993. This included a 1.1354 trillion yuan investment, or a 34.2-percent increase in the investment of state-owned units (including state-owned units, Sino-foreign joint ventures, partnerships, and share system investment. The same applies hereinafter). Investment in collective economy projects totaled 275.8 billion yuan, up 23.6 percent. City and countryside individual investment totaled 181.4 billion yuan, up 22.9 percent.

As part of the investment of state-owned enterprises, investment in capital construction totaled 628.7 billion yuan, up 35.3 percent; investment in renovation and technological transformation came to 284.2 billion yuan, up 29.6 percent; investment in housing and real estate totaled 179.6 billion yuan, up 41.3 percent; and other investment came to 49.2 billion yuan, for a 24.8-percent increase. Investment in central government projects totaled 354.4 billion yuan, up 30.7 percent, and investment in local projects totaled 601.5 billion yuan, up 34.5 percent.

Newly begun capital construction, renovation, and technological transformation projects requiring an investment of 50,000 yuan or more numbered 76,492, 1,768 fewer than during 1993. Nevertheless, investment in fixed assets remained somewhat high in the aggregate scale of investment in construction. Year-end capital construction in progress, and planned renovation and technological transformation projects took an investment of 3.0574 trillion yuan, 31.4 percent more than in 1993.

The pattern of investment continued to improve. The percentage of state investment in energy industries rose from 20.7 to 21.8 percent, and its investment in raw and processed materials industries took 11.9 percent of investment, about the same percentage as in 1993. State investment in posts and telecommunications climbed from 4 to 5.3 percent, but the percentage of its investment in agriculture continued to decline, amounting to only 2.9 percent, or 0.3 percentage points less than in 1993. Investment in the transportation industry fell from 16.2 percent in 1993 to 15.4 percent.

New advances were made in key construction. During the year, 105.1 billion yuan was invested in 151 key construction projects that are part of state plan. This was more than the planned amount. Seventy-two of the programs and individual projects were completed and went into production. A total of 137 large and medium-sized capital construction projects, and 224 above-norm renovation and technological transformation projects were completed and went into production nationwide.

Nationwide, capital construction added major new production capacity including the mining of 4.77 million tons of coal, an installed electric power unit generating capacity of 15.27 million kilowatts, the extraction of 15.45 million tons of petroleum and 1.134 billion cubic meters of natural gas (including the capacity added by renovation and technological transformation and other investment), 810,000 tons of iron smelting, the manufacture of 92,200 motor vehicles, 480,000 tons of chemical fertilizer, and the felling and movement of 148,000 cubic meters of timber. A total of 278.6 kilometers of newly built railroad main lines were turned over for operation; 1,342 kilometers of newly built railroad multiple tracking was turned over for operation; coastal port cargo handling capacity increased by 25.8 million tons; municipal telephone installed capacity increased by 16,220 lines; long distance optical cable was extended 30,000 kilometers; 10,000 kilometers of microwave circuits were newly built; and 483 kilometers of new expressways were built.

Transportation, Posts, and Telecommunications

The production of communication and transportation maintained increase, 224.7 billion yuan of added value being completed during the year in a 6-percent rise over 1993. Nevertheless, imbalance between transportation capacity and demand continued.

X, 28 Feb 1995.

XIV ENVIRONMENT

AFFORESTATION PROGRAMS, 1994–1995

Forest Programs

Four decades of afforestation have yielded impressive results in China. New forests have been planted over vast areas of the nation, protecting crops, reducing soil erosion in agricultural areas, providing a source of local timber and fuelwood, and reducing pressure on China's mature forests. But the program has not been an unalloyed success. Until the late 1970s, emphasis was put on the quantity of trees planted rather than their survival; as a result of this, and widespread pest infestations and forest fire damage, only about 30 percent lived. Since the 1980s, when the program was adjusted, the survival rate has apparently improved.

Estimates of China's total forest cover, depending on how that is defined, vary from 11 to 14 percent. Ministry of Forestry officials put forest cover at 13.6 percent (131 million hectares) in 1992, up from 8.6 percent in 1949. Massive reforestation projects are under way in the north,

continued...

AFFORESTATION PROGRAMS, 1994–1995 (continued)

the upstream and midstream regions of the Chang Jiang River, the plains, and the Taihang Mountains, as well as along the coast. The largest single such effort, being undertaken in southeast China, also involves a conversion of degraded natural forests to exotic tree species such as slash and loblolly pine from the United States.

During the 1990s, the government hopes to plant an additional 57.2 million hectares of forest. Of this total, 39.6 million hectares will be planted by hand and cultivated. Assuming a 70 percent survival rate, the program would bring total forest cover to about 168 million hectares, or roughly 17 percent of China's total area.

These aggregate figures disguise some disturbing trends. Increases in forest cover are primarily due to new tree plantations, while natural forests continue to decline. Natural tropical forestland in Hainan, for example, declined from 25 percent of the island's total area in 1956 to 8.5 percent in 1981. For the country as a whole, it is estimated that virgin forest shrank from about 98 million hectares in 1973–1976 to about 86 million hectares in 1984–1988. Forests were selectively logged for commercially valuable species, then cleared and planted with monoculture species such as larch in the northeast and rubber in Hainan. (Chinese officials say that now only degraded lands are used for rubber plantations. Thus, while total forest cover may be expanding, the native populations and the genetic diversity of China's natural forestland continue to decline.

During the 1980s, in a sample of 11 counties, the proportion of forests in high-quality timber declined from 78 percent to 61 percent. These woods were replanted in orchards and protection forests. Compared with natural forest, they have less biomass, less absorptive soil, less diversity of flora and fauna, and poorer ground cover.

With demand for wood still outpacing supply by about 28 to 30 million cubic meters, the pressure on natural forestland should continue. One opinion is that the annual timber harvest far exceeds incremental growth, and that the shortfall will probably not be made up by new plantation production in this century. Total forest area has likely expanded somewhat over the past decade, but timber volume has declined. Of the country's 140 forest bureaus, 25 have almost run out of forest reserves and 61 report that trees are being felled at unsustainable rates.

Protected Areas

The giant panda, the most visible symbol of China's endangered wildlife, is only one species in a nation that ranks among the top 10 in the world for the diversity of their mammal, bird, amphibian, and flowering plant species. Many other species in China are also endangered, including the tiger, snow leopard, white-lip deer, golden monkey, and green turtle, plus plants such as the Korean pine and dragon spruce.

Loss of habitat from human population pressure is a major threat to China's plants and wildlife. Animal populations continue to be depleted by over-hunting and collecting for taxidermy and medicine. China, aware of these problems, is moving rapidly to create a system of nature reserves. Beginning with 59 reserves in 1979, the system had 606 totaling 40 million hectares by 1990. The government plans to add another 10 million hectares by the end of the century.

In a 1992 World Wide Fund for Nature/Ministry of Forestry workshop on conservation priorities, it was estimated that there were 820 existing or proposed protected areas in China. Forty were deemed exceptionally significant for reasons such as biodiversity, endemic species, ecosystem intactness, uniqueness and sustainability, and size. These 40 areas actually include 118 existing or proposed sites that could be linked by habitat corridors to form larger conservation units. Five of the proposed areas could be joined with conservation units across China's borders. Workshop participants concluded that there are several important gaps in the current system, particularly in the Tian Shan region in the northwest, the southeastern stretch of the Himalayas, and the central part of northern China.

With so many protected areas sprouting up, management has been understandably strained. Typically, managers have limited funds and little decision-making authority. For

continued...

AFFORESTATION PROGRAMS, 1994–1995 (continued)

example, the Ministry of Forestry controls pandas in the wild, while the Ministry of Construction manages their captive counterparts, a situation that invites conflict and breeds reluctance to share information and resources. Six different national agencies have administrative responsibility for some sites, and not all agencies have expertise in nature conservation.

World Resources, 1994–1995.

CHINA'S USE OF FORESTS, 1990–1995 (percent)

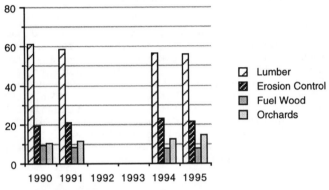

China Facts & Figures Annual, 1995

GOVERNMENT FIGHTS DESERTIFICATION, 1995

At a conference on desert-control research Minister of Forestry Xu Youfang said China would organize joint studies of some key technological issues concerning desert control and make optimal use of the existing technology. Since 1991 China had controlled desertification of 2.2 million hectares of arid areas and reclaimed 100,000 hectares of arable land from the desert.

In 1995 China had 1.5 million square km of land in desert. This was an area equal to one sixth of China's total land area. Such areas were expanding at 2,100 sq km annually, affecting the lives of 170 million people.

X, 17 Jan 1995.

TAPPING THE YELLOW RIVER TO ENHANCE AGRICULTURE, 1995

According to deputy head of the Ningxia Hui Autonomous Region's water resources department, the region has reaped tremendous economic benefits out of water resources from the river.

With the Qingtongxia Water-Control Project now under way, more and more mountainous land is being irrigated and changed from desert to oasis.

At present, the region has 920,000 ha of arable land, with a total grain output of 2.012 billion kg last year. The irrigated land has been enlarged fivefold compared to 1949, and the output of aquatic products reached 17,000 tons last year, the highest rate in northwest China.

Ningxia is located on the middle reaches of the Yellow River. The total length of the river flowing across the region is 397 km. So far, the region has a total length of 1,550 km of man-made water channels.

Some 150,000 poverty-stricken people in remote mountainous areas have been relocated to irrigated areas.

continued...

TAPPING THE YELLOW RIVER TO ENHANCE AGRICULTURE, 1995 (continued)

Government sources said that the region will move one million people to a newly developed irrigated area, at a cost of three billion yuan, within six years. The project will have a grain output capacity of 800 million kg upon completion.

Another water-control project is also under preparation to irrigate more arable land, the sources said. Overseas funds have been and will be used in such projects, they said.

X, 3 Apr 1995.

HOW DAMMING THE YELLOW RIVER WILL AFFECT THE COASTAL SYSTEM, 1994

Effect on the Coastal System

Future decrease of flow and sediment of the Yellow River to the sea will have a profound effect on the coastal system. Among the most important is the progradation of the present Yellow River Delta. Since 1976, the present delta is rapidly prograding to the sea. Between 1976 and 1989, 453 sq km of new land were formed (E of 118°59′E), averaging about 35 sq km per year. Detailed study of satellite data reveals that the present delta advanced or retreated with variation of the river's sediment discharge to the sea. The delta prograded 1.4-2.6 km in 1984 and 1985 when the sediment load at Lijin was 8.45×10^8 t/yr. It retreated 0.4-3.3 km in 1986 and 1987 when the sediment load at Lijin was 1.34×10^8 t/yr, but advanced 3.1 km again in 1988 when the sediment load at Lijin was 8.6×10^8 t (Fang and Guo 1992). It seems likely that over the next 20-30 years, with the reduction of the river's flow and especially of sediment the delta will be prograding at a much slower rate than at present or may even cease to advance.

GeoJournal 33.4, 1994.

MAP OF THE YANGTZE AND YELLOW RIVER INTERBASIN PROJECT, 1994 (Western route)

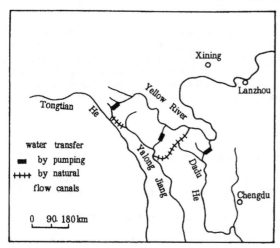

GeoJournal 33.4, 1994.

SOCIAL IMPACT OF THREE GORGES DAM, 1995

In April 1992, the National People's Congress approved construction of the Three Gorges hydroelectric project on the Chang Jing (Yangtze) River as part of China's 10-year development program. Much of the controversy over the project centered on the dam's social impact. Chinese officials estimate the reservoir will inundate 2 cities, 11 counties, 140 towns, 326

continued...

SOCIAL IMPACT OF THREE GORGES DAM, 1995 (continued)

townships and 1,351 villages. So many people, 1.1 million, would have to be resettled that it would account for one third of the project's US$ 10 billion cost. Some critics believed resettlement would fail based on China's past record of resettlement efforts. Plans called for rebuilding cities and towns, reclaiming wasteland for cash crops, and housing resettlers on hillside surrounding the area.

In addition there was concern among ecologists inside and outside China about the dam's impact on the Yangtze dolphin population.

The dolphin is one of the world's rarest species.

Other concerns targeted the decreasing quality of Shanghai's municipal and industrial water once the dam was in place. Further, critics maintained, trapped silt would deprive downstream regions and the river's estuary of vital nutrients. It was also believed that silt buildup behind the dam might impede power generation.

China Facts & Figures Annual, 1995

MAP OF AREA OF CHINA AFFECTED BY FLOODS AND DROUGHT, 1970–1990 (mn ha)

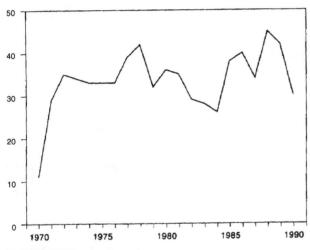

X, 13 Jun 1995.

AREA OF CHINA AFFECTED BY FLOODS AND DROUGHT, 1970–1990 (mn ha)

No.	US CAS-No.	Use	Degree of Restriction	H.S. Code Preparation	H.S. Code Pure Substance
1	12001-28-4	Industry	Banned		2524.0090
2	1336-36-3 59080-40-9	Industry	Severely Restricted [SR]		2903-6990
3	27858-07-7 13654-09-4	Industry	SR		2903-6990
4	126-72-7	Industry	SR		2919-0000
5	545-55-1	Industry	SR		2933.9000
6	107-13-1	Industry	SR		2926.1000
7	107-27-7 62-38-4	Agriculture	Banned		2805.9000
8	309-00-2	Agriculture	Banned	3808.1000	2903.6990

continued...

AREA OF CHINA AFFECTED BY FLOODS AND DROUGHT, 1970–1990 (mn ha) (continued)

No.	US CAS-No.	Use	Degree of Restriction	H.S. Code Preparation	H.S. Code Pure Substance
9	60-57-1	Agriculture	Banned	3808.1000	2910-0000
10	72-20-8	Agriculture	Banned	3808.1000	2910.0000
11	50-29-3	Agriculture	Banned		2903.6200
12	608-73-1	Agriculture	Banned	2808.1000	2903.5100
13	76-44-8	Agriculture	Banned	3808.1000	2903.6990
14	118-74-1	Agriculture	Banned		2903.6200
15	13121-70-5	Agriculture	Banned	3808.1000	2931.0000
16	106-93-4	Agriculture	Banned	3808.1000	2903.3000
17	640-19-7	Agriculture	Banned	3808.1000	2924.1000
18	93-76-5	Agriculture	Banned	3808.1000	2918.9000
19	96-12-8	Agriculture	Banned	3808.1000	2903.4029
20	298-03-3	Agriculture	Banned	3808.1000	2930.9090
21	57-12-5	Agriculture	Banned		2837.0000
22	57-47-9	Agriculture	SR	3808.1000	2903.6990
23	6164-98-3	Agriculture	SR	3808.1000	2921.4200
24	76-06-2	Agriculture	SR	3808.1000	2904.9090
25	7440-38-2	Agriculture	SR		2811.2900
26	87-86-5	Agriculture	SR	3808.1000	2908.1090
27	88-85-7	Agriculture	SR	3808.1000	2908.9090

X, 13 Jun 1995.

CHANGING FUEL SOURCES TO CONTROL AIR POLLUTION, 1995

China hopes to reduce emissions as well as transportation problems associated with its dispersed coal network by converting more coal to clean electricity and distributing this by electrical grid. A program is already well under way to construct coal-fired generating plants that are larger and more efficient than older, smaller units. Many of these units will be built adjacent to coal mines, with power sent by high-voltage lines to circumvent coal transportation bottle-necks. The potential for such plants is limited by a poor water supply in the coal-rich areas of Shanxi, Shaanxi, and Inner Mongolia, which contain 60 percent of China's coal reserves and almost all of its higher-quality coal.

Reforming Urban Energy Use

To continue along the path toward efficiency and cleaner city air, China plans to modernize urban coal technology. Replacing and refitting small and outdated industrial boilers is a high priority, though that effort has been stymied by the surge in urban demand for electricity.

Another priority is to reform residential coal use by encouraging cogeneration and the construction of gas lines and large central heating systems (district heating). City dwellers have traditionally used inefficient coal stoves for cooking, and many residential buildings depend on small, wasteful boilers for heat, resulting in serious indoor and outdoor air pollution. The switch to gas appears likely in many cities.

Measures such as coal washing and molding coal into briquettes will also be stepped up. Coal briquettes burn up to 30 percent more efficiently than raw coal and, in residential use, produce 70 percent less carbon monoxide, 60 percent less dust, and 50 percent less sulfur dioxide (SO^2).

Addressing the Rural Fuelwood Shortage

China intends to continue its effort to upgrade rural stoves and undertake a massive refores-tation program to increase fuelwood supplies. To date, 150 million families—two thirds of the nation's rural households— are using stoves that are 30 percent more efficient than older

continued...

CHANGING FUEL SOURCES TO CONTROL AIR POLLUTION, 1995

stoves. Of the 38 million hectares that have been reforested in China over the past four decades, almost 6 million hectares were planted specifically as fuelwood plantations.

In addition, for two decades, China has promoted a rural biogas program employing concrete digesters that convert animal and human waste into sludge for fertilizer and a methane-rich gas for cooking. Some 5 million digesters were in operation by 1989. Feedstock shortages have slowed biogas generation, however, and, in many cases, digesters are used to produce high-quality fertilizer rather than biogas. In the northern provinces, moreover, cold temperatures make digesters impractical for household heating.

Promoting Development of Renewables

China's interest in renewables, especially to meet rural energy needs, is growing. Though investment in this field is a tiny fraction of total energy investment, substantial progress has already been made in applying solar, wind, and even tidal technology to electricity production. For example, 12 Chinese factories now produce photovoltaic (PV) modules, and small 20- to 50-watt PV kits have become popular at remote sites. Larger installations are few but growing; a 20-kilowatt system was scheduled to be completed in 1992.

Wind energy shows great potential. About 100,000 microwind units designed to power household lighting and television have been installed in remote northern and western provinces. About 10,000 wind pumps are in operation to extract groundwater in northern China and surface water in the south and east. In addition, six wind farms with a capacity of over 4 megawatts have been connected to electric grids in various parts of the country.

Rationalizing Energy Prices

China has promised to stop subsidizing energy within five years, which could help raise the capital needed.

World Resources, 1994–1995.

MAP OF TIBET'S NATURE PRESERVES AND NATIONAL PARKS, 1992

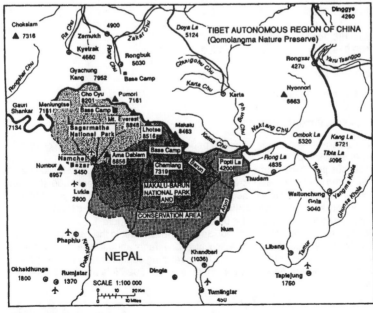

GeoJournal 27.1, 1992.

WATER TREATMENT, 1995

Lanzhou—Australia's Memtec, a water treatment concern, said its US$1 mn joint venture with China National Lanxing Chemical Cleaning was now in operation. The new firm, Lanzhou Blue-Star Memtec Water Treatment Technology, focuses on industrial water treatment for pharmaceutical and beverage companies in particular, and providing drinking water to communities of up to 50,000 people. The facility at Lanzhou, Gansu went into operation in May 1994.

The joint venture aims at combining Memtec's technical experience with Lanxing's office network to provide water treatment equipment service for China, and also to supply treatment chemicals for boiler feedwater and cooling tower circuits. Equipment is manufactured at both the Lanzhou facility and at Memtec's Australian facility.

China Business, 19 Sep 1995.

XV POPULATION

OVERALL POPULATION GROWTH, 1982–1994

	Total Population	Growth Rate (percent)	Birth Rate (percent)	Death Rate (percent)	Net Migration (percent)
1982	1,059,802,000	1.4			
1983	1,033,970,000	1.2			
1984	1,041,346,000	0.9			
1985	1,045,537,000	0.8			
1986	1,064,147,038	0.9			
1987	1,072,330,000	1.6	21.2	6.4	
1988	1,096,140,000	1.6	20.8	6.6	
1989	1,111,910,000	1.6	20.1	6.5	1.0
1990	1,121,511,000	1.6	21.0	6.7	0.1
1991	1,151,486,981	1.6	19.7	6.7	0.1
1992	1,169,619,601	1.6	22.0	7.0	0.3
1993	1,185,100,000	1.5	19.1	7.8	
1994	1,201,098,535	1.0	22.2	7.6	0.5

China Facts & Figures Annual, 1995

CHINA'S POPULATION FUTURE, 1995

The fate of China's environment may ultimately depend on the pace of population growth and China's ability to stabilize it.

The 1990 census put China's total population at 1.13 billion. With about 17 million people added every year, the population will increase to about 1.3 billion by the year 2000. If the total fertility rate remains at the 1990 level, the population will reach 2 billion by the year 2050 and continue to grow thereafter. If the fertility rate falls slightly, the population could level off at about 1.5 billion by 2050 and then decline to 1.4 billion by 2100. (See Figure 1.)

China is making remarkable strides in reducing the growth rate. In the period from 1990 to 1995, the population is expected to increase at an average annual rate of 1.4 percent, substantially below the 2 percent average rate for developing countries as a whole. Whereas China now has 37 percent of Asia's population, by the year 2025 it is projected to have 31 percent of the total.

continued...

CHINA'S POPULATION FUTURE, 1995 (continued)

China's demographic face is changing in several significant ways. For example, the population is aging. The number of people 65 or older is expected to be 90 million in the year 2000 and 167 million by 2020, compared with the elderly population of 66 million in 1990. This change has many important economic implications, particularly as most rural elderly have no old-age pensions and must rely on adult children for support.

The population is also becoming more urban. Using a relatively conservative definition of urban population, the 1990 census estimated China's at 297 million, an increase of nearly 90 million since 1982. Beijing's population increased by 17 percent and Shanghai's by 13 percent during this period. The rate of natural increase was estimated at 8 percent in Beijing and 5 percent in Shanghai; the rest of the growth was due to in-migration, reflecting, in part, mounting population shifts following the economic reforms of the 1980s and the decollectivization of agriculture.

During the mid-1960s, agricultural collectives provided the funds for a new rural health system that included a network of more than 1 million trained paramedics, popularly known as barefoot doctors, plus town and county health clinics that placed a high priority on family planning and provided free contraceptive services. These new services, coupled with heightened political pressure to limit family size, led to a dramatic halving of the fertility rate in the 1970s.

During the 1980s, the family planning program changed substantially. When agricultural collectives were dismantled, the government had to establish a new system of family planning clinics at the town and county levels to replace the communal health system. It was then that the government began to promote the one-child family, providing financial rewards to couples who limited themselves to one child. The program was unpopular in rural areas, where the preference for sons was still strong and the shift to private farming motivated people to have more than one child. Minority populations have always been exempted from the program. The one-child campaign is still strictly implemented in urban areas, but the government, trying a different tack in its attempt to curb growth, is now putting more emphasis on elevating the status of women, providing old-age security, and improving family planning and maternal-child health services.

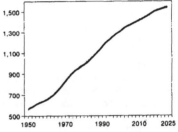

Figure 1: China's Population, 1950–2025 (mn)

World Resources, 1994-1995.

CHANGING POPULATION PROBLEM, 1995

[Editor's note] The new circumstances of China's population problem require a new understanding: fewer births are not everything. The basic strategy for solving the population problem must emphasize "manpower theory" as well as "population theory" and must "open a channel" as well as "reduce the flow." There are two possible negative effects of fertility control: an excessive haste effect and an over-emphasis effect. We must watch out for the predicament of "controls without development or not conducive to development." China needs population control which can be implemented within the framework of sustained development, a "broad population concept" essential for the age of comprehensive management, and a "five-in-one" population development strategy.

Authors: Gu Baochang, born in 1945, earned a Ph.D. in sociology at the Population Studies Center of the University of Texas in the United States in 1986, and is currently a researcher at and deputy director of the China Population Information and Research Center.

continued...

CHANGING POPULATION PROBLEM, 1995 (continued)

Mu Guangzong, born in 1964, is a lecturer at the Population Research Institute in the Demography Department at China People's University. [end editor's note]

Why is there a need for a new understanding of the population problem in China? This is really not a statement designed to shock. Historical developments have reached this stage: Under new historical conditions, we need to undertake some reflection to achieve a deeper and more comprehensive understanding and thus adopt more timely and efficient policies.

China's population problem is not static. The population problem is a function of economic development. The tumultuous process of change in China during the late 20th century is necessarily reflected in every aspect of the population problem. From a macroeconomic point of view, there are at least the following historical background points, which cannot be ignored when looking for a new understanding of China's population problem.

First is that China has had more than ten years of experience of market-induced socioeconomic changes, particularly while the establishment of a socialist market economic system was clearly being promoted during the nineties. These revolutionary changes in the system environment and the market-induced process of change have had and must continue to have profound effects on the population dynamic and on population work. These effects are multifaceted. If one keeps the general goal in sight, these are first manifested in that the living environment of the Chinese people has begun to restructure itself to resemble those of market economy societies in that the traditional living environment based on a culture of the "family as primary unit" is gradually being replaced by the modern "individual as primary unit" culture as the spirit of the living environment. The Chinese people's traditional way of thinking, which does not consider cost, is beginning to change. The changes, which this has induced in modernizing the traditional fertility aspirations of the people and the birth culture and the transition to a modern population all have far-reaching implications. In addition, the production elements, including the working population, required for the development of a market economy must be deployed in an optimal fashion. An unprecedented tide in population movement and the rise of an urbanization movement with modern significance have begun to shape a trend of "country in the city and city in the country, the city and the country cannot be separated and the city and the country are mixed together." This foretells the inevitable future replacement of the dual model of split management of rural and urban situations. A Chinese population on the move also expands and transfers the problem in its mobility. For example, the "workers' tide" problem has a certain significance in relieving the severe degree of excess population in rural areas. So-called "blind movement" is actually not "blind." The people are clearly motivated to escape poverty and seek prosperity. Their migration toward areas rich in opportunities and potential demonstrates a strong pattern. In addition, many changes have occurred in the countryside. The trends toward industrialization of the countryside and urbanization of towns are especially pleasing. These trends could also be called "localized urbanization" or "self-urbanization." Although the residences of this urbanized population has not changed, and their "household registration status" has not changed, the lifestyle and values of these people have changed deeply. Their marriage and childbirth values and behavior are currently changing in ways conducive to family planning. More and more Chinese peasants have begun to reshape themselves into a generation of new peasants who enjoy modern urban culture and can join in the process of modernization with the attitudes of modern people. All of the above situations have transformed the causal mechanisms, means of manifestation, and consequences of China's population problem.

Second is that since China began promoting family planning policies in the early seventies, outstanding achievements have been made in the area of population control. The population of China has entered a period of low growth within certain restrictive conditions. During the past 20 years, the birth rate in China has dropped from 33.43 percent to 18.24 percent. The natural growth rate has fallen from 2.6 percent to 1.16 percent, and the aggregate fertility rate has fallen from 5.81 percent to 2.31 percent, a level which approaches a replacement rate. The momentum of excessively rapid population growth has basically been brought under control. But at the same time that the population growth rate has been declining, the momentum of expansion of

continued...

CHANGING POPULATION PROBLEM, 1995 (continued)

the total population numbers is still difficult to check. This is because the already existing population base is huge and continues to grow. It is estimated that the population increases by about 14 million each year and it is predicted that by the end of this century the population of China will reach approximately 1.3 billion. When the fertility rate decreases to a rate approaching replacement level, the periodic growth volume of the population will reach an unprecedented level due to the effects of population inertia. This is the so-called "low fertility rate and high growth volume" contradiction which will be the basic characteristic distinguishing the nineties from the seventies and eighties. In addition, the unexpected wave of population aging will become a raging tide not to be underestimated. Shanghai, Beijing, and other metropolitan societies will gradually become societies of aging populations. The rapid aging of the population and the many problems associated with it have already become one of the important social issues currently of great concern to our countrymen. Although the ratio of elderly people to the entire Chinese population, when compared with that in other countries, is not one of the highest in the world, the number of elderly people is nearly 100 million. Furthermore, in contrast with developed countries, where population aging follows the industrialization and modernization of the country, population aging in China has arrived "in advance," when the industrialization and modernization of China have still not reached a high level. This exacerbates the seriousness of the problem. One can be certain that the expansion of the total numbers and aging of the age structure are contradictions which will carry over into the next century.

Thus, on the one hand a series of constantly changing external variables are making an impact on dynamic of the population growth. On the other hand, the internal patterns operating within the population will bring us into a period of population problems that are even more complex. We are coming closer and closer to the maximum limits of control of the population numbers, and the conflict between limiting the numbers and adjusting the population structure is becoming more severe. How will we "choose the lesser of two evils or the greater of two goods?"

What will the next century be like? What will be the fate of the Chinese people? Western sinologists, as objective observers, have warned us repeatedly that the main "submerged reef" in the path of economic reform and development in China is still China's swollen population. Actually, under the immense pressure of excess population, the implementation of even the finest development theory or the most outstanding strategic thinking is rife with difficulties. Of course, this does not mean that there is nothing we can do except lament. Professor Wu Cangping once gave others an inspiring comment on this: "We have no reason to resent the huge population created by history, but we must face reality and transform negative factors into positive factors to inspire a positive attitude among all the people. As to whether a large population and large labor resources can increase the overall national strength, the keys are whether 1.1 billion people can be united and in the quality of the population and labor." (Wu Cangping: "A View of the National Situation and Strength from the 1990 Census," Qun Yan, 1991 p 1)

Looking at the manifestations of this issue, it is the huge annual population increase which most attracts the attention of the common people. With an instinctive fear of a continued population expansion in the future, the issues of more births or fewer births have weighed heavily on us for a full 20 years now. Population control is without question the choice of history and the only way for the Chinese nation to live the dream of a strong country. However, the question is, will decreasing births solve everything?

The seriousness of population planning has been emphasized during the past few years, with an emphasis on the one-vote veto system. This has some good aspects but also some biases—it seems that family planning is seen as getting a grasp on population planning. If only population planning is completed, then everything will be all right. So-called population planning is summed up in the number of children born. "Fewer births is everything" is a very common and strongly felt mood. This raises a fundamental question. What after all is the fundamental goal of family planning work?

continued...

CHANGING POPULATION PROBLEM, 1995 (continued)

We believe that "the goal of family planning is not only to decrease births by a certain number but, more importantly, to provide the best possible population characteristics, status, and environment for the modernization of China. In other words, we seek not only to modernize fertility but also to modernize the population." (Liu Jing: "Population Modernization and Priority Development of Education," Renkou Yanjiu, 1992 p 2; Gu Baochang: "On Fertility and Changes in Fertility: Numbers, Timing, and Gender," Renkou Yanjiu, 1992 p 6; Mu Guangzong: "A Few Issues in Fertility Modernization," Renkou Yanjiu, 1993 p 2) Of course, whether it is "fertility modernization" or "population modernization," there is still much investigation and discussion to be done on the definition of concepts and the identification of the issues.

Indeed, the historical mission of population control has not yet been completed. The characteristics of China have determined that family planning will carry over into the next century. Our view, however, that "fewer births is not everything" is based on the following reasons:

First, "fewer births is everything" implies a kind of pessimism similar to population determinism and is rashly irrational. The development and spread of this type of atmosphere has easily caused local governments to take short-sighted actions (such as surprise raids on "big bellied women") and has caused the implementing institutions to rely excessively on the use of administrative methods and to ignore effective ways of using economic methods and cultural measures based on guidance and shared interests. Specifically, family planning work during the past few years has demonstrated an unhealthy trend which emphasizes "planning" and "legal control" and ignores "education" and "service."

Second, we need a philosophy which combines "reducing the flow" with "opening a channel" to resolve the problem of excess population in China. On the one hand, it is true that reducing the additional volume of excessive population as much as possible and achieving "fewer births" through family planning are means of "reducing the flow." On the other hand, the retention (from a static point of view) and flux (from a dynamic point of view) of excess population must be reduced as much as possible and the only routes to resolving this problem are: First, to develop the economy so that as many varied employment opportunities as possible are provided to satisfy the employment demand of excess labor; second, to use population movement to rationally redistribute labor power, or to allow the movement of manpower resources and other production elements to carry out the maximization of resource allocation; and third, to use essential labor capital investment systems (develop common education, professional education, and special training) to guarantee the quality of the labor supply in expectation of reducing as much as possible gaps between supply and demand caused by labor quality problems.

"Reducing the flow" and "opening a channel" actually are issues of emphasizing both "population theory" and "manpower theory." Comparatively speaking, however, "opening a channel" may actually be more practical and more urgent than "reducing the flow." The question of how to develop and utilize existing population resources (total population) and manpower resources (working population) amply, effectively, and rationally has always been a serious topic which we must face sincerely at the same time that we control the population. The study of population movement, migration, and distribution can be very useful for this aspect. Have our efforts in this area been adequate? The problem is still that fewer births do not mean no births. Regardless of how much we reduce births, the population of China will still expand tremendously in the foreseeable future. One can imagine that if the basic national policy of family planning had not been implemented, the population problems we face today would be even more odious.

Third, controlling the population numbers is important, of course, but when emphasized to the point of "fewer births is everything," it may cause biases in the implementation of population policy, even to the extent of deviating from the basic aims of the policy. For example, omissions in reporting result in inaccurate statistics and threaten the understanding of the national situation and policy making. In addition, the reduction of room for choice in fertility has caused many people to seek every means possible to select male children. This has become a major factor in the imbalance in the gender ratio of infants born.

continued...

CHANGING POPULATION PROBLEM, 1995 (continued)

Population control and the healthy development of the population are not completely compatible but conflict to a certain degree. This is a point which we gave little consideration to in the past. Now that we are puzzled by "low fertility, high increases," we should have enough scientific rationality and courage to face the negative effects of population control.

Broadly viewed, one of these is that excessive haste blocks goals. It cannot be denied that population control in China is a control model guided by administrative coercion. This type of control in the beginning is based on the premise of countering the forces against control. It can be said that the stronger the coercion, the stronger the force against control and the stronger the counter resilience. Thus, the current decline in fertility in China is still not stable. Latent counter resilience cannot be ignored. From the beginning of population control to now, we have had many lessons on the ineffectiveness of excessive haste. In the final analysis, the lack of a true scientific understanding or failure to grasp the internal patterns of population dynamics was demonstrated in a hasty desire for rapid success.

Second is excessive attention to one aspect at the expense of another. Broadly viewed, as everyone has seen, a decline in the fertility rate is very closely associated with a dramatic aging of the population age structure. Because this aging of the population structure brings many unprecedented challenges, we must seek demographic solutions to ameliorate the extent of population aging. This is unquestionably related to family planning. At this lime the new issue before us is how to modify reproduction policies for the turn of the century. The effect of excessive attention to one aspect at the expense of another is also demonstrated in the gender imbalance in births, counterelimination of population (partial), and tense relations between cadres and the masses.

Just as economic growth is not the same as economic development, population growth is not the same as population development. Population control is a necessary condition for fertility modernization and population modernization, but it is not the only condition. In consideration of the objective existence of the effect of excessive attention to one aspect at the expense of others in population control, we must be cautious about slipping into the predicament of "control without development" or "control not conducive to development." So-called control without development or not conducive to development refers to population control which has not brought about or has been detrimental to the healthy population and socioeconomic development which we expected. It should be said that population control has to a great degree furthered the healthy development of population, society, and the economy. However, "control without development or not conducive to development" does exist. It is just like a person who is dieting to lose weight. The dieter absolutely must control his intake of food and drink, but if the control is too severe, too extreme, and too strict, then the dieter may overemphasize the approach and miss the goal, damaging his health and perhaps even threatening his life. By the same reasoning, population control as a desire or a policy should not be opposed but given full support. Much study, however, still needs to be done to determine whether maxim of the stricter the better applies to population control. All reforms have some negative effects. Why should population control not have negative effects? It would not be a scientific approach to claim that there are none. Of course, studying the negative effects is not intended to "blacken" the current policies or "pick on" the implementing agencies. On the contrary, it is only with the attitude of seeking truth from facts that we can further discuss how to eliminate various negative effects and then rationally and effectively utilize "population control" to achieve the goal we expect— not only to limit the momentum for rapid population growth but actively to bring about the positive effects of population control.

There is a system of evaluation standards for population control. This is a reference system which encompasses multiple socioeconomic, cultural, and political aspects. As a framework for evaluation, cost-benefit analysis is a more commonly used method, but it appears that applying this method to the population control arena is very sensitive. In many people's minds, the concept of population control is a mandatory choice, so the results of population control should be or must be positive benefits. This type of thinking undoubtedly creates barriers to comprehensive and scientific analysis. Theoretically speaking, there should be three types of net gain

continued...

CHANGING POPULATION PROBLEM, 1995 (continued)

from population control. These are positive gains, neutral gains, and negative gains. Therefore, when the historical evolution and regional differences in population control are considered, are there no differences in the gains (positive, neutral, negative)? Furthermore, population control is a huge social systems engineering project which involves a multitude of aspects. In addition, the costs paid are always current whereas the benefits to be gained are anticipated. There is a great degree of uncertainty. Most of the benefits of population control are vague and indirect and can only be described on the basis of certain hypothetical conditions. For example, the theory of "two hundred million fewer births in 20 years" is built upon the hypothesis of sustaining the fertility rate of the early seventies with no change.

We have mentioned above the dangerous tendency of "control without development or not conducive to development." In the final analysis, we must be reminded to pay attention to overcoming or eliminating the negative effects of population control. Development here includes two levels of meaning. The first is balanced development within the population system. The second is harmonious, sustained development of the large social system. Thus there are the expressions "lesser development" and "greater development," but the two are, of course, very closely linked. From a demographic point of view, "control without development or not conducive to development" is not just a groundless rumor. For example, the practice of many years of "you have over-quota births, I fine you, everybody takes what they need and does what they have to do" is adequate proof of this. The "fines for over-quota births" have even become a source of wealth for some units and individuals. We believe that the way to eliminate "control without development or not conducive to development" is to cease control for the sake of control and fewer births for the sake of fewer births and the short-term behavior of adhering to quotas as the only aim. In other words, what we urgently need is a strategic view and population control to be implemented within the framework of sustained development. That is, at the same time that we carry out the engineering of lowering the fertility rate, we must also consider not allowing excessive aging of the population or excessive imbalance in the gender ratio in births and not create serious threats to sustained socioeconomic development. "In other words, what we need is a broad population concept."

This essay has not yet raised the question of the strategic development of China's population. As explained above, population development and population growth are two concepts which are related but different. Therefore, population development strategy is not limited to population numbers. It is based on the varied nature of the national situation in China and the scope of "population development" itself. Thus, China's population development strategy into the next century should include the following five aspects: 1) control of population numbers; 2) raising the population quality; 3) adjusting the population structure (gender, age); 4) rational population distribution; and 5) development of population resources. These five aspects, however, are not simply a list. "Raising the population quality, adjusting the structure, rational distribution, and ample, effective, and rational development of population resources (the subject is manpower resources, the kernel of which is latent resources) must all be carried out on the basis of control of the population numbers in order to provide a beneficial population environment for the realization of modernization in China. This is the underlying aim of the 'five-in-one' population development strategy." It can be seen from this that population development strategy is absolutely not simply population control and does not only relate to population growth but is a greater population strategy closely related to socioeconomic development to be carried out within the greater framework of sustained development. Without the guidance of this strategic direction, any operational level may commit a directional error in tactics and, within the multitude of interlocking difficult choices, finally fall into the predicament of "control without development or not conducive to development."

The discussion above, summed up briefly, is how to gain a new understanding of the basic nature of the "population problem" and how to define the basic issues in the field of vision of current and historical demography. Population problems are demonstrated in many complex ways. Thus, how can the category of the "population problem" ultimately be defined? Here we

continued...

CHANGING POPULATION PROBLEM, 1995 (continued)

are raising a view to correct everyone—the so-called population problem refers to the imbalances, conflicts, and contradictions caused in the development of the economy, society, and the environment by changes in the numbers, quality, structure, and distribution in the population system as it operates. This is the fundamental reason for the establishment of the conclusion that "the basic nature of the population problem is a development problem." It must be pointed out that the "population problem" as a philosophical category is eternal. Classical historical philosophy has told us long ago that there are contradictions in this world and that there are contradictions among things and that development arises through contradictions. In this way, at a philosophical level, the dynamic nature of the population system is based on the contradiction between the population system and that which is not the population system. Balance between the population system and that which is not the population system is temporary, and there are frequent imbalances during actual development. Thus, viewed historically, resolution of population problems is always relative and the existence of these problems is absolute. It is just that the characteristics of the population problems which appear in different phases of socioeconomic and cultural development are different. Each era has its own mission. Each era has its own population problems to resolve (Mu Guangzong: "On Population Problems", Renkou Yanjiu, 1992 p. 2).

Of course, population problems as concrete issues will be manifested differently under different time conditions. For example, China currently, and for a fairly long time in the near future, faces a major problem of overpopulation pressure. Therefore, the feeling about population growth is "if it's low it's good." But after not too many years, as population aging progresses, the problems of an aging population will become prominent and the feeling of "if it's low it's terrible" will quickly spread. At the same time, the problem of over-concentration of population in developed areas and urbanized societies caused by the "workers' tide" will attract the broad concern of all aspects of society. The questions of how low quality population will adapt to the building of a socialist market economy and how to make the transition from a labor-intensive model to a capital-intensive model of production are also very challenging issues.

Viewed in this way, as history evolves, population problems are also changing and transforming. The cumulative and proliferating nature of the population problem itself has already propelled us into a time of "overflowing population problems." We are increasingly deeply aware that at the same time that the population problem develops, monolithic population control methods have clearly not met our expectations. This is the significance of the question of a new understanding of China's population problem and a new definition of the current and historical field of vision of demography.

Now a calm and accurate judgment is needed of our current historical period of population problems. Some scholars have subtly become aware that as society makes a transition, the population problem also makes a transition from being a problem dominated by total numbers to one of a comprehensive set of complications. China faces the challenge of finding a comprehensive solution to population problems under the condition of lower fertility. The era of population adjustment and comprehensive population solutions has arrived, and the curtain is gradually closing on the era of monolithic population control.

Of course, this absolutely does not mean that the historical mission of population control in China has been completed. There is still much work for us to do on the issue of how to decrease births. The basic nature of this issue is such that it is determined by the still undeveloped state of China's economy and quality of life, which is still not very high. Currently, however, we are beginning to face the problem of population control with low fertility rates (apart from old revolutionary areas and minority, border, or impoverished areas) which is the conflict explained above of "low fertility rate, high growth volume." Therefore, although the basic national policy cannot be allowed to waver, population control will be a long-term action, a heavy burden to carry down a long road, and specific strategies must adapt to the current situations and opportunities.

continued...

CHANGING POPULATION PROBLEM, 1995 (continued)

It must be observed that the low fertility rate currently occurring is still not stable. This is a very important conclusion. How can we solidify existing achievements? How can we further exploit the potential for even lower fertility rates? And how can we maintain the fertility decrease within reasonable limits in the expectation of reaching our goal of sustained development within the conditions of population control? These kinds of questions begin to arise one after the other and push their way onto our agenda.

One common understanding has been accepted by everyone. That is that creating a socioeconomic environment and modern fertility mechanism with a stable and decreasing fertility rate is the only choice. We know that the characteristic of the traditional fertility culture of "give birth to sons, give birth early, have many children" is extremely tenacious and deep-rooted. Cultural scholars long ago cautioned those who are concerned about China that the traditional culture with the family as the basic unit has a deep influence on Chinese fertility behavior. Sometimes it is difficult to form a complete answer from an economic point of view on why Chinese peasants are so deeply committed to fertility. When explaining fertility from the point of view of the fertility culture, recreating a fertility mechanism truly has a deep meaning. Theoretically, the turning point for the revolution in the fertility culture is the recreation of the living environment. The living environment illuminated by modern civilization treats the individual as the basic unit, and the living environment encompassed under traditional civilization treated the family as the basic unit. (Li Yinhe, Chen Junjie," The Individual as Unit, the Family as Unit, and Fertility Concepts," Shehuixue Yanjiu, 1993 p 2)

We believe that the success or failure of population control will not be determined solely by whether the population control goals are met smoothly, but even more so by the extent and progress towards the modernization of fertility concepts. Taking a long-term view, internal factors will determine everything. The transformation of fertility aspirations, or the modernization of the fertility culture, is the most important internal factor in the successful creation of modern fertility mechanism. If we can broadly divide fertility cultures into three types—high fertility culture, lower fertility culture, and no fertility culture—then the so-called "modernization of the fertility culture" refers to the process of the gradual disappearance of high fertility culture and the gradual emergence of low fertility culture and no fertility culture as the mainstream fertility cultures, within the process of socioeconomic modernization. Examining the modernization of the fertility culture in terms of the historical background of the nineties, speaking only of population control methods, guidance-type propaganda and education and high-quality service work will play an increasingly important role. (Mu Guangzong: "The Southern Jiangsu Model in the Transition to Modernized Population," Nongcun Jingji Yu Shehui, 1993 p 2)

Demographers have all noticed that the decline in China's fertility rate during the eighties experienced many fluctuations. There was even a resurgence in the fertility rate during several years in the late eighties (if exaggerated statistics are considered; the actual statistics would be even worse than the ones currently before us). Why does the fertility rate exhibit fluctuations as it decreases to approach replacement levels? Is it because the potential for a decline has already been completely exploited (internal factor) or because the intensity of controls has weakened (external factor)? People are unable to agree which is correct. Of course we could make a list of many factors, but this probably would not assist us in determining the true source among many linked concepts. We need to break away from minute factors and look at the broad framework to explain the characteristics of the changes in the fertility rate since the eighties.

As everyone knows, the mechanism for decline in China's fertility rate is based mainly on coercion. Coercion here primarily refers to relatively direct administrative control with the aim of completing or implementing family planning goals. This type of control is called coercion because it includes harsh restrictions on the control goals. This situation has determined an inevitable internal resistance to China's fertility rate. Considering that the decline in the fertility rates in most of rural China was accomplished through widespread restrictive conditions dominated by coercion, in theory the fertility rate in the majority of rural areas in China still has a relatively strong resistance. Just as mentioned above, the low fertility rates currently achieved are still quite unstable. Therefore, if the fertility rate exhibits fluctuations or resurgence during

continued...

CHANGING POPULATION PROBLEM, 1995 (continued)

the nineties this should not be puzzling. World population history has shown clearly that when high fertility rates begin to drop, the decline is quite rapid, but when the fertility rates begin to approach replacement levels, it is very difficult to continue the decline and fluctuations appear. There is a pattern to this phenomenon. This phenomenon has also appeared in China. If a theoretical analysis is attempted, this could be seen as related to the function of the "rule of maximums" in population control. The so-called rule of maximums can generally be described as follows: The closer an extreme gets to the goal, the greater the number of difficulties encountered, the less correlation between effort and achievement, and efforts tend to bring progressively fewer results. As the fertility rate in China approaches replacement levels, it is also approaching an extreme goal. Control achievements made against the backdrop of strong resistance tend to decrease progressively. The greater the effect the greater the recoil certainly will be. One fact has gradually been acknowledged by the people. This is that the effectiveness of population policies has weakened. There is not much hope for continued decline in fertility rates by relying solely on the effectiveness of government policy.

It is logical that the new problem we face is that of population control with a low fertility rate. The essence of the problem is whether a smooth transition can be made from a fertility decrease mechanism based on coercion to one based on self-awareness. In other words, it would be very difficult to continue using coercion alone to force a fertility decrease to the extent that the fertility rate could exhibit an unknown degree of resistance. As a general theoretical model, we have set forth a hypothesis on fertility rate decline based on control strength. This is the so-called "three divisions under heaven" hypothesis.

We believe that overall there are generally three types of control. These include the spontaneous control which arises from economic development and social change; guidance control led by family planning propaganda and superior service; and coercive control centered on planning restrictions and administrative controls. The first type implies that development is also a type of control. Increases in average incomes, improvements in the quality of life and changes in social roles all indirectly alter people's fertility aspirations and behavior. The second type refers to using a series of propaganda, education, and superior service measures conducive to family planning to create incentive mechanisms based on interests to cause people to accept family planning more consciously. The last type refers to a series of administrative control measures which guarantee the implementation of population planning. If we view the directly functioning coercive control as a "visible hand," then the indirectly functioning spontaneous control and guidance control are two "invisible hands." The distinction is that the former type directly regulates fertility behavior, whereas the latter two types indirectly guide fertility aspirations. The secret to any region which has successfully achieved population control goals is the ample activation of these three types of force. The coordinated use of all three types to create population control quite different from the run-of-the-mill approach. One area which has offered successful experience of this type is southern Jiangsu. Demographic circles have the expression the "southern Jiangsu model" to refer to modern population change.

As we enter the nineties, all localities are more mature in their experience with population control. Each successful population control model has its own characteristics, but the secret shared by all has become clearer. To control population effectively, all types of economic, cultural, and administrative methods must be fully brought to bear. So-called "comprehensive treatment" is actually the comprehensive utilization of the three forces described above. The goals of implementing modern population control cannot be reached without the role of coercion, but what is even more important is a profound influence upon the fertility aspirations of the childbearing age group of people. The experience of southern Jiangsu and other areas has provided evidence that the control phase dominated by coercion is preliminary. To solidify and deepen the results of population control, the role of spontaneous control and guidance control must be continually strengthened, while coercion is maintained, to allow population control to enter a mature, sophisticated phase. In addition, as modern fertility mechanisms begin to emerge, fertility decline mechanisms make a transition from a coercion type to a

continued...

CHANGING POPULATION PROBLEM, 1995 (continued)

spontaneous type. Perhaps it is only then that we will deeply accept the conclusions "develop-ment is a type of control" and "the best government is one with the fewest restrictions." The reason the so-called three-in-one path of "fewer births, faster wealth, more civilization" is successful is that the maturing of spontaneous and guidance forces alter traditional fertility aspirations. From a microeconomic level this demonstrates the formation of a self-restraint mechanism on the family size.

There are two ways of understanding population growth. The first is by the growth of relative numbers. Everything can be understood in a glance at the changes in the "population growth rate." The second way is by the growth in absolute numbers. This can be reflected in the changes in the "total population numbers." At this time, the so-called "continued inflation of the Chinese population," accurately speaking, should refer to the inflation of the absolute numbers and not the relative numbers. But we cannot help but see that circumstances make this type of population inflation unavoidable because the huge existing population base numbers are an unalterable historical fact, a determined historical condition which we cannot but accept. The facts are that even if population growth rates are maintained at a relatively low level, due to the huge base population figures, particularly the large numbers of people who will enter the marriage and child-bearing years during the nineties, the net annual increase in population is very large, estimated at around 14 million. But from the point of view of numbers control, due to the impact of the third peak in births, population work during the early nineties has been extremely difficult.

From the point of view of control of population figures, there are clearly two points which we must pay attention to.

The first is the problem of rural population control. Particularly in the "former revolutionary, minority, border, and impoverished areas," population control duties are still very difficult and strenuous. Indeed, rural population control has always been the emphasis and central focus of population control in China. The new topic, however, faced by all levels of local government in the nineties is how to more effectively control the population under the conditions of a market economy. In certain ways, the family planning mission in the nineties in China is even more difficult. One objective aspect is the huge population base numbers and shocking potential fertility. Additionally, during the social transition, many socioeconomic variables drifting within and outside the market have a counterattack effect on family planning. Subjectively, family planning troops may have relaxed a bit, with the leadership busy working on the economy and neglecting family planning work somewhat. This has made an impact on the strength and effectiveness of population control. Therefore, although China has entered a market economy society, it is still not a mature one. The overall development of the rural economy still has a long ways to go before the fertility rate will decline spontaneously. It is no wonder that scholars want to issue warnings. At the moment, the market economy has given us more challenges than good tidings. We need to be cautious about a resurgence in fertility and emphasize the transformation of the fertility decline mechanism in order to prevent the possible resistance of the fertility rate.

Second is the issue of redistribution of the population. This primarily refers to redistribution of the working population between urban and rural areas and among different regions. With the backdrop of reform and opening, China's population problem has overflowed. This is related to the historically unprecedented movement of population. Due to the effects of population movement, the population problem has silently been transformed. The problem of "over-urbanization" has figured prominently in the nineties due to the rise of the "worker tide." The cities are becoming ever more crowded, the air and the environment are polluted, hygiene conditions are deteriorating, housing is scarce, employment is difficult to find, slum areas are appearing in the cities (especially at the edges of cities), and a gangster problem which cannot be ignored has appeared in the inner cities, among other problems. The many types of "urban illness" actually reflect the quality problems associated with urbanization. With this historical background of promoting urbanization in China, should we now consider "the quality of urbanization?" How should we choose between extent and quality of urbanization? How should

continued...

CHANGING POPULATION PROBLEM, 1995 (continued)

the population be rationally distributed between urban and rural areas and among different regions? These issues all await sincere exploration by the academic community.

In addition, the hidden dangers of low-qualify population have evolved into a series of alarming social evils such as prostitution, thievery, murder and mugging, trafficking in kidnapped people, etc. Low-quality population damages the economic order and social stability and even threatens gains already achieved by reform. If the low quality population, without any organizational affiliation or professional ambition, become mobilized, they will form a significant detrimental force which could not be ignored. Actually, a large hoodlum class has already been formed. The issue of population quality needs to be reexamined at a higher level, within a broader background context. We want to raise this warning for a flourishing society: All of the dreams of modernization could vanish like bubbles in a low-quality population. The historical mission for the turn of the century is to educate the people, to make them a united, strong people with self-discipline and self-respect and respect and appreciation for work.

As change deepens, the population problem needs to be constantly reevaluated. The breadth and depth of China's population problem must be reexamined in connection with the new socioeconomic background and systems environment. As the socialist market economy is built up and perfected, China's population problem needs comprehensive treatment more than during any other period in the past. A "greater population concept" must be created in order to solve China's population problem.

First, the control of the population numbers and quality must be combined. Population quality control must be considered as much as possible while population numbers are being controlled. This means that at the same time that birth rates are controlled, the quality of newborns must also be strictly guaranteed. The birth of inferior fetuses must be checked. A set of measures on optimal birth and death must be implemented for newborns to raise the fertility quality of the entire people.

Secondly, population control (blocking the flow) and manpower development (developing sources) must be combined. Population is the locus of a type of natural consumption force. Indeed, we do not need a greater consumption force than that of 1.2 billion people. At the same time, however, the existing population must somehow enter our scope of consideration. Although the population control problem and the development of manpower resources appear to be closely related over a long process, we have also discovered that, fixed at one particular historical moment, these two issues are very different in nature and thus require different policies. Comparatively speaking, manpower development is more intensely practical but demographers are far more concerned about population control. The population is actually a unique resource, a "resource" that can develop other resources. From the point of view of resources, population resources, manpower resources, and talent resources form a pyramidal structure of relationships. The prominent aspect of the development and use of population resources is the development and use of manpower resources (especially the development and use of talent resources). The question of how to optimize the deployment of manpower resources under the conditions of a market economy is an issue of concern. This includes, for example, how labor migrates and how to achieve in that mobility optimal deployment with other production elements. If research is done at the macroeconomic level, then it must involve labor migration, the quality, structure, and amounts of labor, as well as the age, gender, etc., of the working population. Therefore, it is not a purely demographic, economic, or sociological topic, but a comprehensive one which involves many academic disciplines.

This essay mainly includes framework concepts and primarily raises questions in anticipation of in-depth discussion by everyone. Our intent here is to lay out preliminary ideas to inspire more enlightened comments, as an effort to inspire work on a new understanding of China's population problem under new historical conditions.

Population Research No. 5, Sep 1995.

REPORT ON FAMILY PLANNING, 1995

The State Family Planning Commission (SFPC) is now striving to combine birth-control work with economic development, with the object of helping farmers get rich and at the same time promote cultural progress in the countryside.

The new approach, first carried out in northeast China's Jilin Province, has been praised by Peng Peiyun, State Councilor and minister in charge of the SFPC, as a "road of hope for rural family planning".

At a meeting held at the end of 1994 in Sichuan, the most populous province in China, the approach won support from family planning officials from throughout the country, and a decision was made to carry it out nationwide as a basic principle for the current and future population-control work.

Senior SFPC officials said that they believed that the new principle will be helpful for breaking out of the vicious circle of "poverty-more children-poverty" and for triggering a revolution in people's attitudes towards birth control through economic development.

They said that so far the governments at all levels have started to formulate preferential policies in accordance with the new concept, giving couples who practice family planning special treatment in supplying fine seeds, information, technical training and funds so as to raise their incomes to a level higher than the local average.

The move is aimed at helping farmers solve the problem of supporting the elderly while inducing more couples to practice family planning, the officials noted.

In Yancheng County, in east China's Shandong Province, local family planning departments have helped farmers grow more gingko trees which have a fruit-bearing period of 300 to 1,000 years. A five-year-old gingko is able to produce fruit worth about 1,000 yuan a year.

According to the program, China will strive to hold its population at 1.23 billion by the end of this year, and 1.3 billion by the year 2000, when the population's natural growth rate will drop to one percent.

Official figures show that by 1993 the population's natural growth rate had dropped from 1970's 2.5 percent to 1.1 percent, and women's total fertility rate from 5.8 percent to two percent. The latest statistics show that the Chinese mainland's population will hit 1.2 billion by mid-February this year.

The program says that the more than 20 years of birth control efforts have been critical to the nation's rapid economic growth and the improvement of the people's life in recent years.

However, the program reminds that the birth of some 21 million people every year still keeps severe pressure on the nation's environment, resources, employment and infrastructure, and that the birth rate in rural area is very likely to rise if control loosens, as a further change in farmers' view of the desirability of having lots of children will come only as a result of further economic development.

The burgeoning floating population produced by the economic expansion also poses a new threat to the government's birth control efforts, because the floating population is often outside the population management networks, the program points out.

The program calls on family planning departments at all levels to give top priority to propaganda and education in their work. It calls for the opening of courses in demography in schools, short-term classes for citizens, and programs on population matters on all the major radio and television networks by the year 2000.

The program requires that the present nationwide family planning service networks be further improved in both personnel and equipment to provide better contraception and related services.

The program urges local family planning departments to expand their services, that is, to co-operate with other government bodies in helping farmers get rich; this, they believe, will lead to a change in the traditional rural view that having more children is better.

The program admits that there have been some discrepancies in the demographic statistics. It therefore calls for the better training of census personnel and better evaluation of data.

continued...

REPORT ON FAMILY PLANNING, 1995 (continued)

To improve the quality of census and population management, the program demands that a computer data system be established in all county family planning departments by the year 2000.

The idea of bearing no children which was once popular in Western developed countries has spread over a large area in China especially in major cities. The number of young couples who prefer to live in their own world without children is increasing.

According to a survey in 1991, the number of well-educated couples who did not wish to have children was about 20 percent of the total and such trend went upwards year after year. Statistics also showed that between 1980 and 1990 there were over 350,000 couples who chose not to give birth to children for the whole life. It is believed that the figure will continue to rise by the turn of the century and well into early next century.

Most of the couples who do not want to have children for their whole life are aged around 35 and 68 percent of this group are below 35. Many of them felt that they could neither achieve great success in their career nor shoulder the burden on bringing of children. In order to lead a better life and enjoy themselves, they choose to live in a world of two without any burden on children.

When husbands and wives are divorced, their children would suffer the most because they will have to lose either one of their parents. In Beijing, the number of single-parent children comes up to 20,000 every year. According to a sample survey conducted by a social group on marriage and family, 16.8 percent of the married couples found it difficult to get divorced because of their children. About 14.1 percent had their divorce delayed for a long period because they were concerned about the future of their kids. Cases of unhappy marriage have alerted some young couples and they finally decided to give up bearing children.

However, it runs against the Chinese tradition by not extending one's next generation. Couples who do not want to have children are under great pressure and are criticized for pursuing their own pleasure at the expense of the social responsibility.

For the older generation who is very eager to see the family tree prosper, they feel so sad to find that their sons have decided not to give birth to children and they are afraid that it would come to an end of their family history. According to a sample survey, aging persons from about 80 out of 102 families choosing no children totally opposed the "no child" decision while those from 16 others expressed their understanding but still gave no consent to such decision. There were a mere six households whose aging members kept silent or "left the decision to the young couples on giving up bearing children.

The matter of small family of a mere couple sees the pros and cons. It seems, however, irreversible that the role of bearing and bringing up children seen in the marriage is weakened and there are more young couples in China choosing not to have children.

X, 13 Feb 1995.

REPORT ON ILLEGAL EMIGRATION, 1995

China's public security and border defense units adopted measures to prevent criminal activities associated with illegal emigration. A person in charge of the border defense bureau of the Public Security Ministry said that in 1994 the nation's public security and border defense units arrested a total of 6,838 people trying to cross the nation's borders illegally. In addition, authorities said that 200 "ringleaders" within China and in other countries were arrested. Among those arrested 1,897 were stopped at land borders, 2,437 in coastal areas and 2,504 at ports representing an increase of 23 percent in the total numbers over 1993.

X, 14 Jan 1995.

PROVINCIAL MAP OF CHINA, 1994

Maps on File, 1994.

NAMES OF PROVINCES, 1994

Characters	Pinyin	Pronunciation
安徽	Anhui	ahn-way
北京	Beijing	bay-jing
福建	Fujian	foo-jee_en
甘肃	Gansu	gahn-soo
广东	Guangdong	g_wong-doong
广西	Guangxi	g_wong-she
贵州	Guizhou	g_way-joe
海南	Hainan	hi-nan
河北	Hebei	huh-bay
黑龙江	Heilongjiang	hay-loong-jee_ong
河南	Henan	huh-nan
湖北	Hubei	hoo-bay
湖南	Hunan	hoo-nan
江苏	Jiangsu	jee_ong-su
江西	Jiangxi	jee_ong-she
吉林	Jilin	jee-lynn

Characters	Pinyin	Pronunciation
辽宁	Liaoning	lee_ow-ning
内蒙古	Nei Mongol	nay-mung-goo
宁夏	Ningxia	ning-she_ah
青海	Qinghai	ching-hi
陕西	Shaanxi	shun-she
山东	Shandong	shahn-doong
上海	Shanghai	shong-hi
山西	Shanxi	shahn-she
四川	Sichuan	ssu-ch_wan
天津	Tianjin	te_en-jin
新疆	Xinjiang	shin-jee_ong
西藏	Xizang	she-dzong
云南	Yunnan	yu_oon-nan
浙江	Zhejiang	juh-jee_ong
台湾	Taiwan	tie-wan

World Resources, 1994–1995.

TOP AQUATIC PRODUCT PRODUCING PROVINCES, 1994

Ranking	Province	Output (th tn)	Ranking	Province	Output (th tn)
1	Shandong	3,506.5	6	Liaoning	1,677.0
2	Guangdong	3,128.1	7	Hubei	1,269.0
3	Zhejiang	2,469.0	8	Guangxi	761.5
4	Fujian	2,266.1	9	Hunan	741.4
5	Jiangsu	1,780.0	10	Jiangxi	694.8

CEI Database, 8 Mar 1995.

TOP MILK PRODUCING PROVINCES, 1994

Ranking	Province	Output (th tn)	Ranking	Province	Output (th tn)
1	Heilongjiang	1,415.2	6	Shanxi	236.8
2	Inner Mongolia	423.0	7	Beijing	222.0
3	Xinjiang	408.3	8	Shanghai	206.4
4	Hebei	285.5	9	Qinghai	193.8
5	Sichuan	277.9	10	Shaanxi	173.9

CEI Database, 8 Mar 1995.

TOP MEAT PRODUCING PROVINCES, 1994

Ranking	Province	Output (th tn)	Ranking	Province	Output (th tn)
1	Sichuan	5,021.0	6	Hebei	2,121.0
2	Shandong	3,173.6	7	Jiangsu	2,000.5
3	Hunan	2,723.9	8	Guangdong	1,828.0
4	Henan	2,223.9	9	Jiangxi	1,780.0
5	Hubei	2,139.4	10	Guangxi	1,643.6

CEI Database, 8 Mar 1995.

NORTHEAST REGION STATISTICAL COMMUNIQUE, 1994

The year 1994 was a year in which our country accelerated the pace of building the basic frame of the socialist market economic system. Under the leadership of the provincial party committee and the provincial government, all people of the province worked closely in line with the central major task of "grasping favorable opportunities, deepening reform, expanding the scale of opening up, promoting development, and maintaining stability"; implemented the provincial party committee's economic development ideas and strategic targets; positively promoted the reform of the financial and tax, banking, and foreign trade systems; accelerated the pace of developing the national economy; noticeably improved the livelihood of the urban and rural people; and made headway in various social undertakings, including those in the scientific, educational, cultural, public health, and sports spheres. The initial calculations showed: The annual gross domestic product reached 160.4 billion yuan, an increase of 8.7 percent. Of this, the added value of the primary, secondary, and tertiary industries respectively increased by 8.9 percent, 8.8 percent, and 8.6 percent, respectively accounting for 19.6 percent, 52.9 percent, and 27.5 percent of the total gross domestic product. The province made a good start in pioneering the "second battle field" of the economic development. The added value of the nonstate sectors of the economy increased by 11.8 percent, and the rate of contributions to the economic growth made by the nonstate sectors of the economy reached 56.3 percent. The major problems in economic operation were the excessive price hikes, the more serious

continued...

contradictions caused by the restrictions of markets, and some state-owned enterprises still had difficulties in production and management.

1. Agriculture

In 1994, the province deeply implemented the guidelines of the central rural work conference and the provincial party committee's rural work conference; successively worked out a series of policy measures for strengthening the rural work, consolidating agriculture's role as the foundation of the national economy, and protecting the interests of the peasants; mobilized the broad masses of the peasants' enthusiasm for production; increased the input in agriculture; and accelerated the pace of agricultural production. In 1994, the total agricultural output value of the province reached 53.22 billion yuan, an increase of 12.6 percent over the previous year, and the added value of agriculture reached 31.44 billion yuan, an increase of 8.9 percent, respectively increasing 10.3 percentage points and 4.1 percentage points over the previous year, higher than the figures in the past few years.

The cropping structure was reasonably readjusted. The total grain output surpassed 25 million tons. In 1994, the peasants across the province took markets as an orientation; developed high-yield, high-efficient, and good-quality agriculture; and scientifically and reasonably readjusted the cropping structure in line with actual conditions and according to the principle of stabilizing crop-sown areas, ensuring total output, increasing efficiency, and increasing revenues. The province's grain crop growing areas reached 748,000 hectares, a drop of 57,000 hectares from the previous year. Of this, the paddy rice growing areas reached 748,000 hectares, an increase of 13,000 hectares; the corn growing areas reached 1.964 million hectares, an increase of 187,000 hectares; and the soybean growing areas reached 2.796 million hectares and the wheat growing areas reached 1,195,000 hectares, respectively decreasing 184,000 hectares and 142,000 hectares. The total grain output reached 25.787 million tons, showing an increase of 1.879 million tons or 7.9 percent over 1993 when the province reaped bumper grain harvests and set another historical record. The major cash crop growing areas reached 665,00 hectares, an increase of 84,000 hectares over 1993. Of this, the oil-bearing crop growing areas reached 174,000 hectares, the flax growing areas reached 82,000 hectares, and the sugar beet growing areas reached 344,000 hectares, respectively increasing 18,000 hectares, 19,000 hectares, and 59,000 hectares; and the flue-cured tobacco growing areas reached 66,000 hectares, a drop of 12,000 hectares from the previous year. The output of major agricultural products was as follows:

	1994	Percent Over 1993
Grain (mn tn)	25.787	7.9
Of this: Paddy rice (mn tn)	4.104	5.7
Wheat (mn tn)	2.753	-19.0
Corn (mn tn)	11.464	19.8
Chinese sorghum (tn)	864,000	17.9
Food grains other than wheat and rice (tn)	477,000	70.0
Soybean (mn tn)	5.136	4.5
Potato (tn)	746,000	-13.3
Oil-bearing crops (tn)	155,000	-3.5
Flax (tn)	217,000	27.3
Sugar beets (mn tn)	3.227	8.0
Cured tobacco (tn)	89,000	-23.6
Vegetables (mn tn)	6.722	same
Fruit (tn)	99,000	7.2

New headway was made in forestry and greenery. In 1994, the added value of forestry reached 680 million yuan, an increase of 0.6 percent over the previous year. Some 283,000

continued...

NORTHEAST REGION STATISTICAL COMMUNIQUE, 1994 (continued)

hectares were afforested, an increase of 13.8 percent over the previous year. The afforestation quality was ceaselessly improved, the prevention of forest fire was strengthened, and the rate of wooded areas increased.

The development of animal husbandry was accelerated. The added value of animal husbandry was 5.13 billion yuan, an increase of 30.0 percent over 1993. The output of major livestock products and the number of animals kept in stock were as follows:

	1994	Percent Over 1993
Meat (mn tn)	1.087	28.9
Of this: Pork (tn)	656,000	20.8
Beef (tn)	180,000	62.0
Mutton (tn)	24,000	32.6
Poultry and eggs (tn)	602,000	22.1
Milk (mn tn)	1.415	5.5
Sheep wool (tn)	13,000	16.4
Pigs slaughtered (mn head)	7.887	22
Domestic poultry slaughtered (mn head)	126.923	29.6
Large animals in stock (year-end figure, mn head)	5.19	17.7
Of this: Milk cows (head)	732,000	9.3
Pigs in stock (mn head)	9.094	14.7
Sheep in stock (mn head)	3.997	22.1

The fishery industry continued to develop. The added value of fishery was 530 million yuan, an increase of 8.2 percent. The output of aquatic products was 209,000 tons, an increase of 10.2 percent. Of this, the output of breeding aquatics reached 158,000 tons, an increase of 11.3 percent.

Agricultural production conditions were improved. In 1994, 1.085 million tons of chemical fertilizer were applied (100 percent effective content equivalent), an increase of 8.3 percent. Rural consumption of electricity was 2.29 billion kw hours, an increase of 4.1 percent. The aggregate power of farm machinery was 11.9 million kw, an increase of 0.4 percent. There were 82,000 large and medium-sized tractors, a drop of 3.3 percent; and 405,000 small tractors, an increase of 4.7 percent. The irrigation and drainage equipment had a total power capacity of 1.341 million kw, an increase of 1.2 percent. There were 81,000 power-driven threshers, an increase of 5 percent; and 145,000 farm-use water pumps, an increase of 1.9 percent. Effectively irrigated areas reached 1.022 million hectares, a drop of 12.2 percent from the previous year. The development of nonagricultural industries was accelerated in the rural areas. In 1994, the total output value of the nonagricultural industries, including the rural industry, building industry, transportation, commerce, and catering trade, reached 59 billion yuan, an increase of 77 percent. The proportion of the total output value of the nonagricultural industries in the total output value of the rural areas rose from 50.3 percent in 1993 to 52.7 percent. Town and township enterprises made noticeable achievements in carrying out the project of "making extraordinary development." The total output value of the province's town and township enterprises reached 60 billion yuan, an increase of 66.4 percent; their business income reached 58.71 billion yuan, an increase of 61 percent; their profits reached 3.18 billion yuan, an increase of 37 percent; and the taxes handed over to the higher levels by these enterprises reached 1.52 billion yuan, an increase of 37 percent.

2. Industry and Construction Undertakings

In 1994, the province started to conduct enterprise reform with the core of establishing modern enterprise systems. The role played by the market mechanism was apparently enhanced. Industrial production showed a stable increase. The total output value of all industrial enterprises

continued...

NORTHEAST REGION STATISTICAL COMMUNIQUE, 1994 (continued)

totaled 177.82 billion yuan and showed an 8.9 percent increase over 1993. Of this total output value, that of state-owned enterprises totaled 127.93 billion yuan and showed a 0.3 percent increase over 1993; that of non-state-owned enterprises totaled 49.89 billion yuan and showed a 29.6 percent increase over 1993. The proportion of output value scored by these non-state-owned enterprises increased from 27.6 percent in 1993 to 28.1 percent in 1994. Of the output value scored by these non-state-owned enterprises, that scored by collectively owned ones totaled 32.32 billion yuan and showed a 24.3 percent increase over 1993. Of the output value scored by these collectively owned enterprises, that scored by township industrial ones totaled 9.18 billion yuan and showed a 69.3 percent increase over 1993; that scored by village-run industrial ones totaled 8.64 billion yuan and showed a 47.5 percent increase over 1993; that scored by industrial enterprises jointly and cooperatively run by both urban and rural areas totaled 660 million yuan and showed a 47.9 percent increase over 1993; that scored by individual-run industrial enterprises in both urban and rural areas totaled 10.06 billion yuan and showed a 47.5 percent increase over 1993; and that scored by the "three categories of foreign-funded industrial enterprises" and the industrial enterprises belonging to other economic sectors totaled 7.51 billion yuan and showed a 23.8 percent increase over 1993. Of the output value scored by these foreign-funded enterprises and the enterprises belonging to other economic sectors, that scored by the state-owned holding enterprises totaled 5.37 billion yuan and showed a 5.6 percent increase over 1993. The output value scored by large and medium-sized enterprises across the province totaled 116.56 billion yuan and showed a 2.5 percent increase over 1993, that scored by small enterprises totaled 61.26 billion yuan and showed a 22.8 percent increase over 1993, that scored by heavy industrial enterprises totaled 127.12 billion yuan and showed a 4.1 percent increase over 1993, and that scored by light industrial enterprises totaled 50.7 billion yuan and showed an 18.6 percent increase over 1993. The added value scored by industrial enterprises in the year totaled 76.15 billion yuan and showed a 9 percent increase over 1993. The output of key industrial products is as follows:

	1994	Percent Over 1993
Chemical fiber (tn)	122,000	1.4
Cloth (mn m)	107.265	-35.1
Flax cloth (mn m)	41.412	27.3
Woolen goods (mn m)	4.378	25.1
Sugar (tn)	150,000	-63.1
Dairy products (tn)	119,000	-3.6
White wine (tn)	255,000	10.1
Beer (tn)	890,000	12.1
Cigarettes (cases)	789,000	0.5
Machine-made paper, paper-board (tn)	492,000	-5.8
TV sets	223,000	182.3
Color TV sets	212,000	179.8
Synthetic detergent (tn)	22,000	-1.5
Plastic products (tn)	87,000	-7.9
First energy production (standard fuel mn tn equivalent)	137.779	1.6
Raw coal (mn tn)	76.405	3.9
Crude oil (mn tn)	56.005	0.2
Natural gas (bn cu m)	2.33	4.5
Power output (bn kwh)	37.82	7.5
Steel (mn tn)	1.106	-11.3

continued...

NORTHEAST REGION STATISTICAL COMMUNIQUE, 1994 (continued)

	1994	Percent Over 1993
Rolled steel (tn)	985,000	-10.1
Rolled aluminum (tn)	36,000	-18.1
Timber (mn cu m)	11.143	1.5
Cement (mn tn)	6.784	-2.9
Plate glass (mn tn)	5.575	14.2
Sulfuric acid (tn)	69,000	-7.3
Soda ash (tn)	60,000	-17.7
Synthetic ammonia (tn)	607,000	13.6
Ethylene (tn)	310,000	-0.5
Tire (mn)	1.922	1.4
Power generating equipment (mn kw)	4.11	10.7
Metal cutting tools (sets)	2,318	-38.1
Motor vehicle	24,000	42.5
Small tractor	34,000	52.7

Production was connected with marketing in a basically normal way, and economic efficiency picked up somewhat. In 1994, the industrial enterprises at or above the township level that exercise independent accounting obtained 130.92 billion yuan from selling their products, an increase of 11.2 percent over the previous year, and realized 25.49 billion yuan in profits and taxes, an increase of 38.4 percent. The composite index of the province's industrial economic efficiency was 119.0 percent, up by 5.4 percentage points. Of the six economic efficiency indexes that are under appraisal, the product marketing rate was 95.5 percent, a drop of 1.0 percentage point; the profit- and tax- yielding rate of capital was 13.9 percent, up by 3.3 percentage points; the profit-yielding rate of cost was 10.3 percent, a drop of 0.9 percentage points; the per capita labor productivity was 16,114 yuan/person, an increase of 29.3 percent; the turnover frequency of floating capital was 1.30 times, a reduction of 0.2 times; and the added value rate was 44.2 percent, an increase of 0.1 percentage point. However, the deficits sustained by enterprises remained very serious. The amount of deficits sustained by money-losing enterprises was 4.63 billion yuan, an increase of 10.4 percent, with the range of deficits reaching 22 percent, up by 1 percentage point. The funds tied up by finished products were relatively more, and the loans owed to each other were in a relatively serious situation.

Construction trade developed steadily. In 1994, the added value of construction trade was 8.7 billion yuan, up by 7.7 percent over the previous year. The area of the completed houses built by state-owned construction enterprises was 5.07 million square meters, up by 11.8 percent, and its per capita labor productivity was 29,477 yuan/person, up by 20.0 percent.

3. Investment in Fixed Assets
In 1994, under the situation that the state increased the dynamics of macroeconomic regulation and control, the increase speed of the province's investment in fixed assets was somewhat slower from the previous year, maintaining the trend of stable increase. The completed investment in fixed assets was 39.65 billion yuan, up by 24.1 percent, with the increase margin dropping by 12.3 percentage points. Of this, the investment in local projects was 20.41 billion yuan, up by 16.2 percent, with the increase margin declining by 30.6 percentage points. Of the total, the investment of state-owned units was 35.77 billion yuan, an increase of 22.9 percent; that of collective units, 1.09 billion yuan, up by 24.4 percent; and that of individual residents, 2.79 billion yuan, up by 41.3 percent. The capital construction, equipment renewal, and technological transformation projects conducted by state-owned units, each with a value of 50,000 yuan or more, numbered 3,240,479 fewer than the previous year, of which, the newly started projects numbered 1,983,586 fewer than the previous year.

continued...

NORTHEAST REGION STATISTICAL COMMUNIQUE, 1994 (continued)

The investment structure was improved somewhat. Of the investment in fixed assets made by state-owned units, investment in capital construction was 16.64 billion yuan, up by 14.6 percent; and that in equipment renewal and technological transformation projects was 9.84 billion yuan, up by 42.5 percent, thus changing the long-standing situation in which the increased speed of investment in equipment renewal and technological transformation projects was slower than that in capital construction projects. Investment in other fixed assets was 5.4 billion yuan, up by 39.6 percent. Investment in real estate was 3.98 billion yuan, up by 2.2 percent. Of the total investment in fixed assets of state-owned units, investment in the primary industry was 570 million yuan, with its proportion in total investment rising from 1.3 percent in 1993 to 1.6 percent in 1994; the investment in the secondary industry was 18.92 billion yuan, with its proportion rising from 59.1 percent to 52.9 percent, of which, the investment in the energy resources industry was 14.87 billion yuan, with its proportion rising from 40.2 percent to 41.6 percent; and the investment in the tertiary industry was 16.29 billion yuan, with its proportion rising from 39.7 percent to 45.5 percent, of which, the investment in transport, post, and telecommunications was 4.82 billion yuan, with its proportion rising from 8.4 percent to 13.5 percent.

New headway was achieved in construction of key projects. In 1994, the large and medium-sized capital construction projects and the key projects under construction in the province numbered 44, and the above-norm equipment renewal and technological transformation projects numbered 42, respectively amounting to 7.19 billion yuan and 1.36 billion yuan of investment, or showing an increase of 3.7 percent and 10.2 percent. The large and medium-sized and key construction projects that were completed and put into production in 1994 included the first-phase formaldehyde project of the Jiamusi Chemical Industrial Plant, the second-phase mountain pear alcohol project of Mudanjiang Pharmaceutical Factory, and the Tangwanghe Shaving Board Plant. The above-norm equipment renewal and technological transformation projects that were completed and put into production in 1994 included the 200,000-set radial tire project of the Hualin Group General Company, the pulp water project of the Harbin Papermaking Mill, and four other projects. The major annual newly added production capacity included 12,000 kilowatts of electricity, 55,700 tons of raw coal, 4.247 million tons of oil, 125,000 cubic meters of timber, 50,000 tons of refined steel, 50,000 tons of cement, and 22,000 tons of beer. The newly added supply capacity also included the daily 23,000 tons of tap water and 1 million cubic meters of gas in cities.

4. Transportation, Post, and Telecommunications

Transportation, post, and telecommunications service developed steadily. The 1994 added value of Heilongjiang's transportation, post, and telecommunications industries totaled 6.97 billion yuan, up 7.7 percent from the preceding year. The volume of transportation by various means is as follows:

	1994	Percent Over 1993
Volume of freight transport (bn tn/km)	85.64	0.9
Railway (bn tn/km)	73.02	0.7
Highway (bn tn/km)	5.7	1.9
Waterway (bn tn/km)	1.85	3.5
Airway (mn tn/km)	90	-17.9
Pipeline (bn tn/km)	4.98	1.4
Volume of passengers		
Transport (bn person/km)	22.41	-0.6
Railway (bn person/km)	17.07	0.8
Highway (bn person/km)	4.29	-0.3
Waterway (mn person/km)	20	-24.0
Airway (bn person/km)	1.04	-19.9

continued...

NORTHEAST REGION STATISTICAL COMMUNIQUE, 1994 (continued)

The annual transactions of post and telecommunications service totaled 1.85 billion yuan, up 48.5 percent from the preceding year. Letters totaled 168.91 million, up 2.0 percent; letters for express delivery 1 million, up 67.5 percent; long-distance calls 234.14 million, up 62.7 percent; pager subscribers 283,000, up 67.4 percent; telegrams 6.84 million, down 30.1 percent; newspapers and magazines 518.47 million copies, down 22.9 percent; and the capacity of local program-controlled switchboards 1.56 million lines, up 1.1 times. Telephone subscribers totaled 971,000, up 58.1 percent.

5. Commerce and Commodity Prices

In 1994, Heilongjiang accelerated the establishment of the market system and built a new open and multi-layered market network in its initial form, which took wholesale markets as the mainstay and country fairs as the foundation, and which consisted of both composite markets and specialized markets and both wholesale and retail markets of all sizes. Commodity supplies were sufficient in the market, the supply and demand were by and large in balance, and sales grew steadily. The annual retail sales of consumer goods totaled 53.89 billion yuan, up 20.7 percent; of which 38.26 billion yuan was registered in urban areas, up 21.8 percent, and 15.63 billion yuan in rural areas, up 18.0 percent. In terms of ownership, the consumer goods retail sales of the state-owned economy accounted for 39.7 percent, those of the collective economy 17.3 percent, and those of other economies 33.3 percent. Urban and rural country fair markets increased to 1,893 in the country, and transactions totaled 15.07 billion yuan, up 36.7 percent. The retail sales of peasants to nonagricultural population rose by 37.6 percent.

The sales of the means of production were sluggish. Material supply and marketing departments throughout the province purchased 9.31 billion yuan worth of means of production in 1994 and sold 9.69 billion yuan worth of means of production, both down 30.6 percent from the preceding year. Judging from the sales of major materials, the sales of motor vehicles grew by 24.4 percent, and those of rolled steel, coal, timber, and machinery and electric equipment declined. The stockpiles of rolled steel and motor vehicles rose by 7.6 and 12 percent, respectively; and those of coal, timber, cement, and machinery and electric equipment showed a substantial decrease.

Price reform was expedited, and prices rose by a large margin. Following the price reform conducted in the past few years, the state executed a series of price adjustment measures one after another in 1994, raising the grain purchasing and marketing prices by a large margin and adjusting and raising the prices of a large number of commodities under the state or provincial control, such as electricity, crude oil, refined oil, chemical fertilizer, and transportation, post, and telecommunications service. This played a positive role in rationalizing the relations between various sectors in terms of prices, changing the long-standing low prices of basic products, and gradually establishing the market-oriented price mechanism, but it also led to a large increase in prices. The annual general retail price index rose by 20.7 percent from the preceding year, and the growth rate was 6.1 percentage points higher than in the preceding year.

The following were the changes in prices in 1994 compared with the previous year:

	Increase Over 1993
Cost of living prices for residents	21.9
Of which: urban areas	22.0
Rural areas	21.3
Of which: medical and health-care	6.8
Means of transportation and telecommunications	5.1
Housing	18.1
Service items	13.7
Retail prices of commodities	20.7
Food	32.3
Grain	45.5
Meat, poultry, eggs	38.5
Clothing, shoes, hats	18.5

continued...

NORTHEAST REGION STATISTICAL COMMUNIQUE, 1994 (continued)

	Increase Over 1993
Daily necessities	14.0
Cultural and sports articles	10.2
Books, newspapers and magazines	36.6
Chinese and Western medicines and medical goods	10.5
Building and decoration materials	17.0
Fuels	7.3
Machinery and electric products	same
Transaction prices of farm products	30.3
Prices of agricultural means of production	25.9
Purchasing prices of raw materials, fuels and power equipment	19.3
Factory prices of industrial goods	28.9
Prices of products for investment purpose	9.0

6. Foreign Economic Relations and Tourism

The accelerated pace in reforming foreign trade and the fixing of the exchange rate in 1994 brought new changes to the structure of foreign trade. The structure of imports and exports changed from that of dealing primarily with traditional bartering to sporting the exchange trade. The total value of foreign imports and exports during the year came to $3.09 billion, up 1.1 percent over the previous year, of which, the value of imports totaled $1.25 billion, up 7.2 percent, and that of exports, $1.84 billion, a decline of 2.6 percent. Judging from the foreign trade pattern, the total value of imports and exports during barter trade came to $1.64 billion, a decline of 21.7 percent, and its proportion in the total volume of imports and exports dropped from 68.4 percent in the previous year to 53.0 percent; the total value of imports and exports of the spot exchange trade came to $1.45 billion, up 50.4 percent, and its proportion in the total volume of imports and exports increased from 31.6 percent in the previous year to 47.0 percent.

New progress was made in foreign economic and technological cooperation. In 1994, we successfully held the fifth "Harbin Trade Fair." The volume of capital introduced from foreign countries signed in the agreements declined, and the volume of foreign funds actually used, rose. During the year, 706 agreements on using foreign capital were signed, a decline of 59 percent from the previous year, the volume of contracted use of foreign capital totaled $760 million, a decline of 30.1 percent (of which $610 million came directly from foreign businessmen, a decline of 38.3 percent). The actual use of foreign capital totaled $490 million, up 63.9 percent. Along with the unceasing expansion in the sphere of opening up, by the end of 1994, 3,781 "three types of foreign-funded" enterprises registered an increase of 26.8 percent over the previous year in the industrial and commercial departments.

Jilin Ribao, 19 Apr 1995.

MAP OF NORTHEAST REGION, 1994

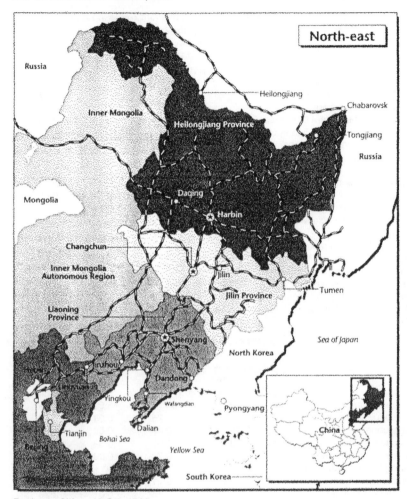

Business China, 19 Sep 1995.

JILIN TERTIARY INDUSTRIAL SURVEY, 1992

A. The situation regarding financial revenues and expenditures of tertiary industrial enterprises.

The data from the general survey of the tertiary industry shows that the business income of tertiary industrial enterprises across the province in 1992 (including enterprises implementing the enterprise accounting system as well as business administrations) was 25.372 billion yuan, up 21.6 percent over 1991; business costs or expenses totaled 22.216 billion yuan, up 20.5 percent over 1991; sales (business) taxes totaled 1.335 billion yuan, up 24 percent over 1991; and business profits totaled 1.921 billion yuan, up 33.4 percent over 1991.

continued...

JILIN TERTIARY INDUSTRIAL SURVEY, 1992

Classify According to Different Trades in 1992 (bn yuan)

	Business Income	Business Cost or Expenses	Sales (business) Taxes	Profits
Total	253.72	222.16	13.35	18.21
Agriculture, forestry, animal husbandry, fishery and service trade	1.23	1.14	0.02	0.07
Geological prospecting and water resources management industries	1.71	1.63	0.04	0.04
Communications, transport, storage, post, and telecommunications	49.29	47.29	1.92	0.08
Wholesale, retail trade, catering industry	80.62	81.86	7.33	-8.57
Banking and insurance industries	86.75	57.86	3.09	25.80
Real estate industry	11.94	11.13	0.32	0.49
Social service industry	12.08	11.24	0.39	0.45
Public health, sports, social welfare undertakings	1.33	1.67		-0.34
Education, cultural, art, radio, film, television undertakings	4.18	3.77	0.07	0.34
Scientific research, and comprehensive technical service industry	1.45	1.34	0.09	0.02
State organs, political party organs, and mass organizations	0.58	0.77		-0.19
Other industries	2.56	2.46	0.08	0.02

Classify According to Economic Sectors in 1992 (bn yuan)

	Business Income	Business Cost or Expenses	Sales (business) Taxes	Profits
State economy	197.90	174.79	9.77	13.34
Collective economy	43.12	38.71	3.02	1.39
Private economy	0.33	0.25	0.04	0.04
Pooling economy	0.48	0.42	0.02	0.04
Stock economy	3.29	1.90	0.39	1.00
Foreign-invested economy	0.87	0.72	0.09	0.06
Hong Kong-Macao-Taiwan-invested economy	0.29	0.21	0.02	0.06
Other economic sectors	7.44	5.16	0.01	2.28

B. The situation regarding financial revenues and expenditures of business administrations of the tertiary industry.

In 1992, the revenues of business administrations of the tertiary industry (including business administrations and enterprises implementing the business administrative accounting system) was 10.906 billion yuan, up 20.9 percent over 1991. Of this, the appropriation receipt totaled 4.981 billion yuan, up 17.2 percent over 1991; business income totaled 3.285 billion yuan, up 21.6 percent over 1991; and receipts not covered in the budget totaled 1.444 billion yuan, up 30.4 percent over 1991.

Expenditures in 1992 totaled 10.611 billion yuan, up 21.9 percent over 1991. Of this, appropriation expenditures totaled 4.236 billion yuan, up 17.7 percent over 1991; business expenditures totaled 3.318 billion yuan, up 23.6 percent over 1991; and extra-budgetary expenditures totaled 1.318 billion yuan, up 30.1 percent over 1991.

continued...

JILIN TERTIARY INDUSTRIAL SURVEY, 1992 (continued)

Classify according to different trades in (1992) and calculated in (billion yuan)

	Gross income	of which			Gross expenditure			
		Appropriation receipt	Business income	Extra-budgetary income		Appropriation expenditure	Business expenditure	Extra-budgetary expenditure
Total	109.06	49.81	32.85	14.44	106.11	42.36	33.18	13.18
Agriculture, forestry, animal husbandry, fishery, service trade	3.48	1.0	1.37	0.71	3.37	0.98	1.25	0.66
Geological prospecting, water resources management	4.04	2.14	1.06	0.28	3.73	1.84	0.92	0.38
Communications, transport, storage, post, and telecommunications industries	4.56	2.18	3.37	0.61	4.43	1.81	1.32	0.63
Wholesale, retail sale trade, and catering industry	0.15	0.03	0.05	0.03	0.15	0.03	0.05	0.02
Banking, insurance	0.02		0.01		0.01		0.01	
Real estate industry	2.42	0.27	1.69	0.20	2.33	0.20	1.66	0.10
Social service industry	4.73	1.32	2.36	0.35	4.78	1.25	2.25	0.35
Public health, sports social welfare undertakings	18.23	3.92	12.45	0.70	17.77	2.54	13.38	0.63
Education, cultural, art, radio, film, television undertakings	22.90	14.97	1.03	5.10	22.23	14.80	1.32	4.59
Scientific research comprehensive technical service industry	4.50	1.77	1.44	0.64	4.10	1.20	1.95	0.44
State organs, political party organs, and mass organizations	42.89	21.95	9.36	5.76	42.27	17.46	8.60	5.32
Other Trades	1.14	0.26	0.66	0.06	0.94	0.25	0.47	0.06

Jilin Ribao, 14 Mar 1995.

MONGOLIA REGION STATISTICAL COMMUNIQUE, 1994

The output of major farm products is as follows:

	1994	Percentage Increase Over 1993
Grain	10.835 million tonnes	-2.2
of which: wheat	2.348 million tonnes	-21.3
corn	4.823 million tonnes	6.3
rice	305,000 tonnes	-7.6
soybeans	940,000 tonnes	4.3
tubers	553,000 tonnes	-13.3
Oil-bearing crops	650,000 tonnes	-10.5
Beets	2.336 million tonnes	-16.2

The production and construction of forestry made new headway. In the entire year, 371,900 hectares of land were afforested and the shelterbelts in north, northeast, and northwest China yielded notable results. Forest-fire prevention, disease and insect pest control, resources management, and ecological protection were continuously strengthened.

Another good harvest was recorded in animal husbandry production. The number of livestock recorded during the animal husbandry fiscal year totalled 57.113 million, up 2.4 percent over the same period the previous year, the highest record in history. The number of livestock by the end of the year totalled 44.506 million, up 5.2 percent over the previous year. The number of large animals, sheep, and hogs slaughtered during the year amounted to 1.03 million, 10.111 million, and 4.593 million, respectively; the rate of livestock slaughtered reached 15.1 percent, 33.3 percent, and 62 percent, respectively. Continued efforts were made to improve livestock strains and the proportions of fine strains, and improved strains of large animals and sheep were enhanced. The output of major animal products and livestock numbers were as follows:

	1994	Increase over 1993 (%)
Pork, beef and mutton	693,000 tonnes	5.0
of which pork	436,000 tonnes	10.3
beef	105,000 tonnes	-0.9
mutton	152,000 tonnes	-4.4
Milk	458,000 tonnes	8.5
Sheep wool	58,000 tonnes	0.1
of which sheep wool	56,000 tonnes	1.0
cashmere	2,614 tonnes	8.0

Large animals in stock during mid-year	7.566 million	-2.0
during year end	6.824 million	-0.5
Sheep in stock during mid-year	40.389 million	2.5
by year end	30.281 million	5.9
Hogs in stock during mid-year	9.158 million	6.0
by year end	7.402 million	7.9

A continued increase was registered in the production of aquatic products. The output of aquatic products during the year totalled 42,000 tonnes, up 10 percent over the previous year. An accelerated development trend in freshwater aquatic products was maintained throughout the entire region.

The conditions for agricultural and animal husbandry production were further improved. By the end of the year, the total power of farm machinery amounted to 8.583 million kw, up 2.9 percent over the previous year; there were 36,000 large and medium tractors, a decline of 6.2 percent; 305,000 small tractors were up 6.1 percent; there were 12,000 heavy-duty trucks for agricultural use, a decline of 0.4 percent; mechanized farming areas totalled 3.184 million hectares, up 2.5 percent; and the electricity consumption of the rural and pastoral areas totalled 1.55 billion kwh, up 14.8 percent. The application of chemical fertilizers (100 percent effective content equivalent) totalled 447,000 tonnes, a decline of 1.5 percent. Continued efforts were made to strengthen the construction of farmland and water conservancy projects. Irrigation and drainage equipment at the end of the year totalled 1.462 million kw, up 0.8 percent over the year-end figure of the previous year; there were 193,000 power-operated wells, up 2.7 percent; and effectively irrigated farming areas increased, totalling 1.755 million hectares.

II. Industry and Building Industry

In 1994, the entire region's industrial production continued to increase quite rapidly. The added-value of industry during the year totalled 20.31 billion yuan, up 13.9 percent over the previous year, of which the added-value of light industry totalled 5.45 billion yuan, up 18.9 percent, and that of heavy industry 14.88 percent, up 11.8 percent; this showed that the increase in light industry was quicker than that of heavy industry. Of the entire industry, the added-value of state-owned industry increased by 8.9 percent, and that of nonstate industry by 30 percent. The growth rate of nonstate industry was quicker than the state-owned industry by 21.1 percentage points. The proportion of the added-value of nonstate industry to the total added-value of the entire industry rose from 23.6 percent in the previous year to 26.9 percent.

continued...

MONGOLIA REGION STATISTICAL COMMUNIQUE, 1994 (continued)

The output of major industrial products was as follows:

	1994	Percentage Increase Over 1993
Chemical fiber	7,000 tonnes	-7.5
Yarn	19,000 tonnes	7.0
Cloth	90.980 million meters	8.0
Knitting wool	4,000 tonnes	14.0
Machine-made paper and paperboard	144,000 tonnes	6.5
Sugar	179,000 tonnes	-32.1
Salt	1.063 million tonnes	-2.9
Cigarettes	303,000 boxes	-4.7
Synthetic detergents	12,000 tonnes	11.8
Color television sets	305,000	33.2
Video sets	4,000	100.0
Coal	55.120 million tonnes	7.1
Crude oil	1.588 million tonnes	57.2
Electricity	25.94 billion kwh	10.5
Steel	3.358 million tonnes	-2.6
Rolled steel	2.609 million tonnes	6.6
Ten kinds of nonferrous metals	82,000 tonnes	12.7
Rare-earth concentrate	23,000 tonnes	65.5
Cement	3.008 million tonnes	-15.8
Timber	4.623 million cubic meters	-1.9
Plate glass	3.829 million heavy boxes	12.3
Sulfuric acid	90,000 tonnes	10.7
Soda ash	157,000 tonnes	44.7
Synthetic ammonia	108,000 tonnes	28.6
Chemical fertilizers (100 percent of effective composition)	173,000 tonnes	27.8
Plastics	10,000 tonnes	7.2
Alternating electric motors	429,000 kw	-16.9
Small tractors	5,000	20.6

Although the increase rate of regional industrial production was fairly rapid, the economic returns of industrial enterprises were not good enough. In 1994, the composite efficiency index of industrial enterprises at or above the township level that exercised independent accounting was 80.55, lower than the level of the previous year. Stockpiles of industrial products were fairly greater, the number of enterprises sustaining losses was relatively great, and the defaults owed to each other were comparatively serious. Therefore, efforts are needed to improve the economic efficiency of industry with a view to effecting simultaneous increases in production and efficiency.

Affected by the control over investment demands, the increase rate of construction production slowed down. In 1994, the added value of the construction industry was 5.30 billion yuan, up 7.9 percent over the previous year. The total floor space of buildings under construction by state-owned construction enterprises was 4.659 million square meters, a decrease of 13.7 percent, with 1.81 million square meters completed during the year, a decrease of 10.4 percent. The overall labor productivity was 21,274 yuan per person, a decrease of 12.4 percent

III. Investment in Fixed Assets

Investment in fixed assets was put under effective control. The regional investment in fixed assets in 1994 came to 24.94 billion yuan, an increase of 14.7 percent over the previous year (or a real increase of 7.5 percent allowing for price increases), with the increase margin declining by 31 percentage points from that of the previous year. Of this, the investment in projects of state-owned units, Chinese-foreign joint ventures, and cooperative units amounted to 12.26 billion yuan, up 10.8 percent, while that of the collective sector of the economy amounted to 720 million yuan, up 5.9 percent; individual investment made by urban and rural residents totalled 3.07 billion yuan, up 54.1 percent. The relatively rapid decline in the increase rate of investment resulted from the restriction on the investment scale in local and central projects. As regards the investment of state-owned units, Chinese-foreign joint ventures, and cooperative units, the investment in capital construction was 14.90 billion yuan, up 11.6 percent; that in technological transformation and equipment renewal projects was 5.2 billion yuan, up 27.5 percent; and that in real estate development was 820 million yuan, a decline of 30.7 percent.

Notable results were achieved in the macroeconomic regulating and control measures. We started 1,868 new capital construction and technical transformation projects in the year, a decline of 36 percent from the preceding year. The investment pattern was adjusted in such a way that priority of investment was given to energy, raw material, transportation, warehouse storage, post, and telecommunications industries. In the investment of state-owned enterprises, Chinese-foreign joint ventures, and associated enterprises, the investment in the energy industry rose from 35.3 percent in the preceding year to 37.1 percent, of which the investment in the electric power industry rose from 37.7 percent to 50.3 percent; that of the raw material industry increased from 16.5 percent to 20.9 percent, of which the investment in the equipment renewal and technical transformation of the metallurgical industry increased from 40.3 to 57.2 percent; and that of transportation, warehouse storage, post, and telecommunications industries grew from 13.9 percent to 14.7 percent. However, the investment in agriculture declined, accounting for merely 0.4 percent, down 0.1 percentage point from the preceding year.

continued...

MONGOLIA REGION STATISTICAL COMMUNIQUE, 1994 (continued)

Key construction projects made new headway. Forty-six large and medium-sized capital construction projects were under construction in the year, an increase of one from the preceding year. Of them, three whole projects and 13 single-item projects were completed and commissioned. Thirty-three equipment renewal and technical transformation projects, whose investment exceeded the stipulated norms, were under construction, an increase of four from the preceding year. Of them, 13 whole projects were completed and commissioned. New production capacity resulting from the major projects that were completed and commissioned totally or partly included the 1 million tonnes of oil extracting capacity of the Horqin Oil Field and the 200,000-kilowatt generating capacity of the Haibowan Power Industry Company Limited.

A new increase was registered in the overall production capacity. In the whole year, 1,843 capital construction, equipment renewal, and technical transformation projects were completed and commissioned. They increased the coal mining capacity by 1.5 million tonnes, oil extracting capacity by 1 million tonnes, power generating capacity by 420,000 kilowatts, timber production capacity by 110,000 cubic meters, iron smelting capacity by 10,000 tonnes, cement production capacity by 150,000 tonnes, caustic soda production capacity by 4,770 tonnes, beer production capacity by 10,000 tonnes, and railways by 145 km.

IV. Transportation, Post, and Telecommunication

Transportation continued to grow. The annual added value of transportation was 4.89 billion yuan, up 11.3 percent from the preceding year. However, the restrictions imposed by transportation on economic development still existed.

The volume of transportation is listed as follows:

	1994	Percentage Increase Over 1993
Volume of freight transport		
Railway	60.79 billion tonne/km	11.2
Highway (transportation departments)	370 million tonne/km	-24.5
Volume of passenger transport		
Railway	7.8 billion person/km	4.8
Highway (transportation departments)	2.1 billion person/km	-51.6
Civil airlines	1.02 billion person/km	1.3times

Post and telecommunications service developed rapidly. The annual added value was 650 million yuan, up 45.0 percent from the preceding year. Total business transactions grew by 48.9 percent. Letters to and from other places of the country, foreign countries, Hong Kong, and Macao totaled 108.578 million, and long-distance calls totaled 76.228 million, up 13.80 and 57.0 percent, respectively, from the preceding year. Both paging and mobile telephone service increased by over 100 percent. Program-controlled local telephone exchanges accounted for 88.2 percent. The year-end number of telephone subscribers totaled 409,000, up 62.95 percent; of which private telephone subscribers reached 266,000, up 1.2 times. Computerized management of postal work was also upgraded to a new level in Inner Mongolia.

V. Domestic Trade and Market Prices

The domestic consumer goods markets were quite stable. The retail sales of consumer goods in society during the year totaled 24.4 billion yuan, up 20.7 percent over the previous year, showing an actual increase of 1.2 percent if the price factors were deducted. Of this, the retail sales of consumer goods in the urban areas totaled 14.62 billion yuan, up 21.8 percent; and the retail sales of consumer goods in counties and below totaled 9.78 billion yuan, up 19.1 percent.

The retail sales of consumer goods in various economic sectors increased comprehensively, and in particular, the nonstate commercial units enjoyed brisker sales. The retail sales of consumer goods of state-owned commercial sector increased by 9.7 percent over the previous year, that of collective commercial sector, 15.8 percent, that of private commercial sector, 23 times, and that of other commercial sectors, 37.6 percent. In the total retail sales of consumer goods in society, the proportion of nonstate commercial sector rose from 52.5 percent in the previous year to 56.8 percent, and that of the state-owned commercial sector, dropped from 47.5 percent to 43.2 percent.

Of the sales of various kinds of major consumer goods sold by domestic large and medium-sized commercial enterprises, the sales of food commodities increased, of which grain increased by 15.5 percent, edible cereal oil, 30 percent, and fresh eggs, five times; and the sales of clothing and durable consumer goods declined, of which, the sales of all kinds of clothes, dropped by 13.2 percent, color television sets, 25.7 percent, refrigerators, 11.7 percent, washing machines, 22.3 percent, and bicycles, 12.8 percent.

The market for the means of production was quite stable. The sales of the means of production in society during the year totaled 9.5 billion yuan, up 37.9 percent over the previous year, showing an actual increase of 18 percent if the price factors were deducted.

Owing to the issuance of some policy-related price adjustments of the state and some macroeconomic reform measures that affected the commodity prices, affected by the stagnant situation resulted from the overly rapid increase in the social demands of the

continued...

MONGOLIA REGION STATISTICAL COMMUNIQUE, 1994 (continued)

previous two years, buffeted by commodity prices outside the region, and caused by the imperfect price management mechanism and various factors, the general price level continued to rise by a large margin and became the most prominent problem in the economic life.

The Percentage Increase in Prices of Commodities in 1994 Over Previous Year

1. Cost of living prices for residents	22.9
of which, urban areas	24.3
rural and pastoral areas	21.3
2. Retail prices of commodities	19.3
of which, urban areas	19.6
rural and pastoral areas	18.8
of which, food	33.3
grain	42.7
edible cereal oil	72.2
clothing, shoes, hats	17.2
textile products	11.6
article for daily use	10.6
cultural and recreational articles	9.1
books, newspapers, magazines	32.4
medicines and medical goods	11.4
building and decoration materials	9.3
fuels	4.9
3. Service prices	
of which, urban areas	38.8
rural and pastoral areas	32.6
4. Retail prices of means of agricultural production	22.6
5. Producer's prices of manufactured goods	12.1
6. Purchasing prices of energy, raw materials	16.8

VI. Foreign Economic Exchange

Affected by various factors, foreign trade declined. In 1994, the total volume of import and export was $1.06 billion, a drop of 12 percent from the previous year. Of this, the volume of export was $590 million, a drop of 9.2 percent; and that of import, $470 million, a drop of 16 percent. Spot exchange trade witnessed a powerful trend of increase. In 1994, the export volume of spot exchange trade was $410 million, up by 46.9 percent.

Some results were achieved in the utilization of foreign capital. In 1994, 226 new agreements were signed in the region on the utilization of foreign capital, involving a total value of $187.79 million. By the end of 1994, 926 foreign-invested enterprises of the three types had registered in the region, 192 more than the figure at the end of the previous year.

New progress was made in economic and technological cooperation with foreign countries. In 1994, construction projects and labor service projects contracted by the region with foreign countries totaled 22, involving $3.96 million in value. The business volume completed by these projects totaled $1.335 million.

Tourism developed with remarkable results. In 1994, the region received 317,000 foreigners, overseas Chinese and Chinese compatriots from Taiwan, Hong Kong, and Macao for sightseeing, visits, business, or other activities, of whom, 312,000 were foreigners. Income of foreign exchange from tourism amounted to $87.50 million. All these figures doubled those of the previous year.

VII. Finance, Banking, and Insurance

Noticeable results were achieved in increasing revenues and reducing expenditures. In 1994, the region's financial revenues totaled 6.81 billion yuan (excluding the special revenues from the power facilities construction fund and the social insurance fund), an increase of 16.8 percent over the previous year, if calculated in terms of the same price. Of this, the revenues organized by localities amounted to 3.63 billion yuan, up by 20.9 percent over the previous year (industrial and commercial taxes amounted to 2.55 billion yuan, up by 14.4 percent); and the revenues from consumption tax and added value tax that were handed over the central authorities amounted to 3.18 billion yuan. The region's expenditures totaled 9.28 billion yuan (excluding the special allocations used as the power facilities construction fund and the social insurance fund), an increase of 5.2 percent over the previous year. Of this, the allocations for capital construction projects amounted to 590 million yuan, a drop of 4.6 percent, the allocations for tapping potentials of enterprises and for carrying out technological transformation amounted to 1.03 billion yuan, a drop of 20.9 percent; the expenses in administration operation amounted to 1.30 billion yuan, up by 20.0 percent; the funds allocated for aiding agricultural production and for operating agricultural, forestry, water conservancy, and meteorological departments amounted to 1.05 billion yuan, up by 11.5 percent; the appropriations for operating scientific, educational, cultural, and public health undertakings amounted to 2.52 billion yuan, up by 20.4 percent; and the allocations for price subsidies amounted to 610 million yuan, a drop of 10.1 percent.

The banking situation was increasingly stable, and remarkable increases were registered in both savings deposits and loan issuance. By the end of 1994, the savings deposits of banks in the region totaled 45.38 billion yuan, an increase of 11.16 billion yuan over the figure at the beginning of 1994, or an increase of 32.6 percent over the figure at the end of 1993. Of this,

continued...

MONGOLIA REGION STATISTICAL COMMUNIQUE, 1994 (continued)

savings deposits of enterprises totaled 10.21 billion yuan, an increase of 2.19 billion yuan over the figure at the beginning of 1994, or an increase of 27.2 percent over the figure at the end of 1993. By the end of 1994, loans issued by various banks amounted to 67.41 billion yuan, an increase of 14.46 billion yuan over the beginning of 1994, or an increase of 27.3 percent over the figure at the end of 1993. By the end of 1994, savings deposits of urban and rural residents amounted to 31.88 billion yuan, up by 8.86 billion yuan over the figure at the beginning of 1994, or up by 37.3 percent over the figure at the end of 1993. In 1994, the cash revenue of banks totaled 95.65 billion yuan, up by 40.6 percent over 1993, and the cash expenditure of banks amounted to 105.46 billion yuan, up by 38.0 percent. In addition, the money supplied in 1994 totaled 9.81 billion yuan, up by 16.9 percent over the previous year.

Further development was made in insurance service. The annual premium income of insurance companies totaled 710 million yuan, up 29.1 percent from the preceding year; and domestic and foreign insurance coverage totaled 121 billion yuan, up 7.6 percent. Over 17,000 enterprises, 180,000 motor vehicles, 737,000 families, and 4.759 million people participated in various categories of insurance programs. Total assets of various insurance properties reached 75.3 billion yuan, up 5.6 percent. Insurance companies of various categories and at various levels took 199,000 cases of claims of property loss, up 51.9 percent; and they paid an indemnity of 300 million yuan, up 64.7 percent. They paid another 110 million yuan as reparations in life insurance programs, down 15.5 percent.

VIII. Science and Technology, Education, Culture, Public Health, and Sports

Scientific and technological undertakings continued to develop. Thanks to the increasingly close coordination of science and technology with economic construction, science and technology played a more and more important role in Inner Mongolia's economic development. The region won 380 scientific and technological achievements in the year, of which 139 were significant achievements and 139 were awarded by regional-level departments. We received 731 patent applications in the year and approved 337. Science and technology markets became increasingly vigorous in the region, with 1,654 science and technology contracts worth 190 million yuan signed. Of these contracts, 670 contracts worth 56.35 million yuan were signed between the departments in the region. We carried out 95 technology export projects worth 17.66 million yuan, and 889 technology import projects worth 120 million yuan. The year-end number of technology trade organizations engaged in technological development, technology transfer, technical consultation, and technical service was 769, and they were staffed with 21,000 personnel, up 46.5 and 31.3 percent, respectively, from the year-end figures of 1993. The contingent of scientific and technical personnel was expanded continuously. By the end of the year, Inner

Mongolia's state-owned units had 458,000 technical personnel of various specialties, up 0.7 percent from the year-end number of 1993. Of the total, 99,000 were scientific personnel of minority nationalities, up 3.1 percent from the 1993 year-end number; and 351,000 were engaged in natural sciences, up 61 percent.

Educational undertakings of various categories continued to be consolidated and developed, and the education of minority nationalities was further intensified. We enrolled 163 new postgraduate students in the year to make the year-end number of postgraduate students 390, an increase of 18 over the 1993 year-end figure. Regular schools of higher learning enrolled 11,000 new students to attend regular and specialized courses, making the year-end number of college students 39,000, of whom 8,749 were students of minority nationalities, and 7,942 were students of Mongolian nationality. In the year, 9,695 students graduated from schools of higher learning, an increase of 1,032 from the preceding year. Adult schools of higher learning had 17,000 students, of whom 3,576 were students of minority nationalities. Adult secondary specialized schools and technical training schools had 1.349 million students, of whom 8,558 were students of minority nationalities. Secondary specialized schools enrolled 18,000 new students in the year, 15,000 students graduated from these schools, and the year-end number of students at these schools was 55,000, of whom 14,000 were students of minority nationalities. Secondary vocational schools had 140,000 students, of whom 55,000 were students of vocational senior high schools. The compulsory education was extended gradually. At the end of the year, ordinary senior high schools had 228,000 students, ordinary junior high schools had 944,000 students, and primary schools had 2.352 million students. Among these three categories of schools, 35,000, 192,000, and 520,000, respectively, were students of minority nationalities. Conditions were also improved for running primary and high schools. The school attendance rate of school-age children totaled 98.5 percent.

Cultural undertakings developed rapidly. By the end of the year, the region as a whole had 1,054 film institutes and organs with 7,571 employees; produced two feature films and dubbed 33 Mongolian films. There were 951 film projecting units of various kinds by the end of the year, 173 art institutes and organs with 6,966 employees, and 118 art performing troupes, of which, 61 were red cultural teams. There were 101 cultural centers, 16 museums, and 137 large archives. At the end of the year, the region as a whole had 42 radio stations, 47 radio transmission and relay stations, and the radio coverage rate reached 75 percent. The region also had 29 television stations, 951 television transmission and relay stations, and the television coverage rate reached 75 percent. The autonomous region as well as the leagues and cities published 166.92 million copies of newspapers during the year, of which, 792 copies were of Mongolian edition; published 10.86 million copies of magazines of various kinds, of which, 147 copies were of Mongolian

continued...

MONGOLIA REGION STATISTICAL COMMUNIQUE, 1994 (continued)

edition; published 52 million copies of books, of which, 7.47 million were of Mongolian edition.

Public health undertakings were steadily developed. By the end of the year the region as a whole had 4,918 public health organs, of which, 2,000 were hospitals of Chinese traditional medicines, an increase of 13 hospitals over the previous year, and 1,608 hospitals in the rural and pastoral areas. The whole region had 63,000 hospital beds in the medical and health-care units by the end of the year, of which, 33,000 hospital beds were in the medical and health-care units in the rural and pastoral areas. By the end of the year there were 102,000 medical and health workers, of whom, 90,000 were high-grade health workers, representing an increase of 2 percent and 3.4 percent respectively over the previous year. Among the high-grade health workers, 49,000 were doctors, up 4.3 percent over the previous year, of whom 3,000 were Mongolian doctors.

Gratifying results were made in sports undertakings. In the major competitions at home and abroad during the year, our athletes won 85 championships. At the 12th Asian Games held in Hiroshima, we sent 10 athletes to participate in the competitions, and won seven medals, of which, two were gold medals, one was silver, and four were bronze. Our athletes broke nine regional records during the year. A total of 1.91 million people met the "National Standards for Physical Exercise" and 1,810 athletes were graded as athletes, of whom, 329 were athletes of minority nationalities.

IX. Population and People's Living Standards

Good results were made family planning work and the natural population growth rate was effectively brought under control. The region's birth rate during the year reached 18.98 per 1,000, the death rate, 6.50 per 1,000, and the natural population growth rate, 12.48 per thousand, up 0.83 percentage points over the previous year. The population of the whole region during the end of the year totalled 22.605 million, an increase of 280,000 people over the year-end figure of the previous year, up 1.25 percent.

The income of urban and rural residents continued to increase and the people's living standards unceasingly enhanced. The annual average per-capita income for living expenses of the urban residents totalled 2,275 yuan, up 32.9 percent over the previous year, showing an actual increase of 6.9 percent if the price rise factors were excluded. The annual average per capita net income of peasants and herdsmen totalled 1,062 yuan, up 28.1 percent over the previous year, showing an actual increase of 4.8 percent if the price rise factors were deducted. Of this, the average per-capita net income of peasants was 970 yuan, up 24.7 percent, and that of herdsmen, 1,664 yuan, up 43 percent, showing an actual increase of 1.8 percent and 18.3 percent, respectively, excluding the price rise factors.

The number of durable consumer goods owned per 100 urban and rural households were as follows:

	Urbanite		Peasant		Herdsman	
	1994	1993	1994	1993	1994	1993
Television sets	107	104	79	72	64	62
Color TV sets	78	80	14	12	11	10
Refrigerators	40	39	1	0	1	0
Electric fans	34	31	3	2	0	0
Washing machines	85	84	17	15	11	7
Tape recorders	61	67	26	24	62	61
Motorcycles	7	5	2	1	39	31

New headway was made in employment. Contingents of staff members and workers steadily developed. Jobs were arranged for some 89,000 urbanites during the year. There were 3.882 million staff members and workers by the end of the year, a drop of 1.2 percent from the previous year. Of this, 3.056 million staff members and workers were employed by state-owned units, up 0.5 percent; and 770,000 staff members and workers by collective units, a drop of 11.6 percent.

Staff members and workers' wages further improved. The total annual volume of wages for workers totaled 13.64 billion yuan, up 25.5 percent. Of this, that of workers at state-owned units reached 11.46 billion yuan, up 27 percent (bonuses reached 1.44 billion yuan, up 7.2 percent); and that of workers at collective units, 2.01 billion yuan, up 11.8 percent. The per-capita wages of the region's staff members and workers reached 3,493 yuan, an increase of 26 percent. Of this, the per capita wages of the workers at state units reached 2,759 yuan and those at collective units reached 2,451 yuan, up 25.9 percent and 20.9 percent, respectively.

Urban and rural dwellers' housing conditions continued to improve. Some 2.013 million square meters of houses were built during the year. Some 7.805 million square meters of houses in rural and pastoral areas were built, up 21.4 percent.

Social welfare undertakings developed with each passing day. There were 20,200 beds in social welfare homes of various categories, caring for 15,000 people, both registering. an increase of 0.3 percent. State relief helped 1.749 million people in the region's urban and rural areas, a drop of 4 percent. The staff and worker old-age insurance covered 39.6 percent of the whole society.

Environmental protection undertakings further developed. At the end of the year, the region's environmental protection system had an employment of 2,000 people and the region had 61 environmental monitoring stations at various levels and 1,200 environment monitors. There were 13 nature-preservation areas, including four state-level ones and 9 regional-level ones. Fifty smoke and dust control areas covering 155 square kilometers were built by the end of the year. Thirty-six areas, covering 112.8 square kilometers, attained noise-free standards. A total of 107 projects for improving environmental pollution were completed within fixed time, and 16.53 million yuan were invested in these projects.

Neimenggu Ribao, 10 Mar 1995.

INNER MONGOLIA COMMUNIQUE ON TERTIARY INDUSTRY, 1992

In June 1993, the State Council decided to conduct the first survey on the tertiary industry throughout the nation. Thanks to the unified leadership of the autonomous regional government, the great attention given by the people's governments at all levels, the great coordination of relevant departments, and the hard efforts and the diligent work of the large number of workers for the survey, notable achievements were won in Inner Mongolia's survey on the tertiary industry for the designated period. Spot inspections showed that the quality of the data provided by the survey was up to the stipulated requirements. The first group of data on the region's survey on the tertiary industry are given as follows:

1. The Number of Units of the Tertiary Industry

Materials collected from the survey on the tertiary industry showed that by the end of 1992, the region's units engaged in the tertiary industry had totaled 330,300, 100,400 of which were enterprises, institutions, and administrative units, and 229,900 were urban and rural private household businesses. Among these enterprises, institutions, and administrative units, those exercising independent accounting numbered 60,900, and those whose accounting was done individually numbered 39,500. Compared with 1991, the number of the units engaged in the tertiary industry throughout the region increased by 18.80 percent, with the increase in those exercising independent accounting registered at 6.87 percent, those whose accounting was done individually registered at 8.21 percent, and those in urban and rural individual household businesses registered at 24.57 percent.

In terms of ownership, among the units engaged in the tertiary industry throughout the region, 54,400 were state-owned, accounting for 16.48 percent of the total; 1,500 were collective, accounting for 12.57 percent; and 500 were private, accounting for 0.14 percent, by the end of 1992. Compared with 1991, state-owned units grew by 5.56 percent, collective units by 9.56 percent, and private units by 94.04 percent.

	1992 Number	1992 Percentage	1991 Number	1991 Percentage
Total	330,000	100.00	278,069	100.00
State-owned sector	54,438	16.48	51,573	18.55
Collective sector	41,514	12.57	37,893	13.63
Private sector	456	0.14	235	0.08
Individual sector	229,961	69.61	184,607	66.39
Joint management sector	93	0.03	48	0.02
Share-holding sector	54	0.02	27	0.01
Foreign-funded sector	12	...	6	...
Hong Kong-, Macao-, and Taiwan-funded sector	19	...	6	...
Other sectors	3,786	1.15	3,674	1.32

In terms of the branches of the tertiary industry, state organs, party and government organs, and social groups accounted for the largest part, 31.53 percent, of all the 12 branches (excluding urban and rural individual household businesses).

	Number	Percentage
Total	100,372	100.00
Agricultural, forestry, animal husbandry, fishery service	5,258	5.24
Geological survey and water conservancy management	1,218	1.21
Transportation, warehouse, and post and telecommunication	2,630	2.62
Wholesale and retail trade and catering service	26,893	26.79
Financial service and insurance	4,004	3.99
Real estate service	486	0.49
Social service	4,605	4.59
Health, sports, social welfare	4,499	4.48
Education, culture, art, and radio and television service	17,023	16.96

continued...

INNER MONGOLIA COMMUNIQUE ON TERTIARY INDUSTRY, 1992 (continued)

	Number	Percentage
Scientific research and multipurpose technical service	798	0.80
State organs, party and government organs, social groups	31,651	31.53
Others	1,307	1.30

Among the individual household businesses engaged in the tertiary industry, those engaged in commerce accounted for the largest number—51.72 percent—in 1992.

	Number	Percentage		Number	Percentage
Total	229,961	100.00	Service trade	20,690	9.00
Transportation	51,535	22.41	Repair trade	14,448	6.28
Commerce	118,933	51.72	Other trades	5,677	2.47
Catering trade	18,678	8.12			

In terms of the year the units opened, 223,800 units opened businesses in 1990 or before, 47,600 in 1991, and 58,900 in 1992.

2. The Number of Employees of the Tertiary Industry

By the end of 1992, 2,503,200 persons were engaged in the tertiary industry in Inner Mongolia. Of the total, 2,135,200 were employees of enterprises, institutions, and administrative units, and 368,000 were employees of urban and rural individual household businesses. Among the employees of enterprises, institutions, and administrative units, 1,657,900 belonged to the units exercising independent accounting, and 477,300 belonged to those whose accounting was done individually. Compared with 1991, the total number of the employees of the tertiary industry rose by 8.53 percent, with those of the units exercising independent accounting increasing by 5.48 percent, those of the units whose accounting was done individually increasing by 7.35 percent, and those of individual household businesses increasing by 26.85 percent.

In terms of ownership, by the end of 1992, 1,630,800 persons belonged to the state-owned sector, accounting for 65.15 percent of the total; 484,500 persons belonged to the collective sector, accounting for 19.36 percent; and 4,900 persons belonged to the private sector, accounting for 0.20 percent. Compared with 1991, the employees of the state-owned sector grew by 4.88 percent, those of the collective sector by 8.63 percent, and those of the private sector by 81.48 percent.

	1992 Number of Employees	Percentage	1991 Number of Employees	Percentage
Total	2,503,200	100.00	2,306,500	100.00
State-owned sector	1,630,800	65.15	1,554,900	67.41
Collective sector	484,500	19.36	446,000	19.34
Private sector	4,900	0.20	2,700	0.11
Individual sector	368,000	14.70	290,100	12.58
Joint management sector	1,300	0.05	600	0.03
Shareholding sector	1,100	0.04	600	0.03
Foreign-funded sector	300	0.01	100	...
Hong Kong-, Macao-, and Taiwan-funded sector	1,300	0.05	900	0.04
Other	11,000	0.44	10,600	0.46

In terms of the 12 branches of the tertiary industry, wholesale and retail trade as well as catering trade had the largest number of employees, who accounted for 26.08 percent of the total, in 1992.

	Number of Employees	Percentage
Total	2,135,200	100.00

continued...

INNER MONGOLIA COMMUNIQUE ON TERTIARY INDUSTRY, 1992 (continued)

	Number of Employees	Percentage
Agricultural, forestry, animal husbandry, and fishery service	70, 100	3.28
Geological survey and water conservancy management	49,800	2.33
Transportation, warehouse, and post and telecommunication	278,200	13.03
Wholesale and retail trade and catering service	556,800	26.08
Financial service and insurance	69,800	3.27
Real estate service	12,400	0.58
Social service	109,500	5.13
Health, sports, social welfare	124,400	5.83
Education, culture, art, and radio and television service	405,700	19.00
Scientific research and multipurpose technical service	33,900	1.59
State organs, party and government organs, and social groups	363,900	17.04
Others	60,700	2.84

Among the individual household businesses engaged in the tertiary industry, those engaged in commerce had the largest number of employees, accounting for 47.69 percent of the total, by the end of 1992.

	Number of Employees	Percentage		Number of Employees	Percentage
Total	368,000	100.00	Service trade	32,700	8.89
Transportation	73,600	20.00	Repair trade	19,300	5.24
Commerce	175,500	47.69	Others	9,200	2.50
Catering trade	57,700	15.68			

In terms of the year the businesses were opened, 2,233,000 persons belonged to the units that opened in or before 1990, 110,600 persons belonged to those opened in 1991, and 159,600 persons belonged to those opened in 1992.

3. Income and Expenditure of the Tertiary Industry

Results of the survey showed that in 1992, the business income of enterprises (including the institutions which implemented the accounting system of enterprises) totaled 18.641 billion yuan, up 18.60 percent from 1991; their sales (business) taxes totaled 971 million yuan, up 17.70 percent; and their business profits totaled 1.563 billion yuan, up 0.32 percent. The expenditure of administrative units and institutions totaled 9.119 billion yuan in 1992, up 16.43 percent from 1991.

In the situation of individual household businesses, the business income of the individual household businesses engaged in the tertiary industry totaled 3.504 billion yuan in 1992, and their tax payment totaled 279 million yuan, up 41.52 and 42.35 percent, respectively, from 1991.

Neimenggu Ribao, 1 Jan 1995.

TIANJIN'S STATISTICAL COMMUNIQUE, 1994

In 1994, the people on all fronts of the municipality worked with one heart and soul and through arduous struggle under the leadership of the municipal party committee and government and fulfilled all targets and tasks well. The national economy developed in a sustained, fast, and healthy manner, and the development of the national economy ranked the province among the country's best. A key breakthrough was made in reform and opening up. Key progress and achievement were made in implementing the "three-five-eight-ten" goal and "two-two-two project." Society was stable, all undertakings were developed comprehensively, and the people's livelihood was further improved. The municipality's gross domestic product was

continued...

TIANJIN'S STATISTICAL COMMUNIQUE, 1994 (continued)

expected to reach 72.119 billion yuan, up 13.5 percent over 1993 and reaching a record high in the past 10 years. Of this, the added value of the tertiary industry was 26.801 billion yuan, up 14.4 percent and accounting for 37.2 percent of the gross domestic product. Revenues came to 9.599 billion yuan, up 31.2 percent over 1993 and at a peak year since the implementation of the reform and open policies. Major economic problems were that the municipality failed to make a fundamental breakthrough in enlivening state-owned enterprises, the agricultural foundation was comparatively weak, the prices of major foodstuffs rose excessively, and some staff members and workers and the peasants of the poverty-stricken villages still lived a hard life.

1. Agriculture
Agricultural production developed in a sustained way. The added value of agriculture came to 4.578 billion yuan, up 5 percent over the previous year. Despite the comparatively serious natural disasters, the municipality reaped a fairly good grain harvest. The total grain output reached 1,903,200 tons. Noticeable achievements were made in building the "vegetable basket" project. The output of major food items increased by a big margin.
The output of major farm and sideline products was as follows:

	1994	Percent Increase Over 1993		1994	Percent Increase Over 1993
Grain (tn)	1,903,200	-4.7	Milk (tn)	98,600	3.3
Cotton (tn)	9,300	22.5	Aquatic products (tn)	128.300	12.6
Oil-bearing			Of this: fresh-		
crops (tn)	40,300	-9.3	water pro-		
Fruits (tn)	172,500	8.7	ducts	106,900	12.9
Vegetables (tn)	4,078,600	15.1	Hogs in stock at		
Meat (tn)	184,500	19.5	year end		
Of this: pork	105,500	14.5	(head)	905,200	18.4
Poultry and			Hogs slaugh-		
eggs (tn)	249,300	15.9	tered (head)	1,395,600	11.7

Agricultural production conditions further improved. The aggregate capacity of farm machinery reached 5,043,400 kilowatts, up 7.3 percent over the previous year; there were 25,300 trucks, up 5.9 percent; and the rural areas' power consumption volume reached 2,506 million kilowatt hours, up 8.4 percent.
The rural economy comprehensively developed. In 1994, the total output value of the municipality's rural society came to 91.8 billion yuan, up 41.5 percent over the previous year. Of this, the total agricultural output value was 6.525 billion yuan, up 7.8 percent. The total output value of town and township enterprises reached 76 billion yuan, up 40 percent.

2. Industry and Building Industry
Industrial production increased at a faster speed. In 1994, the added value of the municipality's industry was 37.28 billion yuan, up 14.7 percent over 1993. Total industrial output value reached 154.2 billion yuan, up 23.7 percent. To suit the demands for the development of the market economy, the municipality comprehensively developed various sectors of the economy. The output value of the state-owned industrial enterprises (including the three types of foreign-funded enterprises, shareholding enterprises, and integrated enterprises with Chinese investment) increased by 14.3 percent; that of three types of foreign-funded industrial enterprises, 94.8 percent; that of the township-run industrial enterprises, 41.5 percent; and that of large and medium-sized industrial enterprises, eight percent.
The industrial composition was further adjusted. In 1994, the output value of the industries at and above the town ship level totaled 99.297 billion yuan, up 18.3 percent from the preceding year. Of the total, the output value of heavy industry came to 55.08 billion yuan, up 13.8 percent; and that of light industry 44.217 billion yuan, up 24.4 percent. The ratio of light industry to heavy

continued...

TIANJIN'S STATISTICAL COMMUNIQUE, 1994 (continued)

industry changed from 42.3 percent to 57.7 percent in the preceding year to 44.5 percent to 55.5 percent.

The output of the major industrial products was as follows:

	1994	Percent Increase Over 1993
Natural gas (mn cu m)	746	14.3
Crude oil (mn tn)	5.888	13.8
Crude salt (tn)	2, 135,600	-3.9
Electricity (bn kwh)	12.54	2.3
Pig iron (tn)	1,511,700	0.4
Steel (tn)	1,850,700	-14.3
Steel products (tn)	1,956,900	-6.2
Cement (tn)	1,557,400	-0.3
Plate glass (mn weight boxes)	4.07	83.8
Soda ash (tn)	628,200	0.5
Caustic soda (tn)	287,400	1.7
Machine-made paper and paperboard (tn)	207,600	-10.8
Chemical fertilizer (tn)	93,900	8.7
Plastics (tn)	159,400	5.2
Plastic products (tn)	72,200	0.6
Dyestuff (tn)	20.900	-53.3
Chemical fiber (tn)	88,600	6.5
Synthetic detergents (tn)	92,300	-6.9
Metal-cutting machine tools	925	-44.4
Program-controlled exchanges (lines)	1,025,200	31.0
Computers	88	-27.9
Cars	122,500	13.4
Of which: Xiali cars	58,500	22.2
Motorcycles	108,200	2.7x
Elevators	3,988	19.3
Internal-combustion engines (kw)	3,027,000	-0.2
Yarn (combined figure, tn)	110,500	-9.5
Knitting wool (tn)	5,539	13.9
Cloth (combined figure, mn m)	351	2.1
Clothes (mn pieces)	96	-11.2
Cigarettes (crates)	243,100	10.9
Cameras	78,000	16.4x
Sewing machines	132,000	14.7
Household washing machines	648,300	11.8
Household refrigerators	50,300	1.6x
Television sets	1,240,200	-8.1
Of which: Color sets	803,700	9.7
Recorders	136,300	86.5
Bicycles (mn)	2.822	-14.9

Development of new products made rapid headway. Industrial enterprises put 1,524 new products into production in 1994, which yielded 9.04 billion yuan in output value, an increase of 26.1 percent over the preceding year. The rate of new product output value rose from 15 percent in the preceding year to 16.7 percent.

continued...

TIANJIN'S STATISTICAL COMMUNIQUE, 1994 (continued)

The economic efficiency of industry was improved, and fairly good results were achieved in reducing deficits and increasing profits. The sales income of the industrial enterprises subject to independent accounting at and above the township level across the municipality totaled 101.276 billion yuan, up 32.3 percent from the preceding year; the marketing rate of their products was 97.34 percent; the profits and taxes they produced totaled 10.697 billion yuan, up 44.4 percent, of which profits stood at 4.616 billion yuan, up 57.1 percent; the profit rate of sales income rose from 3.88 percent in the preceding year to 4.56 percent; and the deficits of loss-making enterprises declined by 7.3 percent.

The building industry was further developed. In 1994, the added value of the building industry was 3.46 billion yuan, up 6.8 percent. The output value of the municipality's construction and decoration enterprises reached 11.868 billion yuan, up 54.3 percent; 10,370,300 square meters of houses were being built, up 24.5 percent; and 4,926,200 square meters of houses were completed, up 25.5 percent.

3. Domestic Commerce and Market Goods Prices

In 1994, along with the acceleration of the setup of the market system, the commodity circulation scale was further expanded, there was an ample supply of goods, and sales were brisk. The added value of the wholesale and retail sale trades and the catering trade reached 7.338 billion yuan, up 23.5 percent over the previous year.

Retail sale markets were brisk. The volume of retail sales of consumer goods totaled 30.113 billion yuan, showing an increase of 32.4 percent and registering a real increase of 14.5 percent when price factors were deducted. Of this, the volume of retail sales of food commodities increased by 49.3 percent; that of clothes, 23.4 percent; and that of daily necessities, 23 percent.

Commodity wholesale trading markets developed rapidly. The transaction volume of the wholesale trading markets of various categories reached 164.6 billion yuan, increasing by 600 percent. Of this, the transaction volume of 19 wholesale trading markets for means of production, such as Beiyang steel product market, iron and steel and furnace burden market, coal market, chemical industrial product market, textile raw material market, and vehicle market, totaled 159.457 billion yuan, increasing by 650 percent over the previous year. The transaction volume of 15 consumer goods wholesale trading markets, such as Beifang sugar market, grain market, and Dahutong Department Store, reached 5.114 billion yuan, increasing by 140 percent over the previous year. The municipality's retail sale prices were comparatively low when compared with those of the country's large and medium-sized cities.

The 1994 price index was as follows (fixing the 1993 figure as 100):

1. Urban dwellers' consumption price index	124.0
Of this: Food	128.5
Clothes	110.0
Household equipment and daily necessities	106.7
Medical treatment and health care	121.9
Transportation and communication means	100.9
Entertainment and teaching articles and stationery goods	111.4
Housing	109.1
Service items	158.4
2. Urban commodity retail sale index	115.6

4. Foreign Economic Relations and Regional Cooperation

In 1994, our municipality made a new breakthrough in opening to the outside world. The scale of using foreign capital was further expanded. International large companies and large groups vied with one another to make investment in Tianjin. In 1994, the municipality as a whole signed 1,890 items on development of three types of foreign-funded enterprises. These items involved $3.502 billion foreign capital, up 55.3 percent over the previous year; and the increase in this regard ranked the municipality first in the whole country. The number of large items noticeably

continued...

TIANJIN'S STATISTICAL COMMUNIQUE, 1994 (continued)

increased. A total of 100 items, each involving $5 million or so, were signed during the year, increasing by 120 percent over 1993. As of the end of 1994, the municipality had 8,026 foreign-funded enterprises of three types and signed agreements involving a total $7.772 billion in foreign capital. In 1994, the municipality used $1.776 billion in foreign capital, up 90.7 percent over 1993 and was at the fore of the whole country in terms of increases in this regard. Of this, $1.015 billion were directly invested by foreign businessmen, up 87.5 percent. As of the end of 1994, a total of $5.793 billion foreign capital were really used by the municipality, including $2.233 billion direct foreign investment.

Construction of the new seaside area was accelerated. Investment made in the fixed assets of this area totaled 9.999 billion yuan in 1994, up 43.7 percent from the preceding year. The gross domestic product it produced in the whole year came to 16.135 billion yuan, up 28.1 percent from the preceding year; and its industrial output value was 25.08 billion yuan, up by 42.8 percent. The development momentum of the development zone and the bonded zone remained strong. The development zone signed 487 contracts concerning the three types of foreign-funded enterprises in 1994, and the amount of foreign capital agreed upon stood at $1.523 billion, up 23.3 percent from the preceding year. The annual gross domestic product generated by the development zone showed an increase of 75.3 percent over the preceding year, the industrial output value 94 percent, and the volume of exports 86.2 percent. The bonded zone imported and exported $677 million worth of goods.

Imports and exports witnessed further development. The total value of imports and exports through the Tianjin customhouse was $16.167 billion, up 29.3 percent from the preceding year. Of the total, imports stood at $7.487 billion, up 26.9 percent, and exports $8.681 billion, up 31.5 percent. The growth rate of Tianjin's exports was the highest since the 1980's. Its annual export value totaled $2.382 billion, up 23.6 percent from the preceding year. Of this, the exports of specialized foreign trade companies came to $1.23 billion, up 8.9 percent; those of industrial and foreign trade integrated companies $333 million, up 35.5 percent; and those of the three types of foreign-funded enterprises $711 million, up 69.2 percent, and they accounted for 29.8 percent in Tianjin's entire exports as against 22.5 percent in the preceding year.

Economic and technological cooperation with foreign countries continued to develop. In 1994, 521 contracts worth $94.26 million were signed concerning construction projects and labor service cooperation abroad. Transactions totaling $60.29 million were realized.

International tourism saw rapid development. Tianjin received 128,100 overseas tourists, up 17.1 percent from the preceding year, of whom 95,500 were foreign tourists, up 30.7 percent.

Regional economic cooperation and lateral economic ties developed even more rapidly, and notable results were achieved in bringing in domestic funds through the lateral ties at home. In 1994, 765 contracts worth 4.09 billion yuan were signed concerning the cooperation at home, of which 3.345 billion yuan came from other places of the country, up 2.5 times from the preceding year.

5. Transportation, Post, and Telecommunication

Tianjin's transportation, post, and telecommunication showed further development in 1994. The annual added value of Tianjin's transportation, post, and telecommunications services totaled 6.322 billion yuan, up 15.5 percent from the preceding year.

The volume of transportation by various means was as follows:

	1994	Percent Increase Over 1993
Volume of freight (tn)	233,269,000	10.0
Of which: railway (Tianjin area, mn tn)	26.336	0.6
Highway (tn)	192,700,000	11.7

continued...

TIANJIN'S STATISTICAL COMMUNIQUE, 1994 (continued)

	1994	Percent Increase Over 1993
Waterway (mn tn)	14.21	5.5
Civil air (tn)	23,000	27.8
Turnover of freight (bn tn/km)	132.34	-1.2
Of which: railway (bn tn/km)	22.49	-14.9
Highway (bn tn/km)	4.59	0.7
Waterway (bn tn/km)	105.26	2.2
Volume of passengers (mn)	33.667	4.5
Of which: railway (Tianjin area, mn)	18.626	2.8
Highway (long-distance, mn)	14.63	6.0
Civil air	411,000	43.2
Cargo handled at the harbor (mn tn)	46.52	25.1
Of which: exported cargo (mn tn)	35.07	38.8
Imported cargo (mn tn)	11.45	-3.5

An important and great breakthrough was made in the development of post and telecommunication undertakings. Total business volume of 1994 reached 1.32 billion yuan and showed a 36.1 percent increase over 1993. Of this volume, that of postal business reached 160 million yuan and showed a 20.7 percent increase over 1993; and that of the telecommunication business reached 1.16 billion yuan and showed a 38.5 percent increase over 1993. The municipality handled 97.36 million domestic long-distance calls in 1994, which showed a 38.3 percent increase over 1993. At the end of 1994, the capacity of program-controlled telephone exchanges reached 1,137,700 lines and showed a 572,000 line increase over the figure scored at the end of 1993. The number of telephone sets totaled 960,000 and showed a 47.5 percent increase over 1993. The number of telephone sets possessed per 100 people across the municipality totaled 10.78 and showed a 3.43 fold increase over 1993.

6. Finance and Insurance Business
The undertakings of finance and insurance achieved new progress. The added value of financial and insurance business in 1994 totaled 5.726 billion yuan and showed a 15.1 percent increase over 1993. At the end of 1994, the number of various financial institutions totaled 1,987. Financial markets achieved faster development and raised 50.158 billion yuan in funds for the whole year. The volume of stock business totaled 80 billion yuan. The total volume of funds used for regulating foreign exchanges totaled $1.773 billion.

By the end of 1994, the volume of various deposits received by the financial institutions across the municipality totaled 80.056 billion yuan and showed a 21.985 billion yuan increase over the figure scored at the beginning of 1994 and a 10.009 billion yuan increase over the same period of 1993.

Tianjin Ribao, 10 Mar 1995.

HAINAN REGION STATISTICS, 1995

With the comprehensive improvement of the infrastructure, further headway was made in transport, post, and telecommunications. Added value in 1994 amounted to 2.322 billion yuan, a 14.7 percent increase over 1993.

The opening of the East Line Expressway and Fenghuang Airport to traffic and acceleration of the building of the oceangoing fleet rapidly enhanced the capacity of land, sea, and air transportation. Added value in 1994 reached 1.846 billion yuan, up 10.6 percent. The volume of transportation by various means was as follows:

continued...

HAINAN REGION STATISTICS, 1994 (continued)

	1994	Percentage Increase Over 1993
Volume of freight transport (bn tn-km)	18.92	5.5
Railway (bn tn-km)	0.207	-8.9
Highway (bn tn-km)	3.018	8.9
Waterway (bn tn-km)	15.67	5.0
Airways (bn tn-km)	0.025	120.0
Volume of passenger transport (bn person-km)	8.496	12.0
Railway (bn person-km)	0.056	18.1
Highway (bn person-km)	6.40	1.1
Waterway (bn person-km)	0.22	-2.2
Airways (bn person-km)	1.82	85.2
Volume of cargo handled by ports (mn tn)	15.12	11.4

Post and telecommunications were further modernized and the sphere of business was expanded. Added value in post and telecommunications totaled 476 million yuan, an increase of 31.2 percent over the previous year. By the end of the year, the province's postal services reached 91,700 km and 20,300 km in rural areas. Hainan had 9,800 lines for long-distance calls and 220 lines for cable. With a capacity of 315,000 switchboards in urban areas there are 216,600 urban telephone subscribers, 19,500 mobile telephone users, and 227,500 pagers. The volume of post and telecommunications trade amounted to 867 million yuan, an increase of 60.5 percent over 1993

The urban and rural markets remained brisk, with an ample supply of commodities, and consumption by inhabitants was steady. The volume of retail sales totaled 9.347 billion yuan, an increase of 28.5 percent (a real growth of 5.5 percent allowing for price hikes). Of the total, retail sales in urban areas amounted to 7.259 billion yuan, up 27.8 percent, while sales in rural areas reached 2.088 billion yuan, up 31 percent. The volume of transactions in urban and rural fairs trade was 4.763 billion yuan, up 30.2 percent. Thanks to their flexible operation, the growth in retail sales of the private and individual sectors far exceeded that in the state and collective sectors. Foreign businessmen also started to invest in the retail business. By the end of the year, Haikou had several large shopping malls which ended the history of Hainan having no large department stores. The volume of sales by various trades was as follows:

	1994 (bn yuan)	Percentage Increase Over 1993		1994 (bn yuan)	Percentage Increase Over 1993
Wholesale	5.475	21.6	Sales by farmers		
Catering	1.003	18.8	to urban		
Manufacturing	0.388	14.6	inhabitants	1.602	39.8
Other trades	0.879	99.6			

Market prices, which rose sharply along with the country's general trend, dropped gradually in the latter half of the year. The increase in retail prices was still below the national average. Compared with the previous year, the increase in prices of various products was as follows:

	Average Percentage of Price Raises in 1994	Price Increases in December Compared With Same Period Last Year
1. Retail prices	21.6	16.3
Farm materials	38.2	23.5

continued...

HAINAN REGION STATISTICS, 1994 (continued)

	Average Percentage of Price Raises in 1994	Price Increases in December Compared With Same Period Last Year
2. Inhabitants consumption	26.7	21.1
Food	32.4	23.9
Clothing	13.3	14.8
Household equipment and articles	22.4	16.3
Medicines, tonics	5.2	7.3
Transport	13.4	8.6
Amusement	7.6	5.7
Housing	21.8	16.2
Services	37.4	36.4

Foreign Trade, Economic Cooperation, and Tourism

Making the most of the advantages in the structure, Hainan opened itself wider to the outside world in 1994 and launched large-scale activities to attract foreign investors, effectively promoting Hainan's external economy and tourism.

Imports and exports continued to increase. The volume of imports and exports reached $2.697 billion in 1994, an increase of 5 percent over the previous year. Of the total, exports amounted to $0.987 billion, up 9.5 percent while imports reached $1.71 billion, up 2.6 percent.

The utilization of foreign capital was fruitful. The number of new contracts signed with foreign businessmen was fewer than in the previous year but the number of large enterprises and groups holding talks on investing in big projects increased. The projects were properly implemented and a large scale was maintained in the actual utilization of foreign capital. Hainan approved 810 contracts on the utilization of foreign capital, of which 802 were direct investments made by foreign businessmen and eight were foreign loans. The new agreements signed by Hainan on the utilization of foreign capital involved a total of $1.566 billion, of which $1.225 billion was directly invested by foreign businessmen. Foreign capital actually utilized during the year amounted to $1.289 billion, an increase of 0.2 percent, including $0.898 billion directly invested by foreign businessmen and $0.391 billion in foreign loans, an increase of 64.3 percent. Foreign government loans came from five countries. Hainan also issued 14.5 billion yen in treasury bonds in Japan. The funds were used mainly in infrastructure, agriculture, and environmental protection projects.

The field of international economic and technological cooperation was further expanded. A good beginning was made in investing and running enterprises abroad, offering labor services abroad, and contracting for foreign projects. Good achievements were also attained in the utilization of gratuitous foreign aid. Technological exports, which started from scratch, increased.

The system for direct registration of enterprise corporation further improved and fairly good results were achieved in introducing the method of annual inspection of enterprise corporations. A total of 810 foreign-funded enterprises, with a registered capital of $875 million, underwent industrial and commercial registration. The interior provinces established 1,314 enterprises in Hainan, with a registered capital of 5.617 billion yuan. According to the records of Hainan's industrial and commercial registration, there were 8,200 foreign-funded enterprises, with a registered capital of $10.722 billion, and 18,400 enterprises set up by interior provinces, with a registered capital of 53.716 billion yuan, by the end of 1994.

Building was accelerated in tourism. By the end of 1994, Hainan had 149 hotels and guest houses serving foreign tourists, of which 30 received star levels. There were three four-star hotels and 11 three-star hotels, with a total of 26,700 beds, an increase of 32.3 percent,

continued...

HAINAN REGION STATISTICS, 1994 (continued)

including 25,500 air-conditioned bedrooms, up 40.3 percent. In 1994, Hainan's hotels and guest houses (including tourist ships) received 2.896 million tourists, an increase of 3.6 percent. The number of tourists received in the year was as follows:

	1994	Percentage Increase Over 1993
International tourists	247,300	3.2
Foreigners	48,500	15.6
Overseas Chinese	10,100	67.5
Hong Kong and Macao compatriots	127,700	-8.3
Taiwan compatriots	61,000	16.5
Domestic tourists	2,648,700	3.7

Income from foreign tourism came to 496 million yuan ($58.78 million), an increase of 40.9 percent. This included 399 million yuan from commodities, up 46.8 percent and 97 million from labor services, up 21 percent.

Finance and Insurance
Banking developed steadily in the course of financial reform and savings deposits recovered. The balance of savings deposits totaled 49.617 billion yuan by the end of 1994, up 11.1 percent. The banks granted 46.725 billion yuan in loans in 1994, an increase of 28.5 percent. The balance of savings deposits in state banks was 36.938 billion yuan, up 8.8 percent, including 16.147 billion yuan in enterprise savings deposits, down 1.6 percent, and 18.097 billion yuan in urban savings deposits, up 25.1 percent. The state banks granted 36.212 billion yuan in all sorts of loans, up 20.6 percent, including 26.056 billion yuan of mid- and short-term loans, up 19.1 percent, and 7.454 billion yuan in mid and long-term loans, up 34.2 percent. The state bank savings deposit balance was 726 million yuan, 3.214 billion yuan less than in 1993. Hainan's state bank put 9.005 billion yuan of currency into circulation, an increase of 8.2 percent.

The balance of savings deposits by urban and rural inhabitants was 23.291 billion yuan by the end of 1994, a 26.6 percent increase.

Further development was made in insurance services. The Hainan People's Insurance Company offered 43.084 billion yuan in insurance coverage to domestic units, an increase of 37.8 percent; received 252 million yuan of premiums, up 13 percent; and paid out indemnity of 137 million yuan, down 9.4 percent. The company offered $5.019 billion in insurance coverage to foreign companies and enterprises, up 10.4 percent; received $5.14 million in premiums, up 34.5 percent; and paid out indemnity of $2.18 million, up 86.3 percent.

Science, Technology, Education, Culture, and Sports
Science and technology made further headway. In 1994, Hainan implemented five state-level torch projects and 10 spark projects; seven provincial-level torch projects and 14 spark projects; and won three state-level research projects established by the State Science Commission, nine projects subsidized by the local fund of the State Natural Science Fund, 28 projects established by the Hainan Natural Science Fund, and eight projects for trial production and evaluation of key state-level new products. In 1994, Hainan won two first-class, five second-class, 13 third-class, and eight fourth-class scientific and technological progress awards and three spark plan awards.

The work of protecting intellectual property rights was strengthened. In 1994 Hainan received 196 applications for patents and approved 64. Progress was made in spreading scientific and technological results, scientific and technological information services, training scientists and technicians, and in international scientific and technological exchanges.

The contingent of scientists and technicians continued to expand. By the end of 1994, Hainan's state enterprises and institutions had 112,800 special technical personnel of various trades, of which 3,353 obtained senior titles and 24,600 obtained intermediate titles.

continued...

HAINAN REGION STATISTICS, 1994 (continued)

Weather forecasting vigorously served production and construction, forecasting the seven tropical storms and typhoons in the year. By the end of 1994, the seismic units had made new achievements in the work of monitoring the effect of the Beibuwan earthquake on the island.

Education developed enormously. Coverage of the nine year compulsory education expanded; the conditions for primary and secondary schools improved; the reform of college internal management, enrollment, and placement systems was promoted; and a new situation emerged in education run by society and nongovernmental organizations. The number of students enrolled and in schools was as follows:

	1994	Percentage Increase Over 1993
Students enrolled by colleges	3,553	4.1
Students in college	11,600	13.4
Students enrolled by secondary technical schools	9,359	3.4
Students in secondary technical schools	21,400	8.3
Students enrolled by senior high schools	14,600	-2.9
Students in senior high schools	40,500	-8.4
Students enrolled by vocational schools	3,800	-1.9
Students in vocational schools	8,600	-4.9
Students in junior high schools	255,200	11.0
Pupils in primary schools	1,102,300	3.2
Children in kindergartens	133,400	5.5
Students enrolled by adult colleges	1,524	-7.4
Students in adult colleges	2,884	-1.3
Students in adult secondary schools	9,444	-2.4

Culture, art, radio, television, news, and publications flourished. In 1994, Hainan had 23 artistic troupes, 17 cultural centers, three mass art galleries, 19 public libraries, 303 cultural centers in towns, 123 cultural centers in townships, 25 archive centers, 21 radio stations, five television stations, and 57 television transmission and relay stations. The province had five book and video publishing houses, 19 news agencies, and 40 magazines, which published 13.22 million copies of 562 kinds of books; 15 kinds of newspapers, with a circulation of 124.17 million; 2.418 million copies of 31 kinds of magazines; and 788,000 boxes of video tapes. Literature and art creation and performance were lively. The first nationality orchestral music concert and the elegant performance by the Central Philharmonic Orchestra and the Central Song and Ensemble Troupe in Hainan were unprecedentedly successful. The "International Practice Book Series" and other books were well received by the readers.

Striking headway was scored in sport. In 1994 Hainan organized 18 delegations comprising over 100 athletes to take part in national games on 18 occasions, including the sports meet for youngsters. The province won 22 gold, 16 silver, and 17 bronze medals at these events. In the national tournaments, championships, and competitions, Hainan's athletes won two gold and two silver medals and broke two records on two occasions at the national children's games. Good results were achieved in sailing, skateboarding, track and field events, swimming, and weightlifting. Hainan held 240 county level games and 22 provincial level games. The masses and enterprises were also enthusiastic in sponsoring sports. A traditional nationality sports meet was held during the "3 March" Li and Miao Art Festival. The first games for staff members of the provincial organs attracted extensive attention from various social circles. During the year some 662,000 people throughout the province reached the state's physical training standards.

IX. Public Health and Environmental Protection
Public health was strengthened, medical conditions further improved, and remarkable achievements were attained in medical and health work. By the end of 1994, the province's hospitals and clinics had 22,700 beds and 31,100 medical personnel, including 907 practicing Chinese

continued...

HAINAN REGION STATISTICS, 1994 (continued)

medicine, 6,566 practicing Western medicine, 3,858 practicing Chinese and Western medicine, 7,914 nurses, and 594 midwives. The activities to prevent poliomyelitis were further strengthened. In the nationwide drive to enhance immunity, 2.8 million children in Hainan were given the vaccine.

Hainan Ribao, 14 Apr 1995.

MAP OF HAINAN, 1994

FEER, 2 Jun 1994.

SHANXI DEVELOPMENT STATISTICS, 1994

Shanxi Province scored marked successes in reform and development in 1994. Under the correct leadership of the provincial party committee and people's government, the province adhered to economic construction as the center; conscientiously implemented the centrally formulated principle of "grasping opportunities, deepening reform, expanding opening up, promoting development, and maintaining stability"; emancipated the minds and sought truth from facts; worked hard and in a down-to-earth manner; made fresh strides in the reform, opening up, and modernization drive; and improved and strengthened macroeconomic regulation and control, thereby registering a sustained national economic growth, continued improvement in people's livelihood, and an energetic development of social undertakings. Preliminary statistics show that domestic output value reached 85.2 billion yuan, up by 9.3 percent. The major problems uncovered in the course of development were as follows: High commodity prices in the market, operational difficulties encountered by certain state-owned enterprises, a rather weak agricultural basis, generally low economic efficiency, and so on. We are now confronted with the arduous task of how to further improve macroeconomic operation quality

I. Agriculture

In 1994, the province registered a steady agricultural, forestry, animal husbandry, and fishing industry growth and a robust rural economic growth. Newly added agricultural output value reached 12.307 billion yuan, up 4.5 percent and accounting for 14.4 percent of total domestic output value. Of the newly added agricultural output value farming, forestry, animal husbandry, and fishing industrial output values accounted for 8.088 billion, 891 million, 3.283 billion, and 45 million yuan respectively.

In 1994, we reaped a good grain harvest and raised cotton, oil crops, and other farm crop outputs by a large margin. However, a serious, prolonged, and unprecedented autumn drought

continued...

SHANXI DEVELOPMENT STATISTICS, 1994 (continued)

caused enormous damage to agricultural production. Under the leadership of the party committees and people's governments at all levels, we made energetic efforts to resist natural calamities and provide disaster relief, succeeding in reducing disaster losses to a minimum and bringing about steady agricultural growth. A sample survey showed that total grain output reached 8.904 billion kg, just 998 million kg short of, or a 10.1 percent drop from, the record grain output of 9.902 billion kg registered in 1993. Thus, it can still be said that we reaped a good grain harvest in 1994. Of the total grain output, summer grain output stood at 3.048 billion kg, just 316 million kg short of, or a 9.4 percent drop from, 1993, while autumn grain output stood at 5.856 billion kg, just 682 million kg short of, or a 10.4 percent drop from, 1993. Cotton production rapidly recovered, picked up,. and reversed a two-year downward turn in output. As a result, the total cotton growing area reached 1.936 million mu, thereby overfulfilling the quota listed in the provincial people's government plan. Total cotton output reached 84.804 million kg, up by 14.804 million kg or 21.1 percent. Oil crops output reached 438 million kg, up 40 million kg or 10.4 percent. The province also succeeded in raising beet and vegetable outputs by a large margin.

The major farm product outputs are as follows below:

	1994	Percent Increase
Grain (mn tn)	8.904	-10.1
Cereal (mn tn)	7.5928	-10.7
Legume crops (tn)	547,200	-5.2
Potatoes (tn)	764,000	-6.9
Oil crops (tn)	437,800	-10.4
Cotton (tn)	84,800	21.1
Flax (tn)	3,047	17.0
Flue-cured tobacco (tn)	10,974	-38.7
Beet (tn)	695,800	3.3
Vegetables (mn tn)	4.945	13.5
Fruits (tn)	867,500	43.7

Afforestation work made gratifying progress and statistics show that the afforestation area reached 299,910 hectares, up by 22.7 percent. The province built 112,580 hectares of economic forests, up by 31.5 percent. The provincial people's government demanded that seven counties and cities, namely, Zuoyun, Huguan, Yangcheng, Yicheng, Xiangyuan, Hongdong, and Huozhou, should basically fulfill their own afforestation quotas by raising funds through various channels and by guiding peasants to actively participate in afforestation work to build more tree and forest networks around farmland. We scored gratifying results in building five "million-mu afforestation projects," including a "three pines" base in the Yantongshuo area, a dry fruit and economic forest base in Luliang area, an ecological economic forest demonstration project in the Xinshuihe Valley, an afforestation demonstration project on Mount Taihang, and a paulownia kiri production base in southern Shanxi.

Animal husbandry also developed by leaps and bounds. Thanks to implementation of the spirit of a series of "vegetable basket project" conferences held by the central and provincial authorities, as well as a general rise in livestock product prices, the province succeeded in keeping a large amount of livestock, replenishing the total amount of livestock kept in stock in a timely fashion, and significantly raising livestock output.

Main livestock product outputs were as follows:

	1994	Percent Increase
Meat (tn)	503,500	16.3
Pork, beef, and mutton (tn)	460,400	16.5

continued...

SHANXI DEVELOPMENT STATISTICS, 1994 (continued)

	1994	Percent Increase
Poultry (tn)	29,100	18.9
Milk (tn)	236,800	18.7
Sheep wool (tn)	6,658	7.9
Slaughtered pigs (mn)	4.6163	14.9
Pigs in stock at end of year (mn)	4.8219	13.8
Sheep in stock at end of year (mn)	8.0453	10.0
Large livestock in stock at end of year (mn head)	3.1844	4.5

The fishing industry developed steadily. Efforts were redoubled to develop an intensive breeding industry by raising fish in "small net boxes" with the result that the aquatic products industry developed rapidly with its output reaching 15,700 tons, up by 10.8 percent.

We further improved agricultural production conditions by putting into operation more machinery and electrical equipment. By the end of 1994, the total power of agricultural machinery was 12.9836 million kw, up 7.1 percent. The province had 26,700 large and medium tractors, down 4.8 percent; 214,300 small tractors, up 0.7 percent; and 49,900 farm trucks, up 6.9 percent. Total irrigation and drainage capacity was 1.4108 million kw, down 0.7 percent. The province's rural areas used 714,400 tons of chemical fertilizer, up 6.1 percent, and 4.145 billion kwh of electricity, up 10.6 percent. Moreover, the province also stepped up farmland water conservancy construction and raised the effective irrigation area by 12,130 hectares.

Township and town enterprises registered a high rate of growth and management department statistics show that the enterprises obtained an operational income of 87 billion yuan, up 46.2 percent.

II. Industry and Building Industry

Industrial production developed relatively quickly. To attain the general goal of building a modern enterprise system, the province accelerated enterprise operative mechanism transformation; conducted relevant experiments in some 50 large and medium state-owned enterprises with an eye to instituting a modern enterprise system; and made new breakthroughs in reforming some small and medium enterprise proprietorships by resolutely implementing to the letter the two relevant central regulations with the result that a batch of pacesetters like Shuozhou City, Yuci City, and so on emerged. The province successfully made an inventory of assets and capital in some 3,879 enterprises and conducted proprietorship reform experiments in four cities in light of the local realities. Thanks to these reforms, the province successfully invigorated the enterprises and steadily raised the industrial output value. Newly added industrial output value realized at and above the township level reached 29.348 billion yuan, up 8.4 percent. Industrial output value realized at and above township level reached 68.199 billion yuan (calculation based on constant prices in 1990 with industrial output value realized at and below village level excluded), up 8.4 percent. Of the industrial output value realized at and above township level, light industrial output value stood at 13.654 billion yuan, up 3.0 percent, and heavy industrial output value was 54.545 billion yuan, up 9.9 percent. The province raised state-owned enterprises output value by 3.8 percent, collectively owned enterprises output value by 17.0 percent, township-run industrial enterprises output value by 25.4 percent, and other types of industrial enterprises by 20.3 percent. Large and medium enterprises output value went up 3.4 percent. The total industrial output value reached 124.085 billion yuan, up 24.5 percent.

The major industrial outputs were as follows:

continued...

SHANXI DEVELOPMENT STATISTICS, 1994 (continued)

	1994	Percent Increase
Raw coal (mn tn)	325.433	5.1
Washed and refined coal (mn tn)	34.043	24.6
Coke (machine processed coke, mn tn)	9.542	20.6
Generated electricity (bn kwh)	44.77	9.9
Pig iron (mn tn)	13.444	24.7
Steel (mn tn)	3.28	7.4
Finished steel products (mn tn)	1.756	8.0
Alumina (tn)	439,000	20.6
Cement (mn tn)	10.025	5.6
Plate glass (mn standard boxes)	1.646	-12.4
Sulfuric acid (tn)	469,000	23.1
Caustic soda (tn)	91,000	16.0
Chemical fertilizer (purified, tn)	846,000	9.3
Program controlled telephone (sets)	25,000	-12.6
Yarn (tn)	71,000	-17.5
Cloth (mn m)	340	-19.3
Machine-made paper, cardboard (tn)	356,000	4.0
Sugar (tn)	81,000	25.6
Beer (tn)	107,000	40.6
White spirit (tn)	122,000	9.3
Cigarettes (boxes)	186,000	-14.7
Synthetic detergent (tn)	96,000	34.5
Household washing machines (sets)	342,000	13.5

The industrial economic efficiency showed further improvement. The comprehensive industrial economic efficiency index gathered from industrial enterprises practicing independent accounting at and above the township level stood at 87.15 percent, up 2.56 percentage points with the calculation based on comparable prices. The industrial sales value stood at 83.691 billion yuan (with calculation based on prevailing prices), up 17.7 percent; the industrial sales rate was 94.76 percent; the all personnel per-capita labor productivity was 9,786 yuan, up 27.3 percent; the profits and tax rate at 9.03 percent, up 0.25 percent; the cost and profit rate at 5.78 percent; and capital turnover at 1.25 times. However, some 1,620 industrial enterprises practicing independent accounting at and above the township level, accounting for 14.8 percent of the total, sustained some 1.162 billion yuan in losses, up 7 percent.

The building industry registered continued and rapid growth. State-owned urban construction enterprises and collectively owned urban construction enterprises raised output value by 3.38 billion yuan, up 48.1 percent. State-owned urban construction enterprises completed 96.56 million square m of construction and built 26.28 million square m of apartments. The building industry's all-personnel labor productivity rose by 42 percent and per capita profits and taxes reached 2,023 yuan, up 25.2 percent, with the calculation based on the industry's total output value.

The geological survey also made much headway with the geological and mining departments conducting 42,967 m of drilling, discovering four mineral deposits, and verifying several new mineral deposits, including 44.32 million ton of coal, 4.03 million ton of quartz, and 168.06 million ton of cement rock.

III. Investment in Fixed Assets

The province conscientiously implemented such centrally formulated macroeconomic regulation and control policies as increasing investment in fixed assets and strictly controlling construction of auditoriums, office buildings, hotels, guest houses, real estate projects, and other non-urgent projects, thereby successfully checking investment expansion and effectively readjusting investment structure.

continued...

SHANXI DEVELOPMENT STATISTICS, 1994 (continued)

Investment expansion slowed down a large margin, with fixed assets investment totaling 29.68 billion yuan, up 18.9 percent but suggesting a growth rate 26.5 percent lower than the previous year. With price hikes factored in, fixed asset investment rose by 8.3 percent in real terms. State-owned units invested 23.9 billion yuan in fixed assets, up 23.2 percent and collectively owned units invested 1.92 billion yuan, down 20.6 percent; urban residents invested 2.8 billion yuan, up 4 percent; and central authorities invested 11.98 billion yuan, up 13.2 percent. The state-owned units invested 14.76 billion yuan in capital construction projects, up 18.5 percent; 5.88 billion yuan in renovation and transformation projects, up 12.2 percent; 1.17 billion yuan in commodity housing projects, down 9 percent; and 1.42 billion yuan in other types of projects, up 100 percent. State-owned units launched 3,386 capital construction, renovation, and transformation projects, down 447, and completed and commissioned 1,702 projects, 50.3 percent of the total. In 1994, newly added fixed assets were valued at 13.2 billion yuan, some 64 percent of which were made available to users.

The investment structure was further improved. As regards fixed assets investment, some 100 million yuan was invested in primary industry, down 29.2 percent and accounting for 0.3 percent of the total as against 0.6 percent, while some 14.42 billion yuan was invested in secondary industry, up 1 percent and accounting for 48.6 percent of the total as against 56.8 percent. Of the secondary industry investment, some 12.43 billion yuan was in the energy and raw and processed materials industries, up 23.6 percent and accounting for 41.9 percent of the total as against 30.6 percent. Tertiary industry investment stood at 15.16 billion yuan, up 41.7 percent and accounting for 51 percent of the total fixed assets investment as against 42.6 percent. Of the tertiary industry investment, some 6.02 billion yuan was invested in the communications, transportation, and post and telecommunications industries, up 77.6 percent and accounting for 20.3 percent of the total as against 13.5 percent.

Marked successes were scored in the "three constructions." The province energetically and successfully pressed ahead with the "three constructions," namely, highways construction, farmland capital and water conservancy works construction, and key projects construction. The province started building five key highways (Taijiu Expressway, Taiyuan-Dongshan Transit Highway, Taiyuan-Changzhi High-Grade Highway, Fenyang-Liulin Highway, and Yuncheng-Fenglingdu Highway) as well as some other highways in various counties and townships at a fast speed. In addition, asphalt roads were built in some 29 towns, highways in some six townships, and roads suitable for vehicles in some 408 administrative villages across the province. Some 480 million people were also mobilized for farmland capital construction on many occasions; 1.24 billion cubic m of earth and stone were excavated; another 200,000 mu of farmland were put under irrigation and 1.12 million mu of farmland were put under economical irrigation; and soil erosion was harnessed on 3.61 million mu of farmland. Insofar as capital construction is concerned, by firmly adhering to the principle of guaranteeing key projects, commissioning projects on schedule, and ensuring efficiency, the province completed a number of key projects and invested 8.68 billion yuan in 31 key projects, including 4.43 billion yuan in 10 key state projects and 4.25 billion yuan in 21 key local projects. The province built and commissioned five large and medium capital construction projects and built a large number of key projects, including the Shanxi Aluminum Plant Phase Two Project, Jianshan Iron Mine, Dongqu Coal Washing Plant in Gujiao Mining Area, Second Taiyuan Power Plant's second generating unit boasting an installed capacity of 200,000 kw, Yushe Power Plant's first generating unit boasting an installed capacity of 200,000 kw, Shanxi Cement Plant boasting an experimental annual output of 600,000 ton, Taiyuan Railroad Station's elevated waiting hall, Taiyuan Airport's waiting hall, Houyue Electric Railroad, electrification of Northern Changzhi-Gaoping section of Taijiao Railroad, Fenglingdu Highway Bridge linking Shanxi, Shaanxi, and Henan Provinces, and some other key projects.

Capital construction resulted in raising the coal output by 3.9 million ton, the electric power generation capacity by 412,000 kw, and the smelted iron output by 30,000 ton. The province also renovated and completed 103 km of highways, including 17 km of high-grade highways, and raised the telephone switchboard capacity by 200,000.

continued...

SHANXI DEVELOPMENT STATISTICS, 1994 (continued)

IV. Energy
The energy industry witnessed rapid growth and made fresh headway in both the production and processing sectors. The province conscientiously carried out a series of macroscopic coal and coke management measures mapped out by the provincial government; comprehensively rectified existing small coal mines; basically put a stop to unauthorized coal mining by private operators; and comprehensively rectified order at 479 coal distribution centers, thereby improving coal transportation and marketing order by a large margin, basically unifying coal prices, and putting a stop to such abnormal coal market competition as indiscriminately lowering coal prices. The energy industry developed steadily and invested 7.32 billion yuan in the state-owned energy sector, up 3.1 percent, of which 4.17 billion yuan was invested in the coal industry, down 3.9 percent, and 2.66 billion yuan in the electric power industry, up 1.1 percent. The province also succeeded in raising coal output by 4.96 million ton and installed electric power generation capacity by 417,000 kw. The province fruitfully implemented the strategy of turning the province from being solely a coal supplier into a coal and electric power supplier; energetically stepped up raw coal transformation and intensive processing; and also accelerated secondary energy sources development. The primary energy (converted into standard coal) output stood at 278 million ton, up 5.3 percent, and secondary energy (converted into standard coal) output at 86 million ton, up 36.0 percent.

Over the past year, Shanxi has supplied other parts of the country as well as other parts of the world with 224 million tons of coal, the same amount as that of the previous year or 68.7 percent of the annual coal output. The province exported 15.84 million ton of coal to foreign countries or regions, up 21.4 percent, and supplied other parts of the country with some 12.875 billion kwh of electric power, up 19.38 percent, accounting for 28.74 percent of annual electrical energy output.

V. Communications, Transportation, Post and Telecommunications
Communications and transportation developed steadily, thereby continually alleviating tension in the province's transportation industry. Railroad transportation mileage was 2,617 km, of which local railroad transportation mileage stood at 286 km, The province's highway transportation mileage was 32,863 km, of which first-grade highway transportation stood at 99 km and second-grade highway transportation at 3,413 km. Civil aviation transportation mileage also registered a rapid growth with the result that Taiyuan City, capital of Shanxi Province, commissioned 41 flight routes to more than 30 hinterland cities. By the end of 1994, the freight volume achieved by all types of transport methods was 625.47 million ton, up 5.3 percent, of which railroad freight volume was 256.98 million ton, up 0.3 percent, and highway freight volume was 367.86 million ton, up 9.1 percent.

	1994	Percent Increase
Cargo turnover volume (bn tn/km)	70.109	5.7
Railroad (bn tn/km)	53.406	4.1
Highway (bn tn/km)	16.689	11.1
Aviation (mn tn/km)	10.33	0.8
Passenger turnover volume (bn passenger/km)	17.102	6.1
Railroad (bn passenger/km)	8.46	4.6
Highway (bn passenger-km)	8.119	7.8
Aviation (mn passenger/km)	523.34	5.4

The province also raised transportation efficiency by a large margin. In 1994, the railroad sub-bureaus of Taiyuan City, Datong City, and Linfen City raised freight loading capacity by 0.9, -0.6, and 1.8 percent respectively and transportation income by 7.3, 2.4, and 8.2 percent respectively.

continued...

SHANXI DEVELOPMENT STATISTICS, 1994 (continued)

Rural communications conditions also saw marked improvement. By the end of 1994, 99.84 percent of the townships and towns had highways, 96.07 percent of them had asphalt roads, and 99.98 percent of administrative villages had roads suitable for vehicles.

Post and telecommunications undertakings developed further with volume reaching 919 million yuan, up 51.4 percent. Telephones became a new popular commodity for residents and, by the end of 1994, the province's residential telephone lines numbered 243,000, an increase of 139,000 and the pager clients and cellular phone users also went up by a large margin.

VI. Domestic Trade and Market Prices

The consumer goods market remained stable thanks to a rich supply of commodities. As a result of production growth and implementation of state macroeconomic regulation and control measures, the province enjoyed sufficient market supplies of commodities so that residents' consumption remained stable while urban and rural markets remained brisk. The annual social consumer goods retail volume was 29.271 billion yuan, up 20.2 percent, of which cities social consumer goods retail volume stood at 16.895 billion yuan, up 18.2 percent, counties' social consumer goods retail volume 6.41 billion yuan, up 15.6 percent; and social consumer goods retail volume below county level of 5.966 billion yuan, up 32.3 percent. Of the province's social consumer goods retail volume, the state-owned economic sector realized 11.385 billion yuan, up 2.9 percent, the collectively owned economic sector 6.83 billion yuan, up 16.0 percent, and the individually or privately owned economic sector 7.937 billion yuan, up 18.1 percent.

The means of production purchase and sales took a downward turn. Goods and materials supply and marketing enterprises purchased 12 billion yuan's worth of means of production, down 18.8 percent, and sold 13 billion yuan's worth of the means of production, down 14.3 percent.

Commodities prices rose sharply. The province constantly attached importance and devoted energetic efforts to inflation control and succeeded in bringing unbridled commodities prices under control. However, insofar as price indexes are concerned, the general market price level still remained relatively high. The prices of grain, poultry, poultry products, vegetables, aquatic products, garments, services, and of other daily necessities all rose too quickly.

The 1994 Price Indexes (1993 price indexes taken as 100)

1. Residents 'living expenses'	124.2
Of which: Urban	125.9
Rural	124.4
2. General commodities retail	121.6
Of which: Food	131.6
Grain	134.9
Vegetable oil	172.7
Poultry eggs	136.5
Fresh vegetables	136.4
Garment, shoes, and hats	121.1
Textiles	114.7
Daily necessities	115.4
Stationery and sports goods	111.5
Books, newspapers, and magazines	148.4
Chinese and Western medicines and chemical reagents	116.7
Building and decoration materials	116.7
Fuel	116.8
3. General services	134.0
4. General producers' industrial products	120.1
5. General agricultural production means retail	122.4
6. General farm and sideline products purchase	139.9
7. General fixed assets investment	108.3

continued...

SHANXI DEVELOPMENT STATISTICS, 1994 (continued)

VII. External Economy

The export volume was $802.64 million, up 26.6 percent, and import volume was $177.40 million, down 12.6 percent. The province exported products to some 95 foreign countries and regions. The province held a series of export trade fairs in some foreign countries and regions with fruitful results, including the United States, France, and so on and in some hinterland regions, including Tianjin, Xiamen, Harbin, and so on. For instance, at a Shanxi Export Trade Fair held in Paris, 24 foreign trade enterprises and six large state-owned enterprises exhibited more than 500 commodities, thereby fully displaying Shanxi's economic strength and prospects.

The province signed agreements on using some $480 million in foreign funds, down 51.9 percent, and on absorbing some $210 million of direct foreign investment, down 46.5 percent. 241 new enterprises run using "three types of capital," namely, foreign capital, overseas Chinese capital, and both Chinese and foreign capital, were registered in the province. By the end of 1994, foreign-invested enterprises registered in the province numbered 1,323, an increase of 254.

The province also conducted numerous tourism promotion activities, including International Drift Month at the Huanghe's Hukou, International Tourism Month on Wutai Mountain, and so on. Some 53,000 foreigners, overseas Chinese, and Hong Kong, Macao, and Taiwan compatriots visited Shanxi as tourists, down 20.2 percent. However, tourism-generated foreign exchange income was $14.957 million, up 130 percent.

VIII. Financial, Banking, and Insurance Undertakings

The province successfully furthered financial and taxation systems reform, basically secured a smooth transition from an old structure to a new structure, established a new financial system under which provincial finance controls prefectural finance and city finance, set up different institutions for handling state revenue and local revenue, and maintained a basic balance between expenditure and revenue.

Shanxi Ribao, 18 Feb 1995.

YUNNAN PROVINCE STATISTICAL COMMUNIQUE, 1994

In 1994, under the leadership of the provincial party committee and government, the people of all nationalities in Yunnan comprehensively carried out the guiding principle of the CPC Central Committee of the CPC—"seize opportunity, deepen reform, open wider to the outside world, promote development, and maintain stability." As a result, great progress was made in reform and opening up; positive effects were achieved in macroeconomic regulation and control; the national economy maintained its sustained, rapid, and healthy development: and new accomplishments were scored in all social services including education, science and technology, culture, public health, physical training. According to initial statistics (Note: The figures listed in this communique are bulletin ones), the GNP for the whole year was 86.7 billion yuan, an increase of 11 percent (Note: With the GNP and the added values of various industries, the absolute amounts are calculated according to current prices while their growths are worked out according to comparable prices, chiefly including remuneration for workers, profits, tax revenue, and depreciation charges but excluding various intermediate consumption values such as energy and raw materials), which includes growth in the primary, secondary, and tertiary industries, of 3, 15. and 16.1 percent respectively. The major problems in the operation of the economy are insufficient effective demand in the rural market, the slow development of prefectural and county industries, and the still relatively great pressure from inflation.

I. Agriculture

With a bumper harvest in agricultural production, the rural economy developed comprehensively. Despite the relatively grave natural calamities which befell some areas, however, a

continued...

YUNNAN PROVINCE STATISTICAL COMMUNIQUE, 1994 (continued)

bumper harvest in agricultural production was achieved in 1994 through the efforts by the cadres at various levels and the masses of the people. The 1994 agricultural output value rose to 23.449 billion yuan, up 3 percent. Grain output hit a historical record. The outputs of major industrial crops increased to different degrees, except for flue-cured tobacco, which decreased owing to the reduction in the cultivated area.

The outputs of major agricultural products were as follows:

	1994	Percent Increase
Grains (tn)	11,464,700	5.6
Including: Cereals (tn)	9,961,700	6.4
Beans (tn)	721,100	-5.8
Tuber crops (tn)	781,900	8
Oil-bearing crops (tn)	139,500	4.5
including: Rape-seed (tn)	90,600	0.2
Sugarcane (tn)	9,280,000	3.1
Flue-cured tobacco (tn)	592,300	-32.3
Tea (tn)	63,800	4.6
Fruit (tn)	501,400	5.1

Relatively good achievements were scored in afforestation and forestry production. In 1994, the afforestation area in the whole province reached 350,000 hectares, overfulfilling the plan. The output of principal forest products recorded increases, with natural rubber output reaching 113,100 tons, a growth of 18.3 percent. Owing to the improvement in forest protection and fire prevention, the forest cover rose slightly. Sustained growth was registered in animal husbandry production. The number of slaughtered pigs throughout the province increased by a large margin, while the output of meat, milk, poultry, and eggs. grew to varying degrees.

The outputs of major livestock products and the number of livestock were as follows:

	1994	Percent Increase
Meat (tn)	1,125,000	10.0
Including: Pork (tn)	991,900	10.4
Milk (tn)	94,600	1.7
Slaughtered pigs (head)	12,330,000	10.9
Year-end live pigs (head)	21,930,000	1.1
Year-end live sheep (head)	6,650,000	6.0
Year-end live draught animals (head)	9,460,000	0.7

Fishery production developed steadily. The output of aquatic products was 68,500 ton, up 17.5 percent. The conditions of agricultural production improved further. By the end of 1994, the province boasted 8.5 million kw of farm machinery power, up 8 percent; 10,600 large and medium-sized tractors, down 9.4 percent; 27,200 trucks, up 20 percent; and 743,000 kw of power generating machines for irrigation and drainage, up 1.5 percent. The rural power consumption went up to 1.937 billion kwh, up 15.2 percent. Farmland under effective irrigation increased by 80,000 hectares. Nevertheless, the ability of agriculture to resist natural calamities was still weak and the task of capital construction on farmland and water conservation was still very arduous. Township and town enterprises developed rapidly. In 1994, the total revenue of township and town enterprises in Yunnan amounted to 38.4 billion yuan, up 70.5 percent, effectively promoting the development of the rural economy.

II. Industry and Building Industry
Industrial production rose rapidly and economic returns continued to improve. Propelled by the deepening reform, the industrial sectors in Yunnan worked hard to open up new markets and

continued...

YUNNAN PROVINCE STATISTICAL COMMUNIQUE, 1994 (continued)

overcome difficulties so that they were able to maintain a good momentum of rapid development. The industrial added value was 38.013 billion yuan, up 15.2 percent, including a 16 percent growth in state-owned industry, 9 percent growth in collective industry, and a 20 percent growth in private industry and in industries of other economic types. With the advantages of "two famous-brand cigarettes" more fully exploited, the tobacco processing industry increased its total output value by 21.4 percent. Owing to the adjustment in both industrial set-up and product mix, there were fast increases in the output of major energy products and raw materials; however, the output of most light industrial products dropped to varying degrees as a result of market changes.

The outputs of major industrial products were as follows:

	1994	Percent Increase
Raw coal (tn)	25,713,000	7.1
Generated energy (bn kwh)	20.091	16.8
Including: hydropower (bn kwh)	13.145	38.3
Steel (tn)	1,336,700	14.6
Finished steel (tn)	1,381,400	22.2
Ten nonferrous metals (tn)	327,200	12.3
Cement (tn)	8,568,300	17.0
Industrial timber (cu m)	1,440,700	-1.3
Plate glass (weight cases)	1,534,900	16.7
Sulfur (tn)	657,700	6.9
Chemical fertilizers for farming (in terms of 100% ingredients, tn)	985,900	4.8
Metal cutting machine tools (sets)	7,493	-9.3
Small tractors (sets)	18,000	-21.2
Yarn (tn)	35,000	-9.2
Cloth (m)	130,000,000	-24.3
Sugar (tn)	806,000	-10.4
Crude salt (tn)	406,200	-1.9
Cigarettes (cartons)	6,023,300	13.2
Baked tea (tn)	42,600	-14.1
Machine-made paper and paper-board (tn)	247,600	13.5
Bicycles (sets)	120,200	-61.0
Television sets	99,400	-21.6
Domestic washing machines	47,400	-4.0
Domestic refrigerators	35,500	-2.2

The economic returns of industry continued to improve. The composite index of the economic returns of all the independent accounting industrial enterprises at or above the township level was 204.6, an increase of 40.49 percentage points. Of this, the sales rate of industrial products was 96.35 percent, down 1.05 percentage points; the profit rate on cost and expenses was 19.62 percent, up from 9 percent; the rate of industrial added value rose from 45.36 percent to 50.27 percent; the per capita labor productivity calculated according to added value rose by 20.8 percent; and the turnover of circulating funds slowed down from 2 to 1.67 times.

The construction industrial production developed in a sustained way. Building enterprises completed 4.698 billion yuan in added value, up 13.6 percent. The floor space under construction by state-owned building enterprises was 8,110,300 sq m, up 24.4 percent, while the floor space completed was 3,037,700 square m, up 3-percent. The per capita labor productivity was 37,639 yuan, up 3 percent and the tax revenue delivered was 170 million yuan, up 20.6 percent.

continued...

YUNNAN PROVINCE STATISTICAL COMMUNIQUE, 1994 (continued)

New results were achieved in geological prospecting. In 1994, the units under the provincial geology and mineral resources bureau accomplished a total of 127,500 m in drilling work, discovered five new mines, and verified a new staple mineral reserve.

III. Investment in Fixed Assets

The growth in fixed assets investment dropped. Some 33 billion yuan was invested in fixed assets, up 31.3 percent (with price factor deducted, the actual growth was 15.5 percent). The growth margin fell by 47.4 percentage points. This included 24.5 billion yuan invested by state-owned units, up 35.1 percent; 4.3 billion yuan by units under collective ownership, up 15.3 percent; and 2.63 billion yuan by urban and rural inhabitants, up 14.3 percent. Of the investment by state-owned units, 14.5 billion yuan was invested in capital construction, up 34.3 percent; 7 billion yuan in upgrading and transformation, up 29.2 percent; 2.38 billion yuan in the development of real estate, up 63 percent; and 0.62 billion yuan in other projects, up 31.9 percent. In terms of subordination, investment in central projects was 6.8 billion yuan, up 54.9 percent, and that in local projects was 17.7 billion yuan, up 28.7 percent. The state-owned invested projects under construction numbered 6,850 in 1994, virtually the same as in 1993. Among these projects, 4,018 were started in 1994, a rise of 9.1 percent.

The investment by state-owned units included 3.185 billion yuan in energy industry, up 52.6 percent, while the proportion of investment rose from 11.8 to 13 percent; and 4.165 billion yuan in transportation and post and telecommunications, up 2.5 percent, while the investment proportion dropped from 22.9 to 17 percent.

Remarkable accomplishments were scored in key construction projects. A total of 8.03 billion yuan was invested in 57 key projects under construction, some of which were either completed or put into operation during the year, such as the Manwan Power Station with an installed capacity of 500,000 kw, the project to divert water from the Er Hai to Binchuan County, the Second-class Anning-Chuxiong Highway specially for motor vehicles, the Second-class Baoshan Airport, the Dianxi Cement Plant, the microwave telecommunication line, and some other projects. All these have added great momentum to the economic development in Yunnan.

IV. Transportation and Post and Telecommunications

Production in transportation and post and telecommunications developed steadily, In 1994, the transportation and post and telecommunications industries gained an added value of 3.681 billion yuan, up 22.9 percent, but the inadequate vitality of state-owned professional transport enterprises remains an outstanding problem.

The performances of transportation undertaken by various transport systems were as follows:

	1994	Percent Increase
Volume of freight transport (bn tn/km)	11.85	-1.8
Railway transport (bn tn/km)	10.802	1.7
Highway transport (bn tn/km)	0.962	-28.7
Water transport (bn tn/km)	0.06	-22.1
Air transport (bn tn/km)	0.026	8.3
Volume of passenger transport (bn head/km)	8.573	-0.7
Railway transport (bn head/km)	2.443	6.9
Highway transport (bn head/km)	4.440	-7.3
Water transport (bn head/km)	0.019	-20.8
Air transport (bn head/km)	1.671	9.3

The post and telecommunications undertakings developed rapidly. The volume of business in post and telecommunications in 1994 reached 0.914 billion yuan, up 63.5 percent. Throughout 1994, a total of 8,556 long-distance telephone lines were added and telephone exchanges with a handling capacity of 45,900 terminals were installed. There were 802,500 city telephone

continued...

YUNNAN PROVINCE STATISTICAL COMMUNIQUE, 1994 (continued)

subscribers, up 444,500, among which the program controlled telephone subscribers numbered 760,100, up 502,100. There was a total of 561,700 telephone sets in the province and 107 counties (cities) have been connected to the nationwide long-distance automatic telephone trunk network.

V. Domestic Trade and Market Prices

The domestic consumer goods market grew steadily. The volume of retail sales of consumer goods totaled 30.5 billion yuan, up percent (the actual figure basically equals that of 1993 if the price factor is deducted). The total amount includes 14.75 billion yuan in cities, up 25 percent; 8.37 billion yuan in counties and towns, up 7.3 percent; and 7.38 billion yuan in areas below the county level, up 11.8 percent. The total volume of retail sales by the state-owned commercial sector was virtually equivalent to that in 1993, while the collective sector increased by 9 percent and the individual, private and other commercial establishments by 44.2 percent. The volume of retail sales to nonagricultural inhabitants by peasants grew by 26.9 percent.

The purchase and sales volumes by material supply and marketing enterprises somehow declined but the sales volume of agricultural materials went up to some degree. The means of production purchased by the material supply and marketing enterprises at or above the county level were valued at 12.71 billion yuan, down 7.1 percent, While the sales volume was 14.11 billion yuan, down 4.8 percent. The volume of retail sales of agricultural means of production amounted to 3.9 billion yuan, up 17 percent (the actual growth was 2 percent if the price factor was deducted).

The general level of market prices started at a high point and rose substantially. The retail prices of commodities rose by 16 percent, rising by 13.8 percent in cities and towns and by 17.9 percent in rural areas. The inhabitant consumer prices grew by 19.2 percent, rising by 17.3 percent in cities and towns and by 19.9 percent in rural areas.

The percentage rises in the various prices were as follows:

1. Residents' consumer price	19.2
Including: in cities and towns	17.3
In rural areas	19.9
Including: prices of various services	19.9
2. Commodity retail price	16.0
Including: in cities and towns	13.8
In rural areas	17.9
Including: foodstuffs	27.2
Cereals	46.4
Oils	50.5
Garments, footwear and hats	9.2
Daily-use articles	13.0
Stationery and sport goods	4.7
Publications	29.5
Chinese and Western medicines	12.3
Building and decorative materials	0.3
Fuels	-4.8
3. Retail price of agricultural means of production	14.6
4. Purchase price of capital goods	10.3
5. Ex-factory price of industrial products	16.7

VI. Foreign Economic Relations

Import and export trade grew by a large margin. The trade volume of imports and exports in 1994 amounted to $1.344 billion, up 60 percent, including $0.91 billion in export volume, up 74 percent, and $0.434 billion in import volume, up 36.9 percent. In terms of export product mix, machinery and electrical products were valued at $151.74 million, up 482 percent, and their

continued...

YUNNAN PROVINCE STATISTICAL COMMUNIQUE, 1994 (continued)

proportion in export products dropped from 19.6 to 16.7 percent. The export volumes of 18 products exceeded $10 million.

Border trade continued to expand, its volume amounting to 3.577 billion yuan (including 1.36 billion yuan in the total volume of imports and exports on an agency basis), up 24.5 percent. This included 2.17 billion yuan in export volume, up 12.8 percent and 1.41 billion yuan in import, up 48.3 percent.

Tourism developed vigorously. The number of foreign tourists, overseas Chinese, and compatriots from Hong Kong, Macao, and Taiwan visiting Yunnan was 522,000, up 28.8 percent, and the foreign exchange revenue from tourism was $124 million, up 19.2 percent.

The utilization of foreign capital grew steadily. Foreign funds actually utilized amounted to $314 million, up 38.9 percent. This included $203 million in direct foreign investment, up 12.8 percent. Throughout the year, some 262 foreign-funded enterprises were registered.

Relatively great progress was made in foreign economic and technical cooperation. The total amount for contracts entered into with foreign partners with respect to contracted projects, labor service cooperation, designing, and consultation was $105 million, up 1.56 times, and the turnover actually realized was $21.52 million.

VII. Banking and Insurance Services

The banking institutions throughout Yunnan seriously carried out the fiscal policies formulated by the central government and, as a result, the bank deposits kept growing noticeably and the size of loans was controlled within the framework of state planning.

At the end of 1994, various deposits at the national banks amounted to 68.487 billion yuan, up 41.8 percent. This included 30.619 billion yuan in institutional deposits, up 39.9 percent and 35.14 billion yuan in urban and rural residents' deposits, up 39.3 percent. The loans granted by national banks within the year totaled 60.604. billion yuan, up 30.1 percent. This includes 46.482 billion yuan in short-term loans, up 35.3 percent, and 8.7 billion yuan in loans for capital construction and technical innovation, up 18.6 percent. The money supplied throughout the year amounted to 4.158 billion yuan, up 1.37 times, and the year-end currency in circulation was 13.55 billion yuan, up 44.2 percent.

Foreign exchange deposits grew quite rapidly. At the end of 1994, the foreign exchange deposits at national banks amounted to $543 million, up 20.6 percent.

Insurance services developed rapidly. The insurance amount covered was 200.103 billion yuan, up 43.7 percent, with insurance premiums totaling 1.105 billion yuan, up 30.5 percent. The total insured amount includes 99.556 billion yuan in domestic property insurance, up 24.5 percent, and 0.559 billion yuan in insurance premiums, up 35.6 percent. Some 12,600 enterprises and other institutions joined the enterprise property insurance program, 2,858,900 households joined the family property insurance program, and 7,518,700 individuals joined the life insurance program. Insurance companies handled 96,200 claims for domestic property, paying out 325 million yuan for the cases settled and 66.38 million yuan to 129,000 individuals with life insurance cover.

VIII. Science, Education, Culture, Public Health, and Sports

New results were achieved in science and technology. In 1994, 180 projects in Yunnan obtained provincial Scientific and Technological Progress Awards and 34 projects the Spark Awards. Throughout the year, 883 applications for patent were processed and 439 approved. Yunnan also signed 1,794 contracts on technical and economic cooperation, with a transaction amount of 119 million yuan. Scientific and technological units transferred 300 scientific and technological achievements to industrial enterprises at a value of 25.6 million yuan. The province approved the setting up of a state engineering and technological research and development center and a provincial-level pilot base.

New advances were made in educational undertakings. In 1994, the educational institutions enrolled 323 postgraduates, up 17.5 percent. Regular universities and colleges in Yunnan enrolled 15,800 new regular and junior college students, up 3.8 percent, and the undergraduates numbered 51,300, up 3.4 percent. The students at secondary specialized schools

continued...

YUNNAN PROVINCE STATISTICAL COMMUNIQUE, 1994 (continued)

numbered 94,300, up 11.3 percent; the students at regular senior middle schools 175,200, down 1.8 percent; students at regular junior middle schools 1,242,700, down 1.9 percent; and primary school pupils 4,506,100, up 1.5 percent. The attendance rate of school-age children was 96.9 percent and the enrollment rate of primary school graduates rose from 67.6 to 71.2 percent. Adult education developed rapidly. The students in adult colleges numbered 33,400, up 14.9 percent; at adult secondary vocational schools, 33,400, up 12.1 percent; and at adult primary schools, 442,100, up 28.7 percent. In 1994, 350,000 adults became literate.

Cultural undertakings continued to develop. By the end of 1994, Yunnan boasted 134 art galleries, 128 cultural centers, 148 public libraries, 24 museums, 160 archive establishments, 13 radio stations, 41 medium- and short-wave transmitting and relay stations, 15 TV stations, 29 TV transmitting and relay stations of 1 kw and above, and 12,200 satellite ground stations for TV reception. Four feature films and two documentary films were produced by Yunnan in 1994, while 153 new films were distributed by the provincial film corporation.

Steady progress was made in medical care and health protection. Hospital beds in the province numbered 83,400 by the end of 1994, up 1.1 percent. Professional medical personnel totaled 110,900, up 2.9 percent, including 57,700 doctors, up 3.9 percent.

New accomplishments were made in sports activities. Yunnan athletes won three gold and one bronze medal at the Asian Games and 13 gold, 8 silver, and 15 bronze medals at the National Games; one athlete broke an Asian record, thus winning honor for Yunnan as well as China.

IX. Population and People's Livelihood

According to a sample survey regarding population changes in Yunnan, the birth rate was 21.8 per mille, death rate 8 per mille, and natural growth rate 13.8 per mille. The population of Yunnan totaled 39.392 million at the end of 1994, up 540,000.

The residents' income increased steadily. A sample survey revealed that the per capita income of urban residents was 3,109.96 yuan, up 30.9 percent; after allowing for the price rise factor, the actual growth was 11.6 percent. The per capita income of peasants was 803 yuan, up 19 percent; after allowing for the price rise factor, the actual growth was 4.6 percent.

There was a further rise in workers' wages. The total payroll for workers was 13.24 billion yuan, up 35 percent; the average wage was 4,279 yuan, up 33.2 percent and, after allowing for the price rise factor, the actual growth was 13.6 percent.

Continued improvement was made in the housing conditions of urban and rural residents. In 1994, houses with a total floor space of 6.35 million and 16 million square m were built in cities and towns and in rural areas respectively.

Constant advances were made in social welfare. There are 729 social welfare institutions with 16,600 beds accommodating 9,162 people throughout the province. A total of 4.799 million people received government relief in urban and rural areas on different occasions.

Fairly great developments were made in environmental protection. By the end of 1994, there were 1,800 people working with the environmental protection institutions throughout the province. There were 86 environmental monitoring stations at different levels and four state level natural reserves, Within the year, with a total investment of 51.971 million yuan, 70 projects for controlling environmental pollution within a specified time were completed, At the end of 1994, 30 smoke and dust control zones with an area of 116.53 square km were established in six provincial cities, and 37 environmental noise control zones with an area of 74.4 square km had been set up in three cities.

• The base period figures used in the comparisons of various indexes are all based on the official statistics published in the "Yunnan Statistics Yearbook."

Yunnan Ribao, 15 Feb 1995.

ZHEJIANG STATISTICAL COMMUNIQUE, 1994

In 1994, people throughout the province earnestly implemented the guidelines of the 14th National CPC Congress and the Third and Fourth Plenary Sessions of the 14th CPC Central Committee to tighten and improve macroeconomic control, seize opportunity, deepen reform, open up wider to the outside world, promote development, and maintain stability, achieving positive results in these respects. Implementation of the reform measures for taxation, banking, foreign exchange, and foreign trade progressed smoothly; the provincial economy maintained a favorable trend of sustained, rapid, and healthy development; the people's life continued to improve; and more progress was made in science, technology, education, culture, public health, sports, family planning, and other social undertakings. According to preliminary statistics, the gross domestic product [GDP] for the whole year was 265 billion yuan, up 21.3 percent over the previous year. The added value of the secondary industry was 141.5 billion yuan, up 27.2 percent, while that of the tertiary industry was 82 billion yuan, up 16.5 percent. The major problems in economic operations were higher increases in market prices, much difficulty faced by some enterprises in production and operations, and the weak agricultural foundation.

1. Agriculture

In agricultural production, we intensified comprehensive development; continued to develop the agriculture that "produces higher economic returns, and better and greater yields"; and stepped up restructuring. The added value of farming, forestry, animal husbandry, and fishery for the whole year was 41.5 billion yuan, up 4.4 percent from 1993.

We managed to reap rather good harvests in crop cultivation despite natural disasters, with the per ha grain yield increasing 73 kg from the previous year. Among the major farm products, the output of fruits increased considerably from the previous year, while grain, cotton, oil-bearing crops, and tea showed different degrees of decline.

The output of major farm products are as follows:

	1994 (tn)	Percent Increase Over 1993
Grain (mn)	14.040	-2.2
Of which: Cereals (mn)	13.176	-2.4
Cotton	55,000	-4.3
Oil-bearing crops	346,000	-10.4
Of which: rapeseed	319,000	-12.2
Tea	107,000	-12.6
Fruits (mn)	1.759	18.1
Sugarcane	701,000	-11.5
Jute, bluish dogbane	49,000	-42.1
Silkworm cocoons	134,000	1.4

While intensifying our efforts to prevent forest fires, and the effort to prevent and control plant diseases and insect pests, we made new progress in afforestation and attained the goal of cultivating barren hills in the whole province ahead of schedule. In 1994, the province afforested 58,000 ha land and steadily improved the quality of afforestation.

Continued development in animal husbandry production helped to basically guarantee the supply of meat, poultry, eggs, and other animal products. However, the number of pigs slaughtered and the number of pigs we had by the end of the year continued to drop.

The output of major animal products and the amount of livestock we had by the end of the year are as follows:

	1994	Percent Increase Over 1993
Meat (mn tn)	1.147	2.2
Of which: pork, beef, and mutton (tn)	981,000	0.4

continued...

ZHEJIANG STATISTICAL COMMUNIQUE, 1994 (continued)

	1994	Percent Increase Over 1993
Poultry (tn)	164,000	14.5
Eggs (tn)	331,000	7.9
Cow milk (tn)	97,000	-10.7
Pigs slaughtered (mn heads)	13.317	-2.3
Pigs in stock (year-end figure, mn head)	12.797	-3.6
Sheep and goats in stock (year-end figure, mn head)	2.060	7.6
Large animals in stock (year-end figure, head)	507,000	-6.2

Good progress was made in fish production, and a new record was set in aquatic production. Aquatic production for the whole year was 2.580 million tons, up 36.3 percent from the previous year, with the output of freshwater products increasing 7.5 percent to 357,000 tons, and the output of marine products increasing 42.4 percent to 2.227 million tons.

The condition for agricultural production was improved. In 1994 a total of 300 million workdays were invested in constructing water conservancy works and capital construction on farmland, resulting in the construction of structures using 260 million cubic meters [m] of earth and stone. By the end of the year, the total power of farm machinery reached 14.969 million kw, up 5.6 percent from the figure at the end of 1993. Rural consumption of electricity for the whole year was 14.7 billion kwh, up 27.4 percent; the amount of chemical fertilizers (in terms of pure content) [zhe chun 2124 4783] applied was 882,000 tons, up 3.0 percent. However, incidents which obstruct steady progress in agricultural production, such as wanton occupation of arable land and abandoning barren land, were still prominent.

2. Industry and Construction

Industrial production continued to grow rapidly. In 1994 the provincewide industrial added value reached 125.6 billion yuan, up 27.3 percent from the previous year. Among the industrial sectors, state-owned enterprises grew 8.2 percent; collective-owned enterprises grew 30.2 percent, with township-run industry growing 38.5 percent; industrial businesses run by individuals grew 91.2 percent; Sino-foreign joint ventures, Sino-foreign contractual joint ventures, and foreign-invested enterprises grew 67.0 percent; and large and medium-sized enterprises grew 28.9 percent. The light and heavy industries achieved comprehensive growth, with light industry growing 28.7 percent and heavy industry 25.3 percent.

Enterprises obtained more decisionmaking power. The vast number of enterprises actively readjusted their product mix according to market demands—enterprises at and above the township levels invested 12.5 billion yuan in technological upgrading, and developed 18,000 new products.

The output of major industrial products are as follows:

	1994	Percent Increase Over 1993
Yarn (tn)	204,000	-11.5
Cloth (bn m)	1.40	16.7
Silk (tn)	27,000	3.4
Silk fabrics (bn m)	1.68	17.4
Chemical fiber (tn)	202,000	34.2
Machine-made paper and paperboard (mn tn)	1,409	10.9
Beverages and wine (mn tn)	2.011	4.1
Cigarettes (boxes)	758,000	0.8

continued...

ZHEJIANG STATISTICAL COMMUNIQUE, 1994 (continued)

	1994	Percent Increase Over 1993
Television (mn sets)	4.107	30.0
Of which: color television (sets)	653,000	53.0
Household washing machines (units)	852,000	40.2
Household refrigerators (units)	457,000	28.5
Air conditioners (units)	219,000	13.5
Freezers (units)	661,000	40.6
Bicycles (mn)	5.444	8.3
Raw coal (mn tn)	1.325	-4.4
Electricity (bn kwh)	32.76	9.9
Processed crude oil (mn tn)	5.253	30.8 (tn)
Steel (mn tn)	1.289	-10.5
Rolled steel (mn tn)	1.519	9.3
Sheet glass (mn crates)	3.033	12.2
Cement (mn tn)	25.81	16.3
Sulfuric acid (tn)	409,000	5.5
Chemical fertilizers (in terms of pure content, tn)	710,000	2.9
Chemical insecticides (in terms of 100% effective content equivalent, tn)	33,000	16.7
Internal-combustion engine (commodity supply, mn kw)	4.047	-15.2
Metal cutting machine (units)	48,000	-29.9
Motor vehicles (units)	20,000	-6.3
Small tractors (units)	63,000	61.3

Industrial economic efficiency dropped from 1993, but had gradually improved. The six comprehensive economic efficiency indices, which the state assesses, fell from the previous year's 107.9 percent to 105.8 percent. Among others, the sales rate of industrial products dropped from 96.01 percent to 94.01 percent; the profit capital ratio fell from 13.93 percent to 11.44 percent: the industrial value-added rate dropped from 25.53 percent to 24.86 percent; the profit-cost ratio dropped from 4.88 percent to 4.45 percent; and the turnover period of circulating funds dropped from 2.14 to 1.82 times. However, the all-personnel labor productivity (calculated in terms of added value) rose from the previous year's 14,945 yuan per person to 19,782 yuan per person. In addition, the rate of decrease of the total energy consumption required for each 10,000-yuan output value dropped from 17.58 percent to 13.46 percent, and the percentage of loss-making enterprises increased from 16.2 percent to 17.8 percent.

The construction sector continued to progress rapidly in production and operations. In 1994 the added value of the construction sector was 15.9 billion yuan, up 27.0 percent from the previous year. State-owned enterprises carried out construction on land totalling 7.546 million square m and completed 3.064 million square m floor space of buildings, up 19.2 percent and 25.3 percent respectively from the previous year. Construction enterprises continued to improve their economic efficiency. The all-personnel labor productivity (calculated in terms of added value) for state-owned and collective-owned city and town construction enterprises for the entire year was 9,790 yuan per person, up 29.0 percent from the previous year.

New achievements were made in geological survey. The geological industry completed 202,000 m machinery core drilling, discovered one mining site, and added six more minerals to our mineral reserves.

continued...

ZHEJIANG STATISTICAL COMMUNIQUE, 1994 (continued)

3. Investment in Fixed Assets
Investment in fixed assets was controlled, resulting in a significant drop after the increase last year. In 1994, 100 billion yuan was invested in social fixed assets in the entire province, up 46 percent from the previous year. Of the amount, state-owned and other units invested 50 billion yuan, up 52 percent; collective-owned units, 33 billion yuan, up 36 percent; and individual investment by urban and suburban residents, 17 billion yuan, up 50 percent. Of the investment by state-owned and other units, capital construction took up 21.8 billion yuan, up 58 percent; technological upgrading, 8 billion yuan, up 5.3 percent; and real estate development, 15.6 billion yuan, up 67.7 percent. State-owned and other units carried out 7,702 capital construction and technical-upgrading projects in the entire year, which was 844 less than the previous year, but the total investment, 106.6 billion yuan, was 63 percent more than the previous year.

Of the investment by state-owned and other units in capital construction and technical upgrading, investment in primary industry went down 3 percent from the previous year to 220 million yuan, or a decrease from 1.1 percent to 0.7 percent in the share of total investment. The investment in secondary industry went up 26.9 percent to 13.27 billion yuan, or a decrease from 48.9 percent to 44.5 percent in the share of total investment, although the share given to the energy sector rose from 14.3 percent to 14.6 percent. The investment in tertiary industry went up 52.6 percent to 16.32 billion yuan, or a decrease in the share of total investment from the previous year's 50 percent to 54.8 percent [sic], of which the investment in transportation and telecommunications went up 67.1 percent to 6.24 billion yuan, or an increase from 17.5 percent to 20.9 percent in the share of total investment.

Key construction projects progressed smoothly. For the whole year, 6.36 billion yuan, or 100.8 percent of the planned annual investment, was invested in 47 state and provincial-level key construction projects. Completed and put into operation were these key construction projects: The first phase of the Xiaoshan Power Station, generating unit No. 2 of the Beilun Power Station, the epoxy propane project of the Zhejiang Chemical Plant, the Beilun Harbor for loading and unloading ores, the Quhua caustic soda project, and other projects. Intensified efforts were made to construct the Jinhua-Wenzhou railway, Hangzhou-Ningbo highway, and other projects.

In 1994, state-owned units constructed and put into operation 3,005 capital-construction projects, including seven large and medium-sized projects; 1,321 technical upgrading projects were also carried out. New increases in production capacity, generated through capital construction and technical upgrading projects, for the entire year are: 857,000 kw generator capacity, 270 km of new highways, 518 km of reconstructed highways, 10.98 million-ton handling capacity from new (expanded) wharves, 350,000-tons of cement, 460,000 automatic telephone switchboards in cities, and 438,000 tons of daily tap water supply.

4. Transport, Posts, and Telecommunications
Transport, postal, and telecommunication services registered steady progress. The value added by the sector was 14.7 billion yuan, an increase of 22.3 percent over the previous year. However, the sector still failed to meet the needs of the rapidly developing national economy.

The volume of transportation by various means is as follows:

	1994	Percent Increase Over 1993
Volume of freight transport (bn tn/km)	63.09	2.1
Of which:		
Railway (bn tn/km)	18.16	1.1
Highway (bn tn/km)	17.16	6.9
Waterway (bn tn/km)	27.72	0.0
Volume of passenger transport (bn person/km)	43.35	8.7
Of which:		
Railway (bn person/km)	10.84	10.5

continued…

ZHEJIANG STATISTICAL COMMUNIQUE, 1994 (continued)

	1994	Percent Increase Over 1993
Highway (bn person/km)	31.5	9.3
Waterway (bn person/km)	1.01	-20.3
Cargo handled at major ports (mn tn)	90.63	7.6
Volume of air passenger transport (mn persons)	1.5	8.7

Total postal and telecommunication business transactions in 1994 totalled 4.29 billion yuan, an increase of 56.0 percent over the previous year. By the end of 1994, the number of telephone subscribers in urban and rural areas had reached 2.41 million, an increase of 57.0 percent over the previous year; of the total figure, the number of urban subscribers was 1.535 million, up 48.6 percent; that of rural subscribers, 875,000, up 74.3 percent. By the end of the year, the number of mobile telephone subscribers had reached 92,000, an increase of 1.8 times over the previous year, and the paging telephone business had increased 1.1 times. The share of program-controlled exchanges was 99.9 percent.

5. Domestic Trade, Supply and Marketing of Goods and Materials, and Prices

Both the urban and rural markets were brisk in 1994. The total volume of retail sales of consumer goods for the year was 97.06 billion yuan, an increase of 39.6 percent over the previous year (an actual increase of 14.7 percent after allowing for price rises). Of this total, the sales at urban markets hit 61.54 billion yuan, up 41.2 percent, while the sales in rural areas was 35.52 billion yuan, up 37.1 percent. In terms of different economic types, the retail sales of state-owned units hit 23.05 billion, an increase of 27.6 percent; the total retail sales of collectively owned enterprises and institutions was 17.97 billion yuan, an increase of 34.7 percent, while the total retail sales of privately owned and shareholding enterprises was 56.04 billion yuan, up 47.0 percent. In 1994, The total retail sales of peasants to non-agricultural population was 15.16 billion yuan, up 36.9 percent. The total volume of transactions at urban and rural fairs was 148.1 billion yuan, an increase of 1.3 times.

A substantial increase in the sales of various types of consumer goods was registered. Food consumer goods increased 37.0 percent over the previous year; clothing consumer goods, 38.7 percent; and other consumer goods for use, 45.3 percent.

Reform of commercial enterprises was deepened, and their management was strengthened. The volume of profits and taxes generated by the commercial and supply and marketing systems for the whole year was 1.83 billion yuan, up 7.6 percent over the previous year.

The market for the means of production was dull. The volume of capital goods marketed by supply and marketing cooperatives at and above the county levels for the year was 84.7 billion yuan, a decline of 0.8 percent over 1993.

New progress was made in pricing reform. In 1994, the prices of crude oil, petroleum products, and electricity distributed by the state for industrial use were raised; the prices of coal distributed by the state were decontrolled; and the gap between prices for a number of important capital goods within planned quotas and those in excess of them was eliminated. At the same time, price control was strengthened by monitoring the prices of 24 types of daily necessities and services and by requiring the display of price tags for commodities and services, thus increasing the transparency of market commodity prices.

Market prices rose by a large margin. In particular, those of grain, fresh vegetables, and poultry, as well as poultry products, and of services rose fairly sharply.

The increase in prices over 1993 are as follows:

Rate of Increase for 1994 Prices Over Previous Year (percent)

Consumer prices	24.8
Urban areas	24.7
Rural areas	24.9
Food	32.2

continued...

ZHEJIANG STATISTICAL COMMUNIQUE, 1994 (continued)

Grain	51.8
Fresh vegetables	47.1
Poultry and poultry products	41.7
Clothing	19.1
Household facilities and articles	11.0
Medical and health care	4.6
Transportation and telecommunication	5.7
Educational, recreational, and	
cultural facilities	13.3
Housing	20.8
Service	31.0
Of which: urban areas	31.2
Rural areas	31.02
Retail prices	21.7
Urban areas	20.0
Rural areas	24.83
Raw and semifinished materials	
purchasing prices	24.8
Producers' prices of manufactured products	17.5
Retail prices for agricultural capital goods	26.5
Purchasing prices for farm and	
sideline products	36.8
Prices of investment in fixed assets	12.5
Of which: prices of investment in	
construction and installation projects	13.4

6. Foreign Economic Relations

The development of foreign trade was rapid. Customs statistics show that the value of Zhejiang's exports in 1994 was $6.9 billion, an increase of 40.8 percent over the previous year, and the value of imports was $2.9 billion, up 20.6 percent. The structure of exports was further improved, with the share of machinery and electronic products rising from 15.7 percent in 1993 to 17.4 percent. The value of exports by foreign-funded enterprises for 1994 was $1.29 billion, up 51.2 percent; its share in Zhejiang's total volume of exports rose from 19.2 percent in 1993 to 20.4 percent. Export markets were added. While maintaining the steady development of the traditional export markets in Hong Kong, Japan, and the United States, export markets were opened in the Middle East, Latin America, and the CIS.

New progress was made in the utilization of foreign capital. In 1994, new contracts on utilization of foreign capital worth $3.13 billion were concluded, a decrease of 22.6 percent over 1993. Foreign capital actually utilized amounted to $1.36 billion, up 11.9 percent. Of the total amount of $3.13 billion, $2.89 billion was in the form of direct foreign investment, a decrease of 22.8 percent; the actual invested amount was $1.14 billion, up 10.8 percent. In 1994, approval was given for the establishment of 2,528 foreign-funded enterprises.

Economic and technical cooperation with foreign countries made considerable progress. Contracts on construction projects, labor service projects, and designing and consultation services contracted by Zhejiang with foreign countries in 1994 reached $180 million, an increase of 92.2 percent, and the accomplished operations revenue was $86.66 million, up 92.0 percent.

International tourism made steady progress. In 1994 Zhejiang received 613,000 foreigners, overseas Chinese, and Chinese compatriots from Taiwan, Hong Kong, and Macao who came to Zhejiang as tourists or for visits, business or other activities, a decrease of 15.9 percent over the previous year. Of the total number of people who visited Zhejiang last year, 330,000 were foreign tourists, up 13.8 percent. Foreign exchange income from tourism for the year was $180 million, up 54.6 percent over 1993.

continued...

ZHEJIANG STATISTICAL COMMUNIQUE, 1994 (continued)

7. Banking and Insurance

Good progress was made in banking reform, the separation of policy-oriented from commercial banks was speeded up, and savings deposits of various forms in banks increased on the whole. At the end of 1994, savings in various forms in banks in the entire province was 36.35 billion yuan more than the end of 1993, including an increase of 15.94 billion yuan of savings by enterprises. The amount of loans of all sorts in the possession of banks was 20.87 billion yuan more than the previous year, including an additional 16.38 billion yuan in short-term loan, and 3.75 billion yuan in middle and long-term loans. Savings deposits of residents in urban and suburban areas at the end of 1994 was 99.03 billion yuan, 32.54 billion yuan more than the previous year.

We continued to make progress in the insurance service. Provincewide in 1994, 57,000 enterprises bought the enterprise property insurance, 2.981 million residents the home property insurance, and 11.680 million people the life insurance. The total amount of coverage for all types of property insurance for the whole year was 475.29 billion yuan, up 23.7 percent from the previous year. Insurance companies handled 553,000 domestic life insurance claims and paid 1.44 billion yuan indemnities. They handled 1.430 million life insurance claims and paid 760 million yuan indemnities.

8. Science, Education, Culture, Public Health, and Sports

Scientific and technical personnel grew in number. By the end of 1994 the province had 697,000 professionals and technicians, or 3.0 percent more than the number in 1993, who specialize in all fields in local state-owned enterprises and institutions, and 168,000 of them, or 16.2 percent more than the previous year, held high and mid-level positions. There were 162 state-owned independent research and development institutions at and above the county level in the entire province; 234 research institutions affiliated to universities; and 650 research institutions affiliated to large and mediumsized industrial enterprises. A total of 67,000 people were involved in scientific and technological activities in these institutions.

Financial input for scientific and technological activities increased. The expenditures of such units as research institutions, universities, and large and medium-sized industrial enterprises on scientific and technological activities in 1994 reached 2.16 billion yuan, up 25.2 percent from the previous year. Of the amount, 560 million, or an increase of 30.0 percent, was used in research and development.

New achievements were made in scientific undertakings. In 1994, 1,560 scientific achievements were appraised with the approval of the provincial science and technology commission, and 300 provincial awards for scientific progress and 43 provincial spark program awards were given out. Also handled in 1994 were 3,495 patent applications, 4.6 percent more than the previous year, of which 2,028 were approved and patented.

Markets for technological transfer were active. In 1994, 14,436 technological contracts, which involved a transaction value of 720 million yuan, up 6.7 percent from the previous year, were signed.

Undertakings related to survey and drawing, quality inspection, standard measurement, and meteorology continued to progress. In 1994, surveying and cartography departments conducted surveying and drawing of 15,000 topographical maps of various measuring scales, up 12.5 percent from the previous year. By the end of 1994, there were 139 product quality inspection and supervision organs, and 158 provincial-level public measuring standards of 44 types in 10 categories were formulated or revised. By the end of 1994, there were 65 super-shortwave transmitting stations in the weather warning and service system, and two weather forecasting and early warning stations.

More progress was made in various educational undertakings. In 1994, institutions of higher learning took in 1,571 postgraduate students, up 14.6 percent from 1993, and the total number of students taking graduate courses was 3,993, up 19.6 percent. Colleges and universities took in 31,000 undergraduates and students for professional courses, up 9.0 percent, and the total number of enrolled undergraduate students was 87,000 people, up 18.0 percent. In institutions

continued...

ZHEJIANG STATISTICAL COMMUNIQUE, 1994 (continued)

of higher learning, 776 students finished postgraduate studies and 18,000 students finished their undergraduate and professional courses, up 11.5 percent from the previous year. Secondary vocational schools took in 49,000 students, up 36.8 percent from the previous year; had 109,000 enrolled students, up 28.2 percent; and produced 23,000 graduates, up 1.7 percent.

We continued to strengthen elementary education, and further promoted the nine-year compulsory education. In 1994 there were 3.662 million students in primary schools and 1.687 million students in junior secondary schools. The enrollment rate of primary school-age children was 99.7 percent, and the proportion of primary school graduates rose from the previous year's 92.5 percent to 95.3 percent in 1994. The dropout rates in primary and junior secondary schools respectively fell from the previous year's 0.6 percent and 5.6 percent to 0.1 percent and 3.8 percent in 1994. The nine-year compulsory education program was implemented in 1,560 townships and towns in the province, as well as other areas populated by 38.85 million people.

New progress was made in adult education and secondary vocational and technical education. In 1994, institutions of adult higher learning took in 20,000 new students for undergraduate and professional courses, up 27.9 percent from the previous year, and produced 6,000 graduates. Adult secondary vocational schools took in 36,000 students, up 40.1 percent, and produced 10,000 graduates, while adult technical training schools trained 2 million students. A total of 77,000 people in their thirties to fifties became literate. By the end of the year, secondary vocational and technical schools had 304,000 enrolled students (including 39,000 students in training schools for technicians), accounting for 54.5 percent of the total student enrollment in senior middle schools.

Steady progress was made in cultural undertakings. In 1994, the province produced three feature films and eight short films, distributed 163 new movies, and produced eight television dramas totalling 38 series. By the end of 1994, there were 89 cultural and art performing groups, 12 mass art centers, 84 cultural centers, 82 public libraries, 58 museums, 111 archives, 3,327 movie houses, 44 radio broadcasting stations, and 62 television stations at the county level or above. We published 1.07 million copies of newspapers, 10 million copies of magazines, and 210 million books in the entire year.

Sustained progress was made in public health undertakings. By the end of 1994, there were 106,000 hospital beds in 8,718 hospitals and clinics, up 1.6 percent over the end of 1993. There were 145,000 professional health workers and technicians, up 3.7 percent, of whom 64,000 were doctors, up 3.7 percent, and 32,000 nurses, up 3.9 percent.

New achievements were made in sports, and mass sports and games developed vigorously. In 1994, our athletes won 70 gold medals in major competitions inside and outside China (including four in world championships and 16 in Asian championships). A total of 92.1 percent of our schools promoted the National Standards for Physical Exercises, whose requirements were met by 92.0 percent of their students.

9. Population and People's Life

A sampling on population changes showed that the birth rate in 1994 was 13.24 per thousand and the death rate was 6.60 per thousand, resulting in a natural growth rate of 6.64 per thousand. If we extrapolated from these figures, the total population in the province by the end of 1994 would be 43.64 million people (with 42.94 million permanently residing here), representing an increase of 290,000 people over the end of 1993.

The incomes of urban and rural residents and the income level of workers improved further. According to a sampling, the annual per-capita income for living expenses of urban residents was 4,691 yuan in 1994, up 39.1 percent over the previous year, or real growth of 11.6 percent when allowed for price hikes. The net per-capita income of rural residents was 2,225 yuan, up 27.4 percent, or real growth of 4.1 percent when allowed for price hikes. The total wages of workers in the whole province was 25.20 billion yuan in 1994, up 27.4 percent from 1993, and the average wage of workers was 5,100 yuan, up 26.6 percent.

continued...

ZHEJIANG STATISTICAL COMMUNIQUE, 1994 (continued)

Living conditions for urban and rural residents continued to improved. By the end of 1994, the average living space for each urban resident was 10.8 square m, up 2.9 percent from the previous year, and the housing space for each rural resident was 32.8 square m, up 0.5 percent.

The pace of labor reform was stepped up, and more progress was made in the labor employment service. By the end of 1994, there were 726 employment agencies at all levels in the province, and 47,000 unemployed people in urban areas were given jobs. At the end of 1994, the urban unemployment rate was 2.7 percent. Provincewide at the end 1994, there were 5.015 million workers—9,000 less than at the end of 1993—of which 1.32 million were employed under the contract system, up 8.0 percent. In urban areas, there were 813,000 self-employed and private-enterprise workers, up 54.8 percent.

Social welfare work continued to develop. At the end of 1994, there were 1,325 social welfare institutions and units with 28,000 beds and 20,000 inmates. A total of 1.369 million urban and rural people who required various forms of social relief received relief funds from the state. Old-age social insurance under unified planning continued to expand, and the number of workers and retirees who joined the old-age insurance program increased to 3.534 million people by the end of 1994, up 1.5 percent form the end of 1993.

More progress was made in environmental protection. At the end of 1994, there were 92 environmental monitoring stations of all levels in the province's environmental protection system; 397 projects to control environmental pollution within certain stipulated period was completed with a total investment of 79.676 million yuan in 1994; and 63 smoke and dust conlrol zones covering 500.4 square km were established in cities, and noise pollution was controlled under a specific level in 86 zones covering 69.4 square km.

•All figures in this communique are preliminary figures for the year.
•In the communique, the absolute number of the GDP and the added values of various industries are calculated in terms of current prices, and growth rates are calculated in terms of comparable prices.

Zhejiang Ribao, 5 Mar 1995.

MAP OF ZHEJIANG, 1993

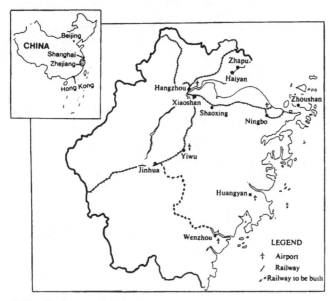

Beijing Review, 12 Jul 1993.

FUJIAN STATISTICAL COMMUNIQUE, 1994

Under the leadership of the provincial party committee and the provincial government, the people of the whole province adhered to the general policy of "seizing the present opportunity, deepening reform, opening the country wider to the outside world, promoting development and maintaining stability," implemented the measures of the Central Committee for the strengthening and improvement of macro-control, and made big strides forward in the reforms of the financial, taxation, banking, foreign exchange, pricing, and circulation systems in 1994. The national economy saw sustained and rapid development. The comprehensive strength of the province further increased, and the province was opened to the outside world on a higher level and on a broader and deeper scale. Science, technology, education, culture, public health and other social undertakings developed in an all-round way, and the livelihood of the people in the urban and rural areas further improved. According to preliminary statistics, gross domestic product for the year was 168.5 billion yuan, an increase of 21.2 percent over the previous year. Of this total, the value added of primary industry was 36.5 billion yuan, up 10.8 percent; that of secondary industry was 72 billion yuan, up 31.7 percent; while that of tertiary industry was 60 billion yuan, up 15.4 percent. The main problems in economic development were: The margin of increase in market prices was too wide, the agricultural foundation was weak, and some state-owned enterprises had difficulties in production and management.

I. Agriculture

In spite of extraordinarily serious floods and water-logging and other natural disasters, the province reaped satisfactory harvests in agricultural production. The total area under crops was 42,014,600 mu. Of this total, the sown area of grain was 30,033,700 mu, 1.8 percent or 525,600 mu more than in 1993. The mix of economic crops was readjusted, with increases in the sown areas of vegetables, fruits and peanuts and decreases in the sown areas of tobacco, medicinal herbs and sugar cane.

The output of major farm products as follows:

	1994 (tn)	Percent Increase Over 1993
Grain	8,874,000	2.1
Oil-bearing crops	216,000	4.5
Of which: Peanuts	200,800	5.6
Sugarcane	2,767,700	-0.9
Cured tobacco	60,600	-51.2
Edible fungus	292,800	32.9
Tea	82,400	7.0
Fruits	1,981,300	28.9

Steady progress was made in forestry production. The new afforested area in 1994 was 684,600 mu. The forest coverage rate was 52.4 percent, the highest in the country.

Overall growth was made in animal husbandry production, and the production of meat, poultry, eggs and milk registered increases of various degrees.

The output of major animal products and livestock as follows:

	1994	Percent Increase Over 1993
Pork, beef and mutton (tn)	926,800	11.5
Of which: Pork (tn)	902,600	11.2
Cow milk (tn)	59,200	1.7
owl eggs (tn)	230,200	19.5
Pigs delivered to slaughter houses (head)	11,207,300	9.7
Pigs in stock (head)	10,623,600	4.0
Large animals in stock (head)	1,303,400	0.3

continued...

FUJIAN STATISTICAL COMMUNIQUE, 1994 (continued)

Continued progress was made in fishery production. The output of aquatic products in 1994 was 2,266,100 tons, an increase of 19.0 percent over the previous year. Of this total, the output of freshwater products was 262,000 tons, up 37.9 percent, and that of marine products was 2,004,100 tons, up 16.9 percent.

Further improvement was made in the conditions for agricultural production, and the agricultural foundation was still weak. By the end of 1994, the total power of the province's farm machinery was 7,297,000 kilowatts, an increase of 5.2 percent over the previous year.

There were 4,000 large and medium-sized tractors, a drop of 6.6 percent; 158,400 small and walking tractors, up 3.5 percent; and 18,200 trucks for agricultural use, up 10.0 percent. The total capacity of electric irrigation and drainage machinery for agricultural use was 619,700 kilowatts, up 0.9 percent. A total of 1,014,500 tons of chemical fertilizers (100 percent effective content equivalent) were applied in 1994, up 10.0 percent. Rural consumption of electricity in the year was 3.604 billion kwh, up 23.6 percent. Irrigation and water conservancy facilities in the rural areas were further reinforced, and the acreage of farmland with effective irrigation system was increased by 109,800 mu.

II. Industry and Construction

Industrial production continued its rapid growth. In 1994, the total value added of industry reached 61 billion yuan, an increase of 33.1 percent over the previous year. Of this total, the value added of state-owned enterprises was 12.240 billion yuan, up 2.2 percent (including state-owned holding enterprises, up 3.1 percent); that of collective enterprises was 27.371 billion yuan, up 44.2 percent; while that of foreign-invested enterprises was 12.151 billion yuan, up 48.0 percent.

The growth of light industry exceeded that of heavy industry. In 1994, the value added of light industry was 39.495 billion yuan, an increase of 38.0 percent over the previous year; that of heavy industry was 21.505 billion yuan, up 24.5 percent.

The output of major industrial products as follows:

	1994	Percent Increase Over 1993
Yarn (tn)	65,900	3.9
Cloth (mn m)	210	-4.1
Chemical fibers (tn)	39,600	23.0
Sugar (tn)	179,600	-40.7
Salt (tn)	682,500	-19.1
Cigarettes (cases)	827,600	-3.7
Beer (tn)	789,200	13.8
Canned food (tn)	227,100	-0.9
Machine-made paper and paperboard (tn)	653,000	4.1
Plastic products (tn)	186,900	11.3
Bicycles	1,263,900	20.5
Color TV sets	1,594,000	2.7
Videotape recorders	300,300	6.8
Coal (tn)	9,758,000	-0.7
Electricity (bn kwh)	22,893	16.9
Gasoline (tn)	599,100	-2.3
Diesel oil (tn)	545,200	-1.7
Cast iron (tn)	671,600	0.6
Steel (tn)	556,900	-8.6
Rolled steel (tn)	750,300	5.0
Timber (cu m)	5,737,400	2.4
Cement (tn)	9,643,500	11.4

continued...

FUJIAN STATISTICAL COMMUNIQUE, 1994 (continued)

	1994	Percent Increase Over 1993
Plate glass (weight cases)	1,475,400	32.7
Sulfuric acid (tn)	274,800	11.6
Soda ash (tn)	52,200	6.3
Caustic soda (tn)	103,200	8.2
Chemical fertilizers (tn)	491,200	11.8
Chemical insecticides (tn)	8,000	21.2
Metal cutting machine tools (units)	1,650	-34.8
Loading machinery (units)	2,493	5.7
Internal combustion engines (kw)	1,447,800	7.0
Motor vehicles	4,909	21.9
Small tractors	50,800	11.2
Agricultural transport vehicles	51,500	-5.9
Power-generating equipment (kw)	119,500	64.1

The economic efficiency of industrial enterprises improved month after month, but the overall level still needed further improvement. In 1994, the volume of sales by industrial enterprises at and above the township level was 120.755 billion yuan, an increase of 25.7 percent over the previous year. The rate of sales of manufactured products was 95.87 percent, exceeding the planned target. The composite economic efficiency index of industrial enterprises with independent accounting at and above the township level was 100.45, a drop of 8.04 percentage points compared with the previous year.

The export of manufactured products increased by a wide margin. The volume of export products delivered by industrial enterprises at and above the township level was 35.481 billion yuan, an increase of 64.3 percent or 13.885 billion yuan over the previous year.

The construction industry continued to develop. In 1994, the value added of construction was 11 billion yuan, an increase of 20.1 percent over the previous year. The total floor space of buildings under construction by state-owned construction enterprises was 8,602,000 square meters, with 2,899,000 square meters completed during the year, up 20.7 percent and 27.1 percent respectively.

New progress was achieved in geological prospecting. In 1994, six mineral deposits were discovered, and major progress was reported in the survey of three areas. The newly discovered reserves included 10.1 tons of gold metals, 1.51 million tons of manganese, 3.112 million tons of pyrite, 27.583 million tons of clay, and 20.663 million tons of limestone. Another 15 sites were reported for further surveys, while 1:50000 regional geological surveys were completed on 5,095 square km of land and 1:20000 regional gravity surveys were completed on 7,300 square km of land.

III. Investment in Fixed Assets
Growth in investment in fixed assets dropped markedly, and there was a decline in the number of new projects started. Total investment in fixed assets in the province amounted to 54.397 billion yuan, an increase of 47.6 percent over the previous year (or a real growth of 37.6 percent after allowing for price rises). The growth rate was 39.1 percentage points lower than that in the previous year. Of this total, investment made by state-owned units (including joint ventures, cooperative enterprises and shareholding enterprises with investment by the state, same below) was 36.208 billion yuan, up 55.3 percent; investment made by collective units was 4.246 billion yuan, up 9.6 percent; and investment by individuals in the urban and rural areas was 10.894 billion yuan, up 43.8 percent. As regards investment in capital construction and technical innovation and transformation, a total of 2,235 new projects were launched, 259 projects less than in the previous year. The new projects accounted for 50.4 percent of projects under construction.

continued...

FUJIAN STATISTICAL COMMUNIQUE, 1994 (continued)

Of the total investment by state-owned units, investment in capital construction was 17.664 billion yuan, an increase of 49.4 percent over the previous year; that in technical innovation and transformation was 6.662 billion yuan, up 38.9 percent; that in real estate was 10.198 billion yuan, up 67.4 percent; and in other projects was 1.684 billion yuan, up 176.6 percent. In investment in capital construction and technical innovation and transformation, investment in projects of the central government was 5.752 billion yuan, up 59.7 percent, while investment in projects of the local governments was 18.574 billion yuan, up 42.7 percent.

The investment structure was improved, and construction of energy, transportation, post and telecommunications and other infrastructural projects was further strengthened. In the total investment made by state-owned units, investment in energy industry was 4.974 billion yuan, an increase of 44.6 percent over the previous year; investment in raw and semi finished materials industry was 1.630 billion yuan, up 80.5 percent; while investment in transportation, post and telecommunications was 8.499 billion yuan, up 122.1 percent.

Further progress was made in key construction projects. In 1994, the 13 key construction projects under guarantee were completed and put into operation or partially completed and put into operation according to plan. The "pioneering project" in highway construction achieved rapid progress and good results, and the Fujian-Xiamen-Zhangzhou Highway extension and renovation project was completed without a hitch. New headway was made in the construction of the Hengnan Railway, a key state project, and the Zhang-Quan-Xiao Railway, a key provincial project. Good progress was made in the development of the power industry. The Numbers 2, 3 and 4 generators of the Shuikou Hydropower Plant, the Numbers 1, 2 and 3 generators of the Shuidong Hydropower Plant, and the Numbers 3 and 4 generators of the Zhangping Power Plant, were completed and put into operation.

The newly increased production capacity in the province through capital construction projects included 4.08 million tons of cargo-handing capacity at new coastal ports; 968,800 kilowatts of power generation (or 1.013 million kilowatts if technical innovation projects were included); 2.23 million kilovolt-amperes of power transformation equipment; 147,000 tons of dally water supply; 600 million cubic meters of reservoir capacity; 190,000 places for students at various levels; 260,000 urban telephone circuits; and 1,048 km of newly constructed or renovated highways.

IV. Transport, Post and Telecommunications

Transportation and post and telecommunications services continued to grow. The value added of these sectors was 14.2 billion yuan, an increase of 17.0 percent over the previous year.

The volume of transportation by various means as follows:

	1994	Percent Increase Over 1993
Volume of freight transport (bn tn/km)	58.156	9.8
Railways (bn tn/km)	14.002	2.9
Highways (bn tn/km)	13.900	21.2
Waterways (bn tn/km)	30.228	7.2
Airways (mn tn/km)	26	8.3
Volume of passenger transport (bn person/km)	28.600	10.5
Railways (bn person/km)	6.801	9.2
Highways (bn person/km)	19.452	9.6
Waterways (mn person/km)	241	-30.9
Airways (bn person/km)	2.106	35.5
Cargo handled at coastal ports (mn tn)	30.0233	12.1

Post and telecommunications services developed rapidly. Total business transaction in 1994 was 3.648 billion yuan, an increase of 50.8 percent over the previous year. The capacity of long-distance exchanges reached 101,000 terminal circuits, up 21.1 percent. The capacity

continued...

FUJIAN STATISTICAL COMMUNIQUE, 1994 (continued)

of exchanges in the urban and rural areas was 2.646 million circuits, up 83.6 percent, 99.1 percent of which were program-controlled exchanges. By the end of 1994, the total number of telephone subscribers in the urban and rural areas was 1.177 million, up 57.0 percent. There was a net increase of 309,000 telephone subscribers in the cities and 118,000 subscribers in the rural areas. Mobile telephone business also developed rapidly. At the end of 1994, there were 69,000 mobile telephone subscribers, 150 percent more than the 1993 figure, representing a net increase of 41,000 subscribers; the number of radio paging subscribers was 818,000, up 95.7 percent, or a net increase of 400,000 subscribers.

V. Domestic Trade and Market Prices

The consumer market was brisk. In 1994, the total value of retail sales of consumer goods was 51.964 billion yuan, an increase of 33.6 percent over the previous year, or a real growth of 8.6 percent after allowing for price rises. Of this total, sales at urban markets reached 36.426 billion yuan, up 29.2 percent, while sales in the rural areas amounted to 15.538 billion yuan, up 45.3 percent. All-round growth was achieved in different economic sectors. Retail sales of consumer goods in state-owned commercial units totaled 11.826 billion yuan, an increase of 9.2 percent over the previous year; sales in collective commercial units totaled 8.729 billion yuan, up 47.8 percent; while sales in private commercial undertakings totaled 22.8 billion yuan, up 38.5 percent.

The market for the means of production was slow. In 1994, total purchases of the means of production by purchasing and marketing enterprises were 9.13 billion yuan, a drop of 24.6 percent compared with 1993; total sales were 9.5 billion yuan, a drop of 27.2 percent. Among the principal means of production, sales of rolled steel totaled 1,027,000 tons, a drop of 27.7 percent; sales of cement totaled 1,445,000 tons, a drop of 22.4 percent; while sales of motor vehicles totaled 15,000, basically the same as in 1993.

Due to policy-oriented price adjustments and the introduction of macroeconomic reform measures which affected market prices, coupled with the excessive growth of social demand and excessive price hikes, particularly soaring grain prices, the retail price index for commodities in 1994 was 123.0 (or 122.7 if agricultural means of production were included).

Prices in 1994	Percent Increase Over 1993
1. Retail prices of commodities	23.0
Of which: Urban areas	22.6
Rural areas	23.7
2. Consumer prices	25.3
Of which: Urban areas	25.1
Rural areas	25.5
Of which:	
Food	31.5
Grain	56.7
Poultry and poultry products	37.7
Edible vegetable oil	56.7
Eggs	26.0
Aquatic products	26.5
Fresh vegetables	24.6
Clothing	19.9
Household equipment and articles	11.1
Medical and health care products	11.7
Transportation and telecommunications	6.4
Recreational, educational and cultural facilities	8.1
Housing articles	20.1
Service price	24.1

continued...

FUJIAN STATISTICAL COMMUNIQUE, 1994 (continued)

Prices in 1994	Percent Increase Over 1993
3. Retail prices of agricultural means of production	17.8
4. Purchasing prices for energy and raw and semi-finished materials by industrial enterprises	15.2
5. Producers' prices of manufactured goods	16.9
6. Purchasing prices for farm and sideline products	28.1
7. Prices of investment in fixed assets	7.3

VI. Foreign Economic Relations

The development of foreign trade was rapid. Foreign trade statistics showed that the combined value of exports and imports of the province was US$13.332 billion, an increase of 35.1 percent over the previous year. Of this total, the value of exports was US$8.234 billion, up 41.3 percent, while the value of imports was US$5.098 billion, up 26.1 percent. Exports by foreign-funded enterprises totaled US$4.151 billion, an increase of 38.2 percent over the previous year, or 50.1 percent of the total value of exports of the province. Exports by the Xiamen Special Economic Zone accounted for 38.7 percent of the total export value of the province.

New achievements were made in the utilization of foreign capital. In 1994, a total of 3,026 contracts for the utilization of foreign capital amounting to US$7.232 billion were signed, a drop of 35.8 percent and 36.6 percent compared with their respective 1993 figures. Foreign capital actually utilized amounted to US$3.764 billion, including US$3.712 billion in direct investment, both representing an increase of 29.5 percent over the previous year. On average, each contract involved foreign capital amounting to US$2.39 million, the highest figure in the country. By the end of the year, 8,005 foreign-invested enterprises had been completed and put into operation.

Economic and technological cooperation with foreign countries continued to develop. Construction projects and labor service projects contracted by China with foreign countries in 1994 totaled 2,562 in number. The value of the contracts signed amounted to US$709 million, an increase of 4.3 percent over the previous year. Business revenue of these projects totaled US$472 million, up 19.0 percent. At the end of the year, 34,200 people were engaged in labor services outside the country, up 15.1 percent.

Fujian received 844,500 overseas tourists in 1994, a drop of 4.1 percent compared with the previous year. Of this total, 199,400 were foreigners, up 3.3 percent, while 616,000 were compatriots from Hong Kong, Macao and Taiwan, a drop of 7.9 percent.

VII. Banking, Insurance and Taxation

The financial situation was basically stable. At the end of the year, savings in various forms in financial institutions totaled 111.786 billion yuan, an increase of 29.349 billion yuan, or 35.6 percent, over the end of 1993. Of this total, savings by enterprises amounted to 38.011 billion yuan, an increase of 9.206 billion yuan, or 32.0 percent, over the end of the previous year; while savings by residents in the urban and rural areas amounted to 55.873 billion yuan, an increase of 16.468 billion yuan, or 41.8 percent, over the end of 1993. Loans in various forms extended by financial institutions totaled 97.040 billion yuan, an increase of 19.575 billion yuan, or 25.3 percent, over the end of 1993. Of this total, short-term loans amounted to 69.869 billion yuan, an increase of 14.463 billion yuan, or 26.1 percent; while intermediate- and long-term loans amounted to 18.072 billion yuan, an increase of 2.739 billion yuan, or 17.9 percent.

Rapid progress was made in insurance services. In 1994, the total accepted amounts of various kinds of insurance was 382.7 billion yuan; insurance premiums amounted to 2.091 billion yuan; and income from reserve assets amounted to 274 million yuan. A total of 21,000 enterprises and 1,005,000 families had taken out property insurance; 9,235,000 people had taken out personal insurance of various kinds; and 433,000 motor vehicles were insured. In 1994, some 375,000 claims by domestic and foreign claimants were processed. These

continued...

FUJIAN STATISTICAL COMMUNIQUE, 1994 (continued)

included 80,000 claims for reparations in property insurance and 280,000 claims for repara-tions in personal insurance from domestic claimants, and 8,000 claims for reparations in foreign business insurance. Insurance services played a positive role in maintaining social stability, promoting production, and ensuring stable livelihood.

New achievements were made in taxation work. In 1994, industrial and commercial tax collected amounted to 13.09 billion yuan, an increase of 34.5 percent over the previous year. Of this total, tax on foreign firms amounted to 2.4 billion yuan, up 46.4 percent; tax on private businesses amounted to 1.464 billion yuan, up 8.4 percent; and personal income tax amounted to 364 million yuan, up 32.8 percent.

VIII. Science and Technology, Education, Culture, Public Health, and Sports

Remarkable progress was achieved in science and technology. In 1994, a total of 175 scientific and technological achievements won awards at and above the provincial level. Research on solid-state materials, surface science and other key disciplines reached domestic and interna-tional advanced standards. State-level high and new industrial development zones were established in Fuzhou and Xiamen, while provincial-level development zones were established in Quanzhou, Nanping, Sanming and Zhangzhou. The ability of enterprises to develop science and technology increased. In 1994, investment in technological transformation in enterprises amounted to 4.202 billion yuan, an increase of 35 percent over the previous year. Scientific and technological personnel also increased in numbers. At the end of 1994, there were 499,800 specialized technological personnel in local state-owned enterprises and institutions, an increase of 15,600 people compared with the figure at the end of 1993. A total of 5,992 contracts on the transfer of technology were signed, involving an agreed value of 251 million yuan and a realized value of 208 million yuan. The provincial authorities also approved 20 technological imports, and contracts worth US$24.93 million were signed.

Further improvements were made in technological supervision, patent applications, survey-ing and mapping, and so on. In 1994, a total of 162 products produced by 102 enterprises were produced in accordance with international standards and certified to be up to international advanced standards or international standards. The ratio of qualified products per inspected batch was 72.1 percent, while the ratio of qualified commodities per inspected batch was 63.0 percent. A total of 1,510 patent applications were accepted, an increase of 18.8 percent over the previous year. Of this total, 733 applications were approved, a drop of 13.8 percent. The mapping departments completed a total of 131,000 work days of surveying and mapping work.

Educational undertakings developed at a faster pace. In 1994, the enrollment of new graduate students was 806, an increase of 294 over the previous year. The total number of students taking graduate courses was 1,967, an increase of 595. Institutions of higher learning took in 22,600 new undergraduate students, a drop of 1,273. The total number of enrolled undergraduate students was 69,300, an increase of 5,190; the total number of graduates was 16,900, an increase of 369. There were 86,100 students studying in secondary specialized or technical schools, 44,200 students studying in technical workers' training schools, and 144,500 students studying in secondary vocational schools. The total number of secondary school students in the province was 1.3621 million, an increase of 82,400 over the previous year, while the total number of primary school students was 3.7198 million, an increase of 81,300. The enrollment ratio of school-age children was 99.97 percent, while the rate of primary school leavers entering schools at a higher level was 82.63 percent. There were 1.0089 million children in kindergartens.

New achievements were made in adult education. In 1994, institutions of adult higher education took in 15,700 new students in undergraduate and special courses. Total enrollment in these institutions was 37,700, and 5,300 students graduated in 1994. There were 64,500 students in adult secondary specialized schools. Illiteracy among young and able-bodied people dropped to 5 percent.

continued...

FUJIAN STATISTICAL COMMUNIQUE, 1994 (continued)

Cultural and art undertakings continued to make steady progress. By the end of 1994, there were 2,778 film projection units, 90 cultural centers and galleries, 76 public libraries, 90 performing groups, and 64 museums and memorial halls, in the province. Television and radio broadcasting also developed rapidly. There were 43 radio broadcasting stations, 36 medium- and short-wave radio transmitting and relay stations, and 102 frequency-modulation radio transmitting and relay stations, as well as 13 television stations and 3,065 television transmitting and relay stations, including 15 television transmitting and relay stations each with a capacity of over 1,000 watts. Initial success was achieved in the building of satellite up-link stations, and there were 3,135 satellite ground stations in the province. Cable television networks were built, and there were 1.32 million cable television terminals in the province. A total of 492 million copies of newspapers, 40.0350 million copies of magazines, and 197 million copies of books were printed in 1994.

New progress was made in public health undertakings. The three-level medical network and epidemic prevention system in the urban and rural areas gradually took shape and improved. By the end of 1994, there were 4,537 public health institutions of various types in the province. These included 1,260 hospitals, 2,896 outpatient departments and clinics, 12 sanitariums, 67 mother-and-child health clinics (stations), and 97 health and epidemic-prevention stations. There were 91,200 full-time health workers in the province, including 38,000 doctors and 24,100 nurses. There were 72,800 beds in public health organs in the province at the end of 1994.

New achievements were made in sports. Mass sports activities vigorously developed. Athletes from our province won 76 gold medals, 34 silver medals and 26 bronze medals in world championships. At the end of 1994, over 2.9 million people met the requirements of the National Standards for Physical Exercises; there were 19 advanced sports counties in the province.

IX. Population and the People Lives

According to sample surveys, at the end of 1994 the birth rate was 16.24 per thousand and the death rate was 5.95 per thousand, resulting in a natural growth rate of 10.29 per thousand. The total permanent resident population at the end of the year was estimated to be 31.83 million, an increase of 330,000 over the end of 1993.

Household income in the urban and rural areas increased steadily. According to a sample survey, annual per capita income of urban households for living expenses was 3,508 yuan, an increase of 35.0 percent over the previous year, or a real increase of 7.7 percent after allowing for price rises. The per-capita net income of rural households was 1,578 yuan, an increase of 30.3 percent over the previous year, or a real increase of 4.5 percent after allowing for price rises.

Reform in the field of labor accelerated, and the labor and employment system further improved. There were 1,191 employment agencies at various levels at the end of 1994, and 132,500 people were given jobs in cities and towns. At the end of the year, the number of jobless was 76,000, and the rate of unemployment was 1.9 percent. A total of 11,000 enterprises and 1.35 million staff and workers in the province had joined unemployment insurance programs.

The number of staff and workers continued to increase. At the end of 1994, there were 3,514,000 staff and workers in cities and towns, an increase of 66,000 over the figure at the end of 1993. The number of staff and workers was 2,176,000 in state-owned units, 662,000 in collective units, and 676,000 in units under other ownership systems. Total wages of staff and workers in 1994 amounted to 16.679 billion yuan, an increase of 43.1 percent over the previous year.

Fujian Ribao, 30 Mar 1995.

XVII CITIES AND URBANIZATION

BASIC INDICATOR OF URBAN HOUSEHOLDS INCOME EXPENDITURE BY CITIES, 1995 (yuan)

	Total Income	Income Available for Living	Expenditure Available for Living
National total	354.65	335.25	291.65
Beijing	411.36	391.93	319.39
Tianjin	330.75	315.60	239.22
Shijiazhuang	276.82	261.04	215.51
Taiyuan	253.64	233.18	194.67
Hohhot	219.48	207.75	202.36
Shenyang	269.86	252.33	247.14
Dalian	353.20	334.55	296.90
Changchun	216.69	207.19	178.96
Harbin	242.05	223.67	223.68
Shanghai	459.46	443.53	369.72
Nanjing	320.49	302.72	290.41
Hangzhou	410.08	400.77	347.18
Ningbo	459.92	426.85	311.92
Hefei	269.10	249.79	262.44
Fuzhou	330.74	296.12	322.84
Xiamen	436.36	412.76	347.76
Nanchang	261.96	241.70	199.05
Jinan	328.84	314.78	265.86
Qingdao	325.59	319.35	277.94
Zhengzhou	369.04	350.99	277.88
Wuhan	309.13	294.81	253.19
Changsha	310.92	280.03	262.11
Guangzhou	611.24	581.70	492.26
Shenzhen	854.30	806.26	751.86
Nanning	346.78	320.63	327.52
Haikou	440.15	417.87	319.25
Chengdu	308.23	289.09	262.86
Chongqing	253.27	233.53	228.37
Guiyang	248.30	224.44	221.32
Kunming	314.43	294.29	268.66
Xian	257.49	241.94	243.42
Lanzhou	273.41	257.77	217.25
Xining	216.98	193.46	213.94
Yinchuan	389.39	364.27	284.41
Urumqi	283.10	267.75	229.06

World Facts, Jun 1995.

PROPORTION OF LIVING EXPENDITURE OF URBAN HOUSEHOLDS OF 35 CITIES, 1995 (percent)

	Living Expenditure	Food	Grain	Meat and Related Products	Eggs	Aquatic Products
National total	100.00	51.77	6.50	10.47	2.38	3.99
Beijing	100.00	46.84	4.56	9.54	2.08	1.52
Tianjin	100.00	53.93	6.58	9.63	3.49	3.14

continued…

PROPORTION OF LIVING EXPENDITURE OF URBAN HOUSEHOLDS OF 35 CITIES, 1995 (percent) (continued)

	Living Expenditure	Food	Grain	Meat and Related Products	Eggs	Aquatic Products
Shijiazhuang	100.00	46.69	5.55	8.13	3.56	1.49
Taiyuan	100.00	53.83	9.92	7.63	3.76	0.77
Hohhot	100.00	45.30	11.08	7.86	2.21	0.61
Shenyang	100.00	51.52	8.35	7.57	3.70	2.08
Dalian	100.00	49.94	5.54	8.67	3.41	4.61
Changchun	100.00	51.23	7.91	9.18	2.90	1.48
Harbin	100.00	54.11	9.03	8.26	4.14	2.66
Shanghai	100.00	52.64	4.65	10.68	1.59	7.88
Nanjing	100.00	50.92	5.01	12.35	2.48	5.11
Hangzhou	100.00	50.64	5.04	9.27	1.35	6.78
Ningbo	100.00	53.55	5.09	8.40	0.94	12.99
Hefei	100.00	48.79	6.33	11.67	2.75	3.38
Fuzhou	100.00	53.60	7.26	10.39	2.07	10.75
Xiamen	100.00	55.17	5.20	12.78	1.84	10.10
Nanchang	100.00	60.56	8.93	15.43	3.22	3.36
Jinan	100.00	49.43	5.72	9.34	3.69	1.64
Qingdao	100.00	52.60	6.31	10.37	3.97	6.29
Zhengzhou	100.00	45.14	9.13	7.44	3.42	1.38
Wuhan	100.00	55.60	6.57	10.34	2.68	3.43
Changsha	100.00	52.80	7.02	9.00	2.04	2.77
Guangzhou	100.00	54.29	6.04	12.15	1.25	5.20
Shenzhen	100.00	40.93	4.67	9.68	1.01	3.36
Naming	100.00	53.98	8.60	18.80	1.50	2.77
Haikou	100.00	64.41	5.68	18.52	0.87	9.62
Chengdu	100.00	57.72	6.43	14.40	3.59	1.35
Chongqing	100.00	57.72	7.97	12.97	3.37	1.87
Guiyang	100.00	60.70	8.14	14.25	2.57	1.85
Kunming	100.00	56.01	9.56	10.59	1.84	2.32
Xian	100.00	47.59	6.39	6.70	3.04	0.94
Lanzhou	100.00	53.93	10.28	7.53	1.65	1.10
Xining	100.00	51.47	14.32	7.62	2.20	0.91
Yinchuan	100.00	36.94	6.18	6.34	1.92	0.85
Urumqi	100.00	49.89	7.72	10.15	2.94	1.67

	Clothing	Household Facilities Appliance and Services	Medicine and Medical Services	Traffic and Communications	Recreational, Educational and Cultural Services	Durable Consumer Goods for Recreational
National total	12.17	10.11	2.83	5.03	7.33	1.88
Beijing	15.94	10.99	2.62	5.44	9.24	2.37
Tianjin	13.82	6.51	1.86	7.68	5.40	0.86
Shijiazhuang	17.68	11.45	2.50	4.45	8.03	2.27
Taiyuan	16.30	6.51	4.27	2.33	5.32	0.04
Hohhot	18.01	10.21	3.60	4.74	7.92	3.64
Shenyang	19.68	5.76	2.71	2.26	6.28	1.00
Dalian	17.73	4.21	2.35	8.75	6.77	1.76

continued...

PROPORTION OF LIVING EXPENDITURE OF URBAN HOUSEHOLDS OF 35 CITIES, 1995 (percent) (continued)

	Clothing	House-hold Facilities Appliance and Services	Medicine and Medical Services	Traffic and Communi-cations	Recrea-tional, Educa-tional and Cultural Services	Durable Consumer Goods for Recrea-tional
Changchun	19.09	5.45	4.24	3.36	5.70	0.28
Harbin	15.42	4.04	3.86	2.34	9.86	0.02
Shanghai	10.35	14.69	1.86	6.24	4.92	0.25
Nanjing	10.68	6.06	1.15	16.47	6.46	0.65
Hangzhou	11.20	11.97	2.44	4.87	8.78	4.76
Ningbo	10.68	10.04	3.89	2.84	7.76	0.62
Hefei	14.60	11.89	1.47	9.80	3.58	0.34
Fuzhou	8.01	19.01	2.77	2.12	5.79	0.19
Xiamen	9.76	3.95	1.80	9.95	6.42	0.09
Nanchang	9.37	5.70	3.37	1.19	5.16	1.86
Jinan	10.94	11.44	2.78	3.82	10.91	7.04
Qingdao	17.11	4.11	3.15	2.43	9.39	1.80
Zhengzhou	13.12	11.67	2.32	4.41	12.52	5.08
Wuhan	13.11	9.84	2.82	3.03	4.25	0.23
Changsha	14.49	4.71	2.38	10.08	7.40	0.84
Guangzhou	5.17	15.79	2.89	3.17	9.49	3.10
Shenzhen	7.18	12.47	5.24	7.20	9.50	4.76
Nanning	7.18	13.87	1.54	6.44	5.14	1.97
Haikou	5.95	6.07	2.02	5.67	3.38	0.00
Chengdu	11.52	10.02	1.79	1.49	7.78	0.06
Chongqing	10.12	9.15	2.65	4.11	7.72	2.37
Guiyang	10.39	8.13	2.39	2.22	6.30	3.63
Kunming	12.42	3.86	4.96	2.33	10.28	3.50
Xian	10.60	15.36	5.50	3.10	7.83	2.16
Lanzhou	10.65	2.08	0.00	0.00	0.90	0.85
Xining	13.68	7.49	12.04	2.43	4.73	0.25
Yinchuan	15.11	8.03	2.71	12.08	13.60	6.94
Urumqi	18.68	9.22	3.22	3.19	5.26	0.01

	Education	Cultural and Recreation	Residence	Housing	Water, Electricity and Fuel	Other
National total	2.87	2.60	6.03	2.25	3.76	4.32
Beijing	3.28	3.59	4.58	2.20	2.39	4.34
Tianjin	1.57	2.97	5.04	1.32	3.72	5.75
Shijiazhuang	3.41	2.35	4.17	1.30	2.87	5.04
Taiyuan	3.75	1.52	7.21	3.22	4.00	4.23
Hohhot	1.69	2.58	3.34	1.56	1.78	6.89
Shenyang	4.39	0.89	7.26	2.92	4.34	4.55
Dalian	3.28	1.73	5.75	1.07	4.69	4.50
Changchun	3.25	2.17	6.89	2.56	4.33	4.04
Harbin	4.54	5.31	6.34	1.50	4.84	4.01
Shanghai	2.03	2.63	5.06	1.50	3.56	4.24
Nanjing	3.17	2.65	5.48	1.41	4.07	2.77
Hangzhou	2.14	1.88	6.64	1.84	4.80	3.47

continued...

PROPORTION OF LIVING EXPENDITURE OF URBAN HOUSEHOLDS OF 35 CITIES, 1995 (percent) (continued)

	Education	Cultural and Recreation	Residence	Housing	Water, Electricity and Fuel	Other
Ningbo	4.84	2.30	6.79	3.17	3.62	4.45
Hefei	1.81	1.42	4.15	0.88	3.27	5.71
Fuzhou	3.89	1.71	5.24	0.67	4.57	3.47
Xiamen	4.30	2.03	8.61	2.54	6.08	4.33
Nanchang	1.67	1.63	12.41	8.98	3.43	2.22
Jinan	2.11	1.77	6.25	1.92	4.32	4.44
Qingdao	4.06	3.53	5.42	1.81	3.61	5.79
Zhengzhou	4.13	3.31	6.69	3.44	3.25	4.13
Wuhan	2.19	1.83	7.13	2.20	4.93	4.22
Changsha	3.66	2.90	5.46	1.72	3.74	2.67
Guangzhou	3.18	3.21	5.88	2.28	3.59	3.32
Shenzhen	1.93	2.81	13.50	8.24	5.25	3.98
Nanning	1.47	1.70	8.22	3.43	4.78	3.64
Haikou	1.70	1.68	6.45	1.31	5.14	6.05
Chengdu	5.15	2.57	6.07	2.29	3.78	3.60
Chongqing	3.14	2.21	5.20	1.45	3.75	3.34
Guiyang	0.63	2.04	5.32	1.47	3.85	4.55
Kunming	4.51	2.27	4.13	0.52	3.61	5.97
Xian	2.48	3.19	4.60	1.08	3.53	5.42
Lanzhou	0.03	0.86	1.82	0.79	0.17	0.00
Xining	2.69	1.79	3.20	0.62	2.59	4.96
Yinchuan	2.27	4.39	3.29	1.05	2.24	8.24
Urumqi	1.82	3.43	4.31	1.93	2.37	6.24

World Facts, Jun 1995.

BASIC INDICATORS OF URBAN HOUSEHOLDS BY REGION, 1995 (person)

	Number of Surveys (home)	Number of Persons of Family	Number of Employees	Employment Rate (percent)	Number of Dependents Per Employee	Number of Retire
National total	35,020.00	3.28	1.88	57.45	1.74	0.31
Beijing	500.00	3.16	1.97	62.35	1.60	0.38
Tianjin	500.00	3.15	1.75	55.66	1.80	0.53
Hebei	1,598.37	3.19	1.93	60.47	1.65	0.22
Shanxi	1,150.01	3.46	1.93	55.84	1.79	0.26
Inner Mongolia	1,400.01	3.43	1.88	54.63	1.83	0.27
Liaoning	3,000.00	3.21	1.93	60.21	1.66	0.34
Jilin	1,350.04	3.26	1.89	57.79	1.73	0.30
Heilongjiang	1,200.00	3.29	1.82	55.22	1.81	0.39
Shanghai	500.00	3.09	1.70	55.10	1.81	0.64
Jiangsu	2,020.06	3.24	1.91	59.06	1.69	0.43
Zhejiang	1,510.00	3.07	1.94	63.23	1.58	0.29
Anhui	1,289.99	3.26	1.89	58.06	1.72	0.31
Fujian	1,249.95	3.31	1.93	58.34	1.71	0.33
Jiangxi	750.00	3.24	1.90	58.58	1.71	0.31
Shandong	2,080.06	3.22	1.96	61.07	1.64	0.24
Henan	2,200.00	3.37	1.90	56.40	1.77	0.36

continued...

BASIC INDICATORS OF URBAN HOUSEHOLDS BY REGION, 1995 (person) (continued)

	Number of Surveys (home)	Number of Persons of Family	Number of Employees	Employment Rate (percent)	Number of Dependents Per Employee	Number of Retire
Hubei	1,330.00	3.24	1.96	60.53	1.65	0.24
Hunan	1,000.00	3.17	1.87	59.12	1.69	0.24
Guangdong	1,550.06	3.64	2.08	57.30	1.75	0.32
Guangxi	1,000.00	3.32	1.89	56.85	1.76	0.19
Hainan	200.00	3.99	2.05	51.45	1.94	0.23
Sichuan	2,000.00	3.07	1.77	57.65	1.73	0.29
Guizhou	830.01	3.11	1.72	55.31	1.81	0.36
Yunnan	950.00	3.19	1.83	57.28	1.75	0.28
Tibet						
Shaanxi	1,400.00	3.19	1.74	54.45	1.84	0.36
Gansu	880.00	3.32	1.80	54.05	1.85	0.29
Qinghai	450.00	3.53	1.79	50.61	1.98	0.21
Ningxia	550.00	3.25	1.88	57.63	1.74	0.22
Xinjiang	590.00	3.46	1.89	54.56	1.83	0.24

World Facts, Jun 1995.

BASIC INDICATORS OF URBAN HOUSEHOLDS INCOME AND EXPENDITURE BY REGION, 1995 (yuan)

	Total Income	Income Available for Living	Expenditure Available for Living
National total	257.79	236.87	211.85
Beijing	397.93	376.89	322.93
Tianjin	305.61	288.16	251.64
Hebei	235.29	218.49	189.20
Shanxi	197.28	178.64	149.17
Inner Mongolia	183.37	170.13	152.57
Liaoning	237.44	215.32	197.91
Jilin	194.66	173.81	154.69
Heilongjiang	197.16	176.40	163.05
Shanghai	443.86	418.86	360. 59
Jiangsu	261.30	240.02	230.07
Zhejiang	358.31	334.83	297.33
Anhui	217.51	199.66	187.76
Fujian	253.44	226.94	232.11
Jiangxi	215.84	198.54	163.38
Shandong	262.56	246.70	198.87
Henan	198.24	183.34	164.22
Hubei	250.49	225.90	196.91
Hunan	285.03	250.37	230.42
Guangdong	470.07	442.46	389.11
Guangxi	282.33	257.66	242.32
Hainan	282.10	256.36	220.03
Sichuan	229.48	209.06	203.64
Guizhou	213.85	184.72	168.88
Yunnan	270.83	247.10	218.14
Tibet			

continued...

BASIC INDICATORS OF URBAN HOUSEHOLDS INCOME AND EXPENDITURE BY REGION, 1995 (yuan) (continued)

	Total Income	Income Available for Living	Expenditure Available for Living
Shaanxi	200.38	186.60	164.42
Gansu	208.48	194.85	156.14
Qinghai	196.08	181.48	172.66
Ningxia	231.41	211.93	192.23
Xinjiang	232.88	211.07	191.52

World Facts, Jun 1995.

COMPARISON OF NATIONAL URBAN, RURAL PRICE INDICES, 1994

	Commodity Retail Price Index	Household Consumer Price Index		Commodity Retail Price Index	Household Consumer Price Index
January	119.0	121.1	July	121.4	124.2
February	120.9	123.2	August	123.5	125.8
March	120.2	122.4	September	124.6	127.2
April	119.5	121.7	January-Sep-		
May	118.9	121.3	tember	120.9	123.3
June	120.0	122.6			

X, 17 Feb 1995.

CHINA URBANIZATION COMPARED TO THAT OF LARGE COUNTRIES, 1995

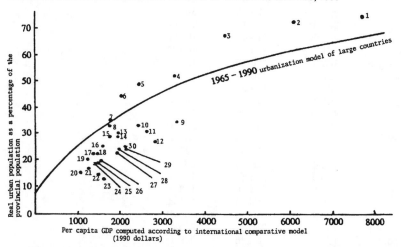

Key:—1. Shanghai—2. Beijing—3. Tianjin—4. Liaoning—5. Heilongjiang—6. Jilin—7. Inner Mongolia—8. Shanxi—9. Guangdong—10. Xinjiang—11. Jiangsu—12. Zhejiang—13. Qinghai—14. Hubei—15. Ningxia—16. Jiangxi—17. Shaanxi—18. Gansu—19. Anhui—20. Guizhou—21. Guangxi—22. Yunnan—23. Tibet—24. Henan—25. Sichuan—26. Hunan—27. Hebei—28. Hainan—29. Shandong—30. Fujian.

X, 27 Apr 1995.

CHINA'S EMPLOYMENT REFORM MODEL, 1994

China will control the unemployment rate in cities to within 3 percent.

According to the official data, at the end of last year, there were 4.8 million unemployed people in cities and towns, and the unemployment rate was 2.9 percent, figures which exclude the several million workers who had to receive subsidies to supplement their income.

This year, the focal point of reform in China is the state-owned enterprises which do not have full employment. Enterprises with long-term losses and cannot pay off their debts will be suspended, reorganized or even be made bankrupt. In last year's economy, state-owned enterprises fared better, but the losses of some enterprise still increased heavily. 34.3 percent of state-owned enterprises showed losses.

The experts concerned think that the economy in urban areas not only has to accept the laborers who have left state-owned enterprises but also the 30 million farmers who have left their land. The main solution to these problems is to provide employment opportunities in rural areas.

China Business, 8 Aug 1994.

COMPARISON OF URBANIZATION PROGRESS OF PROVINCES, 1991

Province Name	Urban Nonfarm Population Proportion (%)	Nonfarm Worker Percentage	Real Urban Population Proportion (%)	Per Capita GNP (1991, yuan)	Per Capita GNP (1990, dollars)	Great-Nation-Model Estimated Value (%)	Difference Between Real Value and Estimated Value (%)	Deviation Rate (%)	Classified Jurisdiction
National	19.2	40.2	27.8	1,725	2,073	38.3	-10.5	-27.4	Generally Lagging
Beijing	61.3	86.4	72.8	5,106	6,136	62.6	10.2	16.3	Generally Leading
Tianjin	55.1	80.2	66.5	3,711	4,460	55.4	11.1	20.0	Generally Leading
Hebei	13.5	40.3	23.3	1,544	1,856	36.1	-12.8	-35.5	Severely Lagging
Shanxi	21.1	52.9	33.5	1,462	1,757	35.0	-1.5	-4.3	Appropriate
Inner Mongolia	28.8	44.4	35.8	1,469	1,765	35.1	0.7	2.0	Appropriate
Liaoning	41.1	65.5	51.9	2,690	3,232	48.0	3.9	8.1	Appropriate
Jilin	38.0	52.0	44.5	1,690	2,031	37.9	6.6	17.4	Generally Leading
Heilongjiang	39.3	61.7	49.2	2,047	2,460	41.9	7.3	17.4	Generally Leading
Shanghai	63.3	88.7	74.9	6,401	7,693	67.5	7.4	11.0	Appropriate
Jiangsu	19.0	52.4	31.6	2,172	2,610	43.2	-11.6	-26.9	Generally Lagging
Zhejiang	15.8	47.7	27.5	2,341	2,813	44.9	-17.4	-38.8	Severely Lagging
Anhui	13.4	31.4	20.5	1,041	1,251	29.0	-8.5	-29.3	Generally Lagging
Fujian	15.3	42.4	25.5	1,812	2,178	39.3	-13.8	-35.1	Severely Lagging
Jiangxi	15.9	34.7	23.5	1,193	1,434	31.3	-7.8	-24.9	Generally Lagging
Shandong	16.1	38.4	24.9	1,830	2,199	39.5	-14.6	-37.0	Severely Lagging
Henan	11.6	31.6	19.1	1,133	1,362	30.4	-11.3	-37.2	Severely Lagging
Hubei	21.1	39.7	28.9	1,557	1,871	36.3	-7.4	-20.4	Generally Lagging
Hunan	13.8	28.6	19.9	1,266	1,521	32.3	-12.4	-38.4	Severely Lagging
Guangdong	23.7	51.0	34.8	2,765	3,323	48.6	-13.8	-28.4	Generally Lagging
Guangxi	11.6	24.5	16.9	1,048	1,259	29.1	-12.2	-41.9	Severely Lagging

continued...

COMPARISON OF URBANIZATION PROGRESS OF PROVINCES, 1991 (continued)

Province Name	Urban Nonfarm Population Proportion (%)	Nonfarm Worker Percentage	Real Urban Population Proportion (%)	Per Capita GNP (1991, yuan)	Per Capita GNP (1990, dollars)	Great-Nation-Model Estimated Value (%)	Difference Between Real Value and Estimated Value (%)	Deviation Rate (%)	Classified Jurisdiction
Hainan	18.5	31.4	24.1	1,622	1,949	37.1	-13.0	-35.0	Severely Lagging
Sichuan	12.9	28.5	19.2	1,179	1,417	31.1	-11.9	-38.3	Severely Lagging
Guizhou	11.2	22.1	15.7	873	1,049	26.2	-10.5	-40.1	Severely Lagging
Yunnan	10.6	22.1	15.3	1,145	1,376	30.6	-15.3	-50.0	Severely Lagging
Tibet	8.6	20.8	13.4	1,351	1,624	33.5	-20.1	-60.0	Severely Lagging
Shaanxi	17.3	37.1	25.3	1,281	1,540	32.6	-7.3	-22.4	Generally Lagging
Gansu	15.4	35.9	23.5	1,119	1,345	30.2	-6.7	-22.2	Generally Lagging
Qinghai	23.0	40.1	30.3	1,599	1,922	36.8	-6.5	-17.7	Generally Lagging
Ningxia	22.4	37.9	29.1	1,405	1,689	34.3	-5.2	-15.2	Generally Lagging
Xinjiang	28.0	40.1	33.5	2,005	2,410	41.5	-8.0	-19.3	Generally Lagging

X, 27 Apr 1995.

URBANIZATION LEVEL COMPARED TO ECONOMIC DEVELOPMENT, 1995

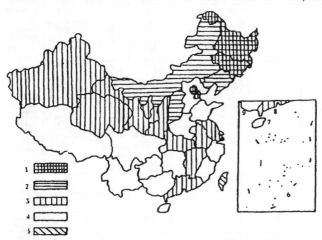

Key:—1. Generally advanced region—2. Appropriate—3. Generally lagging—4. Severely lagging—5. Insufficient data—6. Spratlys—7. Hainan—8. Guangdong—9. Guangxi.

X, 27 Apr 1995.

BEIJING URBAN CONSTRUCTION, 1995

In the heart of Beijing between the southern end of Wangfujing and Dongdan, the attention of anyone passing by is drawn to a large site where demolition work has come to a halt. A month or so ago, the sound of construction machinery of all descriptions was still rumbling on this site. According to a BEIJING WANBAO report on 18 November 1994, the foundation work being carried out at this site was for the Hong Kong-funded Oriental Plaza. Why has work now come to a standstill?

It is understood that one of the reasons why work at the Oriental Plaza has come to a halt is that the scale of construction and the design proposal for the project are at variance with the relevant Beijing urban planning regulations. At present, the design proposal for the project is being readjusted in accordance with the requirements of the "Overall Urban Planning for Beijing" and the project is being reviewed for approval in line with the prescribed procedures. The controversy over this project has aroused much public concern. People are interested in how urban construction can be brought onto the track of the legal system.

Planning Rules and Regulations Are Being Heavily Pounded

The Oriental Plaza project, funded by a consortium headed by Hong Kong's Cheung Kong Holdings, is a huge commercial development, which incorporates business and office premises and recreational facilities. According to the design proposed by the developers, the Oriental Plaza will be over 480 m from east to west. It will be built on a 90,000-square-m site. When completed, the project will have a floor space of over 700,000 square m and will be over 70 m in height.

This design proposal met with objections as soon as it was announced, because its height greatly exceeds the limits prescribed in the 1991-2010 "Overall Urban Planning for Beijing," which was approved by the State Council. The document lays down the following requirements for the protection of this historical cultural city: "With the Imperial Palace and the old imperial city at the center, there are to be graded height limits for all surrounding buildings. The old imperial city should be kept open and spacious, with height limits gradually increasing outwards. High-rise buildings may be permitted along Changan Street and Qiansanmen Avenue, the inner part of the two ring roads, and some sections of the main roads. The general height limit is 30 meters, or 45 meters in individual places." The written reply given by the State Council on the "Overall Urban Planning for Beijing" clearly pointed out: "The principles, measures, and contents laid down in the 'Overall Urban Planning' are feasible and must be implemented in real earnest.... The relevant requirements on distribution, density, and height limits must be strictly adhered to and must not be breached." The Oriental Plaza project exceeds the height limits of the "Overall Urban Planning for Beijing" by 30 to 40 m and is obviously in contravention of the instructions by the State Council.

The proposed Oriental Plaza development, together with the east wing of Beijing Hotel, which is 120 meters wide and over 80 m high, will create a massive concrete block stretching for 600 m and standing 70 to 80 m tall. Its presence will not only overwhelm the Imperial Palace but will affect the landscape of Tiananmen Square, which is only 1.2 km away, fundamentally ruining the features of the ancient capital. The average height of the Great Hall of the People is 31 m; it is 40 m high in some places and has a total floor area of 170,000 square m. The Tiananmen Tower is 35 m high, while the Monument of People's Heroes is 38.29 m high. The Oriental Plaza, which will be four times the size of the Great Hall of the People, will overwhelm these historical buildings which are the embodiments of the nation's political center, making them look relatively small. This will put the city off center and upset the layout of the capital city with Tiananmen Square as its center.

According to the plan for Changan Street mapped out in 1985 by the Beijing CPC Committee, the Committee for Planning and Construction in the Capital, and the Beijing Municipal People's Government, "the Youth Theater and Children's Cinema on the northern side of the intersection between Wangfujing South and Dongdan will be renovated and expanded to become the cultural center of the eastern section of Changan Street." According to the design proposal for Oriental Plaza, the theater and cinema will be torn down and relocated at a new

continued...

BEIJING URBAN CONSTRUCTION, 1995 (continued)

site in Dongdan. If the plaza is built according to the original design, traffic in the Wangfujing and Dongdan areas will also be further aggravated. The development will only provide 1,500 parking spaces, less than half the minimum requirement of 4.5 parking spaces per 1,000 square m for commercial buildings in Beijing.

Protection of the Ancient Capital: A Common Historical Mission
On 23 August 1994, Zhou Ganshi [0719 1626 1492], Wu Liangyong [0702 5326 6978], Zhang Kaiji [1728 7030 3444] and three other architectural experts submitted a joint petition questioning the design proposal for the Oriental Plaza. In their opinion, the design "will alter the level and spacious traditional set-up and special quality of the old city center and will outshine Tiananmen Square and the Great Hall of the People. The traffic problem this development is likely to create is also difficult to resolve." They proposed that efforts be made to "strengthen unified leadership over the planning and development of Changan Street. The redevelopment of the old city cannot be based on the economic returns of isolated sites alone. We must adhere to planning and take into consideration the long-term environmental and cultural impacts. We must not go after high capacity and returns one-sidedly. Hong Kong and Macao experts and developers have experience in high-density and high-capacity developments but comrades in China should recognize soberly that it is not universally applicable to all parts of China, being particularly unsuitable for the city center of the ancient capital."

On 24 October, Luo Zhewen [5012 0772 2429], Xie Yuchen [6200 7183 6591], Fu Xinian [0265 3588 1628], and two other Chinese People's Political Consultative Conference [CPPCC] delegates submitted a joint motion, pointing out that the design proposal for the Oriental Plaza "will ruin the features of Beijing—the famous historical and cultural city of China and the world and is a grave violation of the stipulations made in the 'Overall Urban Planning for Beijing' already approved by the State Council." The CPPCC delegates proposed that the following actions be taken: "1. It is necessary to do things according to law. Work can only proceed when the project has been examined and approved in accordance with the plan submitted by the municipal government and approved by the State Council. 2. The feasibility of the project should be discussed by experts and the views of experts should be widely solicited. 3. It is inadvisable to one-sidedly go after high-capacity and high returns in the redevelopment of the old city. The experience of Hong Kong and Macao developers in high-density and high-capacity developments is unsuitable for China, particularly for historical cultural cities and the ancient capital city of Beijing, and should be treated with great care."

On 26 October, Zheng Siyuan [6774 1835 6678], Shan Shiyuan [0830 1102 0337], Wang Dingguo [3769 1353 0948] and three other historical relics experts submitted a joint petition calling for more efforts to protect the traditional look of the capital. "The pressing task now is that on no account must we do further damage and launch new construction projects that are not in accord with the urban planning for the capital. The Oriental Plaza project is at the central part of the ancient capital. If it is allowed to proceed according to the existing design proposal, the features of the ancient capital will be seriously affected, which is not in accord with the provisions of the law." They proposed that the following actions be taken: "1. The Oriental Plaza should be relocated away from the heart of the old city and redesigned in order to preserve the features of the ancient capital. 2. In future, all large-scale developments in central Beijing must be planned in a unified way and must be examined and approved in strict accordance with laws and regulations as well as urban planning requirements."

Although the proposals put forward by experts have different points of emphasis, they share a common desire to preserve the ancient appearance of Beijing in urban development. They also share the view that decisions on the redevelopment of the ancient city should be reached on a democratic, scientific, and legal basis.

On 22 November, some leaders of the Capital Planning and Construction Committee heard the proposals put forward by Xie Chensheng [6200 6591 3932], Zheng Siyuan, Shan Shiyuan, Wang Dingguo, Chai Zemin [2693 34193046] and Zhao Jing [6392 7234]. At the meeting, the six experts urged that adjustments be made to the height and size of the Oriental Plaza project

continued...

BEIJING URBAN CONSTRUCTION, 1995 (continued)

in order to protect the grand vista of Tiananmen Square. They said that all overseas investors alike must abide by urban planning requirements and the law when they invest in development projects in Beijing, as this is a matter of dignity. Modernization must be integrated with the protection of historical cultural cities and all buildings must blend in well with their surrounding environment. They said that all projects must be incorporated in the urban planning of the capital and that he who puts in the money does not necessarily have the final say.

What is particularly moving is that 75-year-old Chen Gan [7115 1626], a leading town planner who had taken part in the drafting of the "Overall Urban Planning for Beijing" at various stages, and who completed the first planning for Tiananmen Square after the founding of new China and chose the place to erect the pole for the national flag, died on 30 November after busily going around trying to make the Oriental Plaza project conform with the overall city plan in spite of his great age and feeble condition. At the time of his death, he was still thinking of the planning and development of Changan Street.

The Solemnity of Urban Planning Regulations Is Beyond Doubt

In addition to problems with the project itself, the Oriental Plaza development has drawn many objections also because people have come to realize that they must face the problem at issue: In their pursuit for high returns, foreign investors who have come to invest in the redevelopment of the old city and other real estate projects in Beijing have ignored Beijing's urban planning regulations and demanded that height and capacity limits be extended. This not only poses a great threat to the appearance of the ancient capital but puts Beijing's urban planning regulations in danger of being abandoned altogether.

Will foreign investors be unable to make money if they abide by Beijing's urban planning regulations? The answer is in the negative. Some experts have made calculations on the basis of the current land cost, relocation, and other expenses, and come up with the following conclusion: Foreign investors can expect returns of over 100 percent if they develop real estate in accordance with Beijing's urban planning regulations. The profits are amazingly good. It is understood that returns on real estate developments in Hong Kong are 10 to 20 percent, while returns are even lower in other countries and regions. For example, returns are only 6 percent in Sydney, 5 percent in Singapore, and 2 percent in Japan.

Regrettably, violations of urban planning regulations similar to those committed by the Oriental Plaza developers can be found to varying degrees in many other parts of Beijing. Some foreign investors have defied urban planning regulations by increasing the height and dimensions of their property developments and have made demands on the basis of the east wing of the Beijing Hotel, which has long been regarded as an "eyesore." The Beijing Urban Planning Regulations have been repeatedly bent under the unreasonable demands made by a small number of foreign investors. High-rises are set to sprawl all over the heart of the old city. In view of this situation, many urban construction experts have made strong appeals during their interviews, for law and discipline to be more strictly enforced. They said they could not but doubt the solemnity of the legal system if the Oriental Plaza project was allowed to proceed according to its existing design proposal. They were afraid that if others followed, Beijing's overall urban planning would be rendered useless and the features of the ancient city would not be preserved.

According to experts, in most countries where there is a legal system, urban planning regulations which have been examined and approved are legally binding. No one is allowed to modify these regulations without authorization and all violations are punished according to law. In real estate developments where foreign investment is involved, whether or not urban planning is respected by foreign investors is a matter which concerns the dignity of sovereignty and one must not be vague on such matters.

By comparison, the authority of urban planning is really poor in some places in our country. Although urban planning regulations which have been reviewed and approved by local people's governments are legally binding, they are just a slip of paper in the eyes of some of the leaders concerned. When concrete problems arise and decisions can be made at will, urban planning regulations will be modified. This has become a prominent problem in foreign-invested real

continued...

BEIJING URBAN CONSTRUCTION, 1995 (continued)

estate development projects in recent years. In some cities, the leaders only care about absorbing foreign investment during their term of office. They are afraid that they will scare foreign investors away if they enforce the urban planning regulations to the letter. They have not made a conscientious effort to study the intrinsic laws of urban construction and do not make it their first priority to defend the overall and long-term interests of their cities. This gives foreign investors the opportunity to make all sorts of demands.

Experts pointed out: The market economy is an economy based on the legal system and urban planning regulations are the most important macrocontrol measures of government departments. If you look at countries of the West where the market economy is well developed, can you find any country which does not grasp planning, does not grasp the legal system, and does not grasp macrocontrol?

Modernization and the Protection of Cultural Heritage Are Not Mutually Exclusive

The history of modern urban development shows that the damage done to historical cultural cities by economic construction is even more devastating than that done by war. It is precisely for this reason that, after the impact of modernization, an increasing number of cities in the world have come to see the problem and are making all-out efforts to protect the historical features of their cities. The reason is that the style and features of a city are priceless and the age-old history and glamorous civilization which the city embodies are things that no money can buy.

China should and can learn from the experience of urban development in other countries to avoid inflicting "disaster" upon our cultural heritage in the name of economic construction.

The old imperial city of Beijing, which dates to the Ming and Qing Dynasties, has four distinct features: It is "symmetrical, level and spacious, distinct in silhouette, and well-paced in arrangement." Looking down from high vantage points, we can see the glittering palaces surrounded by gray compounds in the shade. Such a magnificent and well-planned capital city is indeed a miracle in the history of man's civilization. Noted Danish architect and urban planner (Luosimusen) [5012 2448 4476 2773] praised Beijing as a marvelous monument, the cream of a great civilization. Nancy Yi-shi-wen-si [2496 0670 2429 2448], daughter of General Stilwell, even exclaimed: "Of all famous cities above latitude 40 degrees north, Beijing is the only capital which has not gone into decline after a history of 3,000 years. It has more places of historic interests than Rome and is more magnificent than Paris.... I hope that Beijing will forever retain its features as an ancient capital because it is a pot of wealth that cannot be created again."

Beijing has seen significant progress in its urban construction since the 1950's and today, it has an urban area of 1,040 square km. With an area of 62 square km, the old imperial city of the Ming and Qing Dynasties is just a tiny part of the capital but it is a place which is rich in cultural heritage. Over 70 percent of the capital's heritage protection units at and above the city level are found there. Moreover, after more than 40 years of development, the old city has become extremely congested, with the population soaring from 1.2 million in the early 1950's to the present 1.7 million. The way to fundamentally preserve the old look of the ancient capital is to develop new districts for the resettlement of the population of the old city. Efforts should be made to avoid bringing in too many huge projects in the already saturated inner city. The solution adopted by London for this problem was as follows: After World War Two, London implemented the "Greater London Plan" to reduce the population density of the inner city by developing new districts and satellite towns. This helped preserve the city's historical features and made it possible to have the best of both the new and the old.

Of course, the old city of the Ming and Qing Dynasties is not an unearthed legacy which is hands-off for everyone and which needs no further development. According to some experts, the important thing is that new buildings must blend well with the traditional atmosphere. This refers to both the dimensions of buildings and their external appearance. Most important is that the dimensions of buildings must be in harmony with their surroundings and must not be too tall or too large. If the dimensions are too outrageous, even the most ingenious external design cannot help. They also talked about some of the profound lessons which Beijing has learned in this respect. For example, with a towering 180-meter chimney standing by its side, the ancient

continued...

BEIJING URBAN CONSTRUCTION, 1995 (continued)

Liao Pagoda at Tianning Temple looks dwarfed and has lost its imposing quality. The monstrous east wing of the Beijing Hotel, built in the 1970's and standing over 80 m tall, has greatly affected the landscape east of the Imperial Palace. The development of such a tall building in the heart of Beijing's old city was criticized by the then Premier Zhou Enlai and by urban construction experts. Premier Zhou had repeatedly instructed during his lifetime that height limits must be imposed on buildings in the old city of Beijing.

The "Building Height Control Plan for the City of Beijing" promulgated in 1985, marked the introduction of a legal system in height control for buildings in Beijing. Height control is the most effective measure for protecting the looks of a city, as has been proved by the experience of many cities abroad. In Washington DC, buildings cannot be taller than the US Congress. In Paris, the building of a high-rise office block in the downtown area attracted so much criticism that the municipal government was compelled to promulgate regulations against the construction of tower blocks in the city center and to locate the business district at La Defense some 5 km away from downtown Paris. This succeeded in preserving the city's historical appearance without affecting its economic development. Even a city like Hong Kong, which boasts such a high density of tower blocks, is not without height control regulations. In Hong Kong's urban planning, the general requirement is that buildings may not be taller than the mountain ridges, which run from Mount Davis in the east to Mount Porringer in the west. This is to prevent the city landscape from being destroyed by tall buildings which break the silhouette of the island.

The future of a city lies in its modernization but the charm of a city lies in the civilization and tradition upon which it is built. In the present-day world where culture is becoming more homogeneous, things which have national and individual characteristics will receive ever greater respect and attention. In their efforts to maintain a proper balance between modernization and the protection of cultural heritage, historical cities like Paris, London, and Rome have paid a high price but they have also won the acclaim of the world's cultural circles and left a rich legacy to mankind.

Beijing has quickened its pace in becoming an international metropolis in recent years but its features as an ancient capital are facing a grim challenge. Will Beijing lose the attractive halo of its ancient civilization and its throne as the capital of oriental culture in its march toward modernization? As we ponder over this weighty issue, we cannot but hope in all sincerity that urban construction will quickly be brought onto the track of the legal system. Only in this way will we be able to give an answer that will not put our history to shame.

Liaowang No. 3, 16 Jan 1995.

MAJOR OFFICE DEVELOPMENTS IN SHANGHAI, 1995

Development	Location	Floor Area, sq m	Gross Average Price US$/sq m	Completion
Universal Mansions	Jingan	28,000	3,683	Aug 1995
Walton Plaza Office	Xuhui	8,182	2,554	Sep 1995
Tomson Financial Building	Pudong	51,000	2,500	Dec 1995
Lucky Target Square	Huangpu	30,000	2,631	Jun 1996
World Center	Pudong	70,000	1,700	Jun 1996
Shanghai Plaza	Hongqiao	40,000	3,450	Jun 1997

EIU, 12 Aug 1995.

MAP OF SHANGHAI DEVELOPMENT ZONE, 1995

NYT, 7 Jul 1995.

SHANGHAI'S GROSS INDUSTRIAL OUTPUT, 1991–1993 (per calendar month)

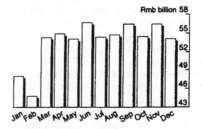

January-February: Chinese New Year
July-August: Summer
October: National Day and Moon Festival

China Business, 8 Aug 1994.

XVIII EDUCATION

CASS ANNOUNCES MAJOR RECONSTRUCTION, 1995

The Chinese Academy of Social Sciences (CASS) announced here today that it will focus on certain branches of learning while canceling dozens of subjects.

According to a draft plan published at its ongoing annual working conference, fields that will receive preferential support include the following:

The theory of building socialism with Chinese characteristics; socialism and Marxism abroad; the socialist market economy and ethics; management of the press; religion in contemporary China; socialist political economy; investment and the market; the rural economy; foreign trade; population and development; issues of ethnic groups; criminal law; international law; social welfare; government administration; the modern and ancient Chinese language; history of the Soviet Union; relations between the countries of the Asia-Pacific region; politics and economics in the Asia-Pacific region; and forecasts of international political and economic situations.

Subjects to be canceled, restricted or merged include:

continued...

CASS ANNOUNCES MAJOR RECONSTRUCTION, 1995 (continued)

Rural sociology; enterprise management; accounting; auditing; handling of goods and materials; the tourism industry; agriculture and land; industrial technology; comparative politics; comparative law science; Tibetan Buddhism; history of the media; studies of Lu Xun; literature in Taiwan and Hong Kong; modern literature; eastern European literature; comparative literature; and overall Chinese history.

CASS's Institute of Journalism will be re-built into the Institute of Journalism and Mass Communications, the working conference revealed. Meanwhile, the South Africa Research Center will be set up to replace the Section of African Studies under the Institute of World Economics and Political Studies.

The field work of a few archaeological teams attached to the academy has been suspended.

"A new-look CASS is necessary to meet the needs of the ongoing modernization drive," said Wang Renzhi, deputy president of the academy.

Some experts said the measures will also save money.

The readjustment will result in the shrinking of the number of branches of learning from 300 to 260, and of research departments from 210 to 180, according to the draft plan.

X, 16 Feb 1995.

LI RUIHUAN VIEWS EDUCATION AT CPPCC MEETING, 1995

The current Standing Committee meeting of the Chinese People's Political Consultative Conference [CPPCC] National Committee is devoted to discussing the issue of education. Vice Premier Li Lanqing delivered an important speech. Vice Chairman [of the CPPCC National Committee] Qian Weichang gave a special report. Those in attendance aired many constructive views and suggestions. I would like to put forth the following thoughts concerning the development of the basic education in China.

I.
Basic education, including preschool, primary, and secondary education, occupies a vital position in the national educational undertaking. To do a good job of basic education, especially the nine-year compulsory education, is of the utmost importance in developing education in China for some time to come.

Basic education is the foundation of higher education. To accomplish the modernization drive we need large numbers of scientists and engineers, as well as professionals in all fields. The training of these talented people hinges upon higher education, whose root originates in basic education. Even people who have become talented through self-study and without going through schools of higher learning also depend on the knowledge and skills they learned during the stage of basic education. Only a firmly rooted tree can grow luxuriant leaves. Therefore, only by ensuring good basic education will there be a reliable foundation for higher education.

Basic education is crucial to improving the quality of the whole work force. China's national condition allows only a small number of people to advance to higher education after completing a basic education. Our basic education is primarily aimed at training competent workers for all trades and professions. Workers are the most fundamental element of productive forces. Without relatively high quality workers, it is impossible to convert any advanced science or technology into practical productive forces; and it will be difficult to increase labor productivity, guarantee product quality, and raise economic efficiency of any trade or profession. Judging from both the immediate situation and long-term perspective, the fundamental factor dictating the development of China's national economy and in all fields of endeavor lies in the quality of the whole work force. Knowledge learned through basic education is an internal component of qualified workers, as well as the basis for their further advance.

Basic education is the fundamental condition for promoting a society's progress in civilization. Science knowledge and work skills imparted by basic education contribute to society's progress in civilization, as do ideas, morality, and physical and mental qualities nurtured by

continued...

LI RUIHUAN VIEWS EDUCATION AT CPPCC MEETING, 1995 (continued)

basic education. Knowledge acquired during the stage of basic education provides the conditions for further assimilating mankind's achievements in civilization. Children and teenagers are the target of basic education. Education received in this period influences the development of life and world outlooks, the development of a healthy personality, and a person's lifetime. In a broader sense, it influences the entire Chinese nation's quality. We often say that we should start training children in the basics when grooming new citizens who have lofty ideals, moral integrity, a good education, and a strong sense of discipline. This means we should start with basic education.

Basic education is an important task encompassing the entire society. Among various levels and types of education, only basic education is mass education. Nine-year compulsory education, in particular, is something that every citizen must receive in accordance with the law. Basic education affects numerous households and attracts attention from all segments of society. Because our country implements the family-planning system, the proportion of only children among primary and middle school students is sizable. These children have generally become the focus of attention in their families, and represent the hopes of several generations of their families. Nothing affords parents greater pleasure than letting their children receive education in a well-run school In fact, providing a good basic education has become an important means for doing practical turns for the people wholeheartedly. This has special significance for and plays a special role in fostering closer ties between the party and people, generating goodwill among the masses, and safeguarding social stability.

II.

In recent years, China's basic education has developed very rapidly, leading to tremendous achievements. The ever-expanding scale of education, steady improvements in educational quality, marked improvements in school conditions, the ever-growing pool of teachers, and gradually deepening educational reform are apparent to all. Nonetheless, China's basic education still falls short of the requirements for promoting material and spiritual civilization, and it continues to face many difficulties and problems that demand prompt solution.

The tasks in promoting basic education are very arduous. China leads the world in the number of people who belong to the age group that should receive basic education. It also has an alarming number of adult citizens who have not completed their compulsory education. On average, people receive only 5.4 years of education. There are 180 million illiterates who are 15 years or older, and they account for 22.25 percent of the people in the same age group. More than 52 million of these illiterates are young and middle-aged people. Despite the party and government's unflagging efforts to eradicate illiteracy, illiterate people join the work force by the millions each year. Over the past two years, in particular, primary and middle schools in quite a few areas have experienced an upswing in dropout rates, giving rise to an even grimmer situation in universalizing compulsory education.

There is a serious shortage of funds for basic education. Although funds for China's basic education have grown significantly in recent years, they still fall far short of what is needed for developing basic education. In 1993 China allocated 2.66 percent of its gross national product, or $12.92 in per capita terms, to education. These figures were not only much lower than those of the developed nations, but were also considerably smaller than the developing countries which earmarked an average 4.1 percent, or $42 on a per capita basis, for education. As required by the central government, educational spending at the provincial level should account for more than 20 percent of financial expenditures. Thus far, only four provinces have actually met this requirement. Another problem is that most of these already inadequate inputs are used to pay for personnel expenses. According to statistics, 82.81 percent and some 90 percent of the funds budgeted by China for education in 1993 were used to pay for personnel expenses in ordinary middle schools and primary schools, respectively, leaving little for educational purposes.

The salaries of teachers involved in basic education are still too low. At present, there is a vast salary gap between primary and middle school teachers in many areas, especially those

continued...

LI RUIHUAN VIEWS EDUCATION AT CPPCC MEETING, 1995 (continued)

in rural areas, and people engaged in other lines of work. Teachers in civilian-run schools nationwide draw an average monthly salary of just 80 to 100 yuan. The problem in some areas of deferring the payment of teachers' salaries has yet to be solved once and for all. Primary and middle school teachers draw scanty benefits and face many problems in housing, medical care, and employment for their children. The shortage of teachers for basic education has grown more worrisome with each passing day.

Courses and teaching methods used in basic education need to be changed. Currently, quite a few problems that warrant close examination and earnest solution exist in China's primary and middle school education. There exist serious problems arising from outdated teaching materials, irrationally structured curricula, failure to serve the needs of most students who will soon join the work force, undue emphasis on raising the rate of admission into higher grades, and unscientific teaching methods such as cramming and rote learning. The excessive workloads of primary and middle school students have affected their all-round development—morally, intellectually, and physically.

III.

As the development of basic education is a complex undertaking, we must proceed from China's reality, encourage joint efforts by people in all circles, keep exploring things during the course of practice, work in a down-to-earth manner, and proceed in a planned and step-by-step fashion in accordance with the "Program for China's Educational Reform and Development."

First, leaders should devote their genuine attention. As local governments are responsible for running different levels of schools that provide basic education, and for administering such education, whether or not leaders at all levels pay attention to this matter is vitally important. In the absence of leadership attention it would be impossible to accord due priority to basic education so that relevant issues will be examined and discussed on a regular basis; it would also be impossible to take effective measures to solve practical problems in earnest, especially the problem of allocating funds for education on a priority basis. Practice shows that only if leaders, especially key leaders, pay attention to this matter can they encourage their counter-parts at each succeeding level and in relevant departments to do the same in what amounts to a joint effort to promote education. We should earnestly organize leaders to study Comrade Deng Xiaoping's theory on education, help leaders at all levels improve their understanding of the importance of basic education, and firmly foster the guiding ideology that "education is the most important among projects of vital and lasting importance." We should vigorously publicize and commend leading cadres who value education, earnestly practice what they advocate, and carry out fruitful work in this respect; we should criticize or even punish those bureaucrats who are extremely irresponsible and who engage in empty talk and cause harm to education. This is to draw a clear distinction between merits and demerits, and between right and wrong. We should include the development of basic education in our list of criteria for evaluating the performance of leading cadres at all levels, making it an important criterion for evaluating, promoting, and appointing cadres.

Second, people in all circles should lend full support. China's huge population is one of its national conditions. A huge population breeds many problems whose solution needs the joint efforts of many people. In an economically underdeveloped large country like China, it is impossible for the government to monopolize educational undertakings. Instead, people in all circles must make joint efforts. We should run schools through various means. While letting local governments assume primary responsibility for basic education, we should continue to encourage enterprises, institutions, mass organizations, community-based organizations, civic collectives, and individuals to run different types of schools. In running schools, people in all circles should strictly abide by relevant state laws and regulations, principles, and policies. For their part, the departments concerned should cherish the initiative and respect the au-tonomy of people in all circles in running schools. We should raise funds through various channels. We should continue to mobilize and support people in all circles at home and abroad to finance basic education, and try our best to make good use of the funds they donate. We

continued...

LI RUIHUAN VIEWS EDUCATION AT CPPCC MEETING, 1995 (continued)

should give wide publicity to various magnanimous acts of running schools and supporting education and commend advanced individuals who are keen on education so that China's fine tradition of respecting teachers and setting great store by education will be promoted, and so that activities launched in society to support education will become an established and institutionalized practice. Activities launched in recent years, such as "Project Hope" and the "Plan of Spring Buds," have generated very good results. We should sum up, promote, and improve on our experiences in this respect. We should better coordinate efforts in various sectors. Schools, society, and families are jointly responsible for providing the next generation with a good education. Press, publishing, radio, cinema, television, literary, and art departments should actively provide beneficial spiritual fare for young people, and create a fine social environment for their healthy growth. Parents have a duty to ensure that their children will complete nine-year compulsory education in accordance with state laws. Working in conjunction with schools, they should also guide their children along the path of healthy development. In a nutshell, people in all circles should join forces in undertaking the task of educating the next generation.

Third, educational workers should work hard. In the final analysis, it is the hard work of educational workers that counts if basic education is to succeed. Over the past several decades, educational workers have worked their hearts out without complaint under harsh conditions, making tremendous contributions to educational development. The party and people are eternally grateful to them. Along with economic development and social progress, the conditions in which basic education is provided will improve, and teachers' material benefits and salaries will also improve gradually. Difficulties and problems, however, cannot be solved in the immediate future. Educational workers should foster lofty ideals, take pride in the educational profession, and devote their entire lives to the sacred cause of educating people in the face of hardship and poverty for the sake of national development and the motherland's future. They should encourage thrifty practices in promoting education, tap potential, create conditions, and do a good job of running schools and educating students. They should carry forward their spirit of dedication; tailor their work to the four modernizations, the world, and the future; strengthen their own political training; work hard to gain professional proficiency; constantly reform curricula and teaching methods; and groom new citizens who have lofty ideals, moral integrity, a good education, and a strong sense of discipline in keeping with the requirements of modernization.

Fourth, work should be done vigorously. At the national educational work conference in May 1985, Comrade Deng Xiaoping pointed out that to make educational work a success, we must "spend less time on idle talk and more on real work," and change the "bad habit of doing nothing but issuing instructions and indulging in empty talk." At present, some areas suffer from serious bureaucratism and rampant formalism, and are given to making empty talk, spouting platitudes, telling lies, holding too many meetings, issuing too many documents, and spending too much time on social intercourse. These have adversely affected cadre-people relations and progress in many fields of work. Too many thorny problems that exist in basic education can only be solved if we take specific action to deal with them regularly and repeatedly. We must change our work style, and, in keeping with Comrade Xiaoping's exhortation, conscientiously "take practical steps" and "take educational work seriously and do it well."

It is a fine tradition of the Chinese People's Political Consultative Conference [CPPCC] to pay attention and lend support to the cause of education. Many CPPCC members are quite conversant with educational work because they have chronically worked on the frontline of education. Speeches and proposals regarding education made at annual CPPCC sessions and its Standing Committee meetings have played an excellent role in reforming and developing China's education. It is hoped that in the future, you will continue in-depth investigations and study, practice what you advocate, and make new contributions to promoting China's education.

X, 14 Jan 1995.

REFORMS CHANGE HIGHER EDUCATION, 1995

Educational reforms have brought the number of Chinese universities and colleges to more than 2,200 over the past four years, the State Education Commission (SEC) has said.

In the process, at least 70 universities have merged to cut costs, and 200 are being run as "joint operations", according to the SEC officials.

"We have no plans to build more universities around the turn of the century, because the national economy could not bear it," explained an SEC official in charge of higher education.

The country is planning on choosing some 100 "key universities" which are expected to grow into megaversities that can help China compete on the world stage, he noted.

X, 26 Sep 1995.

XIX HEALTH AND WELFARE

PUBLIC HEALTH SURVEY, 1995

According to findings of the National Health Service Investigation released by the Ministry of Public Health the ailments the Chinese suffer most from are colds, gastroenteritis, tonsillitis and tracheitis. The two year investigation was conducted through random sampling among public health organizations in 90 counties and cities, covering 50,000 households and more than 200,000 people in the country. It was first survey of its kind to be conducted in China.

The survey found that as the economy developed and living conditions improved, both urban and rural people's health service demands increased. Residents in urban and rural areas received more medical care in 1995 than in years before, with an increase of 63 percent in rural areas and of 35.9 in urban areas when compared with the health care services provided in the 1980s.

X, 17 Jan 1995.

MEDICAL ADVANCES, 1995

China made great strides during 1995 toward vaccinating its total population. At year's end, doctors and medical technicians had vaccinated 63 percent of the urban population and 37 percent of the rural population. Officials viewed this as a major aid to reducing long range medical costs. Much of China's medical cost and care were expended treating patients with debilitating diseases. China has one of the world's highest incidences of polio and tuberculosis. Officials hope education and prevention programs will lower the incidence and cost of treating these diseases.

Other medical advances included the opening of more rural clinics. Most clinics were staffed by paramedical personnel because of a lack of enough qualified physicians.

While many in the West were turning toward traditional Chinese medicine there was a move within China toward Western medical techniques, and hospitals improved the quality of care and types of treatments available.

China Facts & Figures Annual, 1995

IMPORTED MEDICAL PRACTICES AND INSTRUMENTS, 1990–1995 (percent)

	MDs Using Western Medicine	MS Schooled in West	Imported Instruments in Use		MDs Using Western Medicine	MS Schooled in West	Imported Instruments in Use
1990	69	44	39	1993	71	47	41
1991	69	46	43	1994	73	48	43
1992	71	47	41	1995	73	48	44

China Facts & Figures Annual, 1995

LIFE EXPECTANCY, 1986–1994

	Males	Females	Infant Mortality (per th)	Fertility Rate (per woman)
1986	68			
1987	68			
1988	68			
1989	68	70	34	2.5
1990	68	72	33	2.3
1991	69	72	32	2.3
1992	69	72	32	2.3
1993	69	72	31	2.3
1994	69	72	31	2.3

China Facts & Figures Annual, 1995

SPREAD OF AIDS, 1995

Officially, China Ministry of Public Health said there were 2,428 reported cases of H.I.V. infection nation-wide in 1995, but few people have been tested and health officials privately estimated that China had twice that number of carriers of the virus. More than half were believed to be in Yunnan Province, which borders with Myanmar, Laos and Vietnam and where needle sharing drug use, as well as unprotected sex spread the disease. By the end of 1995, the Academy of Medical Science estimated that the number of H.I.V. infections could exceed 6,000 by the year 2000. While this is far from the worst rate in Asia, incipient growth in a country whose blood supplies remain unscreened for the virus is a major concern. In late 1995 the Health Ministry undertook a large scale public education campaign for AIDS prevention and a program to enforce hospitals to abide by the blood-screening code.

NYT, 28 Nov 1995.

MAP OF AIDS INFECTED AREAS, 1995

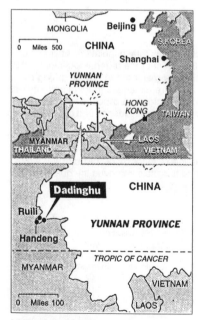

NYT, 28 Nov 1995.

MAJOR TECHNOLOGY PROJECTS THROUGH 2000, 1994 (continued)

23	Agricultural Development Along the West Bank of the Yellow River in Gansu Province	Comprehensive agricultural development across the Shule River valley
24	Agricultural Development in South-West China	Agricultural development and elimination of poverty in Guizhou, Guangxi and Yunan

ENERGY

25	Third-Phase Jiujiang Power Plant in Jiangxi Province,	Installed capacity; 2×300 mw
26	Sanhe Power Station, Beijing	Installed capacity: 2×350 mw
27	Wangpuzhou Hydropower Station, Hubei Province	Installed capacity: 4×27.5 mw
28	Xiaolangdi Key Water Control Project, Henan Province	Reservoir capacity; 12.6 billion cubic meters; Installed capacity: 1560 mw
29	Second-Phase Daqi Power Plant, Inner Mongolian Autonomous Region,	To introduce key equipment for 2×300 mw power generating unit
30	Ertan Hydropower Station, Sichuan Province	Installed capacity: 6×550 mw
31	The First-Class Tianshengqiao Hydropower Stations	Installed capacity: 4×300 mw and its auxiliary transmission line and transformers
32	First-Phase Ezhou Power Plant, Hubei Province	Installed capacity: 2×300 mw
33	Hejin Powr Plant, Shanxi Provaince	Installed capacity: 2×300 mw
34	Second Phase Storage Power Station,	Guangdong Province installed capacity: 4×300 mw
35	Qitaihe Power Plant, Heilongjiang Province	Installed capacity: 2×300 mw
36	Hongjiadu Hydropower Station, Guizhou Province	Installed capacity: 3×180 mw
37	Mianhuatan Hydropower Station, Fujian Province	Installed capacity: 4×150 mw
38	East China Sea Natural Gas Development, Shanghai	To develop Pinghu Gas Field and to build up gas pipe line and urban pipe networks
39	Lingjintan Hydropower Station, Hunan Province	Installed capacity: 8×30 mw
40	Longtan Hydropower Station, Guangxi Zhuang Autonomous Region	Installed capacity: 7×600 mw
41	Yangzhou Power Plant, Jiangsu Province	Installed capacity; 2×600 mw
42	Beilungang Power Plant and Transmission Network renovation, Zhejiang Province	Installed capacity: 2×600 mw for the second-phase project and the provincial transmission networks renovation
43	Tuoketuo Power Plant, Inner Mongolian Autonomous Region	Installed capacity: 2×600 mw
44	Second-Phase Huaneng Dalian Power Plant,	Installed capacity: 2×350 mw, to introduce Japanese technology and jointly manufacture generators
45	Second-Phase Qinshan Nuclear Power Plant,	Key equipments for 2×600 mw generating units

COAL

46	Huojitu Pit and Its Corollary Equipment, Dongsheng Mining Area of Shenfu Coal Mine	Annual production of raw coal: 5 million tons, and the matching transportation and water supply facilities
47	Jining No.2 Coal Mine, Yanzhou Mining Area, Shandong Province	Annual production of raw coal: 4 million tons
48	Jining No.3 Coal Mine, Yanzhou Mining Area, Shandong Province	Annual production of raw coal: 5 million tons
49	Xuchang Coal Mine, Yanzhou Mining Area, Shandong Province	Annual production of raw coal: 1.5 million tons
50	Daizhuang Coal Mine, Yanzhou Mining Area, Shandong Province	Annual production of raw coal: 1.5 million tons
51	Fucun Coal Mine, Tengnan Mining Area, Shandong Province	Annual production of raw coal: 3 million tons
52	Anjialing Opencut Coal Mine, Pingshuo Mining Area, Shanxi Province	Annual production of raw coal: 15 million tons
53	Chensilou Coal Mine, Yongcheng Mining Area, Henan Province	Annual production of raw coal: 2.4 million tons
54	Cheji Coal Mine, Yongcheng Mining Area, Henan Province	Annual production of raw coal: 1.8 million tons

continued...

MAJOR TECHNOLOGY PROJECTS THROUGH 2000, 1994

AGRICULTURE

No	PROJECT NAME	SUBJECT AND CAPACITY
1	Comprehensive Development of Agriculture in Henan Province	To improve 4.5 million *mu* (15 *mu* = 1 hectare) low-yield farmland along the Yellow River and to expand irrigated area to 2.4 million *mu*
2	Comprehensive Development of Agriculture in Sichuan Province	Conveyance system of Wudu-Shengzhong irrigation project which irrigates 2.4 million *mu* of farmland, a project of supporting the poor in eastern Sichuan Province
3	Enhancing Irrigation for Agriculture in the Basins of the Yellow River, Huaihe River and Haihe River	To develop grain production facility and to improve conveyance irrigation systems in Jiangsu, Shandong and Anhui provinces
4	Irrigation Works in the Southern Part of Xinjiang Uygur Autonomous Region	To open up 1.2 million *mu* of wasteland and transform 1.8 million *mu* of low-yield farmland
5	Tongyuhe River Project in Northern Jiangsu Province	River course extends 245 km and 1.85 million *mu* of farmland are put under irrigation.
6	The Development of Water Conservancy Works in Hunan Province	Agricultural development and perfect auxiliary water conservancy facilities in the Dongting Lake area
7	Development of Agricultural Irrigation Works in Hubei Province	To develop agriculture in Jianghan plain, to improve supporting water conservancy facilities and to develop forestry
8	Comprehensive Agricultural Development in Jilin Province and Changchun City	Comprehensive development of crop plantation, animal husbandry and the processing industry for agricultural products in Baicheng, Qianguo and Fuyu prefectures and Changchun city
9	Comprehensive Agricultural Development in Liaohe Plain, Liaoning Province	Comprehensive agricultural development of crop plantation, aquaculture and agricultural and sideline products
10	Agriculture Technology Popularization Service Project	To spread seeds and livestock technologies
11	Tropical Crops Development in Guangdong Province	Cultivation and processing of rubber-plant, sugarcane, etc.
12	Bohai Bay Aquatic Products Development	Farming and processing of marine.
13	Comprehensive Development of Agriculture in Hainan Province	Cultivation and processing of agricultural products
14	Comprehensive Developmet of Agriculture in Western Henan Province	Fruit tree planting, livestock breeding and processing
15	Comprehensive Development of Agriculture in Fujian Province	Cultivation and processing of agricultural products
16	Flood Control Project at Taihu Lake Valley	Comprehensive flood control and water-logging drainage
17	Second-Phase National Afforestation Project	To plant over 0.5 million hectares fast-growing and windbreak forests
18	Fodders Development	To develop the production of forage additives and feed-processing production
19	Grain Distribution	Grain storage and transportation facilities and grain market construction
20	Second-Phase Red Soil Rehabilitation	Water and soil transformation of the red soil and comprehensive development of agriculture in five provinces of South China
21	Loess Plateau Transformation	To comprehensively control soil erosion on the middle reaches of the Yellow River
22	Second-Phase Seed Development	To build up bases for improved variety and processing

continued...

MAJOR TECHNOLOGY PROJECTS THROUGH 2000, 1994 (continued)

TRANSPORTATION

55	Fourth-Phase Project of the Special Coal Quay at Qinhuangdao Harbour, Hebei Province	3 deep-water berths with a handling capacity of 30 million tons
56	Jilin Highway Construction	136 km expressway from Changchun to Siping
57	Nenjiang River Bridge, Qiqihar City Heilongjiang Province,	1,620 meters for the main bridge
58	Hefei-Tongling Highway and Tongling Yangtze River Highway Bridge	136 km for the second-class road and 1,900 meters for the main bridge
59	The Last 6 Berths of the First-Phase Construction at Dayaowan Port Area, Dalian Harbor	Annual handling capacity: 3.1 million tons
60	Second-Phase Construction of Rizhao Harbor, Shandong Province	Five deep-water berths with an annual handling capacity of 2 million tons
61	Extention of Dadong Port, Dandong Harbor, Liaoning Province	3 sundry goods berths for ten thousand tons weight vessels with an annual handling capacity of 950,000 tons
62	Highway, Zhejiang Province	138 km, expressway from Hangzhou to Ningbo
63	Yingkou Port, Liaoning Province	To purchase loading and unloading port facilities
64	Yantai Harbor, Shandong Province	2nd phase, 6 berths at Xigangchi port area with an annual handling capacity of 3.4 million tons
65	Extention of Shanghai Harbor	To construct two coal berths at Luojing port area for 25,000-ton-class vessels, first-phase construction of Waigaogiao port and the reconstruction of the old harbor
66	Highway, Hebei Province	270 km expressway from Shijiazhuang to Anyang
67	Highway, Fujian Province	80 km expressway from Xiamen to Quanzhou
68	Highway, Hunan Province	50 km expressway from Changsha to Xiangtan
69	Highway, Guangdong Province	300 km, first-class highway from Shenzhen to Shantou and from Foshan to Kaiping
70	Shuji wharf, Qinhuangdao Harbor	7 sundry goods berths with an annual handling capacity of 3 million tons
71	The First-Phase Construction at Xugou Port Area, Lianyungang harbor	6 sundry goods berths with an annual handling capacity of 2.1 million tons
72	Highway, Shaanxi Province	145 km first-class highway from Xian to Baoji
73	Highway, Henan Province	121 km, expressway from Anyang to Xinxiang
74	Highway, Xinjiang Uygur Autonomous Rigion	290 km, special highway from Turpan to Urumqi and to Dahuangshan
75	Development of Inland Water Transportation	To improve the channels of Xiangjiang River in Hunan Province, Xijiang River in Guangxi Zhuang Autonomous Region and Beijing-Hangzhou Grand Canal, Zhejiang section
76	Shanghai-Hangzhou Highway	140 km expressway
77	Highway, Liaoning Province	108 km expressway from Tieling to Siping
78	Highway, Heilongjiang Province	580 km, 2nd-class highway from Harbin to Tongjiang
79	Highway, Yunnan Province	207 km, 2nd-class highway from Chuxiong to Dali
80	China Transportation Communication Center	Global sea mishap and security system

RAILWAY

81	Railway Construction of the 7th Group	946 km electrified railway from Harbin to Dalian, 1,064 km railway electrification from Wuhan to Guangzhou
82	Zhangping-Quanzhou-Xiaocuo Railway, Fujian Province	97 km from Hutou of Zhangping to Quanzhou, 58 km from Quanzhou to Xiaocuo
83	Railway Construction of the 6th Group	1,742 km electrified railway from Beijing to Zhengzhou, Chengdu to Kunming, and the transformation of railway communication and singaling systems
84	Xian-Ankang Railway	274 km, annual transportation capacity: 20 million tons
85	Railway Connecting Shuoxian and Huanghua Harbor	

continued...

MAJOR TECHNOLOGY PROJECTS THROUGH 2000, 1994 (continued)

	and the Construction of Huanghua Harbor	586 km, annual short-term transportation capacity: 35 million tons, 3 berths, annual handling capacity: 30 million tons
86	Double-Line Construction of the Railway from Zhejiang to Jiangxi Province	938 km, double-line construction from Zhuzhou to Hangzhou and to increase 10 million tons of transportation capacity annually
87	Xuzhou Railway Hub Construction	Auxiliary equipment for the hub
88	Railway from Guangzhou to Meixian and Shantou, Guangdong Province	427 km, local railway
89	Railway from Hefei to Jiujiang	300 km, first-class railway with an annual transportation capacity of 16 million tons
90	Railway from Nanning to Kunming	To build an 870 km new railway, with an annual short-term transportation capacity of 10 million tons
91	Railway from Hengshui to Shangqiu	To build a 396 km new railway with an annual short-term transportation capacity of 16 million tons
92	Railway from Beijing to Kowloon, HK	The section in Jiangxi Province and its signaling systems
93	Railway from Guangzhou to Zhuhai	147 km, from Guangzhou to Zhuhai

CIVIL AVIATION

94	Xiamen Airport (2nd phase)	To import key equipment and some building materials
95	Civil Aviation Routes Construction	The renovation of the navigation control for the main air routs, navigational communications and meteorological systems
96	Jingdezhen and Ganzhou Airports, Jiangxi Province	Airport extension for the taking-off and landing of MD-82 and Boeing 737 aircrafts alike
97	Lukou Civil Airport in Nanjing, Jiangsu Province	To introduce navigational equipment
98	Zhengzhou Airport, Henan Province	To introduce navigational equipment
99	The Extension of Beijing Capital Airport	To construct a new terminal building with a floor space of 122,000 square meters and its auxiliary facilities

POST AND TELECOMMUNICATIONS

100	Program-Controlled Telephone Exchangers for Nine Provinces and Cities	To import digital exchangers with a total line of 760,000 and digital exchangers with 31,000 long distance lines (among which, 125,000 lines for Tianjin and Guangdong each, 120,000 lines for Shanghai and Jiangsu each, 60,000 lines for Harbin, Xian and Zhejiang each, 50,000 lines for Fujian and 40,000 lines for Changchun)
101	Infrastructure Facilities for Huangdao Island construction, Qingdao City	Digital exchanger with 80,000 lines. 85 km first-class road construction and sewerage treatment equipment with an annual capacity of 35,000 tons
102	Equipment for Post Offices in Heilongjiang, Hunan, Fujian, Jiangsu provinces and Chongqing City	Digital exchanger with 2 million lines
103	Beijing Administration Bureau of Telecommunications	Digital exchanger expansion
104	Optical Fibre Communications	Beijing-Wuhan-Guangzhou and Beijing-Taiyuan-Xian trunk optical fibre cable lines
105	Optical Fibre Communications	Beijing-Hohhot-Yinchuan-Lianzhou trunk optical fibre cable line
106	Optical Fibre Communications	Fuzhou-Guiyang-Chengdu trunk optical fibre cable line

PETROLEUM

107	Gas Exploration and Development in Sichuan Province	Gas exploration and development, reconstruction of the old gas fields, laying new gas pipelines for additional 2.5 billion cubic meters/year
108	Development of Gaotaizi Oil Reservoir at the Section 2 of Sanan District of Daqing Oilfield	1.5 million tons of crude oil/year

continued…

MAJOR TECHNOLOGY PROJECTS THROUGH 2000, 1994 (continued)

109	Development of Gaotaizi Oil Reservoir at the Section 3 of Sanan District of Daqing Oilfield	1.5 million tons of crude oil/year
110	Development of Thick Oil Reserve Area of Dongying Nanxiepo, Shengli Oilfield, Shandong Province	1.5 million tons of crude oil/year
111	Development of Shallow Sea Oil Reserve Area, Shengli Oilfield	1.5 million tons of crude oil/year
112	Development of Thick Oil Reserve Area of Hongshanzui Oilfield, Xinjiang Uygur Autonomous Region	1 million tons of thick oil/year
113	Development of Thick Oil Reserve Area, Section 6, Karamay Oilfield, Xinjiang Uygur Autonomous Region	600,000 tons of thick oil/year
114	Development of Xinmin Oilfield, Jilin Province	550,000 tons of crude oil/year
115	Development of Wubei Oil Reserve Area, Dagang Oilfield, Tianjin	1 million tons of crude oil/year
116	Development of Zhangjuhe Oil Reserve Area, Dagang Oilfield, Tianjin	300,000 tons of crude oil/year
117	Development of Huanxiling-Shuguang Oil Reserve Area, Liaohe Oilfield	1.4 million tons of crude oil/year
118	Development of Rongxingtun-Lengdong Oil Reserve Area, Liaohe Oilfield	1.1 million tons of crude oil/year
119	Development of Wenwei Oil Reserve Area, Zhongyuan Oilfield, Henan Province	1 million tons of crude oil/year
120	Development of Changqing-Ansai Oilfield, Shaanxi Province	600,000 tons of crude oil/year
121	Development of Jiergalangtu Oil Reserve Area at Erlian, North China	600,000 tons of crude oil/year
122	Development of 13-1 Block, Hainanya Gasfield, Guangdong Province	3.25 billion cubic meters of gas/year
123	Yushulin Oilfield, Daqing	400,000 tons of crude oil/year
124	No. Ken 90 Block, Huanxiling Oil Reserve Area, Shengli Oilfield	500,000 tons of crude oil/year
125	No. Qian 12 Block, Huanxiling Oil Reserve Area, Liaohe Oilfield	530,000 tons of crude oil/year
126	Wenliu Oil Reserve Area of Zhongyuan Oilfield, Henan Province	210,000 tons of crude oil/year
127	Zaoyuan Oilfield at Shenusi District, Dagang, Tianjin	170,000 tons of crude oil/year
128	No. 218-133 Well Drilling Area, Xinli Oilfield, Jilin Province	100,000 tons of crude oil/year
129	Offshore Oilfield Exploration, Offshore Oil General Co.	Additional 100 billion cubic meters of natural gas reserve, additional 100 million tons of crude oil
130	Daqing Oilfield Polypropylene Amide	50,000 tons of polypropylene amide/year, and import of equipment

CHEMICAL INDUSTRY

131	Wengfu Phosphate Fertilizer Factory, Guizhou Province	800,000 tons of double superphosphate/year
132	Yanshan Di-phenol Complex	30,000 tons of di-phenol/year
133	Enviromental Protection and Chemical Plant Revamp in Southern Jiangsu	Sewerage treatment, chemical plant's enviromental protection and technical renovations
134	Kaifeng Carbon Steel Factory, Henan Province	30,000 tons of high power graphit electrode/year
135	Honghe Chemical Plant, Sichuan Province	To increase its caustic soda production from 50,000 tons/year to 70,000 tons/year
136	Xuanhua Chemical Fertilizer Factory, Hebei Province	240,000 tons of diammonium hydrogenphosphate and 400,000 tons of sulphuric acid/year
137	Jilin Chemical Fertilizer Factory	300,000 tons of ammonia and 520,000 tons of urea/year
138	Polyester Slice, Shantou Haiyang Audio-Video Co., Guangdong Province	40,000 tons of polyester slice/year
139	Yunnan Chemical Plant	Expansion project with an additional production of 50,000 tons of caustic soda/year

continued...

MAJOR TECHNOLOGY PROJECTS THROUGH 2000, 1994 (continued)

140	Dagu Chemical Plant, Tianjin	80,000 tons of PVC/year
141	Nanhua (Group) Chemical Corporation, Nanjing	300,000 tons of ammonia and 520,000 tons of urea/year
142	Beijing United Chemical Corporation	Production plant with an annual production capacity of 40,000 tons of EVA resin
143	Pingdingshan Nylon-66 Salt, Henan Province	30,000 tons of nylon-66 salt/year
144	Nanning Titanium Dioxide Plant, Guangxi Zhuang Autonomous Region	15,000 tons of titanium dioxide/year
145	Maluping Phosphate Mine, Kaiyang, Guizhou Province	To import the advanced equipment and to increase the production capacity to 1 million tons/year
146	Nantong, Jiangsu	20,000 square meters of ion membrane
147	Chuandong Salt Chemical Co., Sichuan Province	60,000 tons of caustic soda/year

ENVIRONMENTAL PROTECTION

148	Comprehensive Environmental Protection, Hebei Province	To solve waste water, slag and gas pollution problems in Chengde and Tangshan cities through enterprises' technical renovation and environmental protection
149	Dalian Water Supply	Extension project of water supply from Biliuhe River, 1.2 million tons/day
150	Port Environmental Protection	To enhance the ability of solving the port pollution in using the grant from the Global Environment Protection Fund

EDUCATION

151	Development of Important Education Subjects	Facilities for 132 laboratories under Chinese Academy of Sciences and the State Education Commission
152	Basic Education in the Underdeveloped Areas	To strengthen the education work in 6 provinces where economic conditions are comparatively weak
153	Professional Education (Second Phase)	To equip and strengthen the work on some of the vocational and technical secondary schools
154	Medical Education	To strengthen a number of medical vocational schools and some medical colleges
155	Teachers' Trainning Program, Second Phase	With emphasis on equipping and strengthening some of the teachers' trainning colleges

BUILDING MATERIALS

156	Ningbo Cement Grinding Mill	690,000 tons of No.525 portland cement/year
157	Renovation of Nanjing China Cement Plant	To build up a new dry kiln with a production capacity of 2,000 tons of cement/day
158	Kaoline, Zhanjiang, Guangdong Province	Net increase of production capacity per year: 0.1 million tons
159	Wulan Cement Plant, Inner Mongolia Autonomous Region	700,000 tons of cement
160	Hebi Cement Plant, Henan Province	600,000 tons of cement
161	Yaohua Glass Plant, Qinhuangdao, Hebei Province	Expansion of floating glass production line

MACHINERY

162	Renovation of Tianjin Machinery and Electronic Industry	The technological upgrading of some enterprises in the four industries of machine tool, engineering machinery, electric elements and auto spare parts
163	Renovation of Shenyang Machinery and Electronic Industry, Liaoning Province	Transforming machine tool factories for the production of numerical control and numerical display tools, etc.

continued...

MAJOR TECHNOLOGY PROJECTS THROUGH 2000, 1994 (continued)

ELECTRONICS

164	Development of Electronics Industry	The development and transformation of electronic device

FORESTRY

165	Particle Board Project, Wuchagou Forest Bureau, Xingan Prefecture, Inner Mongolia Autonomous Region	Annual processing capacity of 45,000 cubic meters of partical board
166	Yibin Wood Processing Plant, Sichuan Province	Annual processing capacity of 30,000 cubic meters of MDF
167	Eucalyptus Pulp and Paper Making Mill in Leizhou City, Guangdong Province	50,000 tons of pulp/year and high grade art paper

LIGHT INDUSTRY

168	The Technological Transformation of Shanghai's Industry (Second Phase)	The technological transformation of light industry, machinery, electronics, medicine, chemical industry, medical apparatus industry, etc.
169	Simao Paper Mill, Yunnan Province	Commercial wooden paste for bleaching powder: 50,000 tons/year
170	Shanghai Dingfang Xingye Co. Ltd	Producing 20 million pieces of fast fluorescent lamp
171	The Expansion Project of Qingzhou Paper Mill, Fujian Province	Importing bleaching equipment
172	Yuzhou Paper Mill, Chongqing City	Bamboo paste production: 20,000 tons/year, paper production: 15,000 tons/year
173	TDI Project in Cangzhou, Hebei Province	Producing TDI with an annual capacity of 20,000 tons
174	Jinggangshan Pulp Mill, Jiangxi Province	Importing key technology and equipment for paper making
175	Nanning Paper Mill	Producing chemical wood pulp for bleaching powder with a capacity of 100,000 tons/year

TEXTILE

176	Tangshan Chemical Fibre Plant, Hebei Province	Producing viscose staple fibre with a capacity of 20,000 tons/year
177	Shaanxi No.2 Printing and Dyeing Mill	To introduce the production line for printing and dyeing super wide decoration cloth
178	Weifang No.2 Printing and Dyeing Mill, Shandong Province	To introduce the production line for printing and dying super wide decoration cloth
179	Xinxiang Printing and Dyeing Mill, Henan Province	To introduce the production line for printing and dyeing super wide seer sucker
180	Liaoyang Chemical Fibre Plant, Liaoning Province	Producing 6,000 tons of PET filament/year
181	Beihai Chemical Fibre Plant, Guangxi Zhuang Autonomous Region	To import equipment for producing artificial fibre pulp with an annual capacity of 50,000 tons
182	Kaishantun Chemical Pulp Mill, Jilin Province	Producing 20,000 tons of viscose staple fibre/year
183	Yizhen Chemical Fibre Complex, Jiangsu Province	Technology and equipment for third phase project: 250,000 tons of PTA/year, 20,000 tons of filament/year, 60,000 tons of polyester/year
184	Jilin Chemical Fibre Plant	Annual Production capacity of 30,000 tons of acrylic fibre
185	Shaoxing PET Fibre Plant, Zhejiang Province	Annual production capacity of 60,000 tons of polyester

PHARMACEUTICS

186	Penicillin Project, Jining Antibiotic Factory, Shandong Province	1,200 tons of penicillin industrial salt/year and other serial products
187	Penicillin Project, Northeast Pharmaceutical Group Company in Shenyang	1,200 tons of penicillin industrial salt/year and serial products
188	North China Pharmaceutical Factory in Shijiazhuang,	

continued...

MAJOR TECHNOLOGY PROJECTS THROUGH 2000, 1994 (continued)

Hebei Province	2,000 tons of penicillin G Potassium industrial salt and the serial products
189 Cafalexini Project in Jinzhou, Liaoning Province	Producing 110,000 tons of cafalexini/year
190 Wuhan Pharmaceutical Factory	50 tons of cmorxacin materials/year and its preparation
191 Tianjin Amino Acid Company	Amino acid infusion and peritonacum infusion
192 Jilin Pharmaceutical Factory	Aspirin 4,000 tons/year and 200 tons of diolosenae sodium/year

METALLURGY

193 Third Phase Project of Baoshan Iron and Steel Works	To increase the production capacity of various types of steel by 3 million tons/per year, power station with an installed capacity of 350,000 kw and the matching harbor
194 Second Phase Project of Baoshan Iron and Steel Works	Improvement of hot rolling mill and spare parts and reserve products
195 Taiyuan Iron and Steel Co.	Slab continuous caster, secondary metallurgical, vacuum treatment
196 Benxi Iron and Steel Company	To build up a slab continuous caster and matching auxiliary facilities
197 Baotou Iron and Steel Company	Hot metal pre-treatment, surplus heat quench treatment facilities

URBAN CONSTRUCTION

198 Baotou Huajiangyingzi Water Supply Project in the Inner Mongolia Autnomous Region	300,000 cubic meters of water supply per day
199 Shenzhen Urban Light Track Railway	To import key equipment
200 Guangzhou Subway Project	Preliminary construction length: 18.1 km
201 Qingdao Subway Project	Total length: 14.1 km
202 Shanghai Urban Traffic Project	Renovation and extension of urban roads
203 Chongqing Underground Light Track Railway	To import key equipment
204 Beijing Subway Project	The section from Bawangfen to Tongxian County

PUBLIC HEALTH

205 Beijing Union Hospital	To import key medical equipment
206 The Prevention and Treatment of Infectious Diseases	The prevention and treatment of schistosomiasis in seven provinces (regions) in south China

NONFERROUS METAL INDUSTRY

207 Zhongzhou Aluminium Plant, Henan Province	Alumina calciner
208 Zhuzhou Hard Alloy Plant	500 tons of additional production capacity of hard alloy
209 Shanghai Smeltery	To renovate the electrolytic copper foil production and introduce key equipment to produce 1,000 tons of copper foil/year

METEOROLOGY

210 State Bureau of Meteorology	Meteorological satellite comprehensive application system

Beijing Review, 4 Dec 1994.

ANALYSIS OF TECHNOLOGY UPDATES AND INVESTMENT, 1995

From an analysis of the data, we can see that the products of a considerable group of large and medium-sized state enterprises conform to state industrial policy, have a rather good management base, and have had a rather good enterprise image. In the last few years, however, they have clearly lacked vitality. In studying the causes, a very important factor is antiquated equipment and the low technology content of products. In addition, the funds invested are far short of the funds needed for enterprise technology updates. This causes products to be high in cost, low grade, and clearly lacking in market competitiveness. Compared to that, an outstanding characteristic of the enterprises that are models for converting mechanisms is placing the emphasis of expanded reproduction on the development of new products, technology updates, and increased equipment investment. The annual depreciation and new product development amounts can be seen from 100 randomly selected sample enterprises (50 of them stock system enterprises and 50 contract system enterprises) (see table).

Analysis of Technology Updates and Investment

| | | Stock System Enterprises | | Contract System Enterprises | |
		Total	Average Indicators	Total	Average Indicators
Annual Depreciation					
(10,000 yuan)	1991	47,181.3	1,003.857	480,189.2	9,603.783
	1992	58,180.12	1,212.086	560,425.7	11,208.51
	1993	160,432	3,274.123	683,510.2	13,949.10
New Product Development Fund					
(10,000 yuan)	1991	15,575.49	623.0196	32,639.34	796.0815
	1992	70,061.48	2,694.672	50,556.09	1,203.716
	1993	78,868.06	2,719.588	75,378.36	2,355.574

First, the annual depreciation and new product development funds of both stock system enterprises and contract system enterprises exhibited year to year growth. The increases in depreciation and new product development funds for stock system enterprises in the three years were 340 percent and 506 percent, respectively, and those of contract system enterprises were 142 percent and 230 percent, respectively. Second, with the marketization of funds currently rather low and enterprises' own funds limited, these enterprises mainly relied on active reserve assets to expand increases. Third, most of the model enterprises have a definite status in their industry and enjoy rather complete investment policy-making authority. They use this advantage to accelerate the replacement of old generation products with new ones. Several score enterprises, like Shanghai Zhong Textile Machinery, Shanghai Sanwei Pharmacy Company, Harbin Electrical Machinery Factory, Shanghai Shuangli Appliances, Tianjin Tianci Company, Guangdong Kelong Appliances, and Guangdong Fotao Group, have placed their investment emphasis on developing highly scientific and technical, high value added productive items to increase the products' competitive strength.

X, 20 Dec 1995.

REPORT ON SATELLITE EXPLOSION, 1995

According to a source, when gathering the remains of the exploded "Apstar 2" satellite and the "Long March" rockets at the Xichang Satellite Launching Site, the order of the scattered remains of the two objects gives strong, clear evidence that the remains of the wreckage of the satellite were first spotted before those of the wreckage of the second-stage and first-stage rockets and the booster. In accordance with the regular relay work form, the booster should have been spotted first and then the first-stage and second-stage rockets and the satellite entering the orbit. This precisely reverse scattering phenomenon has led people to reach the only possible inference that the satellite exploded before the rockets.

continued...

REPORT ON SATELLITE EXPLOSION, 1995 (continued)

The wreckage of the US-made satellite were taken back to the United States on 13 February by a Boeing 747 dispatched by the US side.

This newspaper took a batch of photos to consult an expert in astronautics science and technology about the cause of the satellite-rocket explosion at Xichang Satellite Launch Center on 26 January. After carefully studying the photos, the expert said that at least three points were certain through analysis: First, abnormal flames first emerged from the part where the satellite was placed. Second, even when the rocket head was burning, the first stage of the rocket was still working normally. Third, from the light given off by the explosion, the shape showing that at the very moment of explosion, the structure of the rocket was still in good condition and no abnormality existed within the rocket.

Could one say then that the flame at the head of the rocket came from the satellite? The expert replied: The head of the rocket is composed of two parts. One part is a shell or cowl to protect the satellite, made of special waterproof, fireproof, and pressure-proof material. The other part is the satellite itself, which carries its own engine. Inside the satellite engine, there is fuel and the fuel is the only combustible item at the head of the rocket.

In addition, could the flame at the head of the rocket be caused by a leakage of rocket fuel? The first two stages of the Long March 2E rocket comprised two connected cylinders, the second stage being closer to the part on fire. The second stage did not carry any fuel, and only carried combustion-supporting oxidants. Only the first stage, or the bottom of the rocket carried fuel. If there was any leakage of the rocket fuel, flames would have arisen from the middle part of the rocket because, while the rocket was flying at high speed, even if the fire spread rapidly it would only spread downward and would never spread upward to the head of the rocket.

"This means that the fire at the head of the rocket could only come from the satellite," he said.

The expert said: The two satellites, exploding in late 1992 and last month, were both HS601 satellites made by Hughes Corporation of the United States. According to rough statistics, Hughes has so far produced 18 satellites of this type and these 18 satellites have been launched separately by France, the United States, and China. France's Ariana launched 10 with nine successes with only one satellite failure, "PanAm-3," which fell into the Atlantic Ocean five minutes after liftoff together with the rocket. It was said that the accident was caused by the rocket. The United States itself launched four with three successes. One satellite failed to enter its orbit due to rocket problems. China has launched four satellites of this type with two successes and two failures. The two failures were caused by the satellites.

It has been learned by these reporters from other sources that, after the satellite made by Hughes, the one to be launched on 26 January, was shipped to China, the US side demanded that 12 guards be assigned to strictly watch the satellite day and night according to the arrangement made in advance, and no Chinese technician was allowed to approach the satellite, to prevent the advanced satellite technology from being "stolen." In order to respect the demand of the cooperation partner, China treated the HS601 satellite in the same way as other US-made satellites launched by China and all customs inspections were exempted as the satellite was shipped into China and transported directly to Xichang Satellite Launch Center. At the same time, all tests of crucial importance, including the "vibration test," were given up according to the instructions from the US side. According to China's practice, when a China-made satellite is to be launched, it has to undergo many vibration tests together with the rocket to see whether or not the satellite and the rocket match each other well.

Although the rocket and the satellite exploded, according to international practice and the terms of the contract, China can still get the launch fee as the rocket carried the satellite and lifted off from the launcher. At the same time, Hughes may also get the order to make another satellite of the same model as a result of the launch failure. Only Hong Kong's Asia-Pacific Communications Satellite Company and China's Pacific Insurance Company directly suffered losses, because Asia-Pacific Communications Satellite Company will have to postpone the use of Apstar-2 to develop its satellite communications services in China, Australia, and some Asian and African countries, and Pacific Insurance would have to make $162 million of compensations.

continued...

REPORT ON SATELLITE EXPLOSION, 1995 (continued)

At present, the satellite launching contractor, China's Chang Cheng Industrial Corporation, and the rocket manufacturer, China's Carrier Rocket Technology Research Academy, are discussing with Hughes Corporation the responsibility issues. It is believed that a conclusion, different from the vague conclusions drawn in 1992, will be reached this time.

Ta Kung Pao, 20 Feb 1995.

INVESTMENT FULFILLMENT OF TECHNICAL UPDATING AND TRANSFORMATION PROJECTS, 1994

	Real Fulfillment		Increase of the Same Period of Last Year		Percentage (based on national total=100)	
	Jan-Jun	Same Period of Last Year	Absolute Number	+/- (percent)	Jan-Jun	Same Period of Last Year
Total (100 mn yuan)	712.09	521.84	190.25	36.5	100.0	100.0
Administrative level						
Central government projects	190.41	117.11	73.30	62.6	26.7	22.4
Local projects	521.69	404.73	116.95	28.9	73.3	77.6
Purpose						
Increasing production	272.31	182.76	89.55	49.0	38.2	35.0
Energy saving measures	14.81	12.62	2.19	17.4	2.1	2.4
Other saving measures	8.62		8.62		1.2	
Increasing variety of products	105.21	82.50	22.71	27.5	14.8	15.8
Improving quality of products	42.88	34.65	8.23	23.7	6.0	6.6
Environmental protection	9.19	7.48	1.71	22.9	1.3	1.4
Other	259.07		259.07		36.4	
Uses of funds						
Construction	283.01	218.70	64.31	29.4	39.7	41.9
Installation	59.65	38.69	20.96	54.2	8.4	7.4
Purchase of equipment and instruments	320.96	226.97	93.99	41.4	45.1	43.5
Among: used technical updating and transformation equipment	44.91	34.70	10.21	29.4	6.3	6.6
Type of construction						
New construction	53.30	31.99	21.31	66.6	7.5	6.1
Expansion	368.74	254.53	114.21	44.9	51.8	48.8
Replacement	258.78	205.84	52.93	25.7	36.3	39.4
Purpose						
Resident	42.94	32.16	10.79	33.5	6.0	6.2
Newly increased fixed assets (100 mn yuan)	134.20	94.90	39.31	41.4	18.8	18.2
Floor space of buildings (10,000 m²)						
Floor space of buildings under construction	6,618.13	6,341.69	276.44	4.4		

continued...

INVESTMENT FULFILLMENT OF TECHNICAL UPDATING AND TRANSFORMATION PROJECTS, 1994 (continued)

	Real Fulfillment		Increase of the Same Period of Last Year		Percentage (based on national total=100)	
	Jan-Jun	Same Period of Last Year	Absolute Number	+/- (percent)	Jan-Jun	Same Period of Last Year
Among: Resident	2,438.58	2,061.04	377.54	18.3		
Floor space of buildings completed	572.37	538.47	33.90	6.3		
Among: Residents	247.46	208.50	38.96	18.7		

China Statistics, Jun 1994.

NEW CONSTRUCTION INVESTMENT FULFILLMENT OF TECHNICAL PROJECTS BY REGION, 1994

	Type of Projects (100 mn yuan)				Percentage		
	Total (100 mn yuan)	New Construction	Expansion	Transformation	New Construction	New Expansion	Transformation
National total	712.09	53.30	368.74	258.78	7.48	51.78	36.34
Beijing	57.32	1.07	39.07	14.03	1.87	68.15	24.47
Tianjin	31.73	4.98	12.80	13.80	15.70	40.36	43.50
Hebei	35.61	2.58	15.30	16.61	7.26	42.96	46.65
Shanxi	7.31	0.15	2.18	4.87	2.11	29.81	66.60
Inner Mongolia	14.35	0.13	12.37	1.73	0.89	86.20	12.04
Liaoning	46.89	3.49	22.24	20.78	7.45	47.43	44.33
Jilin	12.57	0.03	7.86	4.06	0.21	62.50	32.26
Heilongjiang	18.32	0.25	12.57	3.97	1.36	68.58	21.65
Shanghai	75.25	6.09	20.61	39.81	8.09	27.39	52.90
Jiangsu	57.93	6.98	31.43	18.46	12.05	54.25	31.87
Zhejiang	23.63	1.63	11.95	8.96	6.89	50.56	37.91
Anhui	16.96	2.27	8.51	5.75	13.35	50.19	33.92
Fujian	19.15	3.00	11.93	3.67	15.68	62.26	19.18
Jiangxi	16.11	0.85	12.52	2.42	5.29	77.70	15.03
Shandong	39.26	1.30	18.59	18.19	3.31	47.35	46.34
Henan	31.04	2.76	16.84	10.65	8.90	54.26	34.30
Hubei	24.01	1.16	15.00	5.80	4.85	62.46	24.18
Hunan	21.41	0.71	12.47	8.04	3.34	58.26	37.57
Guangdong	54.61	5.50	33.40	14.03	10.07	61.16	25.70
Guangxi	11.87	1.38	7.49	2.56	11.59	63.10	21.54
Hainan	1.39	0.04	0.86	0.11	3.16	61.85	7.68
Sichuan	33.55	1.36	16.36	14.75	4.06	48.76	43.96
Guizhou	7.27	0.84	2.44	3.71	11.53	33.61	51.04
Yunnan	18.43	1.89	9.22	5.65	10.27	50.02	30.66
Tibet							
Shaanxi	15.29	1.35	7.41	5.67	8.82	48.44	37.09
Gansu	5.71	0.23	1.79	3.52	4.02	31.41	61.63
Qinghai	1.18	0.01	0.45	0.64	0.43	37.65	54.40
Ningxia	2.89	0.79	1.49	0.44	27.29	51.62	15.34
Xinjiang	8.41	0.47	3.61	3.45	5.59	42.96	41.07
Non-region	2.63			2.63			100.00

China Statistics, Jun 1994.

GUANGDONG BUILDS SECOND AND THIRD NUCLEAR POWER PLANTS, 1995

Guangzhou, 17 Feb (TA KUNG PAO)—Zhang Minling, deputy director of the Guangdong Power Industry Bureau, said today that Guangdong has already signed a memorandum with France on building the province's second nuclear power plant. If preparations are made properly, Guangdong probably will proceed with the building of its second and third nuclear power plants synchronously.

Zhang said that the Daya Bay nuclear power plant operated normally in 1994. By the end of 1994, the plant generated 12.263 billion kwh of electricity, of which 7.78 billion kwh were transmitted to Hong Kong.

Zhang continued by saying that the power-generating installed capacity put into operation in Guangdong totaled 4,850 megawatts, an increase of 23 percent over the previous year, which is record growth. The generating units that have been built and have gone into operation include: The first and second generating units of the Daya Bay nuclear power plant, the fourth generating unit of Guangzhou's pumped energy storage plant, the fourth generating unit of the Qingxi hydropower plant, the first generating unit of the Zhanjiang power plant, and the second generating unit of the Mawan power plant. By the end of the year, Guangdong's installed generating capacity totaled 19,610 megawatts, ranking first among the cities and provinces throughout the country for two successive years. Of Guangdong's power stations, the Daya Bay nuclear power plant and the first phase project of the Guangzhou pumped energy storage plant were built and completed in a quality fashion, at high speed, and in light of international standards, which won appraise from the trade overseas.

Zhang stated that Guangdong now is drafting a power plan for the Zhujiang delta economic region, which includes establishing a large power network conforming to international standards; maintaining a balance of energy, transportation, capital, equipment, and environmental capacity; and allocating a large amount of funds to build a 500,000-volt large transformer substation in Guangdong. In the near future, efforts will be made to step up construction of the Taishan and Zhuhai power plants, and the preparation of Guangdong's second nuclear power plant, as well as the thermal power plants in Huilai and Shanmei.

Zhang said that Guangdong will strive to develop international and domestic energy-supply channels, and will take a diverse road for energy development. Nuclear power, which is one of the channels for developing power, is required for a rational and scientific distribution. The Guangdong Nuclear Power Group Corporation is now established. The second nuclear power plant will be built at a location 4 km from the Daya Bay nuclear power plant, while the third will be built in Zhanjiang.

Ta Kung Pao, 18 Feb 1995.

CAS REBUILDS SCIENCE TOWN, 1995

The Chinese Academy of Sciences (CAS) announced its ambitious blueprint of rebuilding Zhongguancun, the best-known science town in China, here today.

The announcement was jointly made by Professor Zhou Guangzhao, CAS president, and Li Qiyan, mayor of Beijing at a working conference this afternoon.

Professor Zhou said that the rebuilding project will be open to international bidding.

In the first half of this year, the rebuilding plan will be chosen from the designs submitted by seven universities including two Hong Kong universities, Zhou said.

"And in the later half of this year, we will announce our specific projects for international investment and biddings," he said.

Observers believe that the project, which will start next year and take 15 years to complete, is expected to cost billions of yuan.

X, 23 Oct 1995.

CHINA CANCELS DEAL FOR SELLING IRAN TWO REACTORS, 1995

In a move that sped up the recovery of the troubled relationship between Washington and Beijing, China told the United States that it had decided to cancel its contract to sell two nuclear power reactors to Iran. In March, 1995, Chinese officials stated that despite US protests China intended to go forward with their deal with Iran. Iranian officials were greatly unsettled by China's pullout at the last moment and stated they would endeavor to change the situation to their favor. Although China's nuclear technology was less than that of other major world powers it was far superior to that of Iran. This deal was to allow Iran access to the world nuclear community, a community in which China was a minority citizen.

China Facts & Figures Annual, 1995

SHANGHAI SCIENTISTS DEVELOP ROBOT, 1995

Scientists in the eastern city of Shanghai developed a robot which is used to lift objects. The robot successfully put up a steel antenna, with a weight of 460 tons and a length of 118 meters, at the top of the Oriental Pearl Television Tower. According to officials, using the robot for the installation of the antenna saved 200 million yuan in investment funds. So far contracts for the purchase of the robots, which were developed by researchers at Tongji University and the Machinery Engineering Company of Shanghai, from at home and abroad amounted to 1.5 billion yuan.

China Facts & Figures Annual, 1995

COMMUNICATIONS RESEARCH CENTER ESTABLISHED IN SHANGHAI, 1995

An advanced communications center was jointly established by an enterprise and a university in Shanghai 1 March 1995. The Guo Mai-Fudan Research Center, jointly established by the Shanghai Guo Mai communications Company Ltd. and Fudan University, plans to keep up with the latest scientific and technological developments by using the economic strength of Guo Mai and the know-how of Fudan.

Guo Mai, with assets of one billion yuan, will spend one-five-thousandth of its sales volume on communications research. In addition, it will help Fudan establish a communications laboratory.

X, 1 Mar 1995.

COMPUTER SMUGGLING, 1995

The General Customs Administration and the Electronics Industry Ministry today signed a "Memorandum on Cooperation in Cracking Down on Illegal Activities Involving the Smuggling of Computers, Peripherals, and Other Electronic Products."

In recent years, computer smuggling was quite serious in our country. According to the Electronics Industry Ministry's analysis, 718,000 computers were sold in computer markets nationwide in 1994, and some 60 percent of them were illegal imports. This not only caused the state some 2 billion yuan in lost customs and value-added tax revenues, but also disrupted normal trading order in the computer field, and posed a great threat to the domestic computer industry's survival and development.

According to the cooperation memorandum signed today, the Electronics Industry Ministry will provide timely information to customs offices on industrial policies, domestic and overseas supply and demand, and prices regarding computers, peripherals, and other electronic products, as well as leads on the smuggling of these products. The General Customs Administration will provide timely information on the export and import of these products to the other party, and lay out plans for cracking down on smuggling. Both parties also agreed to adopt measures to encourage enterprises and individuals in the industry to provide leads on smuggling to customs offices. Moreover, they suggested that relevant state departments tighten supervision and management over domestic markets for computers and other electronic products, and ban illegal imports from the market.

X, 14 Jun 1995.

CHINA SOFTWARE SALES, 1995

Country/ Region	Q4 Revenues (mn)	Percent Change	1995 Revenues (mn)	Percent Change
Thailand	3.1	155	11.6	277
China	1.1	95	4.6	189
India, Pakistan	4.6	-91	10.6	124
Taiwan	7.7	28	37.9	75
Malaysia	4.3	52	13.4	60
Hong Kong	6.5	23	30.7	45
Japan	231.8	83	757.8	45
Singapore	10	-38	42	44
Korea	8.9	41	34.4	40

MacWeek, 27 May 1996, 6.

TECHNOLOGY INCREASES RICE YIELD, 1995

This port city in north China has achieved an extra 164,000 tons of rice and 8,872 tons of lean-pork as a result of the use of advanced technology over the past three years.

In 1992 Tianjin started a plan to apply advanced technology in growing about 33,000 ha of rice and raising 500,000 lean-pork pigs.

Over 500 scientists and technicians in 12 counties and districts around Tianjin took part in the plan, saving about 100 million yuan in production costs and increasing economic returns by 394 million yuan.

Advanced technology has been applied to over 70 percent of the paddy fields, enhancing the output per ha to 7,785 kg from 6,150 kg. About 80 percent of the pigs have benefited from the advanced technology, with the result that the lean-pork rate has been increased to 57.3 percent from 50 percent.

The application of advanced technology has also fostered a large number of farmer-technicians.

The past three years have seen Tianjin send over 10,000 pamphlets containing information on agricultural technology and related materials to thousands of rural families. In addition, classes and lectures have been held to train 47,000 farmers in advanced techniques.

X, 3 Apr 1995.

XXI COMMUNICATIONS

CHINA'S CABLE TELEVISION INDUSTRY, 1983–1993

	Operators	Subscribers
1983	na	70,000
1988	500	na
1990	1,096	11.1m
1993	744*	32m

* Operators relicensed.

Hong Kong University Telecoms Research Project, 1994.

GOVERNMENT SPENDING ON TELECOMMUNICATIONS, 1995

China will inject 80 billion yuan (about 9.4 billion US dollars) into the infrastructure construction of posts and telecommunications this year, said Wu Jichuan, minister of posts and telecommunications.

Wu told a national work conference here yesterday that the country poured about 68.3 billion yuan into the industry last year, up 28 billion yuan from the 1993 figure.

Last year saw seven trans-province optical cables and 14 satellite ground stations go into operation, and the capacity of long-distance automatic switching expand to 2.2 million channels, 994,000 channels more than in 1993. Meanwhile, the number of trunk telephone lines reached 687,000 in 1994, an increase of 267,000 lines over the previous year.

By the end of last year, the capacity of the country's telephone network had surpassed 61.62 million lines, thanks to the addition of 18.9 million lines.

Moreover, the country boasts a public packet switching system with 60,000 terminals, as well as a public data network with over 3,300 terminals.

Attributing the rapid development of the postal service to its upgrading of facilities, Wu said that the country has opened six trans-province high-speed postal routes in dozens of provinces.

At present, 15 cities have a total of 25 automatic mail-sorting systems.

The minister said that this year the country will fix its focus on the construction of long-distance cables, especially optical ones.

The capacity of the telephone switching system is expected to be enhanced by 14 million lines this year, as well as by some 300,000 trunk telephones, and 18 more postal routes will be available by the end of this year.

Furthermore, Wu said, China will quicken the development of digital microwave systems, satellite telecommunications and long-distance exchange systems.

The country will raise funds abroad to ensure the completion of those infrastructure projects, according to the minister.

He disclosed that foreign capital will occupy a 10 percent to 18 percent share among the investment in the fixed assets of the posts and telecommunications industry.

Statistics show that the industry has used overseas funds totaling six billion US dollars over the past 15 years.

X, 18 Jun 1995.

CHINA'S SATELLITE PARTNERS, 1995

Name	Owner (14.3% each)
China Telecommunications Broadcast Satellite Corp.	Ministry of Posts and Telecommunications (China)
China Yuan Wang (Group) Corp.	State Commission of Science, Technology and Industry for National Defense (China)
Ever-Victory System Co.	China Aerospace Industry Corp. (formerly Ministry of Aerospace Industry) (China)
Orient Telecom & Technology	Charoen Pokphand (Thailand)
China Travel Fok Tai	China Travel Service (China), Ng Fok (Macao)
Singapore Telecom	Temasek Holdings (Singapore)
Kwang Hua Development & Investment	Ruentex Industries; China Development Corp. (Taiwan)

FEER, 18 Aug 1995.

POSITION OF CHINA'S TELECOMMUNICATIONS SATELLITE IN COMPARISON TO OTHER LARGE COUNTRIES, 1995

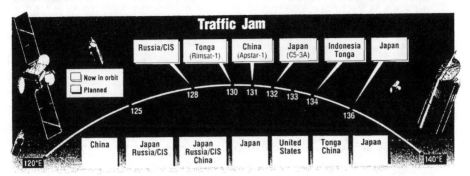

FEER, 18 Aug 1995.

MEDIA OUTLETS, 1994

PRINCIPAL NEWSPAPERS

Anhui Ribao (Anhui Daily): Anhui Province; Editor-in-Chief QIAN LIN.

Beijing Ribao (Beijing Daily): 34 Xi Biaobei Hutong, Dongdan, Beijing 100743; tel. (1) 5132233; fax (1) 5126581; f. 1952; organ of the Beijing municipal cttee of the CCP; Dir MAN YUNLAI; Editor-in-Chief LIU HUSHAN; circ. 700,000.

Beijing Wanbao (Beijing Evening News): 34 Xi Biaobei Hutong, Dongdan, Beijing 100743; tel. (1) 5132233; telex 283642; fax (1) 5126581; f. 1958; Editor LI BINGREN; circ. 800,000.

Chengdu Evening News: Qingyun Nan Jie, Chengdu 610017; tel. 664501; fax 666597; circ. 700,000.

China Daily: 15 Huixin Dongjie, Chaoyang District, Beijing 100029; tel. (1) 4220955; telex 22022; fax (1) 4220922; f. 1981; English; coverage: China's political, economic and cultural developments; world, financial and sports news; also publishes *Beijing Weekend* (f. 1991), *Shanghai Star* (f. 1992), *21st Century* (f. 1993); Editor-in-Chief CHEN LI; circ. 150,000.

Dazhong Ribao (Masses Daily): 8 Jinshi Lu, Jinan 250014, Shandong Province; tel. 648980; telex 9993; fax 262400; f. 1939; Editor-in-Chief LIU HONGXI; circ. 550,000.

Fujian Ribao (Fujian Daily): Hualin Lu, Fuzhou, Fujian Province; tel. 57756; daily; Deputy Editor-in-Chief HUANG ZHONGSHENG.

Gongren Ribao (Workers' Daily): Liupukang, Andingmen Wai, Beijing; tel. (1) 4211561; telex 210423; fax (1) 4214890; f. 1949; trade union activities and workers' lives; also major home and overseas news; Editor-in-Chief QU ZUGENG; circ. 2.5m.

Guangming Ribao (Guangming Daily): 106 Yongan Lu, Beijing 100050; tel. (1) 3010636; telex 20021; fax (1) 3016716; f. 1949; literature, art, science, education, history, economics, philosophy; Editor LIU LUSHA; circ. 6m.

Guangxi Ribao (Guangxi Daily): Guangxi Region; Dir and Editor-in-Chief YANG ZHIQING.

Guangzhou Ribao (Canton Daily): 10 Dongle Lu, Renmin Zhonglu, Guangzhou, Guangdong Province; tel. 8887294; fax 8862033; f. 1952; daily; economic and current affairs; Editor-in-Chief HUANG YONGZHAN; circ. 482,000.

Guizhou Ribao (Guizhou Daily): Guiying, Guizhou Province; tel. 627779; f. 1949; circ. 300,000; Editor-in-Chief LIU XUEZHU.

Hebei Ribao (Hebei Daily): Yuhuazhong Lu, Shijiazhuang 050013, Hebei Province; tel. 646753; f. 1949; Editor-in-Chief YE ZHEN; circ. 500,000.

Heilongjiang Ribao (Heilongjiang Daily): Heilongjiang Province; Editor-in-Chief ZHANG GUOCHANG.

Henan Ribao (Henan Daily): Henan Province; Editor-in-Chief YANG FENGGE.

Hubei Ribao (Hubei Daily): 4 Dongting 2 Lu, Wuhan 430077, Hubei Province; tel. 814531; telex 5590; f. 1949; Editor-in-Chief LU JIAN; circ. 800,000.

Jiangxi Ribao (Jiangxi Daily): Nanchang, Jiangxi Province; tel. 772133; f. 1949; Editor-in-Chief DUAN FURUI.

Jiefang Ribao (Liberation Daily): 274 Han Kou Lu, Shanghai 200001; tel. (21) 3221300; fax (21) 3221300; f. 1949; Chief Editor DING XIMAN; circ. 1m.

Jiefangjun Bao (Liberation Army Daily): Beijing; f. 1956; official organ of the Central Military Comm.; Dir XU CAIHOU; Editor-in-Chief SUN ZHONGTONG; circ. 800,000.

Jingji Ribao (Economic Daily): 277 Wang Fujing Dajie, Beijing 100746; tel. (1) 652018; fax (1) 5125522; f. 1983; financial affairs, domestic and foreign trade; Editor-in-Chief YANG SHANGDE; circ. 1.59m.

Liaoning Ribao (Liaoning Daily): Liaoning Province; Editor-in-Chief ZHU SHILIANG.

Nanfang Ribao (Nanfang Daily): 289 Guangzhou Da Lu, Guangzhou 51061, Guangdong Province; tel. 763998; f. 1949; Editor-in-Chief LIU TAO; circ. 1m.

continued...

MEDIA OUTLETS, 1994 (continued)

Nongmin Ribao (Peasants' Daily): Shilipu Beili, Chao Yang Men Wai, Beijing; tel. (1) 5005522; telex 6592; f. 1980; 6 a week; circulates in rural areas nation-wide; Dir XU JING; circ. 1m.

Renmin Ribao (People's Daily): 2 Jin Tai Xi Lu, Beijing; tel. (1) 5092121; telex 22320; fax (1) 5091982; f. 1948; organ of the CCP; also publishes overseas edn; Editor-in-Chief FAN JINGYI; circ. 3m.

Shaanxi Ribao (Shaanxi Daily): Shaanxi Province; Editor-in-Chief QIAN GUOZHENG.

Shanxi Ribao (Shanxi Daily): 24 Shuangtasi Jie, Taiyuan, Shanxi Province; tel. 446561; fax 441771; Dir WANG XIYI; Editor-in-Chief ZHAO KEMING; circ. 300,000.

Shenzhen Tequ Bao (Shenzhen Special Zone Daily): 4 Shennan Zhonglu, Shenzhen; tel. 244566; f. 1982; reports on special economic zones, as well as Hong Kong and Macau; Editor-in-Chief O HUIWEN.

Sichuan Ribao (Sichuan Daily): 70 Hongxing Zhonglu, Chengdu 610012, Sichuan Province; tel. 678900; fax 665035; f. 1952; Editor WANG XUEMEI; circ. 8m.

Tianjin Ribao (Tianjin Daily): 32 Shanxi Lu, Heping Qu, Tianjin 300020; tel. 700264; fax 701168; f. 1949; Editor-in-Chief LU SI; circ. 600,000.

Wenhui Bao: 149 Yuanmingyuan Lu, Shanghai; tel. (21) 3211410; telex 33080; f. 1938; Editor-in-Chief ZHANG QICHENG; circ. 1.7m.

Xin Min Wan Bao (Xin Min Evening News): 839 Yan An Lu, Shanghai 200040; tel. (21) 2791234; fax (21) 2473220; f. 1929; Dir (vacant); Editor-in-Chief DING FAZHANG; circ. 1,625,789.

Xinhua Ribao (New China Daily): 55 Zhongshan Lu, Nanjing 210005, Jiangsu Province; tel. (21) 741757; fax (21) 741023; Editor-in-Chief LIU XIANGDONG; circ. 900,000.

Xinjiang Ribao (Xinjiang Daily): Xinjiang Region; Dir TIAN YUMIAN.

Xizang Ribao (Tibet Daily): Tibet; Editor-in-Chief LI CHANGWEN.

Yangcheng Wanbao (Yangcheng Evening Post): 733 Dongfeng Donglu, Guangzhou, Guangdong Province; tel. 7776211; f. 1957; Editor-in-Chief GUAN GUODONG; circ. 1.73m.

Yunnan Ribao (Yunnan Daily): Yunnan Province; Editor-in-Chief WANG ZIMING.

Zhejiang Ribao (Zhejiang Daily): Zhejiang Province; Editor-in-Chief JIANG PING.

Zhongguo Qingnian Bao (China Youth News): 2 Haiyuncang, Dongzhimen Nei, Beijing 100702; tel. (1) 4032233; fax (1) 4083961; f. 1951; 4 a week; aimed at 14–25 age-group; Dir and Editor FENG AIYING; circ. 1.5m.

Zhongguo Xinwen (China News): 12 Baiwanzhuang Nanjie, Beijing; tel. (1) 8315012; f. 1952; daily; Editor-in-Chief WANG XIJIN; current affairs.

SELECTED PERIODICALS

Ban Yue Tan (Fortnightly Review): Beijing; tel. (1) 668521; f. 1980; in Chinese and Wei Wuer (Uygur); Editor-in-Chief MIN FANLU; circ. 6m.

Beijing Review: 24 Baiwanzhuang Lu, Beijing 100037; tel. (1) 8326628; telex 222374; fax (1) 8326628; weekly; edns in English, French, Spanish, Japanese and German; also Chinafrica (monthly in English); Editor-in-Chief GENG YUXIN.

BJ TV Weekly: 2 Fuxingmenwai Zhenwumiao Jie, Beijing 100045; tel. (1) 3262388; fax (1) 3262388; circ. 1m.

China TV Weekly: 15 Huixin Dong Jie, Chaoyang Qu, Beijing 100013; tel. (1) 4214197; telex 22022; circ. 1.7m.

Chinese Literature Press: 24 Baiwanzhuang Lu, Beijing 100037; tel. (1) 8326010; fax (1) 8326678; f. 1951; quarterly; in English and French; contemporary and classical writing, poetry, literary criticism and arts; Exec. Editor TANG JIALONG.

Chinese Science Abstracts: Science Press, 16 Donghuangchenggen Beijie, Beijing 100707; tel. (1) 4018833; telex 210247; fax (1) 4012180; f. 1982; monthly in English; science and technology; Chief Editor LI RUIXU.

Dianying Xinzuo (New Films): 796 Huaihai Zhonglu, Shanghai; tel. (21) 4379710; f. 1979; bi-monthly; introduces new films.

Dianzi yu Diannao (Electronics and Computers): Beijing; f. 1985; popularized information on computers and microcomputers.

Elle (China): Lane 955, 14 Yanan Lu, Shanghai; tel. (21) 4311890; fax (21) 4335100; f. 1988; fashion; Editor LOU ZHAOTIAN; circ. 100,000.

Family: 14 Shieng Lu, Xinhepu, Dongshan Qu, Guangzhou; tel. 7750899; monthly; circ. 2.47m.

Feitian (Fly Skywards): 50 Donggan Xilu, Lanzhou, Gansu; tel. 25803; f. 1961; monthly.

Guoji Xin Jishu (New International Technology): Zhanwang Publishing House, Beijing; f. 1984; also publ. in Hong Kong; international technology, scientific and technical information.

Guowai Keji Dongtai (Scientific and Technical Trends Abroad): Institute of Scientific and Technical Information of China, 15 Fuxing Lu, Beijing 100038; tel. (1) 8515544; telex 20079; fax (1) 8514025; f. 1965; monthly; scientific journal; circ. 20,000.

Hai Xia (The Strait): 27 De Gui Xiang, Fuzhou, Fujian Province; tel. (1) 33656; f. 1981; quarterly; literary journal; Prin. Officers YANG YU, JWO JONG LIN.

Huasheng Bao (Voice of Overseas Chinese): 12 Bai Wan Zhuang Nan Jie, Beijing 100037; tel. (1) 8315039; fax (1) 8315039; f. 1983; 2 a week; intended mainly for overseas Chinese and Chinese nationals resident abroad; Editor-in-Chief ZHOU TI.

Jianzhu (Construction): Baiwanzhuang, Beijing; tel. (1) 8992849; f. 1956; monthly; Editor FANG YUEGUANG; circ. 500,000.

Jinri Zhongguo (China Today): 24 Baiwanzhuang Lu, Beijing 100037; tel. (1) 892190; fax (1) 8328338; f. 1952; fmrly China Reconstructs; monthly; edns in English, Spanish, French, Arabic, Portuguese, German and Chinese; economic, social and cultural affairs; illustrated; Dir and Editor-in-Chief MENG JIQING.

Liaowang (Outlook): 57 Xuanwumen Xijie, Beijing (1) 3073049; f. 1981; weekly; current affairs; Gen. Man. ZHOU YICHANG; Editor CHEN DABIN; circ. 500,000.

Luxingjia (Traveller): 23A Dong Jiaomin Xiang, Beijing; tel. (1) 552631; f. 1955; monthly; Chinese scenery, customs, culture.

Meishu Zhi You (Friends of Art): 32 Beizongbu Hutong, East City Region, Beijing; tel. (1) 5122583; telex 5019; f. 1982; every 2 months; art review journal, also providing information on fine arts publs in China and abroad; Editors PENG SHEN, BAOLUN WU.

Nianqingren (Young People): 169 Mayuanlin, Changsha, Hunan Province; tel. 23610; f. 1981; monthly; general interest for young people.

Nongye Zhishi (Agricultural Knowledge): 21 Minziqian Lu, Jinan 250100, Shandong Province; tel. 832238; f. 1950; monthly; popular agricultural science; Dir YANG XIANFEN; circ. 730,000.

Qiushi (Seeking Truth): 2 Shatan Beijie, Beijing 100727; tel. (1) 4011155; telex 1219; f. 1988 to succeed Hong Qi (Red Flag); every 2 months; theoretical journal of the CCP; Editor-in-Chief YOU LIN; circ. 1.83m.

Renmin Huabao (China Pictorial): Huayuancun, West Suburbs, Beijing 100044; tel. (1) 8411144; f. 1950; monthly; edns: 2 in Chinese, 4 in minority languages and 15 in foreign languages; Dir and Editor-in-Chief FING YAN.

Shichang Zhoubao (Market Weekly): 2 Duan, Sanhao Jie, Heping Qu, Shenyang, Liaoning Province; tel. 482983; f. 1979; weekly in Chinese; trade, commodities and financial and economic affairs; circ. 1m.

Shufa (Calligraphy): 83 Kangping Lu, Shanghai 200030; tel. (21) 4377711; telex 5928; fax (21) 4311905; f. 1977; every 2 months; journal on ancient and modern calligraphy; Chief Editor LU FUSHENG.

Tiyu Kexue (Sports Science): 8 Tiyuguan Lu, Beijing 100061; tel. (1) 7614477; telex 22323; f. 1981; sponsored by the China Sports Science Soc.; every 2 months; summary in English; Chief Officer ZHANG CAIZHEN; in Chinese; circ. 20,000.

Wenxue Qingnian (Youth Literature Journal): Mu Tse Fang 27, Wenzhou, Zhejiang Province; tel. 3578; f. 1981; monthly; Editor-in-Chief CHEN YUSHEN; circ. 80,000.

Xian Dai Faxue (Modern Law Science): Chongqing 630031, Sichuan Province; tel. 961671; f. 1979; bi-monthly; with summaries in English; Dirs XU JINGCUN, XIE XOUPING.

Yinyue Aihaozhe (Music Lovers): 74 Shaoxing Lu, Shanghai 200020; tel. (21) 4372606; telex 33384; fax (21) 4332019; f. 1979; every 2 months; music knowledge; illustrated; Editor-in-Chief CHEN XUEYA; circ. 50,000.

Zhongguo Duiwai Maoyi (China's Foreign Trade): 1 Fu Xing Men Wai Jie, Beijing; tel. (1) 863770; telex 22315; fax (1) 8011370; f. 1956; monthly; edns in Chinese, English, French and Spanish; carries information about Chinese imports and exports and explains foreign trade and economic policies; Editor-in-Chief LIU DEYU.

Zhongguo Ertong (Chinese Children): 21, Xiang 12, Dongsi, Beijing; tel. (1) 444761; telex 4357; f. 1980; monthly; illustrated journal for elementary school pupils.

Zhongguo Funu (Women of China): 24A Shijia Hutong, Beijing; tel. (1) 551765; f. 1956; monthly; women's rights and status, marriage and family, education, family planning, arts, cookery, etc.; Editor-in-Chief Ms WANG XIULIN.

Zhongguo Guanggno Bao (China's Advertising): Editorial Dept, Beijing Exhibition Hall, Xizhimen Wai, Beijing; tel. (1) 890661; f.

continued...

MEDIA OUTLETS, 1994 (continued)

1984; weekly; all aspects of advertising and marketing; offers advertising services for domestic and foreign commodities.

Zhongguo Guangbo Dianshi (China Radio and Television): 12 Fucheng Lu, Beijing; tel. (1) 896217; f. 1982; monthly; sponsored by Ministry of Radio, Film and Television; reports and comments.

Zhongguo Jin Rong Xin Xi: Beijing; f. 1991; monthly; economic news.

Zhongguo Sheying (Chinese Photography): 61 Hongxing Hutong, Dongdan, Beijing 100005; tel. (1) 552277; f. 1957; monthly; photographs and comments; Editor LIU BANG.

Zhongguo Zhenjiu (Chinese Acupuncture and Moxibustion): China Academy of Traditional Chinese Medicine, Dongzhimen Nei, Beijing 100700; tel. (1) 4014411; telex 210340; f. 1981; 2 a month; publ. by Chinese Soc. of Acupuncture and Moxibustion; abstract in English; Editor-in-Chief Prof. WEI MINGFENG.

Other popular magazines include **Gongchandang Yuan** (Communists, circ. 1.63m.), **Nongmin Wenzhai** (Peasants Digest, circ. 3.54m.), and **Jiating** (Family, circ. 1.89m.).

NEWS AGENCIES

Xinhua (New China) News Agency: 57 Xuanwumen Xidajie, Beijing 100803; tel. (1) 3073767; telex 22316; fax (1) 3073735; f. 1931; offices in all Chinese provincial capitals, and about 95 overseas bureaux; news service in Chinese, English, French, Spanish, Arabic and Russian, feature and photographic services; Pres. GUO CHAOREN; Editor-in-Chief NAN ZHENZHONG.

Zhongguo Xinwen She (China News Agency): POB 1114, Beijing; f. 1952; office in Hong Kong; supplies news features, special articles and photographs for newspapers and magazines in Chinese printed overseas; services in Chinese; Dir WANG SHIGU.

Foreign Bureaux

Agence France-Presse (AFP) (France): 11–11 Jian Guo Men Wai, Diplomatic Apts, Beijing 100600; tel. (1) 5321992; fax (1) 5322371; Bureau Chief PIERRE LANFRANCHI.

Agencia EFE (Spain): 2-2-132 Jian Guo Men Wai, Beijing 100600; tel. (1) 5323449; telex 22167; fax (1) 5323688; Rep. ENRIQUE IBÁÑEZ.

Agenzia Nazionale Stampa Associata (ANSA) (Italy): 1–11 Ban Gong Lu, San Li Tun, Beijing; tel. (1) 5323651; telex 22290; fax (1) 5321964; Bureau Chief FRANCO VASELLI.

Allgemeiner Deutscher Nachrichtendienst (ADN) (Germany): Jian Guo Men Wai, Qi Jia Yuan Gong Yu 7-2-61, Beijing 100600; tel. (1) 5321115; telex 22109; fax (1) 5321115; Correspondent Dr LUTZ POHLE.

Associated Press (AP) (USA): 7-2-52 Qi Jia Yuan, Diplomatic Quarters, Beijing; tel. (1) 5323743; telex 22196; fax (1) 5323419; Bureau Chief KATHY WILHELM.

Deutsche Presse-Agentur (dpa) (Germany): Ban Gong Lu, San Li Tun, Apt 1–31, Beijing 100600; tel. (1) 5321473; telex 22297; fax (1) 5321615; Bureau Chief ANDREAS LANDWEHR.

Informatsionnoye Telegrafnoye Agentstvo Rossii—Telegrafnoye Agentstvo Suverennykh Stran (ITAR—TASS) (Russia): 6-1-41 Tayuan Diplomatic Compound, Beijing; tel. (1) 5324821; telex 22115; fax (1) 5324820; Correspondent GRIGORIY ARSLANOV.

Inter Press Service (IPS) (Italy): c/o ISTIC, Room 209, n. 15, Fu Xing Lu, POB 3811, Beijing; tel. (1) 8014046; telex 20079; fax (1) 8014025; Dir WANG LIANHAI.

Jiji Tsushin-Sha (Japan): 9-1-13 Jian Guo Men Wai, Waijiao, Beijing; tel. (1) 5322924; telex 22381; fax (1) 5323413; Correspondent KENZO SHIDA.

Kyodo News Service (Japan): 3-901 Jian Guo Men Wai, Beijing; tel. (1) 532680; telex 22324; fax (1) 5322273; Bureau Chief KAZUYOSHI NISHIKURA.

Magyar Távirati Iroda (MTI) (Hungary): 9-2-52 Tayuan, Beijing 100600; tel. (1) 5321744; telex 22106; Correspondent GYÖRGY BARTA.

Prensa Latina (Cuba): Qi Ji Yuana 6-2-12, Beijing; tel. (1) 5321831, ext. 539; telex 22284; Correspondent MARÍA ELENA LLANA CASTRO.

Reuters (UK): 1-42 Ban Gong Lou, San Li Tun, Beijing; tel. (1) 5321921; telex 22702; fax 5324978; Chief Representative C. K. CATLIN.

United Press International (UPI) (USA): 7-1-11 Qi Jia Yuan, Beijing; tel. (1) 5323456; telex 22197; Correspondents DAVID R. SCHWEISBERG, SCOTT SAVITT.

The following are also represented: Korean Central News Agency (Democratic People's Republic of Korea), Rompres (Romania), Tanjug (Yugoslavia) and VNA (Viet Nam).

PRESS ORGANIZATIONS

All China Journalists' Association: Xijiaominxiang, Beijing 100031; tel. (1) 6023981; telex 222719; fax (1) 6014658; Exec. Chair. WU LENGXI.

Association of Newspaper Industry: Beijing; Pres. BAO YUJUN.

The Press and Publication Administration of the People's Republic of China: 85 Dongsi Nan Dajie, Beijing 100703; tel. (1) 5124433; telex 22024; fax (1) 5127875; Dir YU YOUXIAN.

Publishers

In 1991 there were 465 publishing houses in China. A total of 89,615 titles were published in 1991.

Beijing Chubanshe (Beijing Publishing House): 6 Bei Sanhuan Zhong Lu, Beijing 100011; tel. (1) 2012339; telex 8909; fax (1) 2012339; f. 1956; politics, history, law, economics, geography, science, literature, art, etc.; Dir ZHU SHUXIN; Editor-in-Chief TAO XINCHENG.

Beijing Daxue Chubanshe (Beijing University Publishing House): Beijing University, Haidian Qu, Beijing 100871; tel. (1) 2561166; telex 22239; f. 1979; academic and general.

Dianzi Gongye Chubanshe (Publishing House of the Electronics Industry): 27 Wanshou Lu, Beijing 100036; tel. (1) 815245; f. 1982; natural sciences; Dir LIANG XIANGFENG; Editor-in-Chief ZHANG DIANGE.

Falü Chubanshe (Law Publishing House): POB 111, Beijing 100036; tel. (1) 815325; f. 1980; current laws and decrees, legal textbooks, translations of important foreign legal works; Dir LAN MINGLIANG.

Gaodeng Jiaoyu Chubanshe (Higher Education Publishing House): 55 Shatan Houjie, Beijing 100009; tel. (1) 4014043; fax (1) 4014048; f. 1954; academic; Pres. YU GUOHUA; Editor-in-Chief YANG LINGKANG.

Gongren Chubanshe (Workers' Publishing House): Liupukeng, Andingmen Wai, Beijing; tel. (1) 4215278; f. 1949; labour movement, trade unions, science and technology related to industrial production.

Guangdong Keji Chubanshe (Guangdong Science and Technology Press): 11 Shuiyin Lu, Huanshidong Lu, Guangzhou 510075, Guangdong; tel. (20) 7769412; fax (20) 7764169; f. 1978; natural sciences, technology, agriculture, medicine, popular science, video and audio tapes; Dir OU YANGLIAN.

Guoji Shudian (China International Book Trading Corporation): POB 399, Chegongzhuang Xilu 35, Beijing; tel. (1) 8414284; telex 22496; fax (1) 8412023; f. 1949; foreign trade org. specializing in publs, including books, periodicals, art and crafts, microfilms, etc.; import and export distributors; Pres. LIU CHUANWEI.

Haitun Chubanshe (Dolphin Books): 24 Baiwanzhuang Lu, Beijing 100087; tel. (1) 8326332; telex 22475; fax (1) 8326642; f. 1986; children's books in Chinese and foreign languages; Dir JIANG CHENGAN.

Heilongjiang Kexue Jishu Chubanshe (Heilongjiang Science and Technology Press): 41 Jianshe Jie, Nangang Qu, Harbin 150001, Heilongjiang; tel. (451) 3642127; fax (451) 3642127; f. 1979; industrial and agricultural technology, natural sciences, economics and management, popular science, children's and general.

Huashan Wenyi Chubanshe (Huashan Literature and Art Publishing House): 45 Bei Malu, Shijiazhuang, Hebei; tel. 22501; f. 1982; novels, poetry, drama, etc.

Kexue Chubanshe (Science Publishing House): 16 Donghuangchenggen Beijie, Beijing 100707; tel. (1) 4019821; telex 210247; fax (1) 4012180; f. 1954; science and technology.

Lingnan Meishu Chubanshe (Lingnan Art Publishing House): 11 Shuiyin Lu, Guangzhou 510075, Guangdong; tel. 7779158; fax 7771049; f. 1981; works on classical and modern painting, picture albums, photographic, painting techniques; Editor-in-Chief LIANG DINGYING.

Minzu Chubanshe (Nationalities Publishing House): 14 Hepingli Beijie, Beijing 100013; tel. (1) 4211261; f. 1953; books and periodicals in minority languages, e.g. Mongolian, Tibetan, Uygur, Korean, Kazakh, etc.; Editor-in-Chief ZHU YINGWU.

Qunzhong Chubanshe (Masses Publishing House): 14 Dongchangan Jie, Beijing 100741; tel. (1) 5121672; telex 2831; f. 1956; politics, law, judicial affairs, criminology, public security, etc.

Renmin Chubanshe (People's Publishing House): Dir XUE DEZHEN.

Renmin Jiaoyu Chubanshe (People's Education Press): 55 Sha Tan Hou Jie, Beijing 100009; tel. (1) 4035745; fax (1) 4010370; f. 1950; school textbooks, guidebooks, teaching materials, etc.

Renmin Meishu Chubanshe (People's Fine Arts Publishing House): 32 Beizongbu Hutong, Beijing 100735; tel. (1) 5122371; fax (1) 5122370; f. 1951; works by Chinese and foreign painters, picture albums, photographic, painting techniques; Dir CHENG YUNHE; Editor-in-Chief LIU YUSHAN.

continued...

MEDIA OUTLETS, 1994 (continued)

Renmin Weisheng Chubanshe (People's Medical Publishing House): 10 Tiantan Xi Li, Beijing 100050; tel. (1) 755431; f. 1953; medicine (Western and traditional Chinese), pharmacology, dentistry. public health; Pres. DONG MIANGUO.

Renmin Wenxue Chubanshe (People's Literature Publishing House): 166 Chaoyangmen Nei Dajie, Beijing 100705; tel. (1) 5138394; telex 2192; f. 1951; largest publr of literary works and translations into Chinese; Dir and Editor-in-Chief CHEN ZAOCHUN.

Shanghai Guji Chubanshe (Shanghai Classics Publishing House): 272 Ruijin Erlu, Shanghai; tel. (21) 4370013; f. 1978; classical Chinese literature.

Shanghai Jiaoyu Chubanshe (Shanghai Educational Publishing House): 123 Yongfu Lu, Shanghai 200031; tel. (21) 4377165; telex 3413; fax (21) 4339995; f. 1958; academic; Dir and Editor-in-Chief CHEN HE.

Shanghai Yiwen Chubanshe (Shanghai Translation Publishing House): 14 Xiang 955, Yanan Zhonglu, Shanghai 200040; tel. (21) 2472890; fax (21) 2475100; f. 1978; translations of foreign classic and modern literature; philosophy, social sciences, dictionaries, etc.

Shangwu Yinshuguan (Commercial Publishing House): 36 Wangfujing Dajie, Beijing; tel. (1) 552026; f. 1897; dictionaries and reference books in Chinese and foreign languages, translations of foreign works on social sciences; Pres. LIN ERWEI.

Shaonian Ertong Chubanshe (Juvenile and Children's Publishing House): 1538 Yan An Xi Lu, Shanghai 200052; tel. (21) 2513025; telex 5801; fax (21) 2512851; f. 1952; children's educational and literary works, teaching aids and periodicals; Dir ZHOU SHUNPEI; Editor-in-Chief REN DALIN.

Shijie Wenhua Chubanshe (World Culture Publishing House): Dir ZHU LIE.

Waiwen Chubanshe (Foreign Languages Press): 24 Baiwanzhuang Lu, Beijing 100037; tel. (1) 8326642; telex 222475; fax (1) 8326642; f. 1952; books in 20 foreign languages reflecting political and economic developments in People's Republic of China and features of Chinese culture; Dir XU MINGQIANG.

Wenwu Chubanshe (Cultural Relics Publishing House): 29 Wusi Dajie, Beijing 100009; tel. (1) 4014662; fax (1) 4010698; f. 1956; books and catalogues of Chinese relics in museums and those recently discovered; Dir YANG JIN.

Wuhan Daxue Chubanshe (Wuhan University Press): Wuhan University, Wuchang, Hubei; tel. (27) 712661; fax (27) 720651; f. 1981; academic; Pres. and Editor-in-Chief Prof. NIU TAICHEN.

Xiandai Chubanshe (Modern Publishing House): 504 Anhua Li, Andingmenwai, Beijing 100011; tel. (1) 4210403; telex 210215; fax (1) 4214540; f. 1981; directories, reference books, etc.; Dir ZHOU HONGLI.

Xinhua Chubanshe (Xinhua Publishing House): 57 Xuanwumen Xidajie, Beijing 100803; tel. (1) 3073885; telex 22316; fax (1) 3073880; f. 1979; social sciences, economy, politics, history, geography, directories, dictionaries, etc.; Dir ZHANG WANSHU; Editor-in-Chief CHENG KEXIONG.

Xuelin Chubanshe (Scholar Books Publishing House): 120 Wenmiao Lu, Shanghai 200010; tel. (21) 3777108; f. 1981; academic, including personal academic works at authors' own expense; Dir LEI QUNMING; Editor-in-Chief LIU ZHAORUI.

Youyi Chubanshe (Friendship Publishing House): Editor-in-Chief HUO BAOZHEN.

Zhongguo Caizheng Jingji Chubanshe (China Financial and Economic Publishing House): 8 Dafosi Dongjie, Dongcheng District, Beijing; tel. (1) 4011805; f. 1961; finance, economics, commerce and accounting.

Zhongguo Dabaike Quanshu Chubanshe (Encyclopaedia of China Publishing House): 17 Fuchengmen Bei Dajie, Beijing 100037; tel. (1) 8315610; f. 1978; specializes in encyclopaedias; Dir MEI YI.

Zhongguo Ditu Chubanshe (China Cartographic Publishing House): 3 Baizhifang Xijie, Beijing 100054; tel. (1) 3014136; fax (1) 3014136; f. 1954; cartographic publr; Dir ZHANG XUELIANG.

Zhongguo Funü Chubanshe (China Women Publishing House): 24A Shijia Hutong, 100010 Beijing; tel. (1) 5126986; f. 1981; women's movement, marriage and family, child-care, etc.; Dir LI ZHONGXIU.

Zhongguo Qingnian Chubanshe (China Youth Publishing House): 21 Dongsi Shiertiao Hutong, Beijing 100708; tel. (1) 4032266; telex 4357; fax (1) 4031803; f. 1950; literature, ethics, social and natural sciences, youth work, autobiography; also periodicals; Editor-in-Chief QUE DAOLONG.

Zhongguo Shehui Kexue Chubanshe (China Social Sciences Publishing House): 158A Gulou Xidajie, Beijing 100720; tel. (1) 4031534; telex 1531; fax (1) 4031542; f. 1978; Dir ZHENG WENLIN.

Zhongguo Xiju Chubanshe (China Theatrical Publishing House): 52 Dongsi Batiao Hutong, Beijing; tel. (1) 4015815; telex 0489; f. 1957; traditional and modern Chinese drama.

Zhonghua Shuju (Chung Hwa Book Co): 36 Wangfujing Dajie, Beijing; tel. (1) 554504; f. 1912; general; Pres. DENG JINGYUAN.

PUBLISHERS' ASSOCIATION

Publishers' Association of China: Beijing; f. 1979; arranges academic exchanges with foreign publrs; Chair. WANG ZIYE; Sec.-Gen. WANG YEKANG.

Radio and Television

At the end of 1992 there were 812 radio broadcasting stations, 714 medium- and short-wave radio transmitting and relay stations, 591 television stations and 1,018 television transmitting and relay stations with a capacity of over 1,000 watts. There were an estimated 213.0m. radio receivers and 35.8m. television receivers in use in 1991.

Ministry of Radio, Film and Television: Fu Xing Men Wai Jie 2, POB 4501, Beijing; tel. (1) 862753; telex 22236; fax (1) 8012174; controls the Central People's Broadcasting Station, the Central TV Station, Radio Beijing, China Record Co., Beijing Broadcasting Institute, Broadcasting Research Institute, the China Broadcasting Art Troupe, etc.

RADIO

China National Radio (CNR): Fu Xing Men Wai Jie 2, Beijing 100866; f. 1945; domestic service in Chinese, Zang Wen (Tibetan), Min Nan Hua (Amoy), Ke Jia (Hakka), Hasaka (Kazakh), Wei Wuer (Uygur), Menggu Hua (Mongolian) and Chaoxian (Korean); Dir TONG XIANGRONG.

China Radio International (CRI): 2 Fu Xing Men Wai Dajie, Beijing 100866; tel. (1) 6092266; telex 222271; fax (1) 8513174; f. 1947; fmrly Radio Beijing; foreign service in 38 languages incl. Arabic, Burmese, Czech, English, Esperanto, French, German, Indonesian, Italian, Japanese, Lao, Polish, Portuguese, Russian, Spanish, Turkish and Vietnamese; Dir ZHANG ZHENHUA.

TELEVISION

China Central Television Station: Bureau of Broadcasting Affairs of the State Council, Beijing; f. 1958; operates three channels; Dir YANG WEIGUANG.

By December 1993 China had more than 500 cable television stations, with networks covering 30m. households. Satellite services are available in some areas, and by 1993 millions of satellite receivers were in use. In October of that year the Government approved new regulations, attempting to restrict access to foreign satellite broadcasts.

Statistical Survey Directory, 1994.

CHINA AND AMERICA'S AT&T SIGN AGREEMENT, 1994

Guangzhou—AT&T, an American telecommunications firm, signed a US$500m long-term partnership agreement with the Guangdong Province Posts and Telecommunications Administrative Bureau and the Guangdong Machinery Import-Export Corp.

The agreement states that AT&T will provide network infrastructure equipment over the next five years to Guangdong province. The equipment includes digital switching systems, optical transmission systems, wireless systems and operations systems. In addition, comprehensive training programs for the bureau's senior managers and engineers augmented by a technical support center will be provided.

continued…

CHINA AND AMERICA'S AT&T SIGN AGREEMENT, 1994 (continued)

AT&T expects to receive over US$150m in orders this year from the bureau. These will include orders for HESS-2000 switching systems, synchronous digital hierarchy transmission systems, digital cross-connect systems, and operations systems.

Currently, AT&T has nine joint ventures in China and offices in the following cities— Beijing, Shanghai, Guangzhou, Qingdao.

China Business, 21 Dec 1994.

CHINA'S ADVERTISING BUSINESS GROWS, 1995

As household income grew in 1995 consumers became eager to buy goods and advertisers were just as eager to tell them which goods they should buy. China's advertising market quadrupled from 1992 to 1995 to US$3 billion and is expected to soar to US$22 billion by the year 2000. In addition to 43,000 Chinese advertising agencies there were also 167 foreign joint ventures with local partners. The government did not stand still while advertisers were busy capturing the consumer's attention. In 1994 the unregulated business advertised everything from patent medicine to wrinkle removing cream. On February 1, 1995 laws were enacted to rein in extravagant product claims. These laws required all advertising claims be backed by statistics and provable facts. This proved a headache for foreign agencies, and that coupled with discriminatory pricing which favored Chinese advertisers, left most foreign agencies operating at a loss. Most said they would not profit until late 1997. But even with all the drawbacks none of the foreign agencies, hungry for a piece of worlds largest consumer pie, planned to discontinue its China operations.

China Facts & Figures Annual, 1995

CHINA'S ADVERTISING SPENDING, 1994

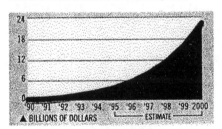

Business Week, 23 Oct 1995.

ADVERTISING INDUSTRY TURNOVER, 1994 (bn Rmb)

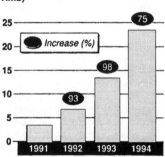

China Trade Report, 1994.

POSTS AND TELECOMMUNICATION GROW, 1994

The posts and telecommunications industry maintained high-speed growth. A total of 69.3 billion yuan worth of posts and telecommunications jobs were completed during the year, 50.2 percent more than in 1993. New city and countryside telephone customers broke the 10 million mark, 3.2 percent of the country having telephone service. Public communications capacity continued to improve, local exchange switching capacity reaching 48.78 million lines, and long distance switching capacity reaching 2.2 million circuit terminals. The technical level of the entire network improved greatly, the percentage of digitalization of long-distance relays reaching 80 percent, and the percentage of programmed urban telephone switching reaching 97 percent. Packet switching networks and public digital data networks are already equipped with

continued...

POSTS AND TELECOMMUNICATION GROW, 1994 (continued)

the communications capacity to meet the information needs of the national economy at the present time. Postal routes have been increased by 29,000 kilometers, and computer control of postal tasks has been upgraded.

Zhongguo Xinxi Bao, 18 Apr 1995.

CHINA'S PAGER MARKET, 1990–1995

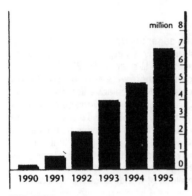

EIU, 1994.

CONDITIONS FOR WOMEN JOURNALISTS, 1995

A recent survey shows that conditions for women journalists in China are good in terms of gender equality, equal pay, attitudes toward their work, psychological and physical health, and married life.

The news was released at a press conference held here today by the All-China Journalist Association and the Institute of Journalism under the Chinese Academy of Social Sciences (CASS), which conducted the survey.

Chen Chongshan, head of the survey group, said that women journalists in China have played an important role in reporting on the economy, society, culture, education, and women.

The survey revealed that, out of 200,000 journalists in China, about one third are women, with an average age of 35. Women journalists with professional titles account for 29,000, and about 84 percent have received higher education.

The survey was funded by the United Nations Educational, Scientific and Cultural Organization (UNESCO) to give a clearer picture of women in journalism, among press organizations, in their work environment and achievements, health, individual qualities, and other basic characteristics.

The survey was said to have provided some advice from the perspective of women journalists for the Chinese government for the Beijing Declaration and the Platform for Action of the Fourth World Conference on Women of United Nations, which ended just ten days ago in Beijing.

The survey said that women can be found reporting on various issues, with nearly 40 percent of them being economic reporters, and more than 41 percent of them holding junior professional titles. But only 6.7 percent of them have senior professional titles, 9.2 percentage points below men.

continued...

CONDITIONS FOR WOMEN JOURNALISTS, 1995 (continued)

Chen noted that "there is a long-standing social tendency of discrimination against women" which needs greater effort to overcome. She also expects women journalists to increase their self-awareness and work ability.

Over 70 percent of the women journalists are satisfied with their jobs and the decision-making opportunities, as well as the harmonious work environment. At the same time though, they are asking for more training and chances at promotion.

On average, more than 87 percent of women journalists believe that they are treated as equals of men in getting their work published, selecting good news stories, professional titles, and salary increases.

The survey also showed that over 85 percent of the women journalists said that they are "full of energy" and nearly 97 percent of them described themselves as "optimistic and responsible".

Among those women journalists who are married, more than 85 percent described their married life as "very good" or "fairly good."

The survey was conducted from April 1994 to June 1995 with 4,033 women journalist across the country taking part.

X, 25 Sep 1995.

TV PRODUCER REGULATIONS, 1995

The Ministry of Radio, Film and Television has strengthened regulations governing units producing and releasing television programs and plays.

Those wishing to establish such units should seek permission beforehand from the administrative departments in charge of radio, film and television at or above provincial level, as required by newly published ministry regulations.

Only with certificates of permission from the relevant departments may units apply for registration at the commercial and industrial departments.

Shen Xiangjun, an official with the Ministry of Radio, Film and Television, disclosed that the applying unit should be staffed by at least five permanent qualified personnel and should have at least 500,000 yuan ($60,241) as registered capital.

Besides a fixed studio and equipment, the unit should have a department to examine and approve its annual production, as stipulated in the regulations.

Units currently producing and releasing television programs should apply for permission certificates before the end of this year, otherwise they will have to close down, have all their programs blocked and be fined twice their revenue.

The provincial departments in charge of radio, film and television are required to make an annual inspection of units producing television programs and plays to ensure they are running their businesses in accordance with the regulations.

Permission certificates can be revoked if the units produce indecent or low-grade material.

The regulations also stipulate that individuals or private enterprises are not encouraged to set up units producing television programs and plays.

No foreign organization or individual is allowed to establish such units in China either unilaterally or with domestic partners.

China Daily, 12 Dec 1995.

XXII TRANSPORTATION

VOLUME OF TRANSPORTATION, 1994

Item	Unit	Volume	Percent Increase Over the Same Period of 1993 (Jan-Jun)
Freight traffic (tn)	1,000,000	229	0.7
Railways	1,000,000	133	3.0
Highways	1,000,000	43	-9.2
Waterways	1,000,000	53	4.1
Civil Aviation	1,000	66	18.5
Volume of freight traffic (tn/km)	1,000,000	223,857	7.0
Railways	1,000,000	102,432	5.5
Highways	1,000,000	2,597	-4.7
Waterways	1,000,000	118,672	8.6
Civil Aviation	1,000,000	156	11.8
Passenger traffic (persons)	1,000,000	379	-1.1
Railways	1,000,000	84	5.1
Highways	1,000,000	280	-2.5
Waterways	1,000,000	12	-9.6
Civil Aviation	1,000,000	3.21	15.7
Volume of passenger traffic (persons/km)	1,000,000	48,379	4.6
Railways	1,000,000	27,212	6.9
Highways	1,000,000	15,726	0.1
Waterways	1,000,000	1,154	-8.4
Civil Aviation	1,000,000	4,287	11.8
Cargo handled at major seaports (tn)	1,000,000	55	5.4
Total traffic volume of civil aviation (tn/km)	1,000,000	469	11.8
Postal and telecommunication services (yuan)	1,000,000,000	5.95	49.3

China Statistics, Jun 1994.

THE STATUS OF COMPLETED TRANSPORTATION, 1994

	1994	Percentage Increase Over 1993
Freight turnover volume (tr tn/km)	3.3275	9.1
Railroads (tr tn/km)	1.2462	4.4
Highways (bn tn/km)	448.1	10.1
Water transportation (tr tn/km)	1.5704	13.9
Civil aviation (bn tn/km)	1.95	17.4
Pipelines (bn tn/km)	60.8	0
Tourist turnover volume (bn tn/km)	849.2	8.1
Railroads (bn tn/km)	363.7	4.45
Highways (bn tn/km)	363.7	4.4

continued…

THE STATUS OF COMPLETED TRANSPORTATION, 1994 (continued)

	1994	Percentage Increase Over 1993
Water transportation (bn tn/km)	17.5	-10.8
Civil aviation (bn tn/km)	53.3	11.6
Main coastal ports cargo handling volume (mn tn)	730	6.2
including: Foreign trade cargo handling (mn tn)	270	11.1

Zhongguo Xinxi Bao, 18 Apr 1995.

CHINA'S HIGHWAYS AND ROADS, 1983–1994 (km)

	All Types	Paved	Gravel Improved	Gravel Unimproved
1983	900,000		288,000	350,000
1984	1,001,000	170,000	581,000	250,000
1985	1,001,000	190,000	540,000	260,000
1986	950,000	150,000	540,000	240,000
1987	930,000	150,000	540,000	240,000
1988	962,000	196,000	566,000	200,800
1989	980,000	162,000	617,200	200,800
1990				
1991	980,000	162,000	617,000	200,800
1992	1,029,000	170,000	648,000	211,000
1993	1,031,000	173,000	648,000	211,000
1994	1,034,000	175,000	624,000	213,000

China Facts & Figures Annual, 1995

CHINA'S INLAND WATERWAYS, 1983–1994 (km)

	Total	Navigable			Total	Navigable
1983	138,600	100,000		1989	138,600	109,500
1984	138,600	136,000		1990		
1985	138,600	108,900		1991	138,600	109,800
1986	138,600	108,900		1992	138,600	109,800
1987	138,600	109,300		1993	138,600	109,800
1988	138,600	109,500		1994	138,600	110,000

China Facts & Figures Annual, 1995

CHINA'S MERCHANT MARINE FLEET, 1990–1994

	Total Ships	1,000 GRT	DWT	Other Registry
1990	1,333	12,950,719	19,509,375	159
1991	1,421	14,010,317	21,223,170	183
1992	1,454	13,887,312	20,916,127	194
1993	1,454	13,887,312	20,916,127	194
1994	1,456	13,889,312	21,917,124	195

China Facts & Figures Annual, 1995

MAIN TRANSPORTATION ROUTES, 1994

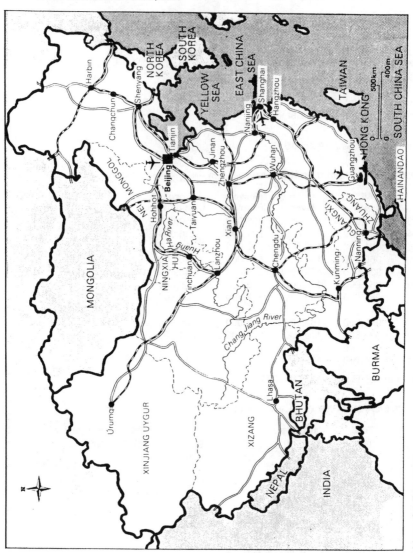

Maps On File, 1994.

TRUCK ROUTES PLANNED FOR YEAR 2000, 1994

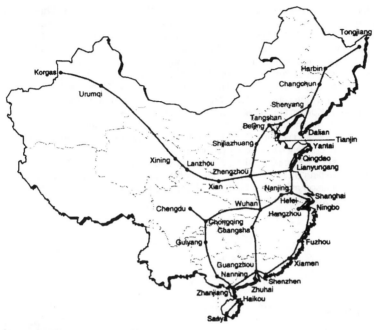

Business China, 13 Jun 1994.

SALES OF DOMESTIC CARS, 1993

Model	Sales 1993	Sales 1992	Percent Difference	Percent Market Share 1993
SVW (VW Santana)*	100,030	65,952	51.7	44.9
Tianjin (Daihatsu Charade)	47,811	30,158	58.5	21.4
FAW (Audi 100)*	17,703	14,992	18.1	7.9
FAW (VW Jetta)*	12,603	7,626	65.3	5.7
Fukang (Citroen ZX)	4,797	663	623.5	2.2
Guangzhou Peugeot (505)	16,075	15,666	2.6	7.2
Beijing Jeep (Cherokee)	13,307	19,435	(31.5)	6.0
Norinco (Suzuki Alto)	10,423	5,566	87.3	4.7
Skylard (Subaru Rex)	230	0	—	0.1
Total	222,979	160,058	39.3	100.0

*   Volkswagen models.

EIU, 1995.

CHINA'S "DETROIT", 1995

Polluted and stranded at the heart of one of China's most inefficient rail networks, Changchun has been put on the map by its famed First Auto Works (FAW), the nation's number one truck producer since the 1950s. Today the vehicle industry accounts for around 40% of the city's industrial output, and ambitious officials tout the provincial capital as "China's Detroit".

Before Volkswagen sunk US$400 mn into a joint venture in 1991, the city's economy was stagnant and unimaginative. But now, foreign investment—most of it in automotive-related ventures—is transforming one of the nation's most conservative cities. Recent arrivals include, car part firms following in the wake of Volkswagen's manufacturing and licensing operations with FAW. Taiwan and Korean firms predominate, but the USA's Owens-Corning and Britain's Pilkington Glass made the mix a little more cosmopolitan when they arrived in the first half of 1994. Pilkington Glass joined with the Changchun Glass Factory in April 1994 in a three-way joint venture to produce safety glass for Volkswagen Jettas and Audi 100s.

Outside the auto sector, PepsiCo of the USA has signed a contract with the Changchun No. 2 Food Factory, committing US$11.5 mn to set up a bottling plant. Construction is due to begin this month with completion scheduled for 1996. Malaysia's Kerry Group and Thailand's CP Pokphand also have projects in the city.

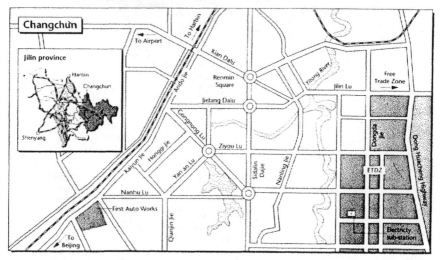

Business China, 3 Oct 1995.

ATTACK ON ILLEGAL AUTO IMPORTS, 1995

According to Chien Ping, deputy general manager of China Trading Center of Imported Automobiles the number of smuggled automobiles decreased somewhat in 1994 but it still constitutes a serious threat to China's auto market and the problem of illegal auto assembling also remains serious.

Ping said that in 1994 China's official imports of automobiles were 237,000 and the total number was well over 300,000 if confiscation of smuggled automobiles were counted. He said that according to 1995 programs the number of automobiles to be imported during the year is estimated to remain at 1994 levels. He also said that most of 1995's imported cars will go to taxi companies or township enterprises.

X, 14 Jan 1995.

VOLKSWAGEN'S PRODUCTION IN CHINA, 1991-2000 (th vehicles)

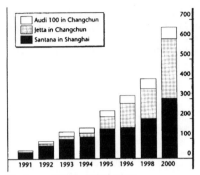

Business China, 3 Oct 1995.

CHINA AIRLINE PROFITS DECLINE, 1989-1993

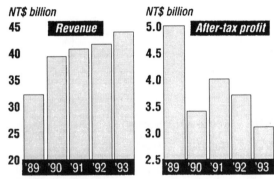

FEER, 16 Jun 1995.

AIRPORT IMPROVEMENT, 1994

More than 60 airports across China are either under construction or were being expanded in 1994, with nine already completed, according to a spokesman of the Civil Aviation Administration of China.

China has built nearly 50 airports for both civil and military uses, pushing the total number of airports in operation to more than 120.

Major airports completed last year include Phoenix Airport in Sanya, Hainan Province, Zhangjiajie Airport in Dayong, Hunan Province, Tianhe Airport in Wuhan, Hubei Province, Bomda Airport in Qamdo, Tibet, and Bailian Airport in Liuzhou, Guangxi Zhuang Autonomous Region.

To accelerate the construction of airports, China's airport investment structure has moved from sole investment by the central government to multi-sources such as local governments and enterprises. Overseas investment started to enter China's airport construction last year following the country's policies encouraging foreign investment in civil aviation infrastructure facilities.

A new aviation network has begun to take shape with medium-sized or large cities such as Beijing, Guangzhou, and Shanghai as centers. These airports now handle more than 85 percent of the total transport volume. The number of passengers in Beijing, Shanghai, and Guangzhou alone approached 10 million, the spokesman said.

X, 21 Jan 1995.

NEW SMALL AIRCRAFT BUILT BY XIAN AIRCRAFT COMPANY, 1994

China's Xian Aircraft Company began building the Eaglet-100 a high quality, low cost small aircraft in 1994. The Eaglet-100 was the first aircraft on its kind in China. According to the company it had a length of 5.51 meters and a wingspan of 9.75 meters. It carried two people and could take off and land on only 20 meters of runway either hard surface or grass. The Eaglet-100 had a price US$13,000. It was used for tourism, flight training and photography.

X, 27 Jan 1995.

CHINESE AIR TRAVEL GROWTH, 1985–1993 (mn passengers)

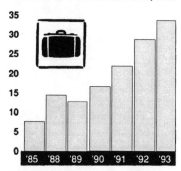

China Trade Report, Sep 1995.

CHINA'S AIRPORTS, 1983–1994

	Total	Total Usable	Runways Paved Surface	Runways 3,500 Meters	Runways 2,500 Meters
1983	340		272	11	61
1984	325			13	63
1985	322		263	13	66
1986					
1987	325		266	11	80
1988	330	330	260	10	90
1989	330	330	260	10	90
1990					
1991	330	330	260	10	90
1992	330	330	260	10	90
1993	336	336	262	11	90
1994	336	336	262	11	90

China Facts & Figures Annual, 1995

NATION'S LARGEST AUTO MAKER, 1995

The second-phase project of the Shanghai Volkswagen Automobile Corporation has recently gone into operation, pushing its annual production capacity to 200,000 and making this Sino-German joint venture China's largest auto maker.

As another important event for the corporation, the Santana 2000 car series, jointly developed by international experts and Shanghai Volkswagen, the first such collaboration project between China and the rest of the world, has been put into production.

continued...

NATION'S LARGEST AUTO MAKER, 1995 (continued)

The new motor vehicle series, which has cost the company 100 million yuan for development, is considered comfortable and technologically advanced and competitive compared with other cars of the same feature in the domestic market.

According to corporate sources, the company plans to build 30,000 such series of cars with daily production capacity of 280 by the end of this year, pushing the total number of Santana series to 160,000 this year.

To expand production, the corporation has also decided to increase another 1.1 billion yuan in investment to build a new engine plant and expand the annual sedan production capacity to 300,000.

A joint venture between China and Germany, the Shanghai Volkswagen Automobile Corporation was established in the early 1980s with an investment of 160 million yuan. To date, the joint venture has developed into a large auto enterprise with 2.3 billion yuan of registered capital and five billion yuan in fixed assets.

Over the last ten years, the Sino-German auto joint venture has produced a total of 420,000 cars and paid seven billion yuan in taxes to the state. At present, 86 percent of the auto parts are made in China as against 2.7 percent ten years ago.

X, 24 Apr 1995.

TERRORIST THREAT TO AIRPORT, 1994

Kai Tak Airport was on full alert when terrorist bomb threats grounded one aircraft and stopped another from landing. Security measures were strengthened after a United Airlines flight from Hong Kong to San Francisco was evacuated and searched. The incident was surrounded by fear that a bomb had been planted by Islamic fundamentalist who have targeted United States airlines flying Asian routes.

Hong Kong Eastern Express, 16 Jan 1995.

XXIII LAW AND CRIMINAL JUSTICE

COURT WORK REPORTS, 1993–1994

	1994	1993	Percent Increase
Overall			
Suspects detained	688,771	607,945	13.3
Suspects formally arrested	598,633	532,394	12.4
Suspects charged	699,111	574,176	16.5
Suspects tried	570,693	479,860	18.9
Serious Crimes			
Suspects arrested	247,435	153,764	61.9
Suspects arrested and tried	232,216	137,523	68.8

Eastern Express, 11 Mar 1995.

CHINA'S ILLEGAL DRUG PROBLEM, 1995

The area surrounding China's tropical rain forests became a haven for drug trafficking. Since 1990 China seized more heroin than any other country. The Chinese authorities captured more

continued...

CHINA'S ILLEGAL DRUG PROBLEM, 1995 (continued)

than four tons of heroin in each year since 1993. Since 1989 seizure of heroin increased tenfold. Most of the heroin comes from Myanman which was the source of two-thirds of the world's heroin supply. Although 80 percent of drug arrests and half of China's registered drug addicts were in Yunnan province, the problem was not confined to that area. The government estimated that there were millions of heroin users in the country in 1995. The year between 1994 and 1995 the number of registered addicts went from 250,000 to 380,000. Graft at all levels of law enforcement was a problem because of low police pay. Investigators believed the increasing availability of consumer goods tempted officials to take money when it was offered by drug traffickers.

China Facts & Figures Annual, 1995

MAP OF DRUG AFFECTED AREA, 1995

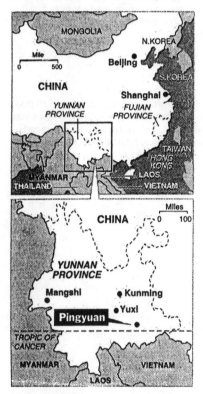

NYT, 2 Nov 1995.

ACHIEVEMENTS IN DRUG CONTROL, 1985–1994

	1985–1990	1991	1992	1993	1994
Drug cases cracked	30,000	8,344	14,701	26,191	38,033
Offenders involved		18,479	28,292		
Including overseas offenders		829	561		

continued...

ACHIEVEMENTS IN DRUG CONTROL, 1985–1994 (continued)

	1985–1990	1991	1992	1993	1994
Opium seized (kg)		1,980	2,660	3,354	1,700
Heroin seized (kg)		1,919	4,489	4,459	3,881
(for 1988 and 1989)	2,120				
Marijuana seized (kg)		328	910		
Morphine seized (kg)		33			
Deoxy ephedrin seized (kg)		308	655		
Chemical elixirs for making drugs (tn)		49	58.5		
Arrests	20,800	8,080	7,025	7,677	10,434
Offenders sentenced	16,000	5,285	6,588		7,883
Including life imprisonment or death penalty and death sentences with reprieves		866	1,354		
Drug abusers registered nationwide		148,539	250,000		
Compulsory drug abstinence institutions		232	252		
Number of drug addicts under compulsory drug abstinence		41,227	46,000	50,000	
Number of illegal drug users punished		12,060	20,000		

• The aforementioned statistics were published by the Narcotics Control Office of the Ministry of Public Security.

X, 15 Dec 1995.

PROBLEM OF RISING CRIME, 1994

In dealing with the issue of public security at present (this mainly refers to the issue of the rising crime rate), theoreticians and professionals have different views. The focal point of people's conversation during their leisure time is on the issue of public order. It looks like the masses and the National People's Congress deputies are not so satisfied about the current rising crime rate. Theoreticians have characterized the current public security issue in four sentences: "The situation is basically stable. It remains relatively normal. There are serious hidden perils. We should not become optimistic." Officials who are relatively authoritative said that the overall situation remains stable, and this helps promote the reform and opening-up program and develop the economy. Right now, the number of crimes, particularly serious cases, is still rising. In some localities, public order is indeed not so good, and criminals are becoming more rampant. The masses have complained a great deal about this situation. Although the aforementioned two groups of people differ in their views, their differences are not so significant in terms of actual content.

We believe that to evaluate the current situation in public order and correctly understand the issue of the rising crime rate, we must set a standard. People's views cannot be the same, when their standards are different.

1. We must understand whether or not the increasing number of criminal cases will affect social stability and to what extent it does. Here we have to examine the following three aspects:

Firstly, is there any riot or turmoil in certain areas or in the whole country stirred up by the rising crime rate? That includes the psychological pressure created among the populace by this situation in public order.

continued...

PROBLEM OF RISING CRIME, 1994 (continued)

Secondly, has the rising crime rate affected production, life, work, scientific research, and economic order in society?

Thirdly, have major gatherings or activities of a mass nature, such as sports meetings, economic and trade activities, or major festivals, been jeopardized or affected by the increasing number of criminal cases?

As seen from the situation in promoting the reform and opening-up program and economic development in the past several years, major serious crimes have always been under the control of the police, although the number of such cases is on the rise. This crime has not yet affected social stability in an overall manner. This is to say that the rising crime rate has some harmful effects, but it has not completely endangered social, political, economic, and cultural order and development.

2. To understand the crime rate, we must look at the incidence and rate of growth of serious crimes. We should start to analyze this issue by comparing China with other countries and analyzing the crime rates in various cities in the country. When we compare China's crime rate with that of other countries, China's advantage of a lower rate of serious crimes no long exists., With the exception of some countries with a high crime rate, such as the United States, all other nations have lower rates of serious crimes as compared with China. Let us take the example of murder cases. In proportion with a nation's population, the annual rate of such crimes is 1.5 per 100,000 in the EC, 7.5 per 100,000 in the United States, and 1.3 per 100,000 in Japan, but that in China is 1.9 per 100,000, a rate much higher than Japan, EC, Hong Kong, and other nations and districts. As for cases involving robbery, the annual rate of such crimes is 4.9 per 100,000 in the EC, 1.6 per 100,000 in Japan, and 1.66 per 100,000 in Indonesia, but this rate has already reached 7.5 per 100,000 in China. When we compare the crime rates in various cities in China, the crime rate in our nation was low in the fifties and sixties. The number of serious crimes in the early eighties was less than 50,000. This rose to 530,000 in 1993, an increase of more than 10 times. The incidence of such crimes in some relatively developed cities such as Hainan, Shenzhen, and Zhuhai is even higher. The number of serious crimes in Shenzhen in 1991 rose by 229 times over 1980. In proportion to the city's population, Shenzhen's annual rate of serious crimes in 1991 was 41.8 per 10,000. The number of serious crimes in Zhuhai City in 1993 was 2,810, an increase of 71.1 times over 1980.

Renmin Gongan Bao, 8 Feb 1995.

CRIMINAL LAW REFORM, 1994

The symposium on national market economy and revision and perfection of criminal law and the 1994 academic forum sponsored by the Criminal Jurisprudence Research Society of the China Jurisprudence Society were held in mid-October in Nanning. Participants comprehensively discussed issues on the development of market economy, the revision and improvement of criminal laws, and on determining and punishing economic crimes. Here is a summary of the relevant academic viewpoints:

I. Basic Concept of Improvement of Criminal Law
1. The criminal law should be revised with emphasis on economic crimes.

2. The criminal law should be revised while paying attention to crimes and non-crimes and to punishments and non-punishments.

3. The criminal law should be revised with both traditional and modern methods.

4. The criminal law should be revised by studying Chinese and international legal concepts.

5. In revising the criminal law, we must avoid oversimplification. However, we must also avoid spending too much time on nitty-gritty details. We should strike a balance between the two.

6. In determining punishments, we must follow the guiding thought of not being harsh or lenient. We must not punish criminals too severely or too lightly.

continued...

CRIMINAL LAW REFORM, 1994 (continued)

II. Keep or Abolish the Analog System

Most of the theses presented at the aforementioned symposium and the forum advocate the abolishment of the analog system. They pointed out: 1) The criminal law of the day demands abolition of the analog system. 2) The values of legal system decide that the analog system be abrogated. 3) Judicial practice after the promulgation of the criminal law prove that the analog system has already lost its value. 4) The existence of the analog system runs counter to the principle of legally prescribing all punishments. 5) Strengthening legislation in criminal law may help plug the loopholes it created by the use of the analog system. There are also some articles which stress the need to keep the analog system. Their main reasons are: China lacks experience in legislation. In practice, it is hard to legally prescribe all punishments. China has only started to establish the market economic system, and it has not yet begun to reform its political system.

III. Improvement of Legislation Against Crimes Committed by Legal Persons

Some of the theses believe that the current criminal law has not enough coverage on crimes committed by legal persons. They have made the following suggestions to improve the criminal law:

1. Crimes committed by legal persons should be included in the general provisions of the criminal law.

2. Standards must be set for determining punishment for crimes committed by legal persons.

3. Standards must be clearly set for imposing fines to legal persons who commit crimes, and types of punishments in this connection be diversified.

IV. Improvement of Death Penalty Provisions

Those who attended the symposium and the forum also expressed their views on improving the criminal law regarding the death penalty.

1. It is necessary to avoid imposing unnecessary death sentences as in cases involving crimes of speculation.

2. In applying the death sentence, it is essential to avoid emphasizing the use of death penalty as in the current criminal law and using the death penalty as an absolute legally prescribed punishment.

3. It is necessary to restrict and gradually abolish death penalties for those who commit non-violent crimes.

4. It is essential to restrict and abolish death sentences to some of the offenders who commit violent crimes.

5. Efforts must be made to improve legislative techniques in reducing the number of death sentences.

6. The death penalty should ultimately be abolished.

V. Legislative Improvement on Fines

Some of the theses made the following suggestions on legislative improvements on fines:

1. Allow more offenders to pay fines.

2. Clearly specify the amount of fines.

3. Improve the system of collecting fines, and add the following systems:

A) allowing offenders to perform free labor services in lieu of fine;

B) paying fines in installments;

C) delaying fine payment;

D) imposing fines in lieu of imprisonment.

VI. Legislative Improvement of Criminal Charges

Some of the theses made the following suggestions on improving legislation concerning criminal charges:

1. Change the legislative concept on criminal charges.

continued...

CRIMINAL LAW REFORM, 1994 (continued)

2. Follow the legislative principle on criminal charges such as the principle of paying attention to the lawful, scientific and comprehensive nature in carrying out specific operations.

3. Standardize the legislative procedure on criminal charges.

4. Eliminate conflicts and redundancies among offenses of the same criminal charge listed in several laws, and make criminal charges more specific.

VII. Legislative Improvement on Crimes of Dereliction of Duties

Some of the theses expressed their views on crimes of dereliction of duties as follows:

1. Change crimes of dereliction of duties into "crimes of dereliction of duties by government functionaries."

2. Crimes of dereliction of duties should be given priority in the Special Provisions of the Criminal Law.

3. Make the necessary revisions and deletions of the legislative contents on crimes of dereliction of duties.

4. Establish the system of making criminal charges against those who take advantage of their office to commit crimes.

5. Improve the mechanism in punishing those who commit crimes of dereliction of duties. We should mainly carry out the following tasks:

(1) Expand the range of giving heavier punishments to those who commit crimes by not merely taking advantage of their office.

(2) Give more severe punishments to those who commit some crimes of dereliction of duties as mentioned in the Special Provisions of the Criminal Law.

(3) Pay attention to punishing those who take advantage of their office to commit crimes with the property penalty (cai chan xing 6299 3934 0438) and the qualification penalty (zi ge xing 6327 2706 0438).

VIII. Legislative Improvement on Crimes of Corruption

Some theses did some research work or carried out special topic discussions on legislative improvement on crimes of corruption. They mainly discussed the following topics:

1. In light of the theories in the academic field on abolishing, consolidating and retaining crimes of corruption in the Criminal Law, most of the scholars opted to retain such crimes in this Law. While keeping such crimes, they hoped to add the crime of embezzlement on the list of crimes.

2. All theses opted to narrow the scope of such crimes. However, their views differed as to what extent the scope of such crimes should be narrowed. Some academicians opted to limit the crimes of corruption to "state personnel and those in the collective economic sector," while others sought to limit offenders to "personnel working for party and government organs and judicial and procuratorial organs who perform official duties for the state." Activities carried out by non-state personnel to steal or seize public properties by cheating or taking advantage of their jobs should be included into crimes of larceny and fraud. The crimes of embezzlement should be added in the Criminal Law in dealing with those who appropriate public properties.

IV. [as numbered] Legislative Improvement on Crimes of Misappropriation of Public Funds

Some of the theses carried out special topic discussions on legislative improvement for crimes of misappropriation of public funds. Their discussions mainly involved the following issues:

1. They unanimously named the charge as "Crimes of Misappropriation of Public Funds and Properties." some scholars even suggested that the situation described in Article 126 of the Criminal Law be regarded as a serious one and that it be given severe punishment.

2. Some scholars suggested to include words "relatively large amount" as an important condition for committing such crimes. The use of misappropriated public funds should only be used as a factor to determine whether heavier or lighter punishment be given to the offender. It should not be used as an important condition for committing such crimes. Other scholars suggested to raise the legally prescribed punishment of these crimes to life imprisonment.

continued...

CRIMINAL LAW REFORM, 1994 (continued)

3. They also discussed the issue of changing misappropriation of public funds into corruption. Some scholars believed that the practice of classifying those who are able to return misappropriated funds but refuse to do so and those who seek to return such funds but cannot afford to do so into the same category runs counter to the principle of evaluating and determining a crime both subjectively and objectively. They suggested that only the latter can be construed as crimes of misappropriation of public funds but may be treated as a serious case and that a heavier punishment be given to the offender.

4. In connection with the "two high's," some theses expressed different views on the issue of misappropriation of public funds for use by a unit. They believe that in practice, it is difficult to determine whether the misappropriation of public funds is made "in the name of an individual" or "in the name of a collective." As long as the main subject which commits the crime misappropriates public funds for use by another unit, this act constitutes a crime of misappropriation of public funds.

X. Legislative Improvement of Crimes of Fraud

1. Classification of crimes of fraud. Some scholars believed that from the macroscopic point of view, we might consider putting crimes of fraud in an exclusive chapter. However, from the microscopic point of view, we might either retain the current classification in the existing Criminal Law or add crimes of economic frauds in the list such as contract frauds, loan frauds, advertisement frauds and insurance frauds.

2. Impose heavier legally prescribed punishment for crimes of frauds.

3. The issue of crimes of frauds committed by a unit with the status of a legal person. Some scholars suggested to legislatively define the scope of erring units with the status of a legal person which should be held responsible for criminal liabilities, while other scholars suggested to legislatively specify the need to prosecute those personnel in charge of or directly responsible for the seriously defrauded unit for their criminal liabilities.

XI. Legislative Improvement of Crimes of Bribery

Some theses carried out special topics discussions on crimes of bribery and commercial bribery. Some scholars suggested to revise the scope of the main subject of the crime of bribe-taking as "personnel of state organs." These personnel should be referred to as "personnel of state organs of power, administrative organs, judicial organs and military organs, who are engaged in public service according to law." With the exception of the aforementioned personnel, others who accept bribes will be given sanctions under the crimes of commercial bribery. Some scholars suggested to add words "or influence" after words "take advantage of their office." All scholars suggested to expand the connotative and denotative definition of the word "bribery." However, they remained divided between the "Theory of Material Benefits" and the "Theory of Benefits." Some of the scholars suggested to regard the issue of "seeking benefits for others" as a major subjective condition for such crimes; while others suggested to add the fine penalty and the qualification penalty to the list of penalties against those who accept bribery. Some of the theses expressed the following views on crimes of commercial bribery:

1. It is necessary to carry out legislative work in a centralized and decentralized way.

2. Facts about a crime should be clearly specified and a definite charge made. Commercial bribery may be divided into crimes of commercial bribe-offering, crimes of commercial bribe-taking and crimes of acting as a go-between in commercial bribery.

3. It is necessary to set up legally prescribed punishments. Firstly, the offender should be sentenced to a lesser punishment as compared with an ordinary crime of bribery. Secondly, it is essential to strictly enforce economic sanctions. Thirdly, qualification penalty should be added to the list of penalties.

Fazhi Ribao, 15 Dec 1994.

COURT OFFICIAL ON EXECUTION OF CORRUPT OFFICIALS, 1995

Liu Jiachen, Supreme People's Court vice president, today announced the verdicts that the court pronounced on two large corruption and bribery cases in Guizhou, noting that two degenerate elements guilty of serious criminal offenses have been harshly punished by the law:

Yan Jianhong, former member of the Guizhou Provincial Committee of the Chinese People's Political Consultative Conference [CPPCC] Standing Committee and chairman of the Guizhou Provincial International Trust and Investment Company, was sentenced to death and had her political rights deprived for life after being found guilty of corruption, misappropriation of public funds, speculation and profiteering, and accepting bribes; Yan was shot in Guiyang this morning; and Guo Zhengmin, former director of the Guizhou Provincial Public Security Department, was sentenced to death, with a two-year reprieve, and had his political rights deprived for life after being found guilty of accepting bribes.

At a news briefing called by the Supreme People's Court, Liu Jiachen briefed the press on the crimes committed by Yan Jianhong and Guo Zhengmin. He said: On five occasions from December 1992 to July 1993, Yan Jianhong, 61, took advantage of her office and embezzled her company's income and unregistered cash—totals that were 650,000 yuan and $14,300. From June to September 1993, she and some other people also misappropriated 1.5 million yuan of public funds by concealing the company's income.

On 21 September 1992 and 5 July 1993, Yan Jianhong misappropriated her company's public funds, 2.64 million yuan and $50,000 in all, for other people for their private use. In July 1992, Yan collaborated with a person with the surname of Chen in speculating on the cigarette trade. She provided Chen with the purchasing documents and received from Chen 400,000 yuan from the profits Chen made through reselling the 1,000 bills of lading for Red Tower Hill cigarettes. Moreover, from November 1992 to February 1993, when Yan extended loans to a foreign businessman with the surname of Jin, she received from him 10,000 Hong Kong dollars, a videodisk player, a leather hunting jacket, a woolen overcoat, and other gifts worth more than 17,000 yuan.

When he served as director of the Guizhou Provincial Public Security Department, Guo Zhengmin, 52, became acquainted with Jin in September 1992 through a third person. At Jin's request, Guo got from another location two permits for Jin's wife and her business partner to go to Hong Kong and Macao. Guo gave the permits to Jin on 4 December of the same year. In the evening, Guo received from Jin a gift of 30,000 yuan. Later, Guo, at Jin's request, continued to seek illegitimate interests for Jin and, on 20 March and 7 May 1993, received from Jin bribes totaling 140,000 yuan. To cover up the facts, Guo, on 3 December of the same year, spent 130,000 yuan of the bribes in the name of official expenditures, and instructed the recipient to write the receipt with the date of 26 March.

After verifying the facts, the Guiyang Intermediate People's Court found Yan Jianhong guilty of corruption, misappropriation of public funds, speculation and profiteering, and accepting bribes; at the first trial, it sentenced her to death and deprived her of her political rights for life because of all these crimes; and it found Guo Zhengmin guilty of accepting bribes and, at the first trial, sentenced him to death and deprived him of his political rights for life. Both defendants disagreed with the verdicts and appealed. The Guizhou Provincial Higher People's Court rejected Yan Jianhong's appeal and upheld the original judgment. In accordance with the law, it referred the verdict to the Supreme People's Court for reexamination. On 12 January, the Supreme People's Court approved Yan's death sentence and the deprivation of her political rights for life.

When handling Guo Zhengmin's appeal during the second trial, the Guizhou Provincial Higher People's Court maintained that because of the enormous amounts of bribes Guo received from foreign businessman as well as the seriousness of the case, the argument in Guo's appeal that the money he received did not constitute a crime could not be established, and that the ruling issued in the first trial of sentencing him to death and depriving him of his political rights for life was a proper one. However, in view of Guo's significant contributions during the second trial in terms of reporting other people's criminal offenses, the punishment

continued...

COURT OFFICIAL ON EXECUTION OF CORRUPT OFFICIALS, 1995 (continued)

could be reduced. Thus, in accordance with the law, Guo was sentenced to death with a two-year reprieve and had his political rights deprived from him for life.

Liu Jiachen stated in the news briefing that the people's court will, as always, firmly prosecute all economic crimes, especially major crimes such as corruption and accepting bribes. He said: Whoever offends the laws of the state will be harshly punished. The court will pronounce heavy punishments or even death sentences on those who deserve them, and the court will never tolerate these people.

X, 16 Jan 1995.

OFFICIAL EXECUTED FOR GRAFT, 1995

In January of 1995 eighteen government officials were executed after standing trial for "graft and corruption". During 1993 and 1994 there was growing concern over the amount of corruption at all levels of government. This led to stronger laws against corruption in general and graft in particular and to investigations of all officials suspected of such crimes. Authorities stated that corruption had to be controlled before the economy could move forward and reforms could be effective.

When one official was executed by firing squad, people observing the event applauded.

China Facts & Figures Annual, 1995

SECRET SOCIETIES PLAGUE PUBLIC SECURITY, 1995

Secret societies also known as triads continued to infiltrate the Chinese mainland from Taiwan and Hong Kong. In Shenzhen alone 400 members of the societies were arrested in cases involving robbery, rape, extortion and other crimes. Despite increased efforts by the public security apparatus secret societies continued illegal activities. In an apparent reprisal against the anti-triad operations a deputy director of Shenzhen was shot to death while on duty 5 December 1994.

China Facts & Figures Annual, 1995

ILLEGAL GUNS CONFISCATED, 1995

As of the end of January 1995, public security organs at all levels nationwide had confiscated 260,000 guns of various kinds and 780,000 round of ammunition and cracked down on 1,573 dens for manufacturing and selling guns and ammunition. Thirteen criminals were arrested by Zhejiang authorities, which organized a unified action to crack down on illegal elements who tried to promote the sales of steel-ball guns by sending advertising fliers all over the country. Guangxi and Yunnan authorities carried out raids in border areas where smuggling and selling guns were rampant and confiscated 5,174 guns.

Beijing Central Television, 22 Feb 1995.

PIRATES ARE A PROBLEM, 1995

Piracy against commercial and fishing vessels was a problem in Chinese controlled waters. Most of the attacks were directed at Russian vessels sailing those waters but other ships were not exempt. Asian countries, Japan in particular, made formal protests to the Chinese government about the problem of piracy. It is estimated that one in twenty vessels which operated in the affected waters were boarded by pirates, the crews killed and the vessels either sunk or stolen. In response China stationed more naval and police ships and boats in the area to protect those traversing what had become dangerous waters.

China Facts & Figures Annual, 1995

MAP OF PIRATE AFFECTED AREA, 1994

FEER, 16 Jun 1994.

XXIV SOCIETY

FINANCIAL INCOME AND EXPENDITURES, 1981–1995 (100 mn yuan)

Year	Total Income	Total Expenditures	Nominal Deficit	Liability Income	Actual Deficit
1981–1985	66,830.8	6,952.0	121.2	403.6	524.8
1986–1990	13,517.7	13,978.3	460.6	1,237.2	1,697.9
1991–1995	23,905.6	25,708.9	1,803.3	4,545.3	6,348.6
1991	3,610.9	3,813.6	202.7	461.4	664.1
1992	4,153.1	4,389.7	236.6	669.7	906.3
1993	5,114.8	5,319.8	205.0	739.2	944.2
1994	5,181.8	5,819.8	638.0	1,175.0	1,813.0
1995	5,845.0	6,366.0	521.0	1,500.0	2,021.0

X, 19 Dec 1995.

GALLUP POLL SURVEY OF POSSESSIONS OWNED AND DESIRED, 1995

Color televisions remain the most coveted possession of Chinese citizens, most of whom have ambitions to "work hard and get rich," according to an unprecedented nationwide Gallup survey.

Behind color TVs—now owned by 40 percent of Chinese people and wanted by 32 percent more—on the shopping list came washing machines, which can be found in 36 percent of homes and are dreamed about in another 21 percent, the survey, conducted from May to September 1994, found.

The findings were at odds with many surveys conducted by Chinese organizations that have concluded that citizens have now moved on from items like televisions to focus on purchasing cars, computers and even their own home.

The discrepancy no doubt arises from the Chinese tendency to focus on booming coastal cities while neglecting the habits of residents of the vast interior:

The US market research giant, whose findings were released this week, instead sent people out "on foot, on horseback and even on camel from Shenzhen to the Gobi desert" to quiz one adult from 3,400 randomly selected households [as received], said Beijing-based employee Mike Van Buskirk.

The survey is "very, very accurate"—with a margin of error of 1.7 percent—thanks to sophisticated sampling methods introduced by Gallup at 23 field stations nationwide, he said.

The most widely owned product among Chinese citizens is—unsurprisingly—the bicycle (81 percent), followed by an electric fan (63 percent), radio (58 percent), black-and-white TV (54 percent) and tape recorder (48 percent).

Some 45 percent of those sampled said they were satisfied with their homes, while 44 percent were not, the survey found, putting the average Chinese residence at 260 square meters (2,800 square feet) with four rooms.

Of the households surveyed, 95 percent had electricity, 47 percent running water, 26 percent gas, 24 percent cable television and nine percent a telephone. The proportions rise to 99 percent, 88 percent, 65 percent, 48 percent and 30 percent in urban areas.

"Sixty eight percent (of Chinese) want to work hard and get rich," a summary of the survey said, but added that the figure fell to just 35 percent in Beijing where, it noted, "they are more often government employees."

The survey indicated that foreign and domestic firms had a lot to do to win the loyalty of Chinese customers, with only 14 percent—mostly residents of Guangzhou and Shanghai—able to name an advertised product or company unaided.

Japanese companies came to mind most frequently, with Panasonic topping the list, it found, adding that some individuals mentioned US firms such as Coca-Cola, Marlboro and—more surprisingly—Head and Shoulders dandruff shampoo.

The survey is aimed at helping "multinationals gain some real insight into the hearts and minds of Chinese consumers" and to show what Gallup—which officially launched its China joint venture in January 1994—can do on a nationwide scale, said Van Buskirk.

He said the reaction of Chinese interviewees had been "very very positive."

"Obviously we're limited to covering market research, we don't do politics. But if you're not talking politics, then Chinese people are very open and friendly about their ideas," he said, comparing them favorably with westerners who have become fed up with being asked questions.

Hong Kong AFP, 16 Feb 1995.

LABOR EMPLOYMENT, 1990–1995

Year	1990	1995
Population (bn)	1.14333	1.22265
Population of working age (men 15–59, women 15–54) (mn)	685.19	727.92

continued...

LABOR EMPLOYMENT, 1990–1995 (continued)

Year	1990	1995
Actual labor force (mn)	567.40	629.11
Staff and workers (whole-people, collective, other) (mn)	140.59	155.01
Individual laborers in urban areas (mn)	6.71	17.03
Rural laborers (mn)	420.10	457.07
Retired laborers (mn)	23.01	30.33

X, 5 Mar 1995.

MIGRANT LABORERS' CONTRIBUTIONS, 1995

In recent years, there have been more and more migrant laborers appearing everywhere in China. When people talk about the migrants, they always mention the problems these laborers have brought about, and seldom remember the positive contributions made by these people. In fact, the migrant laborers have made great contributions to society.

According to statistics, 60 percent of the workers in the 500 largest township enterprises in the whole country are migrant farmers. Among the farmers who go to work in Guangdong, 70 percent of them work in township enterprises. The 130,000 migrant laborers in Wuxi of Jiangsu Province make up a quarter of the nonagricultural labor force. In 1988, Baoan in Shenzhen employed more migrant laborers than local people. In other words, the cheap labor force provided by farmers has supported the development of rural enterprises as well as foreign-funded enterprises. The rapid economic development in prosperous regions is closely connected with the contributions of the labor force provided by migrant farmers.

These migrant farmers have also contributed to their hometowns. In 1993, the total income of migrant farmers in Sichuan was over RMB [Renminbi] 10 billion. Their remittance received through the post office was over RMB 5 billion, which was one-sixth of the total income of the farmers in the whole year. After several years' hard work, these wage-earners return to their villages to start their own business, thus becoming the backbone for the development of township enterprises. In Fuyang of Anhui, there are more than 700 enterprises run by returned migrant laborers. In some counties, their output value, profit, tax and absorption of the remaining agricultural labor force represent a quarter of those of local township enterprises.

Zhongguo Xinwen She, 7 Mar 1995.

UNEMPLOYMENT PROBLEM, 1995

Many economic authorities viewed China's unemployment rate as a two edged sword. On the front side, according to Western nation's standards China with an unemployment rate of just 3% had full employment. There were two problems with that theory: 1) Only apparent unemployment was taken into account. 2) Unemployment in China meant urban unemployment not total unemployment. On the back side of the unemployment sword, even if the true rate equaled 3% it would mean in excess of 156 million unemployed workers. Unemployed rural workers added another 170 million to that number. In an effort designed to control unemployment Chinese government officials attempted to control population growth and shorter term to retrain workers for industrial jobs. In early 1995 it was uncertain as to what effect those measures would have.

China Facts & Figures Annual, 1995

TOP TEN REGIONS IN SOCIAL DEVELOPMENT, 1995

Prece-dence	A	B	C	D	E	F	G	H	I	J
1	JS	BJ	SH	BJ	BJ	BJ	SH	BJ	BJ	TJ
2	BJ	TJ	GD	SH	TJ	SH	BJ	SH	SH	HEB
3	TJ	SH	HN	ZJ	SH	JL	IM	TJ	TJ	IM
4	SH	LN	BJ	TJ	JL	LN	TJ	JS	HN	AH
5	HL	HL	TJ	GD	QH	HL	HL	JL	GD	HEN
6	HEB	ZJ	FJ	FJ	GD	TJ	HN	LN	SD	SN
7	SD	JL	ZJ	JS	LN	JS	GD	FJ	JL	SX
8	GD	GD	JS	LN	SX	SD	JL	SD	LN	GS
9	ZJ	SD	LN	SD	FJ	HB	NX	GD	IM	GS
10	AH	JS	SD	HEB	HL	XJ	LN	SN	HUN	HL

Note 1: A stands for environment; B stands for population; C stands for economic base; D stands for income distribution; E stands for labor employment; F stands for social security; G stands for hygiene and health care; H stands for education, science, and technology; I stands for culture and physical science; and J stands for social order.

Note 2: JS stands for Jiangsu, BJ stands for Beijing, SH stands for Shanghai, TJ stands for Tianjin, GD stands for Guangdong, HEB stands for Hebei, HN stands for Hainan, ZJ stands for Zhejiang, JL stands for Jilin, IM stands for Inner Mongolia, LN stands for Liaoning, AH stands for Anhui, HL stands for Heilongjiang, QH stands for Qinghai, HEN stands for Henan, FJ stands for Fujian, SD stands for Shandong, SN stands for Shaanxi, SX stands for Shanxi, NX stands for Ningxia, GS stands for Gansu, XJ stands for Xinjiang, and HUN stands for Hunan

X, 14 Feb 1995.

SURVEY ON PUBLIC ATTITUDE TOWARD REFORM, 1994

In 1994, the central government put forth a series of macroeconomic reform measures aimed at establishing a socialist market economic system. This made the characteristics of China's system conversion even clearer. At the same time, it also signaled that reform had entered a key period of conversion, that is, principally overall systematic innovation. In this period, what clear changes occurred in the social psychological environment, what were the causes that triggered these changes, and what effect these changes will have on the next group of changes that will be promoted as well as on social stability, are all actual unavoidable questions for reform and important information and a basis for us to analyze and judge the social situation of reform. At the end of 1994, the State Commission for Restructuring the Economy Social Survey System, based on the survey observations of a succession of previous years, again conducted a national survey by sending questionnaires to households.

The scope of the survey involved all 29 provinces, municipalities, and autonomous regions, and 55 cities. A total of 2,500 households were surveyed and 2,392 valid questionnaires were returned for an effective return rate of 96 percent.

I. General Characteristics of the Current Social Psychological Environment

(1) Generally speaking, the current social psychological environment is not as relaxed as in 1992 and 1993, but the fundamental attitude of the public tends to be peaceful.

The above judgement is supported by two aspects of the survey data. In one respect, although the public's dissatisfaction and frustrations are rather strong, they are all specifically directed. Most of the public's complaints and dissatisfactions are expressed toward those specific aspects that are closely related to their individual lives, and they do not have any strong negative reactions in their overall evaluation of society. In a second respect, the public's expectations for the future social environment also are rather stable. There are some estimates of the future situation that are not optimistic, but most people do not at all believe that things will get worse and worse. (See Table 1, Table 2). The survey data listed in Table 1 and Table 2 indicate that most people's overall feelings toward the situation are positive reactions.

continued...

SURVEY ON PUBLIC ATTITUDE TOWARD REFORM, 1994 (continued)

Table 1. The Public's Basic View of the Social Psychological Environment of the Current Reform (percent)

Very Stable	Rather Stable	Basically Stable	Very Unstable	Unclear
4.0	24.5	45.8	19.2	6.6

Table 2. The Public's Expectations for the 1995 Social
Environment (percent)

More Stable	No Change	Not as Good as 1994
30.7	48.0	21.3

(2) In their overall evaluation of reform, the public
still expresses rather strong approval of the value
and significance of reform.

The public's overall evaluation of reform reflects the
most basic attitude that they hold toward reform. The
direction that this attitude takes is one of the core indicators conditioning the social psychological environment.
So, it is one of the essential bases that this survey system uses to form a judgement. The results of the 1994
survey reveal that 80.7 percent of the public hold a favorable attitude on the general direction of reform (see
Table 3).

Table 3. The Public's Evaluation of the "General Direction of Reform" (percent)

Very Correct	Rather Correct	Generally Correct	Incorrect	Very Incorrect
33.1	47.6	15.3	3.3	0.7

Despite the fact that on specific issues such as evaluation
of the results of reform and the speed of reform, the
public exhibited different reactions and some people
held a negative evaluation, there tended to be rather
consistent approval in their overall judgement of the
general direction of reform.

(3) Most people are confident about the intensification of reform and have a positive attitude about the
prospective goal of "establishing a socialist market
economy," but a considerable share also lack confidence in this.

The survey reveals that 61.4 percent of the public
expresses confidence in the goal of "establishing a
socialist market economy" (see Table 4).

Table 4. The Public's Attitude About the Goal of Achieving a "Socialist Market Economy" (percent)

Ex-tremely Confident	Rather Confident	Generally Confident	Lack Confi-dence	Not the Slightest Confi-dence
16.8	44.6	25.9	10.1	2.6

Reform is concrete action and not abstract concepts. In
the questionnaire, this question was designed beginning
from specific, manageable goals to measure the public's
confidence toward reform goals. The results of measuring specific goals often are better able to reflect the
public's true feelings. We discover from the data of Table 4 that while most people are confident of the goal
of intensifying reform, 12.7 percent of the people lack
confidence in this goal. This is a percentage that bears
watching.

II. Abrupt Changes in Public Attitudes

By a systematic analysis of the data obtained from this
survey and comparison with social psychological survey
data since 1991, we have discovered that there are
some obvious changes in the 1994 social psychological
environment. Linking the analysis with the results of
surveys since 1991, these changes to a certain extent
have significance as turning points and require a great
deal of attention from various sectors.

(1) As regards the level of psychological demand
and concern, generally speaking, the public for the
first time made social stability the primary goal and
put the goal of increased income in second place.
Problems that people are generally concerned about
are further inflation, followed by corrupt social
values and social chaos.

Survey data reveals that the public's demand for social
stability rose from 69.4 percent in 1993 to 76.9 percent
in 1994, but the demand for increased income fell
from 71.2 percent in 1993 to 68.5 percent (see Table
5). When Chinese reform first began, especially when
urban reform began in 1984, people expected a very
high income and most people equated reform with
increased income. At the same time, reform also caused
obvious increases in most people's income. In turn, this
further solidified the superficial understanding of the

continued...

SURVEY ON PUBLIC ATTITUDE TOWARD REFORM, 1994 (continued)

people of that time toward reform. But 10 years later, even though people's demand for increased income still is rather strong, they have placed the goal of social stability in first place. This change indicates that the public has experienced the throes of converting systems and changing the form of society and hopes that by maintaining smooth change in the type of society, they can realize their desire of increasing their income.

Table 5. The 1994 Public Social Psychological Demand Situation (percent)

	Very Strong	Generally Strong	Undeter-mined
Stable Social Environment	76.9	18.3	4.8
Increased Income	68.5	28.5	3.0
Improved Social Position	33.9	49.4	16.7
Awareness of Major National Decisions	33.4	47.0	19.6
A Voice in Public Affairs	25.3	48.1	26.6

The public expression of a strong demand for social stability in a period of transition is not just because stability can satisfy their desire for increased income, it comes more importantly from the bitter memories produced after undergoing social unrest. The vast majority of the people in the survey (92.4 percent) believe that "the results of social unrest always are grief for the common people." It is precisely based on this tendency to rationally understand and realistically consider the consequences of social unrest that people first pursue a stable social environment. This is a demand for stability to produce an increase in individual income as well as a demand for stability produced when individual members of society feel that unstable social factors are increasing somewhat and are psychologically repelled by social unrest.

What type of motivation does the specific structure of the demand for social stability of individual members of society have on their actions. That is to say, what are the actions of people in the psychological state described above. This is most significant for social stability. Our survey reveals that the Chinese people have invented a distinctive structural form suited to current social conditions so they can seek a balance between stability and risk. That is using the family as a unit to resolve unstable factors.

In a family, the husband and wife act as a whole to make the appropriate corresponding adjustment to social transformation. The survey reveals that as of the end of 1994, 26 percent of families had become families of the "mutually beneficial systems type." That is, one of the marriage partners works in a state unit and the other works in a unit outside the system with a greater risk. The occupational structure that this type of couple has selected can satisfy the demands for stability of the family unit and, at the same time, it can satisfy the demand for increased family income. The emergence of one fourth of the families as the "mutually beneficial systems type" can eliminate the unstable influence brought on by system conversion rather well. Currently the numbers of this type of family still are increasing, and it is forecast that before 1997 at the current rate, they could reach one third. This undoubtedly will help to reduce resistance to social reform and increase social stability.

The problems that the public are most concerned about are, in order: inflation, corrupt social values, social turmoil, a worsening law and order situation, and a widening gap between poor and rich. The most pronounced change compared with 1993 survey data is that the concern for inflation rose from second place in 1993 to first place in 1994. We should say that from the national rush to purchase in 1988, people began to experience inflation, and as far as the major social groups are concerned, their tolerance gradually increased. We discovered in a July 1992 survey that 64.0 percent of the people at that time were accustomed to rising prices. But two years later in 1994, why have prices again become the issue that people are most concerned about? By conducting a cross-analysis of the data, we discovered that, besides the fact that inflation was excessive in 1994, people are most concerned about prices for the following three reasons:

1. The 1994 price rises occurred with a background of increased personal expenditures. Since July 1992, with the advancement of public health reform, housing reform, education reform, and reform of the old-age insurance system, individual expenditures began to increase. This caused most members of society to feel that they could not bear the burden or it was difficult to bear. For example, 82.3 percent of the people believe that the portion of health care expenses that individuals bear is unbearable or difficult to bear (see Table 6).

continued...

SURVEY ON PUBLIC ATTITUDE TOWARD REFORM, 1994 (continued)

Table 6. The Public's Ability to Bear Various Expenses (percent)

	Unbearable	Difficult to Bear	Just Right	Not Heavy to Bear	Undetermined
Individual Health-care Expenses	57.8	24.5	6.2	6.9	4.6
Individual Housing Expenses	43.8	31.7	11.0	7.3	6.2
Individual Education Expenses	42.3	35.2	7.1	7.5	7.9
Individual Old-age Insurance Expenses	36.6	33.6	9.4	10.3	11.2

2. The public lacks confidence in the government's ability to control prices. The 1994 survey data reveal that 69.2 percent of the public lacks confidence (49.2 percent) or has no confidence (19.7 percent) in the government's capability to control prices. On this point, the general lack of confidence in the government in society, with the background described above, makes public anxiety toward price rises even greater.

3. Serious forecasts for price rises in 1995. Because there is a lack of confidence in government control of prices, the vast majority of people (84.9 percent) expect great (42.5 percent) or small (42.4 percent) price increases in 1995. On the other hand, only 3.5 percent believe that prices will fall slightly compared to 1994.

It should especially be pointed out that by further analysis of the data, we discovered that there is a very strong relationship between confidence and the expectation that prices will rise. Those who have the least confidence in government control of prices expect the greatest price rises in 1995. This indicates that people ascribe price rises in part to weak government control.

(2) Continual worsening of the price situation, consumer product quality, and corrupt social values are major causes leading to society's psychological environment rather lacking. Generally speaking, the public in one respect has a positive attitude about the living environment of society's taking a favorable turn in the next year; but, in another respect, they have a negative attitude about improvement in the corrupt social values of society, the price situation, and the gap between poor and rich. A considerable number of people lack clear expectations regarding changes in opportunities to earn money and economic order in the next year, and frustrations are beginning to increase.

The survey reveals that 81.8 percent of the people believe that dissatisfaction in the life of society will increase very much (37.3 percent) or will increase somewhat (44.5 percent), and only 10.3 percent of the people believe that there will be no change. Another 7.9 percent of the people believe that dissatisfaction will decrease somewhat or very much. Moreover, 74.4 percent believe that the current phenomenon of "being right, but not speaking out" is very widespread. Table 7 compares the numbers of people from different occupational groups who believe that "dissatisfaction will increase very much." The data also reveal that, of the 14 occupational groups surveyed, the increase in the value of dissatisfaction for nine groups exceeds the average value (37.3 percent). Among these, the worker group and the individual household group are the highest, 43.9 percent and 43.8 percent respectively. In addition, compared with other groups, workers, individual households, and the military group also have the deepest feelings about the current phenomenon of "being right, but not speaking out." Among them, 80.5 percent, 81.7 percent, and 82.6 percent respectively believe that the current phenomenon of "being right, but not speaking out" is very widespread.

In addition, in the survey we also discovered that 55.6 percent of the people believe that "although they do not have a problem, in their hearts they generally feel ill at ease." This data tells us that with dissatisfaction continuously congealing, a considerable number of people believe that "being right, but not speaking out" is a widespread phenomenon in the social environment and more than half the people have formed a feeling of dissatisfaction that will be hard to reconcile. The so-called settled feelings are feelings that have built up to form a rather firm attitude.

continued...

SURVEY ON PUBLIC ATTITUDE TOWARD REFORM, 1994 (continued)

Table 7. The Share of People in Various Occupational Groups Who Believe That "Dissatisfaction Will Increase Very Much" (percent)

Workers	43.9
Scientific Research Personnel	42.9
Cadres at the Assistant Department Level and Above	39.4
Professional Personnel	42.1
Cadres at Section Level and Below	40.4
Individuals	43.8
Middle and Elementary School Teachers	40.2
Irregular Professionals	41.7
Scientific and Technical Personnel	37.8

So, what are the causes leading to the widespread dissatisfaction of various major social groups? From analysis, we believe that the principal reason is that the public persists in a negative evaluation of the living environment of society. In the survey questionnaire, we listed a total of 18 aspects of the life of society and allowed the interviewees to evaluate their satisfaction or dissatisfaction with the current situation of each. The results revealed that there was satisfaction with the current situation in only five (using in excess of 50 percent as the dividing line). They were, in order: international status (63.5 percent), market supply (62.8 percent), municipal government development (55.5 percent), opening to the outside (53.9 percent), and cultural life (51.5 percent). But there were eight dissatisfactory items. They were, in order: the price situation (90.0), consumer product quality (88.9 percent), corrupt social values of society (86.5 percent), the gap between poor and rich (79.7 percent), the law and order situation (76.1 percent), handling affairs according to the law (67.2 percent), environmental protection (58.1 percent), and economic order (56.2 percent).

Compared with the same data for 1993, the most obvious change was that dissatisfaction with the price situation and consumer product quality changed from second and third place in 1993 to first and second place in 1994. Although dissatisfaction with corrupt

social values of society and the law and order situation declined slightly (an average decline of 4 percent), people's dissatisfactory evaluation of market supply and the truth of news reporting exhibited an obvious rise, increasing by 14.1 percent and 10.0 percent respectively.

How does the public regard the prospects for changes in the living environment of society? We let the interviewees forecast the changes in 1995 for various aspects of the life of society. The results indicate that the size of the share forecasting improvement or worsening is standard. On the one hand, people have a positive attitude about improvement in the life of society for most in 1995, but on the other hand, people have a negative attitude about improvement in corrupt social values, the price situation, and the gap between poor and rich.

In the analysis we noticed that people lacked clear expectations about prospects for changes in such things as opportunities to earn money, economic order, and the truth of news reporting, 43.1 percent, 40.2 percent, and 40.0 percent of the people respectively, selected "Do not know" in answer to expectations for these categories. This indicates that a considerable number of people personally feel that society is in the midst of a rather large change and the undecided factor is increasing with that. But it should be pointed out that with the impetus of the demand for increased individual income, society, on the one hand, bears the squeeze of the double heavy pressures coming from price rises and increases in individual expenses. On the other hand, their prospects for change, especially prospects for changes in the ability to provide opportunities for earning money and economic order, are very uncertain. This is bound to increase the psychological tensions of individual members of society and, in this way, produce rather strong feelings of frustration. For this we should proceed from a standard economic order as quickly as possible and appropriately expand employment opportunities, thereby causing individual members of society to be able to have rather clear expectations about this to reduce the feelings of frustration produced by increased psychological tension, so that social stability can create a good psychological environment.

(3) Compared with the previous few years, while one fourth of the objects of the survey subjectively feel that their standard of living has declined, the share of people who believe that reform is speeding up has begun to increase.

Considered from the perspective of residents' subjective evaluation of various aspects of their individual lives, the share who believe that the standard of living has declined has greatly increased compared to 1993 and

continued...

SURVEY ON PUBLIC ATTITUDE TOWARD REFORM, 1994 (continued)

1992. In 1994 the share of members of society who subjectively felt that the standard of living has declined is 25.2 percent (of those, 19.2 percent believe that it has declined slightly and 6.0 percent that it has declined very much). In 1993 this share was 18.8 percent and in 1992 this share was 10.9 percent (of those, 9.7 percent believed that it had declined slightly and 1.2 percent that it had declined very much). In the past three years, the share of people believing that the standard of living has declined continuously increased, and by 1994, one fourth of the people feel that their own standard of living is not as good as before (see Table 8).

Table 8. Public Feeling About Changes in the Standard of Living (percent)

	Greatly Im- proved	Slightly Im- proved	No Change	Slightly De- clined	Greatly De- clined
1992	5.7	62.3	21.1	9.7	1.2
1993	5.5	49.1	26.6	15.2	3.6
1994	3.3	44.3	27.2	19.2	6.0

In further inquiring regarding the specific level of residents' lives, we discovered that the tendencies described above still exist. The survey data of Table 9 prove this point.

Table 9. Share of the People Believing That Their Individual Standard of Living Has Declined (percent)

	Income Reduced	Savings Reduced	Bonds and Stocks Reduced	Consump- tion of Expensive Goods Reduced
1992	7.0	12.4	—	6.9
1993	12.6	21.3	8.3	7.8
1994	16.2	27.8	14.8	12.3

In the indicators described above, the share of people with negative feelings continually increased in the past three years. A considerable part of this was by no means an absolute decline in various aspects of individual income, such as consumption of expensive goods, but it was their decline in comparison with wealthier people around them. This is a subjective feeling of comparative

deprivation. This comparative evaluation of the public regarding their own lives does not need to be fair and objective, but this unhappy feeling of theirs is real and strong.

This subjective feeling has a very strong influence on their attitude. So, correspondingly the rate of people's support for reform also has exhibited a slide. The share of people expressing great approval for reform declined from 57.2 percent in 1992 to 44 percent in 1994, a slide of 13.2 percentage points, and the share of people expressing disapproval of reform rose from 2.9 percent in 1992 to 4.6 percent in 1994, increasing nearly two percentage points. The share of people expressing great satisfaction with reform also declined from 28.6 percent in 1992 to 12.5 percent in 1994, an actual decline of 16.1 percentage points. At the same time, the share of people expressing dissatisfaction and great dissatisfaction toward reform rose from 6.1 percent in 1992 to 25.1 percent in 1994, a total increase of 19 percentage points. And the decline in the share of people with a positive attitude about the prospects for reform declined most clearly, from 52.5 percent in 1992 to 25 percent in 1994, a total decline of 27.5 percentage points. The share believing that reform has no hope changed from 3.1 percent in 1992 to 8.9 percent in 1994.

While the public's attitude toward reform was changing, how did they judge the rate of progress of reform? The survey reveals that the share believing that the rate of reform is too fast and comparatively fast increased by a total of 23.4 percent, and the share who believe that the rate of reform is just right declined from 36.2 percent in 1992 to 23.6 percent in 1994 (see Table 10). People from different living standards, educational levels, and occupational groups also expressed clearly different attitudes toward reform:

1. The more people have the subjective feeling that the standard of living is improving, the more they support and are satisfied with reform, and the more they believe that reform has a future.

2. The higher the education level of people, the lower their satisfaction with reform, but compared with people with a lower level of education, they support reform more.

3. As regards occupational groups, scientific research personnel, teachers, party and government organization cadres, and enterprise cadres support reform more than military personnel and people from individual households. People from individual households are the most lacking in optimism regarding the prospects of reform and the confidence of workers and people from individual households regarding reform is the weakest.

continued...

SURVEY ON PUBLIC ATTITUDE TOWARD REFORM, 1994 (continued)

Table 10. Public Evaluation of the Rate of Reform (percent)

	Too Fast	Comparatively Fast	Just Right	Comparatively Slow	Too Slow
1992	5.6	28.2	36.2	25.9	4.1
1993	13.0	31.8	25.7	10.0	19.6
1994	15.0	42.2	23.6	16.3	2.9

4. Workers and party and government organization cadres at the section level and above believe that the rate of reform is too fast, but military personnel, members of individual households, and workers all generally believe that the social environment of reform is very unstable.

In the early period of reform, the public, under huge influence from government mass media publicity, mostly looked forward to magnificent prospects. In the middle period, the vast majority of the residents also actually obtained benefits such as great increase in income from the prosperity brought on by reform and the growth of the economy. But when reform entered the offensive stage and touched on the actual interests of a great many people, and with the gap between poor and rich appearing and continually widening in recent years, people expressed stronger dissatisfaction with the current situation and somewhat reserved support for reform was a normal social psychological phenomenon. But the three year continuous decline in the general rate of support for reform by major social strata and occupational groups undoubtedly is a signal that cannot be underestimated.

Management World No. 4, 24 Jul 1995.

PETITION ON HUMAN RIGHTS SUBMITTED, 1995

Some 26 prominent dissidents and intellectuals sent a formal petition Monday to the Chinese parliament, demanding an improvement in human rights and social justice.

Exercising their right under the constitution to petition the National People's Congress (NPC) which holds its annual plenary session next month, the petitioners, including dissidents Wang Dan, Ma Shaohua and Ma Shaofang, decried the "extremely backward" human rights situation in China.

"We believe that the defense of human rights and social justice is a fundamental principle sought by all humanity," the petition said, listing three individual cases where the rights of Chinese citizens had been abused.

It was the second such petition submitted to the NPC within a week, following one signed by 12 prominent intellectuals that called for measures to curb corruption within the Chinese leadership.

The signatories, including leading dissident Chen Ziming and two former senior editors of the official Communist Party newspaper, the People's Daily, insisted that a free press and the creation of independent judicial bodies were necessary to wipe out graft in Communist Party and government organs.

Both petitions are significant given the heavy government crackdown on dissident activity in the past year, which effectively silenced those activists not already imprisoned or forced into exile.

Similar petitions calling for widespread democratic reforms were submitted to the NPC's last annual session.

Monday's petition called on the NPC to investigate the case of Wang Wanxing, who has been detained in a Beijing psychiatric hospital since June, 1992, after being arrested for unfurling a banner in Tiananmen Square.

The banner condemned patriarch Deng Xiaoping and other leaders for the 1989 massacre of pro-democracy demonstrators.

It also highlighted the case of Hua Huiqi, a factory worker who the petition said was beaten and detained by police in January because of his Christian beliefs.

"We sincerely hope the NPC will use its power under the constitution to reinforce surveillance of the law and to protect fundamental human rights and defend social justice," the petition said.

Hong Kong AFP, 27 Feb 1995.

YOUTH SURVEY, 1994

Table 1: How Do You Rate the Changes in 15 Year of Reform in the Following Areas?

Evaluation Items	Operating State and Evaluation			
	Good Operations (Favorable Evaluation)	Neutral Operations (Uncertain Evaluation)	Poor Operations (Negative Evaluation)	Grade Average
1. Overall National Might	94.11%	2.93%	2.96%	4.30
2. Market Supply	90.33%	4.21%	5.47%	4.25
3. China's International Standing	86.35%	9.74%	3.90%	4.12
4. National Economic Situation	87.03%	5.98%	6.94%	4.06
5. Material Living Standards	89.37%	6.23%	4.41%	4.05
6. Chance To Make Money	85.27%	8.07%	6.66%	4.01
7. Cultural Living Standards	78.68%	11.22%	10.09%	3.95
8. Chance To Get Rich	73.77%	14.93%	11.31%	3.73
9. National Cohesion	51.44%	21.97%	26.58%	3.32
10. Government Administrative Efficiency	35.31%	30.93%	33.75%	2.96
11. Public Order	37.86%	7.44%	54.70%	2.79
12. Ethical Practice	29.26%	13.10%	57.65%	2.66
13. Government Honesty	25.21%	16.17%	58.62%	2.43

Having done a factor analysis of the evaluation results reflected in Table 1, we have discovered that the youth evaluation of all social aspects in 15 years of reform can be divided roughly into the three categories of the "social conformity factor," the "material and cultural living standards factor," and the "national economic situation and overall national might factor." After 15 years of reform, Youth rank changes in the "national economic situation and overall national might factor" highest, with an average grade of 4.16; second is the "material and cultural living standards factor," with an average grade of 4.00; and lowest is the "social conformity factor," or the one that is tied most closely to our spiritual civilization establishment, with an average grade of 2.85.

This analysis shows that urban Chinese youth, when evaluating social developments over 15 years of reform, express a strong attitude orientation: In all cases where items are tied closely to our society's material civilization establishment, the youth evaluation is higher; in all cases where items are linked closely to our society's spiritual civilization establishment, the youth evaluation is lower. This highly regular pattern of change in the youth evaluation of social developments shows the objective reality of our hard line on one the hand, and soft on the other, in the course of social development over 15 years.

Youth acknowledge the "moral decline" during the changeover period, and the arrival of a golden age for a "moral reconstruction project."

Since reform and opening, as to the changes that have occurred in the public mindset and values, the society and intellectuals mostly approve of them as positive, while lacking a clear enough understanding of the various unhealthy social mindsets (materialism, vulgarism,

rashness, and utilitarianism) and value orientation (the pernicious expansion of individualism) that have appeared during these changes, as well as of their disruptive impact on social conformity.

This poll found that nearly 60 percent of youth (57.65 percent) acknowledge the phenomenon of a "moral decline" during our social changeover period. This fact proves that the social and psychological grounds for a "moral reconstruction project" exist, so that a golden age for such a project has arrived.

An historical comparison of youth evaluations shows that youth are more satisfied with reform and social realities than in 1988 or 1991.

When evaluating market supply change, the percentage of youth holding it to be favorable in 1994 (90.33 percent) was 37.93 points higher than in 1988 (52.4 percent), and 21.53 points higher than in 1991 (68.8 percent).

When evaluating the change in the national economic situtation, the percentage of those holding that it had improved in 1994 (87.03 percent) was 46.73 points higher than in 1988 (40.3 percent), and 35.53 points higher than in 1991 (51.5 percent).

When evaluating the change in the chance to make money, the percentage of those holding that it was greater in 1994 (85.27 percent) was 21.17 points higher than in 1988 (64.1 percent), and 23.47 points higher than in 1991 (61.8 percent).

When evaluating the change in China's international standing, the percentage of those holding that it was improved in 1994 (86.35 percent) was 21.15 points higher than in 1988 (65.2 percent), and 21.15 points higher than in 1991 (65.2 percent).

Zhougguo Quingnian Bao, 21 Jan 1995.

GUANGXI COMMENDED FOR ARRESTING SALES OF WOMEN AND CHILDREN, 1995

Recently the State Council Working Commission for Women and Children commended Guangxi's public security office for its efforts against the abduction and selling of women and children. Since 1993, Guangxi's public security apparatus has focused its efforts on prevention and rescue. In November 1994, the regional public security office conducted an experimental large-scale assault on trafficking in women and children in Qingzhou city. By 15 January 1995 it had

continued...

GUANGXI COMMENDED FOR ARRESTING SALES OF WOMEN AND CHILDREN, 1995 (continued)

rescued 68 women and apprehended 40 buyers and sellers. During 1993 and 1994, Jingxi county apprehended 308 traffickers and broke up 10 gangs involving 36 criminals. Throughout Guangxi, three special efforts were undertaken in 1993 and 1994. Security officials apprehended 3,886 criminals, breaking up 595 gangs whose membership was 2,007 people. In the process, 2,861 women and 134 children were returned to their homes.

Renmin Gongan Bao, 16 Feb 1995

FIFTEEN YEAR DEVELOPMENT PLAN, 1995

China is drafting a blue print for social development for the next 15 years, said Hao Jianxiu, vice minister of the State Planning Commission, today.

The Outline Program for National Social Development for the trans-century period between 1996 and 2010, will summarize the achievements in social development in the past 45 years, set new tasks and goals, and stipulate related policies and measures, said Hao, who also acts as vice chairman of the Chinese preparatory committee for the UN world summit for social development.

She said that under the guidance of the outline program, governments at various levels will work out their own plans to cover various fields of social development.

Hao, who has been serving as a high-ranking official since 1977, said that China has made outstanding achievements in social development while seeking quick economic growth in the past 16 years.

She said that economic development is the prerequisite and basis for social development and that social development is the result and goal of economic growth.

"China's national development strategy is to properly coordinate changes in the population, the economy, the society, the environment and resources and follow the road of sustainable development," she said.

She said that since China, a developing country, has a big population, lacks resources, and is relatively backward in science and technology, only when its economy develops to a certain level can poverty be gradually alleviated, people's living standards be raised and social development upgraded.

She said, China has made good progress in overall social development in the past 16 years, during which China's gross national product grew an annual average of nine percent.

The official added that the family planning policy has proved successful in reducing the birth rate, pulling down the natural population growth rate to 11.45 per thousand from 25.83 per thousand in 1970, and extending the average life expectancy from 65 years in the mid-1970s to the present 70 years.

During the past 16 years, she said, China has used seven percent of the world's farmland to feed 22 percent of the world's population, and reduced the number of the impoverished in China's rural areas to the current 80 million from 250 million people.

Meanwhile, China has paid great attention to the development of education, she said.

According to statistics, the school attendance rate of school-age children has reached 97.7 percent, primary education was basically universal in the country, and junior secondary education was basically universal in big cities and economically developed regions. Pre-school education and special education for disabled children also advanced steadily.

The vice-minister said that China has also made progress in environmental protection. She said that China regards environmental protection as a basic national policy, and has adopted a series of measures in controlling environmental pollution and preventing damage to the ecological conditions.

In health care, China has also made significant progress, she said, adding that some major hygienic and health indices are placed in the front ranks among countries with similar levels of economic development and the gap between China and developed countries in this regard is being narrowed.

continued...

FIFTEEN YEAR DEVELOPMENT PLAN, 1995 (continued)

At the same time, she said, China has kept the rate of unemployment in cities and towns below three percent for the past 16 years and has also improved the social welfare system and social insurance system.

X, 26 Feb 1995.

UNDERGROUND SEX INDUSTRY IS BIG BUSINESS, 1995

According to Chinese sexual sociologists, the sex industry on the mainland, including prostitution, the sale of sex related services and pornography was big business in 1994–1995. Pan Suiming, Director of the Institute for Sexual Sociology at China People's University said the proliferation of pornography, gambling and drugs would indicate that people were ignoring the law.

Pan Suiming estimated sex related services to be a 600 million yuan business and put the total sales of pornographic products at 1.9 billion yuan. According to Pan Suiming, the medical departments of 26 provinces and municipalities discovered over 180,000 cases of sexually transmitted disease in 1992. Add to that the cases in some large cities which did not report and the actual number was closer to 280,000. This means, according to Pan Suiming, that 14 million yuan were spent on treating these cases in 1992 and probably over 20 million yuan in 1993.

Ming Pao, 10 Nov 1995.

TEXT OF BEIJING DECLARATION ON WOMEN, 1995

Following is the full text of the Beijing Declaration adopted today at the closing session of the UN Fourth World Conference on Women.

Beijing Declaration

1. We, the Governments, participating in the Fourth World Conference on Women,

2. Gathered here in Beijing, in September 1995, the year of the fiftieth anniversary of the rounding of the United Nations,

3. Determined to advance the goals of equality, development and peace for all women everywhere in the interest of all humanity,

4. Acknowledging the voices of all women everywhere and taking note of the diversity of women and their roles and circumstances, honoring the women who paved the way and inspired by the hope present in the world's youth,

5. Recognize that the status of women has advanced in some important respects in the past decade but that progress has been uneven, inequalities between women and men have persisted and major obstacles remain, with serious consequences for the well-being of all people,

6. Also recognize that this situation is exacerbated by the increasing poverty that is affecting the lives of the majority of the world's people, in particular women and children, with origins in both the national and international domains,

7. Dedicate ourselves unreservedly to addressing these constraints and obstacles and thus enhancing further the advancement and empowerment of women all over the world, and agree that this requires urgent action in the spirit of determination, hope, cooperation and solidarity, now and to carry us forward into the next century.

We reaffirm our commitment to:

8. The equal rights and inherent human dignity of women and men and other purposes and principles enshrined in the Charter of the United Nations, to the Universal Declaration of Human Rights and other international human rights instruments, in particular the Convention on the Elimination of All Forms of Discrimination against Women and the Convention on the Rights of the Child, as well as the Declaration on the Elimination of Violence against Women and the Declaration on the Right to Development;

continued...

TEXT OF BEIJING DECLARATION ON WOMEN, 1995 (continued)

9. Ensure the full implementation of the human rights of women and of the girl child as an inalienable, integral and indivisible part of all human rights and fundamental freedoms;

10. Build on consensus and progress made at previous United Nations conferences and summits—on women in Nairobi in 1985, on children in New York in 1990, on environment and development in Rio de Janeiro in 1992, on human rights in Vienna in 1993, on population and development in Cairo in 1994 and on social development in Copenhagen in 1995 with the objectives of achieving equality, development and peace;

11. Achieve the full and effective implementation of the Nairobi Forward-looking Strategies for the Advancement of Women;

12. The empowerment and advancement of women, including the right to freedom of thought, conscience, religion and belief, thus contributing to the moral, ethical, spiritual and intellectual needs of women and men, individually or in community with others and thereby guaranteeing them the possibility of realizing their full potential in society and shaping their lives in accordance with their own aspirations.

We are convinced that:

13. Women's empowerment and their full participation on the basis of equality in all spheres of society, including participation in the decision-making process and access to power, are fundamental for the achievement of equality, development and peace;

14. Women's rights are human rights;

15. Equal rights, opportunities and access to resources, equal sharing of responsibilities for the family by men and women, and a harmonious partnership between them are critical to their well-being and that of their families as well as to the consolidation of democracy;

16. Eradication of poverty based on sustained economic growth, social development, environmental protection and social justice requires the involvement of women in economic and social development and equal opportunities and the full and equal participation of women and men as agents and beneficiaries of people-centered sustainable development;

17. The explicit recognition and reaffirmation of the right of all women to control all aspects of their health, in particular their own fertility, is basic to their empowerment;

18. Local, national, regional and global peace is attainable and is inextricably linked with the advancement of women, who are a fundamental force for leadership, conflict resolution and the promotion of lasting peace at all levels;

19. It is essential to design, implement and monitor, with the full participation of women, effective, efficient and mutually reinforcing gender-sensitive policies and programs, including development policies and programs, at all levels that will foster the empowerment and advancement of women;

20. The participation and contribution of all actors of civil society, particularly women's groups and networks and other non-governmental organizations and community-based organizations, with full respect for their autonomy, in cooperation with Governments, are important to the effective implementation and follow-up of the Platform for Action;

21. The implementation of the Platform for Action requires commitment from Governments and the international community. By making national and international commitments for action, including those made at the Conference, Governments and the international community recognize the need to take priority action for the empowerment and advancement of women.

We are determined to:

22. Intensify efforts and actions to achieve the goals of the Nairobi Forward-looking Strategies for the Advancement of Women by the end of this century;

23. Ensure the full enjoyment by women and the girl child of all human rights and fundamental freedoms, and take effective action against violations of these rights and freedoms;

24. Take all necessary measures to eliminate all forms of discrimination against women and the girl child and remove all obstacles to gender equality and the advancement and empowerment of women;

25. Encourage men to participate fully in all actions towards equality;

continued...

TEXT OF BEIJING DECLARATION ON WOMEN, 1995 (continued)

26. Promote women's economic independence, including employment, and eradicate the persistent and increasing burden of poverty on women by addressing the structural causes of poverty through changes in economic structures, ensuring equal access for all women, including those in rural areas, as vital development agents, to productive resources, opportunities and public services;

27. Promote people-centered sustainable development, including sustained economic growth through the provision of basic education, life-long education, literacy and training, and primary health care for girls and women;

28. Take positive steps to ensure peace for the advancement of women and, recognizing the leading role that women have played in the peace movement, work actively towards general and complete disarmament under strict and effective international control, and support negotiations on the conclusion, without delay, of a universal and multilaterally and effectively verifiable comprehensive nuclear-test-ban treaty which contributes to nuclear disarmament and the prevention of the proliferation of nuclear weapons in all its aspects;

29. Prevent and eliminate all forms of violence against women and girls;

30. Ensure equal access to and equal treatment of women and men in education and health care and enhance women's sexual and reproductive health as well as education;

31. Promote and protect all human rights of women and girls;

32. Intensify efforts to ensure equal enjoyment of all human rights and fundamental freedoms for all women and girls who face multiple barriers to their empowerment and advancement because of such factors as their race, age, language, ethnicity, culture, religion, or disability, or because they are indigenous people;

33. Ensure respect for international law, including humanitarian law, in order to protect women and girls in particular;

34. Develop the fullest potential of girls and women of all ages, ensure their full and equal participation in building a better world for all and enhance their role in the development process.

We are determined to:

35. Ensure women's equal access to economic resources including land, credit, science and technology, vocational training, information, communication and markets, as a means to further the advancement and empowerment of women and girls, including through the enhancement of their capacities to enjoy the benefits of equal access to these resources, inter alia, by means of international cooperation;

36. Ensure the success of the Platform for Action which will require a strong commitment on the part of Governments, international organizations and institutions at all levels. We are deeply convinced that economic development, social development and environmental protection are interdependent and mutually reinforcing components of sustainable development, which is the framework for our efforts to achieve a higher quality of life for all people. Equitable social development that recognizes empowering the poor, particularly women living in poverty, to utilize environmental resources sustainably is a necessary foundation for sustainable development. We also recognize that broad-based and sustained economic growth in the context of sustainable development is necessary to sustain social development and social justice. The success of the Platform for Action will also require adequate mobilization of resources at the national and international levels as well as new and additional resources to the developing countries from all available funding mechanisms, including multilateral, bilateral and private sources for the advancement of women; financial resources to strengthen the capacity of national, subregional, regional and international institutions; a commitment to equal rights, equal responsibilities and equal opportunities and to the equal participation of women and men in all national, regional and international bodies and policy-making processes; the establishment or strengthening of mechanisms at all levels for accountability to the world's women;

37. Ensure also the success of the Platform for Action in countries with economies in transition, which will require continued international cooperation and assistance;

continued...

TEXT OF BEIJING DECLARATION ON WOMEN, 1995 (continued)

38. We hereby adopt and commit ourselves as Governments to implement the following Platform for Action, ensuring that a gender perspective is reflected in all our policies and programs. We urge the United Nations system, regional and international financial institutions, other relevant regional and international institutions and all women and men, as well as non-governmental organizations, with full respect for their autonomy, and all sectors of civil society, in cooperation with Governments, to fully commit themselves and contribute to the implementation of this Platform for Action.

X, 15 Sep 1995.

XXV CULTURE

TRAINING FOR YOUNG WRITERS, 1995

Zhai Taifeng, deputy head of the Propaganda Department of the Chinese Communist Party Central Committee called on the Chinese Writers' Association to train more writers under the age of forty. Zhai stated that the country would suffer a serious lack of outstanding writers by 2000 if some action weren't taken. He said that writers under age forty account for only eight percent of the institute's 5,000 members. Further, he said the training programs would lay a solid basis for the prosperity of socialist culture into 2000 and beyond.

China Facts & Figures Annual, 1995

FIRST WESTERN ROCK CONCERT IN A DECADE, 1995

The members of Swedish pop band Roxette were the first foreign performers allowed into China from a place other than Hong Kong or Taiwan since rock group Wham! played a sell-out concert in Beijing in 1985. World renowned pop/rock idols Madonna and Michael Jackson were denied permission to perform in China. According to officials the Chinese wanted something cleaner. "Roxette," said the official, "is a traditional rock group which is not in any way offensive."

Hong Kong Eastern Express, 15 Feb 1995.

HISTORIC FILMS BEGUN, 1995

Shooting began on the serial movies depicting the Chinese communist revolutionary war— "Great Turning Point" and "Titanic March." Each film when complete will contain five volumes of ten parts. The project is overseen by Yu Yongbo, member of the Central Military Commission (CMC) and director of the General Political Department of the People's Liberation Army (PLA). According to Yu, "CMC Chairman Jiang Zemin attached great importance to and showed deep concern for the production of these movies." Projected completion date of the project is 1 August 1997, to coincide with the 70th anniversary of Army Day.

China Facts & Figures Annual, 1995

VATICAN URGED TO SEVER TAIWAN TIES, 1995

Chinese officials once again issued a call to the Vatican to break diplomatic ties with Taiwan, just hours before a radio message by Pope John Paul II to Chinese Catholics.

"Our position has not changed. The Vatican should sever its so-called diplomatic relations with Taiwan and recognize the People's Republic of China as sole legal government of China,"

continued...

VATICAN URGED TO SEVER TAIWAN TIES, 1995 (continued)

said a foreign ministry spokesman. "The Vatican must not interfere in China's internal affairs, including religious affairs," the spokesman added in a telephone interview.

China severed relations with the Vatican in 1957 after the Holy See recognized Taiwan which Beijing considers a renegade province. The mainland then set up an official church, known as the patriotic church, under state control, but an estimated three to ten million Chinese Catholics remained faithful to Rome. They are members of the so-called silent church which is supported by the Vatican and regularly persecuted by the communist regime.

Hong Kong AFP, 14 Jan 1995.

BEAUTY PRODUCTS BUSINESS GROWS, 1994

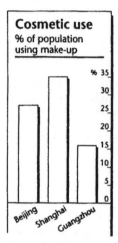

Cosmetic use
% of population
using make-up

Business China, 8 Aug 1994.

RAPID GROWTH OF CULTS, 1995

An inconspicuous story about an obscure sect that was run in a provincial newspaper last week tells much about the grim reality of China. Authorities in Sichuan Province have started to take action against a crypto-Christian underground organization called the Society of Disciples, according to a district-level paper. The society was set up in early 1989 by an educated peasant of nearby Shaanxi Province called Ji Sanbao, who, apparently styling himself after Jesus, had initially recruited 12 apostles.

Police in Sichuan expressed surprise that by sheer word of mouth, the denomination had snowballed to more than 10,000 converts by the end of last year. While the bulk were Sichuanese, believers could be found in provinces including Shaanxi, Hebei, Shandong, Yunnan and even Xinjiang. Security officials said the movement had at first escaped attention because of its secretive and highly disciplined nature.

The society has a seven-tier structure: an "overall organization"; an assembly; branch societies; small societies, small sub-societies; small sub-society stations; and the churches. And it has flourished not just in villages, where illiteracy levels are high, but also in the suburbs of cities including Chongqing, Changshou, Dazhu Rongchang and Jiangjin.

An elaborate underground communications network was set up to link the far-flung "house churches". Emissaries talk through codes. Internal documents described the clandestine priests as luring converts through a combination of vulgarized Christian beliefs, feudal superstition, and febrile attacks against the Communist administration. The sect's adherents claimed

continued...

RAPID GROWTH OF CULTS, 1995 (continued)

that "the end of the world" would come in the year 2000, and only their God could save the country. They also asserted that with the deity in their hearts, converts could stay alive with a mere mouthfuls of rice every day and that illnesses could be cured through saying prayers.

Most disturbing for the Chinese Communist Party (CCP), the priests decried its corrupt, "dark rule", which would soon be knocked down by God. Society affiliates persuaded factory laborers to stop working, farmers not to sell their produce to state buyers, and villagers not to observe the one-child policy. While the authorities have ridiculed the sect for its "rank superstition", they must have realized that its fast growth was predicated upon the underground prelates' ability to exploit the people's dissatisfaction at their standard of living and grievances against the administration.

The fact that local governments tolerated the rebellious grouping for five years suggests a dangerous disintegration of state authority at the regional level. Phenomena such as the Society of Disciples are the tip of the iceberg. Cadres in provinces including Hunan, Hubei, Shaanxi, Sichuan, Yunnan and Jiangxi have conceded that large chunks of their territories have been overrun by illegal organizations including clandestine churches and sects, clans, triads and assorted "feudal kingdoms". Triads and other underground elements have spread to the richer provinces along the coast in the wake of the waves of migrant labor.

Most alarmingly, many local governments lack the resources and authority to stamp out the "evil forces". Very often the underworld bosses are allowed to run their fiefdoms after professing perfunctory allegiance to the local Communist Party committees. The CCP knows full well what is at stake: the clans and sects not only cause severe law-and-order problems but could pose a lethal threat to Beijing's rule. After all, the Communist Party swept to power in the late 1940s through building bases first in the mountains and then the cities. Looking further back, the Qing Dynasty was almost wrecked by a quasi-Christian order led by "peasant visionary" Hong Xiuquan, one of Chairman Mao's heroes. Since last winter, China's political agenda has largely consisted of two issues: preparing for the post-Deng era, moping up the secret societies and mollifying the peasants. The two are interrelated. Underground organizations could see in the death of Mr. Deng an opportunity to unleash a full-blown challenge to the administration of President Jiang Zemin.

Late last year, the CCP announced a three-year program to resuscitate and strengthen its 800,000-odd cells in the villages and towns, an estimated 35 percent of which are "in a state of paralysis". The lofty mission is to lure peasants and townsfolk from triad dens and house churches back to the Communist embrace. Last week, the party's Central Commission on the Comprehensive Management of Social Security proclaimed a blitz against "ruffians, gangsters and village warlords" in rural areas. Officials who failed to crush enough underground rings— or who might have been co-opted by them—would be severely punished.

Law and order has dominated the provincial and municipal people's congresses that have been held nationwide during the past week. Guangzhou, 80 percent of whose crimes are committed by gang members and other outlaws from other provinces, is due to set up a 24-hour patrol police force of 3,000. Premier Li Peng indicated on Monday that his Government Work Report, to be delivered at the National People's Congress early next month, would be revised to "help achieve better social order this year". Mr. Li called the maintenance of social order a "burning issue", conceding that "many problems still exist".

Cases like the Society of Disciples, however, show that the chances of the CCP restoring control over the villages and small towns are not high. In spite of efforts by Beijing to oblige the richer provinces as well as nouveau riche entrepreneurs to make donations to pockets of rural poverty, discontent remains high. Officially, the ratio between the per capita income in rural and urban areas was 1:2.55 last year. However, given the fact that farmers are not entitled 'to subsidies available to city folk, and that much of their income is siphoned off in the form of taxes or re-investment in the land, their real income is at least four times less than urbanites.

As many as 200 million unemployed or underemployed farmers are set to inundate the cities in the next few years. Those remaining are game for sects like the Society of Disciples that offer a solution beyond the party's tried-and-untrue formulas.

South China Morning Post, 22 Feb 1995.

CHURCH ACTIVIST ARRESTED, 1995

Beijing's Kuanjie Protestant church held an emergency meeting after authorities formally charged an activist member under laws believed to be reserved for the control of dissidents.

Hua Huiqi was detained during a visit to Beijing by the US human rights envoy, John Shattuck.

Friends believed Hua's detention was linked to fears of Beijing religious authorities about growing independence among the city's official Protestant churches, particularly the Gangwashi and Kuanjie churches.

Dozens of dissidents, including a number of Christian activists, were followed during Shattuck's visit although Hua is the only one known to have been arrested.

Eastern Express, 22 Jan 1995.

RELIGIOUS ISSUES IN TIBET, 1994

["The Golden Bridge Across the New Century—Lecture Materials for Publicizing the Guidelines of the Third Forum on Work in Tibet—Compiled by the Tibet Autonomous Regional CPC Committee's Propaganda Department"]

Properly carrying out nationalities and religious work is of extremely important significance to safeguarding stability and promoting development. The main task in our region's current nationalities work is to work with fraternal nationalities and fraternal provinces, autonomous regions, and municipalities across the country in seeking common development, in jointly moving toward a fairly well-to-do living standard, in achieving common prosperity, and in waging arduous struggles, expediting economic development, promoting social progress, and improving and raising the material and spiritual lives of people across the region with the support of people of all nationalities across the country.

We should continue to uphold and improve the system of regional autonomy for minority nationalities. The system of regional autonomy for minority nationalities is our party's basic system for solving our country's nationalities problems, including those in Tibet. It is the only correct path that completely accords with our country's national conditions and that possesses strong vitality. In the future, we must unswervingly continue this system and comprehensively implement the "Law on Regional Autonomy for China's Minority Nationalities." The system of regional autonomy for minority nationalities that we implement is conducive to both making the people the masters of their own destiny and to safeguarding the country's unity because it combines ethnic and regional factors, as well as political and economic factors. To practice regional autonomy for minority nationalities, we must safeguard the country's unity and ensure that the Constitution and laws will be observed and carried out in Tibet's localities. To ensure that the Constitution and laws will be observed and carried out in Tibet's localities, we must uphold and implement the principles of equality, unity, mutual assistance, and common prosperity for all nationalities, and oppose big-nationality chauvinism as well as local nationalism. The so-called "Greater Tibet Area" and "high degree of autonomy" advocated by the Dalai clique are essentially different from our autonomy for minority nationalities because they are essentially an attempt to promote independence, semi-independence, or independence in disguise.

We should constantly strengthen inter-ethnic contacts to promote great unity between various nationalities. Along with the development of the commodity economy and the establishment of the socialist market economic system, contact and cooperation between Tibetans themselves, between the Tibetans and Chinese, and between other nationalities are bound to increase, and Tibet's relations with the Han and other nationalities based on mutual assistance, mutual dependence for existence, common progress, and inseparability from each other are bound to strengthen. This is an objective requirement for and an inevitable trend in economic and social development, as well as in nationalities' progress. We should welcome and promote this trend. Problems of one kind or another in economic and cultural exchanges between different regions and between members of different nationalities should be dealt with according

continued...

RELIGIOUS ISSUES IN TIBET, 1995 (continued)

to their nature if they constitute contradictions between the people. We should not treat everything as a nationality problem. We should promptly expose and criticize actions that undermine unity between forces and separatists outside of China who use religion to engage in activities of infiltration and sabotage. We should squarely face the reality that the Dalai clique is using religion to engage in separatist activities, and we should expose the Dalai's political face under the religious veil. Cadres along with party members, the people, and Buddhist monks and nuns in temples should firmly make a clean break with the Dalai clique in the political arena. We should promptly expose and handle in accordance with the law a handful of people who carry out separatist activities under the guise of religion.

We should strengthen the management of religious affairs in accordance with the law. We should place religious activities within the framework of the Constitution, laws, regulations, and policies. Moreover, we should support and assist patriotic religious organizations in carrying out activities on their own in light of their distinctive features and rules, and give full rein to their role and initiative. The main task of the moment is to strengthen the management of temples and Buddhist monks and nuns in accordance with the law. We should earnestly implement the relevant laws and regulations promulgated by the State Council, intensify our efforts to formulate implementation rules, and draw up rules and regulations so that there are laws and regulations to go by in managing religious affairs. We should set the number of monks and nuns permitted in a temple, and step up the management of temples, especially problem-prone ones. Democratic management committees are grassroots organizations that help the government manage temples. We should do a good job of selecting members of the democratic management committees of temples so that the reins of leadership will be truly placed in the hands of religious figures who love their country and religion, abide by the law, and observe canons. We should step up education on patriotism and the legal system among Buddhist monks and nuns. We should intensify our efforts to draw up specific implementation procedures in accordance with the relevant State Council provisions on Tibetan Buddhism and the reincarnation of living Buddhas, and in light of our region's reality. We should teach and guide practitioners of Tibetan Buddhism to reform themselves in keeping with the socialist society. As required by Tibet's development and stability, and in accordance with the law of religious development, we should reform canons and religious rituals that are unsuitable for the socialist society. [passage omitted on party building in Tibet and nationwide support for Tibet]

Xizang Ribao, 2 Nov 1994.

XXVI TOURISM

CHINA'S INTERNATIONAL TOURISTS ARRIVALS, 1992–1994

Continent of Origin	Year	Number of Entries	Continent of Origin	Year	Number of Entries
Africa	1992	9,630	Australia	1992	36,024
	1993	13,629		1993	48,535
	1994	15,312		1994	52,796
Americas	1992	17,412	Europe	1992	152,948
	1993	23,186		1993	273,333
	1994	25,392		1994	278,402
Asia	1992	328,791	Total	1992	544,805
	1993	536,857		1993	895,540
	1994	601,498		1994	973,400

China Facts & Figures Annual, 1995

TOP TOURISTS HOTELS, 1994

#	Name	Location	Business Volume (Rmb million)	#	Name	Location	Business Volume (Rmb million)
1	Garden Hotel	Guangzhou, Guangdong	339.67	16	Century Plaza Hotel	Shenzhen, Guangdong	131.48
2	China Hotel	Guangzhou, Guangdong	331.87	17	Shanghai JC Mandrin	Shanghai	127.98
3	White Swan Hotel	Guangzhou, Guangdong	258.85	18	Jingguang Centre	Beijing	125.08
4	China World Hotel	Beijing	243.47	19	Portman Shangri-La Shanghai	Shanghai	124.80
5	Holiday Inn Lido Beijing	Beijing	210.56	20	Friendship Hotel	Beijing	123.45
6	Dongfang Hotel	Guangzhou, Guangdong	205.08	21	Jinjiang Tower	Shanghai	121.90
7	Hilton International	Shanghai	195.95	22	Shenzhen Bay Hotel	Shenzhen, Guangdong	119.20
8	Jinling Hotel	Nanjing, Jiangsu	179.81	23	Zhuhai Holiday Resort Hotel	Zhuhai, Guangdong	117.82
9	Palace Hotel	Beijing	169.63	24	Sheraton Hua Ting Hotel	Shanghai	114.07
10	Beijing Hotel	Beijing	151.92	25	Kunlun Hotel	Beijing	110.58
11	Garden Hotel	Shanghai	144.69	26	Xiyuan Hotel	Beijing	108.17
12	Changfugong Centre	Beijing	142.93	27	Beijing International Hotel	Beijing	104.45
13	Great Wall Sheraton Hotel	Beijing	135.41	28	Furama Hotel	Dalian, Liaoning	103.80
14	Liuhua Hotel	Guangzhou, Guangdong	132.01	29	Shangri-La Hotel Beijing	Beijing	101.99
15	Zhuhai Hotel	Zhuhai, Guangdong	131.75	30	Airport Hotel	Guangzhou, Guangdong	101.24
31	Baiyun Hotel	Guangzhou, Guangdong	97.74	67	Hong Kong Macao Centre Hotel	Beijing	56.51
32	International Guide Hotel	Shanghai	97.18	68	New Dadu Hotel	Beijing	56.08
33	Yindu Hotel	Zhuhai, Guangdong	93.38	69	Traders Hotel	Beijing	55.97
34	Zhongshan International Hotel	Zhongshan, Guangdong	92.54	70	Guangdong Mansion	Guangzhou, Guangdong	55.89
35	Jinjiang Hotel	Shanghai	91.25	71	Ocean Hotel	Shanghai	55.49
36	Fulin Hotel	Shenzhen, Guangdong	90.29	72	Mingha Hotel	Jinan, Shandong	55.46
37	Foshan Hotel	Foshan, Guangdong	88.60	73	Hot Spring Hotel	Zhongshan, Guangdong	55.28
38	Jianguo Hotel	Beijing	86.90	74	Peace Hotel	Shanghai	55.01
39	Yangjiang Hotel	Shenzhen, Guangdong	85.27	75	Golden Dragon Hotel	Kunming, Yunnan	54.76
40	Haitian Hotel	Qingdao, Shandong	82.76	76	Silver Star Hotel	Shanghai	54.04
41	Yangtze New World Hotel	Shanghai	81.54	77	Sanyu Hotel	Guangzhou, Guangdong	53.79
42	Fuhua Hotel	Zhongshan, Guangdong	80.69	78	Dongzhimen International Apartments	Beijing	52.44
43	Jinglan Hotel Beijing-Toronto	Beijing	79.66	79	Grand Hotel Beijing	Beijing	52.44
44	Dragon Hotel	Hangzhou, Zhejiang	78.14	80	Kempinski Hotel Beijing Lufthansa Centre	Beijing	52.07
45	Huaxia Hotel	Guangzhou, Guangdong	74.45	81	Capital Hotel	Jiangmen, Guangdong	51.28
46	Shangri-La Hotel	Hangzhou, Zhejiang	73.75	82	Huatian Hotel	Changsha, Hunan	50.98
47	Holiday Inn Dalian	Dalian, Liaoning	73.58	83	Galaxy Hotel	Shanghai	50.46
48	Oihao Hotel	Shenzhen, Guangdong	72.97	84	Minzu Hotel	Beijing	49.79
49	Peace Hotel	Beijing	71.37	85	Chengdu Hotel	Chengdu, Sichuan	49.78
50	Gonghei Palace Hotel	Zhuhai, Guangdong	69.90	86	Taiwan Hotel	Beijing	48.86
51	Liancheng Hotel	Shenzhen, Guangdong	69.34	87	Xiqiaoshan Hotel	Nanhai, Guangdong	48.75
52	Shiyan Lake Hot Spring Holiday Country Hotel	Shenzhen, Guangdong	68.83	88	Rainbow Hotel	Shanghai	48.32
53	Holiday Inn City Centre	Guangzhou, Guangdong	67.72	89	Xuanwu Hotel	Nanjing, Jiangsu	48.20
54	Panyu Hotel	Guangzhou, Guangdong	65.95	90	Diaoyutai State Guest House	Beijing	47.84
55	Landmark Complex	Beijing	65.41	91	Jincheng Hotel	Foshan, Guangdong	47.55
56	Nanfang International Hotel	Shenzhen, Guangdong	64.35	92	Railway Station Hotel	Guangzhou, Guangdong	47.12
57	CVIK Hotel	Beijing	63.93	93	New Century Hotel	Beijing	47.04
58	Nanhai Hotel	Shenzhen, Guangdong	63.86	94	Park Hotel Shanghai	Shanghai	46.99
59	Guangdong Guest House	Guangzhou, Guangdong	62.39	95	Huatai Hotel	Guangzhou, Guangdong	46.99
60	Hyatt Tianjin	Tianjin	61.73	96	Overseas Chinese Mansion	Foshan, Guangdong	46.52
61	Hotel Oriental Regent	Shenzhen, Guangdong	61.72	97	Pan Pacific Wuxi Grand Hotel	Wuxi, Jiangsu	46.12
62	Westin Shanghai	Shanghai	61.49	98	Huanyu Hotel	Shenzhen, Guangdong	46.05
63	Moslem Mansion	Beijing	61.45	99	Guangzhou Hotel	Guangzhou, Guangdong	45.14
64	Jinjiang Hotel	Chengdu, Sichuan	61.30	100	Shanghai Mansion	Shanghai	45.10
65	Century Hotel	Shunde, Guangdong	59.15				
66	Longhu Hotel	Shantou, Guangdong	56.61				

China Trade Report, Apr 1995.

LAW TO REGULATE TOURISM, 1995

China's top tourism administration is drafting rules to tighten management of the overseas tourism business.

The regulation, "Temporary Provisions on Chinese Citizens Traveling Abroad at their own Expense," aims to meet the needs of Chinese people wishing to travel overseas, and to ensure a healthy tourism industry.

Travel services in other countries and regions are forbidden to organize Chinese citizens traveling overseas or acting as their agent, according to the new rule.

continued...

LAW TO REGULATE TOURISM, 1995 (continued)

The nine chapters of rules also stipulate that first-class travel services with approval of the China National Tourism Administration (CNTA) can solicit and organize visitors and check their passports and exit and entry formalities at public security departments.

Those travel services can also entrust other first- and second-class travel services to be their agents under contract.

A spokesman said that CNTA plans to approve at least one travel agency in every province within two or three years.

Under the rule, if a travel service organizes visitors going overseas without approval of CNTA, it will be fined 100,000 yuan ($11,900). Its income from overseas tourism can be confiscated and its travel business terminated.

While more and more foreigners are traveling here as tourists, more domestic visitors are similarly bound for overseas destinations, compared with previous decades.

As the market-oriented economy develops, more people from coastal regions, especially Guangdong and Fujian provinces, see travel overseas as one way to spend their holidays, according to Zhang Zhifang, an official with CNTA.

China has opened several travel routes to Thailand, Singapore, Malaysia, Philippines, Hong Kong and Macao.

Last year, an estimated 700,000 people traveled overseas, a slight decrease compared with 1993's 723,600 people, said Li Chengrong, an official with CNTA.

China imposed rigid control over citizens' applications to go abroad for personal reasons before reforms began in 1979.

Only 210,000 applications were approved between 1949 and 1978.

Since China has opened to the outside world, more citizens have been allowed to go to other countries or regions for education, visits with friends and relatives, business, travel and other personal affairs.

Many travel services, however, rushed headlong into organizing trips overseas without government approval. CNTA allowed only nine big travel agencies, such as China International Travel Service, China Travel Service and China Youth Travel Service, to start overseas tour business.

China Daily, 4 Mar 1995.

FROM ACADEMIC INTERNATIONAL PRESS*

THE RUSSIAN SERIES Volumes in Print

2 **The Nicky-Sunny Letters, Correspondence of Nicholas and Alexandra, 1914-1917**

7 Robert J. Kerner **Bohemia in the Eighteenth Century**

14 A. Leroy-Beaulieu **Un Homme d'Etat Russe (Nicholas Miliutine)...**

15 Nicolas Berdyaev **Leontiev** (In English)

17 **Tehran Yalta Potsdam. The Soviet Protocols**

18 **The Chronicle of Novgorod**

19 Paul N. Miliukov **Outlines of Russian Culture Vol. III** Pt. 1. The Origins of Ideology

20 P.A. Zaionchkovskii **The Abolition of Serfdom in Russia**

21 V.V. Vinogradov **Russkii iazyk. Grammaticheskoe uchenie o slove**

22 P.A. Zaionchkovsky **The Russian Autocracy under Alexander III**

23 A.E. Presniakov **Emperor Nicholas I of Russia. The Apogee of Autocracy**

25 S.S. Oldenburg **Last Tsar! Nicholas II, His Reign and His Russia** (OP)

28 S.F. Platonov **Ivan the Terrible** Paper

30 A.E. Presniakov **The Tsardom of Muscovy**

32 R.G. Skrynnikov **Ivan the Terrible**

33 P.A. Zaionchkovsky **The Russian Autocracy in Crisis, 1878-1882**

34 Joseph T. Fuhrmann **Tsar Alexis. His Reign and His Russia**

36 R.G. Skrynnikov **The Time of Troubles. Russia in Crisis, 1604–1618**

38 V.V. Shulgin **Days of the Russian Revolutions. Memoirs From the Right, 1905–1907.** Cloth and Paper

40 J.L. Black **"Into the Dustbin of History"! The USSR From August Coup to Commonwealth, 1991. A Documentary Narrative**

41 E.V. Anisimov **Empress Elizabeth. Her Reign and Her Russia, 1741–1761**

44 Paul N. Miliukov **The Russian Revolution** 3 vols.

THE CENTRAL AND EAST EUROPEAN SERIES

1 Louis Eisenmann **Le Compromis Austro-Hongrois de 1867**

3 Francis Dvornik **The Making of Central and Eastern Europe** 2nd edition

4 Feodor F. Zigel **Lectures on Slavonic Law**

THE ACADEMIC INTERNATIONAL REFERENCE SERIES

The Modern Encyclopedia of Russian and Soviet History 58 vols.

The Modern Encyclopedia of Russian and Soviet Literatures 50 vols.

The Modern Encyclopedia of Religions in Russia and the Soviet Union 30 vols

Soviet Armed Forces Review Annual

Russia & Eurasia Facts & Figures Annual

Russia & Eurasia Documents Annual

USSR Calendar of Events (1987- 1991) 5 vol. set

USSR Congress of Peoples's Deputies 1989. The Stenographic Record

Documents of Soviet History 12 vols.

Documents of Soviet-American Relations

Gorbachev's Reforms. An Annotated Bibliography of Soviet Writings. Part 1 1985–1987

Military Encyclopedia of Russia and Eurasia 50 vols.

China Facts & Figures Annual

China Documents Annual

Sino-Soviet Documents Annual

Encyclopedia USA. The Encyclopedia of the United States of America Past & Present 50 vols.

Sports Encyclopedia North America 50 vols.

Sports in North America. A Documentary History

Religious Documents North America Annual

The International Military Encyclopedia 50 vols.

SPECIAL WORKS

S.M. Soloviev **History of Russia** 50 vols.

SAFRA Papers 1985-

*Request catalogs